3.

TO FIND AMONG THE APPREN-
TICES OR ASSISTANT MASTER
BUILDERS ONE WHO COULD
BUILD THERE A DECK SHIP
ALONG THE LINES OF THE BIG
SHIPS HERE. FOR THAT PURPOSE
THERE SHOULD BE SENT WITH
HIM YOUNG SHIP CARPENTERS,
SUCH INSTRUMENTS AS MAY BE
NEEDED, ONE QUARTER MASTER
AND EIGHT SAILORS.

The student of shipbuilding, Fedor
Koslov, is able to build either
decked or open ships if he is furnished with a plan.

D1609308

IT IS NECESSARY TO HAVE AS
NAVIGATOR OR ASSISTANT NAVI-
GATOR ONE WHO HAS BEEN IN
NORTH AMERICA.

4.

LIKEWISE TO FORWARD FROM
HERE ONE AND A HALF SETS* OF
SAILS; BLOCKS, CABLES, AND
SUCH LIKE; FOUR FALCONETS
WITH THE NECESSARY AMMUNI-
TION; AND ONE OR TWO
SAILMAKERS.

Rigging is being sent.

*TWO SETS.

THE REST IS ALL RIGHT.

RUSSIAN
PENETRATION ^{OF}_{THE}
NORTH PACIFIC
OCEAN

В изыскании же Америки может быть следующая великая Государственная полза . . .

Great Imperial benefit may result from searching for America . . .

Count Nikolai Golovin to Empress Anna Ivanovna.
October 1, 1732.

В том следовании искать американских берегов . . . с крайнею прилежностию и старанием . . .

On this voyage you are to search with great diligence and effort for the American coasts . . .

Admiralty College instructions to Vitus Bering.
October 16, 1732

Денис Иванович! Реляцию вашу о сыскании и приведении Мне в подданство неизвестных доныне шести Алеутских островов . . .

Denis Ivanovich! I have read with satisfaction your account of the discovery of six hitherto unknown Aleutian islands which have been brought under My scepter . . .

Catherine the Great to Denis I. Chicherin, Governor of Siberia.
March 2, 1766

RUSSIAN

PENETRATION OF THE

TO SIBERIA AND

NORTH PACIFIC

RUSSIAN AMERICA

OCEAN

THREE CENTURIES OF
RUSSIAN EASTWARD EXPANSION

1700-1797

VOLUME TWO
A DOCUMENTARY RECORD

EDITED AND TRANSLATED BY
BASIL DMYTRYSHYN
E.A.P. CROWNHART-VAUGHAN
THOMAS VAUGHAN

OREGON
HISTORICAL SOCIETY
PRESS
1988

Library of Congress Cataloging-in-Publication Data
Russian penetration of the north Pacific Ocean, 1700–1799.
   (To Siberia and Russian America; v. 2)
   Translated from Russian.
   Bibliography: p.
   1. Soviet Union—Territorial expansion—Sources.   2. Soviet Far East
(R.S.F.S.R.)—Discovery and exploration—Sources.   3. Northwest, Pa-
cific—Discovery and exploration—Sources.   4. Alaska—Discovery and
exploration—Sources.   5. Discoveries (in geography)—Russian—Sources.
I. Dmytryshyn, Basil, 1925–   .   II. Crownhart-Vaughan, E. A. P.,
1929–   .   III. Vaughan, Thomas, 1924–   .   IV. Series.
DK43.T6   1988   Vol. 2   947 s [910'.09'823]   86-18249
ISBN 0-87595-149-X (alk. paper)

Printed in the United States of America.

Endpapers: Paragraphs three and four of Peter the Great's 1724 orders to
Bering for the First Kamchatka Expedition. The left column contains para-
graph three and four. In the right column are holograph comments from the
Admiralty (beginning with "The apprentice" and "The rigging") and by
Peter the Great (beginning with "*It is very," "*Twice," and "Everything").
The left panel of each endpaper is a facsimile of the original document; the
right panel is the translation. *See* Document 15 for details. Golder, *Bering's
Voyages*, I.

The preparation of this volume was made possible in part by a grant from
the Translations Program of the National Endowment for the Humanities,
an independent federal agency.

This volume was designed and produced by the Oregon Historical Society
Press.

The paper used in this publication meets minimum requirements of American National Standard for Information Sciences—Permanence of Paper for
Printed Library Materials, ANSI Z39.48-1986. ∞

This volume is dedicated to
Jane and John Youell
of Portland, Oregon

Since 1967, their confidence in
and generosity toward
this project
have never waned.

NORTH PACIFIC STUDIES SERIES

No. 1   *Explorations of Kamchatka: North Pacific Scimitar.*
Stepan P. Krasheninnikov, [*Opisanie zemli Kamchatki*]
Translated and edited by E.A.P. Crownhart-Vaughan.
1972

No. 2   *Colonial Russian America: Kyrill T. Khlebnikov's Reports, 1817–1832.*
Translated and edited by Basil Dmytryshyn and E.A.P.
Crownhart-Vaughan
1976

No. 3   *Voyages of Enlightenment: Malaspina on the Northwest Coast, 1791/1792.*
By Thomas Vaughan, E.A.P. Crownhart-Vaughan and Mercedes
Palau de Iglesias.
1977

No. 4   *The End of Russian America; Captain P.N. Golovin's Last Report, 1862.*
Translated with introduction and notes by Basil Dmytryshyn and
E.A.P. Crownhart-Vaughan.
1979

No. 5   *Civil and Savage Encounters: The Worldly Travel Letters of an Imperial
Russian Navy Officer, 1860–61.*
By Pavel N. Golovin.
Translated and annotated by Basil Dmytryshyn and E.A.P.
Crownhart-Vaughan, introduction by Thomas Vaughan.
1983

No. 6   *Log of the* Union: *John Boit's Remarkable Voyage to the Northwest Coast
and Around the World. 1794–1796.*
Edited by Edmund Hayes, foreword by Thomas Vaughan.
1981

No. 7   *For Honor and Country: The Diary of Bruno de Hezeta.*
Translated and edited by Herbert K. Beals, foreword by Thomas
Vaughan.
1985

CONTENTS

of God and convert the Kamchadal natives to Orthodox Christianity.

children attend schools and then be assigned to service, and providing pay for them from Kamchatka revenues.

Kodiak Island by Russian Orthodox missionaries.

ILLUSTRATIONS

FOREWORD

B y 1649 the epic overland phase was concluded; a Siberian journey to be remembered forever. Leaving the random authority of Moscow's princes and the topographical demarcations of the Ural Mountains, short-burst advances had moved the Russian presence purposefully eastward. In a dramatically short span—only sixty-eight years—insatiable fur hunters reached the strand of the "quiet ocean," the always restless Pacific. Those who first reached the shore had no way to know that they now faced a sea—the shallow and stormy Okhotsk—and that far below the eastern sea horizon lay the peninsular mass of Kamchatka pointed like a giant sword down toward Sakhalin, the Kurils and the as yet unknown islands of Japan—familiar only to Portuguese and Dutch merchants. Nor were they yet focused to think of the endless ocean waters stretching east, toward Bolshaia Zemlia—the great land—the legendary Alaska, which would possess the dreams of Peter and Catherine.

Among several events, volume II soon discloses to us that for Russian hunters the obsessive drive to capture furs—the lustrous "soft gold"—continued unabated. The seemingly endless Siberian taiga and tundra had been relatively denuded of desirable furs. To secure more—especially the increasingly acclaimed sea otter—demanded new skills, new courage and determination, and a new geographical sense. True, the hunters had penetrated many a riverine puzzle in their conquest of Siberia; but the new fur seekers and their leaders had no experience with the relentless and unforgiving ocean deeps: a different prospect.

Ill-made ships and awkward crews piled up on uncharted rocks and shoals, vanished in terrifying storms, or were killed in tribal encounters among the island labyrinths. Ocean travel demands quite different skills. This becomes dramatically apparent in the wondrous reports that follow—again, powerful stories of bravery, cruelty, sacrifice, fearless and foolish men and enterprises, and some extraordinary examples of womanly determination and courage. The story is once again epochal—but more on the sea than land with a whole new cast of astonishing flesh and blood characters and a new dimension in imperial rivalries. The future combined with trader intrepidness would soon unveil an unbelievable trading opportunity stretching far down the American coast toward temperate latitudes. The Siberian conquest incorporated eleven time zones. The southern thrust toward California now involves an endless imperial dream.

As well we note here, the rise of entirely different business practices was urged on by imperial pride and financial needs. The fur monopoly is formed, successfully, and its innermost workings explained by the canny founders. What their European masters made of their guileful plans and explanations we shall assess in Volume III.

Thomas Vaughan
General Editor
North Pacific Studies Series

PREFACE

In this volume we review records of a continental-maritime expansion which readers must regard with timeless awe.

By the second half of the seventeenth century small raiding bands of cossacks, fur trappers, minor government officials, adventurers and mixed social outcasts had established a Russian presence at several points along the Sea of Okhotsk and the Kamchatka Peninsula. The scattered natives of this vast and forbidding reach were numerically few and technologically primitive. Other European powers had neglected the distant and as yet undescribed reach in their drive toward overseas expansion, and Russia swiftly added the region to her colonial preserves. Throughout the eighteenth century, she launched numerous voyages from Okhotsk and the Kamchatka ports—south to the Kurils and Japan and generally east toward the Aleutian chain and Alaska. It is a study of incessant movement and exploitation.

Russian government officials conceived and carried out many voyages. They had a two-fold objective: to gain new territories for Russia without embroiling the empire in a war with other powers, especially European, and to gather as much information as possible about the new lands, their resources and inhabitants. Most voyages of the eighteenth century, however, were sponsored by merchants and noble entrepreneurs with full support and supervision from the government. Again, there was a two-fold objective: to procure as many furs as possible and to bring the region and its inhabitants under Russian control. Through utilization of entrepreneurs, the throne kept the imperial expansion costs down, while adding substantial revenues to the Treasury through taxes and a range of tributes. Private development further reduced risks of a clash with the colonial powers of Europe.

Regardless of whether these Russian voyages to the North Pacific and to Alaska in the eighteenth century were government sponsored or privately financed but controlled by the government, all were shrouded in secrecy. For Russia these voyages accomplished much. They placed a very large area of North America and the entire North Pacific under Russian control. They transformed the Russian Empire into the largest political entity in history, whose possessions encompassed substantial portions of three continents—Europe, Asia and North America. They brought the Russian government and Russian private entrepreneurs enormous revenues from the sale of furs, taxes and tribute. They provided the first information about the physical setting of the North Pacific, its resources and inhabitants. Finally, because the Russians adhered to their traditional secrecy and refused to share that information fully with other powers of Europe, their voyages aroused Spanish, English, French and then American curiosity that culminated in a series of non-Russian expeditions into Russia's new preserves.

These results were of great historic, scientific, economic, cultural and geopolitical consequence. It is an absorbing epic. Our purpose in this second volume is at last to bring together rare key documents that reveal Russia's empire-building process in the North Pacific and Alaska from 1700 to 1799, to make this fusion of eighteenth century sources available to the English-speaking world for the first time and to stimulate western scholarly interest in this dimly perceived yet dynamic imperative of Russian history. It is a record of great expectations, hardships, cruelty, suffering, and of enormous losses and rewards.

The documents in this volume reflect a vast spectrum of Russian intentions and activities in the North Pacific and Alaska. They include public and secret decrees and directives by Russian rulers, and instructions, memoranda and letters of high government officials in St. Petersburg, Moscow and Siberia, as well as reports of subordinates in the area to their superiors. There are also illuminating reports from principal seafarers, including log records, directives on the treatment of the native population, petitions of Russian entrepreneurs for opportunities and privileges, instructions to Russian religious personnel concerning their responsibilities, Russian descriptions of natives of the North Pacific, complaints from natives about their conditions, accounts of native resistance to domination, documents on Russo-Chinese and Russo-Japanese relations, plus sources on topics for future study.

The originals of these documents are currently held in Soviet archives. Access to them is a privilege, not a right. Fortunately, since the middle of the eighteenth century a number of pertinent documents have been published in Russian in limited and very rare editions such as: *Polnoe sobranie zakonov rossiiskoi imperii s 1649 goda* [First Series, 1649–1825] (St. Petersburg: 1830); 44 volumes; *Pamiatniki sibirskoi istorii XVIII veke* (St. Petersburg: 1882), 2 volumes; A. Pokrovskii, ed., *Ekspeditsiia Beringa: sbornik dokumentov* (Moscow: 1941); S. F. Markov, ed., *Ekspeditsiia Beringa: sbornik dokumentov* (Moscow: 1941); A. I Andreev, ed., *Russkie otkrytiia v Tikhom Okeane i v Severnoe Amerike* (Moscow: 1948); A. V. Efimov, ed., *Iz istorii russkikh ekspeditsii na Tikhom Okeane, pervaia polovina XVIII veke* (Moscow: 1948); V. A. Divin, ed., *Russkaia tikhookeanskaia epopeia* (Khabarovsk: 1979); and N. N. Bashkina et al., eds., *Rossiia i SShA: Stanovlenie otnoshenii 1765–1815*, published simultaneously in Moscow and in Washington, D.C. in 1980. All of the above, and future references, are fully cited, with translated titles, in the Bibliography. The Library of Congress Manuscript Division holds the Yudin and Golder collections of documents, and the National Archives hold the records of the Russian American Company.

Colleagues in many countries have provided most generous assistance in many aspects of our work. Our warmest thanks go to Robert V. Allen of the Library of Congress; the Right Reverend Gregory, Bishop of Sitka and Alaska; Colonel M. J. Poniatowski-d'Ermengard and the late Ivan L. Best, Portland, Oregon; Raymond H. Fisher, Los Angeles; James R. Gibson, Toronto; Helen Wallis, Keeper of the Maps of the British Library; Commander A.C.F. David, Ministry of Defence, Taunton; Elisabeth Tokoi, National Library, Helsinki; John Stephan and Patricia Polansky, Honolulu; Susan Mango, Washington, D.C.; John D. Taylor, St. Paul, Minnesota; Iu. V. Bromley, Nikolai N. Bolkhovitinov, and Svetlana G. Fedorova, Moscow; the late Erna V. Siebert and Mikhail I. Belov, Leningrad; Rostislav V. Kinzhalov, R.G. Liapunova, A.D. Dridzo, G.I. Dzensikevich, E.A. Okladnikova, and E.G. Kushnarev, all of Leningrad. A number of institutions in the USSR have been most helpful: Library of the Academy of Sciences, Leningrad; Saltykov-Shchedrin State Public Library, Leningrad; Lenin Library, Moscow; State Public Scientific Library of the Academy of Sciences, Siberian Section, Novosibirsk; Institute of Ethnography of the Academy of Sciences, Moscow and Leningrad; Geographical Society of the USSR; Moscow State University; Zhadnov State University Library, Irkutsk; Central State Naval Museum, Leningrad; Far East Literary Museum, Khabarovsk; Pacific Institute of Geography of the Academy of Sciences, Far Eastern Scientific Center, Vladivostok; Arctic and Antarctic Institute, Leningrad.

Support for research and publication has come from the National Endowment for the Humanities; the Northwest Area Foundation; The Westland Foundation; and the S.S. Johnson Foundation, as well as from many private benefactors who, under the aegis of the Oregon Historical Society, in 1968 established the Irkutsk Archival Research Group. This group has for the past two decades provided for the support of the scholarship involved in the production of this three-volume series, as well as previous Russian translations published in this North Pacific Studies Series. This vanguard group was first headed by John Youell, then by Samuel S. Johnson. Jane West Youell presently serves as chairman in association with James B. Thayer, past chairman now serving as president of the Oregon Historical Society.

The extensive and ever-growing research collections of the Oregon Historical Society are the backbone of all three volumes.

The design, editing and production of this series is the work of Bruce Taylor Hamilton, OHS Assistant Director-Publications, and the Society's Press staff: Krisell B. Steingraber, Thomas S. Booth, Adair M. Law, Lori R. McEldowney, and George T. Resch. Indexing of the *To Siberia and Russian America* series is done by Jean Brownell.

To all, we give our heartfelt thanks and gratitude.

Basil Dmytryshyn
E.A.P. Crownhart-Vaughan
Thomas Vaughan

This stylized conception of a volcano confirms the earliest reports from Kamchatka, that noted volcanic activity on the peninsula. Activity was and is frequent, especially from the Ava-
chinskaia Volcano, overlooking Petropavlovsk and Avacha
Bay. Private collection.

INTRODUCTION

Russia's expansion to North America from 1700 to 1799 was a natural extension of her drive across northern Asia from 1580 to 1700. The similarity can best be seen in the Russian treatment of the indigenous population, the manner of exploitation of the region's natural resources, the content of official directives to the leaders of various expeditions, the secrecy surrounding Russian plans and activities, and in the deliberate determination to keep other powers in ignorance and away from her ever-expanding colonial domain.

There also are fundamental differences. The most basic, affecting everything else, was the full involvement of the government in the expansion process. Until 1700 the Russian sweep across northern Asia was neither a grand design, nor a clearly coordinated, planned, national undertaking. It was essentially an effort of the following major groups: 1) the *promyshlenniks* [entrepreneurs, trappers, traders], who hunted and trapped fur-bearing animals and obtained pelts from the natives through trade, extortion, theft and tribute; 2) the *sluzhashchie liudi* [state servitors, both civil and military], who protected state and private interests; 3) *Litva* [captured Poles, Swedes, Lithuanians, Ukrainians, Belorussians and other warring Europeans], whom Moscow authorities dispatched to the region for safekeeping; 4) exiled Russian political and religious dissenters, whom colonial administrators used for various assignments, including defense; 5) state peasants, craftsmen and church personnel, who were sent to the region to assist colonial administrators; 6) merchants and their agents, who went to the conquered wilderness voluntarily to seek their fortunes; 7) *guliashchie liudi* [runaway serfs, social misfits and outcasts], who sought refuge in the region and were willing and ready to join in any assignment; and 8) native guides and armed detachments of indigenous people who cooperated with the Russians for various reasons.

For the most part these overland trailblazers, now called by the Russians *zemleprokhodtsy*, were simple, illiterate men. Some were condemned criminals. They crossed northern Asia on foot, by horse, reindeer and dogsled and by small river boat. There was no master plan, no long-term design, no notion of an ultimate destination. Cold, hunger, flight from punishment, lust for wealth and in some cases for native women, and determination to survive and to succeed drove them across mountains and from one puzzling valley and river system to the next. For direction they relied more on local lore and rumor than on compasses, and above all, on information supplied by native guides. To date scholars of Russian expansion, both Russian and non-Russian, have paid little attention to this basic reason for Russian success.

We do not suggest that before 1700 the government in Moscow was dissociated from the expansion process. It was deeply involved. This was mandated by the socio-political nature of the Muscovite state. The Tsar was the ultimate source of all power. Little of importance happened without his knowledge or approval. Yet the involvement of the government in the expansion process was not central. The government joined the enterprise only when it became obvious that the initial push by the Stroganov cossacks across the Urals was a resounding success. Subsequently the government limited its role to collecting a lion's share of tribute from the indigenous population and of taxes from Russian entrepreneurs. It also established administrative machinery, including the building of *ostrogs* [forts] to control and exploit the conquered region and to maintain peace among competing Russians and between Russians and conquered natives. It likewise supplied the zemleprokhodtsy with necessities, including weapons, and rewarded them for their achievements and punished them for failures. Finally, the central government sponsored new expeditions to bring other regions under Russian control and protected the conquered territories from foreign intrusions.

The pattern of Russian expansion into North America during the eighteenth century differed fundamentally from that across Northern Asia in that from beginning to end the entire venture to North America was conceived and expedited by the government. Throughout the whole period the government either sponsored or authorized all major expeditions. It provided all logistics, including weapons, credits, permits, punishments and rewards. It supplied the bulk of manpower and prescribed rules of behavior and conduct toward the indigenous population. Further, the government set out rules for selected private entrepreneurs to collect information, and carefully monitored the activity of foreign competitors. Finally, in 1799 the central government assigned the expansion effort to the Russian American Company. The Company was not a private venture as understood today. The government not only chartered it, but regulated, supplied, controlled and protected it from domestic and foreign competitors. Indeed, in 1867 the government sold the Company's Alaskan domain to the United States. As volume III reveals, the government then dissolved the company even as it created it.

Three fundamental factors seem to have been responsible for the government's domination of Russia's expansion into the North Pacific. Foremost was the drastically altered nature of the expansion enterprise. Until about 1700 Russian expansion across northern Asia had proceeded, with the assistance of native guides, along the region's major rivers and in a few instances along the coast of the Arctic and North Pacific oceans and the Sea of Okhotsk. Although dangerous and full of hardships, this system of overland exploration and conquest required very little financial outlay and only minimal technological expertise. Once the zemleprokhodtsy reached the rugged coast of the Sea of Okhotsk and the shores of the North Pacific, that system failed. Native guides proved useless here because they themselves had never ventured far out to sea and consequently knew nothing of what lay beyond. Thus, for example, when the Russians reached the Sea of Okhotsk and asked their Tungus guides what body of water it was, the answer was: "*Penzhin,*" that is, "a large body of water." For many decades afterward the Russians called this *Penzhinskoe More* [the Penzhin Sea]. The only exception to this lack of knowledge of what lay beyond the sea horizon was some vague information about contact between the Chukchi of the northeastern tip of Asia and the Eskimos of *Bolshaia Zemlia* [the Big Country], Alaska. The Russians learned of these contacts as early as the 1660's but did not pursue them.

Brought up short by the formidable ocean barrier, some zemleprokhodtsy returned west to their original ostrogs; others scouted the coast on foot and in order to survive built *zimov'es* [winter huts]. A few determined ones felled trees from the nearby forests to build primitive sailing vessels, but violent sea storms usually put an end to their sailing ambitions. Exhausted survivors became easy prey either to malnutrition or to hostile natives. Bitter experience and common sense dictated that exploration of this dangerous and uncharted body of water required a massive infusion of new funds, new skills and new technical knowledge. Because the zemleprokhodtsy themselves had none of these prerequisites, the central government assumed broad authority for Russian expansion across the North Pacific to North America.

In a concomitant development, in the late seventeenth and early eighteenth centuries Russian government and society underwent a profound transformation. This change was spearheaded by Tsar Peter I (1682–1725). Before his reign the government of Russia had very strong Byzantine-Oriental characteristics. In outward appearance the Tsar was a perfect embodiment of these features. He resembled a composite of a Chinese emperor, a Persian shah and a Byzantine patriarch. Because of his close association with the Orthodox Church, life at court as well as some domestic and foreign policies had strong religious overtones.

Peter I changed all that. He moved the capital from Moscow to his newly-built St. Petersburg, donned a military uniform, replaced religious advisors with military men and forced Russian nobles to modernize their outward appearance and their outlook on life. With the aid of numerous West European experts, he reorganized the Russian army, chartered a modern navy, introduced new diplomatic practices, established secular schools and emancipated them from religious control, reorganized the administrative apparatus, redirected the country's economic development and introduced strict supervision over all of his subjects.

So profound indeed were Peter's reforms that within a generation they propelled Russia from a relatively insignificant, although very large, empire to a major world power. Although Peter's successors did not and perhaps could not support every reform, many of his changes were irreversible and became permanent fixtures of Russian life until 1917, and some perhaps after.

The sudden emergence of a new, powerful, dynamic, secretive and expansionist Russia aroused concern and suspicion among other major powers. While this concern expressed itself first in Europe, by the second half of the eighteenth century it also affected the vast North Pacific arena. Spain, Great Britain, France and the United States, in that order, began to monitor as well as to oppose Russian designs there. Their concern and suspicion led to numerous tensions but never to all-out war, because responsible Russian leaders realized that they had overextended themselves and that militarily they could not defend their colonial empire in the North Pacific and in North America against the combined, or indeed individual, forces of the other powers. This realistic assessment of the situation caused the Russians eventually to abandon their extensive colonial interests first in Hawaii (1817), then in California (1839) and finally in Alaska (1867).

THE INITIAL PHASE OF RUSSIAN EXPANSION TO
NORTH AMERICA, 1700–1743

Russian expansion to North America in the eighteenth century falls into three distinct phases. The first was the initial phase by the government, 1700 to 1743. The second was a carefully government-controlled and monitored phase of private interests, 1743 to 1799. The final phase, 1753 to 1795, in part concurrent with the second phase, consisted of a series of secret government-sponsored expeditions to promote and defend Russian interests in the North Pacific. The initial phase included a series of carefully planned information-gathering expeditions. Russian literature in the pre- and post-revolutionary period claims that it was the Russians, not foreigners, who supplied the initiative for these pioneering undertakings. It is immaterial who persuaded Peter the Great to initiate these ventures—that is, whether it was the Dutch writer and traveler, Nicholas Witsen, or the German scientist-philosopher Gottfried Leibnitz, or members of the Academy in Paris, or the Russian "unofficial consul" in London, Fedor S. Saltykov. What really matters is that Peter committed himself to the dispatch of costly expeditions which, in their basic organization, embraced the new principles of scientific inquiry.

The first took place between 1719 and 1722 and was led by two young geodesists, Ivan Evreinov and Fedor Luzhin. Peter's order, dated January 2, 1719, instructed the two men to proceed to Tobolsk and then to Kamchatka and beyond. There they were to survey and describe local places of interest, ascertain whether Asia was linked by land to America, and to map all of their findings. Some scholars maintain that Peter also gave the two men secret instructions, the content of which has never been discovered. This is not an unreasonable assumption. Evidence clearly reveals that throughout the seventeenth century Russian explorers received elaborate instructions concerning their assignments, behavior, and the type of information they were to obtain for authorities in Moscow. Sea storms prevented Evreinov and Luzhin from fulfilling their assignments as instructed. They visited the northern Kuril Islands aboard an antiquated vessel, and while in Kamchatka they questioned veteran cossacks and other zemleprokhodtsy about rivers, lakes and adjacent territories, as well as about islands and distances between various points. The only concrete result of their efforts, however, was a map which they had prepared and which Evreinov personally presented to Peter upon his return in 1722.

Because Peter was apparently only partially satisfied with these findings, on December 23, 1724 he signed a decree ordering a new expedition to the same area under the command of a Danish captain in Russian service, Vitus Bering (1681–1741). The stated objective of this First Kamchatka Expedition was brief and ambiguous, which subsequently gave rise to varied interpretations of the aim of that mission. According to Peter's terse instructions, Bering was to go to Kamchatka or to any place under Russian control, where he was to build one or two boats with decks. With these boats he was then to sail "near the land which goes to the north, which (since no one knows where it ends), it seems is part of America."

Peter instructed Bering to search in that region for a place where that land was joined to America. He was also to sail to any town belonging to a European power, and if he encountered any European ship en route, he was to inquire the name of the nearest coast, go ashore personally, obtain first hand information about it, locate the site on a map and return to Russia.

In accordance with Peter's orders, Bering and his crew left St. Petersburg on February 5, 1725. Because they had to carry all of their equipment, their progress across northern Asia was very slow and filled with hardship and delays. Bering reached Okhotsk on October 1, 1726. His associate, a Dane named Martyn Spanberg, arrived early in January, 1727. The second-in-command, the Russian naval Lieutenant Aleksei I. Chirikov, at the head of the first detachment to leave St. Petersburg, arrived in July of that year.

In Okhotsk the crew built the *Fortuna*, a *shitik* [a decked boat with side planking "sewn" with willow wands and leather strips instead of nails or pegs], and repaired an old vessel. In early August they sailed for Kamchatka, where by mid-1728 they built and launched another boat, the *Sv. Gavriil*. On July 13, 1728, Bering in the *Sv. Gavriil*, with a year's supply of provisions for the 44-man crew, put out to sea to carry out Peter's instructions.

The expedition sailed north parallel to the coast of northeast Asia. In early August they rounded the Chukotsk Peninsula and a few days later, without realizing it, passed through the fog-covered strait that separates Asia from America.

On August 15 they reached 67°18′ northern latitude. There Bering consulted Spanberg and Chirikov on their further sailing. The council revealed differences of opinion. Spanberg advised that the expedition return to Kamchatka, while Chirikov urged that they continue sailing either west to the mouth of the Kolyma River or east to search for Bolshaia Zemlia. Bering sided with Spanberg and ordered a return course to Kamchatka by the same route they had just taken. Fog again prevented the crew from sighting America. On September 1, the *Sv. Gavriil* returned safely to Nizhnekamchatsk.

Apparently Bering was dissatisfied with the outcome of his mission, for during the winter he sought out many veteran seafarers, listened to their travel experiences and solicited their information. In June, 1729, he again put out to sea in search of the coast of North America, but a severe storm forced him to abandon his plans. On July 2, he landed at Bolsheretsk, and twenty days later was in Okhotsk. Returning overland, he arrived in St. Petersburg in January, 1730. There he prepared a report about his voyage. There, too, he soon discovered that he had many admirers but also critics—a situation that has influenced all subsequent scholarly treatments of his efforts.

During the years of Bering' first voyage, Russian authorities also organized a minor expedition into the uncharted regions of the North Pacific. The undertaking was led by Afanasii Shestakov and Dmitrii Pavlutskii. They were killed in a fight with the Chukchi, so the task fell on a Dutchman, Jacob Hens, and two Russians, Ivan Fedorov and Mikhail Gvozdev. In 1732 the trio put out to sea from the mouth of the Anadyr River aboard Bering's vessel *Sv. Gavriil* and sailed above 65° northern latitude.

They may have been the first Europeans to see Alaska's shores. Disunity among the leaders and sickness among the crew forced the expedition to return to home base. Their report about the voyage failed to attract official attention until 1741.

In 1733 the Russian government organized a new expedition known variously as the Second Kamchatka, Second Bering, Great Northern and First Academic Expedition. This mammoth undertaking had as its major objective to map the entire northern coastline of the Russian Empire from Arkhangelsk to the Chukchi Peninsula, take an inventory of Russian possessions in northern Asia, map the Kurils and the Japanese islands, sail to the Pacific shores of North America and bring the entire region under Russian control. Again Bering was put in charge of the entire undertaking and of the naval expedition to the shores of North America. Chirikov was his second-in-command. This expedition too was beset with delays, divisiveness and disagreements, shortages, and other problems. Unlike the earlier voyage, however, this expedition had a clearly spelled out objective: to reach and claim for Russia the western shore of North America.

In pursuit of that goal, once preparations had been completed, the expedition sailed in September, 1740 from Okhotsk to Kamchatka. There, during the subsequent winter and spring, the crew completed preparations for the voyage. On June 4, 1741 they put out to sea from the harbor at Avacha Bay (subsequently Petropavlovsk). Bering was accompanied by the naturalist Georg Wilhelm Steller, Lieutenant Sven Waxell and a crew of seventy-five men aboard a packetboat of Baltic design, *Sv. Petr.* Chirikov's command included the astronomer Louis de Lisle de la Croyère and a crew of seventy-three men aboard a packetboat *Sv. Pavel.*

Until June 12 the two vessels sailed south southwest in search of the nonexistent "Gama Land." When they failed to sight land in the supposed location, the expedition changed course to east by north. On June 20 in 40°30' north latitude the two vessels lost sight of one another during a severe storm. On July 16 in latitude 58°14' Bering spotted Alaska's mountains and four days later anchored between the mouth of Copper River and Cape Suckling. There he permitted Steller to go ashore for a few hours to explore and search for ore. Bering then set course for the southwest. He discovered the islands of Kodiak and Ukamok, and later, in August, the group of islands off the Alaska Peninsula later known as the Shumagin Islands to honor the first death in Bering's crew. Scurvy struck many crew members, including Bering himself, forcing the expedition to head back for Kamchatka. Violent storms impeded a progress at best extremely slow and difficult. On November 6, 1741 the *Sv. Petr* was wrecked on one of the Komandorskie Islands, subsequently named Bering Island in honor of Bering, who died there. The forty-six survivors spent nine months building a new vessel from the wreck of the *Sv. Petr*, and aboard this craft they finally reached Avacha Bay on August 26, 1742.

Chirikov had better success. Separated from Bering, he searched for two days for his commanding officer and failing to find him, sailed east. On July 15 the Russian naval officer sighted and approached the coast of Alaska where he spent eleven days cruising off shore. On July 23 he dispatched a landing party. The ten crew members failed to return, as did a smaller party sent to rescue the first. On July 26 the *Sv. Pavel* commenced its westward journey along the south side of the Alaska Peninsula and the Aleutian Islands. By mid-September scurvy had weakened most of the crew, including Chirikov. From that point on the *Sv. Pavel* was in the hands of navigator I. F. Elagin, who brought her safely to Avacha Bay on October 10, 1741, minus twenty-one crew members who had died en route.

On May 25, 1742 Chirikov again put out to sea in search of Bering. He reached the island of Attu. Violent storms forced him to return to Kamchatka, which he reached safely on July 1.

Notwithstanding the human and material cost, delays and other problems, the American Section of the Second Kamchatka Expedition accomplished much. It unlocked the hitherto unknown North Pacific to the world and recorded the first information about it. It discovered and partially described the shores of Northwest America and some of the Aleutian Islands. the Bering-Chirikov thrust also opened a vast and unclaimed area to Russian penetration, which transformed the region rich in fur-bearing animals and other resources into an exclusive Russian preserve for a generation. Finally, in discovering valuable furs, the Second Kamchatka Expedition inaugurated a new phase in Russian Expansion to North America.

The second phase, 1743–1799, of Russian expansion to North America has not, to date, received the attention it deserves. Aside from restricted access to the documents and the difficulty of translating them, the reason for this neglect is not clear, except that the process failed to produce charismatic leaders. Too, it was overshadowed by the earlier efforts of Bering and by Baranov's subsequent designs. Whatever the reasons, scholarly neglect of this movement is unfortunate because the period witnessed two far-reaching achievements: Russian conquest of the Aleutian Islands and the establishment of a number of permanent Russian outposts in Alaska. In response came the slow but determined emergence of Spanish, British, French and eventually American concern and suspicion about Russian activity in the North Pacific.

This second phase began as soon as the Second Kamchatka Expedition had completed its task. The movement was triggered by the arrival of precious furs brought back by surviving crew members. The news spread rapidly throughout the empire and many Russians who were allowed to travel began to move toward Irkutsk, Iakutsk, Okhotsk and Kamchatka. Once there they realized that to strike it rich they would first have to obtain some basic prerequisites: funds to build and provision seagoing ships, employment of reliable crews of promyshlenniks for long voyages, and permits from government authorities in St. Petersburg, Moscow or Siberia to undertake such voyages.

Russian private entrepreneurs solved the first problem by pooling their resources and by organizing themselves into small venture companies. It has been estimated that over forty North Pacific companies operated from 1743 to 1799. Before 1780 each company consisted of from thirty to fifty shareholders who were bound by a contract among themselves and with the promyshlenniks. Each contract stipulated that upon successful completion of a voyage, after giving the government a tenth of the catch, the remaining furs would be divided into three sets of shares. A modest part was to go to the church, local charities and schools, the ship's skipper, the supercargo and the most productive promyshlenniks. The second part was to be divided equally between the promyshlenniks and the original promoters of the undertaking as recompense for their expenses in building and provisioning the vessel. The final set of shares went to the original investor-promoters, who received dividends on the basis of their original investments. If the hunt was rich, everyone profited. If it was poor, the promyshlenniks were the chief losers because they received little for their toil and suffering.

Since so many ships were lost at sea, we cannot estimate the ruble value of all the furs they took. Even so, an early nineteenth century appraisal of the cargo estimated that between 1743 and 1797 these hunting parties returned with furs valued at close to 8,000,000 rubles—an enormous wealth in those days. A few lucky investors became so rich they were able personally or in limited partnerships to finance the cost of a subsequent expedition. This new form of finance reduced the number of companies engaged in hunting in the North Pacific. The company life span now extended beyond a single voyage and the wealthy owners became influential with high officials not only in Siberia but in St. Petersburg. The most noteworthy of these new companies were the Lebedev-Lastochkin, the Kiselev, the Shelikhov-Golikov and the Mylnikov. In 1799 the last two companies merged to form the Russian American Company. As the sole government-supported and supervised monopoly company, it lasted until 1867 when the Russian government sold its colonial holdings in North America to the United States.

Regardless of who financed them, these voyages were costly. It has been estimated that initially it took 20,000 to 30,000 rubles to prepare a ship for a voyage. Subsequently, because of inflation, greater distances and the larger size of ships, the cost more than doubled. However these figures include the cost of building a ship, plus the preparation of provisions for a crew of as many as seventy men for a period of as long as four years. Many supplies had to be brought by pack train from Iakutsk. The cost was exorbitant. The most favored vessel for these voyages was the two-masted shitik, built either in Okhotsk or Kamchatka. A large shitik could accommodate a crew of seventy; a smaller one took a crew of forty. Large or small, half the crew was Russian, the rest usually Kamchadal. This ratio benefitted the entrepreneurs and promyshlenniks, since the Kamchadals received but a small fraction of the profit.

Before it could put to sea, each privately organized voyage

had to secure permission from the Governing Senate or other important agencies in St. Petersburg or from Siberian governors or administrators of key outposts. There were few denials. Officials readily issued such permits because they received a payment upon the completion of every successful voyage and because each voyage increased Russia's possessions in the North Pacific. Those who secured permits pledged to collect *iasak* [tribute in furs] from the natives as a sign of their submission to Russian rule; the iasak was to be handed over to proper authorities in Russia when the ship returned. Permit holders also agreed to surrender a tenth of their furs to the Treasury, and to supply the government with pertinent information about the voyage. They pledged not to mistreat the natives and vowed to convert them to Orthodox Christianity.

To assure full compliance with these pledges, the authorities placed agents aboard almost all outgoing vessels. Their reports, as well as subsequent debriefings of crew members, brought rewards to those who enhanced Russian national interests and punishment to those whose actions were deleterious to Russia's interests. Upon recommendations from Siberian governors, several of the seafarers and a few principal promoters were presented to Catherine II. All of them received special medals, some were granted privileges of nobility, a few were freed from the payment of taxes they owed, and the Shelikhov-Golikov Company even obtained permission to settle several families of exiles on Kodiak Island to enable it to strengthen its enterprise.

The usual voyage commenced either in Okhotsk or Kamchatka, in late summer or early fall. The first stop was uninhabited Bering Island, where crews spent the entire winter procuring sea lion meat and whale blubber for the voyage. The following summer the ship sailed east to Copper Island and the Near Islands, then on to the Rat Islands, Andreanovs, Umnak, Unalaska, Unimak, Kodiak, Afognak and to the Alaska Peninsula. When they reached their destination the promyshlenniks built temporary zimov'es and in order to assure the cooperation of the native population, seized a number of women and children whom they held as hostages. They kept the hostages for the duration of their stay on that island.

After completing these vital preliminaries, the Russian promyshlenniks then divided into *artels* [small hunting groups] to hunt and trap red, black and brown foxes, ermines, martens and beavers. A third of the crew usually stayed behind to guard the hostages, the zimov'e and the ship. This group also forced the natives to hunt sea otters by imposing iasak on all adult males. They also encouraged the natives to hunt by offering them various trinkets for pelts. If the hunt was bountiful on any given island, the Russians returned to home port. If not, they moved on to the next island where they repeated the routine. In either case, before they departed they released their hostages. If the natives had fulfilled their iasak obligation, they received a written receipt.

These voyages and the island hunts in the North Pacific were filled wth hardships. Violent sea storms took a terrible toll of ships and men. Many ships were poorly constructed and were unseaworthy. Moreover, many were commanded by inexperienced skippers. Food was a very serious problem, especially on a voyage lasting several years. Undernourished, overworked and exposed to the inhospitable climate, many Russians fell victim to scurvy and other diseases. And native resistance took such form as ambush, murder, and the burning of ships.

Life in the hostile environment of the North Pacific, as in Siberia, created among the Russian promyshlenniks, regardless of their origin or background, an esprit de corps that enabled some to succeed and survive. Many of course did not survive the miseries. Some who did made handsome profits for themselves and their promoters. And the vision of profit doubtless allayed many sufferings.

Russian expansion across the North Pacific in the eighteenth century, like the seventeenth century counterpart across Siberia, produced many remarkable individuals, both promoters and promyshlenniks. The most outstanding promoters were Nikifor Trapeznikov, a merchant from Irkutsk involved in promoting 18 voyages between 1743 and 1764, who made enormous sums of money but because of later losses and bankruptcies died in poverty; Pavel S. Lebedev-Lastochkin, a merchant from Iakutsk, who organized three permanent settlements in Prince William Sound in Alaska; and Grigorii I. Shelikhov, a merchant from Rylsk who was dubbed the "Russian Columbus" because of his promotion of Russian colonial exploration and expansion.

The most noteworthy Russian seafaring promyshlenniks were Emelian Basov, who initiated the Russian drive across the

North Pacific in 1743; Andreian Tolstykh, who discovered a number of islands in the Aleutian chain between 1746 and 1765, now known as the Andreanovs; Potap Zaikov, who brought considerable wealth to his sponsors in the years between 1772 and 1791; Gerasim A. Izmailov, who sailed to the coast of Alaska in the employ of the Shelikhov-Golikov Company; and Gerasim Pribylov, who, while working for the Lebedev-Lastochkin Company, brought to Okhotsk one of the richest fur cargoes on record—worth 253,018 rubles.

Of course, just as in the Russian drive across Siberia, the voyages in the North Pacific produced villains. Among those recorded are the notorious Illarion Belaev, Gavriil Pushkarev and Ivan Solovev, who killed hundreds of Aleuts.

Scholars agree that Grigorii I. Shelikhov was the leading entrepreneur in Russia's expansion across the North Pacific to North America. Born in Rylsk, Kursk gubernia, Shelikhov came to Eastern Siberia in the early 1770s. There he married a wealthy, energetic, ambitious and intelligent widow, Natalia Alekseevna. Using his newly acquired wealth, Shelikhov joined many merchant-promoters in financing expeditions to the Aleutians and the Kurils between 1775 and 1783. In a long run of luck, each of these ventures brought great financial returns. We know that between 1777 and 1795 Shelikhov had an interest in fourteen of the thirty-six Russian ships venturing in the North Pacific. He became so successful that he was able to build and outfit three ships in 1783 using his own resources. He also was the first major promoter to sail to Kodiak Island—on which voyage he was accompanied by his wife. Upon his return, Shelikhov prepared a lengthy and favorable report about his activities on Russia's behalf. He submitted this to his friend, Ivan A. Pil, governor general of Siberia, who immediately forwarded it with his own personal endorsement to Catherine II. A Russian priest who visited Shelikhov's new settlement a few years later submitted a less favorable report, but the Empress never saw that account.

Because of his great wealth, good luck, excellent connections and grand vision, Shelikhov also established very close rapport with two highly influential personal friends of Catherine, Count Aleksandr R. Vorontsov, head of the College of Commerce, and Count Aleksandr A. Bezborodko, Catherine's secretary. These connections enabled Shelikhov to meet the Empress when he went to St. Petersburg to present and defend his grand designs in the North Pacific, but Catherine rejected Shelikhov's request for an exclusive trade and hunting monopoly in the North Pacific because she was influenced by the writings of Adam Smith. She was preoccupied with dangerous and rapidly unfolding events in Europe, the French Revolution, disturbing developments in Poland and imminent wars with Sweden and the Ottoman Empire. However, she bestowed gold medals upon Shelikhov and his partner, Ivan L. Golikov, a merchant from Kursk, for their efforts in promoting Russia's interests. She also authorized them to employ Russian exiles in their newly established settlements on Kodiak Island. Shelikhov's plans came to a sudden halt with his death in 1795. He was mourned by such celebrated Russian figures as Aleksandr N. Radishchev and the poets Gavriil R. Derzhavin and Ivan I. Dmitriev, who wrote the inscription for Shelikhov's marble headstone in Irkutsk.

After her husband's death, Natalia Shelikhova took over the direction of the company, successfully fended off a hostile takeover attempt and concluded an advantageous merger. Thus, Shelikhov's grand design for Russia's colonial empire became a reality in 1799 when Emperor Paul I granted the Shelikhov-Golikov Company, subsequently the Russian American Company, exclusive rights in the North Pacific.

Although his sudden death prevented Shelikhov from realizing all of his design, during his lifetime he did achieve part of it. In 1784 he established the first permanent Russian settlement in the North Pacific: Three Saints Harbor on Kodiak Island. The new settlement had more than 180 persons and was intended to serve a threefold purpose: to save time and money for the Shelikhov-Golikov Company now that the great distances made each voyage so time-consuming and costly; to assist the company in exploiting the area more completely; and to serve as headquarters for other outposts on key islands in order to assure an incontestable Russian claim. In pursuit of the latter objective Shelikhov set up forts or redoubts on Afognak and Atka islands and in Kenai Inlet. In 1792 the company strengthened its presence by founding St. Paul's Harbor on Kodiak, and increased it further with the 1795 establishment of Slavorossiia in Yakutat Bay on the coast of the Gulf of Alaska.

Lebedev-Lastochkin, once Shelikhov's partner and subsequently his rival, pursued an identical policy. In 1787 he organized Fort St. George in Kenai Inlet, to which he added St. Nicholas redoubt in 1793. That same year he also established St. Constantine redoubt in Chugach Inlet. The Russian government not only approved these steps but also dispatched state peasants from northern regions of European Russia to manifest Russian presence in the area. The assigned number, however, was too small and the area too large and too inhospitable to enable the new transplants to act both as promyshlenniks and as defenders of private and national interests.

THE THIRD PHASE OF RUSSIAN EXPANSION TO THE NORTH PACIFIC: GOVERNMENT SPONSORED EXPEDITIONS, 1753–1792

Concurrently with the monitored ventures by private entrepreneurs, between 1753 and 1792 the Russian government planned and dispatched several of its own expeditions to the region. These were conceived and guided by four departments of government with interests in the area: the College of the Admiralty, the College of Foreign Affairs, the College of Commerce and the Academy of Sciences. High-ranking officials in charge of affairs in Siberia and the North Pacific also played a vital role in the planning and execution of these undertakings. The objectives were to verify information about the region supplied by private entrepreneurs and their employees, ameliorate some of the abuses promulgated by promyshlenniks against natives, gather additional information about the region, establish firm Russian claim and hegemony over the entire area, and fend off all foreign interlopers from Russia's colonial empire. Some of these expeditions were successful, but none could match Bering's Second Kamchatka Expedition in scope and numbers.

The first of these government-sponsored expeditions is known in historical literature as "The Secret Expedition" and as "The Tobolsk Secret Commission" and lasted from 1753 to 1764. The principal promoters were Rear Admiral Vasilii A. Miatlev, governor general of Siberia, and his successor, Fedor I. Soimonov. Miatlev outlined his ideas in a lengthy memorandum to the Governing Senate. He argued that all Russian possessions along the coast of the Sea of Okhotsk and in the North Pacific should be supplied from Irkutsk via the Amur River, rather than over the more torturous route from Iakutsk. He suggested that the Russians gain complete control of the Amur and build and fortify shipyard facilities at its mouth. He made the strategic recommendation that the government develop the more fertile Trans-Baikal region, especially the area around Nerchinsk, to serve as a new agricultural and industrial base to support Russian interests in the North Pacific. He urged that all major tributaries of the Amur be surveyed to determine their navigational capabilities and the possibility that adjacent areas could accommodate Russian settlers. Finally, he insisted that Russian authorities gain firm control over the activities of the promyshlenniks in order to acquire better knowledge of the resources of the North Pacific and to end the reported abuses against island natives.

For several years government authorities in St. Petersburg studied Miatlev's shrewd proposals but did little to implement them. They wished at all costs to avoid a war with China which would have become a reality had Miatlev's suggestions been carried out, and during this period Russian officials focused their attention not on the Far East or the North Pacific, but on events in Europe, where Russia became deeply embroiled in the Seven Years' War (1756–1763). As a result, early in 1764 Catherine lost interest in Miatlev's plan and ordered that the work of the Secret Expedition be suspended.

The second government-sponsored expedition to the North Pacific lasted from 1764 to 1767. It was promoted by Denis I. Chicherin, governor general of Siberia, and Major Frederick C. Plenisner, commanding officer of the port of Okhotsk and a former member of the Second Bering Expedition. The plan, approved by the Admiralty, called for close monitoring of the seaborne fur trade carried on by private entrepreneurs, careful surveying of all islands lying between Kamchatka and America, and a scrupulous determination of their resources. This assignment went to Lieutenant Ivan Sindt, a Baltic German in Russian service. The selection was unfortunate. Although he had been a member of the Second Bering Expedition, Sindt did not have the necessary leadership qualifications for such an assignment. He sailed from Okhotsk in two small galiots to Kamchatka and then on to the North Pacific. At the end of his journey he submitted to the Admiralty a report and a map of the islands in the Bering Sea, a map filled with errors and exaggerations which took years to correct. Perhaps for that reason a full account of Sindt's voyage has never been published.

The third expedition was undertaken in 1764–1769 by two young naval officers, Captain Petr K. Krenitsyn and Lieutenant Mikhail D. Levashev. The principal aim was to verify all recent discoveries by promyshlenniks and to check on reported Russian abuses. All participants were sworn to secrecy. The undertaking was officially designated "An Expedition to Survey the Forests in the Ural Mountains along the Kama and Belaia Rivers." From inception to conclusion, the Krenitsyn-Levashev expedition experienced misfortune. In October 1766 three of their four vessels were wrecked on the run between Okhotsk and Kamchatka. When the expedition resumed in two ships in June 1768, the vessels became separated in a heavy fog. The crews were forced to winter over on two islands, Krenitsyn on Unimak and Levashev on Unalaska. The crews of both ships met hostile native receptions and both suffered from a shortage of food and from scurvy.

Both ships returned to Kamchatka in the summer of 1769 with the missions only partly fulfilled. They had even failed to provide detailed descriptions of Unimak and Unalaska; their map of the Aleutian Islands was inaccurate; and many men were lost, including Krenitsyn, who drowned in the Kamchatka River. The only satisfactory result of this venture which had cost more than 112,000 rubles was Levashev's ethnographic descriptions of the appearance and customs of the natives of Unalaska whom he had had opportunity to observe during the winter of 1768–69.

The fourth of these government-sponsored expeditions to guard Russian interests in the North Pacific was organized in 1786–87. It was planned by the Colleges of the Admiralty, Foreign Affairs, Commerce and the Academy of Sciences. Captain Brigadier Grigorii I. Mulovskii was appointed commander. The objectives were to verify and claim all the discoveries made by the Russians from the southern Kurils to the southern tip of Alaska; to warn Spanish, British and French intruders into northern waters to stay out of Russia's sphere of interest; to establish a permanent Russian naval presence in the North Pacific to ensure the security and safety of Russian rule; to establish commercial relations with China and Japan; and to undertake further scientific investigations.

With Catherine's full support the promoters of this grand venture outfitted five three-masted ships: the *Kolmogor*, 600 tons and 32 guns; *Solovki*, 539 tons, 20 guns; *Sokol*, 450 tons, 16 guns; *Turukhtan*, 450 tons, 16 guns; and the transport vessel *Smelyi*, 14 guns. Mulovskii was given 1,700 iron and copper plates engraved in Latin and Russian proclaiming "This territory belongs to the Russian Empire." He was instructed to bury these plates secretly at various points along the shores of North America and to ignore possible Japanese, English or Spanish protests. A similar scheme was devised by Shelikhov.

The expedition was ordered to sail around Africa and to rendezvous at the Hawaiian Islands. From there two ships were to proceed to the Kurils, two to Alaska and the transport vessel to Kamchatka. On the eve of the fleet's scheduled departure, Catherine, although a firm supporter of the plan, aborted the mission because of imminent war with the Ottoman Empire and Sweden (1787–1792). These efforts were not in vain, however, for the Russians later put this logistical experience to good use in planning their first around-the-world voyage under the command of captains Ivan F. Krusenstern and Iurii F. Lisianskii (1803–1806).

The final government-sponsored expedition to the North Pacific took place (1785–1792) under the command of an English captain, Joseph Billings, who had sailed as a midshipman with Captain James Cook on his North Pacific voyage, and Captain Gavriil A. Sarychev. As with some previous expeditions, this mission too was secret and its aim manifold. The assignment was to map all the islands in the North Pacific; explore the seas between Russia's Asian possessions and North America; correct the map of the Kuril Islands, Japan and the coasts of Korea and China; lay Russia's claim to every known and all newly discovered islands; avoid conflict with foreign vessels, particularly Spanish, English and French; discover a navigable passage eastward from the Lena River to Kamchatka; and to gather geological, astronomical, botanical, linguistic and commercial information.

The Billings-Sarychev expedition had three phases. The first began in May 1787, when two vessels, *Pallas* and *Iasashna*, put to sea from the mouth of the Kolyma River in an effort to reach the North Pacific. Icebergs forced this plan to be aborted. The next phase began in September 1789 and lasted until 1791. It included three vessels: *Dobroe Namerenie*, which was wrecked before it sailed out of Okhotsk; *Slava Rossii*, commanded by Billings, which sailed to Kamchatka and from there to Unalaska, Kodiak, Chugach Bay and the Bay of St. Lawrence; and *Chernyi Orel*, under Lieutenant Robert Hall. This second phase was the most productive because under Sarychev's supervision both Russian and non-Russian expedition members surveyed large areas of the North Pacific and prepared detailed descriptions of places they visited and people encountered. The third phase lasted from the fall of 1791 until August 1792. During this period Billings handed over command of *Slava Rossii* to Sarychev in order to take an overland expedition to map Shelagskii Cape, under extremely difficult conditions.

The Billings-Sarychev Expedition, like the Bering Expedition, accomplished only part of its objectives. Its failure in others was not due to Billings' ineptitude, as some patriotic Russian and Soviet writers have suggested, nor was its success due to Sarychev's abilities. Rather, this had to do with the fact that uninformed officials in St. Petersburg once again assigned overly ambitious tasks to yet another expedition. Natural elements prevented preparation of accurate descriptions of the coast of the Arctic Ocean from the Kolyma River to Bering Strait, and of the Northwest Coast of North America. The expedition did, however, prepare a series of quite accurate maps of the North Pacific, and it also gathered valuable ethnographic and linguistic materials on the Aleuts and the peoples of northeastern Asia.

Scholarly assessment of this phase has been uneven. Patriotic Russian and Soviet scholars have overemphasized the contributions of their seafarers and of the promyshlenniks to the knowledge of geography and ethnography, while others, unfamiliar with the Russian languages and sometimes short on facts, have tried to minimize this. A number of factors have contributed to this problem: the secrecy that surrounded all Russian explorations both private and government; the unwillingness of authorities, both pre- and post-revolution, to publish all pertinent information about these expeditions; restricted access to the archival records; and the loss of many primary sources through fire or neglect. Furthermore, much was never written down, since many promyshlenniks were illiterate.

It is obvious that the Russians and the many West Europeans in Russian service were the first "Europeans" to visit the Kurils, Aleutians and the coast of Alaska. After that the ground is somewhat shaky, especially when the discussion turns to the relative contribution of the promyshlenniks to various branches of learning. Half of these men were Russian and the rest Kamchadal natives. Almost all were illiterate. They often could not know or understand where they were. Their prime objectives were to survive and procure furs. They were scarcely concerned about the accurate placement of an island on a map or studies of various native dialects or customs.

Many skippers possessed practical seamanship rather than professional training. Upon their return they provided only approximate width, length and circumference measurements of the islands visited, so it is difficult to call these finds great scientific achievements or precise contributions to knowledge. They were not. This is the reason concerned authorities in St. Petersburg were forced to dispatch government-sponsored expeditions manned by knowledgeable individuals to verify the findings of the promyshlenniks. Had the Russian government published these corrections the results of their efforts would no doubt have been given universal and deserved recognition similar to that accorded the Spanish, British and French undertakings such as the Cook, Vancouver, Malaspina and La Pérouse voyages.

SPANISH, BRITISH, FRENCH AND AMERICAN RESPONSES TO RUSSIAN ACTIVITY IN THE NORTH PACIFIC

Because they were the first Europeans to penetrate into the remote and inhospitable North Pacific region, the Russians enjoyed an absolute monopoly on that vast area for the first six decades of the eighteenth century, just as they had in Siberia in the seventeenth century. Like all monopolies, this one fell victim to time, ill-advised actions and circumstances. It would appear that the Russians helped to destroy their own monopoly. They did this by the secrecy that surrounded their activity, by their great reluctance to share their discoveries with other nations, and by their disclosure of only partial and often misleading information about their intentions and finds. These practices generated rumors and aroused suspicion and curiosity among the leading maritime powers of Europe which in the late 1760's culminated in an open challenge.

The challenge was spearheaded by Spain. This was to be expected. Spanish officials, both secular and religious, claimed the entire west coast of America as Spain's exclusive royal domain by virtue of first discovery, although no Spaniard had set foot on any area north of San Francisco before 1700. Spanish diplomats, nevertheless, followed very closely all published reports about Russian explorations by Bering and Chirikov and they also studied the subsequent writings of Gerhard F. Müller, a participant in those explorations and the greatest eighteenth century scholar of Russian conquest of Siberia and of Russian explorations in the North Pacific. To gain first-hand knowledge of Russian moves and designs, the Spanish government sent the Marques de Almodovar to Russia as a special envoy and observer in March 1761. At the end of his seven-month assignment, Almodovar prepared a report for Madrid. Based on official and unofficial information he had gathered in Russia, the report was moderate in tone and concluded that because of the inhospitable climate and great problems of navigation and logistics, Russian expansion to the North Pacific did not pose an immediate threat to Spanish interests. Almodovar noted, however, that Russian penetration into "the Spanish lake" posed worrisome threats and ominous portents.

To counter possible Russian advances toward California, the Spaniards decided to move north from Mexico. This decision was energetically pursued by José de Galvez, the newly appointed royal representative in Nueva Espana, Mexico. In 1769 Galvez dispatched five parties to Upper California—two by land and three by sea. Land reconnaissance was led by Gaspara de Portola, and resulted in the founding of such major Spanish missions and presidios as San Diego (1769), Monterey (1770) and San Francisco (1776). Naval reconnaissance was undertaken by Vincente Villa aboard the *San Carlos* and by Juan Perez aboard the *San Antonio*, who sailed to Cape Mendocino between 1769 and 1770. Later Juan Perez and Esteban José Martinez sailed aboard the *Santiago* to distant Nootka Sound in 1774–1775.

Later the Spaniards dispatched a number of other naval expeditions to the North Pacific to check on Russian activity. The most important were those led by Bruno de Heceta y Dudagoitia and Juan de la Bodega y Quadra aboard the galiot *Sonora* to the mouth of the Columbia River, Cape Trinidad and Vancouver (Quadra) Island in 1775; Bodega y Quadra aboard *La Princesa* in 1779 came to the shores of Alaska north of Cape St. Elias; Martinez, aboard the frigate *La Princesa* and Gonzalo Lopez de Haro aboard the packetboat *San Carlos* visited Chugach and Kenai bays and the islands of Kodiak, Shumagin, Umnak and Unalaska in 1788; Martinez reached Nootka Sound in 1789 aboard *La Princesa* and caused a confrontation with the British; scientific circumnavigators Admiral Alejandro Malaspina aboard the corvette *La Descubierta* with Captain José Bustamante aboard *Atrevida* reached Chugach Bay (Prince William Sound) and Yakutat Bay in 1791–1792; and a three-ship Spanish expedition under the leadership of Francisco Eliza and Salvador Fidalgo which sailed to Kenai and Chugach bays between 1790 and 1792. A sizable part of this notable Spanish record is as yet unpublished.

The next to express genuine concern about Russian activity in the North Pacific were the British. This too was natural, since Britain rose to naval supremacy in the world in the eighteenth century. Moreover, like the Spaniards, the British had a vague claim on some of the areas of the west coast of North America by virtue of Sir Francis Drake's visit in the late 1570's to the Oregon coast below Coos Bay and to northern California, which he named New Albion.

The first British effort to check on Russian activity in North Pacific waters came between 1776 and 1780 when captains James Cook, Charles Clerke and John Gore, aboard the *Resolution* and *Discovery* made a historic visit to the capes of Gregory, Foulweather, Fairweather and Suckling; to Nootka Sound (which Cook named King George's Sound); to Kodiak, Unalaska, Unimak and other islands; to Bering Strait; and to the great harbor of Petropavlovsk in Kamchatka. Curious Russian officials in those areas received Cook and his men with due courtesy and offered them generous assistance. Their superiors in St. Petersburg were subsequently annoyed, because Cook had given English names to many places the Russians believed their promyshlenniks had previously visited. Further, Cook had provided accurate locations and descriptions of all the places he had visited and of the natives he had encountered. Cook's presentation, like those of the Spaniards, sharply contrasted with some descriptions brought back by the promyshlenniks. Most of the world accepted Cook's published findings, which revealed much hitherto held secret or unevaluated.

After Cook's historic voyage, many captains flying the British flag, that of the South Seas Company, the British-owned East India Company, or one of convenience, visited Russian preserves in the North Pacific. They checked on Russian activities there but they also traded with the Russians and with various fur-hunting natives of the region.

The most important of these voyages were those under the leadership of Captain James Hanna, who made two voyages from South China to Nootka Sound between 1785–87; captains George Dixon and Nathaniel Portlock, who made a trading voyage to the coast of Northwest America, 1785–88; Captain William Peters, who sailed from Macao to Petropavlovsk in 1786, but lost his ship in a wreck off Copper Island; Captain Henry Laurie, who sailed from Bombay to Prince William Sound and other locations in 1786; captains John Meares, William Tipping and Charles W. Berkeley, who came to Nootka Sound, 1786–7; captains William Douglas, James Colnett and Robert Hudson, who sailed from South China to Northwest America, 1788–9; and Captain George Vancouver and Lieutenant William Broughton, who visited the Pacific Northwest, 1790–92 in the conclusive extension of the Cook search for a northern passage home.

Active French interest in Russian presence in the North Pacific and in Spanish and British concern about this came rather late. This was because the French were increasingly preoccupied with internal problems, especially economic problems, after signing the Treaty of Paris in 1763 which influenced their colonial struggle with Great Britain. Their failure to solve their domestic problems led to revolution in 1789. Yet in spite of the approaching crisis, the French mounted a major naval expedition, 1786–88, sailing to the North Pacific under the command of Count Jean Francois Galaup de La Pérouse. La Pérouse and his men perished on this elaborate voyage but a companion, Baron Jean Baptiste Barthelemy de Lesseps, was earlier put ashore in Kamchatka with many expedition journals and traveled overland to Paris. He subsequently published a four-volume account of that historic voyage. It should also be noted that French interest in the North Pacific was kept alive by translations of all accounts by English and Spanish voyagers to the region. The story of the publication of the La Pérouse maps and descriptions is an epic in itself.

Finally, between 1789 and 1792, the first two American expeditions, commanded by captains Robert Gray and John Kendrick in the *Columbia Rediviva* and *Lady Washington*, sailed from Boston to the North Pacific. In 1790 Gray took a rich cargo of sea otter skins from the Pacific Northwest to Canton. When he sailed in to Boston he was recognized as the first American skipper to circumnavigate the globe. In 1791 Gray returned to the North Pacific and in May 1792, sailed over the treacherous bar and into the elusive river which was later named for his sloop, the *Columbia*. A decade later Thomas Jefferson and the government of the United States launched an overland expedition to the same spot under the leadership of army officers Meriwether Lewis and William Clark (1803–1806).

It is obvious that the combined number of Spanish, British, French, and American voyages to the North Pacific in the second half of the eighteenth century fall far short of the number of Russian sailings to the region. The results, however, were more significant. Three closely intertwined factors contributed to this imbalance. The first was the matter of purpose. Almost all Russian voyages by promyshlenniks had a single purpose: to procure as many furs as possible and in the process to bring the area under Russian control. That single goal determined the Russian view of the area, the treatment of the indigenous population, disinterest in any other matters and fear of foreign intrusion into their sphere of influence. In contrast, non-Russian voyages had diverse goals. Some were sent to check on Russian activity, others to discover new lands, peoples and ocean routes, still others were dedicated to scientific pursuits, and several were basically private trading voyages, such as those of merchant adventurers like Hanna and Gray.

These diverse purposes, in turn, determined the composition of the personnel who sailed to the region. With few exceptions crew members on Russian ships were Russian and Kamchadal, with little or no formal education or intellectual curiosity. Their sole purpose was to procure furs by any means for their government, promoters and themselves. Two notable exceptions were the aforementioned government expeditions, the secret Krenitsyn-Levashev Expedition, and the Billings-Sarychev Expedition, which although more open, still carried long secret instructions. In contrast, the command personnel of all the non-Russian voyages were well-educated and often included doctors, artists, astronomers, botanists, naturalists and other scientists eager to collect new information and record their observations. These were in fact true voyages of enlightenment. The first Russian mission of genuine enlightenment that compared with these European voyages was the first circumnavigation by the British-trained Krusenstern and his second, Lisianskii, 1803–1806.

The final element that distinguishes all Russian voyages from others to the North Pacific during this period is secrecy. Regardless of whether they were sponsored by private entrepreneurs or by the government, all Russian voyages were secret and authorities released very little information about them. All the more reason for the surprise registered by British traders who encountered the Russians in unexpected corners. Information brought back by illiterate promyshlenniks was sparse and imprecise. Some of these accounts given in oral testimony to officials in Okhotsk and Kamchatka still languish in Soviet archives, never published. In contrast, most records of non-Russian voyages to the North Pacific were made public, often in several languages, shortly after the ships returned from their expeditions, except for aspects of Malaspina's accomplishments. By openly publishing these accounts, west European seafarers received credit for several discoveries that, unknown to them or to the world, had actually been made or perhaps had been made much earlier by Russian argonauts.

RUSSIAN RELATIONS WITH AND TREATMENT OF NATIVES OF THE NORTH PACIFIC IN THE EIGHTEENTH CENTURY

When the Russian promyshlenniks landed in the Kurils, the Aleutians and on the coast of Alaska in their quest for "soft gold," they found not only the prized furs but many diverse peoples as well. In the Kuril Islands they met the Ainus, in the Aleutians the various Aleut peoples, and along the coast and on the islands off Alaska they encountered the Chugach in Prince William Sound, the Koniags on Kodiak Island, the Kenais on the Kenai Peninsula and the fierce Tlingit (whom they referred to as *Kolosh*) around Yakutat Bay. The Russians identified these people by the place they inhabited: "Kurils" for Ainus and "Americans" for the inhabitants of Alaska. Frequently, however, they simply referred to them as "savages".

Regardless of where they lived, all the natives the Russians encountered in the North Pacific were technologically primitive. The Aleuts, for example, lived for the most part in earthen iurts covered with prized driftwood, since most of the islands were treeless. Their household goods were grass mats, buckets, bowls and benches formed from driftwood. Their basic tools and weapons were bows and arrows, spears, harpoons and knives made of bone. Their primary occupations were hunting for sea otters, seals and sea lions and fishing for salmon, cod, flounder and halibut. They also ate shellfish, seaweed, berries and roots. Both men and women painted or tattooed their bodies and both sexes wore bone ornaments in their ears, nostrils and lips. They wore two basic pieces of apparel: *parkas*, long shirt-like garments made of birdskins for men or sea animal pelts for women; and *kamleis*, long, waterproof outer garments made from the intestines of sea animals finely sewn with sinew, worn in the rain or during hunting at sea. Their skillful craftsmanship also produced the *baidarka*, a kayak-like craft with a light wooden frame covered with skins of sea animals sewn with sinew and used for hunting at sea or inter-island voyages.

By European estimates all North Pacific natives were primitive, not only technologically, but economically and culturally as well. They had no government system or structures similar to European models. Their most advanced political unit was the tribe, presided over by an elder referred to in Russian contemporary sources as a *toion*. Until the coming of the Russians, even he exercised little authority over his tribesmen. The Russians changed that. In return for gifts, they designated him their official spokesman and made him responsible for the collection of iasak from all adult male members of the tribe.

The state of the economy matched the simplicity of its political counterparts. The natives had few modes of production or distribution. Since food was abundant, they lived on a day-to-day basis. Aside from group singing, dancing, making parkas and baidarkas, they had other skills of which to boast. Their tools belonged to the Stone Age, but they had learned to survive in a very austere environment. They had an oral tradition to account for their genesis; had perfected skills in bone carvings, both for utility and for decoration; and their sophisticated woven baskets even today are among the finest in the world. Above all, they had superb, highly developed hunting skills. The Russians also noted that, given the opportunity, all the natives were able to master quickly "the civilized way of doing things."

Moreover, the Russians would have failed without the expert hunting skills of the Aleuts. There are no reliable figures on the numerical strength of the natives encountered by the Russians in the North Pacific in the eighteenth century. The Russians never took a thorough census of these swiftly diminishing people, and some natives, especially the Aleuts, constantly moved back and forth between islands. Furthermore, numerically strong natives such as the Tlingits, Chugach, Kenais and Koniags would not allow the Russians to count them. Most Russian estimates are vague. The "most reliable" estimate was made in 1763–64 by Andrean Tolstykh, who reported there were 200 males and females on Tanaga Island; 2,400 males on Tagalak; 60 males on Atka and 600 on Amlia.

Regardless of their numbers, these natives soon resented the Russian presence and although there were some peaceful episodes, the record of encounters between natives and Russians, 1743–1799, bristles with great violence. The prime reason was mistreatment and exploitation. Continuing their practice from Siberia, as soon as the Russians arrived at an island, they immediately seized hostages, usually the wives and children of leaders. As in Siberia hostages provided a guarantee that for the duration of the Russian stay on the island the other natives would be peaceful and would assist the Russians in procuring furs, especially sea otters, a skill in which the Aleuts excelled. Finally, the giving of hostages meant acceptance of Russian suzerainty, and the commitment to paying iasak on time.

Natives of the North Pacific had never paid tribute to anyone. They resented this imposition even though the Russians offered trinkets. They hated the new burden because in order to fulfill it the men had to leave their wives and children, who were used and abused by the Russians. Hunting sea otter to pay iasak created other basic problems for the natives, including the inability to use this time to procure food for their own needs. And this meant famine. When that happened the natives subsisted on creatures washed up by the sea. Since these were usually dead and often spoiled, death from food poisoning resulted.

Native opposition to the Russian presence expressed itself in concerted attempts to prevent Russian landings, ambushes of small Russian hunting parties, attempts to burn Russian ships, flights of entire tribes to other islands or into the interior, and deceptively posing as peaceful and loyal subjects in order to gain Russian trust and subsequently murdering the Russians as they slept. These efforts were not altogether successful. While the natives enjoyed numerical power, the Russians had technological superiority. Although they lost many men to Aleut arrows and knives as well as to hunger and scurvy, the Russians triumphed because they had firearms. Whenever they lost one ship, another was on its way. The Aleuts suffered such heavy losses in this uneven battle that by the 1780's the survivors were forced to cooperate with the Russians, and, like the Kamchadals before them, reluctantly they became dependable servants in Russia's expansion to Alaska and northern California.

It should be noted that Russian officials in St. Petersburg and in Siberia regularly ordered the promyshlenniks not to mistreat the natives. To insure correct behavior they assigned government supervisors to every vessel. These measures, however, seldom produced the desired result. Once on land, the promyshlenniks did as they pleased. They crushed all native resistance. The most notorious Russians operating in the Aleutians were Ilarion Belaev, Gavriil Pushkarev and Ivan Solovev. Their excesses were so violent that officials in Siberia formally investigated, but in the end punished no one.

Much of this violence against the Aleuts and the natives of the Kurils derived from the nature of the Russian system of expansion in the North Pacific, which differed from that used earlier in Siberia. There they built ostrogs at various strategic points to serve as permanent centers of control of a given territory, as outposts from which to plan new conquests, and as depositories of the iasak that was collected regularly by government agents. In the Kurils and the Aleutians, the Russians did not build such permanent centers. Every year they sent out ships belonging to various groups whose sole aim was to gain as much profit as possible from furs. In practice this meant that at any time on any island there might be competing groups of Russians hunting and imposing iasak and other obligations on the native population. This was bitterly resented and opposed.

This system of exploitation did not work on Kodiak Island, the Kenai Peninsula, Prince William Sound and Yakutat Bay.

There the natives were numerous, fierce and much better organized. The Russians encountered a hostile reception that continued until the mid-nineteenth century. This forced the Russians to mount formal fortress guards 24 hours a day and prevented them from making any significant advance into the Alaskan interior.

Regardless of where it occurred in the Kurils, Aleutians or along the Alaskan coast—the constant threat created an esprit de corps among the Russians that enabled them to survive and succeed. That spirit was reinforced by hardships due to the harsh climate, violent sea storms, shortages of food, fear, scurvy, long voyages and frustrated visions of profit. These elements forged unity among the Russians, even though their backgrounds were diverse. Some were peasants or petty merchants; others were outcasts or even criminals. About half were Russian, the rest Kamchadal. Evidence indicates that prior to 1780 few of the Kamchadal hunters deserted to join the Aleuts. After that time the rise of powerful companies brought about rivalry, conflict and long-term suspicion. The struggle was particularly bitter between the employees of the Lebedev-Lastochkin Company and those of the Shelikhov-Golikov Company, over control of the richer hunting grounds in Alaska.

In summation, Russian contacts with the natives of the North Pacific produced both negative and positive results. Among the former were outright murder, economic exploitation, the iasak burden, the hostage system, disease, the abuse of women, addiction to tobacco and alcohol and substantial loss of population. The positive results included introducing the natives to technology and to the use of grains, sugar, hemp, seed oil, butter, textiles, beads and iron. As early as the 1760s, some of the Aleuts were converted to Orthodox Christianity. The number of converts increased after the Russians established permanent settlements that included religious missions on Kodiak Island and in Alaska. The conversion process was slow because unlike the evangelical Protestant and Catholic missionaries who proselytized so zealously, the Orthodox clergy used a cautious approach to gain converts. Moreover, there were very few Orthodox missionaries in the North Pacific before 1800.

S cholarly interest in Russian activity in the North Pacific during the eighteenth century has been sporadic. Several factors have contributed to this neglect. High on the list is the initial secrecy which surrounded almost all the Russian undertakings. Next is the failure of Russian and Soviet authorities to publish pertinent information or to allow interested scholars to examine the source material in various archives. Some perhaps have assumed there would be a dearth of rewarding topics for research since most persons involved in the expansion were illiterate. Finally, the remoteness of the region and its inhospitable environment doubtless have been responsible for some of the neglect.

Despite all the secrecy and inadequate documentation, in the end Russian expansion produced many far-reaching results. It gained new territories for Russia, established indubitably an empire whose domains stretched over the continents of Europe, Asia and America, transformed her into a Pacific power and placed at her disposal valuable natural and human resources. This Russian expansion also aroused the curiosity and concern of major European powers and led to numerous expeditions to the region which gathered and formalized a great amount of scientific and ethnographic data. Russian expansion to North America was a profound human adventure. And like all such towering adventures, this enterprise abounded in hopes, hardships, sufferings and cruel tragedies. It produced countless heroes as well as villains. Finally, it gave rise to songs and stories for interested scholars, and created thousands of topics to research and write about.

This is not to imply that little or nothing has been published on Russian expansion to North America. Listings in bibliographies indicate this is not so. But a problem of such magnitude and importance deserves more scholarly attention than it has received thus far.

In the eighteenth century three men kept alive the interest in Russian expansion. In order of importance they were Gerhard F. Müller (1705–1783), Peter S. Pallas (1741–1811) and William Coxe (1747–1828). The first two were Germans who spent many years in Russian service, the last was an Englishman who traveled extensively in Russia.

Müller's importance is crucial. Born and educated in Germany, he came to Russia in 1725 to study and to teach. He soon mastered the language and through a stroke of luck, in March 1733, officials of the Academy of Sciences asked him to join the Second Kamchatka Expedition to describe the history of Siberian natives, their beliefs, customs, languages, social structure, economy and all other pertinent matters. Müller traveled 24,000 miles during the next ten years to carry out his assignment. During that period he met and interviewed many persons, observed a multitude of cultural situations, studied problems and collected and copied vast numbers of important documents, a number of which are translated into English for the first time in Volume I of this series, *Russia's Conquest of Siberia*. The result of his labors, preserved in archives as the Müller Portfolios, are a goldmine on the history of Siberia and its conquest by the Russians and on the Russian thrust toward Alaska.

Subsequently, in his capacity as chief archivist of Russia, Müller used this material and numerous firsthand reports from Russian explorers and officials in Siberia, especially Timofei Shmalev, to prepare his monumental work on the history of Siberia and write three major studies of Russian explorations in the North Pacific. These are: 1) "Opisanie morskikh puteshestvii po Ledovitomu i po Vostochnomu moriiu s rossiiskoi storony uchinennykh" (A description of voyages in the Arctic and Pacific oceans undertaken from the Russian side), which was serialized in 1758 in *Ezhemesiachnye sochineniia* (Monthly Publications). A German translation of this lengthy work appeared in 1758 in Müller's *Sammlung russischer Geschichte* (A Survey of Russian History), Volume III, parts 5–6; an English translation in London in 1761; and a French version in Amsterdam in 1766. 2) "Istoriia o stranakh pri Amure lezhashchikh . . . " (A history of the lands along the Amur . . .), which was also serialized in *Ezhemesiachnye sochineniia* in 1757 and translated into English in 1763 and French in 1766; and 3) "Pismo odnogo russkogo morskogo ofitsera" (Letter from a certain Russian naval officer), which was written in 1752 and published in French that same year and in English and German the following year.

In addition to these works Müller also shared a generous amount of information with Pallas, Coxe and Anton F. Büsching, editor of an informative journal, *Magazin für die neue Historia und*

Geographie (A Journal for New History and Geography), which in 1782 published a long account of Russian exploration entitled "Nachricht von den Russischen Entdeckungen zwischen Asien und Amerika" (A report about Russian discoveries between Asia and America).

After Müller the chief promoter of interest in Russian activity in the North Pacific was Peter Simon Pallas. This brilliant natural scientist, geographer and ethnographer studied in Berlin, Halle, Göttingen and Leyden, and in his lifetime was elected a member of every major scientific academy in Europe. In 1768 through the efforts of Catherine II, he became a professor of natural history in the Imperial Academy of Sciences in St. Petersburg and in that capacity, in spite of poor health, he traveled extensively in Siberia. These travels resulted in a three-volume work entitled *Reise durch Verschiedenen Provinzen des russischen Reichs* (A Journey Through Various Provinces of the Russian Empire), published in St. Petersburg 1771–76. This travel experience also enabled Pallas to realize the importance of Siberia to Russia and to Russian activity in the regions of the North Pacific. On this subject he wrote two important studies. The first, entitled "Erläuterungen Über die im Östlichen Ocean zwischen Siberien und Amerika geschehen Entdeckungen" (Clarifications of explorations undertaken in the Pacific Ocean between Siberia and America), appeared in 1781 in the influential *Nordische Beiträge zur physikalischen und geographischen Erd- und Völker Beschreibung Naturgeschichte und Oekonomie* (Northern Reports on the Physical and Geographic Descriptions of Natural History and Economy of the Earth and People), and discussed the Krenitsyn-Levashev Expedition to the Aleutian Islands. The second, published in 1790 in *Sobranie sochinenii vybrannykh iz Mesiatsoslovov na raznye gody* (A Collection of Works Selected from Monthly Reviews for Various Years), offered a chronological account of Russian voyages to the North Pacific between 1740 and 1780. Because of his great scholarly reputation and access to primary sources, Pallas' works, like Müller's, are considered primary sources themselves, although much is omitted. It should also be noted that Pallas served as a scientific consultant to the Billings-Sarychev Expedition, which named one vessel *Pallas* in his honor, and to the Mulovskii Expedition.

The third eighteenth-century author who provided information about Russian activity in Siberia and the North Pacific was

William Coxe. Born in London, Coxe, in common with a goodly number of his British contemporaries, liked to travel and write. His first major publication, which appeared in 1778, was an account of his journey to Poland, Sweden and Russia. Two years later appeared his *Account of the Russian Discoveries between Asia and America to which are Added the Conquest of Siberia, and the History of the Transactions and Commerce between Russia and China*. Between 1780 and 1803 this work appeared in four editions. It was a popular success because it was based on primary information Coxe obtained from Müller during his stay in Russia. It gave British readers entirely new information and it offered (in a 1787 supplement) a contrast between Russian discoveries and those made by Captains Cook and Clerke. For these reasons most scholars consider this work a classic.

In the nineteenth century the principal writers in this field were Vasilii N. Berkh, Aleksandr S. Polonskii, Aleksandr P. Sokolov and Hubert H. Bancroft. The first three were Russian, the fourth, American. None of these men was an academically trained historian. Each, however, developed a deep personal interest in the problem and each made a significant contribution to its understanding. They were helped enormously both in their research and their writings by two fundamental developments. The first was the publication of many pertinent documents in such multi-volume collections as: *Polnoe sobranie zakonov Rossiiskoi Imperii*, First Series (1649–1825), 44 volumes; *Akty istoricheskie*, 5 volumes; *Dopolneniia k aktam istoricheskim*, 12 volumes; *Pamiatniki sibirskoi istorii*, 2 volumes, and others. The second was the appearance of a number of journals that published articles as well as documents. These included *Syn otechestva*, *Otechestvennye zapiski*, *Severnyi arkhiv*, *Sibirskii vestnik*, *Morskoi sbornik*, *Zhurnal Ministerstva Narodnogo Prosveshcheniia*, *Chteniia v obshchestve istorii i drevnostei rossiiskikh*, *Zapiski imperatorskogo russkogo geograficheskogo obshchestva*, *Zapiski Gidrograficheskogo Departamenta*, *Russkaia starina*, *Magazin zemlevladeniia i puteshestvii* and a number of others.

The first of these nineteenth century writers was Berkh, a naval officer and a member of Lisianskii's complement on the *Neva* on the 1803–06 circumnavigation. Berkh became interested in Russian colonial enterprise during his brief stay in Alaska where he gathered information on the Russian presence there and interviewed many "old timers" and officials of the Russian American

Company. Because of poor health Berkh retired early from naval service but continued to pursue his new interest. This activity produced the following works: *Karta rossiiskikh vladenii v Severnoi Amerike* (A Map of Russian Possessions in North America) in 1812; *Pervoe morskoi puteshestvie rossiian* . . . (The First Russian Sea Voyage) in 1823; "Poslednee pismo o Billinsovoi ekspeditsii," (The Last Letter about Billings' Expedition) in *Otechestvenny zapiski*, (Fatherland Notes) No. 62 in 1820; "Snosheniia russkikh s Iaponiei ili obraztsy iaponskoi diplomatii," (Russian Relations with Japan or Patterns of Japanese Diplomacy) in *Severnyi arkhiv* (Northern Archive) No. 22 in 1826; and *Khronologicheskaia istoriia otkrytiia aleutskikh ostrovov ili podvigi rossiiskogo kupechestva* (A Chronological History of the Discovery of the Aleutian Navy Islands, or the Achievements of Russian Merchants) in 1823. Berkh also produced a study of the Russian Navy. Although he published a good deal, he was a pedantic writer. But because in his writings he utilized unpublished as well as published material, and because he incorporated information gathered from interviews and correspondence with many persons directly involved in the Russian enterprise in the North Pacific, Berkh's works, like those of his eighteenth century predecessors, have become classics.

The second nineteenth century writer to deal with Russian expansion to the North Pacific in the eighteenth century was Polonskii. He became interested in the problem during his almost 20-year stay in Kamchatka, Okhotsk, Iakutsk and Irkutsk, where, as a government official, he had access to local archives. His efforts produced six studies. Four were published in periodicals; two languish in Soviet archives. The published items deal with Gvozdev's expedition to the Bering Strait in 1732, Bering's first expedition and the Kuril Islands. The unpublished manuscripts are "Perechen puteshestvii russkikh promyshlennikov v Vostochnom Okeane s 1743 po 1800 g." (A Survey of Travels by Russian Promyshlenniks in the Pacific-Ocean from 1743–1800) and "Promyshlenniki na Aleutskikh ostrovakh (1743–1800)" (The Promyshlenniks on the Aleutian Islands, 1743 to 1800). According to A. I. Andreev, a Soviet scholar who examined them, Polonskii's manuscripts contain useful information on the life of the Aleuts, their conversion to Christianity and the activity of various Russian companies in the area. Their publication is long overdue and interested scholars eagerly await their availability.

The third writer in this period was Aleksandr P. Sokolov, described by a Soviet scholar as "an indefatigable historian of the Russian navy." Using Russian naval archives, Sokolov published four studies. Two of these deal with the second Kamchatka Expedition; one treats the Krenitsyn-Levashev Expedition; one analyzes the preparation for Mulovskii's circumnavigation. Although Sokolov wrote primarily about the government-sponsored undertakings, his works also include material on the activity of the promyshlenniks.

The fourth person in this group was Hubert H. Bancroft. A San Francisco book dealer, publisher, collector of sources and historian of North America, Bancroft gives his account of Russian activity in this period in his *History of Alaska* which comprises Volume 33 of his works. Although the work is rich in detail, it has no startling revelations, for Bancroft lacked a knowledge of the Russian language and had to base his account on the published works of Müller, Pallas, Berkh, Sokolov and others. He also relied heavily on a Russian-born assistant who was inexperienced in historical research and made certain highly inaccurate translations; indeed at times he produced wholly fictitious accounts. In spite of these shortcomings, Bancroft's *History of Alaska*, like his other works, enjoyed wide circulation and was accepted as a basic reference.

In the twentieth century scholarly interest in this aspect of Russian history has been confined to American, Canadian and Soviet scholars. In the United States and Canada, in chronological order these are Frank A. Golder, Robert J. Kerner, Raymond H. Fisher and James R. Gibson. Golder, a graduate of Bucknell and Harvard, became interested in the problem of Russian expansion to North America after his brief stay in Alaska. His subsequent research at Harvard, and in Paris, Moscow and St. Petersburg, produced the following works: *Russian Expansion on the Pacific, 1641–1850* (Cleveland, 1914); *A Guide to Materials for American History in Russian Archives* (Washington, 1917); and *Bering's Voyages: An Account of the Efforts of the Russians to Learn the Relations of Asia and America*, 2 volumes. (New York 1922–25). Possibly because he did not have full command of the Russian language nor complete access to Russian archives, Golder reached a few erroneous conclusions about the real achievements of such Russian explorers as Semen Dezhnev. These have recently been documented by Fisher. It appears, however, that Golder reached these conclusions not through an intent to minimize Russian achievements, as some Soviet scholars have suggested, but because he did not have all the records at his disposal.

Kerner's contribution to interpreting Russia's push to North America was twofold: his own scholarship, and his training of future scholars in the field. A graduate of Chicago and Harvard, with research experience in European and Russian archives, Kerner published three basic works that deal with Russian expansion to the North Pacific. These were a lengthy article entitled "Russian Expansion to America: Its Bibliographical Foundation" (1931); a two-volume *Bibliography of Northeast Asia* (1939–41); and *The Urge to the Sea* (1946). Kerner also made a great contribution by training at the University of California many future scholars of Russian history, including a few who would specialize in Russian expansion in Asia and in the North Pacific.

One of the most productive of Kerner's students was Fisher. Author of a major monograph on the role of furs in Russian expansion in Asia from 1550 to 1700, Fisher subsequently published several studies in which he corrected a number of previous misconceptions in both Russian and western literature about Russian exploration and activity in the North Pacific. These included his criticism of Golder's skepticism about Dezhnev's successful navigation of the Bering Strait in 1649–51, his questioning of Kerner's thesis about Russian motives in the Amur Basin, and above all his penetrating analysis of the intent of Bering's voyages, *Bering's Voyages: Whither and Why?*

The fourth major western scholar whose publications have stimulated interest in eighteenth century Russian activity in the North Pacific is James R. Gibson. A native of Canada but a graduate of the University of Wisconsin, Gibson has published two important monographs and numerous articles on the Russian involvement in the North Pacific: *Feeding the Russian Fur Trade* analyzes the cost of the Russian colonial enterprise; *Imperial Russia in Frontier America* treats the Russian advance to and retreat from North America. Because he has based his works on extensive archival research in Canada, the United States, the Soviet Union, Japan, Mexico and Europe, scholars have applauded Gibson's works as they did Fisher's.

Since the early 1970s these western efforts in promoting inter-

est in Russian expansion to the North Pacific have been ably sup-
plemented by several translations of basic works. These include
the eighteenth century description of Kamchatka by Stepan P.
Krasheninnikov, a young Russian member of the Second Kamchatka Expedition (translated and edited in 1972 by E. A. P.
Crownhart-Vaughan, Oregon Historical Society); and a number
of Russian and Soviet works edited by Richard A. Pierce and
published by Limestone Press in Canada.

Soviet scholarship on eighteenth century Russian expansion
to the North Pacific has been quite extensive. This is not unexpected, since the bulk of primary source material is located in
Soviet archives. It should be noted, however, that Soviet interest
in this topic began to surge only after 1940. Prior to that time,
interest barely existed. It surfaced in the early 1940s to commem-
orate the bicentennial of Bering's Second Kamchatka Expedition.
World War II muted the celebration, but the postwar period
which witnessed the emergence of the USSR as a superpower,
saw a sharp increase in the volume of Soviet publications on expansion into the North Pacific and North America.

Three outstanding Soviet scholars deserve mention. In chronological order these are: Lev S. Berg, Aleksandr I. Andreev and
Aleksei V. Efimov.

Berg, a graduate of Moscow University, was not exclusively
nor continuously interested in this perod, for he was involved in
many other research projects. During his long career he published over 600 items, of which only a few dealt directly or in-
directly with Russian explorations. These were: 1) "Izvestiia o
Beringom prolive i ego beregakh do Beringa i Kuka" (News from
the Bering Strait and Its Shores before Bering and Cook) in
Zapiski po gidrografii (Notes on Hydrography) (1919); 2) "Iz istorii
otkrytiia Aleutskikh ostrovov," (A History of the Discovery of the
Aleutian Islands) in *Zemlevladenie* (Land Ownership) vol. XXV
(1924): 3) *Otkrytie Kamchatki i Kamchatskie ekspeditsii Beringa, 1725–
1742* (The Discovery of Kamchatka and Bering's Kamchatka Expeditions), which was published in three editions (1924, 1935 and
1946); 4) *Ocherki po istorii russkikh geograficheskikh otkrytii* (A Survey
of the History of Russian Geographic Discoveries), which appeared in two editions (1946 and 1949); and 5) *Ocherk istorii russkoi
geograficheskoi nauki vplot do 1923 goda* (An Outline of the History
of Russian Geographic Science to 1923) (1929).

The second Soviet scholar was Andreev. A graduate of the University of St. Petersburg, Andreev was first interested in the early history of Muscovy, but during the early 1930's he turned his attention to the study of Siberia and Russian expansion to the Pacific. This shift resulted in a number of valuable works: 1) Müller's *Istoriia Sibiri* (2 vols.), which Andreev helped to edit in 1937, and for which he wrote two long introductory articles analyzing Müller's published works and manuscripts. 2) *Ocherki po istochnikovedeniiu Sibiri* (A Survey of Sources on Siberia), a two-volume analysis of sources on Siberian history; 3) *Russkie otkrytiia v Tikhom Okeane—Severnoi Amerike v XVII v.* (Russian Discoveries in the Pacific Ocean and in North America in the Eighteenth Century), a collection of documents that was soon translated into English; and 4) a number of articles on Bering's expeditions, the role of the Russian fleet in geographical discoveries, Russian voyages to the Arctic and Pacific oceans, the first surveyors of the Aleutian Islands and sources on the early history of the Russian American Company and its founders. Andreev's scholarship is impressive both in quantity and quality because he based his works on judicious use of sources.

Efimov was the third leading Soviet scholar in this area. He came to this field in his later years. Prior to that he pioneered Soviet studies of America and from 1957–1971 headed the American sector of the Institute of Ethnography of the Academy of Sciences of the USSR. Efimov's major publications in the field of study of this recent volume include: 1) *Iz istorii russkikh ekspeditsii na Tikhom okeane. Pervaia polovina XVIII veka* (A History of Russian Expeditions to the Pacific Ocean in the First Half of the Eighteenth Century) (Moscow, 1948): 2) *Iz istorii velikikh russkikh geograficheskikh otkrytii v Severnom Ledovitom i Tikhom okeanakh* (A History of the Great Russian Geographic Discoveries in the Arctic and Pacific Oceans) (Moscow, 1950; 3rd ed., 1971); and 3) *Atlas geograficheskikh otkrytii v Sibiri i severo-zapadnoi Amerike, XVII–XVIII vv* (Atlas of Geographic Discoveries in Siberia and Northwest America in the Seventeenth and Eighteenth Centuries) (Moscow: 1964). Efimov's work was based on archival material and received wide acclaim; some of his studies have been translated into foreign languages. For the *Atlas* Efimov received the coveted Dezhnev Prize from the Geographical Society of the USSR. Prior to his death Efimov was working on a project entitled "Atlas russkikh geograficheskikh otkrytii v severo-zapadnoi Amerike XVIII–XIX vv" (An Atlas of Russian Geographical Discoveries in Northwest America in the Eighteenth and Nineteenth Centuries). In addition to these publications, Efimov wrote a number of articles and reviews, edited one volume of documents about Russian overland explorers and polar seafarers in northeast Asia in the seventeenth century, and trained a number of Soviet students in American studies and in history and geography.

It should be remembered that in addition to these major scholars, in the second half of the twentieth century Soviet academic institutions have produced a number of other scholars, whose publications on Russian activity in the North Pacific in the eighteenth century have been well received. In alphabetical order these are Vasilii A. Divin, an expert on Russian voyages; Svetlana G. Fedorova, an eminent historian and ethnographer; Vera F. Gnucheva, who has written of the role of the Academy of Sciences in these explorations; Vadim I. Grekov, a scholar of Russian geographic exploration, 1725–1765; Roza G. Liapunova, an authority on the ethnology of the Aleuts; Dmitrii M. Lebedev, a student of the development of Russian geographical knowledge in the eighteenth century; and Boris P. Polevoi, whose interest in Northeast Asia and Northwest America has resulted in numerous studies.

EDITORIAL PRINCIPLES

In marked contrast to the documents in Volume I of this series, which posed a number of extremely taxing technical problems, including illegibility, the documents in this, Volume II, were for the most part written by reasonably or very literate persons. Our goals as translators, however, remain the same: to retain the original flavor, but ever seeking accuracy in a clear, modern English translation.

Our selection of documents is again guided by a desire to present examples which illuminate the major aspects of each situation, while holding the reports to a reasonable length. To this end we have selected the germane portions of some inordinately long documents. Four selections for which the Russian originals are simply unavailable are adapted from earlier translations, two from the eighteenth century, two from the early twentieth; these are so noted in the citation. Documents which appeared in the Russian publication *Rossiia i SShA: Stanovlenie otnoshenii 1765–1815*, may also be found in the limited edition simultaneous English language publication *The United States and Russia: The Beginning of Relations 1765–1815*, produced in Washington by the Government Printing Office; after some reflection we decided to produce our own translations for this volume for continuing uniformity of usage.

In transliterating Russian words into English we again use the Library of Congress system, slightly modified; we have omitted ligatures and terminal soft signs, but have retained certain internal soft signs: *zimov'e*. We have anglicized plurals of words which have no exact English equivalent: promyshlenniks, ostrogs. The given names of rulers have with some reluctance been anglicized: Peter, Catherine.

Dates are given in accordance with the Julian calendar which was in official use in Russia from 1700 to 1918. In the eighteenth century the calendar was eleven days behind the Gregorian calendar.

The continuing Glossary again contains obscure and arcane words and terms that are so important to the text that we have again placed the Glossary in the front of the volume. You will note the gradual change in meaning and evolution of some words and terms through the three volumes.

Wherever possible we have given the present archival location of each document so interested scholars may themselves use the original document in their research rather than a published version. However, because of the massive reorganization of the entire Soviet archival system in recent years, and because published Soviet finding guides to these often relocated archives are still far from complete, this has not always been possible. On occasion we give reference to an available Russian published source.

Archival acronyms used in this text:

AVPR: Arkhiv vneshnei politiki Rossii [Archive of Russian Foreign Policy]

GAFKE: Gosudarstvennyi arkhiv feodalno-krepostnicheskoi epokhi [State Archive of the Feudal-Serfdom Epoch]

GPBOR: Gosudarstvennaia ordena trudovogo Krasnogo Znameni Publichnaia biblioteka imeni M. E. Saltykova-Shchedrina [M. E. Saltykov-Shchedrin State Public Library, Order of the Red Banner of Labor], Otdel Rukopisei [Manuscript Division]

LOII: Leningradskoe otdelenie Instituta istorii SSSR AN SSSR [Leningrad Branch of the Institute of History of the USSR, of the Academy of Sciences of the USSR]

LOTsIA: Leningradskoe otdelenie Tsentralnogo istoricheskogo arkhiva [Leningrad Branch of the Central Historical Archive]

TsGADA: Tsentralnyi gosudarstvennyi arkhiv drevnikh ak-tov [Central State Archive of Ancient Arts]

TsGVMA: Tsentralnyi gosudarstvennyi voenno-morskoi ar-khiv [Central State Military-Naval Archive], a prerevolution-ary division of the Military-Naval section of the Leningrad Branch of the Central Historical Archive; these holdings now part of TsGAVMF.

TsGAVMF: Tsentralnyi gosudarstvennyi arkhiv voenno-morskogo flota [Central State Archive of the Navy of the USSR]

Archival abbreviations:

Ch.: *chernovik*, draft version

d.: *delo*, item or unit

f.: *fond*, basic unit group of archival records

k.: *konsept*, draft

l.: *list* (plural: ll.), folio, leaf

ob.: *oborotnaia storona*, verso

sb.: *sbornik*, a collection of materials of disparate origin, bound or fastened together

sobr.: *sobranie*, a collection of materials, usually of disparate origin, assembled but unbound.

GLOSSARY

Altyn.   A Tatar word for six; from the fourteenth to the eighteenth century it designated a Russian monetary unit equal to six *dengi* or three *kopecks*.

Arkhimandrit.   The administrative head of two or more monasteries in the Russian Orthodox Church.

Arshin.   A linear measure used in Russia from the sixteenth century on, equal to 28 inches or 71.1 centimeters. An arshin contained four *chetverts* or 16 *vershoks*. Three arshins equaled one *sazhen*.

Artel.   A cooperative work party of Russian men, organized for the purpose of hunting, fishing, harvesting or other labor.

Baidara.   A large open boat with a wooden framework, covered with cured sea-mammal hides fastened with thongs. Similar to the Eskimo *umiak*. Used by Aleutian Island natives for hunting at sea. It could hold as many as 40 persons. Also adapted for use by the Russians, sometimes with a mast, sail, and rudder.

Baidarka.   The Eskimo *kayak*; a long, narrow boat with a wooden framework covered with *lavtaks*. Differs from a baidara in that it is smaller and closed; there is a small round opening for each person; the opening has a drawstring which pulls it close around the body to prevent water from coming in. A baidarka could be made for one, two or three persons. The Russian American Company often used the three-hatch size to transport passengers or to make coastal explorations. Natives used the baidarka for hunting.

Baidarshchik.   The several meanings include skillful steersman; owner of a baidara; overseer of the construction or crew of a baidara; head of an artel; head of a small Russian American Company trading post; an elder in a small Russian American settlement.

Balagan. A Tatar word for a stable, barracks or a temporary shelter for storing goods or equipment; also a summer hut.

Bat, bata. A boat used by Tlingit natives along the Northwest Coast of America; it had a distinct keel, an elevated bow and stern, and could hold up to 40 persons.

Belaia izba. Literally, "white cabin," that is, a log or plank cabin with fenestration to admit light.

Bolshaia zemlia. "Big land." A Russian term, borrowed from the Chukchi of Northeast Asia, to describe Alaska. The Russians used to the term from 1650 to 1750.

Buer. A Dutch word for a small, one-masted cargo vessel; also, an ice boat used in the Arctic.

Chetvert. An old Russian unit of measure. In linear measurement it was equal to seven inches or one-quarter arshin; as a unit of dry measure it varied according to what was being measured from two to four *puds.*

Cossack. A word of Tatar origin (*Kazak*) which originally denoted a free frontiersman. In the period of Russian expansion to the North Pacific the term referred to a member of a garrison in a fortified *ostrog* who performed military service under the jurisdiction of Siberian officials. Cossacks also served as government agents aboard ships that explored the Aleutian Islands and Alaska.

Cossack sotnik. A Russian term for a commander of 100 cossacks.

Dan. A Slavic term meaning tribute paid by the conquered to the conqueror.

Denga. (Plural *dengi*). A Mongol and Russian term for a coin, which in the early eighteenth century was worth ½ kopeck.

Desiatnik. A Russian term for a low-ranking leader of ten cossacks, *streltsy* or other armed men.

Deti boiarskie, syny boiarskie. A term used to describe a large group of impoverished or petty nobles who often became middle-ranking military commanders and civil administrators in Russia as well as in the Russian colonies through the middle of the eighteenth century.

Diachok. A sacristan, sexton or reader in the Russian Orthodox Church.

Diak. A secretary, clerk, assistant or associate of the heads of central and regional departments of Russian administrative, financial, judicial and diplomatic institutions. In the Russian Orthodox Church, a reader and an assistant to the priest; the upper sacristan rank.

Diakon. A deacon in the Russian Orthodox Church.

Doshchanik. A flat-bottomed river boat about 150 feet long, constructed of pine and fir planks. It was used by the Russians for river and coastal transport; it could carry 30,000 to 40,000 puds (540 to 720 tons) of cargo and 40 to 50 persons.

Dvorianin, dvoriane (pl.). A Russian term for a nobleman, a member of the gentry. There were various categories of dvoriane, depending on status in military or administrative service.

Forty. A bundle of precious furs, packed and transported in groups of 40 for convenience in handling and sorting.

Golova. In modern Russian, a leader or head. In the past it referred to a civil administrative official, a military commander or an assistant or secretary to a high-ranking military or civil bureaucrat.

Gramota. A word of Greek origin which referred to a letter, deed, will, charter or any other official or private written document.

Gruz. Weight, load, cargo, freight. Also a linear measure of 3.5 feet.

Guliashchie liudi. A Muscovite term used to describe a person not assigned to any tax (*tiaglo*) category and hence, mobile. This group included runaway serfs, tramps, itinerant workers, and various misfits and unfortunates. Many were hired for work in Russia's Northeast Asia and North American possessions.

Iadritsa. Unground buckwheat; groats.

Iasak. A Mongol-Tatar term meaning tribute paid by the conquered to the conqueror. During the period covered by the present three-volume study, iasak refers to a tribute primarily paid in furs. The practice was widespread in Siberia, introduced briefly in the Aleutian Islands but officially terminated by Tsarist *ukaz* in 1768. Unofficially, however, it continued throughout the eighteenth and early nineteenth centuries in Russia's American colonies.

Ierodiakon. A priest-deacon in the Russian Orthodox Church.

Ieromonk, hieromonk. In the Russian Orthodox Church, a monk who has been ordained as a priest.

Igumen. An abbot; head of a Russian Orthodox monastery.

Ipatka. *Nyorka ferina* or pochard; a duck similar in form and color to the redhead duck.

Iukola. Dried meat or fish, especially salmon, used widely in Siberia and Alaska for winter provisions. The head and backbone were given to dogs; the rest was eaten by natives, also by Russians.

Iurt. A Turkic word for a settlement, camp or dwelling. In Siberia it referred to a dwelling dug into the earth or to a semi-excavated dwelling covered with hides. In the Aleutians and Alaska it referred to any coastal native dwelling.

Izba. In modern Russian, a term for a cottage, hut or peasant dwelling. It could also refer to any structure housing a wilderness station or post.

Kaiur. A Kamchadal word for a post or dogsled driver. In Alaska and the Aleutian Islands, a native worker for the Russian American Company, taken from among native *kalgas* [slaves].

Kalan. Aleut name for the sea otter, *Enhydra lutris.*

Kalga. Aleut, Eskimo or Tlingit captives used as slaves by the native captors, or drafted into service by the Russians.

Kamlei. The upper garment worn by natives of northeast Asia the Aleutian Islands, and coastal Alaska. A hooded waterproof garment made of sea lion throat membrane, seal gut or reindeer hide. It was worn either alone, in summer, or over a fur or feather garment in cold weather.

Kasha. A dish of cooked grain or groats; buckwheat porridge.

Kazarma. A shelter used by Russian hunting parties in the Aleutian Islands and Alaska; semi-subterranean, similar to native structures.

Kazhim. In the Aleutian Islands and coastal Alaska, a communal structure serving as a barracks for men. Often a partially excavated structure similar to but larger than a family dwelling.

Khaskak. A Koniag word for elder.

Kiprei. An edible grass; willow-herb.

Kislitsa. A large-leafed sour grass.

Kitaika. A Russian term for nankeen, a Chinese cotton fabric.

Koch. A small, flat-bottomed sailing vessel for river and coastal use. It generally had a small deck and could carry ten persons along with their equipment and provisions.

Koekchuchami. A Kamchadal word for a male native wearing

women's clothing and performing women's tasks; a male wife; transvestite. In Alaska, the term *akhnuchik* referred to a "changed sex" person.

Koen. A native dwelling in Alaska and the Aleutian Islands.

Kopeck. A small silver coin.

Kovsh. A bowl shaped like a scoop, dipper or ladle; a traditional shape often crafted in silver or gold as an official gift or reward for special service.

Kugakh, kugalch. An Aleut mask worn during festivals.

Kuiak. Alaskan native armor made of bone or hammered metal plates sewn onto a heavy cloth or hide garment.

Kukhta. A Chukchi term for small boat.

Kuklianka. A fur upper garment. Often made of reindeer hide with the fur inside. Generally had sleeves and an attached hood. In extremely cold weather two kukliankas could be worn, one with the fur inside and the other outside.

Lama. A Russian term for an Orthodox priest, a Buddhist monk in Mongolia and later in Tibet. Also a word used to refer to a large body of water such as the Sea of Okhotsk.

Landrat. A German term that came into use in eighteenth-century Russian through German officials from the Baltic region. An official in local administration in charge of matters pertaining to the interests of the nobility.

Lavtak. Cured hides from seal, walrus, and sea lion, used to cover baidaras and baidarkas. A lavtak could also be used as an emergency writing surface.

Litva. A Muscovite term used to designate prisoners of war and other foreigners sent to Siberia as punishment (Poles, Lithuanians, Ukrainians, Belorussians, Germans, and Swedes). Russian officials in Siberia utilized the superior knowledge and skills of the Litva by sending them on missions to difficult areas.

Lodka. A river boat about 30 sazhens (200 feet) long, built of pine or fir planks. It could transport 60,000 to 70,000 puds (1,080 to 1,260 tons) of cargo and 70 persons.

Lushnik, luchnik. An archer; a warrior armed with bow and arrows.

Mauta. Dried strips of seal hide about 30 sazhens long, fastened to the shaft of a harpoon.

Michman. In the Imperial Russian Navy, a midshipman. In the Soviet Navy, a warrant officer.

Mukhomor.   A mushroom of the amanita family, used by certain natives for its intoxicating and hallucinatory affects.

Nagovshki.   Strips of walrus or whale hide worn as ornaments around the wrists or ankles of natives of Russian America.

Namestnichestvo.   A large administrative unit ruled by a governor-general in Russia, Siberia, and Russia's Asian colonies.

Narta.   A sled or sledge, drawn by dogs or reindeer, used to transport cargo, personal belongings and at times, a passenger.

Oblast.   A Russian term for a province, region or administrative district.

Ostrog.   A Russian term with several meanings; fort, fortification, blockhouse, settlement, town.

Ostrozhek.   A small ostrog; blockhouse.

Packetboat.   A three-masted sailing vessel.

Parka.   The upper garment worn by natives of Russian America and Eastern Siberia. Made of birdskin or the pelt of a furbearing animal, worn with the fur on the outside. Especially favored were the pelts of marmot, ground squirrel, seal, sea otter, and newborn reindeer. A similar garment, to be worn in warm or rainy weather, was made of cured gut or fish skin.

Pech.   A brick oven used for heating and cooking in Russian cabins.

Peredovshchik.   A foreman, experienced seaman or pilot of a vessel engaged in the fur trade. Also referred to an experienced guide for hunters and trappers. Within the Russian American Company the term was used for the head of any one of the departments of Russian America.

Piatidesiatnik.   A leader of 50 men, primarily military.

Pirogi.   Tarts or turnovers; small pastries, generally with a hearty filling of meat.

Poddiachi.   A low-ranking clerk.

Pominiki.   A modern Russian term for a funeral repast. In eighteenth century usage it referred to a "gift," usually of furs, exacted by Russians from conquered natives in Siberia and in early explorations in the North Pacific. Also, a bribe from natives to Russian hunters or officials.

Ponomar.   In the Russian Orthodox Church, a sexton, sacristan or lay caretaker.

Prichetnik. In the Russian Orthodox Church, junior deacon; a minor member of the clergy.

Prikashchik. A low-ranking official or agent of the *prikaz*; a town or village administrator; a steward; manager of an estate; a merchant's agent. In Alaska, it also referred to a special agent employed by the Russian American Company. A supercargo.

Prikaz. See *Sibirskii Prikaz.*

Promyshlennik. In Siberia and Russian America, a hunter of fur-bearing animals, fish or birds. In Russian America the term was also used to identify Russians hired as fur trade workers by the Russian American Company. During the period of Russian expansion into the North Pacific, it also referred to an individual Russian hunter, trader or trapper who worked for himself, in a group, or for a wealthy merchant, or government officials on assignments such as exploration, conquest and pacification of natives.

Pud. A Russian unit of weight equal to 36 pounds or 16.38 kilograms.

Purga. A Siberian blizzard; a blinding snowstorm with high winds and intense cold.

Sarana. The martagon or Kamchatka lily (*Fritillaria kamchatcensis*), the root of which was widely used by natives of Siberia and Russian America.

Sazhen. A unit of linear measure equal to seven feet or 2.134 meters.

Sekach. A half-grown male fur seal or sea lion, under five years of age.

Shaitan. A word of Tatar origin used to refer to an idol, statue, devil, demon or Satan.

Shar. A globe or ball. A brick of tea or tobacco. Brick tea was a solid mass of the leaves and stalks from the tea crop, wetted, mixed with bullock's blood, pressed, and dried into a brick. To use, a small amount was chopped off, pounded with stones, mixed with water and the possible addition of sour cream, salt and millet; the concoction was then boiled for half an hour.

Shitik. Literally, a "sewed" seagoing vessel, whose planking was fastened together with twisted willow and fir withes.

Shif. The German *schiff*; a ship, boat or vessel.

Shmaka; *shmiak*; *shniak*.   A fishing boat 4 to 5 sazhens long and 1 sazhen wide.

Shuba.   A fur greatcoat or cloak worn in Siberia or Russian America.

Sibirskii Prikaz.   A department of central Russian government in charge of administration of Siberia. Headed by a noble assisted by diaks and prikashchiks:

Slanets.   Ground cedar or stone pine, a creeping, ground-hugging plant with small edible nuts eaten to prevent and cure scurvy. From stlat, to creep.

Sloboda.   A term used to designate a settlement of low-ranking servitors in Russia, or petty merchants and artisans, or state peasants living on government, church or private lands, who were exempt for a specified number of years, or permanently, from certain taxes and obligations.

Sluzhiaschie Liudi.   Literally, "serving people." We have translated this throughout as "servitor." A low-ranking Russian government employee of the Russian American Company might also be referred to by this term.

Stolnik.   A high-ranking official in Imperial service, with social standing, often entrusted with military, civil and diplomatic assignments. Originally an important boiar or noble who had the right to be present at the table (*stol*) of the Tsar.

Syny boiarskie.   See *deti boiarskie*.

Terpuk.   Rock cod.

Tiulen.   A (marine) seal.

Tiun.   An agent for a nobleman or high church official, assigned to economic, administrative or judicial duties. Also a measure of dry goods.

Toion.   A Iakut term for a native elder, widely used in Siberia. In Russian America refers to the elder of a native settlement, and later to native named as a prikashchik by the Russian American Company.

Tolkusha.   A favorite food of the native peoples of Siberia and Russian America. Dried meat or fish mixed with fat or oil, roots and berries. Often made with the mashed blubber of seals, whales or sea lions.

Toporka.   *Alca arctica*, a member of the auk family.

Tosny.   See *Toion*; a term used for a Koniag toion.

Tselovalnik.   Literally one who kisses. An elected or appointed official in Russia who kissed the cross or the Bible upon taking office. In Russian America they often assisted iasak collectors in the early period, and later assisted administrators.

Uezd.   A Russian term for a district administrative unit that included not only a settlement but the surrounding rural area; a subdivision of a diocese.

Ukaz.   A Russian term for a decree, edict or order issued by the Tsar.

Ulozhenie.   The Code of Laws of 1649.

Ulus.   A Mongol term meaning a settlement, an area inhabited by a native tribe.

Uril.   A violet-green cormorant.

Vedro.   A bucket or pail; 21 pints.

Vershok.   A Russian unit of linear measure equal to 1.75 inches.

Versta.   A verst, a Russian unit of linear measure equal to 3500 feet or 1.06 kilometers.

Voevoda.   An old Slavic term for a military commander. A Tsar-appointed administrator holding military, civil and judicial powers over a region.

Volost.   A rural administrative unit.

Zaimka.   An illegally cleared place in the wilderness used for hunting or agriculture.

Zakazchik.   An overseer.

Zemleprokhodtsy.   Literally "land-crossers," "land penetrators." A term used by Russians to refer to overland explorers in Siberia and Alaska.

Zhupan.   An Aleut male who wore women's clothing and performed the tasks of a wife; a transvestite. Also, a homespun caftan or warm sheepskin coat.

Zimov'e.   A Russian term for a small winter outpost in a newly conquered region.

Zolotnik.   A Russian measure of weight equal to 1/96 of a pound.

Zubatye.   A Russian word for native peoples of the North Pacific who wore ivory or bone teeth or tooth-shaped ornaments in holes pierced in their lips or near their mouths; "Tooth People."

120° 140° 160° 180°

ARCTIC OCEAN

Lena R.

Zhigansk

SIBERIA

Iakutsk

Kolyma R.

CHUKOTS

Aldan R.
Urak R.
Iuodoma R. Iudoma Portage
Maia R.
Okhota R.
Ulia R.
Uda R.

Okhotsk

Anadyr R. An

Shantarskie
Is.

*Shelkhov
Gulf*

Gulf of Penzhina

KAMCHATKA PENINSULA

Oliutora R.

Oliutorsk
Gulf

Cape
Oliutorskii

Amur R.

SEA OF
OKHOTSK

Karaginskii
Is.

Kamchatka R.

Nizhnekamchatsk

BERING IS.

Mednyi Is.

Sakhalin

Lower Kamchatka

Kamchatka Bay

Bolsheretsk

Petropavlovsk

Commander Is.

Avacha Bay

Atru Is.

NEAR IS.

Cape Lopatka

Kisk

Hokkaido
(Japan)

KURIL IS.

Russian Exploration
of Siberia and America
in the 18th Century

RUSSIAN AMERICA
(Alaska)

New Archangel
(Sitka)

Kotzebue
Sound

East
Cape

DIOMEDE IS.

Bering Strait

Yukon R.

Cape Prince
of Wales

Iakutat Bay

St. Elias
(Kayak) Is.

Norton Sound

Cape Chukotskii

Cross

Bay   St. Lawrence Is.

Pavlovsk Har.

St. Matthew Is.

Bristol Bay

PRIBILOV IS.

St. Paul Is.

St. George Is.

Shumagin Is.

Unimak Is.

RING SEA

Umnak Is.

ISLANDS

FOX IS.

UTIAN

ANDREANOV IS.

PACIFIC OCEAN

160°   140°   120°

RUSSIAN PENETRATION OF THE NORTH PACIFIC OCEAN

1

AN ACCOUNT BY THE COSSACK PIATIDESIATNIK, VLADIMIR ATLASOV, CONCERNING HIS EXPEDITION TO KAMCHATKA IN 1697

On February 10, 1701, the Iakutsk cossack *piatidesiatnik* [leader of 50] Vladimir Atlasov came to the Sibirskii Prikaz and made the following report.

Vladimir said that late in August of the year 203 [1697] he left Iakutsk and traveled to the Anadyrsk *zimov'e* [winter outpost] to collect the Sovereign's *iasak* [tribute in furs]. With him were thirteen Iakutsk servitors. From Iakutsk he traveled in boats on the Lena River, then took horsedrawn carts and made his way through forests and meadows to the Aldan River which took three days, making about 30 *versts* [1 verst = approximately 1 kilometer] per day.

He and his men crossed the Aldan in boats, then hired horses and crossed the river a day's journey above its mouth, across from the Tokulan River. The Aldan is about twice the size of the Moscow River. Opposite the Tokulan they went up along the right bank [looking upriver] by horseback, through marshes and rocky places, for eleven days to the headwaters of the river.

Winter caught them at the mouth of the Tokulan, which is smaller than the Moscow River. After crossing the Tokulan they came out onto the upper reaches of the Iana River across the mountain range after one day. Then for two weeks they proceeded down the Iana on horseback until they came to the Verkhoiansk zimov'e.

They hired new horses at the Verkhoiansk zimov'e and went down the Iana, which is wider than the Moscow, and then crossed over to the Tastak. The Tastak is both smaller and shallower than the Moscow River. From the Tastak they proceeded to the small Galiandina River, which falls into the Indigirka River below Indigirsk *ostrog* [fort]. They proceeded along the Galiandina to Indigirsk ostrog on horseback. The entire journey from Iakutsk to the Indigirsk ostrog took between six and seven weeks.

They then hired reindeer and traveled from the Indigirsk ostrog down the Indigirka River for five or six days until they reached the Uiandinsk zimov'e. The Uiandina River falls into the

3

left bank of the Indigirka. From there they traveled to a small place down the Indigirka where they crossed the mountains to reach the Alazeisk zimov'e, which took eight or ten days. From there they again traveled with reindeer across the mountains to the Kolyma River, to the Iarmonga settlement, which took two days. From Iarmonga they proceeded down the Kolyma for ten days with sleds to the lower Kolymsk zimov'e, which is near the mouth of the Kolyma River.

From the Kolymsk zimov'e they went up the Aniui River and across the mountains to the Iablonnaia River, then down that river to the Anadyr and down the Anadyr to Anadyrsk ostrog, a journey of four weeks. In spring when travel is easier it could be done in three weeks. The servitors hire horse and reindeer transport from the iasak-paying natives.

Between the Kolyma and Anadyr rivers there is an impassable cape called Neobkhodimoi Nos which juts out into the sea. On its left side there is ice in the sea in summer, and in winter the sea is completely icebound. On the other side of this cape there is ice in spring but not in summer. Vladimir did not go to Neobkhodimoi Nos. The Chukchi natives who live on the cape and at the mouth of the Anadyr River said that there is an island opposite the cape and in winter when the sea is frozen other natives who speak their same language come to them from that island and bring inferior pelts of a sable which is similar to a polecat. Vladimir saw three specimens of this sable. The tail is about ¼ *arshin* [1 arshin = 28 inches] long and has black and red stripes.

In the Anadyrsk zimov'e Vladimir gathered some 60 servitors and *promyshlenniks* [hunters] and arranged with them where they were to go. This has been set down in Vladimir's report which was sent from Iakutsk, and also in his petition which has likewise been sent from Iakutsk with his signature.

During his travels to and from the land of the Kamchadals his men lived on reindeer and fish which they procured from the natives. They also caught fish themselves, using nets which they had brought with them from Anadyrsk zimov'e.

The fish in the rivers in Kamchatka are ocean fish. One variety is similar to salmon, red in summer, but much larger than salmon. The natives call it *ovechina*. There are many other fish, seven varieties in fact, which are not similar to any fish in Russia. They come into the rivers from the sea in great numbers, but they do not return to the sea. They die in the backwaters of the rivers. Because of the fish there are animals such as sable, fox and river otter along those rivers.

In Kamchatka Vladimir and his men traveled by reindeer in both summer and winter. In winter they harnessed the reindeer to sleds, and in summer they used wooden saddles and rode the reindeer.

Winter in Kamchatka is warmer than in Moscow. There is not much snow there, and even less in the area where the Kuril natives live. In Kamchatka the winter sun shines almost twice as long each day as in Iakutsk. In summer in the land of the Kurils the sun is directly overhead and one's body does not cast a shadow.

In the land of the Kurils there are many ducks and gulls along the seashore in winter, and since the marshes do not freeze over in winter there are many swans. The birds fly away in summer. Only a few remain. The sun is very hot and there is a good deal of rain, thunder and lightning. Vladimir believes that this land extends quite far to the south.

In Kamchatka and in the land of the Kurils there are the red bilberry, birds' cherry and honeysuckle, which are smaller than raisins but sweeter. There is a fruit which grows about a *chetvert* [¼ arshin; 7 inches] above the grass. It is a little smaller than a hen's egg, is green when ripe, tastes like a raspberry and has small seeds like a raspberry. But he did not see any fruit on trees.

There is a grass which the natives call *agatatka*; it grows about knee-high and is withy. The natives pick the grass, peel it, braid the interior, bind it up with bark fiber and dry it in the sun. When it is dry it turns white and can be eaten. It has a sweet taste and when it is ground it is white and sweet like sugar.

One of the trees that grow there is a small cedar, a little larger than a juniper but without nuts. Kamchatka has a great many birch, larch and fir trees. On the side of the Sea of Okhotsk birch and aspen grow along the river banks.

The beardless Koriaks live along the Sea of Okhotsk. Their skin is light in color, they are of medium height and they have their own language. They have no religion but they do have shamans who cast spells when needed by beating drums and shouting. They wear clothing and footwear of reindeer hide; the soles of the boots are made of sealskin. Their *iurts* [camp or dwelling] are made of reindeer hide and deerskin.

5

A timely chart by Arrowsmith (London, January, 1802) reveals the general boundaries of land and sea exploration and exploitation areas contained in Volume II. Sauer, *Billings' Expedition to Russia*. (OHS neg. 80334)

A CHART of the STRAIT between ASIA & AMERICA with the Coast of the TSCHUTSKI, laid down from ASTRONOMICAL OBSERVATIONS, made in the Icy Sea During the Years 1786 &c. to 1794. Drawn by A. Arrowsmith

NORTH AMERICA

SEA of ANADYR

BRISTOL BAY

ISLANDS

Beyond the Koriaks live natives called the Oliutors who have a language quite similar to that of the Koriaks. Their iurts are excavated into the earth and resemble the iurts of the Ostiaks.

Beyond the Oliutors live the Kamchadals, along the rivers. They are not tall; they have moderate beards and their faces resemble those of the Zyrian people. They wear garments made of sable, fox and reindeer pelts, trimmed with dog fur. They live in earthen iurts in winter and in summer inhabit iurts built on posts about three *sazhens* [1 sazhen = 7 feet] above the ground. These are built of planks covered with fir bark. They use ladders to climb into these iurts. The iurts are close together so that in one place there may be anywhere from 100, 200, 300 or even 400 iurts.

These people live on fish and animal meat. They eat fish either raw or frozen. In winter they lay up a supply of raw fish by digging a pit into which they put the fish and cover it with dirt. When the fish is decayed they remove it into a trough where they cover it with water and add hot rocks to heat the water. They then mix the fish with the water and consume it. Fish prepared this way has such a horrible stench that no Russian can endure it.

The Kamchadals make wooden utensils and earthen pottery and they have some dishes made of clay decorated with pigments. They say these latter come to them from an island but they do not know under whose jurisdiction this island is. They have no religion except for shamanism; the shamans differ from other natives by way of wearing their hair long.

The reindeer[-herding] Koriaks live in the mountains of Kamchatka. Whenever the Russians have an opportunity to talk with these Kamchadals they use prisoners as interpreters, for all conversation is carried on in the Koriak tongue. Vladimir cannot speak any Koriak or Kamchadal.

The Kuril natives live beyond the Kamchadals. They are darker in appearance than the Kamchadals and are less heavily bearded. The land of the Kurils is warmer than Kamchatka. The people wear clothing similar to the Kamchadals', except that it is of poorer quality. They do have sables, but they are inferior because the climate is warmer. There are large sea otters and many red fox. No one knows what people live beyond these Kuril natives, nor how far that land extends.

A week's journey up the Kamchatka River from its mouth there is a mountain which looks like a loaf of bread, being quite big and high. Another one near it resembles a haystack and is also very high. It emits smoke, sparks and flames both day and night. The Kamchadals say that halfway up the mountain there is such terrible noise and thunder no one can endure it. People who go more than halfway up the mountain never return and no one knows what happens to them.

The Kliuchevaia River flows from that mountain. The water is green, and if you toss a *kopeck* [small silver coin] into it, you can still see it at a depth of three sazhens.

No one wields power over these natives. They honor and esteem the persons in any given tribe who are the wealthiest. Tribes war and battle against one another. In summer all the men go about naked. In battle they are sometimes very bold but at other times inept and too quick. To the present time no one has managed to collect tribute from them.

These natives may have anywhere from one to four wives. They have no livestock except for dogs which are larger and shaggier than ours, with fur about 1/4 arshin long. They trap sables along rivers where there are many fish, and also shoot other sables in trees, using arrows.

These native tribes war against one another. They are very much afraid of firearms and call the Russians "fire people." They only fight the Russians when they encounter them. They cannot make a stand against firearms and so they run off.

In winter the Kamchadals go to battle on skis, while the reindeer Koriaks use dogsleds, one man driving and another using a bow and arrow. In summer some go into battle on foot and naked, but others wear clothing. Their favorite trade goods are glass beads, lapis beads and knives. For these, one can obtain from them such pelts as sable, fox, sea otter and river otter.

In winter the sea near the Oliutor people has icebergs but does not entirely freeze over. It is not known whether there are icebergs in the sea off the coast of Kamchatka. There is no ice in that sea in summer.

Vladimir sent a cossack along the Kamchatka River to the sea to learn about the natives. The cossack reported that he had seen some 160 fortified settlements belonging to Kamchadal natives along that river, between the Elovka River and the sea. In one winter settlement and in two others, there were between 150 and 200 natives living. The summer iurts are built on posts and each man has his own iurt. Before the Russians came these settlements were smaller, but since then the natives have begun to build larger settlements for security. They fight from these fortified settlements by hurling rocks with slings and by throwing stones using their hands. They also fight with sharp spears and staves. The Russians advance on these native settlements, protected by shields, and set fire to them. Then they take a stand opposite the entrance where the natives run out, and kill many of their native adversaries at those gates.

Where these fortified settlements or *ostrozheks* [small ostrog or blockhouse] are made of earth, the Russians advance and destroy the earthen walls with their spears, and then use firearms to prevent the natives from fleeing:

On the opposite side of the land of the Kamchadals there is no ice in the sea in winter except along the shore from the Penzhina River to the Kygyl River, where there is a small amount; but beyond the Kygyl there is no ice at all. One can go from the Kygyl River to its mouth in three or four days by making a quick march over the mountains to the Kamchatka River. There are many bears and wolves along the seacoast.

The lucky few who survived clawing by the huge Kamchatka bears were called "the flayed ones." Private collection.

10

Opposite the first of the Kuril Islands Vladimir sighted what appeared to be islands in the sea. The natives told him that these are islands and that there are people living there in towns made of stone, but the natives did not know who those people are. From these islands the Kuril natives receive costly plates and dishes, cotton garments, cotton textiles in plaids and bright colors, *kitaika* [nankeen] fabric and kaftans. The Kurils said the dishes and garments are given to them as gifts and they do not have to pay anything for them. But how the people from the islands come to these Kuril people, the natives do not know.

The natives also said that on the east side of Kamchatka above the Kamchatka and Kalansk Beaver rivers, boats come every year. The people in the boats take seal blubber from the Kamchadals, but it is not known what they trade for the blubber.

There are many great whales, seals and *kalan* [sea otters] in the sea. The kalany come into shore during high water and when the water recedes they are left up on the land where the natives kill them with spears. The natives also club them to death by striking them on the nose. The kalany cannot run because they have such short legs. The coast is wooded and is firm land. Vladimir does not know whether the Amur River is far from there.

The Penzhina natives use *baidaras* [hide-covered boats] as crafts for sea voyages. The baidaras are made of seal hide; they are about six sazhens long and one and one-half wide. There are compartments made of wood in the middle. In those baidaras 30 to 40 men can put out to sea to hunt seals for their fur. Vladimir does not know how far out to sea the baidaras go. The Kamchadals have boats which will hold 10 to 20 men, but he did not see any other vessels. He did not observe any vessels while he was with the Kuril people because it was wintertime.

In the land of the Kamchadals and the Kurils it is possible to raise grain because these places have a warm climate and the soil is black and friable; however there are no draft animals to use to cultivate the soil. The natives do not understand anything about cultivation.

Vladimir does not know whether there is silver or any other ore because he is not knowledgeable about ores.

He does not know what language is spoken by the captive who was shipwrecked. His appearance suggests that he is Greek. He is lean and has a small moustache and dark hair. When he saw an icon which the Russians had, he wept a great deal and said that such icons are also found in the land where he came from. This prisoner spoke a little Russian because he had lived with Vladimir for two years. Sometimes he communicated through an interpreter who used the Koriak language, because before he met Vladimir he had spent two years with natives. He said that he was Indian and that his land has much gold and rich palaces and that the Indian tsar has silver and gilded palaces.

From the Kuril natives Vladimir took a silver kopeck which weighed nearly one *zolotnik* [1/96 pound]; the prisoner said this was an Indian kopeck. He also said that his countrymen do not wear sables or any other furs; they wear clothing made of fabrics such as brocade and cotton.

The captive traveled with Vladimir from the Anadyrsk zimov'e on skis for six days. Then his feet began to swell and he fell ill of scurvy and turned back to Anadyrsk zimov'e. When he recovers he will come with the Russians to Iakutsk. This captive is very energetic and intelligent.

Vladimir also took a Kamchadal prince to Moscow with him to provide detailed information about that land. That native spoke Russian, but he died of smallpox in Kaigorodst *uezd* [settlement].

None of the Siberian natives are at all civilized. They are poor and far from clean.

See: N. N. Ogloblin, "Dve 'skaski' Vl. Atlasova ob otkrytii Kamchatki" in *Chteniia v obshchestve istorii i drevnostei rossiiskikh* (Moscow: 1891), Vol. 158, Bk. III, 1–18.

2

INSTRUCTIONS FROM TSAR PETER ALEKSEEVICH (THE GREAT) TO THE
VOEVODA OF ENISEISK, BOGDAN DANILOVICH GLEBOV, PROHIBITING
MERCHANTS AND ALL OTHER PERSONS FROM TRAVELING TO OR PRI-
VATELY TRADING WITH CHINA

From the Great Sovereign Tsar and Grand Prince Peter Alekseevich, Autocrat of all Great and Little and White Russia, to
Our *stolnik* [high-ranking government official] and *voevoda* [mili-
tary governor] in Eniseisk in Siberia, Bogdan Danilovich Glebov,
and to the *poddiachii* [clerk], Ivan Borisov.

We, the Great Sovereign, became aware in the year 1699 that
merchants and persons of other ranks were going from Siberian
towns into the Chinese Empire without Our Great Sovereign's
ukaz [order] and without permission from the Sibirskii Prikaz.
Many went there and thus impinged upon [the government monopoly on] the China trade and created much trouble. In that
year of 1699 Our Great Sovereign's instructions to prohibit this
travel were sent out to all Siberian towns.

Now we, the Great Sovereign, forbid anyone to be sent to
China on any of Our business, the Great Sovereign; neither Eniseisk merchants, promyshlenniks nor persons of other ranks are
to go there with any trading goods. We forbid such persons to be
issued transit papers. This, Our Great Sovereign's *gramota* [written
instructions] shall be recorded in the Prikaz Office in Eniseisk and
henceforth shall be made known to Our other voevodas and Prikaz officials. And in accordance with this, Our Great Sovereign's
ukaz, the Prikaz officials shall notify all ostrogs and *slobodas* [tax-
exempt settlements] and *zaimkas* [clearings] and zimov'es so that
from now, after Our Great Sovereign's ukaz, no one carrying trade
goods, or wishing for any personal reasons to go there, will be
allowed to travel there without Our Great Sovereign's special personal authorization.

Anyone who [disobeys this order and] goes to China with
trade goods shall be condemned to death without mercy.

When you receive this, Our Great Sovereign's gramota, you
will act in accordance with this, Our Great Sovereign's decree,
and do everything precisely as it is written here, without the

slightest deviation from these, Our Great Sovereign's instructions, as detailed above.

However if some person is sent to China on business of Ours, the Great Sovereign, and does not have Our Great Sovereign's ukaz, yet goes on important matters, then such measures will not apply to him.

The Nerchinsk bazaar was a famous commercial site for Russian and Chinese traders, imposing for its volume of trade, unpredictable as it was. It is now remembered for the Treaty of Nerchinsk in 1689, which was the first step toward limiting Russian expansion into China. In the early 18th century commercial travel to China was prohibited to private merchants. Private collection.

We, the Great Sovereign, are to be informed as quickly as possible of anything that is to be sent to China. And a copy of this written report shall be sent to the Sibirskii Prikaz to Prince Matvei Petrovich Gagarin and his associates.

See: A. I. Timofeev, ed. *Pamiatniki sibirskoi istorii XVIII veka.* (St. Petersburg: 1882–85), I, 278–279.

3

A REPORT FROM PETR CHIRIKOV, PRIKASHCHIK OF THE KAMCHATKA
OSTROGS, TO THE VOEVODAS OF IAKUTSK, CONCERNING AN ATTACK
BY OLIUTOR NATIVES.

Petr Chirikov humbly reports to Iurii Fedorovich, Mikhail
Iurevich and their comrades, stolniks and voevodas of the
Great Sovereign Tsar and Grand Prince Peter Alekseevich, Auto-
crat of all Great, Little and White Russia.

On July 20, 1709 I was on my way from one settlement
to another. When I crossed the Karaga River a vast number of
Oliutor bandits, protected by shields, attacked us with bows and
arrows. They fell on us during daylight and seized the cash box
which contained 200 rubles. It was so heavy it had been transferred from the saddlebag of the reindeer to another bag. The
Oliutors killed the *prikashchik* [agent], who was the *syny boiarskii*
[noble] Ivan Paniutin. He had been sent from Iakutsk to the Kamchadal zimov'e. The natives also killed other servitors, ten men in
all, including Ivan Bryzgalov and Ivan Otsyforov. Many others
were mortally wounded. They seized gunpowder and shot and
tradegoods made of copper and tin which a number of cossacks
were taking to Kamchatka. Because of the subsequent scarcity of
powder and shot and because the natives had stolen the dried
meat and other provisions which belonged to the servitors and
me, we had to live without food or clothing in the tundra. When
they attacked us, the natives said, "We will not let you go to Kamchatka by land or by sea. You will never get to Kamchatka."

Now these bandits have forced us to live under siege. Every
night they come to observe our outposts. The powder which Ivan
Paniutin and I brought is unusable in our muskets because it is
compacted. In the future I will report to Iakutsk how much powder and lead and taxes for the state Treasury we are able to collect
in the tundra, if God permits us to reach Kamchatka alive.

We have not heard any news about the Kamchadal ostrog and
the servitors there. On July 22 [1709] a great multitude of these
same Oliutors gathered and came up to our encampment, ready
to do battle. The servitors and I prayed to Christ our Lord for
mercy, and went out from camp and battled the natives. With

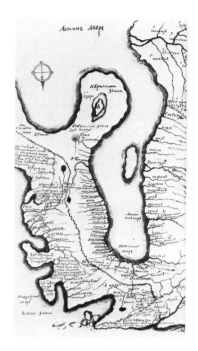

These crude maps of Kamchatka—a 1699 detail with north facing down (left) and a conventionally drawn map with north facing up (right)—are included in A. V. Yefimov's classic *Atlas of Geographical Discoveries in Siberia and America*. They reveal the limited understanding of the 17th and early 18th century fur gatherers and the importance of river systems as avenues of travel. (OHS neg. 80259 and 80256)

God's mercy and the Sovereign's luck we repulsed the Oliutors. We killed two and wounded many and captured five of their baidaras.

At the present time I, Petr, and the servitors, God permitting, plan to take the baidaras and go to our assigned destination by sea. In the future, servitors from Iakutsk should not try to go to the Kamchatka ostrogs unless they are accompanied by guides from Anadyrsk. The natives from the Anadyrsk region are familiar with local conditions. They know the methods of fighting and which places should be avoided as well as which places can safely be used as resting stops.

See: A. I. Timofeev, ed. *Pamiatniki sibirskoi istorii XVIII veka* (St. Petersburg: 1882–85), I, 411.

4

INSTRUCTIONS FROM TSAR PETER ALEKSEEVICH TO THE COSSACK DE-
SIATNIK VASILII SEVASTIANOV CONCERNING THE COLLECTION OF
IASEK IN KAMCHATKA

On September 9, 1710, in accordance with the ukaz of the
Great Sovereign Tsar and Grand Prince Peter Alekseevich,
Autocrat of all Great, Little and White Russia, the stolnik and
voevoda Dorofei Afansevich Traurnikht, under the signature of
the poddiachii Ivan Tatarinov, ordered the Iakutsk cossack *desiatnik* [leader of ten] Vasilii Sevastianov to select men from among
the Iakutsk servitors; with these newly chosen men, whose names
are appended to this instruction, he was to proceed on the service
of the Great Sovereign. They were assigned to the newly constructed ostrogs on the upper and lower parts of the Bolshaia
River in Kamchatka where they were to collect iasak and *pominki*
[gifts of fur] for the Great Sovereign's Treasury in accordance with
the updated iasak collection record books.

A previous gramota of the Great Sovereign dated 1702 and
issued from the Sibirskii Prikaz to Iakutsk, under the signature of
the *diak* [secretary] Afonasii Garasimov, had conveyed orders to
send a prikashchik to the Kamchatka ostrog. He was to take volunteers from Iakutsk with him as well as single cossacks, young
cossacks and promyshlenniks who were reliable and experienced
in military matters, some 100 men in all. Foot cossacks were to
receive a recompense of cash and rations of food from the Great
Sovereign for a period of two years, and one musket each. This
prikashchik was to urge all hostile natives encountered en route to
submit anew to the mighty hand of the Great Sovereign. He was
to do everything possible to persuade them, and he was to bring
in a substantial number to pay iasak. Any servitors who went to
the Kamchatka River and were in any way disobedient, or who
gambled or engaged in unlawful activity were to be apprehended
by their leaders and punished, the severity of the sentence to depend on the offense. Some were to be knouted and whipped, but
any who were sentenced to death were not to be sent to the Great
Sovereign in Moscow because of the great distance; rather, the
death penalty was to be carried out in Iakutsk.

Until an official courier was sent out from Moscow, the pri-kashchik was to use every possible means to establish a significant trade between the Russian and Japanese empires, similar to that between the Chinese and the Russians. The Great Sovereign's trade goods were to be sent out from Moscow to help carry out that aim, in order to create a large profit for the Great Sovereign's Treasury from those newly developed trade relations. The prika-shchik was to ascertain what precious goods were available in Japan, and which Russian goods were in demand there and whether the Japanese would commence trade with the Russians. The prikashchik was also to determine what kind of weaponry the Japanese had, what battle formations they used, how well they performed in battle, and what route might be used to reach them.

[On the basis of these earlier orders] the prikashchik was to ascertain all of this personally and send a detailed written report to Iakutsk immediately upon reaching the Kamchatka ostrog. From Iakutsk the officials were to report to the Great Sovereign in Moscow via the Sibirskii Prikaz.

[The 1710 instructions to Vasilii Sevastianov read] You, Vasilii, when you reach the Kamchatka ostrogs, are to take command of the above mentioned ostrogs, servitors and hostages from the pre-vious prikashchiks, the piatidesiatnik Osip Mironov and Petr Chi-rikov. On the basis of the official lists, indicate any persons they leave behind in the Kamchatka ostrogs after their departure. Ob-tain from Osip and his comrades a written statement of every-thing they hand over to you: cash belonging to the Treasury of the Great Sovereign, trade goods, furs, guns, other weapons, pow-der, shot, official [blank] paper, iasak books, income and expen-diture books, and fish to feed the hostages. When you have this list, send Osip and his comrades and the collected Treasury goods of the Great Sovereign to Iakutsk post haste. Also send to Iakutsk the report with their signature and with yours.

Upon assuming command of the Kamchadal ostrogs you are to invite the Kamchatka servitors and the loyal iasak-paying na-tives to your quarters. When you have assembled them, you are to praise them generously for their service, in the name of the Great Sovereign. Then you are to inspect the ostrogs to ascertain whether they are sound and what manner of fortifications they have. If there are weaknesses you are to make repairs, using all available manpower, so that you and your servitors can live without fear of attack by hostile natives.

In accordance with the above mentioned ukaz and gramota from the Great Sovereign, you are to collect iasak for the Treasury of the Great Sovereign from Kamchadals who have previously paid iasak and from the newly subdued natives. This is to be done on the basis of the iasak books, with the help of the servitors. Collect prime sables with bellies and tails and black, black-brown and brown foxes with paws and tails, all in prime condition and all intact. In addition to the amounts of iasak assessed you are to collect sable *shubas* [coats], *parkas* and *kukliankas* [fur upper garments], also sea otters. You are to pay for these and give a signed receipt.

You will serve the Great Sovereign along the Kamchatka River and other rivers all the way to the sea where the previous prikashchiks Petr Chirikov and Osip Mironov and their men did not travel. You are to bring the various tribes there under the mighty autocratic hand of the Great Sovereign Tsar so they will pay iasak. You are also to go along other new rivers and into lands where other tribes live, entice them through kindness to pay iasak, and collect this iasak from them for the Great Sovereign's Treasury.

All the persons from various tribes whom you bring under His Mighty Tsarist autocratic hand while you are in service, you are to have swear the oath in accordance with their own customs. Make detailed entries into the new assessment books every year about the hostages you take from the various tribes and the amount of iasak you collect from them.

Concerning the inquiry about the Japanese Empire and the possibility of establishing trade there, you are to proceed on the basis of the above mentioned ukaz and gramota from the Great Sovereign.

You are to enter into the iasak books the amount of new iasak you collect and the names of the persons from whom you collect it. Also record the names of princes and leaders of these natives. Show them kindness, greet them and offer them protection [from native enemies] so they will serve the Great Sovereign loyally and willingly and will keep their *ulus* [native settlement] people from engaging in hostile insurgence. They will then also persuade other hostile natives to come under the mighty hand of the Great Sovereign. You are to praise them in the name of the Great Sovereign for such service, and also report the names of all who perform such service. They will be presented with gifts from the Great Sovereign, depending on the nature of their service.

In regard to any of the Great Sovereign's natives whom you may bring under the mighty Tsarist autocratic hand through your service, either peacefully or through battle, ascertain whether those natives pay iasak, what faith they profess and how they previously swore allegiance. Then bring them in to take a new oath in accordance with their own customs, reaffirming that they live under the Great Sovereign's mighty authority in eternal servitude and will pay iasak. Take princes from the newly discovered lands and collect the Great Sovereign's iasak from the iasak-paying natives, depending on their ability to pay, so they will not suffer undue burdens and become hostile. Make a special effort to find other prosperous natives. Learn which rivers fall into the Pacific Ocean. Find out what people live on the islands. Make your inquiries courteously and establish friendship as well as trade.

Obtain the following information about these peoples: What goods and riches do they possess? What goods would they like to receive from Siberia? What form of government do they have, what [armed] forces, what weapons, what customs? Also ascertain under whose suzerainty they are. What is the shortest route to these ostrogs from the Kamchatka track? How can one get there from Iakutsk? Is there a sketch map? Are there any iasak record books for the newly discovered natives? When you return to Iakutsk, prepare and sign a written report with all of this information, and include a sketch map if one is available. Give this to the stolnik and voevoda Dorofei Afansevich Traurnikht and the poddiachii Ivan Tatarinov in the Prikaz Office.

If there are any *guliashchie liudi* [transients] or persons who were born in Anadyrsk or Kolymsk who want to go to Kamchatka with you, Vasilii, you have permission to take such volunteers with you on your service assignment.

The Great Sovereign's 1702 gramota, which was issued from the Sibirskii Prikaz to Iakutsk under the signature of the diak Ivan Cheredeev, ordered that one prikashchik in the Kamchatka land be accompanied by servitors and summon the natives in a courteous and friendly manner to pay iasak. If any natives refused to submit to the Tsarist Majesty's mighty hand and to pay iasak to the Great Sovereign, and if they attempted to rebel, then the prikashchik was to protect himself and the servitors and the Great Sovereign's Treasury and wage battle against them.

[Now you, Vasilii, are to] do this, insofar as Merciful God may help you, so that all of these people will be subdued and be brought under the Great Sovereign's Tsarist hand to pay iasak. However, natives and Russians and servitors who have been sent there previously are not to be subjected to cruelty without cause. You are to be kind to these persons and keep them on friendly terms so they will be more amenable and more willing to perform necessary service.

However any Russians who commit crimes while on this assignment, or who indulge in excessive drinking and gambling and thus cause all manner of troubles, and any who disobey orders, are to be apprehended and punished in accordance with the ukaz and with the *Ulozhenie* [Code of Laws 1649] of the Great Sovereign, depending on the seriousness of their offence. Those who are found guilty are to be knouted. Do not ask Iakutsk [officials] for instructions because the distance is too great. Each punishment is to be based on individual guilt. All of this is to be done in accordance with the ukaz of the Great Sovereign, and with the gramota which is included with this instruction concerning such offenses.

In the year 1706 the prikashchik Vasilii Kolesov wrote from Kamchatka to Iakutsk. In his report he stated that he sent servitors to the land of the Kurils to subdue hostile natives. Upon their return the servitors reported to him that they had explored the lands from the Kuril ostrog all the way to the cape [southern tip of Kamchatka], but that from that point on, there is no terra firma, only sea. In the distance they could see an island in the sea, but since they had no ship or supplies they could not sail out to explore it.

Vasilii, when you are in the land of the Lukhtorskii people near the sea, you are to build ships however you can and make contact with the people on that island. If the island is inhabited you are to use every possible means to bring those people who belong to the Great Sovereign under the Tsarist mighty hand again. Collect iasak from them as courteously as possible. Also, make a sketch map of that land.

In accordance with the ukaz of the Great Sovereign, and on the basis of the above mentioned gramota, 33 servitors are being sent to Kamchatka with you. Their names are appended. They have been issued wages and rations from the Great Sovereign similar to those given to Iakutsk foot cossacks for two years. Each man has been issued a musket, the cost of which is listed below. The muskets which were issued in Iakutsk as part of their pay are to be counted at the end of the two years as part of the future salary of those servitors. Two and one-half *puds* [1 pud = 36.12 pounds] of gunpowder have been sent with you, and two and one-half puds of shot. Do not waste the powder and shot. Use them only when absolutely necessary, and guard them with great care. You have also been sent gifts for natives who pay their iasak. These include 1 pud 20 pounds of tin, 40 arshins of colored fabric and 10 quires of paper on which to record all of the Great Sovereign's business matters.

The servitors who are accompanying you from Iakutsk and from the Aldan, Indigirka, Alazei, Kolyma and Anadyr rivers are not to be allowed to return to Iakutsk nor to halt anywhere. If you permit servitors to return to Iakutsk, or if you leave them anywhere, you will be responsible for making up their unearned wages, Vasilii, and furthermore you will be punished without mercy.

You are personally to report to Iakutsk all the monies and goods which belong to the Great Sovereign which you receive from the prikashchik Osip Mironov and his men. The servitors may keep their money on the basis of the previous premise. Any servitors who have previously earned salaries and those who are being sent with you and will earn salaries while they are with you should receive an advance on their wages from the Great Sovereign in the amount of 5-1/4 rubles per year, each. This money is to be recorded in the book of expenditures with receipts. You are to take over the income and expenditure books for former servitors from the prikashchiks. Do not incur any unauthorized expenses. Do not collect money from servitors from salaries they have received from the Great Sovereign for previous years of service.

When you are replaced you are to hand over to the new prikashchik an inventory and all cash, goods, powder and shot which you still have. Then you and your servitors are to take all the items you have collected for the Great Sovereign to Iakutsk. Hand over the iasak collection books and the Treasury goods, and appear in person at the Prikaz Office before the stolnik and voevoda Dorofei Afonsevich Traurnikht and the poddiachii Ivan Tatarinov.

In 1709 a report was sent to Iakutsk from the rivers beyond the sea [of Okhotsk] from the Kamchatka prikashchik on the Bolshaia River, the syn boiarskii Ivan Paniutin. He reported that only sixteen of his men were still alive. The others had died of scurvy in the Zashiversk and Uiandinsk zimov'es. The survivors are Ivan Nikhoroshkov, Fedor Khitsenkov, Ondrei Zalesov, Gavrilo Trubachev, Nikita Chegus, Iakov Naritsyn, Vasilii Tolstoukhov, Fedor Erofeev, Stepan Lapin, Mikhailo Minozim, Vasilii Grotskoi, Kirilo Chernykh, Gavrilo Istomin, Ivan Volkov, Mikhailo Varaksin and Ivan Khailov.

These men are to be taken to Osip Mironov in Kamchatka. If any of these men who have stayed behind are unwilling to serve the Great Sovereign, you, Vasilii, are to make a careful investigation and punish them, Ivan Nikhoroshkov and his comrades and Osip Mironov's cossacks. Since they remained behind illegally, you are to take away their full salary and have when whipped so that others will observe this and wish to avoid the same punishment. You are to search for others who may have remained behind in Zashiversk and Uiandinsk zimov'es without their prikashchiks. Any such men you find you are to take with you to the Kamchatka ostrogs without delay and order them to serve with your men.

If you fail to take these servitors with you to Kamchatka and this is found out in Iakutsk, then in accordance with the ukaz of the Great Sovereign you will be punished, Vasilii, and the salary which you did not deserve will be taken away from you.

Last year, 1709, the Kamchatka prikashchik Petr Chirikov wrote to Iakutsk from Anadyrsk ostrog that the iasak-paying Parensk natives and Koriak leader Shcherbak and his tribesmen would not permit the Great Sovereign's Treasury collection to come from the Kamchatka ostrogs by sea. When the natives sighted [the Russians] at sea, they took counsel with the Chandonsk natives and many others. They set out wearing their *kuiaks* [armor of bone or metal plates] armed with bows, arrows and spears. They battled the Russians and killed eight servitors. Petr and 20 other servitors were wounded and lived in Aklansk under siege from the Koriaks.

Petr then went to Anadyrsk ostrog and at the bay near Kosu-khin ostrog captured the son of a cossack, Vasilii Permiakov, and the Koriak Akhaino Utkin. In interrogation they testified that the iasak-paying native leaders from the Kamennoi and Kosukhin ostrogs, Avitkin and his brother Shikalev and their tribesmen, had committed treason against the Great Sovereign. They had gathered with their tribesmen and reached an agreement with the rebel Oliutor natives to pillage the Treasury collection of the Great Sovereign. They planned to kill Petr and his servitors and they also planned to kill any future Russians who came to Kamchatka.

Because of these killings over all these years at the Aklansk, Kosukhin and Kamennoi ostrogs by the iasak-paying Koriaks, the route there is dangerous and perilous. When a convoy goes from Anadyrsk to Kamchatka these Koriaks obtain information from the outlaw Oliutors and kill those in the convoy. These Koriaks and Oliutors work together. They pay only a small amount of iasak, do not willingly give hostages, and because of this, the Koriaks year after year wander about at will, live lawlessly and kill the Russians.

Take hostages from the Parensk natives and take these hostages to the Aklansk, Kamennoi and Kosukhin ostrogs. Build zimov'es either in these ostrogs or wherever else you feel it advisable. Leave people there in charge with all the provisions they need. Petr believes that if this is done, the Great Sovereign's Treasury collection will be safe in the future and the Koriaks will be subdued, but *lushniks* [archers] will be needed. It is difficult to control the Koriaks with firearms alone because they are familiar with firearms.

In the year 1709, according to reports from Petr Chirikov and the Anadyrsk prikashchik Efim Petrov, the natives of the Kosu-khin and Kamennoi and Chandonsk ostrogs were punished for their crimes and treason by having all of their fortifications destroyed. You, Vasilii, are to learn the details of all this, so that from these and other ostrogs you and your servitors may proceed along the Kamchatka route without fear of these natives or of those from other ostrogs. You will be able to protect yourself and the servitors, guard the Great Sovereign's Treasury collection which is being sent with you and reach the Kamchatka ostrogs intact. The Kamchatka prikashchiks and servitors are to be informed of the safe route which they are to use to go from Kamchatka to Iakutsk with the Treasury of the Great Sovereign so that they too will be able to go from Kamchatka to Iakutsk with the iasak treasure of the Great Sovereign intact.

Vasilii, when you are on service in those Kamchatka ostrogs in the future, in accordance with your oath, as you swore in the cathedral on the Holy Scriptures, you are to show earnest enthusiasm in your service to the Great Sovereign. You are to collect the same amount of iasak from the peaceful natives as has been collected in the past. If you manage, either peacefully or through battle, to bring hostile natives under the mighty hand of the Great Sovereign so they will pay iasak and be in eternal servitude, and if you fulfill all of your written instructions as detailed in the Sovereign's previous ukaz, you will be rewarded through the Great Sovereign's largesse and your men will also be rewarded.

While you and your servitors are en route from Iakutsk to the Kamchatka ostrogs, Vasilii, you are not to permit any violence or hardships to be inflicted on the iasak-paying natives; neither are you to seize anything from them by force, so that you will not cause complaints or petitions to be brought against you. You are to keep your servitors from causing any trouble. Further, Vasilii, in accordance with the ukaz of the Great Sovereign, insofar as you are able, you are to ascertain the route from the Kamchatka ostrogs to the Touisk and Lama ostrogs across the Lama Sea [Sea of Okhotsk] used by the Russians and the iasak-paying natives. When you find this, write about it to Iakutsk.

In accordance with the ukaz of the Great Sovereign, signed by the stolnik Prince Vasilii Ivanovich Gagarin, 20 Anadyr natives, a guide and an interpreter from Anadyrsk are to be sent to assist the Kamchatka prikashchiks. As their replacements 20 volunteers are to be assigned from among the guliashchie liudi to be sent from Anadyrsk into Kamchatka service. The servitors assigned to the Kamchatka route are to proceed peacefully and not harm the natives. They are to take reindeer from the natives for transport, but only as many as they actually need, and they are not to take anything else from them.

On February 9, 1710, the Anadyrsk prikashchik Fedor Kotkovskii was informed of these 20 Anadyrsk natives and was instructed to send them to Osip Mironov. If Fedor fails to send these 20 natives to Osip, you, Vasilii, are to take them and a guide and an interpreter; all are to be experienced in using the bow and arrow. Take them from the Anadyrsk prikashchik Matvei Skrebykin and give him a signed paper for them. Twenty servitors are being sent to Matvei in place of these natives. Proceed with them and with your servitors from Anadyrsk to Kamchatka with great caution. Go peacefully and do not harm the natives. Take only as many reindeer from them as you need for transport and do not take anything else from them.

Vasilii, you are also to take the [native] cossack Petr Niugut with you from Zashiversk ostrog to Kamchatka ostrog. Send his father and brothers to the camp at Verkhoiansk zimov'e. If Petr refuses to undertake this service or if he deserts en route, the Indigirsk prikashchik is to send him to Iakutsk under guard.

And if you forget your fear of God and the pledge which you swore on the Holy Gospels, and if thereby you cause harm to the servitors and the natives, and because of this cause them to rebel; or if you cause shortages in the iasak collection; or if you fail to bring hostile natives under Russian suzerainty; or if you squander the Treasury funds of the Great Sovereign; or if you fail to prevent the servitors from harming the natives; or if you cause harm or hardship to anyone without reason; or if you do anything contrary to the ukaz of the Great Sovereign and this instruction—for any of the above, in accordance with the ukaz of the Great Sovereign Tsar and Grand Prince Peter Alekseevich, Autocrat of all Great, Little and White Russia, you will be put to death without mercy and all of your possessions will be confiscated by the Treasury of the Great Sovereign with no possibility that they will be returned to you.

See: A. I. Timofeev, ed. *Pamiatniki sibirskoi istorii XVIII veka* (St. Petersburg: 1882–85), I, 417–425.

5

SEPTEMBER 27, 1710

A REPORT TO THE VOEVODA OF IAKUTSK, DOROFEI AFONASEVICH
TRAURNIKHT, FROM THE PRIKASHCHIK OF THE KAMCHATKA OSTROGS,
OSIP LIPIN, CONCERNING HARDSHIPS AND DIFFICULTIES ENCOUN-
TERED ON HIS EXPEDITION TO KAMCHATKA

The prikashchik of the Kamchatka ostrogs, the cossack piati-
desiatnik Osip Lipin, and his servitors, report to the stolnik
and voevoda of the Great Sovereign Tsar and Grand Prince Peter
Alekseevich, Autocrat of all Great, Little and White Russia,
Dorofei Afonasevich [Traurnikht], and to the poddiachii Ivan
Tatarinov.

On March 28 of this year, 1710, I reached Anadyrsk ostrog in
desperate straits because the newly recruited servitors were inexperienced and slow on the trail and were not accustomed to a diet
of fish. Many contracted scurvy en route and could not proceed
any farther. These include Gavriil Koltsov, Ivan Podshivalov,
Iakov Naritsyn, Grigorii Ivanovskikh and Ivan Lebedev. Gavriil
Koltsov and Ivan Lebedev remained at Anadyrsk. Both have muskets, but muskets were taken away from Ivan Podshivolov, Iakov
Naritsyn and Grigorii Ivanovskikh and were given to more experienced servitors until they reached the Kamchatka ostrogs.
These muskets are to be kept in the Kamchatka ostrogs until the
Great Sovereign's ukaz is received.

The cossack Andrei from Verkhotur'e did not go to Anadyrsk
by way of Kamennoi ostrog because of a *purga* [Siberian bliz-
zard]. He took his musket and became separated from his comrades and then was lost. As of April 27 of this year, 1710, they
still had not found him.

That same day I sent 40 servitors from Anadyrsk to the Penzhina River to build small seagoing vessels. I instructed them to
sail on these vessels from the Penzhina to the Kamchatka [River]
side along the coast. At the mouth of the Penzhina there are two
ostrogs near the sea, Kosukhin and Kamennoi, which Efim Petrov destroyed. These ostrogs are now well fortified, and more
[natives] have settled there than previously, but they have not paid
iasak for 1709 and 1710. I do not know how many [cossacks] will
sail from the Penzhina out to sea, but I think they will not get

28

Tungus reindeer herders raise their iurt for the night to protect against winter purgas. Demand for pack reindeer for the mountainous overland trails between Anadyrsk and Kamchatka reduced herds, and Osip Lipin intensified the search for a reliable route via the Sea of Okhotsk. Sarychev, *Voyage of Discovery*. (OHS neg. 80236)

through without a battle. In previous years the Kamchatka military units were given baidaras for the sea voyage. At the present time a [native] leader, Iulta, has come from the Penzhina, from Aklansk to Anadyrsk. Another leader named Ikilav has come from Kamennoi ostrog, but no one knows why. I asked that they give me their baidaras for the sea voyage, but they refused.

It is impossible to take the overland route from Anadyrsk over the mountains because the servitors who have been sent to go with me to the Kamchatka ostrogs are very poorly equipped. There are no reindeer to use in the mountains, and the minimum requirement for that journey is at least three or four reindeer. In Anadyrsk one reindeer costs five red fox pelts. Because of these shortages our trip from the Penzhina to the Kamchatka will be undertaken by sea in small boats. There are no boats ready for a sea voyage in the newly built Penzhinsk ostrozhek, nor are there any under construction, so we will have to build them ourselves.

In these precarious years I have very few men with me, only 50, including cossacks who had been left behind whom I picked up along the rivers. But God will provide because He, the Creator, knows all.

Last year, 1709, an ukaz was sent from Iakutsk with Iurii Diachkov to Efim Petrov in Anadyrsk, ordering Efim to send 20 reliable servitors, experienced in military matters, from Anadyrsk to Kamchatka to reinforce the servitors who were to be sent to Kamchatka in 1710. But Efim did not carry out these orders. He did not send the servitors and he did not leave any information about the Sovereign's affairs in the box. I, Osip, learned of these ukazes from the Great Sovereign and I made a report to the Great Sovereign and in Anadyrsk I submitted to the prikashchik Fedor Kotkovskii a petition to be given reinforcements of 20 men. Fedor accepted my petition but he would not give me a single man without an ukaz from the Great Sovereign. He would only give me a cossack guide named Kuzma Karmanskii and an interpreter named Spiridon Sidorov.

At the present time I am remaining in Anadyrsk with seven servitors awaiting the Great Sovereign's supplies of shot, powder and gifts, which are being delivered in secret. The Kolymsk prikashchik, Semen Badanin, has sent these supplies by reindeer, which can be done more quietly than by using dogsleds. On the same day that the Great Sovereign's supplies reach Anadyrsk I will move on to the Penzhina. God willing, the journey will not be delayed.

I am sending this report from Anadyrsk to Iakutsk with Zakhar Poniatovskii and Petr Atamanov. I have appended a petition from Gavriil Koltsov and his men. You, stolnik and voevoda, will instruct me on all of these matters.

See: A. I. Timofeev, ed. *Pamiatniki sibirskoi istorii XVIII veka* (St. Petersburg: 1882–85), I, 428–431.

A Tungus couple in summer finery. They represent reindeer breeders who were pressed to sell stock to Russian officials. Prikashchik Petr Chirikov took advantage of his high office to purchase reindeer cheaply from the Tungus then charged his servitors exorbitant prices for them. He paid 3½ kopecks per head and sold at 2½ to 5 rubles. Before the servitor mutinies his profit was 7-14,000 percent! Sarychev, *Voyage of Discovery*. (OHS neg. 80231)

6

A PETITION FOR PARDON TO TSAR PETER ALEKSEEVICH FROM SER-
VITORS AND PROMYSHLENNIKS WHO KILLED THE COSSACK GOLOVA
VLADIMIR ATLASOV IN KAMCHATKA

Reigning Tsar, Merciful Sovereign! In the year 1707, according to information provided by the servitor Danilo Petrov
Beliaev, the cossack *golova* [headman] Vladimir Atlasov had a
prime black-brown fox pelt when the servitors of the Kamchadal
ostrog arrested Vladimir in the Upper Kamchatka ostrog, confiscated his belongings and deposited them in Your warehouse,
Great Sovereign. But they did not find the prime black-brown fox
pelt they had been told of in Vladimir's possessions. In the year
1711 we, Your slaves, learned that Vladimir was keeping that
prime black-brown fox pelt hidden in a secret place in his home.
So when we, Your slaves, reached Lower Kamchatka ostrog, we
went to Vladimir's dwelling with several men. We planned to ap-
prehend Vladimir and question him about this pelt.

However Vladimir fought the servitors in his dwelling. The
servitors defended themselves against Vladimir in his house, and
with our consent they killed him, because they were afraid he
would kill them. Prior to that time Vladimir had stabbed several
of our servitors and had clubbed the Kamchatka ostrog servitor
Danilo Beliaev to death.

After Vladimir was killed we did find a brown fox pelt in his
home. His wife, Stefanida Fedorova, had sewed it into a three-
cornered hat and she had another brown fox pelt hidden in
her bosom. In the Lower Kamchatka ostrog, in the iasak office,
Stefanida stated that her husband Vladimir in the year 1707 had
taken a third prime fox pelt from her niece, the black-brown fox
pelt, and had thrown it into the fire in the *pech* [brick stove]. On
that occasion Vladimir had said, "God forbid that I find you with
such a fine, forbidden pelt again in the future!"

When we, Your slaves, found those two brown fox pelts in
Vladimir's quarters, we submitted them to the prikashchik Kozma
Marmanskii in the iasak *izba* [cabin-office] in Lower Kamchatka
ostrog, and we registered them. We handed over the two brown
fox pelts we had found in the iasak izba at the Upper Kamchatka

ostrog to Your warehouse, Great Sovereign, to the prikashchik Aleksei Aleksandrov. We, Your slaves, also submitted a complaint against Vladimir, stating how he had killed many servitors in the Kamchatka ostrogs, and how he had attacked them with a club and a knife without provocation.

In the year 1710 we, Your slaves, also submitted a complaint to His Holiness, *Arkhimandrit* [administrative head of two or more monasteries in the Russian Orthodox Church] Martinian, against the former prikashchik Osip Lipin on account of the hardships and abuses and dreadful ruin he had inflicted. On the basis of our complaint Father Arkhimandrit sent Osip a spiritual reprimand. When Osip was stationed in the Kamchatka ostrogs with his friend, Petr Chirikov, he did not serve well on Your Sovereign's service. He exploited us, Your slaves, for his personal gain. We will submit a petition against Osip and Petr regarding all of this.

Great Sovereign, we sorrowfully acknowledge our guilt in this killing. Merciful Sovereign, we beg Your Majesty, Great Sovereign, order that the prikashchik servitor Aleksei Aleksandrovykh accept our petition in the Upper Kamchatka ostrog and then send it on to Iakutsk by courier.

We are Your Majesty's lowly slaves, the servitors and promyshlenniks Danilo Iakovlev Antsyforov, Ivan Petrovich Kozyrevskii and 75 comrades.

See: A. I. Timofeev, ed. *Pamiatniki sibirskoi istorii XVIII veka* (St. Petersburg: 1882–85), I, 438–441.

7

APRIL 17, 1711

A PETITION TO TSAR PETER ALEKSEEVICH FROM 75 SERVITORS IN
WHICH THEY DESCRIBE MALFEASANCE AND CRUELTY ON THE PART OF
THE PRIKASHCHIKS OF THE KAMCHATKA OSTROGS, PETR CHIRIKOV
AND OSIP LIPIN, AND CONFESS THEIR OWN GUILT IN KILLING THEM

Ruling Tsar, All Merciful Sovereign! From the year 1701 to
the present year, 1711, we, Your slaves, have been on Your
Great Sovereign service for these many years in the Upper and
Lower Kamchatka ostrogs. During this time we have brought
under Your mighty Sovereign Tsarist hand many non-iasak-
paying natives so they will pay iasak. We, Your slaves, have taken
native leaders prisoner and held them hostage in the Kamchatka
ostrogs. We, Your slaves, gladly collect Your Great Sovereign's
iasak of sable and fox and sea otter in the Kamchatka ostrogs from
the Kamchadals and other peoples. We have been able to do this
because we have taken these hostages.

During the above mentioned years we have been sent on Your
Great Sovereign service to collect the iasak treasury for You, the
Great Sovereign, and we have also been dispatched on campaigns
against hostile natives. On these assignments and campaigns, we,
Your slaves, have suffered cold and deadly famine and we had to
buy our own shot and gunpowder out of our own pockets, at a
high price, which was ten to fifteen fox pelts per pound.

At native fortifications we, Your slaves, were badly wounded
by hostile natives, and in those years many of our fellow servitors
were killed by natives. In the year 1710 we, Your slaves, were
in Kamchatka on the Sea of Okhotsk and on campaign on the
Zhupanova River where we tried to use kindly means to bring
non-iasak-paying natives under Your mighty autocratic Tsarist
hand. We also used force to bring previously hostile natives under
Your control.

In the year 1710 on the Sea of Okhotsk ten men were shipwrecked during a storm. They were citizens of the Empire of
Japan who had sailed into Kaligirsk Bay where they were shipwrecked. Hostile natives sighted them, attacked and killed four of
them and took the other six prisoner. With God's help and Your
good fortune, Sovereign, we, Your slaves, used force to rescue

four of these men from the hostile natives. In this present year of 1711 two of the four men from the Japanese Empire have learned to speak a little Russian while they have been living in the Kamchadal ostrogs. They say that their land is called Yedo and that in their empire there are seven cities quite near one another. Their empire is located opposite the Cape [Lopatka] of Kamchatka; in the Sea of Okhotsk, on an island.

They report that in their empire and in the towns there are both gold and silver and that they produce silk and cotton textiles. We have not been able to learn of other goods they produce, or which ones of ours they would find useful, because they have not yet learned enough Russian.

In the year 1709 we, Your slaves, received Your Great Sovereign's generous wage for our service in the Kamchadal ostrogs. The money was brought in by the prikashchik syn boiarskii Petr Chirikov. Petr was ordered to give us, Your slaves, the full amount of money we had earned, from Your Treasury, Great Sovereign. We were to be paid in cash, not goods, and Petr was not authorized to make any deductions from our pay. He was not authorized in Iakutsk to keep Your Great Sovereign's funds to purchase foreign and Chinese goods. Your ukaz, Great Sovereign, instructed Petr that while he was in the Kamchatka ostrogs he was to collect pelts of sable, fox and beaver from the Kamchadals and other natives for Your Treasury, Great Sovereign, peacefully and without deceit. He was not to cause harm or violence to any natives during the collection of iasak. He was also instructed to be considerate of us, Your slaves, in our desperate need, and not to harm or abuse us. He was not to take advantage of us, Your slaves, for his own personal benefit.

But while Petr was in the Kamchatka ostrogs he began to lead a corrupt life. He lost his fear of God and he also lost sight of the oath he had sworn on the Holy Bible. He was not devoted to You, Great Sovereign, in his service. He stole Your Great Sovereign funds and sable treasury, and in Iakutsk he stole 200 rubles from Your Great Sovereign's sable treasury to buy goods. While Petr was in the Kamchatka ostrogs he traded a two-arshin length of linen for a fox pelt and an arshin of calico for another fox pelt and a zolotnik of tobacco for three fox pelts. With the proceeds from the sale of these goods he acquired 20 *forties* [bundles of 40 pelts each] of sables. Petr put these sables in Your warehouse but registered them as his own property, not as part of Your Treasury, Great Sovereign, although he had acquired them with Your Great Sovereign's money. In addition, he also transferred to his own account the cash from Your Treasury [earmarked for servitors' wages]. He did not give us our full pay in the Kamchatka ostrogs, and instead of cash he forced us to accept twelve arshins of linen as full pay for 5¼ rubles, and in the expense book we had to sign for having received cash, not goods.

Because of the great distance we, Your slaves, did not dare complain, because the prikashchiks threatened to knout us, Your slaves, or to torture us with branding irons.

In the year 1708 while Petr was on assignment in Anadyrsk ostrog he bought 150 reindeer from the cossack piatidesiatnik prikashchik Efim Petrov, and for these reindeer he paid 100 rubles from Your Great Sovereign's Treasury. One hundred of the reindeer cost 22 *altyns* [1 altyn = 3 kopecks] 1 *denga* [½ kopeck] each; the other 50 cost 22 altyns each. Then Petr sold these reindeer to us, Your slaves, at very high prices, not the real prices. He charged us 2½ rubles for each reindeer. He sold other reindeer for fox pelts at the rate of ten or fifteen fox pelts for each reindeer. He put us, Your slaves, into bondage in the name of Ivan Kharitonov. For these reindeer Petr made deductions from our salary from You, Great Sovereign. In the years 1709 and 1710 he deducted 5¼ rubles, and as a result of setting this exorbitant price for the reindeer, he crippled us, Your slaves, with this ruinous imposition.

In June, 1709 Petr wrote to Iakutsk to the stolniks and voevodas Iurii Fedorovich and Mikhail Iurevich and their associates. In his report he said that beyond the Karaga River hostile Oliutor natives attacked in daylight and stole 200 rubles in cash from Your Treasury, Great Sovereign, which money had been sent to Petr in the Kamchatka ostrogs to pay us our salaries. With this clever slyness and evil invention Petr lied in his report, trying to cover up the 200 rubles [he had stolen] from Your Treasury, Great Sovereign.

In the year 1709 while Petr was at the mouth of the Kamchatka River he collected iasak for You, Great Sovereign, in his *balagan* [summer hut], from iasak and non-iasak natives, taking prime sable pelts. He went alone, without servitors, and he did not take any *tselovalniks* [sworn men] with him [to verify] the iasak collection. Then he appropriated Your Great Sovereign's sable treasury for himself, and he criminally misused Your Great Sovereign's Treasury. He gave the iasak natives receipts indicating that they had paid their iasak, but he did not enter into the official books the names of those from whom he had collected iasak while he was alone in his balagan with no servitors present.

Further, in both the Lower and Upper Kamchatka ostrogs Petr pillaged iasak natives, causing them harm, hardship and desperate ruin. He ordered his men to take all the fish, winter provisions, *sarana* [lily root] and *kiprei* [edible grass] from the natives. He also killed a number of iasak native leaders, without cause, for his own advantage. He used knouts and whips to beat them to death. In the year 1710 many iasak natives died in the bitter famine because of Petr's pillaging. Others were so destitute they sold their wives and children to other iasak natives for fish.

Also in 1709 Petr ordered us servitors and promyshlenniks in the Upper and Lower Kamchatka ostrogs to build four *koches* [flat-bottomed boats]. Petr told us, Your slaves, that we were to sail in these koches with the Great Sovereign's Treasury across the Sea of Okhotsk. In accordance with Petr's orders we, Your slaves, finished building the four koches on June 29, 1709. But Petr did not want to go aboard those koches with the Great Sovereign's Treasury, for reasons of his own personal profit and desire. Instead, he kept Your Great Sovereign's Treasury in the Kamchatka ostrogs and thereby caused great loss and ruin to us, Your slaves.

In the year 1710 Petr sent the cossack piatidesiatnik Ivan Kharitonov and his servitors with us, Your slaves, on a campaign on the Bolshaia River. The expedition had very few men, only 40, and was to pacify the traitors among the longtime iasak natives and to use peaceful means to bring the non-iasak-paying natives back under Your Tsarist mighty hand. Ivan was ordered to use military force against those lawless and disobedient persons who would rebel against Your Great Sovereign's ukaz and refuse to pay iasak as previously. But Petr would not issue any powder or shot from Your supply depot, so the servitors had to supply their own powder and shot, enough for five or ten rounds.

Along the Bolshaia River, natives who had earlier been outlaws and rebels as well as native leaders from many other tributary rivers gathered together in large numbers and attacked us in daylight. They severely wounded Ivan [Kharitonov] and many of his servitors and killed eight other servitors. After this native attack, Ivan and the servitors regrouped and fought back and were able to seek shelter in a native ostrozhek which was deserted because of the multitude who had gone off to fight. There Ivan made a written report of everything that had happened to him and to the servitors on the Bolshaia River concerning the native attack and the slaughter. Ivan sent the report to Petr Chirikov at Upper Kamchatka ostrog.

In the report Ivan asked that they be relieved from the siege. Ivan and his men sent the report to the Kamchatka ostrog asking for rapid reinforcements on the Bolshaia River, within five days. But it took four weeks for Ivan to receive a reply from the Kamchatka ostrog. During that time the cossack piatidesiatnik prikashchik Osip Lipin arrived in the Kamchatka ostrogs from Iakutsk. But Petr and Osip did not want to go on Your Great Sovereign's service onto the Bolshaia River to relieve the servitors who were under siege, as Ivan Kharitonov had urgently requested in his written report, because they were drinking very heavily. So Ivan waited for relief on the Bolshaia River which never came. Because of the great multitude of natives and the shortage of gunpowder and shot, for which Petr was to blame, they could not hold out indefinitely in the native ostrozhek. But they managed to get away and at last reached the Kamchatka ostrogs.

In spite of our service and our wounds, Osip tried to take advantage of us, Your slaves, in every possible way. He imprisoned us and threatened us without any justification. He even wanted to knout us, Your slaves. Osip ordered the servitors in the Upper and Lower Kamchatka ostrogs to collect Your Great Sovereign's Treasury, but he himself would not do this. Instead, while the iasak collection was going on, Osip journeyed through native ostrozheks from the Upper to the Lower Kamchatka ostrog. During this journey he caused the iasak natives hardships, making impositions for his personal advantage. He used them however he could, and without any reason he beat many of them to death.

Because of the hardships and abuses inflicted on them by our prikashchiks, in the year 1711 the iasak natives from the Upper and Lower Kamchatka ostrogs plotted rebellion and planned to kill us, Your slaves, who were assigned there to build boats. We, Your slaves, learned about this dangerous situation and the rebellion from iasak native leaders who are loyal to You, Great Sovereign. At the present time we, Your slaves, are guarding Your Great Sovereign's Treasury and hostages in the Kamchatka ostrogs and we are posting sentries to protect the Kamchatka ostrogs against hostile natives.

When we go out on duty in both summer and winter we are constantly beset by hostile natives, yet in spite of our service and our wounds, the prikashchiks Petr Chirikov and Osip Lipin impose great hardships and burdens on us, Your slaves, for their own personal advantage. They have beaten us, and have killed some of us with knouts and whips without cause or investigation. Futhermore, they have not paid us the full amount of money due us from Your Treasury, Great Sovereign, as recompense for our service and for our wounds. Instead of cash Osip gave us six zolotniks worth of tobacco. And whenever he gave us cash, Osip deducted one ruble from that pay, and if any of us, Your slaves, refused to accept Osip's substitute of tobacco for cash, Osip would not give that person any of his wages from the Great Sovereign. And so we, Your slaves, accepted this six zolotniks worth of tobacco in lieu of full pay, and Osip ordered this to be recorded in the expense book as payment in cash, not in tobacco.

In accordance with Your Great Sovereign's ukaz, while we, Your slaves, and Osip were in the Kamchatka ostrogs, he was to obtain information about the Japanese realm and about the new lands which lie beyond the cape across the strait. He was ordered to be zealous in making this investigation. We, Your slaves, asked Osip to let us, Your slaves, familiarize ourselves with this Japanese realm and learn about the new land, in accordance with Your Great Sovereign's ukaz. But Osip would not agree to this and did not show any interest in Your Great Sovereign's orders to obtain information about the new lands. He and his friend Petr Chirikov interpreted our oral petition as mutinous, and because of this he had us, Your slaves, put in a cell where they put us in irons and tortured us by starving us. Osip hoped in this way to extract large bribes from us, Your slaves.

When Osip went to the Kamchatka ostrogs by way of the Sea of Okhotsk, he abandoned six servitors on [another] vessel. The servitors on Osip's vessel urged him to wait for the other boat, which they could see from Osip's vessel, but Osip would not heed their petition to wait. He went on ahead and we, Your slaves, do not know whether those servitors are now alive or dead. Later on in his journey Osip stole the fish catch of the leader of the Oplansk natives, the son-in-law of Iurtin, for his own use. In all, Osip took a great deal from the Oplansk natives.

We, Your slaves, killed these prikashchiks in the Kamchatka ostrogs because they had stolen Your Great Sovereign's Treasury. They had endangered Your Great Sovereign's Treasury in the Kamchatka ostrogs through obstinacy and indifference. They caused iasak natives to rebel because of the oppression and abuse they inflicted on them. They withheld Your Sovereign's generous cash recompense from us, Your slaves, and they subjected us, Your slaves, to endless abuses and great oppression.

Because of the great distance, our complaints against these prikashchiks do not reach You, Great Sovereign. The prikashchiks would not accept petitions sent to the town of Iakutsk because they wanted to prevent incriminating evidence of their theft and lawless conduct from being made known.

We, Your slaves, confess our guilt to You, Great Sovereign, in having killed them.

In the present year, 1711, we submitted a petition to You, Great Sovereign, in the Lower Kamchatka ostrog, to the prikashchik Kosma Marmanskii. In that petition we asked that powder and shot be issued to us from Your Great Sovereign's supply depots so we could carry out Your service assignments, Great Sovereign, and subdue the rebels along the Bolshaia River. We, Your slaves, had no means of subduing the hostile natives or of collecting Your Great Sovereign's iasak from them because we are destitute and could not buy powder or shot.

But Kozma did not show any eagerness to help us in Your service, Great Sovereign, and he would not issue us any powder or shot from Your Sovereign's supply depots. Instead, Kozma wanted to make the decisions regarding Your service, Great Sovereign. So we, Your slaves, took what was due us from the dead prikashchiks, those things they had withheld from us, Your slaves. We had paid a high price, not the standard price, for these items when we bought them from the servitors and promyshlenniks in the Lower Kamchatka ostrog. We bought gunpowder, shot, sleds, dogs, kukliankas and parkas at that price because we did not want to delay going on Your service, Great Sovereign.

The inventory of our own rightful things which we took from the dead prikashchiks, and those things we bought in Lower

The Bolsheretsk settlement in Kamchatka was the site of a fierce servitor mutiny in 1711. The raised structures stored provisions out of reach of the always ravenous dogs, who are too close to the leather sled bindings. Such realities might elude J. Webber, the skillful delineator of James Cook's Third Voyage. Private Collection.

Kamchatka ostrog, and the list of prices paid, is being submitted in detail with this petition.

On April 17, 1711, we, Your slaves, left Upper Kamchatka ostrog for Your Great Sovereign's service on the Bolshaia River to subdue hostile and unfriendly brigands and traitors and to bring them peacefully and willingly under Your mighty Tsarist autocratic authority. We also wanted to subdue other non-iasak-paying natives through war so that through our zealous service the Bolshaia River would be stable and profitable in the future and the hostile natives would become Your peaceful subjects, Great Sovereign.

Great Sovereign, please accept our confession of guilt for this crime. Merciful Sovereign! We beg Your Majesty, Great Sovereign, to order that the prikashchik servitor Aleksei Aleksandrov accept our petition in Upper Kamchatka ostrog and forward it to Iakutsk, under seal, by official couriers.

We are Your Majesty's most humble slaves, servitors and promyshlenniks. This eleventh day of April, 1711.

The inventory of goods taken from the prikashchiks follows.

From Petr Chirikov: 15 forties of sables, 500 red fox pelts and 20 beaver pelts of which 10 are from immature animals.

From Osip Lipin: 20 forties of sables, 400 red fox pelts and 30 sea otters.

For these sables and foxes we bought a pound of powder, paying 10 foxes; dogs and sleds for 20 foxes; kukliankas and parkas for 10 foxes.

The following servitors are petitioners: Danilo Iakovlev Antsyforov, Ivan Kozyrevskii, Matvei Leontev Kiukov, Dmitrii Ivanov Tomskoi, Andrei Kutyn, Aleksei Meledin, Gavrilo Keltiaka, Luka Savinskoi, Aleksei Mikhailov, Vasilii Barashkov and comrades, 75 men in all.

See: A.I. Timofeev, ed. *Pamiatniki sibirskoi istorii XVIII veka* (St. Petersburg: 1882–85), I, 441–451.

8

SEPTEMBER 26, 1711

A PETITION TO TSAR PETER ALEKSEEVICH FROM SERVITORS WHO
KILLED THE PRIKASHCHIKS OF THE KAMCHATKA OSTROGS, A REPORT
OF EXPEDITIONS TO THE KURIL ISLANDS AND AN ACCOUNT OF NATIVE
RESISTANCE

Most Sovereign Tsar, most Merciful Lord! In this year, 1711, we, Your slaves, killed the prikashchiks in the Upper and Lower Kamchatka ostrogs. We explained the reasons for this and our suffering and guilt in two petitions submitted to the prikashchik servitor Aleksei Aleksandrovykh in the Upper Kamchatka ostrog on April 12.

In that month we, Your slaves, went out from the Kamchatka ostrogs to the Bolshaia River to serve You, Great Sovereign, by putting down the rebels who in the years 1707 and 1710 committed treason against You, Great Sovereign. They burned the iasak zimov'e and an ostrog on the Bolshaia River, looted the iasak collection place belonging to You, Great Sovereign, and killed the prikashchik and the servitors. From 1707 until the present time they have killed many servitors every year, looted Your Great Sovereign's iasak treasury, stolen powder and lead and robbed the bodies of all the servitors they have killed.

On April 23 we, Your slaves, were on the Bolshaia River and tried unsuccessfully, using peaceful means, to bring the native leader Kushuga and his tribe to the ostrog to pay iasak to Your Tsarist autocratic authority. Today we, Your slaves, seized Kushuga's stronghold by force. During the attack many of us, Your slaves, were killed and others were injured by rocks. Three servitors were killed. Kushuga was taken from the battlefield as a hostage and now his relatives pay iasak to You, Great Sovereign, [as ransom] for that hostage.

In that same place, to replace the former iasak zimov'e, we, Your slaves, built an earth-reinforced ostrog with a iasak zimov'e inside. We built a log house around the iasak zimov'e. In the name of Your Tsarist autocratic authority, with greetings, in a friendly manner and peacefully, we, Your slaves, brought the former lawless native leader Karimcha Tovach and his comrades to the iasak zimov'e where they paid iasak for eight persons. We collected iasak from them for You, Great Sovereign, and we kept them as hostages.

This year, 1711, on May 21 a lawless native named Kanach from the Bolshaia River amassed his people from the Bolshaia River and from five other settlements. He also gathered many other natives not related to him who lived along various rivers. This multitude attacked the iasak zimov'e and the ostrog. Kanach, who had earlier been deceitful, hoped that with the huge multitude he had with him, he would be able to seize the iasak zimov'e and the ostrog and kill us, Your slaves, and free the hostages from their place of detention. We, Your slaves, who were in the Bolshaia River ostrog and in the iasak zimov'e, defended ourselves from this multitude of hostile and warring natives, although we were outnumbered, and we held the Treasury belonging to You, Great Sovereign, and we also kept the hostages.

We went out from the ostrog to meet them in battle and we repulsed them from the ostrog. In the ensuing battle we killed the wicked Kanach and his band of traitors. The rest of the natives retreated into their strongholds. We, Your slaves, were besieged as we hid ourselves in the Tavacha ostrog from May 21 until July 8. We suffered greatly from hunger and withstood many violent attacks. During these attacks many of us, Your slaves, were mortally wounded in the Tavacha ostrog. But when the natives saw our resolute resistance and determination to hold out, and when they failed to take the ostrog, they fled from their strongholds. Today the rest of the natives have confessed their guilt to You, Great Sovereign. Today their Tavacha stronghold has been captured and destroyed. And the natives from the four other strongholds have been subdued and forced to pay iasak.

Sovereign, when the prikashchik Vasilii Kolesov was in the Kamchatka ostrog in 1706 he sent servitors to the land of the Kurils to put down the warlike natives. While the servitors were in the land of the Kurils, from the Kuril ostrog they could see beyond the strait the land which lies along the Sea of Okhotsk, but they did not go to that land. They could not find out who lives there, what manner of battle they are able to wage or how they make a living.

In this present year, 1711, we, Your slaves, from the Bolshaia River, went on August 1 to the land of the Kurils from Cape Kamchatka. It is a two-day journey from there to the place where the servitors visited the Kuril ostrog. We, Your slaves, sailed from this cape in small boats and baidarkas [the Eskimo *kayak*] to the islands. We reached that land where we, Your slaves, were directed by Your ukaz, Great Sovereign, to visit and to prepare a map.

When we, Your slaves, reached the first island beyond the strait at the mouth of the Kudtugan River, the Kuril men assembled in a multitude and fought a very fierce battle with us. The Kuril men are very skillful in battle. Of all the natives who live from the Anadyr to Cape Kamchatka they are the most warlike.

Through God's mercy and with God's help we killed ten Kuril men and wounded many others and destroyed three of their sea-going boats.

There are neither sables nor foxes nor beavers on their island, but they do catch seals. Their garments are made of sealskin and birdskins with feathers.

Beyond another strait on an island in the Iasovilka River live natives called Ezovitians. A great mass of them assembled but did not give us battle. Through an interpreter we summoned them to submit peacefully to Your Tsarist autocratic authority. The natives told us, Your slaves, that they did not know any people who paid iasak and that no one had ever collected iasak from them. They do not hunt sable or fox, but they do hunt sea otter in January. Before we came they used to obtain sea otter also by trading with natives of other lands, which can be seen as one looks south from their island. They also obtain iron and other goods and textiles of all colors from these people. They [the Ezovitians] do not have any goods with which to pay iasak. They did not tell us, Your slaves, whether they would pay iasak to You in the future, Great Sovereign.

They faced us with their great multitude of warriors and were ready to engage us in battle. We, Your slaves, remained in their land for two days but did not dare attack because we did not have enough men or ammunition.

We, Your slaves, returned from that land to the newly built earthen ostrog on the Bolshaia River on September 18 [1711], and, Sovereign, we prepared a map of that island. We, Your slaves, went by sea to that land beyond the strait in accordance with Your ukaz, Great Sovereign, which was given to the former prikashchiks [Osip Mironov and Petr Chirikov] and which ordered a reconnaissance of the land of the Kurils opposite Cape Kamchatka.

Last year, 1710, we, Your slaves, repulsed an attack by inhabitants of the Japanese Empire and by warlike natives along the Zhupanova River on the Beaver Coast. They say that these people come from the above-mentioned distant land which is in the sea to the south, close to the town of Matmai and the Japanese Empire. We, Your slaves, will pay close attention to Matmai and the Japanese Empire. We, Your slaves, are in Your service, Great Sovereign, and we pledge that we will visit that distant land in the future.

Most Merciful Sovereign, we beseech Your Majesty to accept, Great Sovereign, this our petition given to the prikashchik Vasilii Sevastianov in Upper Kamchatka ostrog, which we have petitioned him to send to Iakutsk with the map.

We are Your Great Sovereign's humble slaves and servitors, Danilo Iakovlev Antsyforov, Ivan Petrov Kozyrevskii, Aleksei Posnikov, Matvei Kiukov, Dmitrii Tomskoi, Andrei Kutyn, Aleksei Meledin, Gavrilo Keltiaka, Vasilii Barashkov, Luka Savinskii, Aleksei Mikhailov and comrades.

See: A. I. Timofeev, ed. *Pamiatniki sibirskoi istorii XVIII veka* (St. Petersburg: 1882–85), I, 459–461.

9

FEBRUARY 17, 1713

INSTRUCTIONS FROM TSAR PETER ALEKSEEVICH TO CAPTAIN PETR
IVANOVICH TATARINOV TO PROCEED FROM TOBOLSK TO TAKE COM-
MAND OF THE KAMCHATKA OSTROGS

In accordance with the ukaz of the Great Sovereign and the
orders of Governor [of Siberia] Prince Matvei Petrovich Gagarin, Captain Petr Ivanovich Tatarinov, captain of the Governor's
squadron, is to proceed from Tobolsk to the Kamchatka ostrogs.
In Kamchatka he is to inform himself about all the servitors and
iasak natives and about Anadyrsk ostrog. While he is there the
captain is to use every means at his command to bring profit to
the Great Sovereign. Likewise, beseeching God's help, he is to
summon hostile natives to come under the Tsarist mighty hand
to pay iasak and he is to take hostages from them. Asking God's
help, he is to give battle to any who will not give iasak or hostages.

If any of the servitors or *deti boiarskie* [petty nobles] or other
subordinates or persons of any rank should be found engaged in
brigandry or violence or other illegal activity, such persons are to
be punished, depending on their guilt, by being whipped and
knouted.

If, in accordance with the ukaz of the Great Sovereign, anyone deserves to be put to death for some serious transgression,
this sentence is to be carried out without reporting to Tobolsk;
however once the sentence has been carried out this matter is to
be reported in writing to Iakutsk.

The captain is also to build churches in Kamchatka and he is
to be very diligent in attracting natives to embrace the Orthodox
Christian faith, in accordance with the ukaz of the Great Sovereign. He is to baptize them and on that occasion distribute the
Sovereign's largesse, as much as possible, to each newly baptized
person, according to his judgment.

He is also to make detailed inquiries and do everything possible to have someone make the voyage from Kamchatka across
the Sea of Okhotsk to the mainland [of Siberia]. He is to ask
God's mercy and send three vessels from Kamchatka on this mission so that at last this route will be established. His Tsarist Majesty has ordered this in a personal ukaz.

If certain natives refuse to submit to the mighty hand of His Tsarist Majesty, he is to attack them with cannon, and use extreme caution in this dangerous situation.

The captain is also to invoke God's help and make a painstaking investigation to search for gold and silver ore deposits. If such ores are found, then he is to send word immediately to Iakutsk to Governor Prince Matvei Petrovich Gagarin.

The captain is also to inspect Anadyrsk ostrog and dispatch prikashchiks and servitors to collect iasak and order them to exercise great care in sending the collection to Iakutsk.

In addition to the above, in Iakutsk, if circumstances permit, the captain is to receive articles signed by the Iakutsk voevoda Colonel Iakov Ageevich Elchin.

While the captain is on this assignment, he is to attend zealously to the affairs of the Great Sovereign, invoking the aid of the Almighty. He is to exercise his best judgment and consider local conditions. He is not to report about this to Iakutsk or to Tobolsk. He is to care for all local matters in accordance with his best judgment and with the enlightenment of the Lord Jesus.

Finally, in addition to the above, if he judges it possible, the captain is to bring profit to the Treasury of His Tsarist Majesty and benefit to Him, the Great Sovereign.

See: A. I. Timofeev, ed. *Pamiatniki sibirskoi istorii XVIII veka* (St. Petersburg: 1882–85), I, 508–510.

10

JULY 3, 1714

AN UKAZ FROM TSAR PETER ALEKSEEVICH TO NAVIGATORS AND TO
IAKUTSK SERVITORS CONCERNING ESTABLISHING A ROUTE TO KAM-
CHATKA AND THE KURIL ISLANDS

On July 3, 1714, in accordance with the ukaz of Peter Alekseevich, Sovereign Tsar and Grand Prince of all Great,
Little and White Russia, and by order of the voevoda Colonel
Iakov Ageevich Elchin and the diak Ivan Tatarinov, the following
instructions are issued to the servitors Kozma Sokolov of Iakutsk
and the navigator and pilot Iakov Neveitsyn and the servitor
Mikhail Krivonosov and their comrades.

You are to proceed from Iakutsk in boats via the rivers Lena,
Aldan, Maia and Iudoma to Iudoma Cross. From the Cross you
are to portage to the Urak River, then proceed along the Urak to
Okhotsk ostrog and to the Sea of Okhotsk, traveling day and
night without delay so you will reach Okhotsk ostrog during the
summer of this year.

The reason for this is that on July 26, 1713 the following
orders were sent to the Iakutsk Prikaz Office via a personal ukaz
of the Great Sovereign signed by the Governor of Siberia, Prince
Matvei Petrovich Gagarin. According to this ukaz of the Great
Sovereign, a syn boiarskii and twelve servitors were to proceed
from Iakutsk to Kamchatka and, invoking God's help, were to
find a feasible route across the Sea of Okhotsk to Kamchatka. On
the basis of this ukaz of the Great Sovereign, a group of deti
boiarskie led by Ivan Sorokoumov were sent on the service.

On May 23, 1714, an ukaz of the Great Sovereign, signed by
Governor Prince Matvei Petrovich Gagarin in Iakutsk, ordered
that seafarers and shipbuilders be sent from Tobolsk to Iakutsk to
build seagoing vessels. Thus Iakov Neveitsyn and seven comrades
are to be sent to find a direct route across the Sea of Okhotsk to
Cape Kamchatka. Having built ships suitable for such a sea voyage, they are to return from Kamchatka via the same route across
the Sea of Okhotsk to Okhotsk ostrog.

According to this ukaz of the Great Sovereign, [you], Kozma
Sokolov and the seafarers, shipbuilders and servitors whose names
are appended to this instruction, are to proceed from Iakutsk by

49

A view of the Aldan in northeast Siberia. The overland route from Iakutsk to Okhotsk utilized boat or ice sled travel on the Lena, Aldan, Maia, and Iudoma rivers with arduous portages between. This scene gives no hint of predictably murderous problems in the endless miles ahead. M. G. Euhler engravings. Private collection.

the above mentioned rivers to the Sea of Okhotsk, traveling day and night. On the shore of the Sea of Okhotsk you are to search for timber appropriate for ship construction, and with the ship-builders who are being sent, you are to build seaworthy vessels, invoking the Lord God for help. You are to sail with these navigators, shipbuilders and servitors across the Sea of Okhotsk to Cape Kamchatka without delay.

If Jesus the Creator aids you and you reach Kamchatka, then you are to lose no time in obtaining information in Kamchatka from government employees and then take the same route from Kamchatka across the Sea of Okhotsk and back to Iakutsk. If through God's mercy you return safely, then in accordance with the Great Sovereign's beneficent promise, all of you will be rewarded generously with His Tsarist Majesty's largesse. You will be promoted in rank and receive an advancement in salary and gifts by order of the Great Sovereign, and in addition you will be richly rewarded.

However, if the will of the Lord Christ is that you lose your life on this assignment, you may expect that our Lord Christ, the Creator of all things, will give you eternal life in the next world. No one can know the moment of his death, but God's Church will always ask Christ's intercession on behalf of those who have been sent [on the Tsar's service], for they have gone on assignment by order of His Tsarist Majesty, without any doubts, and hope that He, Creator of all things, will not abandon them without His help. Wives and children who are left behind will be provided for in accordance with the ukaz of His Tsarist Majesty.

In accordance with the ukaz of the Great Sovereign, the seafarer Iakov Neveitsyn and his men will be assigned to you in Iakutsk, and you will be issued all the marine equipment for the sea voyage as well as gunpowder and shot. The amount and description of the equipment and powder and shot are listed below. The prikashchik and servitors of Okhotsk ostrog have been ordered to deliver these supplies and powder and shot so there will be no delay. You are to proceed to Kamchatka by the route across the Sea of Okhotsk without delay. And if you are negligent on this assignment, or delay for some personal reason, or if you do not serve the Great Sovereign and immediately proceed on the voyage, or if you do not reach Kamchatka, or if when you are in Kamchatka you do not obtain the required information from the government servitors, and return without it, then in accordance with the ukaz of the Great Sovereign you will be executed without mercy because this assignment and your service are imposed on you by the personal ukaz of His Tsarist Majesty, and you are being given special monetary rewards and full issues of provisions.

If Ivan Sorokoumov does not sail across the Sea of Okhotsk with servitors, you are to take from Ivan the servitors who are with him and all the cash and supplies that were issued to him. Ivan is then to be dismissed from service. When you have taken over those servitors, along with the servitors and seafarers and carpenters who are presently being sent to Kamchatka by way of the Sea of Okhotsk, you are all to proceed without any delay. The seal of the Great Sovereign Tsar and Grand Prince Peter Alekseevich, Autocrat of all Great, Little and White Russia is appended to this instruction.

The Port of Okhotsk. Peter the Great dispatched shipbuilders and sailors to the newly established port site. This later view reveals considerable building progress with a fortress, warehouses, churches, and stockades effectively dominating the sea and river mouth approaches. Sauer, *Billings' Expedition to Russia*. OHS neg. 80237)

You, Kozma, and your men, are to record how many days or weeks it takes to sail across the Sea of Okhotsk to Cape Kamchatka, and note whether there are any inhabited islands on that sea route. If there are, make note of what faith the people profess, under whose sovereignty they are, what kind of military force they have and what wealth they possess. Likewise, if there are uninhabited islands, estimate their size, note their number and record whether there are any wild animals on them. Describe everything and make a sketch map.

Upon your return from the land of Kamchatka, you are to proceed to Iakutsk and submit your written description and the map in the Prikaz Office.

The list of seafarers and shipbuilders and servitors follows. Seafarers: Andrei Iakovlevich Bush, Iakov Neveitsyn, Nikita Triaska. Shipbuilders: Kirilo Ploskikh, Varfolomei Fedorov. After the ships have been built on the Sea of Okhotsk, Ivan Kargapol and Mikhail Karmakulov are to be dismissed to return to Iakutsk. Servitors: piatidesiatnik Mikhailo Krivonosov (and twelve men).

The inventory of equipment for the voyage:
Iron anchor, 5 puds
Iron anchor, 4 puds
Iron anchor, 3½ puds
600 arshins of fine sailcloth
4 ropes 110 sazhens long
1 rope 90 sazhens long, total weight 20 puds 20 pounds
5 fine ropes, 110 sazhens, weight 16 puds 10 pounds
2 lengths of fine cord, 110 sazhens long, weight 4 puds
15 pounds of mica for lamps and compasses
4 men received 4 muskets valued at 1½ rubles each
1 pud 20 pounds of gunpowder
3 puds 2 pounds of shot
8 large and medium augers
9 axes
4 chisels
2 picks
3 adzes
5 shackles
20 drills
4 large knives
3 round saws
28 *vedros* [buckets] of tar

See: A. I. Timofeev, ed. *Pamiatniki sibirskoi istorii XVIII veka* (St. Petersburg: 1882–85), II, 37–39.

11

A REPORT FROM ANADYRSK FROM CAPTAIN PETR TATARINOV TO
COLONEL IAKOV AGEEVICH, COMMANDANT OF IAKUTSK, CONCERNING
ATTACKS BY IASAK IUKAGIR NATIVES

Petr Tatarinov humbly reports to the commandant, Colonel
Iakov Ageevich and to the diak, Ivan Sergeevich.

On December 15 of this year, 1714, a servant of Petr Lavrinov of
Anadyrsk, by name of Vasilii, and a iasak Koriak named Oriavin
Anaul came to the Anadyrsk iasak office and brought me a report
from Aklansk ostrog written by the Kamchatka prikashchiks Vasilii Kolesov and Ivan Eniseiskii. That report contains the following information.

On December 2, 1714, two tribes of iasak Iukagirs, the Chiu-
vans and the Khodyns, were en route from Oliutorsk ostrog with
the Great Sovereign's Treasury. At Talovsk Pass near Anadyrsk ostrog they rebelled and stole the entire Treasury of the Great Sovereign and killed the prikashchik Afanasii Petrov as well as Stepan
Kolesov and the tselovalnik Vasilii Zykov. They clubbed others to
death. Some of the servitors escaped, including Petr Lavrinov,
Mikhailo Argunov, Semen Saldat, Iakov Manykin, Foma Kur-
batov, Ivan Chirok, Grigorii Kuznetsov, Fedor Langin, Fedor
Khabarov, Ivan Pavlov and Vasilii Kavanaev. These men are in
Aklansk ostrog under siege. The Iukagirs have surrounded the ostrog. They do not have any powder or shot. The Iukagirs attack
these Aklansk men and life is very hard. They do not know when
and where they might be killed, nor how they might escape to the
Anadyrsk or Oliutorsk ostrogs.

The Iukagirs have stolen from them all the transport reindeer
as well as the ones intended to be slaughtered for food which had
been acquired from the reindeer Koriaks and from the Kamchadals. The Iukagirs have driven off all these reindeer and now they
boast that they will seize Anadyrsk ostrog as well and kill all the
government reindeer and also kill all the servitors. We must reinforce the [loyal] Oliutors who have remained near the ostrog to
guard the Great Sovereign's Treasury.

That report also states that the Aklansk and reindeer Koriaks
should be sent gifts from Anadyrsk in the name of the Great Sov-

ereign. This report does not contain any information on how many servitors were killed with Afanasii Petrov, by the will of God, or what their names are. There is no information as to the circumstances, why the Iukagirs perpetrated such a slaughter, why they stole the Great Sovereign's Treasury, or how the Great Sovereign's Treasury can be retrieved and taken to Aklansk or Anadyrsk, nor do we know how many servitors have been killed. No details are given in the report.

In addition to this report, Vasilii Lavrinov and the Koriak Anaul gave me further information in the iasak office in Anadyrsk. They said that in 1714 Afanasii Petrov, Vasilii Kolesov and Ivan Eniseiskii left Oliutorsk ostrog on December 2 to take the Great Sovereign's Treasury to Anadyrsk. They were accompanied by the servitors whose names were mentioned in the report of Vasilii Kolesov and Ivan Eniseiskii. Vasilii Lavrinov went with them from the upper Talovsk near Argish to the Aklansk ostrog to get provisions.

After they left, the Iukagirs from Anadyrsk ostrog who were transporting the Great Sovereign's Treasury from Oliutorsk killed the prikashchik, Afanasii Petrov, and at least 70 servitors. However Vasilii Kolesov and his men and a man from their iurt who had been shot had gone on ahead because of a fierce storm called a purga, and did not hear about the battle and the slaughter. The Iukagir Sopina Iukalnikov and three men traveled ahead with the Kamchatka prikashchik. After the purga had abated, Vasilii Kolesov and his men decided to return to Argish.

Ivan Pavlov, who lived in Anadyrsk, passed through Argish on his way home and before he reached his home he discovered the bodies of the many servitors. He returned to Vasilii Kolesov and his men to report the massacre. The Iukagir Sopina and his men heard about the killing and returned to Argish. Vasilii Kolesov and Ivan Eniseiskii and the servitors who were with them, all traveling light, together hastened on to Aklansk. On the way the Iukagir bandits caught up with them and stabbed the piatidesiatnik Nikifor Martianov. Vasilii Kolesov and his men ran day and night to escape them. Three days later, traveling by reindeer, they managed to reach Aklansk ostrog. It was the evening of December 5. The next morning 20 Iukagir murderers pursued them to Aklansk, carrying shields and muskets. Each man had two muskets and a bow and arrows.

They told Vasilii Kolesov and Ivan Eniseiskii that they had killed the prikashchik Afanasii Petrov because he had brought on them so many abuses and taxes, and such ruination and despoliation. The Iukagirs had killed all the servitors with him, but promised to return the Great Sovereign's Treasury. They said they would bring it to the Koriaks at Aklansk so it could be sent on to Anadyrsk ostrog. These same Iukagirs have threatened to kill Vasilii Kolesov and Ivan Eniseiskii and all the rest of the servitors in Aklansk ostrog, and will not under any circumstances permit them to come out. They have also vowed they will kill the servitors and the reindeer in Anadyrsk ostrog and will take the ostrog itself.

On December 6, [1714] the servitor Fedor Zershchikov escaped from that bloody slaughter to Aklansk. He reported the same news to Vasilii [Kolesov] and his men, that on December 2 Afanasii Petrov and his servitors were killed during the purga by the Anadyrsk Iukagirs, and that the Great Sovereign's Treasury was now in the hands of the Iukagirs. That same day those traitorous Iukagirs ran off 200 reindeer in Aklansk which were actually draught animals but were intended for slaughter to feed the Kamchatka servitors.

Late at night on December 7 Vasilii Kolesov and Ivan Eniseiskii secretly sent the courier Vasilii Lavrinov and his comrades from Aklansk to Anadyrsk ostrog, traveling by reindeer as quickly as possible with their report. On December 16 I ordered the messenger Vasilii Lavrinov and his comrades to return to Anadyrsk by order of the Great Sovereign. I gave him powder and shot from the Treasury to use in the siege and I sent gifts to the Aklansk and reindeer Koriaks. I sent them with instructions to travel by reindeer as swiftly as possible to Vasilii Kolesov.

On December 17 Vasilii Lavrinov and his comrades reached Anadyrsk ostrog and reported to me that they had left Anadyrsk ostrog and at night reached the reindeer herd. A herder, one of the reindeer Koriaks, was standing near the iurts. When he approached the nearest iurt a Koriak woman came out and said to Vasilii, "The Iukagirs attacked Vasilii [Kolesov] in great numbers. They drove off the reindeer herd and tied up the men and stripped them of all their clothes."

That same night Vasilii heard the shouts of the Iukagirs coming from a distance. He dispersed everyone and killed the reindeer, then took his comrade and the two of them hastened on skis to Anadyrsk, using a roundabout route. On December 19, in accordance with the ukaz of the Great Sovereign, I collected servitors in Anadyrsk and took counsel with the local people. I then sent 30 men from Anadyrsk to search for and capture the rest of the Anadyr Iukagirs, as well as their women and children. I also ordered them to use great care in guarding the Great Sovereign's supplies of gunpowder and gifts which had been left behind with a few of the servitors on the Angarka stream. I ordered that all of this be brought to Anadyrsk.

On December 19 from Anadyrsk ostrog I sent to you in Iakutsk a servitor named Ivan Gabyshev who was to guard this dispatch. At present there are only 40 servitors left in Anadyrsk, a very small number indeed, and this includes 18 men who are old and sick. There is such a shortage of men that there is no one to send from Anadyrsk to Aklansk to help with the warehouse supplies of the Great Sovereign, or to go on an expedition against those outlaw Iukagirs, or to act as replacements for the men who are guarding the Great Sovereign's warehouses. Because of this shortage of manpower in Anadyrsk at present as well as in the future, there will be a very dangerous situation because of those outlaw Iukagirs.

As of December 19 we have not received any information in Anadyrsk from Aklansk because the Iukagirs have blockaded the entire road. In the future I will report to you whatever word I receive about any action these Iukagirs may take, or about any news from Aklansk concerning the servitors and the Great Sovereign's Treasury.

In the year 1713, in accordance with the ukaz of the Great Sovereign, signed by Governor Prince Matvei Petrovich Gagarin, I was authorized to be assigned 60 reliable and experienced men in Iakutsk. On the basis of this ukaz of the Great Sovereign, you sent me 40 men from Iakutsk and you also sent me written authorization to find 11 more men along the rivers and conscript them into service with me. I found one cossack named Andrei Palamoshnoi whom I ordered to proceed to the Anadyr with the rest of the servitors, but I have not been able to find ten more.

I had left my prikashchik, the syn boiarskii Osip Ushnitskii, in Iakutsk [to take charge of the newly assigned servitors]. But Vasilii Ignateev, the Zashiversk prikashchik, would not release to him Andrei Bereskin, Andrei Antipin and Andrei Palamoshnoi, who had been sent to Iakutsk. Consequently these servitors did not report to Anadyrsk. Earlier here in Anadyrsk I received a message from the Oliutorsk ostrog prikashchik Afanasii Petrov saying that because of the shortage of men he planned to leave only 52 men in the newly constructed Oliutorsk ostrog and take the rest with him to Anadyrsk. After he had sent the message to Anadyrsk, he dispatched 100 Oliutorsk and Kamchatka servitors who were reliable men experienced in battle, whom he had rounded up from Iakutsk and from along the rivers. They were all adequately supplied with powder and shot for the expedition and the siege and had enough for replacements. They also carried supplies of official writing paper to report on the Great Sovereign's affairs. Gifts for the iasak Koriaks and Kamchadals, in contrast to previous occasions, were hastily distributed in accordance with the ukaz of the Great Sovereign in order not to delay the Great Sovereign's service.

Thus neither Anadyrsk nor other ostrogs were destroyed or depopulated by these lawless people for want of manpower and the great Kamchatka warehouse of the Great Sovereign has not been lost.

A decree from the Great Sovereign has been sent to Kolymsk, Alazeisk and Zashiversk ostrogs to the prikashchiks, instructing them to send servitors to Anadyrsk ostrog immediately. Also, a report has been sent with Ivan Gabyshev from Anadyrsk to Governor Prince Matvei Petrovich Gagarin. Ivan is to appear before you and deliver it in the Prikaz Office. In accordance with the ukaz of the Great Sovereign, you are to make note of the receipt of this report and send it by post from Iakutsk to Tobolsk.

[signed] Captain Petr Tatarinov

See: A. I. Timofeev, ed. *Pamiatniki sibirskoi istorii XVIII veka*, (St. Petersburg: 1882–85), II, 53–58.

12

1714

A PROPOSAL FROM FEDOR SALTYKOV TO TSAR PETER ALEKSEEVICH
THAT THE COASTS OF THE ARCTIC AND PACIFIC OCEANS BE SURVEYED
AND THAT THE POSSIBILITY OF A SEA ROUTE BE INVESTIGATED FROM
THE NORTHERN DVINA RIVER TO THE PACIFIC OCEAN, TO THE MOUTH
OF THE AMUR RIVER AND TO CHINA

Proposal 1. First order that two or three medium-size seagoing vessels such as a *buer* [ice boat] or a *shmaka* [fishing boat] be built for moving quickly along rivers. One should be built at Arkhangelsk for use on the Dvina, another at Berezovo in Siberia to use on the Ob, one at Iakutsk ostrog to use on the Lena. Beyond Iakutsk ostrog near Sviatyi Nos search out a suitable place on one of the rivers near the mouth of the Amur or at the mouth of the Amur itself, if it is part of Your Empire, of which I am not certain. This should be ascertained, because since peace has been made with the Chinese, they retain control of the mouth of the Amur, and the mouth of that river lies opposite a Japanese island.

2. When these vessels have been built at the mouths of these rivers, a number of naval personnel, both Russian and foreign, should be assigned to those vessels and instructed to survey the coast from the mouth of the Dvina to the mouth of the Ob, from the Ob to the Enisei, from the Enisei to the Lena, and from there to whatever river mouth may be discovered near the Amur, also the mouth of the Amur itself and the coast between Japan and China.

3. When these ships have been outfitted and have put out to sea, their navigators should be instructed to chart the coasts and the estuaries of the rivers they find, also the depth and current of the water in those rivers and a description of the river bottoms as well as the width and depth. They should take compass readings for any recognizable landmarks such as a particular tree, a mountain or some structure or some other object. They should mark the distance, note the climate, which places are suitable for harbors and which are not and what kind of forests may be located nearby.

The river shore should be surveyed and the banks described, as well as peninsulas, sea slopes, sandy beaches and river mouths.

Note should be made of places that have good anchorage possibilities, and the latitude in which various islands in the sea are located. They should also note their lengths and widths, whether they are inhabited, what kind of natural resources they have and what manner of forest, animals and people there are. Rivers on such islands should be described, noting whether there are harbors, where there is fresh water, where there are rocks in the sea, both above and below water. When all of these things have been described, Your Majesty should decree that the description be sent to St. Petersburg for Your Majesty's information.

4. If an open passage can be found to the coasts of China and Japan, Your Empire will receive great wealth and profit for the following reason. Ships are sent to eastern India from all realms such as England and Holland and others, and must cross the equator twice, when they go out and when they return. Because of the great heat in those places many of their people die and there are severe food shortages if they are on their voyage for a prolonged period of time. Thus upon the discovery of a [northern] sea route such as this, they will all wish to use it.

Entrance to the Amur River. Saltykov's proposal to explore and fortify the banks of the Amur was part of a bold, unrealized plan to establish a sea route from the Arctic Ocean around the eastern Siberian headlands to Japan and China. Private collection.

5. If such a route is found, a fortress should be built in the strait of Vaigats in Novaia Zemlia, and another on the mainland that lies opposite Novaia Zemlia. These forts should be built for this reason: once this route is discovered, duty should be imposed on all ships sailing on it, such as there is for example at the Sound [between Denmark and Sweden] in the East Sea, or in the Strait [of Gibraltar] in Spain. This will bring Your Empire great profits in duties and in trade. Forts should also be built in various bays in Siberia, on the Angaman River, on an island in the Amur River and in other such suitable places in straits which may be discovered.

6. It would then be possible to send ships from Your Empire to trade in East India; this would bring great wealth and profit. For trading purposes Your Empire is closer than any other realm.

7. Many persons maintain it is impossible to penetrate some of these places because of ice, but from Your Empire it is possible to try, as suggested above. I believe that it is possible to undertake such a voyage in spring or in summer, even to the coldest places. But no one can successfully do this except from Your Majesty's Empire.

8. An ukaz should be sent to the Governor of Siberia, directing him to send persons to investigate and make descriptions of the people who live beyond Sviatyi Nos along Your Majesty's shores, on which river they live, and what people live beyond that river, under whose suzerainty they are, whether they are subject to China or self-governed, or whether they may be under Your suzerainty. This is important because in that latitude, as is borne out in Japan and on the island of Geteo, very fine silver ore is to be found. When I was in Siberia with my father there were abandoned silver mines and tailings in that latitude. When Fedor Alekseevich Golovin was there he found silver ore and smelted it and sent samples to Moscow to the Sibirskii Prikaz. But the sites were abandoned because of the shortage of manpower; there were only a few workers who settled there. Their number could be increased if a diligent effort were made.

9. Although some difficulties may be encountered in this search, nothing is accomplished without effort. The English and the Dutch search every year for new territories to bring them profit. . . .

[Saltykov's proposals for building fortifications in the upper reaches of the rivers Iaik, Tobol, Irtysh, Angara, Selenga, Enisei and Amur:]

1. A decree should be issued ordering the construction of fortifications in the upper reaches of the Iaik [Ural] River when suitable sites have been found near lakes or tributaries. These forts will be useful in trading with Bokhara and other towns such as Erkent and Terafan. From these forts it would be possible to observe the strength of the area and I hope that in time we might take possession of these regions and carry on trade with them. These realms have copper, iron, cotton and all manner of produce and silk. Instructions should be issued to describe these places and note their latitude in order to prospect for all kinds of minerals. English accounts say that in those places there are deposits of iron, crystal and precious stones, but we have made no attempt to find them. A fort would also serve as a means to control the Bashkirs. From one fort a route should be laid out to the upper reaches of the Irtysh River and small forts built along that way to shelter all the travelers who go there.

2. Forts should also be built at suitable locations near lakes and rivers in the upper reaches of the Irtysh and all the way to the upper reaches of the Amur. The territory there is unpopulated all the way to the frontiers of East India and China. At the present time the Kalmyks and Mongols have nomadic settlements in those places.

In East India and in China there are gold, silver, precious stones of all varieties, spices, porcelains and many kinds of fabrics of silk, cotton and muslin. From forts it would be possible to establish trade with these people. The English and Dutch have made great profit there from such trade, doing business only along the coast and on islands off East India. If we were to establish trade there it could be conducted by water because all the rivers from there flow into Siberia into Your Empire. Instructions should be given to make descriptions and ascertain the latitude in which the headwaters of those rivers lie because according to a description in a geography book, they are located in the same latitudes as Persia and the island of Japan. These lands have very fine goods, as does East India. The regions between the upper reaches of these rivers and India have not yet been surveyed because in those mysterious places live savage peoples such as the Kalmyks and the Mongols.

3. Upon construction of fortresses and the establishment of trade, it would be possible to reap great profit for the Empire, such as England and Holland now have. Further, if such forts were to be built, it would be possible to bring nomadic peoples such as the Kalmyks and Mongols under our control, because they are governed by various rulers, not just by one. Moreover they are constantly in a state of discord and war with one another.

4. Small forts should be built between the headwaters of the various rivers as hospices for travelers and rest stops and protected places for merchants and others.

5. Trade goods from East India and China come to Siberia in caravans. Some also go to the Daurs, as we know for certain. However, nothing has been done to enlarge and strengthen the control of these territories. Obviously this must be done for the national interest, profit and control of these lands.

Reference: TsGADA, Kab. Petra I, otd. II, kn. 13, 11. 958–962.
See: N. Pavlov-Silvanskii, *Proekty reform v zapiskakh sovremennikov Petra Velikago* (St. Petersburg: 1897), 32–35.

13

AN UKAZ FROM TSAR PETER ALEKSEEVICH TO E. P. LIUBAVSKII, COM-
MANDANT OF IRKUTSK, DIRECTING HIM TO AID COLONEL IAKOV
AGEEVICH ELCHIN'S EXPEDITION TO THE ISLANDS OFF THE COAST OF
SIBERIA

On July 12, 1716, in accordance with an ukaz of the Great
Sovereign and on orders from Governor Prince Matvei Petrovich Gagarin, the following instructions were sent to Irkutsk to
the Commandant, the stolnik [E. P.] Liubavskii.

In accordance with the personal ukaz of the Great Sovereign,
Colonel Iakov Ageevich Elchin has been ordered to sail from
Iakutsk to islands in the sea which are visible from the coast, and
to bring hostile natives there under the autocratic mighty hand
of the Great Sovereign and to pay iasak. You are therefore ordered
to select 100 men from among the nobles, deti boiarskie and
servitors in Irkutsk and Udinsk. Send them to Iakutsk where
they will be under the command of Colonel Elchin during his
assignment.

When you receive this ukaz, you are immediately to select
2 nobles, 15 deti boiarskie, 15 mounted cossacks and 68 foot
cossacks from the Irkutsk and Udinsk garrisons. Do not take
mounted men, nobles or cossacks from Irkutsk or Selenginsk.
When these men have been selected and sent to Iakutsk, send a
personal report to Governor Prince Matvei Petrovich Gagarin in
Tobolsk and include a detailed list of the names of the men and
how much salary each is to receive; definitely do not impose this
assignment on anyone.

See: A. I. Timofeev, ed. *Pamiatniki sibirskoi istorii XVIII veka* (St. Petersburg: 1882–85), II, 109.

14

JANUARY 2, 1719

OFFICIAL ORDERS FOR IVAN EVREINOV AND FEDOR LUZHIN TO EX-
PLORE KAMCHATKA AND THE NORTH PACIFIC OCEAN TO DETERMINE
WHETHER NORTHEAST ASIA IS CONNECTED TO NORTHWEST AMERICA

You are to proceed to Tobolsk and obtain guides, then go to Kamchatka and beyond, in accordance with your instructions and make a description of the area. Are America and Asia joined?

This assignment is to be carried out very thoroughly, not only south and north, but also east and west. You are to make an accurate map of everything.

An ukaz has been sent to the Siberian gubernia, to the *Landrat* [official uezd counselor] and other administrative officials concerning your departure from Tobolsk and ordering that you be furnished with transport and guides.

Reference: *Polnoe sobranie zakonov rossiiskoi imperii s 1649 goda.* First series. (St. Petersburg: 1830), V, 607.

15

INSTRUCTIONS FROM TSAR PETER ALEKSEEVICH TO THE ADMIRALTY COLLEGE REGARDING SELECTION OF OFFICERS FOR THE FIRST KAMCHATKA [FIRST BERING] EXPEDITION, 1725–1730.

Concerning the Siberian assignment:
1. Find geodesists who have been in Siberia and have returned. [Response from Admiralty College:] On orders from the Senate the following geodesists were [previously] sent to the Siberian gubernia: Ivan Sakharov, Petr Chichagov, Ivan Evreinov (deceased), Fedor Luzhin, Petr Skobeltsyn, Ivan Svistunov, Dmitrii Baskakov, Vasilii Shetilov and Grigorii Putilov.

2. Find a qualified naval lieutenant or sublieutenant to go with them [geodesists] to Siberia and Kamchatka. [Response:] In the opinion of Vice Admiral Sievers and Rear Admiral Siniavin, any of the following are qualified for such an expedition: lieutenants [M. P.] Spanberg, Sverev or [A. N.] Kosenkov, or sublieutenants [A. I.] Chirikov or [D. Ia.] Laptev. Either Captain [Vitus] Bering or [K. P.] von Verd is recommended as commanding officer. Bering has been in East India and knows conditions, and von Verd has been a navigator.

3. Find a student or an apprentice who can build a decked boat there, similar to the ones here that accompany large ships. For that purpose send with him four young shipwrights with their tools, a quartermaster and eight seamen. [Response:] The apprentice shipwright Fedor Kozlov is capable of building boats either with or without decks, according to designs.

[Note in the margin:] It is very necessary to have a navigator and assistant navigator who have been to North America.

4. For this expedition send from here half again as much [note in margin: Twice as much] sailcloth, pulleys, *shif* [a boat or a vessel], cordage and the like and four falconets with appropriate ammunition and one or two sailmakers. [Response:] The rigging is being sent.

[Note in margin:] Everything else is fine.

5. If such navigators cannot be found in the [Russian] Navy, then immediately write to Holland via the Admiralty Post and

request two men who are familiar with the sea north toward Japan.

[Noted by Vice Admiral Sievers:] If there are any such navigators in the [Russian] Navy they will be sent without delay.

Reference: TsGAVMF, f. 223, op. 1, d. 29, 11. 110–111.
See: V. I. Grekov, *Ocherki iz istorii russkikh geograficheskikh issledovanii v 1725– 65 gg.* (Moscow: 1960), 22.

16

BEFORE JANUARY 28, 1725

UKAZ FROM TSAR PETER ALEKSEEVICH TO PRINCE VASILII LUKICH DOLGORUKII, GOVERNOR OF SIBERIA, CONCERNING ASSISTANCE TO CAPTAIN VITUS BERING ON THE FIRST KAMCHATKA EXPEDITION

We have sent to Siberia Navy Captain Vitus Bering with the requisite number of servitors to organize an expedition. He has been given special instructions regarding what he is to do. When this captain reaches you, you are to render him every possible assistance to enable him to carry out those instructions.

Reference: Library of Congress, Manuscript Division. Yudin Collection, Box 156, Folder 29, (Russia, Archive of the Naval Ministry).

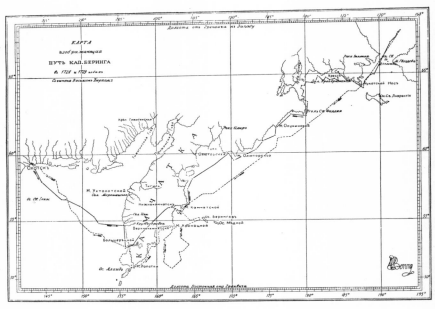

Peter's terse instructions to Bering for the First Kamchatka Expedition resulted in this remarkable voyage of 1728-29. Aboard the *Sv. Gavriil* Bering departed Kamchatka past the Chukotsk Peninsula. He actually sailed through the strait separating Asia from America for which he was to search, but because of heavy weather did not realize what he had accomplished. D. M. Lebedev, *Plavanie A. I. Chirikov....* (OHS neg. 80328)

17

INSTRUCTIONS FROM EMPRESS CATHERINE ALEKSEEVNA TO CAPTAIN
VITUS BERING FOR THE FIRST KAMCHATKA EXPEDITION*

1 In Kamchatka or some other place build one or two boats with decks.

2. On those boats sail near the land which goes to the north which (since no one knows where it ends) it seems is part of America.

3. Discover where it is joined to America, and go as far as some town belonging to a European power; if you encounter some European ship, ascertain from it what is the name of the nearest coast, and write it down and go ashore personally and obtain firsthand information, locate it on a map and return here.

Reference: Russia. *Polnoe sobranie zakonov rossiiskoi imperii s 1649 goda.* First Series. (St. Petersburg: 1830), VII, 413.

---

*These instructions were written by Peter the Great before his death (January 28, 1725) but were given to Bering by Peter's wife and successor, Empress Catherine I.

18

OCTOBER 21, 1727

THE TREATY OF KIAKHTA

Preamble. An ukaz of the Empress of all the Russias, etc. etc. etc. The Illyrian Count Ambassador Sava Vladislavich [Raguzhinskii], who was sent to renew and reaffirm the peace, which was previously concluded between the two Empires at Nipkov (Nerchinsk), agreed with the officials appointed by the Emperor of the Empire called Taidzhin (China), [namely] Chabin, the Imperial Counselor, President of the Mandarin Tribunal and Administrator of the Department of Internal Affairs, and Tegun, Imperial Counselor, President and Administrator of the Tribunal of External Provinces, and Lord of the Red Banner, and Tuleshin, Second President of the Military Tribunal. They reached the following agreement:

ARTICLE I

This new treaty has been concluded specifically so that peace between the two Empires may be stronger and eternal. Henceforth each government is to rule and control its own subjects, revere peace more ardently and control and restrain its own subjects more diligently so that they will not cause any provocation.

ARTICLE II

Now, as a result of the renewal of peace, it is contrary to the spirit [of this treaty] to review previous problems between the two Empires, and it is inappropriate to return those deserters who escaped prior to this time. They are to remain where they are. But in the future any who flee and are not immediately apprehended are to be diligently pursued by both sides; when they are caught they are to be turned over to frontier authorities.

ARTICLE III

The Russian Ambassador, the Illyrian Count Sava Vladislavich, together with the Chinese officials, agreed that the frontiers of the two Empires are very important, and if they are not surveyed, it will be impossible to delineate them. For that purpose, the Russian Ambassador, the Illyrian Count Sava Vladislavich, journeyed to the frontier and there he reached an agreement with Shushak-toroi Kun vam khoksoi Efu Tserin, General of the Chinese Empire, and with Besyg, an official of the Royal Guard, and with Tuleshin, Second President of the Military Tribunal. The frontiers and territories between the two Empires were established as follows: from the Russian guard post, which is on the Kiakhta River, and the Chinese stone marker, which is located on the hill called Orogoitu, the land between these two points was divided equally, and in the middle a marker was emplaced as a sign of frontier delineation. That place was also designated as a meeting ground for merchants of both Empires. From that point officials were sent in both directions to delineate the frontier.

From the above-mentioned place to the east, the frontier lies along the summit of the Burgutei Mountains to the Kiransk guard post, and from the Kiransk guard post to Chiktai, Ara khudara and Ara khadain usu. Opposite these four guard posts, the frontier was delineated along part of the Chikoi River.

From Ara khadain usu to the Mongolian guard post Ubur khadain usu, and from Ubur khadain usu to the marker of the Mongol guard post Tsagan ola, all of these uninhabited regions are equally divided between the lands belonging to Russian subjects and the markers of the Mongols, subjects of the Chinese Empire, as was done in the place called Kiakhta, namely: whenever mountains, hills or rivers are near settlements of Russian subjects, they are to be viewed as border markers. Likewise, when mountains, hills and rivers are near markers of Mongol guard posts, these are also to be viewed as border markers. Areas that do not have mountains or rivers are to be divided equally and there border markers have been placed.

Officials of both Empires who went from the guard post called Tsagan ola up to the bank of the Argun River, and who surveyed these territories which are located beyond the Mongols' markers, unanimously adopted this boundary line. And beginning from the border marker which was emplaced as a delineation of the frontier between the two places, Kiakhta and Orogoitu, proceeding west, [the boundary] lies along the mountains of Orogoitu, Tymen kovnokhu, Bichiktu khoshego, Bulesotu olo, Kuku chelotuin, Khongor obo, Iankhor ola, Bogosun ama, Gundzan ola, Khutugaitu ola, Kovi moulou, Bugutu dabaga, Ekouten shaoii moulou, Doshitu dabaga, Kysynyktu dabaga, Gurbi da-

71

baga, Hukutu dabaga, Ergik targak, Kenze mada, Khonin dabaga, Kem kemchik bom and Shabina dabaga.

Along the summits of these mountains the division was made through the middle and that line is considered to be the frontier. Those mountain ranges and rivers that cross them are to be divided equally so that the north side will be part of the Russian Empire and the south side will belong to the Chinese Empire. The officials sent by both sides described and traced this division and exchanged letters and sketchmaps and took these to their respective superiors. During the time the frontiers between the two Empires were being delineated, certain corrupt persons deserted and illegally laid claim to lands and built their iurts there. These persons have been pursued by officials of both Empires and sent back to their original encampments. In this manner inhabitants of both Empires who have fled back and forth have been apprehended and compelled to live in their own encampments. As a result the frontier area has been cleared.

The Uriankhi [people] who paid iasak consisting of five sables to one side will in the future be left under the jurisdiction of their previous masters. However, those who paid only one sable as iasak will in the future be freed from such obligation for all time, as of the day the frontier treaty takes effect. Everything that was decided upon has been confirmed in writing and presented to each side.

ARTICLE IV

Now that the frontier between the two Empires has been delineated, neither side need hold deserters. In addition, following the establishment of peace, it was resolved with the Russian Ambassador, the Illyrian Count Sava Vladislavich, that trade between the two Empires will be free and that the number of merchants, as in the past, is not to exceed 200. These merchants may travel to Peking once every three years. Because they will all be merchants, they will not receive provisions as previously, nor will duty be collected either from sellers or buyers. When merchants arrive at the frontier they are to announce their arrival in writing. When their letters are received, mandarin officials will be sent to meet them and accompany them for the purpose of trade. If the merchants wish to buy camels, horses and provisions en route, and to hire workers, they may do so at their own expense. The mandarin or leader of the merchant caravan will supervise and administer, and if any quarrel develops, he will resolve it justly. If the leader of the caravan or the supervisor is a man of high rank, he is to be received with dignity.

Goods of all kinds may be sold and purchased, except those which may be prohibited by ukazes of the two Empires. If someone without the consent of the supervisor should secretly try to remain, he will not be permitted to do so. If someone dies of an illness, his remains and possessions will be turned over to the people of his Empire, as the Russian Ambassador, the Illyrian Count Sava Vladislavich stipulated.

In addition to this trade between the two Empires, an appropriate place should be chosen near Nipkov (Nerchinsk) and on the Selenginsk [portion of the] Kiakhta [River] where minor trade can be carried on. Houses are to be built there and surrounded by a fence or palisade, as circumstances may dictate. Anyone who wishes to go to those places to trade is to proceed there by the direct route. If anyone strays from that, and goes to other places to trade, his goods will be confiscated for the Sovereign. Both sides will appoint equal numbers of servitors who will be commanded by officers of equal rank, and will guard the places together and resolve all disagreements. These provisions were agreed upon with the Russian Ambassador, the Illyrian Count Sava Vladislavich.

ARTICLE V

The *koen* or dwelling which is presently available for Russians in Peking will be reserved for Russians who go there in the future so that they may live in that dwelling. All suggestions that the Russian Ambassador, the Illyrian Count Sava Vladislavich has made concerning building a church have been made in this dwelling with the assistance of the officials who supervise Russian affairs. In this house will live one *lama* [Orthodox priest] who is presently in Peking; three more lamas will be added in accordance with the agreement which was reached. When they arrive they will receive provisions as does the current one who arrived here earlier. They will be assigned to that church. The Russians will not be denied the right to pray and to honor their God in accordance with their faith. In addition, four young students and two older ones who know Russian and Latin, and whom the Russian Ambassador, the Illyrian Count Sava Vladislavich, wishes to leave in Peking to study languages, will also be allowed to live in this dwelling and will be issued provisions from the Tsarist account. When they have mastered [their study of languages], they may return freely [to Russia].

ARTICLE VI

For the purpose of communication between the two Empires, passports with official seals are essential. For that reason, whenever official communications are sent from the Russian Empire to the Chinese Empire, they are to have an official seal, either from the Senate or from the Russian tribunal and the Governor of the town of Tobolsk, and they will be given to the Chinese tribunal in charge of external provinces. When similar official communications are sent from the Chinese Empire to the Russian Empire, from the tribunal of external provinces, they will bear official seals and be addressed to the Senate or to the Russian tribunal or to the Governor of the town of Tobolsk. If official letters are sent from the frontiers or from frontier outposts about deserters, thefts and such matters, then they are to be addressed to the chief administrators of Russian frontier outposts. The same procedure applies to the local Chinese frontier officials Tushetukhan, Ovan dzhan torzhi and Ovan tanzhin torzhi. These officials will exchange letters which they are to sign personally and on which, for verification, the official seal is to be placed.

When the Russians write to Tushetukhan, Ovan dzhan torzha and Ovan tanzhin torzha, they will use the same method as mentioned above. All couriers carrying such official letters must travel exclusively via the Kiakhta route, but if some vital matter is concerned or a serious problem arises, they may then take the shortest route. However, if anyone deliberately uses the shorter route (because the Kiakhta route is far away) then the Russian town administrators and commanding officers and the Chinese frontier khans are to exchange letters, and when the matter is resolved, each will punish his own.

ARTICLE VII

Regarding the Ud River and its vicinity, the Russian Ambassador, Fedor Alekseevich [Golovin, negotiator of the 1689 Treaty of Nerchinsk] and Samgutu, an official of the Internal Chamber of the Chinese Empire, agreed that this matter should remain unresolved for the present, but that it will be settled in the future either through the exchange of official correspondence or through ambassadors. This has been written into the protocols. Accordingly, the officials of the Chinese Empire told the Russian Ambassador, the Illyrian Count Sava Vladislavich: because the Russian Empress has sent you with full authority to settle all affairs, we must negotiate this point as well, because your people constantly cross the frontiers into our land at Khimkon Tugurik. If we do not resolve this problem now, there will be a dangerous situation because the subjects of both Empires who live along the frontiers may become involved in quarrels and disputes. And since this would be completely contrary to peace and unity, it must be settled now.

The Russian Ambassador, the Illyrian Count Sava Vladislavich responded as follows: the Empress has not only not given me instructions about this land, but I do not even have any reliable information about it. Consequently, let this matter remain as was agreed previously. If any of our people cross the frontier, we will stop them and forbid it.

The Chinese officials responded to this as follows: if the Empress did not authorize you to negotiate about these eastern territories, we will not continue to press you, and so for the time being we must leave it. But when you return, you must issue a strict prohibition to your people, because if any of your people do cross the frontier and are apprehended, we will certainly punish them and you will not be able to complain that we have violated the peace. If any of our people cross your frontier, you will likewise punish them.

Consequently, since these negotiations do not deal with the matter of the Ud River or other area rivers, these matters are to remain as previously, but your people do not have any more rights to claim these [lands] for settlement.

The Russian Ambassador, the Illyrian Count Sava Vladislavich, upon his return, is to submit a clear report about all of this to the Empress, and explain how officials should be sent there who are knowledgeable about those territories, who could jointly inspect and resolve this problem so that henceforth it will be settled. For if this minor matter remains unresolved, it will be detrimental to peace between the two Empires. An official written statement concerning this matter has been sent to the Russian Senate.

ARTICLE VIII

Frontier officials of both Empires are to resolve each matter under their jurisdiction fairly and without delay. If there is any delay because of personal interest, then each Empire is to punish its own officials according to its own laws.

ARTICLE IX

Whenever an ambassador, regardless of whether his rank is high or low, is dispatched from one Empire to another on official business, when he arrives at the frontier and reveals the nature of his business and his rank, he will wait at the frontier only a short time until someone is sent out to meet him and conduct him. He will be provided with immediate transportation and with provisions, and will be conveyed to his destination promptly. During his stay he will be provided with living quarters and food. But if the ambassador comes in a year when merchandise is not permitted to be brought into the country, then he will not be allowed to bring any in with him.

If one or two couriers arrive on some important matter, then when they have shown their passports with seals, the frontier mandarin officials, without any delay whatsoever, are immediately to provide transportation, provisions and guides, as the Illyrian Count Sava Vladislavich resolved and agreed.

Because communication between the two Empires is extremely important, whether through letters or through envoys, it should not be hindered in any way. In the future if letters are delayed or couriers are detained, and no explanation is forthcoming or if this results in the loss of time, because such actions are not consonant with peace, envoys and merchants cannot be admitted; however, for a time, both envoys and merchants will be detained until the matter is cleared up, at which time they will be admitted as previously.

ARTICLE X

In the future if any subject of either Empire should desert he will be executed in the very place where he is apprehended. If

The Chinese frontier town of Kiakhta as depicted in Coxe's *Account of the Russian Discoveries*. The 1727 Treaty of Kiakhta did not necessarily guarantee Russian entry to the border town. Months might go by while Chinese traders comfortably considered price possibilities for furs offered by Russian winter-bound merchants outside. (OHS neg. 80242)

armed men should cross the frontier and be involved in theft and murder they too will be punished by death. Anyone who crosses the frontier without a passport with an official seal, even though he may not be involved in theft or murder, will nevertheless be meted appropriate punishment. Any servitor or anyone else who robs his master and runs off will be hanged if he is subject to Russian authority. If he is subject to Chinese authority he will be executed right where he is apprehended and any stolen property will be returned to his master.

If anyone crosses the frontier and steals wild animals or domestic livestock, he will be turned over to his chief who will fine him ten times [the amount stolen] for a first offense, twenty times for a second offense and will inflict the death penalty for a third offense. Anyone who hunts near or beyond the frontier for his own profit will have his catch confiscated for the Sovereign. That hunter will also be punished upon investigation by a judge. Dissolute persons who cross the frontier without passports will also have to be punished, as the Russian Ambassador, the Illyrian Count Sava Vladislavich, has stipulated.

ARTICLE XI

The instruments for reaffirming peace between the two Empires were exchanged.

The Russian Ambassador, the Illyrian Count Sava Vladislavich put his signature and appended his seal to copies of the document written in Russian and Latin and presented these to the officials of the Chinese Empire for safekeeping; the Chinese officials signed and appended seals to copies of the document written in Manchu, Russian and Latin and presented them to the Russian Ambassador, the Illyrian Count Sava Vladislavich, for safekeeping. Printed copies of this instrument were given to all frontier inhabitants so they would be informed of this matter.

In the Year of Our Lord 1727, October 21, in the first year of the reign of Peter II, Emperor of All the Russias, etc. etc. etc.

The original was signed by Count Sava Vladislavich and the Secretary of the Embassy, Ivan Glazunov.

[Seal]

Reference: Russia. *Sbornik dogovorov Rossii s Kitaem 1689–1881* (St. Petersburg: 1889), 50–60.

19

A REPORT FROM CAPTAIN VITUS BERING TO EMPRESS ANNA IVANOVNA
CONCERNING THE FIRST KAMCHATKA EXPEDITION

On February 5, 1725, I received from Her Imperial Highness, Empress Catherine Alekseevna, of blessed and eternally deserving memory, instructions written in the hand of His Imperial Majesty, Peter the Great, of blessed and eternally deserving memory, a copy of which is hereby appended. [See Document 17]

I was also given instructions from the former General-Admiral Count Apraksin to request artisans and everything I would need for the expedition from the Tobolsk gubernia office. I was also instructed to report to the State Admiralty College every month.

Prior to receiving these instructions, on January 24 the Admiralty College sent a lieutenant and 26 men who were to be under my command for the expedition. With them were 25 wagons carrying the necessary supplies. In all, there were 33 servitors under my command. I was to join my command in Vologda. In going from St. Petersburg to Tobolsk our route was via the following towns: Vologda, Totma, Ustiug Velikii, Sol Vychegodskaia, Verkhotur'e, Turinsk, Epanchin and Tiumen.

We reached Tobolsk on March 16. We remained there until May 15 because it was too late to travel farther on the winter route. While I was in Tobolsk I requested the necessary supplies for the expedition. On May 15 we departed from Tobolsk and using a water route proceeded down the Irtysh River on four barks called *doshchaniks* [flat-bottomed river boats] in Siberia. On these we loaded all the supplies which we had brought from St. Petersburg and those which we had taken on in Tobolsk. In Tobolsk I also requested and was given an *ieromonk* [a priest-monk in the Russian Orthodox Church], a commissar, non-commissioned officers and 37 soldiers.

From Samarovskaia Iama I sent the naval cadet [P. A. Chaplin] aboard a *lodka* [small river boat] with the orders I had received in the Tobolsk gubernia office. He was to go to the designated towns and arrange for doshchaniks to be readied in Eniseisk and at Uskut, and then he was to proceed on to Iakutsk by water.

From Samarovskaia Iama we sailed up the Ob River to Surgut and Narym, and from there up the Ket River to Makovsk ostrog. From Tobolsk to Makovsk ostrog our route went along rivers where Ostiaks live who were previously idolaters, but who were converted to the Christian faith in 1715 through the efforts of Metropolitan Filofei [Leshchinskii] of Tobolsk. From Makovsk ostrog we journeyed overland to Eniseisk; from there we took four doshchaniks and went by way of the Enisei and Tunguska rivers to the mouth of the Ilim River. There are three rapids and several stretches of shoal water on the Tunguska. Rapids are areas where huge underwater rocks extend across the entire width of the river so that a sailing vessel can only pass through in one or two places; shoals also have underwater rocks as well as some rocks which protrude above the water; shoals differ from rapids only in that shoal water is low and extends for one or two versts. Such places are crossed with no small difficulty. In accordance with the orders given me in Tobolsk I took 30 carpenters and blacksmiths from Eniseisk.

It was impossible to reach the town of Ilimsk by doshchaniks on the Ilim River because of the rapids and shoals, so lodkas were sent from Ilimsk to transport the heavy equipment, and we sent the rest by the winter route.

From Ilimsk I sent Lieutenant [Martyn] Spanberg overland to Uskut on the Lena River with 39 servitors and carpenters. During the winter they built 15 barks to transport provisions and equipment for my entire command down the Lena River to Ia-kutsk. I wintered in Ilimsk with the rest of my command because there were not enough provisions in Uskut. Because of the short-age of convoy people and because of heavy snow and severe cold it was impossible to travel overland to Iakutsk. There are many barren places along that route, and since grain is not grown in Iakutsk, an ukaz was sent out from the Tobolsk gubernia office that our expedition was to receive extra provisions from Irkutsk and Ilimsk. That winter I traveled from Ilimsk to Irkutsk to dis-cuss with the local voevoda how it would be best for us to go from Iakutsk to Okhotsk and on to Kamchatka; we did not have de-tailed information about those regions, and he had previously served as voevoda in Iakutsk and was familiar with that area. Dur-ing the winter all of my men and I went to Uskut where I was given [number missing] carpenters and blacksmiths from Iakutsk

Bering observed that reindeer furnished the Tungus near Okhotsk with summer and winter transport, food, clothing, and hide for shelters. Bering's First Kamchatka Expedition reports were sent to Peter's successor, Empress Anna Ivanovna. Sauer, *Billings' Expedition to Russia*. (OHS neg. 80238)

and two coopers from Ilimsk.

The Tungus people who use reindeer for transport live along the Tunguska, Ilim and Lena rivers as far as the Vitim River. Those who do not have reindeer live near the rivers and eat fish. They use birchbark boats and are idolaters.

In the spring of 1726 we took fifteen barks down the Lena River from Uskut to Iakutsk. Iakuts and a few Tungus natives live along both banks of the Lena. The Iakuts have plenty of horses and cattle which provide them with food and clothing. Those who have only a few head of livestock live on fish. They are idolaters and worhip the sun, moon and certain birds such as swans, eagles and ravens. They hold sorcerers called shamans in high esteem. They have crudely carved little statues they call *shaitans* [devils] which are supposedly of Tatar origin.

Upon reaching Iakutsk I requested additional men to assist my command on boats. When I received them, I sent Lieutenant Spanberg down the rivers Lena, Aldan and Maia and up the Iudoma with thirteen flat-bottomed boats they had built near Uskut. These vessels were loaded with supplies which could not be transported overland, including provisions for the [later] overland and sea travel. I sent these things in the hope that these vessels would be able to reach Iudoma Cross. If they could reach the Cross it would be less expensive than to send them overland by horse. With a small detachment I set out for Okhotsk ostrog on horseback in the local manner. We carried our provisions in packs, putting five puds on each horse. It was impossible to use carts for transport because of the vast swamps and the mountains, and I had personally brought 1600 puds of provisions. [This would indicate 320 horses for Bering's cargo alone]. The Russians have only ten dwellings at Okhotsk ostrog. I left Lieutenant Chirikov to spend the winter in Iakutsk and ordered him to come overland to Okhotsk ostrog in the spring.

In late December, 1726, I received information from Lieutenant Spanberg that the vessels which had been sent by river under his command had not reached Iudoma Cross. They were still 450 versts short of the Cross and icebound in the Gorbeia River. He had built long *nartas* [dogsleds] and loaded the most vital supplies on those. Then he and his men continued on foot, hauling the supplies themselves. I sent some of the men who were with me and some of the people who lived at Okhotsk ostrog to help them with dogs and provisions. Spanberg and his detachment reached Okhotsk ostrog early in January, 1727. They brought no supplies with them, because along the trail on their journey they were all so starved that they ate the horses that died, leather saddlebags and any bit of hide, including their clothing and leather boots. Spanberg cached supplies in four places along the way since no one lives along the trail. At Iudoma Cross they helped themselves to the flour which we had left there; on our overland trek several horses had collapsed and so I had had to leave 159 puds behind.

Along the Aldan and Maia rivers live Iakuts who belong to the same tribe as those on the Lena River and along the Iudoma but not right on it. Seagoing Tungus natives camp around Okhotsk ostrog; in their language they are called Lamuts. They have enough reindeer to use for travel both summer and winter. Domesticated reindeer and wild animals provide them with food and clothing. There are also nomadic Tungus living near the sea and along the rivers who subsist on fish and have the same beliefs as the Iakuts.

Early in February I gathered 90 men and a number of dogs

and sleds and sent them under Lieutenant Spanberg to gather up the materials which had been left behind on the Iudoma River. He returned to Okhotsk ostrog in early April and the others in the middle of the month, but they did not bring all the supplies. I sent another 27 men to Iudoma Cross; they returned in May with the rest of the supplies which they transported on horses. In that region horses are not used to travel from Iakutsk to Okhotsk and other distant places in winter; people go everywhere on foot, which takes from eight to ten weeks. For this reason they use the same dogsleds which our men had when they went on foot from the Gorbeia to Okhotsk; they hauled ten to fifteen puds of supplies on each sled because the snow is very deep there, up to one sazhen, and in some places even more. When they travel in winter they have to shovel the snow off right down to the ground every evening in order to keep warm during the night.

On June 30 I dispatched Lieutenant Spanberg across the sea [of Okhotsk] to the mouth of the Bolshaia River. He took a new vessel and carried all the supplies with him. I ordered him to unload the materials there and to send the apprentice and the shipwrights from our crew to Kamchatka to prepare lumber for the boats. He himself was to return to us.

On July 3 Lieutenant Chirikov arrived from Iakutsk, and following the instructions I had given him, he brought 2300 puds of flour with him.

On August 21 we loaded the flour on the new ship which had returned from Kamchatka and on an old vessel which had been at the mouth of the Bolshaia. I took the men who had been with me at Okhotsk ostrog and sailed across the sea to Bolsheretsk ostrog.

We had left some of the supplies on boats in the Gorbeia River over the winter; I ordered the navigators who had been in charge of guarding these provisions to take some of the men and return to Iakutsk by boat and deliver the supplies to the Iakutsk office and obtain a receipt. Then they were to proceed on to Kamchatka in 1728, bringing with them some of the provisions and iron and tar.

When we reached the mouth of the Bolshaia we ferried the supplies and provisions to Bolsheretsk ostrog on small boats. There are fourteen Russian dwellings at that ostrog. I sent the heavy equipment and part of the provisions up the Bystraia River in small boats. They were taken by water to Upper Kamchatka ostrog, a distance of 120 versts. That same winter we transported everything from Bolsheretsk ostrog to the Upper and Lower Kamchatka ostrogs, using the local means of transport, dogsleds. Every evening we scooped out a shelter in the snow where we could spend the night; we had to cover over the tops because the area is subject to violent storms which people here call purgas. If a storm catches anyone out in the open and he fails to prepare a shelter for himself, then he will be covered by the snow and die.

There are seventeen dwellings in Upper Kamchatka ostrog and fifty in the Lower Kamchatka ostrog. In another place where there is a church, there are fifteen.

During the time we were in Kamchatka, there were not more than 150 servitors living in all three ostrogs to collect iasak from the natives. That fall a whale was washed ashore, and they prepared 300 puds of whale blubber for the natives whom we used for transport from Bolsheretsk. Instead of cash they were paid in Chinese tobacco.

The Kuril people live in the south of Kamchatka and the Kamchadals in the north. Their languages have some words that are different. Some of the natives are idolaters and the rest have no faith at all and are quite devoid of any good habits. Neither the Russians who live in Kamchatka nor the local natives grow grain; the only livestock they keep are dogs, which they use for travel and transport, and whose hides are made into garments. They live on fish, roots and berries, and in summer on wild birds and all manner of sea creatures. At the present time barley, hemp, turnips and radishes grow in the hermitage of Iakutsk monastery, which is about one verst from the Kamchatka church. Many servitors in all three ostrogs grow turnips which in one year grow to a size rarely found in Russia. Four of them will weigh a pud. I took rye and oats to the hermitage, and they planted both while we were there, but I do not know whether they were able to harvest any because there are early frosts. The land was not fertilized because they have no livestock as yet; they plow by hand.

All of the above-mentioned people are subjects of the Russian Empire and pay iasak in furs.

Because of their evil beliefs, all these people are savages. If women or livestock give birth to twins, one of the twins is killed immediately; it is considered a serious sin if one is not killed.

The Kamchatka people are very superstitious. It is customary to take anyone who is very ill and near death, even one's own fa-

84

ther or mother, out into the forest with only enough food for a week, winter or summer, and many die. They do not bury their dead, but take the body into the forest and leave it to be devoured by wild animals. Some abandon dwellings in which a person has died. The Koriak custom is to burn their dead; this is now prohibited, but they do it anyway. When I reached Lower Kamchatka ostrog much of the lumber had already been prepared for building the boats. On April 4, 1728, we laid the keel for one boat (*Sv. Gavriil*) which, with God's help, we completed by July 10. The lumber used to build the boat was transported on dogsleds. We made the tar from local trees called larch. The tar which we had brought had not arrived, and prior to now the local people have not known how to make tar from trees. Likewise because of the hazards of the sea voyage, instead of brewing spirits from grain we followed local custom and brewed from grass. We distilled salt from sea water. Because of a shortage of sea rations, we used fish oil instead of butter and salted fish instead of meat. We loaded the vessel with supplies enough for 40 men for one year, and on July 14, (1728) we sailed out of the mouth of the Kamchatka River into the open sea. I followed the instructions given to me by His Imperial Majesty Peter the Great, in person, as the map which we have drawn up will indicate.

On August 8 we reached 64°30" northern latitude. Eight men in a hideskin boat rowed out to us from shore and asked where we had come from and for what purpose. They told us they were Chukchi (about whom local Russian inhabitants have known for a long time), and when we invited them to come aboard, they inflated the bladder of a large seal, which in Russian is called a *tiulen*, put one man in it and sent him out to us to converse. Later they brought their boat out to our vessel and told us that many Chukchi live along the shore and that the land turns to the west not far from there. They also told us there was an island not far off; we went out to it but could not see anything clearly except dwellings. We named this island after Sv. Lavrentii since it was his feast day. Prior to that we had not seen any people along the shore, although twice I sent the naval cadet from our vessel out in a sloop to search for people.

On August 15 we were in a latitude of 67°18′ where I reached the decision that on the basis of everything we had observed, we had fulfilled the instructions given us by His Imperial Majesty of eternally blessed and deserving memory, because the land does not extend farther to the north, and there is nothing beyond Chukotka or the eastern extremity; and so I turned back. Information was detailed. We sailed some 200 versts but did not see land. We sailed around the southern tip of Kamchatka to the mouth of the Bolshaia River. We charted the tip which had never before been described. From the mouth of the Bolshaia River we sailed across the sea to Okhotsk ostrog. We left 800 puds of flour, groats, dried meat and salt at Lower Kamchatka and Bolsheretsk ostrogs. We left these supplies for the local administrators, under the jurisdiction of the Iakutsk office.

On July 23 we reached the mouth of the Okhota River and handed over the vessel with all necessary supplies and materials to the administrator of Okhotsk ostrog. Then I hired horses and took my men to Iudoma Cross. From there we took boats and rafts on the Aldan River to the Belska crossing and below, from where we again traveled on horseback to Iakutsk.

The entire journey from Okhotsk to Iakutsk took place between July 29 and August 29, and for some it lasted until September 3. On September 10 we left Iakutsk and sailed up the Lena River on two doshchaniks, which took until October 1. We spent the fall in the village of Poledue, because ice prevented us from proceeding further.

On October 29 there was a light snowfall and the banks of the Lena River were covered with ice. We went to Ilimsk, and from there by way of the Tunguska and Enisei rivers to Eniseisk, passing through Russian settlements. From Eniseisk to Tomsk we passed through Russian settlements as well as those of the newly baptized Tatars along the Chulym River. We then went from Tomsk to Chausk ostrog through Russian settlements; then across the Barabinsk steppe from Chausk to Tara; from Tara to Tobolsk we proceeded along the Irtysh river through Tatar settlements. We reached Tobolsk on January 10, 1730, and on the 25th of that month we left Tobolsk for St. Petersburg, traveling the same route which we had earlier taken to go to Tobolsk.

We reached St. Petersburg on March 1 [1730].

Reference: GAFKE, Sibirskie dela, K. No. 1
See: A. Pokrovskii, ed. *Ekspeditsiia Beringa: sbornik dokumentov.* (Moscow: 1941), 59–65.

20

INSTRUCTIONS FROM THE GOVERNING SENATE TO RUSSIAN ORTHO-
DOX MISSIONARIES GRANTING THEM NECESSARY RESOURCES TO
PROSELYTIZE AMONG THE NATIVES OF KAMCHATKA

The Governing Senate has issued the following orders to the *igumen* [abbot] Varfolomei Filevskii, formerly a teacher in the Slavonic-Greek-Latin Academy in Moscow, and also to the ieromonk and *ierodiakon* [priest-deacon] from the Spaskii Monastery school. Her Imperial Majesty [Empress Anna Ivanovna] has authorized that funds be issued to them for their long journey. The igumen is to receive 200 rubles, the ieromonk 150, and the ierodiakon 100 rubles per year. The salary is to be issued to them either in cash or in provisions, whichever they choose, from revenues in Iakutsk. It is also authorized that these funds be sent to them in Okhotsk, since all grants for servitors are sent to Okhotsk.

The College of the Economy is to issue them funds for the coming year and give them transport wagons to Tobolsk. The igumen is to have three wagons, the ieromonk and the ierodiakon will each have two. Funds from the College of the Economy are also to be issued to cover the expenses of the horses for the distance involved. Because of the dangers en route, soldiers are to be assigned from the Sibirskii Prikaz from among those already there on assignment or presently en route. From Tobolsk to Iakutsk and Okhotsk, the Governor of Siberia is to send them by water or overland, whichever is more convenient, together with Captain Commander Bering's men. The Governor is to provide them with transport servitors from one place to another and, in accordance with the ukaz, he is to give them funds for horses for the distance involved.

During their stay in Iakutsk they are to receive the stated annual salary so they will not be in want when they are in such distant places. They are to be transported across the sea from Okhotsk to Kamchatka aboard whatever vessel may be found there. During their stay in Kamchatka and while they are traveling on their assignment to spread the Word of God, they are to receive reindeer or other transport animals, as well as guides

An approximate French rendering of Nizhnekamchatskoi ostrog on the east coast of Kamchatka, on the lower reaches of the Kamchatka River. The ostrog enclosing the Russian Orthodox Church, can be seen on the right. Private collection.

chosen by the officers of the Kamchatka ostrogs. These officers are also to give them every possible additional assistance.

Three times a year they are to send a report on all their activities to the Holy Synod, to civil officials in the Sibirskii Prikaz and to the Senate. For that purpose the Holy Synod has requested that they receive appropriate instructions so their stay in that distant land will not be fruitless, and so that they will not be given the money and provisions to no avail. Finally, they are to be informed that they have the authority to reduce the amount of iasak newly baptized natives must pay, to accept those who wish to enter [Russian] service, and to give them largesse.

Reference: Russia. *Polnoe sobranie zakonov rossiiskoi imperii s 1649 goda.* First series (St. Petersburg: 1830), VIII, 632–33.

21

OCTOBER 1, 1732

A PROPOSAL FROM COUNT NIKOLAI GOLOVIN TO EMPRESS ANNA
IVANOVNA CONCERNING SENDING RUSSIAN SHIPS TO KAMCHATKA TO
ASSIST BERING'S EXPEDITION AND TO CARRY ON INDEPENDENT EX-
PLORATIONS THERE

To Her Imperial Majesty, the Autocrat of All Russia.

1. . . . . Your Imperial Majesty, through Your constant effort and untiring attention, You have already improved Your armies to such efficiency and order that their status is now widely acknowledged and even those inimical to Russia cannot deny this.

2. Your Imperial Majesty, with the same maternal concern, has authorized the creation of a special naval commission to examine the fleet and the Admiralty, and to make recommendations as to what aspects need improvement, and has decreed that any loss that has occurred through thievery by government employees is to be redressed and remedied as well as possible.

The commission has already found that a great deal has been neglected, but as much of this as possible has been corrected by the commission. The commission works on a daily basis making recommendations for the work that needs to be done. The results of that commision will shortly be submitted to Your Imperial Majesty.

Meanwhile, I personally would like to submit most humbly to Your Imperial Majesty a recommendation for a method by which it would be possible to establish useful ways for training young officers and seamen in the Russian fleet so Your Imperial Majesty could rely on them in case of war or an enemy attack on ships belonging to Your Imperial Majesty. They could defend themselves and also protect Your Imperial Majesty's territorial possessions. I am sorry to report that in my judgment they are not in condition to be able to do that at the present time.

3. Your Imperial Majesty has decided to send Captain Commander Bering overland across Siberia to Kamchatka. He is to be accompanied by several naval officers, artisans and sailors, and he is to take with him all supplies necessary for the construction of several seaworthy vessels. He is to search for new lands, sail toward America and the Japanese islands and survey the coastline

of Siberia from the Ob River all the way to Okhotsk and beyond. In this regard I have been authorized by the Admiralty College to draw up a proposal regarding the responsibility of the naval administration, the tasks of the officers, and to prepare appropriate instructions.

In accordance with Your Imperial Majesty's ukaz to the Admiralty College, the proposal and instructions for all this have been prepared and have already been submitted to the Senate. It is to be hoped that the office of the Senate will not delay issuing its instructions, because the route across Siberia and the barren wastelands is very difficult. Information is needed as to the amount of provisions and supplies necessary for so many persons, in order to prevent possible loss to Your Imperial Majesty's Treasury. The journey will require some travel by water and some overland. In some places one will use horses, and in other places people will have to carry all their provisions and other cargo on their backs.

In some areas it is impossible to travel in summer and one must wait to take the winter route, while in other places it is impossible to travel in winter and one must await summer. In the face of such adversities it will take at least two years for these people to reach Kamchatka with all their cargo. And once they arrive there, it will take at least two more years to prepare lumber and build ships. When the ships are ready, Bering will have to spend at least an entire year at sea searching for land and islands. When these have been discovered, he will immediately send word to Your Imperial Majesty in St. Petersburg, but the courier who carries this information will be en route from Kamchatka to St. Petersburg for eight months. This means that in all, it will take at least six years and four months.

Truly, the description of these shores and the search for new lands and islands is absolutely imperative, and will be very beneficial for the glory of Your Imperial Majesty as well as for the expansion of various regions and of the Empire itself. Further, this will add to the knowledge of navigation in those parts. For these and other reasons vital to the Empire, Captain Commander Bering has been ordered to travel overland across Siberia to Kamchatka.

I now find it imperative, nevertheless, to submit an additional proposal to Your Imperial Majesty. Next spring I would like to send two Russian Navy frigates from here [St. Petersburg] to Kamchatka. They would carry all kinds of supplies, enough for a year or more. The plan would be to go from here across the great ocean around the world to the South Sea and between the Japanese islands to Kamchatka. These frigates could make such a voyage in eleven months or less. Every year Dutch vessels sail to the Japanese islands and back in sixteen or eighteen months, and that route is well known to every good navigator and naval officer. There is nothing to fear in these seas except pirates, and each of Your Imperial Majesty's frigates will be armed with 40 guns and will have a double crew of senior and junior officers and an ample supply of ammunition. The frigates will always be in good condition to defend themselves as well as to repel attack. In addition to the required supplies of food it will be possible to load on these frigates enough sea rations for 300 men for two years, over and above the rations for the crew.

Other nations in that region, such as the Japanese and Chinese, do not have vessels such as these with guns. When these frigates reach Kamchatka they could assist Commander Bering and his crew by delivering equipment, ammunition and necessary supplies. When they arrive there they would be able to sail without fear to discover lands and islands. When they return safely, it would be advantageous to send two frigates to Kamchatka every year. They could remain there to explore for new lands and islands, sea straits, harbors, bays and the like. A great deal will be gained in the way of naval experience if this is approved, and considerable benefit will accrue to the Empire.

[The ramifications of the proposals are:]

1. By these means continuous and uninterrupted schooling will result and this will enable us to train young [naval] officers and sailors who will be familiar with conditions in these seas through a variety of experiences during their voyages there and back, such as compass variations, sea currents, changes in the wind and all the things good naval officers must know. In a single voyage these officers and sailors can learn more than they might otherwise learn in ten years.

2. Another great Imperial benefit may result from searching for America. Rich deposits of silver and gold are there which are still largely unknown. The Spanish, English and Portuguese kingdoms presently benefit from these, and the profit to those

kingdoms from this commerce and navigation in those regions is very significant to the present day. Based on this manifest and indisputable evidence concerning these advantages, it is possible that the Russian Empire might derive equal benefit by sending frigates there. In addition, still greater advantage may be gained by making further discoveries. There may develop a situation enabling us to establish genuine commerce with various nations such as the Japanese. We might even reach an agreement with them and conclude a trade treaty. It also might be possible to search for suitable sites for harbors or naval ports where we could build fortresses and settle a number of Russian civilians and military personnel. Many other advantages of great interest to Your Imperial Majesty might be realized from this project.

3. The most important benefit to Your Imperial Majesty from dispatching those two frigates will be that Your Imperial Majesty's subjects will be constantly studying naval sciences. This will result in Your Imperial Majesty's fleet being supplied with reliable and experienced men who, whether admiral or any other officer, in case of war will be able to move against the enemy unhesitatingly, which is not the case at present.

4. If some of the sailors or servitors on this new voyage, or in newly discovered places, should become ill, or even if some should die of illnesses, it will be possible to select young men from local [native] people in Kamchatka or Siberia to become sailors on those frigates to replace those who have died. In six months they could learn seamanship, and when the frigates return, these same sailors could be used to spread the Christian faith among their people.

5. There will be no great expense to Your Imperial Majesty in dispatching these two frigates because at present ships belonging to Your Imperial Majesty are constantly being repaired in all ports. The officers and sailors are being paid, and they are issued uniforms, provisions and all supplies. The frigates are kept in readiness. The only difference will be that there will have to be a very small increase in the rations which will cost about 150 kopecks per man per month.

6. At the present time, thanks to the wise rule and power of Your Imperial Majesty, peace and friendship are maintained with all realms, both those far away and those which border on Your Imperial Majesty's empire. This means that naval vessels are idle

and are falling into disrepair in the harbors and are not being used for Imperial benefit. The officers and ranks regularly receive salaries, uniforms and rations, but are deprived of the opportunity to learn the art and practice of seamanship. A number of them die, and although they are replaced, their replacements are inexperienced in the practical side of seamanship. Many, in fact, have never been to sea. At the same time, regions that border on Russia such as Denmark and Sweden are constantly expanding their maritime commerce. Their young officers and men are sent to East India and other distant places to study every year. In the future they will be reliable, good and experienced, while in contrast, Your Imperial Majesty's subjects do not have any experience at sea and are thus deprived of this direct training at the proper time in their youth. Therefore they know very little and all of them lose the opportunity. For this reason one cannot expect any fruits from their learning in the future.

7. The frigates should be sent from here [St. Petersburg] at an opportune time in the month of July so they could cross the equator at the most ideal time of year. This is the season usually specified, for certain maritime reasons which can be enlarged upon when the plans for this voyage are drawn up.

8. If the means for carrying out these proposals are not immediately perceived, if there is no appropriate time, or if there is a delay of even one year, a number of officers will have forfeited this opportunity. It is possible that there may never be a time as ideal as the present. There may be war with another country, or some powers may become allies of Your Imperial Majesty and we would have to commit our ships to that alliance. In any of these cases, it would be more difficult to carry out this advantageous project.

9. These humble proposals are submitted for the high and all merciful consideration of Your Imperial Majesty. If You approve them, detailed plans will be drawn up as soon as Your Imperial Majesty indicates the route for the expedition, the places the frigates should stop for firewood and fresh water and other necessities, and the instructions to be given the officers aboard the frigates.

10. If Your Imperial Majesty deigns to approve this proposal to permit these frigates to sail, in order to spread the glory of the name of Your Imperial Majesty as well as to bring benefit to the

The sea approaches to Petropavlovsk. The superb harbor in Avacha Bay, Kamchatka was remarkable for its distinct coastline and incessant volcanic activity nearby. Engraving, published by Alexander Hogg, London. Private collection.

entire Russian Empire, then I most humbly propose myself as leader, if no capable officer is found to serve Your Imperial Majesty. It would only be necessary to send several naval officers and sailors to assist me. I would request them from Your Imperial Majesty's fleet, as well as from England, Holland and other countries. These should be men who have been in these places and are familiar with them. The following year these men would be assigned to Your Imperial Majesty's service, for although my naval experience enables me to plan such a voyage very well, nevertheless I have never personally undertaken such a voyage, nor have I experienced these particular difficulties and dangers.

I submit this proposal most humbly, being fully convinced that this is a very necessary and important project, in its initial stages to dispatch Your Imperial Majesty's fleet, and subsequently to learn from the experience, and to increase the number of good naval officers and seamen. I believe all these results will accrue. Because of my ardent service to Your Imperial Majesty, I hope that my humble proposal, as laid out above, will forever bring benefit and Imperial fruitfulness to the Russian Empire.

I am Your Imperial Majesty's most humble servant.

Reference: Library of Congress, Manuscript Division. Golder Collection, Imperial Archives XXIV, No. 1, 1–8.

22

OCTOBER 16, 1732

A STATEMENT FROM THE ADMIRALTY COLLEGE TO THE SENATE CON-
CERNING THE PURPOSE OF THE BERING EXPEDITION

In accordance with the instructions from His Imperial Majesty, Peter the Great, of blessed and eternally deserving memory, instructions which he personally gave to Captain Commander [Vitus] Bering while Bering was in St. Petersburg, the expedition made a search to find whether the land of Kamchatka might be joined to America. However, as Bering reports, he followed that instruction and sailed along the land from Kamchatka north and east to 67° latitude, and as he has indicated on the map he prepared in conjunction with that expedition, there is no joining of the land in that latitude with the coast of America. All information on the map above that latitude, from there north and west to the mouth of the Kolyma River, Bering has taken from earlier maps and records.

Bering indicates on this map that he found no juncture between the two lands. Nevertheless, it must be strongly emphasized that even though he suggests there is no juncture, this has not been proven and should not be accepted as fact. Also, it is possible to voyage along the [Siberian] coast from the Ob River to the Lena and beyond. Nothing is known about some of these places, and consequently it is impossible to describe them precisely because there are no reliable maps or reports. Further, no observations or descriptions have been made about the islands near Japan and a route to the east. Consequently, to fulfill the desire of His [late] Imperial Majesty [Peter] and to bring benefit to the Empire and to enhance the interests of Her Imperial Majesty, the Admiralty College believes with Captain Commander Bering that this matter lies within the jurisdiction of the Admiralty College and submits the following opinion.

On the strength of the above mentioned instructions given by the late Sovereign Emperor Peter the Great, of blessed memory, and by the desire of Her Imperial Majesty, a detailed observation and search should be undertaken, even though Bering has shown that the coast of Kamchatka does not appear to be joined to the coast of America. This should nevertheless be studied in detail, and the American coast should be visited by a naval expedition and explored as thoroughly as possible. Further, a voyage should be made to the islands near Japan, where observations and explorations should be made. The entire expedition should be undertaken in the following manner:

1. To secure first hand information as to whether the land of Kamchatka is joined to America, as well as whether there is a sea route from the mouth of the Ob River to the Enisei and Lena rivers, there should be constructed in sites described below, sloops with 24 oars and a deck. One should be built near Tobolsk on the Irtysh River, and two on the Lena River near Iakutsk, because in regard to local travel and peoples, these places can be most useful. The vessels should be armed with falconets. The one built at Tobolsk should sail to the mouth of the Ob River and then from the mouth east along the coast [of the Arctic Ocean] as far as the mouth of the Enisei. Of those built in Iakutsk, one should go on the Lena River to its mouth and from there west along the coast to the mouth of the Enisei, toward the one instructed to sail [east] from the mouth of the Ob. The other one built in Iakutsk should proceed from the mouth of the Lena River east along the coast to the mouth of the Kolyma River. From the mouth of the Kolyma it should continue east along the coast and round the point which the map indicates is in 73° latitude, and from there, continue along the coast to the mouths of the Anadyr and Kamchatka rivers. Thus the entire [Arctic] coastline from Arkhangelsk will be surveyed in detail. For that purpose another ship should be sent out from Arkhangelsk to survey the coast to the Ob River. Thus, by making several expeditions, the time required for this survey will not be too great.

2. In regard to the exploration of the American coastline: if in Okhotsk, in accordance with point no. 18 of the Proposition submitted to the Senate by General Cavalier Pavel I. Iaguzhinskii, the ships are either being built or are completed, they should be inspected. If they are ready for such a voyage, two should be dispatched. If construction has begun but the ships are not yet completed, then oversee their completion. But if construction has not begun, or if it has commenced but the ships will not be suitable for such a voyage, then do not build others in Okhotsk because of the shortage of trees there. Instead, following Captain Commander Bering's suggestion, since there is a good roadstead in the

Kamchatka River and an abundance of good shipbuilding timber there, build two *packetboats* [three-masted sailing vessels] on the Kamchatka River. Then if, God forbid, one should be ship-wrecked, the other could provide assistance and information. However, if one ship has been started in Okhotsk and appears suitable for the voyage, then finish it and build another packet-boat in Kamchatka. Arm them with guns and outfit them fully, as required. Both should proceed east as winds will permit, even as far as 67° northern latitude. Search for the American coast or is-lands with great diligence and effort.

The expedition should be undertaken with good judgment so the men can return to Kamchatka as they did previously, and will not be so delayed that they might be trapped in the ice. For this reason the expedition should set out immediately after the spring breakup of ice and there should be no delay.

3. For use in exploring and discovering a route to the Japanese islands, there should be built on the Kamchatka River a suitable decked vessel and two sloops, each with 24 oars and a deck. Once these are built and armed, they are to proceed on the designated voyage in accordance with instructions. If there is a vessel left from the previous expedition, in sufficiently good condition that a voyage can safely be undertaken, then there will be no need to build a new decked vessel. It will then only be necessary to build the two sloops.

4. These vessels, according to the judgment of their com-manding officers, should proceed toward America under Captain Commander Bering on one ship and Captain Lieutenant Chirikov on the other. As noted above, they should sail together. During the voyage they are to act in mutual agreement. For that reason they should be given joint instructions. Captain Spanberg is to proceed toward the Japanese islands in command of the ship and the two double sloops which Bering used on his previous ex-pedition. The Admiralty College feels that both Spanberg and Chirikov are completely qualified to undertake this expedition.

Bering's subordinates should be sent to survey the [Arctic] coast from the Ob River to the Lena and beyond, from Tobolsk to the mouth of the Enisei, from Iakutsk to the mouth of the Enisei, and from Iakutsk and the mouth of the Ob [sic. Lena?] east along the coast to the Kolyma and around the cape [Chukotsk penin-sula] to the mouths of the Anadyr and Kamchatka rivers.

Each of these vessels should be staffed as required with subordinate senior and junior naval officers and enlisted men of various ranks. The Governing Senate will receive a special list indicating these assignments. The crew has already been appointed. In accordance with an ukaz from the Governing Senate, some of the ranks have already been sent to Siberia. The names of those who have already been sent are included in the present list, so no others are required for those positions.

5. Captain Commander Bering and the other commanders on these vessels, while at sea, are to receive special instructions from the Admiralty College on their conduct at sea. The Admiralty College will submit these instructions, when they are ready, to the Governing Senate for their review.

6. While Captain Commander Bering is on land during this expedition, he is to proceed as follows. When the expeditions reach the Japanese islands, when they survey the American coastline or islands located near America, and when as they sail from the western [Siberian] rivers and from Arkhangelsk they encounter islands on their way, they should anchor near shore and find out everything possible about the natives there and how to deal with them.

When Captain Spanberg returns to Okhotsk from Japan either he or a staff officer is to return here [to St. Petersburg] with detailed information and a description and a map. The rest of the crew is to remain in Okhotsk until an ukaz is issued. The Admiralty College will transmit all this information to the Governing Senate for its consideration.

7. In this regard the Admiralty College will submit to the Governing Senate its opinion as to whether the construction of the designated ships will be accomplished on time so that artillery and other supplies which can be secured in those towns can be prepared in a reasonable length of time.

In addition, adequate provisions are to be prepared in Iakutsk for the servitors who are sent to Kamchatka and Okhotsk. The Admiralty College will submit a list of the amount of provisions, artillery and other supplies which will be necessary for the ships. On the basis of that list, ukazes are to be sent to those places ordering that all necessary items be prepared in good time. Vessels must be built in Iakutsk to transport these supplies by water. The Admiralty College believes that naval officers should be sent to Iakutsk now to build these vessels and make all necessary preparations. They would have joint responsibility with the local commanding officers for carrying out these instructions without delay, and should send these provisions and supplies on to Okhotsk so that when Captain Commander Bering arrives, everything will be ready for him . . .

Reference: TsGADA, f. Senat, kn. 666, 11. 105–109 ob.

See: V. A. Divin, ed. *Russkaia tikhookeanskaia epopeia* (Khabarovsk: 1979), 168–171.

23

OCTOBER 16, 1732

INSTRUCTIONS FROM THE ADMIRALTY COLLEGE TO CAPTAIN COM-
MANDER VITUS BERING AND CAPTAIN ALEKSEI CHIRIKOV CONCERN-
ING EXPLORATION OF THE NORTHWEST COAST OF NORTH AMERICA

The Admiralty College has given the following instructions:
1. When you reach Okhotsk ostrog with the crew of servitors which has been assigned to you, see if the galiot which has been ordered built has been commenced. If it has, have it completed and also build a packetboat in Kamchatka. If construction has not begun in Okhotsk, do not build it there because of the shortage of timber. Since there is a good roadstead in the Kamchatka River and a goodly amount of timber there, build two packetboats on the Kamchatka River. Then, God forbid, if one is wrecked during the voyage, the other can assist and provide information. These vessels are to be armed and equipped with all necessities, as required.

2. One of these ships is to be under Captain Commander Bering and the other under Captain Lieutenant Chirikov. You are to proceed eastward, together, as winds permit, all the way to 67° northern latitude. On this voyage you are to search with great diligence and effort for the American coast or for [offshore] islands. Also, plan this voyage carefully so that you can return to Kamchatka as you did previously. Do not wait so long that you become icebound. For this reason, set out on the voyage as soon as the ice breaks up in spring. Do not delay.

3. In accordance with naval regulations you are to keep a journal during the entire voyage. Likewise, mark your bearing whenever you have an opportunity and make a description of coasts, islands and channels, following the rules of navigational science, so that this information can be used to prepare a detailed and accurate map.

4. Follow the instructions in the ukaz sent to you from the Governing Senate in regard to your course of action when you finally manage to reach the coast of America or the offshore islands, including what you are to do there and in Kamchatka when you return.

5. Captain Commander Bering, it is incumbent upon you to act in mutual agreement with Captain Lieutenant Chirikov on all matters during the course of this voyage.

6. If in spite of our expectations you cannot reach the American coast or its offshore islands because of great icebergs, then you are to wait until the ice is ready to break up and will no longer pose a problem. Then make the greatest possible effort to proceed on your voyage without losing any time. However, if the ice is such a problem that it still has not broken up after you have waited a considerable length of time, and there is no possibility of making the voyage as planned, then you are to summon your senior and junior officers, announce this situation to them, take

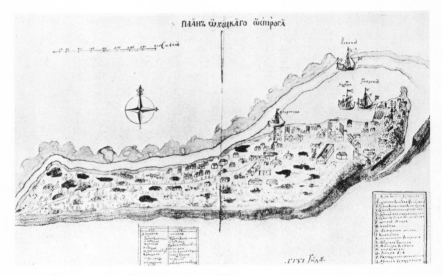

An exceptional 1737 view of Okhotsk ostrog attributed to Spanberg, found in Bering's papers. The exploring ships *Gavriil* and *Nadezhda* are grouped together on the tidal flat protected by the point, strategically occupied as the stronghold. One perceives the usual hierarchy and the hodgepodge problems of a frontier village anywhere, but the key is very informative, as witness: A, church; B, Bering's quarters; C, Spanberg; D, Chirikov; E, Lt. Walton; F, Surgeon; G, Barracks; H, Storehouse; I, Commissary; K, Pilot Petrov. L through S are petty officers; T, Chapel; U, Officers; W, Pisarev's quarters; X, Warehouse; Z, Cemetery. The *Fortuna* and *Mikhail* are anchored to the left and above the others. Golder, *Russian Expansion on the Pacific 1641-1850*. (OHS neg. 80299)

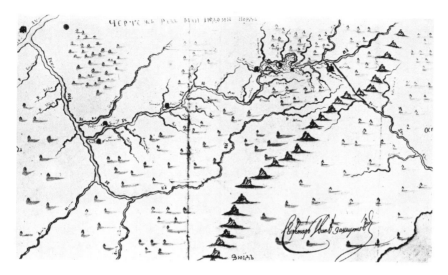

Bering's land crossing is depicted in this sketch map preserved in his papers. The route is from the Maia River to Okhotsk by the treacherous Iudoma Cross and Urak River portage. Golder, *Russian Expansion on the Pacific*. (OHS neg. 80255)

counsel with them and have them sign a statement to verify that this has been done. Then return to your original location without delay and prepare a detailed written report about this.

7. If in spite of our expectations it is impossible for you to carry out this instruction to see and describe everything in the course of one summer, you still are to make a detailed report about everything. You and your crew are to explore and bring the expedition to a conclusion in the following summer, without waiting for an ukaz. However if you decide that because of the amount of ice, this is neither possible nor desirable, then take counsel with your senior and junior officers, return and follow the instructions in paragraph no. 6.

Reference: TsGADA, f. Senat, kn. 666, 11. 113–114 ob.
See: V. A. Divin, ed. *Russkaia tikhookeanskaia epopeia* (Khabarovsk: 1979), 172–173.

24

NOVEMBER 28, 1732

INSTRUCTIONS FROM JOHANN GEORG GMELIN* TO VITUS BERING FOR
MAKING A WRITTEN DESCRIPTION OF THE NATIVE PEOPLES WHO LIVE
ALONG THE ROUTE TO KAMCHATKA

In order to make a description of the history of the peoples
whom Captain Bering will encounter along the route to Kamchatka, it will be necessary to investigate, observe and make notes
on the following points:

1. Where are boundaries of habitation of all these peoples and
where are the limits? Under which constellations are they located—the Ram, the Bull, Andromedes, Perseus or the Corona?
Where do each of these groups of people live? Are they divided
into tribes, do they differ from one group to another in appearance or are they of mixed blood?

2. What is the origin or beginning of each of these peoples?
What legends do they have about their progenitors? What are
their dwellings and settlements like? What weapons do they have?
What items do they make?

3. What is the natural piety, if any, of each of these groups
of people? What are their views about God and about matters
pertaining to salvation? What beliefs do they hold about sacred
things? Do they follow any liturgy or ritual activities in performing ceremonies?

4. All customs and habits must be observed, non-Christian or
heathen activities, domestic, marriage and betrothal ceremonies,
and other traditions of all these people.

5. With whom do these people have amicable relations? With
whom do they trade? What crops do they raise? From what do
they derive income? Do they have any secular learning? What are

_____

*Johann Georg Gmelin (1709–1755), a native of Württemberg, a brilliant
young doctor of medicine and professor of chemistry and natural history,
was already a member of the recently formed Russian Academy of Sciences
and a principal member of the Second Bering Expedition. His botanical
studies during the expedition resulted in the four volumes of *Flora Sibirica*
(St. Petersburg: 1747–69), while his experiences during the expedition
are recorded in his *Reise durch Sibirien, von den Jahr 1733 bis 1743*, 4 vols.
(Göttingen: 1751–52).

their military and battle tactics? What kind of political or civil ruler do they have?

6. What language, form of writing and alphabet does each group use? Bring a sample back to Russia, such as a translation of their prayers to God, or on holidays—that is, the prayers they recite on God's days and on holidays. What numerical system do they use? How do they count? What are the words they use for various things?

7. The names of all countries or provinces, rivers, towns, various natural objects and personal names should all be carefully and correctly written down from an etymological point of view, indicating the correct native dialect of each particular group, if such exists.

8. Make notes on the history of every settlement. When was it founded and by whom? Has its history been written down? If so, why? Or if a particular settlement was previously under the jurisdiction of another ruler, when and how did this happen?

9. Make careful sketches of all buildings or palaces made of stone, either still standing or in ruins, old graves or cemeteries, statues, porcelain, old and new ceramics, idols or images. Make sketches showing the appearance of important towns and indicate the location, fortifications, and the like. Make sketches of other things also, if possible, and bring everything here [St. Petersburg].

10. Make careful drawings of several men and women in each group of people, showing their appearance, what their foreheads and eyes look like, their customary garb and all their costumes. Bring these back to Russia.

Reference: TsGADA, f. Senat, kn. 666, 11. 221–222 ob.
See: V. A. Divin, ed. *Russkaia tikhookeanskaia epopeia* (Khabarovsk: 1979), 173–174.

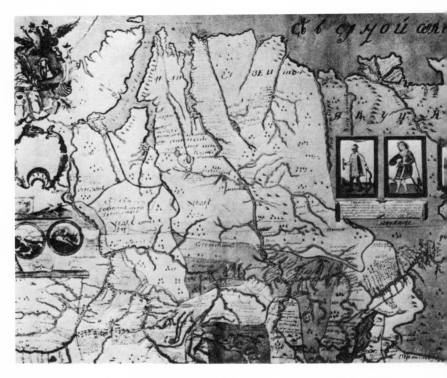

A 1757 ethnographic map of Siberia, with a doubleheaded eagle top left and native chieftains adjacent. To the east, natives of the Iakutsk uezd are depicted, ending with a seagoing baidara above the compass rose. The map based in part on ethnographic data compiled by Gmelin, a pioneer in the field. Yefimov, *Atlas of Geographical Discoveries....* (OHS neg. 80222)

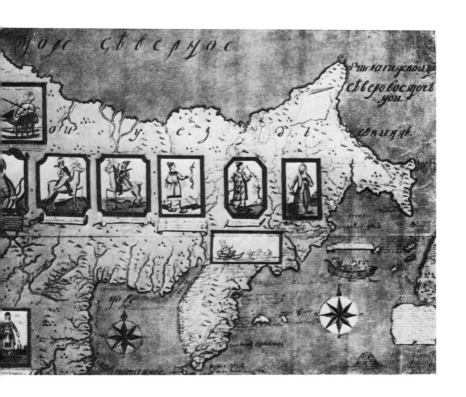

25

DECEMBER 28, 1732

INSTRUCTIONS FROM EMPRESS ANNA IVANOVNA TO VITUS BERING
FOR HIS SECOND KAMCHATKA EXPEDITION, AS PREPARED BY THE AD-
MIRALTY COLLEGE AND THE SENATE

The Senate has heard the extract, report and opinion of the Admiralty College concerning the Kamchatka Expedition and has examined the maps of the region and has also given thorough consideration to the matter so that this expedition will be of genuine benefit to Your Imperial Majesty and to the glory of the Russian Empire (since those distant places as well as areas of northern Siberia are still very little known), and has decided to submit humbly the following for Your Imperial Majesty's gracious approval.

1. Your Imperial Majesty's ukaz of April 17, 1732 has decreed that Captain Commander Bering be sent to Kamchatka again and that the Senate is to review and make a decision regarding his proposals concerning shipbuilding there and other projects to benefit the Empire and enhance Your Imperial Majesty's interests, for which purpose it is necessary to send the requisite number of servitors and equipment. All necessary supplies are to be sent; the Governor of Siberia [Aleksei L. Pleshcheev] and his associates and the Irkutsk Vice Governor are to provide assistance to Bering; and Grigorii Skorniakov-Pisarev, who was assigned to Okhotsk, is to be transferred to this previous assignment where he will remain.

In accordance with Your Imperial Majesty's ukaz concerning dispatching Bering and the naval officers he has requested, appropriate ukazes have already been sent to the Admiralty College and to other places, wherever necessary. Bering himself has received an ukaz indicating that in 1731 it was decided that Pisarev make the necessary preparations in Kamchatka and Okhotsk and in that general region. Subsequently the Senate decided on June 12 that in order to fulfill the goal of the expedition completely, one of the professors who is a member of the Academy of Sciences would be sent with students and with astronomical instruments and other equipment to make astronomical observations.

This professor is to take with him the assayer [S.] Gardebol, who was sent to Kamchatka in 1727 with Captain Pavlutskii's group. The Senate has also decided to send two or three men from the Ekaterinburg mining complexes who will find persons who are knowledgeable about metallic ores. They will take the necessary instruments and equipment so that wherever rich metals or minerals are found they will be able to assay them and determine their quality without delay.

The Academy of Sciences responded that not one but two professors should be sent, who want to go, as well as other master workmen and also students. By Senate decree, twelve students from the Slavonic Latin School in Moscow have been ordered to go to the Academy where they will be given scientific training and practical experience in the natural sciences pertaining to the expedition. In accordance with the ukaz from the Senate, on November 24 the Academy submitted a number of instructions to the Senate regarding the assignment for the professors on the expedition.

In the meantime, on September 12 the Senate decided that in conjunction with dispatching Captain Commander Bering, special detailed instructions should be drawn up for the voyage and other matters. The Senate also decided that a reliable Russian naval captain and several junior officers should be sent. Members of the Admiralty College were invited to the Senate to consult and to present their views on these and all other matters pertaining to this expedition.

The Admiralty College offered its considered opinions to the Senate and advanced the idea that it would be useful to make various observations and explorations at sea during the expedition, not only between Kamchatka and Japan and America, but also in the Arctic, out from the mouths of rivers that empty into the [Arctic] ocean, such as the Ob, Lena and Kolyma, as well as from the town of Arkhangelsk to the mouth of the Ob. There are to be three seagoing vessels and five double sloops. In addition to Captain Commander Bering, the Admiralty College has appointed Captain Spanberg and Captain Lieutenant Chirikov, both of whom were on the first expedition, and also one lieutenant, three second lieutenants and 157 servitors and sailors. Thus in accordance with the above, the expediton will be fully manned and completely equipped.

No qualified officers have been assigned in Okhotsk, where the first harbor for the Pacific and for Kamchatka is located, or in Kamchatka itself. A resolution of May 2, 1732 from the Governing Senate, Point 10, authorizes the Sibirskii Prikaz to appoint a special commanding officer in Kamchatka from among those men who are in Siberia or Kamchatka. Captain Pavlutskii has been recommended for this; he was there with a party in 1727 to subdue natives who had previously paid iasak but who, because of a shortage of [Russian] manpower in Kamchatka, had gone off with other natives not under Russian rule.

Under present conditions, however, it may be impossible for the person who is presently appointed, or who may in the future be appointed under the earlier ukaz, to prepare and correct internal conditions in such a distant, new and boundless region. For that purpose, the commanding officer who is to be sent to Okhotsk should be selected from those here who are experienced. He should be properly recompensed for his service on such a distant assignment, and as commanding officer of Okhotsk he should have Kamchatka under his jurisdiction as well as the entire coastal region. At present all that area is under the jurisdiction of the voevoda of Iakutsk, and a look at the map will clearly show that he has more than enough territory under his control without the addition of the above mentioned.

Concerning all matters that Pisarev and then later Bering were assigned to handle, such as the relocation and settlement of people, the production of grain and livestock and the collection of iasak and liquor revenues, complete instructions should be prepared for the commanding officer of Kamchatka in the Senate because Captain Commander Bering and the others will actually be at sea and there will be no free time in Kamchatka and Okhotsk to care for all the matters relating to his departure from the port and the administration of the local populace. Furthermore, if any emergency should arise during the naval expedition, the Okhotsk commander will be expected to take charge and provide assistance to them and to attend to other matters.

In accordance with the instructions of 1731, 300 of the 1,500 servitors assigned to Iakutsk were ordered to go to the Okhotsk and Kamchatka ostrogs without replacements; peasants were to be transferred to work the land; Tungus and Iakuts were assigned to care for the livestock. In addition to these, exiled convicts have been sent there as punishment, and persons indebted to the Treasury are also being sent there. Gradually these persons will increase the population in the port and in Kamchatka

2. In its review the Admiralty College has submitted the following. In accordance with the instructions issued by the Emperor Peter the Great, of blessed and eternally deserving memory, which He personally gave to Captain Commander Bering, while Bering was on the [first] expedition he searched to see whether or not Kamchatka and America are joined. However, as Bering has reported, on the basis of that instruction he went along the coast of Kamchatka northeast all the way to 67° latitude, and as he has indicated on the map of that expedition, up to that particular degree of latitude there is no land which joins Kamchatka and America. Above that latitude Bering has indicated the region north and west to the mouth of the Kolyma River, but he obtained this information from earlier maps and reports, and thus it is not certain whether or not the continents are joined. It may be possible to voyage along that coast from the Ob River to the Lena and beyond, near the shore. There is no information about some places, and for that reason it is impossible to ascertain. There are neither adequate maps nor reports.

Because of this, the Admiralty College believes that in order to obtain first hand information as to whether or not Kamchatka and America are joined, and whether there is a northern sea route, there should be built double sloops, each with a deck and 24 oars. One should be built in Tobolsk on the Irtysh River and two in Iakutsk on the Lena River. Considering the present routes and the peoples there, these places will be most appropriate.

Falconets are to be placed on these vessels. The one built in Tobolsk is to proceed down the Ob River to its mouth and then continue east along the coast [of the Arctic Ocean] all the way to the mouth of the Enisei. One of the vessels built in Iakutsk is to sail down the Lena River to its mouth and from there is to proceed west along the coast to the mouth of the Enisei, toward the one that will come from the mouth of the Ob. The other is to go from Iakutsk to the mouth [of the Lena River] and sail east along the coast to the mouth of the Kolyma. From there it is to continue east along the coast, and after rounding the point which on the map is located in 73°, it is to sail along the coast to the mouths of the Anadyr and Kamchatka rivers. In the same way the coast of the Arctic Ocean is to be explored from Arkhangelsk to the Ob River. For that purpose a suitable vessel is to be sent out from Arkhangelsk so that no great time will be lost for these various expeditions.

Foreign vessels sail at will beyond Arkhangelsk to the Pechora River, where Pustozersk ostrog is situated, in order to catch salmon. The coast is uncharted beyond the Pechora to the mouth of the Ob River. It is particularly dangerous since between Novaia Zemlia and the natural coast, the map shows the strait as quite narrow.

3. The Admiralty College is of the opinion that officers should be appointed for these double sloops, one second lieutenant for each, and as many other ranks as may be necessary, to be selected from the above mentioned number. In order to have the best possible informed men, search in Siberia for all possible individuals who have been at the mouths of these and other rivers to hunt and fish. Select three or four men who are to be appropriately provided with money and provisions.

The Admiralty College believes that several months' supply of provisions for all the persons assigned to the expedition should be sent to the Governor of Siberia because it would be possible to ship it all down the Ob and Lena rivers. Likewise, small supply depots are to be set up along other rivers which empty between those mentioned above. If, because of ice or other problems, the sloops which are sent out do not reach their destinations, or if they are delayed or have to winter over, then when they arrive they could use the provisions which have been prepared.

To render the best possible assistance to the sloops on their voyages, persons who are being dispatched to collect iasak should be sent out early. These persons should be accompanied by geodesists and guides who should inform all the nomadic iasak natives and promyshlenniks along the coast that they are to watch for these sloops, and in case of any problems give them assistance without delay. They are to prepare beacon lights at the mouths of these rivers and during the months when the ice is moving these should be kept lighted at night as soon as the sloop approaches. They are to inform other settlements about this and report to Tobolsk. When a sloop approaches, the officer should reward the keeper of the beacon light with trinkets up to one ruble in value.

While the geodesists are on that assignment, they should

spend as much time as possible preparing a description as to the degree in which each river mouth or sea cape is located. They should also make notes as to where help may be obtained from iasak natives and from promyshlenniks and where the beacon lights are to be built. When they return with that information they are to prepare maps with a brief description and give this information to the officers in command of the sloops and send the other information to the Senate through the office of the voevoda.

4. The island opposite the mouth of the Kolyma River in the Arctic Ocean is to be located on a map. This has been known as Velikaia Zemlia [Great Land]. Some Siberiaks have been there and have seen people there. They have reported about this in detail to Bering and his men in Iakutsk. If this proves to be true, then the sloops are to put ashore on this island or on other islands or land which they have been sent to explore. On shore they are to investigate as much as possible. If they encounter people, they are to treat them well and not antagonize them in any way. They are to obtain information as to how large these islands and lands are, how far they extend and what they have in abundance.

They are to find an opportunity to entice the natives by giving them small presents similar to the ones given to Siberian princelings and other natives at the time of their first encounter. If these people express willingness to become [Russian] subjects, they are to be accepted, especially those who have been enticed. If necessary, precautions should be taken. These people are not to be abused in any way. Allow them to live among each other as they will. Encourage them to pay iasak but do not interfere much with them. Proceed with the explorations so as not to lose any time.

If they reach a place where the Siberian coast is joined to that of America, for which reason it is impossible to proceed to Kamchatka, then they are to follow the coast which goes north as far as possible. En route they are to treat the people they meet as indicated above. They are to inquire how far across that land it is to the Pacific Ocean. They are then to return to the mouth of the Lena and thence to Iakutsk, as before, without delay, before the ice forms.

If, while they are voyaging along the northern coastline, they unexpectedly reach some possession belonging to a European sovereign, in that case they are to act in accordance with the instructions which Bering and Chirikov are given. If they do not discover any connection to the American lands, they are definitely not to return, but are to round the point and continue on to Kamchatka as noted above.

5. In order to discover the American coast from Kamchatka, if boats are being built in Okhotsk according to the 1731 instructions, or if they have been completed, then they are to be inspected. If they are suitable for the designated voyage, two of the boats are to be used. If they are not complete, finish them. If they have not been started, or if they have been started but are inadequate for such a voyage, then the opinion of the Admiralty College is that they should not be built in Okhotsk because of the lack of timber there.

According to Captain Commander Bering's proposal, there is a suitable roadstead in the Kamchatka River and good forest nearby. Therefore two packetboats should be built on the Kamchatka River. If one is shipwrecked, the other could provide assistance and information. However, if one vessel has been started or completed in Okhotsk and is suitable for the voyage, then build the other one in Kamchatka. When they have been armed and completely outfitted, Captain Commander Bering is to sail on one and Captain Lieutenant Chirikov on the other. They are to sail together and not separate from one another. In this manner they are to search most diligently and zealously for these American shores or islands. They are to act in mutual agreement in all matters, in accordance with naval regulations. They are to take counsel concerning various routes to America with the professors who have been sent from the Academy of Sciences. The Academy has prepared instructions to which Bering and Chirikov are to be privy.

6. In his most recent report from Kamchatka, Captain Pavlutskii stated that the servitor Afanasii Melnikov, who was sent out from Iakutsk in 1725 to explore and to urge the unsubdued natives to come under [Russian] suzerainty and to pay iasak, had just returned from Cape Chukotsk with a small detachment. He reported that in April of 1730, while he was on Cape Chukotsk, two natives came there from an island in the sea. These natives insert walrus teeth into their mouths. They told Melnikov where their dwellings are located and said they live on an island about a day's voyage from Cape Chukotsk. They said it takes one day to

voyage from their island to the next, which is called Bolshaia Zemlia [Big Land] and abounds in wild animals such as sable, fox, beaver, river wolverine, lynx and reindeer. There are also all kinds of trees there. They also said that nomadic reindeer-herding natives live there in great numbers.

Although it is impossible to confirm such reports, nonetheless on this voyage an investigation should be made into people living east of Cape Chukotsk. Sail to those islands which appear to be clearly on the route to America. When you arrive there, treat the people in accordance with point 4 of your instructions and also carry out all your other instructions. Then proceed toward America and explore islands and lands, because with the exception of Pavlutskii's report, there is no other information as to whether there are lands and islands between the known parts of the Kamchatka and American coast, or whether there is simply one sea, which, according to the map of the learned Professor Delisle,* extends from Chukotsk Cape about 45 degrees to the Spanish province of Mexico.

When you reach the American coast proper, act in accordance with the earlier instruction given to Captain Bering by His Imperial Majesty Peter the Great: try to reach some town or settlement under European jurisdiction. If you encounter any European ship, ask what the name of the coast is and make note of this in writing. Then you personally are to go ashore and obtain firsthand information. Locate it on a map and return to the coast of Kamchatka, investigating other new lands or islands en route. Stay out of danger so as not to fall into hostile hands. Do not reveal your route to anyone who is not privy to your assignment.

7. For the purpose of observation and for discovery of a route to Japan, in accordance with the instructions of the Admiralty College, on the Kamchatka River you are to build one boat with a deck and two double sloops, each with 24 oars and a deck, and fit them with guns. Captain Spanberg is then to proceed on the designated voyage for which the Admiralty College appointed him. If there is a vessel left from the previous expedition which is in good enough condition that a voyage could safely be made with it, there would be no need to build a new one, only to build the two sloops mentioned above.

---

*Joseph Nicholas Delisle (1688–1768) French astronomer and cartographer, was named chief astronomer for the Russian Academy of Sciences.

First, proceed to those islands which lie south of Cape Kamchatka toward Japan, some of which are already under Russian jurisdiction. Iasak has already been collected in Kamchatka from the people who live on those islands, but because of the small number of people, the collection is being suspended for the present.

Some years ago the navigator Evreev [I. M. Evreinov?] was sent there and sighted and described six other islands. You are to prepare the fullest possible report and description about these and any other islands you may discover, both those that are inhabited and those that are not. And if you should discover other islands or lands further on toward Japan, which belong to the Japanese ruler or some other Asian ruler, you are to investigate these. Establish friendly relations with the people living there in accordance with point 4, and learn as much as possible about their conditions and everything else. You are not to take any hostile action toward them. After that, proceed on to the coast of Japan itself. While you are there, find out about the government, about ports, and about whether amicable relations can be established with the country.

Captain Commander Bering stated that during his stay in Kamchatka some shipwrecked Japanese had been seen and he ordered an inquiry made. In 1731, in accordance with the order of the Senate, the Russians were not only ordered not to antagonize these Japanese, but to render them every assistance and to send them back to the places from whence they had come, thereby giving an indication of friendship and neighborliness.

If, prior to Bering's arrival, there has been no opportunity to send these shipwrecked Japanese back, and if they can still be found, then they are to be provided with all necessities. Take them with you, and while you are [sailing] along the coast of Japan, reveal as your purpose that you have returned the men who were wrecked on our shores. Then hand them over, if authorities will accept them. However, some accounts say that the Japanese do not save men who are wrecked at sea, because they consider them dead. So if authorities do refuse to accept them, put them ashore so they can return to their own homes.

If you have an opportunity to pick up [other] shipwrecked Japanese along the coast, or if during your voyage you should find wrecked Japanese vessels, then give the men every possible friendly assistance and take them, and their boats if possible, alongside your vessels toward the Japanese coast. Either hand them over or put them ashore as noted above, in order that your friendship may conquer their inveterate Asiatic isolationist attitudes. The more often this happens, the more information you can obtain.

8. While you are along the Japanese coast, or near its possessions, do not linger near the islands nor heed any attempts to delay you, lest they detain you through deceit and ready their own ships to attack you. Instead, make an excuse and return when you have found out everything you can about them. Likewise, during these first encounters you are to be on guard against any possible deception on their part. This is customary with them, for what they cannot achieve through strength they try to attain through flattery and reassurance. They substitute deception for wisdom.

Bering has suggested that during the voyage, because of our shortage of ships, it would be acceptable to take possession of any Japanese ships they may encounter, but this is not to be done. No hostile action is to be taken during these first encounters, either against vessels or against people on shore. As noted above, this is prohibited because if even minor hostility is evidenced at sea, it will be impossible to establish friendly relations on land.

It will be necessary to use interpreters to make inquiries about them. Such inquiries must be made politely, and everything is to be recorded in writing. Kamchadals who know the language of the island people are to be used as interpreters. For the more distant islands, interpreters should be taken from inhabitants of the preceding islands, and people from the most distant island should interpret the Japanese language; moreover, the language can be learned from them if necessary. They are to receive pay and provisions in accordance with your judgment. Any shipwrecked Japanese who may be with you on that voyage can also serve as interpreters.

9. In the past in Siberia, and even now in Kamchatka, both the natives who come under Russian suzerainty and those who were previously local native princelings have received small gifts in the name of Your Imperial Highness when they pay their iasak. These gifts are items such as scarlet fabric, knives, needles, tinware and similar things. For this reason, in the present situation when this is such an important expedition to distant places, it

would be very useful to use the same approach with local people on the new islands and on land, in order to make friends of them. Bering reported that when he was in Kamchatka, they gave the Kamchadals and other natives small amounts of Chinese *shar* [brick] tobacco. He said this was so helpful to him in achieving his goals that he was able to accomplish many things he could not otherwise have done, even with more expensive goods. For this purpose Bering should take with him fabrics purchased from the Sibirskii Prikaz and other small goods which would be useful there, as well as Chinese shar tobacco from Siberia, as much as 2,000 rubles worth. Officers who are sent to explore the Arctic coast should be given some of this, and the rest is to be taken to Okhotsk and Kamchatka. When the sea and land expeditions are sent out, they should take whatever is deemed necessary.

These things should be given as presents to princelings and natives, in accordance with previous custom, because no money circulates among them and they do not need any. They barter furs for whatever they need. Everything that is sent with the expeditions, and all expenses they incur, are to be recorded in special expenditure books.

10. For further expeditions to explore places in the Kamchatka Sea, one or two vessels are to be readied with naval personnel and Siberian servitors who are familiar with those areas. The coast around Okhotsk and the rivers which fall into the sea are to be described, up to and including the Ud River. It is particularly important to learn how far ships can sail, where there are forests along the banks of rivers and where there is land suitable for farming.

Some reports say there are many forested areas there which would have timber suitable for ship construction and that the land is good for agriculture. However, explorations should not be made from the mouth of the Ud to the Tugur River where the Russian Tugur ostrog once stood, which was destroyed by the Chinese, nor beyond the Tugur to the Amur River and farther, even though no opposition is encountered, because the suspicion of the Chinese must not be aroused.

The Chinese rule the lands beyond the Tugur to the Amur and farther, including Korea and other lands. Opposite the mouth of the Ud are the unpopulated Shantar Islands, which have been located on the map. Our information is that there are many sables on these islands and that promyshlenniks have hunted there. For the above reason, do not go to these islands, nor to the Bolshoi Ostrov [Sakhalin] which lies opposite the mouth of the Amur and which is inhabited.

11. In voyaging to all of these places, along new lands and islands, it is essential to look for appropriate sites for harbors and places where one could take refuge during storms or ice at sea. Also look for forested areas which would have lumber suitable for shipbuilding. With this information, in the future, vessels could put into such places for safety or to fulfill other needs. Likewise, wherever it is possible and conditions permit, put the previously mentioned mining experts ashore with appropriate guards. They are to be instructed to prospect for ores.

Wherever rich minerals and metals are found, they are to take small samples of ore, or depending on circumstances, larger samples, and describe such locations in detail. If they find rich mineral deposits in places under Russian jurisdiction, and the large samples they take indicate a profit may be expected, then as soon as they return to Okhotsk they are to inform the commanding officer of Okhotsk, or if they return elsewhere, the commanding officer in that place. These officers will then send experienced men, accompanied by the requisite number of people to protect them and to work. They also will take equipment, supplies and provisions. Every effort must be made to ensure that Your Imperial Majesty's interests will benefit from this. When this is done, the Senate is to be informed in writing and samples of ore are to be sent.

12. The Ud River has its source in the mountains or hills which separate the lake, called the Baikal Sea, from the watershed of the Lena River. Promyshlenniks hunt sable in these mountains, as do iasak natives from the Iakutsk administrative region. It is apparent from looking at the map that these places have not been described in detail. We need to find the shortest route to the Sea of Kamchatka without going to Iakutsk for the purpose of sending small parcels and correspondence. For that reason both geodesists and knowledgeable local Siberians should be sent there immediately, and instructed to describe and survey all the rivers which flow from the east into Lake Baikal, with the exception of the Selenga and the Angara which have already been described. They should also describe the sources of the rivers that flow into the

Lena. If these can be found, then they should also find a route between these rivers and the source of the Ud River, which could be used for both summer and winter travel in order to cut the distance of the present route via Iakutsk.

13. While on these voyages, Captain Commander Bering and the other commanders of the vessels are to conduct themselves in the following manner. Each will receive special instructions from the Admiralty College such as the College has sent to the Senate. These will include additional Senate recommendations. They are to keep these instructions secret and in safekeeping, especially during the voyages. For public disclosure, Bering and Chirikov will sail toward America and Spanberg toward Japan. Special instructions will be issued from the College for these ships and for the sloop which will sail east from the Lena toward Kamchatka. These instructions will indicate that as a result of the request and desire of the Academies [of Sciences] in St. Petersburg and in Paris and other places, the Emperor Peter the Great, of blessed and eternal memory, dispatched an expedition out of curiosity to discover from His own shores whether the shores of America are joined to those of Asia.

Since this quest was not accomplished at that time [during the First Bering Expedition], now Your Imperial Majesty has ordered the present voyagers to be sent out to satisfy the curiosity of these Academies. Upon resolving the question they are to return. If en route they reach some European or Asian power's possessions, or if they discover ships belonging to another power, they are to request friendly assistance and information from them for this quest. At an appropriate time they are to reveal this orally to foreigners, if asked, and show this instruction, since it will contain no compromising information. European powers themselves have sent out such exploring expeditions by sea, and not one of them has yet discovered definitely whether or not the American shores are joined to those of Asia.

The Admiralty College will issue a statement based on its judgment as to how many senior and junior officers and ranks and artisans should be sent with these commanders, and whether men should be selected who have previously been in Siberia and Kamchatka. As far as the lower ranks and artisans are concerned, these should be taken if possible from among Russians living in Siberia. The required number of soldiers and drummers should be taken from the Siberian garrison regiments. Also to be sent from here with a convoy are twelve men and a corporal, selected from the sailors and grenadiers. During the expedition, both on land and at sea, these men could prepare rockets and grenades, not for battle, but to impress primitive people who have never seen or heard such things.

14. The Admiralty College directs that such pieces of artillery and appropriate supplies as can be found there be prepared. The College will obtain direction from Captain Commander Bering on this matter because he has been there and can advise what is available, in what quantity, how much additional is needed and where it is most likely to be obtained. In regard to provisions, the Admiralty College advises that these should be prepared in Iakutsk for the servitors who are being sent to Kamchatka and Okhotsk, in accordance with the appended list. For that purpose, [appropriate] ukazes are to be sent to those places. An adequate number of boats must be built to transport goods from Iakutsk by water, and proper equipment for transporting provisions must be prepared. The Admiralty College believes it is necessary to send officers there now to attend to all these preparations. They will be responsible jointly with the local commanders for rapid preparation. Once everything is ready, the provisions and all other supplies are to be sent out on the route with all possible speed so they will be ready in Okhotsk by the time Captain Commander Bering arrives and his voyage will not be delayed in the least.

The 1731 instructions stipulate the wages and the amount of provisions for the servitors and the amount of equipment. All of this is to be sent by water from Iakutsk to [Iudoma] Cross in good time in spring, using the Iakutsk servitors to transport it. From the Cross all of this is to be delivered to Okhotsk where for the time being the servitors will supervise it.

Vessels that return to Iakutsk are to transport the collected treasury furs. One official will accompany the Iakutsk people so they will not travel in vain over the great distance to Iakutsk, transporting the treasury, and to receive their wages, as has happened in the past. On May 2 of this year this was approved at Bering's request. Consequently, in sending out provisions and other supplies for the present expedition from Iakutsk to Okhotsk, everything is to be done in accordance with the earlier orders. For better and more rapid preparations, and for the dispatching of officers in the future, the Admiralty College will issue instructions in accordance with its own judgment.

15. Because this expedition is the most distant and the most difficult, and never before have men been sent to these unknown places, would it not be appropriate for Your Imperial Majesty to give monetary awards, and to grant everyone on that expedition double pay? Also, the geodesists have never held a rank. Some have been on assignments in Kamchatka and Siberia for many years, and others who are being sent out from here have been in Siberia and on other distant assignments. For this service, they should be given the rank of second lieutenant. Those who are being sent on their first assignment should be given the rank of ensign.

All should receive pay commensurate with their ranks, based on the new military regulations. All of them will be all the more diligent on their assignments for having been better recompensed. When they have accomplished and fulfilled their assignments to the benefit of Your Imperial Majesty's interests, they should return, assured of Your Imperial Majesty's gracious rewards. The designated pay should be given to them upon their departure, either here [St. Petersburg] or in Moscow, for a year in advance, and in Tobolsk and Iakutsk, upon request, for an additional year. Thus in those remote regions where they can neither buy nor be supplied with necessities, they will have been able to obtain these items ahead of time and can proceed fully outfitted.

In regard to their pay for future years, as long as they are on that expedition, the manner in which their pay is sent to them should be detailed in instructions to be sent to the Governor of Siberia and the Irkutsk Vice Governor, on the basis of the requests and proposals from Captain Commander Bering and his associates. These funds should be made to the account of this expedition, because at present there is no exact information about the actual conditions in various places there, and the Kamchatka revenues cannot be ascertained precisely.

16. Professor Ludwig [sic; Louis] Delisle de la Croyère,* of the Academy of Sciences, is responsible for all the astronomical,

---

*Louis Delisle de la Croyère (?–1741), was the younger half-brother of Joseph Nicholas Delisle; because of a somewhat tarnished reputation he had been persuaded to use his mother's name. An astronomer and cartographer like his brother, he was nonetheless much inferior to him as a scholar.

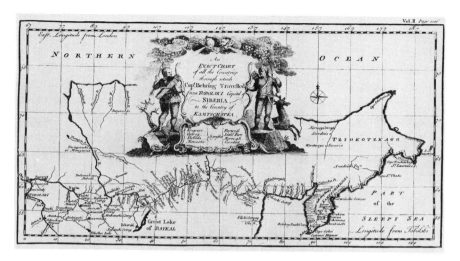

This "exact chart," with its fanciful cartouche of fur clad natives and blizzards scarcely reveals the wicked terrain Bering and his men traversed. The transport of heavy equipment, anchors, ironwork, spikes, and hawsers to Kamchatka for the 1741 voyage took six years. Note the "Sleepy Sea" designation for the Pacific. Harris, *A Complete Collection of Voyages and Travels*. (OHS neg. 80260)

physical and other observations. In accordance with a proposal made by him, the Senate has issued instructions that he is to have the geodesists he especially requested, Semen Popov and Andrei Krasilnikov, who have spent several years studying astronomical observations in the St. Petersburg Observatory. They are to receive astronomical tables with written instructions on how to proceed in preparing new geographical maps. They are to consult with him and use instruments which they have obtained from him and submit written reports about all their observations and activities.

During his voyage with Captain Commander Bering, Delisle de la Croyère is to advise and assist him on all matters pertaining to Your Imperial Majesty's interests and on any needs Bering himself may have. This professor has asked that a good interpreter be sent with the geodesists, one who knows French or Latin, and also a good mechanic who is familiar with the equipment and can repair it if necessary. He will thus serve not only as an interpreter, but also as an instructor to the students of the Slavonic-Latin School who are going on that expedition. The person who is to care for the instruments is to be sent by the Academy.

When Bering reaches Kamchatka he will build the ships for the voyage. By his own request the professor will make astronomical observations wherever appropriate during his free time in Siberia. If such observations are performed by other officers of the command while Bering is there, they are to be assisted and supplied with necessities. In addition, an ukaz is to be issued that such persons are to be given living quarters and assigned appropriate places for making observations. They are also to be provided with guides to take them from one place to another. Wherever artisans and laborers are required, help and assistance are also to be provided.

Likewise, in order to further our knowledge of geography, those who assist the professor are to find answers to his questions and discuss these matters with him. Those to whom he gives barometers or thermometers to record changes in climatic conditions are to send their reports to the voevodas, who will forward the reports to the Senate. The professor is also to send his own observations to the Senate. Communications to him from the Academy of Sciences are to be sent to the Senate, from whence they will be forwarded via the [regular] postal service. As soon as they reach Siberian towns they are to be sent on immediately to wherever the professor is at that time.

The professor is to have ten carts to transport his instruments and books from St. Petersburg to Moscow and on to Tobolsk, and he is also to receive funds for transport. Beyond Tobolsk he is to have carts for overland travel and a boat for water travel, as the Governor of Siberia may deem appropriate. At times the professor will be in remote places where he will not have supplies of his own and where he is unable to purchase them. If government provisions are available in such places, in accordance with the professor's request, he is to be issued everything he needs from the government warehouses at cost, for as long as necessary. He is to be given two years' salary in advance now, and anything due him from the Academy is to be drawn for him on the Academy's account.

The professors and their fellow travelers are to forward information about observations and surveys to the Senate. The reports and letters are to be sent through the Senate office. When letters are received from Siberia from the professors they will be translated into Russian. The translations will be left in the office and the originals sent on to the Academy where in due time books will be prepared in Russian and other languages. Until permits to publish are issued, however, no information is to be revealed, either secretly or openly, anywhere, orally or in writing. This information is not to be available in foreign countries before it is available in this country.

In order to maintain this secrecy the professors and everyone with them on the expedition, as well as professors in the Academy of Sciences and everyone else involved in any way with the expedition, are to be informed in writing that if they reveal any information contrary to this order they will be punished, however ukazes direct. On this matter the Senate requests Your Imperial Majesty's most gracious approval.

Reference: Russia. *Polnoe sobranie zakonov rossiiskoi imperii s 1649 goda.* First series (St. Petersburg: 1830), VIII, 1002–1013.

26

AN EXTRACT FROM A SENATE UKAZ TO THE ADMIRALTY COLLEGE, GIVING THE TESTIMONY OF AFANASII MELNIKOV, A MEMBER OF THE EXPEDITION HEADED BY CAPTAIN DMITRII I. PAVLUTSKII, REGARDING NATIVE REPORTS OF AN ISLAND IN THE SEA OFF THE COAST OF CAPE CHUKOTSK, POSSIBLY IN THE DIRECTION OF AMERICA

In his last report from Kamchatka, Captain [Dmitrii I.] Pavlut-skii reported information brought back by the servitor Afanasii Melnikov, one of a small party of men who had returned from Cape Chukotsk. The group had been sent out from Iakutsk in 1725 to search for unsubdued natives and urge them to come under Russian suzerainty and pay iasak. Melnikov stated that in April, 1730, while he was at Cape Chukotsk, two Chukchi men wearing walrus teeth in their mouths came to Cape Chukotsk from an island in the sea. They told Melnikov about their dwellings on that island, which is located one day's voyage from the great Cape Chukotsk. They said that it takes one day to travel from their island to another island called Bolshaia Zemlia [Alaska], where many animals are to be found, such as sable, fox, river beaver, wolverine, lynx and wild reindeer. There are also many varieties of trees and a substantial number of nomadic reindeer-herding natives.

Although it is impossible to verify this conversation, nevertheless during this voyage one should make inquiries of the Chukchi natives and proceed to these islands to discover whether there are any lands directly en route to America, learn about the people there and about everthing else, as instructed in Point 4 [of the Instructions]. Then they should proceed to America and observe the islands and territories, because except for Pavlutskii's report, there is no other information as to whether there are lands and islands between the known coasts of Kamchatka and America or whether there is open sea, as indicated by the learned Professor Delisle on his map, extending some 45 degrees from Cape Chukotsk to the Spanish province of Mexico.

When they reach the coast of America, they are to follow the earlier instructions given by His Imperial Majesty Peter the

Choris depicted the strong features of the St. Lawrence natives off the coast of the Chukotsk Peninsula, possibly the "island in the sea" reported by servitor Melnikov to Captain Pavlutskii. Choris, *Voyage Pittoresque.* . . . (OHS neg. 80230)

Louis Choris drawing of a typical native dwelling on the island of St. Lawrence shows the finely woven baskets used for cooking and storage, the beautifully sewn parkas, and the tambour-drum used for dancing festivities. Note the prized furs which propelled the activities of Russian traders and explorers. Choris, *Voyage Pittoresque.* . . . (OHS neg. 80252)

Great to Captain Bering in 1725, and sail to some town or settlement belonging to a European power; or if they encounter a European vessel, they are to find out what the name of the coast

Methods of boat construction used by the natives of St. Lawrence Island reveal their sturdy seagoing characteristics basically similar to the Aleut baidara. Choris, *Voyage Pittoresque.* . . . (OHS neg. 80254)

is, make a written description of it and put in to shore. Then, having acquired detailed information, they are to locate it on a map and return to the coast of Kamchatka, using a different route . . .

Reference: TsGADA, f. Dela Pravitelstvuiushchego Senata 1731–1732, d. 664, 11. 135 ob., 136.
See: A. V. Efimov, ed. *Iz istorii russkikh ekspeditsii na Tikhom Okeane. Pervaia polovina XVIII veka* (Moscow: 1948), 212–213.

27

A REPORT FROM THE ADMIRALTY COLLEGE TO THE SENATE CONCERN-
ING INSTRUCTIONS TO BERING TO SURVEY THE AMERICAN COAST,
MAP IT AND RETURN TO KAMCHATKA

In accordance with the personal ukaz of Her Imperial Majesty, on December 31, 1732 the Governing Senate gave orders to Captain Commander Bering and Captain Chirikov, who were sent on the Kamchatka Expedition. The instructions for their expedition to the coast of America orders them to describe the exact moment when the American coast comes into view, because according to the earlier instructions from His Imperial Majesty Peter the Great to Bering in 1725, when [Bering] reached any town or settlement belonging to a European power, or encountered some European ship, he was to ascertain the name of the coast, record it and go ashore in person. When he had secured detailed information and had located the place on a map, he was to return to the coast of Kamchatka.

Now, however, it is the judgment of the Admiralty College that although it was definitely the intention of His Imperial Majesty of Blessed and Glorious Memory to have Bering take his [first] expedition to some such site belonging to a European power, nevertheless at the present time such an expedition is not considered useful, nor is it prudent, for the following reasons:

1. Her Imperial Majesty's all-gracious intention is only that the unknown coast of America be discovered.

2. It is impossible to know how little or how much time an unknown route would require to find the coast of America. Moreover, if from the place where they discover America they were to continue on to European possessions, to would be impossible for them to return to the coast of Kamchatka in the course of one summer.

3. According to the scholarly map which Professor Delisle has prepared, and in the judgment of both Bering and Chirikov, it appears that the distance of a direct route between that province

[America] and Kamchatka is some 5,000 versts, which is no small distance. There is no information about settlements closer than that province in America belonging to a European power.

4. If they were to proceed on, they would have to spend the winter en route, which is thought to be extremely dangerous because it is not known whether they would find places appropriate for wintering over where the ships would be safe. Moreover, it is impossible to obtain enough provisions for two voyages of more than a year's duration.

5. It is considered neither important nor necessary to reach such European possessions, because these places are already known and located on the maps. Furthermore, certain Spanish ships have surveyed the American coast up to 40° of latitude or even above.

6. Finally, there is the danger that they might encounter strong hostility from local officials of European possessions because they are under Spanish protection. History and other information reveal that local peoples in that possession do not carry on trade with anyone without permission through His Royal Spanish Majesty's decree, and that they consider everyone who comes there an enemy.

For these reasons it is the opinion of the Admiralty College that a statement must be included in the instructions for this voyage to the effect that at first they should proceed in accordance with the suggestion and opinion of Professor Delisle, as well as in accordance with their own mutual judgment. When they find the American coast they should remain on the coast and make detailed observations of what kind of people live there, what the name of the place is, and whether it is indeed actually part of the American coast. After they have done this and have verified their observations, they are to locate everything on the map and then proceed, exploring the coast as long as time and circumstances permit, using their best judgment so they will be able to return to the coast of Kamchatka in good time, when the weather is favorable there. They are not to have their hands tied, lest this voyage be without result, as was the case with the first.

Since the Admiralty College cannot order this without an ukaz, it reports this to the Governing Senate and requests an ukaz from Her Imperial Majesty.

[Signed] Naum Seniavin

Golovin

Vasilii Dmitriev Mamonov

Ober-Secretary Vasilii Mikhailov

Reference: TsGADA, f. Senat, kn. 666, 11. 400–401.

See: V.A. Divin, ed. *Russkaia tikhookeanskaia epopeia* (Khabarovsk: 1979), 179–181.

28

APRIL 10, 1741

A STATEMENT FROM THE COSSACK ILIA SKURIKHIN CONCERNING THE VOYAGE OF THE *SV. GAVRIIL* TO THE SHORES OF BOLSHAIA ZEMLIA [AMERICA] IN 1732

On April 10, 1741, the cossack Ilia Skurikhin added the following information to his previous report to the office of the Port of Okhotsk dated April 8.

In the summer of the year 1732 (he says he does not remember the month or the day), the geodesist Mikhail Gvozdev, the navigator's mate and Ivan Fedorov set out from Kamchatka aboard the *Sv. Gavriil* on their voyage. Skurikhin was a member of that expedition.

They left the mouth of the Kamchatka River and sailed to the left, keeping the coast of Kamchatka in sight. In about two weeks they reached the mouth of the Anadyr River. While they were on that expedition, between the mouths of the Kamchatka and Anadyr rivers they saw two islands in the sea to the right, about 1½ or 2 versts distant from their ship. These islands appeared to be about three versts long. They did not see any trees on the islands, except for ground cedar, nor could they see any people living there. No one from the *Sv. Gavriil* went ashore on the islands.

From the mouth of the Anadyr they sailed directly east out to sea. They had sailed about five days with a favorable wind when they sighted land a little to the left of their route. Believing that it was an island, they sailed directly toward it. When they were within half a verst of it they realized it was not an island, but a large land with a coast of yellow sand. There were iurt dwellings on shore and many people walking about. There is a large forest there of larch, spruce and poplar, and there were many reindeer. They sailed along that land to the left for about five days and still did not reach the end of land, nor could they see an end to it. They turned back because when they took soundings the water was not deep enough [for safe navigation].

As they were returning they were becalmed. A naked native paddled out to the vessel from land on an inflated bladder, but [Skurikhin] does not remember his name or sobriquet. Through a servitor who was acting as an interpreter aboard the *Sv. Gavriil*, the native asked where they had come from and where they were going.

The men on the *Sv. Gavriil* replied that they were lost at sea and were looking for Kamchatka. The native asked whether there were many people on the ship, to which they replied that some had died of starvation. Actually, however, some of the men had concealed themselves inside the vessel. The native showed them the direction in which to search for Kamchatka, the same direction from which they had come, and he invited them to put ashore, promising to give them plenty of food. Gvozdev tossed the native a gift packet of needles, thimbles and little bells. The native accepted these and paddled back to shore. Then he came back out from shore on his bladder boat, coming within 30 sazhens of our vessel, and put a small fish skin bladder in the water, then paddled back about 20 sazhens.

One naked man was sent from the *Sv. Gavriil* to pick up the bladder the native had left. When he swam up to the floating bladder, the native, upon seeing this, paddled back to land. On the bladder which the native had brought as a gift there were 2 marten parkas, 3 cross fox pelts and 10 red fox pelts. Gvozdev and the navigator's mate divided the parkas between themselves because they had given the native their own needles, thimbles and small bells. When the native then paddled up to the vessel, he conversed with them. They invited him to come on board the ship, but he would not come very close.

Shortly thereafter they turned back toward Kamchatka with the good weather and sailed along the coast for about five days. Then, leaving the coast, they continued their course to the right toward Kamchatka. When they reached the two islands mentioned previously, the ones they had seen earlier during their voyage, they went up to one of the islands and anchored. They sent a small sloop ashore with the following persons: the geodesist Gvozdev, the servitors Ivan Rebrov, Ivan Zalevin, Grigorii Nekhoroshikh, Mikhail Sharypov, Dmitrii Shchadrin, Efim Permiakov and Vasilii Zyrian, and the sailor Lavrentii Smetanin. They spent about four hours on the island and brought food back to the ship when they returned. They had the carcasses of 10 or 20 young reindeer, which provided enough meat for each of the 40 crew members to have a half or a third of a carcass. He does not remember precisely how much, because a good deal of time has elapsed.

They also brought back about 100 puds of walrus teeth which they sold to a monastery monk for two rubles per pud when they reached Kamchatka, but he does not remember the monk's name. They divided up the money from the sale. When Gvozdev and his men sailed back to the *Sv. Gavriil* from the island on the little sloop, a hundred or more men suddenly appeared on the shore of the island and fired arrows at them but did not wound anyone. In response to this hostility, [the Russians] fired their guns at the natives from the sloops. When the natives saw the gunfire they ran off throughout the island. When the men who had gone to the island returned to the ship, they said that they had found only three iurts on the island and that the inhabitants had run off. They took fawns and young reindeer from these iurts.

Several days after they sailed off from the island there was a heavy storm at sea and their mast broke. With great difficulty, and after a considerable time, they came to the mouth of the Kamchatka River. This happened in the fall, but he does not remember the exact month or day. The large land which they found can be reached in about five days from the mouth of the Anadyr River if the weather is good, and it is possible to reach it in a day or a day-and-a-half from Cape Chukotsk.

At the request of Ilia Skurikhin, the Okhotsk cossack Login Probylov has added his signature to this testimony in 1741. Captain Timofei Shmalev has witnessed this.

Reference: TsGADA, portfeli Millera, No. 528, I, No. 4, ll. 1–2.

See: A. I. Andreev, ed. *Russkie otkrytiia v Tikhom okeane i v Severnoi Amerike v XVIII veke* (Moscow: 1948), 101–103.

29

AN EXTRACT FROM THE REPORT OF ALEKSEI I. CHIRIKOV, SECOND-IN-
COMMAND OF THE BERING EXPEDITION (1735–1741), CONCERNING
HIS VOYAGE AND DISCOVERIES ALONG THE COAST OF AMERICA

September 9, 1741. At 10:00 A.M. we sighted seven small
boats, with one man in each, who appeared to be paddling
out toward us. These boats are about fifteen feet long and three
feet wide in the middle. The bow is very pointed and the stern
rounded. These craft are completely covered with the hides of
seal or sea lions. The decked area is curved and covered with the
same hide as the rest of the boat. Just back of the middle part
there is a circular opening in which the man sits, wearing a long
shirt-like garment with sleeves and a hood made of whale or other
gut, which is worn in place of a hat. He also wears a garment
similar to breeches made from the same hide, which ties around
him completely. Some of the natives had not totally tied up this
garment, so it was possible to see into their little craft and discern
that they had put some rocks inside. They use double-bladed
paddles which are made of birch and are very light. They use the
paddle on both sides of the boat; they proceed very boldly and
without fear of any kind of waves. These little craft are very
swift.

As they approached within 50 sazhens of our vessel they all
shouted, maneuvering around on both sides of our ship, not in
order to converse, but like the Iakut and Tungus shamans move
when they are performing their incantations. We then understood
that the people who were coming to us in their customary way
were performing rituals, or praying and casting a spell so that no
harm would come to them because of us. It was not possible to
learn precisely why they were shouting in such a strange fashion.
After they had shouted for a quarter of an hour, they began to
converse in a normal manner.

We made our appearance pleasant, nodded to them and beck-
oned with our hands for them to come closer to our ship, but they
were hesitant to approach and gestured as if they were using
bows and arrows. We understood this to mean that they were
afraid we would shoot at them. For that reason we made every

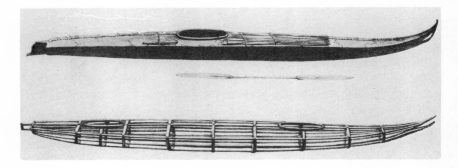

Choris accurately drew the baidarka for one or two occupants, as it was used along the Aleutian chain. Made of skins drawn over light wood and bone frames, this craft weighed less than ten pounds. Choris, *Voyage Pittoresque.* . . . (OHS neg. 80249)

effort to let them know that we would not harm them in any way. Then we put our hands on our chests and indicated that they would be received in friendship.

As a demonstration of kindness I tossed a Chinese cup to them as a token of friendship. One man retrieved it from the water, took it in his hands and waved it in such a manner that we could surmise that he did not need it and wanted to toss it back to us on the ship. We gestured that he should keep it for himself, but he threw it back into the water.

I then ordered two pieces of fabric to be cut, and again invited them to come up to the boat and tossed the fabric onto the water. They picked it out of the water, held it in their hands for a time and threw it back into the water, not keeping it for themselves. Then I ordered that various gifts be brought out such as beads, bells, needles, balls and pipes which they smoke. We showed these to them and summoned them to the ship.

I had only a few of the crew with me on the deck, having ordered the rest to stay below decks with firearms at hand in case of danger. For a long time we could not persuade the natives to come to us, even by using every gesture to let them know we would not harm them in any way if they came. Finally, we emboldened them to come by indicating that we did not have any water or anything else to drink, and wanted them to help us.

At last one of them approached our ship. We gave him Chinese tobacco and a pipe, which he accepted and placed on the deck of his little boat. Seeing this, the rest of them were also emboldened and came to the ship. We gave them little bells and metal trinkets and needles, which they accepted with no great gratitude, obviously unaware of how these things were to be used. It was apparent that they did not know that needles sink, because they let them fall into the water and did not grab them, but watched as they sank.

Then we noticed that some of them would put one hand to the mouth and use the other hand to rub the first, then suddenly pull the hand from the mouth. We realized they were asking for knives, because Kamchadals and other regional natives, when they eat meat or anything else, cut it with a knife right at their mouths. I ordered that they be given one knife from the gift items we had, and when they saw it they were quite overjoyed and grabbed each other and begged for more knives with great persistence.

We indicated that some of them should come onto our ship so as to improve our friendly relations and intentions and to converse. We asked whether they would let some of their men come with us, as stipulated in the instructions which Captain Commander [Bering] had received regarding dealing with such people. However we could not persuade them to agree to do this, because we could not understand each other's language, and thus none of them could be sure that our invitation to visit the ship was well-intentioned.

We gave them a small barrel so they could bring us water from shore, but they decided not to take our barrel and indicated that they had bladders which they would use to bring water out to us. Three of their little boats paddled back to shore and brought us water in the bladders. When they came up to our ship, they handed over one bladder and demanded a knife in exchange for it. I ordered that they be given a knife. But when the native took the knife he would not give us the water. He indicated to a third companion that he should also receive a knife for the same container of water. This indicated that they are persons of no conscience, which was also apparent from other actions.

These men are tall. They have faces like Tatars and they are pale and obviously healthy. They have almost no beard, either by nature or because they pluck it out, we could not tell which. We saw only two or three men who had short beards. All of them had inserted roots in their noses, which made some of them bleed. They gave us some of the same roots, which we ate, seeing them eat them. We took a few roots to be polite and gave them sea biscuits in return. They also brought us some minerals wrapped in seaweed. Aside from these, they had nothing for us in their boats but arrows, of which they gave us four.

On their heads, instead of hats they wear head coverings made of thin pieces of wood painted in various colors and decorated with feathers. Some had little bone figures tied on top. They gave us one of these hats, and we gave them a dull axe in return, which they were overjoyed to receive. We gave them a copper kettle as a token of friendship, but they held it in their hands for a while and then gave it back. After they had spent quite a bit of time at our ship they went back to shore.

In the afternoon fourteen men in similar little boats came out to us, including several who had been with us in the morning. They came up to our ship with the same shouts as previously. They stayed near the ship for three or four hours, but we could not entice even one to come aboard. And although they talked a great deal, our interpreter could not understand anything they said. After a while I gestured to them to return to shore because the wind was coming up, which meant we would be able, albeit with difficulty, to sail out of this bay which we had entered. The wind did help us, but we had difficulties and lost an anchor; however with the help of God we eventually managed to leave, as is apparent from this present journal.

Reference: TsGADA, Gos. Arkhiv, razr. XXIV, d. No. 9, 1732–1733 gg., 11. 38 ob.—40.

See: A. I. Andreev, ed. *Russkie otkrytiia v Tikhom okeane i v severnoi Amerike v XVIII veke* (Moscow: 1948, 106–110.)

30

A REPORT FROM CAPTAIN ALEKSEI I. CHIRIKOV TO THE ADMIRALTY
COLLEGE CONCERNING HIS OBSERVATIONS AND EXPLORATIONS
ALONG THE COAST OF AMERICA

On May 4, 1741, Captain Commander Bering, I, Captain Chirikov, Lieutenant Chikhachev, the navigators Fleet Lieutenants Sven Waxell and Plautin, Astronomy Professor Ludwig [Louis] Delisle de la Croyère, Fleet Master Sofron Khitrov, the administrator Fleet Master Avram Dementev and navigators Andris Ezelberkh and Ivan Elagin familiarized ourselves with the content of the written articles which Captain Commander Bering had received from the State Admiralty College [See Document 25] and especially with articles Nos. 9, 10 and 17. We also studied the written copy of Article 6 attached to those instructions from the ukaz of the Governing Senate which had been especially prepared to supplement the articles dealing with the discovery of the American coast. This stipulated that the following course be taken from the harbor [Petropavlovsk].

First, proceed southeast by east by true compass, then continue along this rhumb if no land is discovered up to 46° northern latitude (because from the present harbor along this rhumb to the 47th degree of northern latitude, according to a map belonging to the Astronomy Professor Delisle de la Croyére, there is a land known as Juan da Gama land which is believed to be part of America. The general maps from California to the place where Juan da Gama land is located indicate the existence of the land, which is also indicated on Professor Delisle de la Croyére's map. For this reason the decision was made to follow this direction, for although Juan da Gama land is not connected to America and may be an island, still, according to the instructions, islands en route to America are also to be surveyed.

If we did not discover any land from that latitude, we were to follow a strict course east by north until we did sight land. Then, when we sighted land lying southeast by east or to the northeast, we were to sail close to the land as it stretched from east to north and from north to west. If it should have extended from south and east, then we were to leave that land and sail east until we sighted land and proceed along that coast to the north, as noted above, up to 65° or, with God's help, as far as time permitted. If we reached 65° in good time, then we were to proceed west until we sighted the land of the Chukchi, in order to ascertain the distance between America and the Chukchi land. From there we were to return to this harbor. If we were to encounter headwinds in that rhumb, then we were to hold close to the rhumb as much as possible. If, with God's help, we sighted land, we were to survey it as indicated in the instructions which had been given to the Captain Commander.

The time of our voyage was to be organized in such a way that we could return to this harbor by the end of September. We decided that perhaps it would be more advantageous for us, if, hopefully, the distance were short, to sail first to the land of the Chukchi and then search for the American coast, as I had suggested in the State Admiralty College prior to our departure from Petersburg. My suggestion was not accepted, however, because of the fear that since it was so early in the summer ice would hinder our voyage to the land of the Chukchi because it is located near 65°.

Therefore we were governed on the basis of the decision and we set out on our projected voyage. We left the harbor of Petropavlovsk for the roadstead in Avacha Bay on May 29. Because of headwinds we remained there until June 4. On that day the wind became calm and we sailed out into the sea and followed the predetermined course for Juan da Gama land. On June 12 we reached 46° northern latitude but did not sight any land. Thus it became evident that there is no Juan da Gama land, because we had sailed right through the place it was supposed to be.

On June 13 we turned to search for the American coast and held to the prescribed course of east and north as close as the wind would permit. On June 20, because of the customary constant storms and fierce winds prevalent in that region (which forced us to lie to under the mizzen) we became separated from the Captain Commander. After the heavy weather passed I searched for him all during the time he had stipulated, but I could not find him. From that time on, I did not sight his packetboat and was therefore forced to follow an appropriate route holding to the prescribed course.

A very informative locative view from the bay entrance looking toward Petropavlovsk with volcanoes in the background.
Krusenstern, *Atlas*. (OHS neg. 67275)

On July 15 I sailed from the mouth of Avacha Bay where we
had built a lighthouse at a place called Vau. We calculated the distance proceeding from 61°51" east, following a bearing east and
north 6°57" to the east 2,178 minutes. In Italian miles or Russian
versts, of which there are 104-1/2 in one degree, the distance is
3,793 versts. According to our calculations when we returned, we
had voyaged a distance of 73°30' [east of Kamchatka].

Following a bearing of northeast 7°38' by east for 2,589 miles
or 4,509 Russian versts, we sighted land which is without doubt
part of America, because according to maps published by the
Nuremberg geographer Johann Baptist Homann and others,
there are certain known American places not far from there. For
clarity, I ordered that certain American places be located on the
map of our voyage and that a description of that land be made and
submitted to the State Admiralty College with the maps of this
same geographer, Homann, as well as with the maps of the astronomy professor, Delisle de la Croyère.

These places are the northern part of California, the mouth of the Mazamblek River [sic, but map shows and names Mississippi River] and part of the interior eastern coast of Hudson Bay. On this map Kamchatka is located equidistant from Tenerife Island and from St. Petersburg, on the basis of the new observations made by the expedition member Delisle de la Croyère.

When we approached land, that same day I looked for a place where I could anchor in order to carry out surveys according to the instructions. As we approached land we took soundings in various places at a distance of three versts or less to discover an appropriate place to anchor, but we could not find one, for everywhere the water was close to 70 sazhens deep or more. The coast there is rugged and there are mountains everywhere. The timber we saw on the mountains was good sized, and in places we saw snow on the mountains. The ship's journal indicates how the land lies and our track parallel to it, but it is more clearly shown on the map we prepared to accompany the journal.

Since I did not find an anchorage, when we sighted a bay I sent the quartermaster Grigorii Trubitsyn and eight servitors ashore in a landing boat to examine the bay to see whether it would be possible for the packetboat to sail in and anchor there, and for that purpose I ordered them to measure the depth.

[Trubitsyn] returned four hours later and made a written report that he had taken soundings about 60 sazhens offshore and found the water to be 40 sazhens deep with a bottom of sand and gravel. He reported it would provide shelter from eastern and northern winds but that there was no protection against winds from the south and west. It is possible to sail in with a small boat. The bay is four or five versts wide from the cape. In sailing near the cape many sea lions were visible on the rocks on the cape. In the mountains there is an extensive coniferous forest of fir, silver fir and pine. Trubitsyn did not see any signs of human habitation, however.

We picked up the longboat, according to the ship's journal, on the 16th of the month at 8:00 P.M. There was no place to anchor, and because of the danger we sailed away from shore that night and moved off from the coast. At 5:00 the next morning there was a favorable wind and so we returned to the north on the same bearing where the last part of the land lay which we had seen in the north the previous evening. At 10:00 A.M. we approached that

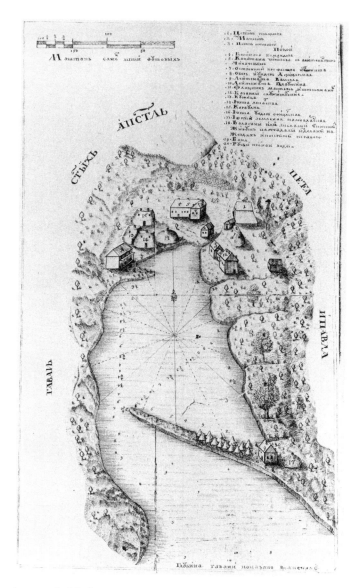

A remarkable location map of Petropavlovsk circa 1741 with a key which indicates Bering's quarters. 1. Mobile field church. 2. Warehouse. 3. Powderhouse. 4. Bering's quarters. 5. Chirikov and Lt. Chikhachev. 6. Not given. 7. Academic quarters. 8. Other officers. 9. Lt. Vaskel. 10. Lt. Plauatin. 11. Fleet master and navigator. 12. Servitor's bunkhouse. 13. Blacksmith. 14 Iurt for medical officer. 15. Guardhouse. 16. Noncommissioned offices. 17. Kamchadal earthen iurt. 18. Balagans for storing provisions. 19. Bathhouse. 20. Stream for potable water. (OHS neg. 80249)

part of the land at a distance of half a verst because it was very foggy. As a result, as we left, we sailed parallel to land, between north and west, until July 18. If we had not had a misfortune, about which I shall report later, I would have expected to describe a good-sized part of America.

On July 18 we were in 58° northern latitude, and on shore saw much more snow on the mountains. Fearing that we would be unable to make an appropriate survey of the land, and being unable to reach a warm climate, in which it is better to make a survey than in a cold climate, that same day at 4:00 in the afternoon I sent Fleet Master Avram Dementev and ten armed servitors ashore in the yawl to examine the bay. All the officers agreed with my decision.

I myself followed the longboat, aboard the packetboat, hoping to approach land opposite the bay where I had ordered the longboat to proceed, and to anchor there or to find some other appropriate anchorage. The coast was very rugged everywhere, with high mountains coming right down to the shore. The water is usually very deep in such places. We took soundings in a number of sites, as is apparent in the journals of all the officers. As we approached within some two versts of the bay we took another sounding, but did not find a depth of less than 65 sazhens. The bottom was gravel everywhere, and we also found that in many places huge rocks protruded above the water. For that reason I did not anchor the packetboat there, but anchored off the bay, took note of the place, took our bearings and then tacked into the wind and drifted.

When I sent Dementev ashore, I reminded him of the instructions we had been given, which he had already read several times. I also gave him my personal orders which stated:

"You are entrusted with command of the longboat and the ten armed servitors aboard it, as well as one bronze cannon and two rockets. You are to invoke God's help, take the boat, and go ashore to do the following:

"1. When you are near shore and see some place where the boat can anchor, stop there. If you do not find such a place, return to the ship and fire the cannon as a signal.

"2. If, with God's help, you land on shore, you are to investigate to see whether there are any people living there. If you see any, show them friendship and give them small presents. For this purpose you are authorized to take from Ensign Choglokov one copper kettle, one iron kettle, 200 small bells, three bricks of tea, one *tiun* of Chinese cotton, one bale of Chinese silk, five leather purses, and a packet of needles. I am personally giving you ten rubles worth of goods to give to helpful local people, using your own judgment. Ask if your interpreter, who speaks the Koriak language, may converse with them. If no one knows that language, then use sign language to ask what land that is, under whose authority the people are, and invite several of the people to come to visit us aboard our ship.

"3. Observe whether there is a suitable place for a ship to enter from the sea and find a safe anchorage. Take soundings of the depth of the harbor and if possible make a sketch map of it.

"4. Observe what trees and grasses grow on shore.

"5. See whether there are any particular rocks or soil which might indicate rich ore. I am giving you a sample of silver ore for reference. If you find anything similar to it, bring a sample back to the ship.

"6. Inquire of the inhabitants, insofar as you are able, how far this land extends, whether there are any rivers which fall into the sea and if so, where.

"7. If the inhabitants become hostile, defend yourselves and return to the ship as quickly as possible but do not harm them or let the servitors abuse them.

"8. Do your best to make all these observations. Return to the ship without delay, the same day if possible, or at the very latest the next day. If, God forbid, there is such dense fog that you cannot see the ship, do not set out in such weather. If the weather is very bad, wait it out. For this purpose take with you enough provisions for yourself and the servitors for an entire week.

"9. When God takes you to shore, fire a rocket so we will know. Also fire a rocket when you leave shore to put back out to sea. While you are ashore build a large fire if you feel we will be able to see it, especially at night, but also during the day, even though we may only be able to see the smoke.

"10. When you are within one verst of shore take a sounding to see how deep the water is and what the bottom is.

"11. Two barrels are being sent with you to fill with water. Conduct yourself in everything as a loyal and true servant of Her Imperial Majesty."

However there were no signals from him. We saw him approach the shore but then we saw nothing after he landed. We waited five days for him to return to us, holding under sail as close as possible to the bay into which he had gone. In the beginning the weather was such that the longboat could easily have come out to us. But then came heavy rains with clouds and strong winds, which carried us away from the bay by as much as 30 minutes.

On July 23 we again approached the bay the longboat had entered and we saw a fire on shore, which we supposed had been built by the servitors we had sent there. We had not seen any other fires for the entire distance we had sailed along the coast, nor had we seen any structures or boats or other signs of life. For that reason we did not think there were any persons living there. Believing the fire was a signal to our ship, since it was stirred up several times, we fired a cannon shot, but they did not come out to us. The time for leaving was just right and we sailed in close to shore. When we fired the cannon, the fire was built up on shore.

On July 24 we decided the boat had been damaged and for that reason could not come out to us, although the weather was favorable. Therefore all the senior and junior officers agreed, and signed a statement, that the small boat should take a carpenter, a caulker and all necessary equipment and go in to repair the longboat. The boatswain Sidor Savelev and others volunteered to take these men in, and the sailor Fadeev volunteered to help row the boat and to go ashore.

I gave orders to the boatswain, a copy of which is appended to this report. I emphasized that he should look for the boat when he reached shore; that he was taking the carpenter and the caulker to repair it; and that he should immediately pick up the navigator Dementev and three or four servitors and return to us. The weather was very calm at that time, so we sent him ashore. We followed and approached very close and observed that the boatswain went onto shore with the small boat at 6:00 P.M. However he did not make the signals I had instructed him to make, nor did he return to us at the time expected, although the weather remained very calm.

On July 25 at 1:00 P.M. we saw two rowboats coming out from the bay where our boat and lodka had been sent. One was small and the other somewhat larger. We hoped that these were our boat and longboat returning. We went to meet them, but realized that the boat was not ours because its bow was very pointed and the oars were not the same. The men rowed with the oars close to the sides, and the boats did not come close enough to our packetboat for us to make out the faces of the men. We did see that there were four men seated in the boat. One was at the rudder and the others were rowing. One man, dressed in red, stood up when they were still some distance away and shouted twice, "Ahai! Ahai!"

They waved their hands and then immediately turned and rowed back to shore. I ordered that white flags be waved and that our men bow, so the others would come up to our ship. Many of our servitors did this, in spite of the fact that the boats were being rowed quickly to shore. We could not pursue them because the wind was calm and their boat was very swift. The other large rowboat, farther from our ship, returned, and then both of them went back into the same bay from which they had come.

We then realized that the servitors we had sent were very likely in trouble since the navigator Dementev had already been gone eight days, and had had plenty of time to return. When we sent the boatswain, we did not leave our position. The weather remained calm, and if they had not encountered some misfortune they would already have returned to us.

We supposed that because the American natives did not dare come up to our packetboat, they had been hostile toward the men we had sent to their shore, and that they had either killed them or taken them captive. We continued sailing in the vicinity until evening, however, waiting for our boats. It was not until night that we moved offshore because of the danger. All during the night we kept the light burning on the stern of the ship in hope that when they saw it they might come out to us at night.

At 11:00 A.M. we turned and held a course toward land between north and west. By the end of July 26 we reached 58°21″ northern latitude. By subsequent calculations we fixed the longitude from Vau at 54°11″. Early on July 27 we took counsel as to whether we could go on, because we no longer had a small boat on our ship either to send ashore on reconnaissance or to take fresh water for our own use.

On the basis of subsequent calculations we were then about 2,000 minutes from this harbor of the Holy Apostles Peter and

Paul [Petropavlovsk], and had only 45 barrels of water left, which was scarcely enough for such a long voyage. We did not know what winds we might encounter, nor did we know whether the barrels were still full of water or whether some had seeped out. (When we returned to the harbor we made a count and found that seven barrels were missing.)

Consequently, with my consent, Lieutenant Chikhachev, the navigator (who held the Navy rank of Lieutenant) Plautin and the navigator Ivan Elagin agreed that for the above reasons we should not continue our voyage and that on that very day we should turn back toward Petropavlovsk. I am appending an exact copy of our decision. We realized that it was still early for us to turn back, and had it not been for the obvious misfortune we could have continued our voyage for some time. However during our return voyage there were almost constant headwinds in one quarter of the compass between northwest and southwest, and we could not know whether some unexpected disaster might not befall our ship on the course we were taking on our return voyage along the land.

In accordance with this mutual decision, that same day we set out on our return and sailed toward this harbor. Along the land where we had been sailing and making observations for some 400 versts, we saw whales, sea lions, walruses, porpoise, white feathered ducks and a multitude of others, some with curved red bills, and many kinds of seagulls. There are high mountains everywhere on that coast. The shore has steep cliffs where it meets the sea in deep bays. In the mountains near the place where we came close to shore, as noted above, there is abundant forest of good size. On some of the mountains we saw snow here and there, and the farther north we went, the more snow we saw. From the place where we turned back we could see very high mountains on shore in a direction north 3/4 east, much higher than any mountain in Kamchatka, and all the mountains were covered with snow.

On August 1 at 5:00 p.m. on our return voyage we sighted land to the northwest and 1/2 west, at a distance of 30 minutes. At the end of that day we took bearings on it. All along the land there was an unbroken chain of mountains covered with snow. We believe that the land from which we returned is not separated from this, because during all the days we saw many birds, gulls, ducks and floating grass which grows along the sea. We did not see these when we were some distance out from shore, except for two or three days when we saw some floating grass and birds, one a day (except for grey gulls and some small birds which resemble the steppe kestrel which we saw in great numbers at sea some distance from shore).

Because of these signs we kept a little south of our regular course, sailing with a favorable wind. Early on July 31 the color of the water changed from the usual hue of seawater found some distance from shore, but we did not see any land that day and I believe it was because for several days fog prevented us from seeing it. On August 2 and 3 land came into view. At the end of the day we took bearings. On August 4 and 5 we took soundings and found the depth of the water to be between 90 and 43 sazhens. There were many birds flying and the color of the water suggested we were near shore but we did not sight land. During the night of August 6 we came to a bank where the water was only 30 sazhens deep. The bottom was sandy with small and large rocks, because of which we had to turn back and proceed on an easterly course. The places we sighted between August 1 and 6 are indicated on the map with the dates beside, for all during our time at sea, we marked wherever we were at the end of the day on the map.

On August 21, realizing that headwinds had been blowing for a long time, with the consent of the officers I ordered that the crew cook *kasha* [buckwheat porridge] only once a day for two days and twice on the third day, for there was a shortage of water. Each man was to receive the smallest possible amount of drinking water. I also ordered that kasha be cooked for the officers only once a day. Whenever it rained the crew collected rainwater from the sails, using pails and other containers. It was bitter and tasted of tar, but the crew willingly drank it because they had tried drinking rainwater previously and said it was healthy, that the bitter tar would cure scurvy.

To prevent the men from becoming weak on the reduced rations, I ordered that on the days when of necessity they had only one serving of kasha (except for senior and junior officers and their servants), they were to be given a cup of straight spirits in addition to their regular rations. Because the headwinds continued, we had no hope of obtaining more water and we were still far distant from this present harbor. I therefore gave the order that the men were to be given kasha only every other day in order to

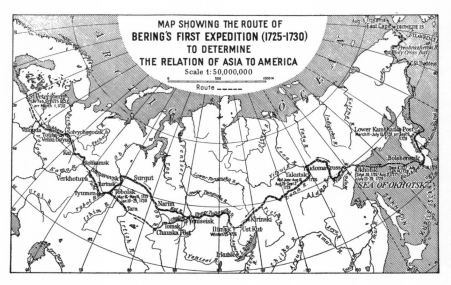

MAP SHOWING THE ROUTE OF
BERING'S FIRST EXPEDITION (1725-1730)
TO DETERMINE
THE RELATION OF ASIA TO AMERICA
Scale 1:50,000,000

Route _ _ _ _ _

Map showing the route of Bering's first expedition. Scale I: 50,000,000. Of the land journey, between St. Petersburg and Okhotsk, both the outward and the return routes are shown; of the sea voyage, between Okhotsk and Bering Strait (overland across Kamchatka), only the outward route is shown. Golder, *Bering's Voyages, I.* (OHS neg. 80261)

conserve water. The men themselves were in favor of this and lived on sea biscuits with butter. On certain days when extra rations were dispensed they had salted meat which they cooked in sea water. From September 14 on, I had to order that kasha be cooked and given to the men only once a week. The other six days they had to eat almost everything cold. However, any of the crew who wished, could use their drinking water ration to cook the sea biscuits, but this would then be the only hot food they would receive.

All the men were already becoming weak and many were ill with scurvy. It was very difficult for the officers and crew to carry out their duties. Some were completely bedridden and could not come up on deck. Because of the shortage of provisions and the weakness of the crew, from September 14 on, in order to keep the men from completely breaking down, I ordered that in addition to the designated ration of straight spirits the crew be given two extra cups per day, and the junior officers one cup.

On September 4 at 7:00 A.M. we sighted land and at the end of that day took bearings. At that time we were on our return voyage, in 52°23′ northern latitude, and from Vau we were distant 32°49′ on a bearing east by south 9°48′, which was 1,186 miles or 2065½ Russian versts. We saw mountains everywhere on land and the highest peaks were snowcapped.

At 8:00 A.M., having observed the land, we left and turned to sail on a course between south and west, so that after we had sailed past the land we held to our usual course. On September 8 there were signs that we were approaching land, flying birds and grass floating on the sea. For that reason, from 7:00 P.M. until 7:00 A.M. we maintained a bearing of one or two compass points south and then held for a short time to the usual compass point. By September 9 it was very foggy and there were indications that we were quite near land, so I ordered that we sail south of our present bearing by one compass point; thus we kept to the west by true compass.

At 7:00 P.M. the wind suddenly calmed, apparently because of God's mercy toward us. We took soundings and found the depth of the water to be 50 sazhens. We prepared to drop anchor, and at that time waves came and carried us in to a depth of 30 sazhens, where the bottom was sandy. We dropped the port anchor and when we let half the cable out, we found the depth at the bow was 38 sazhens and at the stern, 24 sazhens. We could hear the sound of the surf breaking on rocks and on the shore, but because of the dense fog we could not see land. However by 9:00 the next morning the fog lifted a little and we saw the shore to the west at a distance of about 200 sazhens. There were high mountains without trees, but they were green with grass. The shore was broken; to the east the land appeared to be lower at a distance of about 300 sazhens, and near land on both sides there were many rocks both above and below the water which could be seen as the waves broke over them. To the north no land was visible.

At this time we noticed two men walking on shore. We shouted to them in Russian and in the Kamchadal language, calling to them to come out to us. Shortly we heard a voice, calling to us from land, but because of the noise of the waves breaking we could not make out the words. Several times we called both with and without the horn, inviting them to come out to us on the ship.

At 10:00 A.M. seven small hide boats, each carrying one man, came out. They stayed near the ship for quite some time and then went back to shore. After noon on that day, which according to the ship's journal was September 10, fourteen such craft, each carrying one person, came out to the ship. They gave us one of their hats made of birds, the kind they were wearing on their heads, and four arrows. They also gave us a small amount of some mineral wrapped up in seaweed; I believe the mineral was crude antimony or stibnite. I sent it to the master assayer, Gardebol, in Bolsheretsk ostrog for a detailed examination. Unfortunately, to the present time I have not received any response. They also gave us roots of some grass which they all insert in their noses, and we brought some of these roots back with us to display. I am appending copies of journal excerpts explaining how these people came out to us, their appearance, their boats, the dealings they had with us and other such information.

On September 10 at 8:00 P.M. a wind came up from the western shore. Trusting in God's aid, we hoped to sail away without difficulty from the land we had discovered and which was now in a heavy fog. We started to haul in the cable so we could raise anchor, but before we had it on its stock we began to drift toward land which lay east of us about 300 sazhens. I was afraid that as we drifted toward land there might be submerged rocks to the west and so I ordered that the port cable be cut at the hawsehole, although 35 sazhens were still out. We then proceeded under full sail to the southeast. We still had considerable difficulty because the wind coming from the mountains kept changing in strength and direction, but with the help of Almighty God we left without any disaster. The place where we anchored is located in 51°40' northern latitude, distant from Vau, according to our return calculations, on a bearing of east south 6°20', 852 minutes to the east, 1484 Russian versts. As we sailed away from land we started out on a western bearing closer to our proper course, but we were greatly impeded by headwinds.

On September 21 at 8:00 P.M. we saw some small fish swimming near the ship. I gave orders to take a sounding and we found the depth of the water to be 60 sazhens. Because of this we allowed the ship to drift and took further soundings, finding the same depth and a sandy bottom. We did not sight land because it was late in the evening and foggy as well. For fear of running aground during the night we sailed back to the east for two hours, and then lay adrift for the rest of the night until 3:00 A.M. when we resumed sailing. Some time after 9:00 A.M. we sighted land on a bearing of northwest. Realizing that we had not yet reached Kamchatka, we turned in order to pass it to the south. We had a favorable wind and so held a course parallel to shore between south and west. At the end of that day we took the bearing of that land which was in 52°35′ northern latitude, 956 Russian versts from Vau, based on our return calculations. The coast of that land did not appear level anywhere. There were small hills in some places and high snowcapped mountains could be seen in the distance, but there was no snow on the low hills.

At various times near this land we saw four sea otters, which are also found near Kamchatka; however we did not see this animal anywhere else in these places. We had land in view until 6:00 A.M. on September 22. I believe the land which we saw on September 4, 9 and 21 is contiguous, although it was not continuously in view; there was heavy fog, but still there were many indications that we were near land: shore birds, various kinds of marine animals and grass floating on the sea. When the wind forced us to keep our course more to the north, more of these signs appeared. When the course was held more to the south, there were fewer signs, sometimes none at all. As we sailed on, because we were then keeping much more to the south on our return voyage, these signs were almost never seen except for marine animals and a small amount of seaweed, and even that was rare.

I have no doubt that all the land we sighted is contiguous because from August 6 when it was lost from sight until September 4 when we sighted it again, we saw these signs of the proximity of land more frequently. I believe that another major indication that the land is contiguous is the presence of inhabitants on the land where we were on September 9. If this land were an island, distant from the mainland, how would it have been possible for the people to have been there? For that reason, even if it is an island, it is located near mainland and may be considered Bolshaia Zemlia, although I cannot speak from firsthand proof.

By the end of September all the members of the crew were seriously ill with scurvy. Many were bedridden and could not stand watch, and those who did manage to stand their watches did so only by exerting the last of their strength. From September 16 until we came into harbor six men died. The names of those

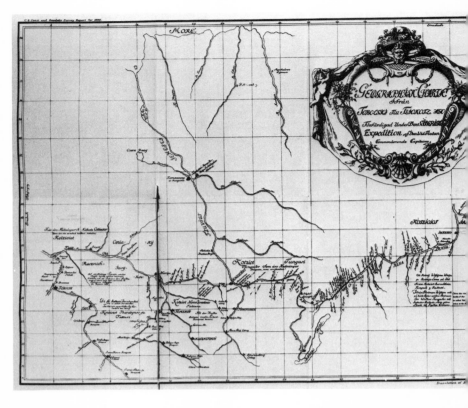

A Danish version of a map of the overland portion of Bering's journey across Siberia from Tobolsk to Kamchatka and the Sea of Okhotsk. The translation is provided by William Dall in *Bering Sea and Strait*. (OHS neg. 80333)

who died and were left in America, and the dates, are recorded in the official register.

On October 6 at 10:00 A.M., by God's will, Lieutenant Ivan Chikhachev died, and on October 8, the navigator Fleet Lieutenant Mikhailo Plautin. They had been too ill to stand watch; Chikhachev for three weeks and Plautin for two weeks. At that time I was also very ill with scurvy and was so weak I did not expect to live. According to custom I was prepared for death. I could not go up on deck from September 21 until our return to harbor. The navigator Ivan Elagin was in command of the ship. Although he himself was very ill he would not give in, and by exerting himself to the utmost he remained almost constantly on deck in command. I gave him as much assistance as I could (since thanks to God's mercy I was of sound mind), and by studying the

154

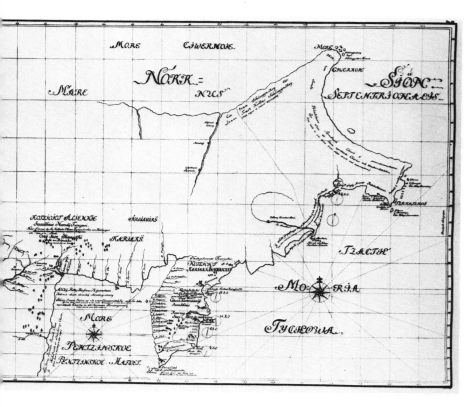

calculations of our voyage from the journal, I advised him what
course to follow. But when the calculations we had kept on the
outward voyage indicated we should have sighted Kamchatka but
the land failed to appear, I ordered him to steer west close to the
parallel of this harbor. If it were not for his great skill and the fact
that God gave him strength, the entire ship might soon have met
with disaster. For his devotion to duty and constant good judgment, as well as to reward him for all his hard work, I promoted
him to the rank of Fleet Lieutenant, for not only had he performed the work of Lieutenant, but he had been in command of
the entire ship.

On October 8 at 7:00 A.M., with God's mercy, we sighted the
land of Kamchatka, and on the 10th at 9:00 p.m. we entered Avacha Bay and lay at anchor. By then we had consumed all the fresh
water we had except for two barrels which we had distilled from
sea water by boiling it in kettles.

At 10:00 A.M. on October 10 the Professor of Astronomy Delisle de la Croyère died. With God's help we reached the present
whether some misfortune has forced him to winter over some-

bay of Petropavlovsk on October 12. The Captain Commander [Bering] had still not returned by that date, and it is not known where. We had enough provisions with us on the packetboats to sustain the crew if necessary for half a year.

A list of the names of the crew members who were with the Captain Commander is appended to this report. I am also submitting to the Admiralty College the journal of our voyage and a Mercator map. Because the difference in longitude between Kamchatka and the American land which we sighted was different on our outward voyage from our return, for that reason on the map of our outward voyage we marked the land we saw in black, and the location of where land was supposed to have been according to calculations made on the return voyage is indicated in red. The difference in length is due to the length of the voyage and the fact that for a long time we were obliged to calculate the difference in length without correction from one certain place from which we had begun our calculations, namely the meridian crossing Vau. During our voyage we did not encounter any land whose longitude we would have known, on the basis of which we would have been able to correct the discrepancey of longitude. Because of the long voyage we undertook and the length of time involved, I realize that even the best navigators cannot avoid errors in calculations.

From the appended map, if it should be desired, the professors in the Academy can prepare a map closer to the truth, on the basis of both calculations or by using other means, judging the evidence we have gathered in our logbook. The reason for the discrepancy which appears in our calculations may have been due to sea currents, because when we were on our outward voyage we twice tried to measure the current, but there was none. Along the American coast there was a current running parallel to shore. On our return voyage, because we did not have our small boats, we could not measure the current.

Our voyage from Kamchatka to the American land lasted six weeks. Although it took place in June and July, by the middle of June we were in 46° latitude and the weather was constantly as cold as it would be in our land late in fall. There were heavy fogs almost every day, some days it would clear off around noon, but there were only three clear days. During our return in August

A seaward view of Petropavlovsk, the port associated with the Bering Chirikov Expedition (1741). The long sandbar running into Avacha Bay became a fortified wall behind which Russian war vessels repulsed a combined British-French flotilla during the Crimean War. Krusenstern, *Voyages Around the World.* (OHS neg. 67274)

and September there were more clear days, and strong winds usually associated with autumn blew more frequently; however, for most of the time the weather was bad along the American coast. In my judgment the best time to sail in those waters is in the month of August and during the first half of September, rather than in June and July.

Our instructions require that an officer who took part in this voyage accompany this report to the Admiralty College. However, as noted above, all the naval officers, by God's will, have died. For this reason I am sending a marine, Semen Plotnikov, overland with this report, for it is now winter. However the trip to Iakutsk is not safe because of hostile natives who travel along the route between the Kamchatka and Kolymsk ostrogs. Russian travelers are often killed there, sometimes robbed and held.

I did not wish to be accused of delay, and so have not dared not to send this present report. But because of the danger of this travel route, I am sending a detailed report with our journal and maps and a list of the names of the servitors and various tables, and copies, to the State Admiralty College with the naval cadet Orlov. He will go by sea to Okhotsk next spring. I will send with him the items which we received from the native inhabitants in the newly discovered land, which I described earlier, so they can also be presented to the State Admiralty College.

I hereby humbly state that in this present report, the days of the month noted in the journal begin at noon, as is customary in all naval journals.

[Signed] Captain Aleksei Chirikov,
humble servant of the
State Admiralty College
December 7, 1741

Reference: TsGVMA, [TsGAVMF] f. gr. Golovina, d. No. 44, 11. 5–14; also GAFKE, Gosarkhiv, XXIV, 1732–1743 gg., d. No. 9, 11. 28–38.
See: A. Pokrovskii, ed. *Ekspeditsiia Beringa. Sbornik dokumentov* (Moscow: 1941), 273–285.

31

A DECREE FROM THE SENATE APPOINTING MISSIONARIES TO KAM-
CHATKA TO SPREAD THE WORD OF GOD AND CONVERT THE KAMCHA-
DAL NATIVES TO ORTHODOX CHRISTIANITY

In order to enable the local [native] population of the Kamchatka territory to have the opportunity to hear the Word of
God, and to convert them and enable them to understand Christian morality, Arkhimandrit Ioasaf Zankevich of Spaskii Monastery in Tobolsk is to proceed there. To assist him in baptizing the
natives, two church-servitor priests and one *diakon* [deacon] who
have been exiled to Okhotsk [are to be sent there]. Also, five
priests, two other diakons, ten *diachoks* [reader-assistants] and a
ponomar [sexton] will be sent to the Kamchatka, Okhotsk and
Anadyrsk ostrogs to conduct church services. Her Imperial Majesty, at the request of the Holy Synod, has designated the following salaries for them: 300 rubles for the Arkhimandrit for the first
year, to be taken from gubernia revenues in Tobolsk; 150 rubles
apiece for the two assisting priests; 100 rubles for the diakon
[from Okhotsk]; 80 rubles apiece for the other priests; 60 rubles
apiece for the other diakons; 40 rubles apiece for the *prichetnik*
[minor churchman], diachoks and ponomar.

The following supplies are also to be issued to them for the
church: sacramental wine, wax, palm branches and flour for the
holy wafers. All of this is to come out of revenues from Okhotsk
ostrog, if they are sufficient. If not, then Iakutsk is to provide
these things every year without any delay so they will not suffer
need and hunger in such a distant land without resources for
food, and so they can conduct church liturgy and carry on church
affairs without delay.

Arkhimandrit Zankevich should be provided transportation
and a guide. He is also to be issued sufficient travel funds for the
journey from Tobolsk to Irkutsk, and from there, for himself and
for the church supplies, to Iakutsk and on to Okhotsk. From that
place he and the designated church servitors are to be sent across
the sea [of Okhotsk] to Kamchatka aboard an appropriate vessel,
taking with them everything else needed for the iconostasis and
the church furnishings.

If the Siberian gubernia office failed to send with the previous igumen, Filevskii, any items specified in the ukaz issued by the Governing Senate in 1732, these things are also to be sent now without any further delay. A guard of three reliable soldiers who can read, taken from church lists, are to be sent with Arkhimandrit Zankevich from the Tobolsk garrison for his protection and assistance. They are to receive appropriate compensation and remain with him constantly as long as he is proselytizing in Kamchatka. They are to obey him implicitly. Wherever necessary, the arkhimandrit is to receive guides and interpreters. Such persons are to be reliable and to have sworn the oath.

Any necessary ukazes regarding this assignment are to be issued and the Holy Synod is to be kept informed of progress. The Holy Synod will decide the question of what financial reward those who choose to be baptized will receive, and the Holy Synod will inform the Governing Senate. Upon receiving Senate approval, the Holy Synod will issue a statement so that the Office for the Newly Baptized in Kazan will issue the appropriate amount of money.

Reference: Russia *Polnoe sobranie zakonov rossiiskoi imperii s 1649 goda.* First
Series (St. Petersburg: 1830), XI, 577–578.

32

SEPTEMBER 1, 1743

THE REPORT OF THE GEODESIST MIKHAIL SPIRIDONOVICH GVOZDEV
TO MARTYN PETROVICH SPANBERG CONCERNING HIS VOYAGE OF EX-
PLORATION TO THE COAST OF NORTH AMERICA IN 1732

In the orders which Your Excellency sent to me under No. 381,
and also in a written memorandum from Your Excellency
from the Okhotsk office, you requested the following information.

"During your voyage [1732] you were on the islands which lie
north of the Kamchatka River toward Bolshaia Zemlia. How far
are these from Kamchatka or from dwellings of the Chukchi?
How far from Anadyrsk? Do you know in what degrees of latitude they are located? How is it possible to reach them—by what
reliable route and by what means of conveyance? How do the islands and the mainland lie? What forests are there? What other
kinds of places? What arable lands? Are there harbors?

"Do people live there, and if so, are they numerous? Who
rules them? One ruler or several? Are their rulers independent, or
do they pay tribute to someone, and if so, what kind of tribute?
What language do they speak? What faith do they profess? Are
they literate? Do they use money? Are they similar in appearance
to other native peoples or are they unique? What do they eat? In
the territory they inhabit are there any agricultural settlements,
or do they still carry on a nomadic way of life? Do they live by
fishing, and if so, is the fishing organized commercially? Do they
have any relations and contact with the Chukchi? Do they help
the Chukchi in battles to kill Russian subjects of Her Imperial
Majesty, and iasak-paying Koriaks? Are there any other lands and
islands beyond this Bolshaia Zemlia which are inhabited by other
people about whom nothing has hitherto been known? If so, what
are they called? What customs and habits do they have? In what
degrees of latitude and longitude are they located?"

It is apparent from this memorandum that you know that in
the year 1732 I sailed from the Kamchatka River on a seagoing
vessel, the *Sv. Gavriil*, with [Ivan] Fedorov as assistant navigator
for the purpose of describing the above-mentioned islands and
Bolshaia Zemlia. For that reason, upon receiving your query, I am
giving you all the information you request, and shall relate every-

thing I saw while I was in that northern region. I have described it as accurately as circumstances permit and have not omitted anything. I am immediately reporting to Your Excellency everything we wrote in our journals and recorded on our maps.

In this report I state the following. On May 1, 1732, in accordance with orders sent to us from Anadyrsk ostrog via a detachment from the exploring party of His Excellency, Major [Dmitrii] Pavlutskii, we were ordered to take a navigator and assistant navigator and sail aboard the *Sv. Gavriil* around the cape of Kamchatka to the mouth of the Anadyr [to the land] opposite the Gulf of Anadyr which is called Bolshaia Zemlia. We were to survey the islands, determine their number, what people inhabit them, and to explore and again try to collect iasak from those who had not previously paid iasak. We were to be especially attentive to the interests of Her Imperial Majesty. In accordance with these orders, together with the assistant navigator Ivan Fedorov we sailed on the *Sv. Gavriil* on July 23, 1732 from the mouth of the Kamchatka River and rounded the cape of Kamchatka on July 27. We reached Anadyr Cape on August 3 and from there continued on our search for the islands.

When his Excellency Captain Commander Ivan Ivanovich [Vitus J.] Bering was on his previous voyage, a sailor named Moshkov was with him when they sighted an island. We took Moshkov and went to find that island. We went to the south side of Cape Chukotsk on August 5. We stood at anchor. The sea was calm and he [Moshkov] took the small sloop in to shore to observe the coast and obtain fresh water. While taking the sloop to shore, the men sighted a small river and took the sloop in and put ashore. The place was unpopulated; there were only roaming reindeer herds. They did see two men with the reindeer who took to the cliffs when they saw our men. When our men had taken two barrels of water, they rowed back out to the vessel.

On August 6 the Chukchi came out to our vessel in two baidaras from another inlet, but they did not come close enough for us to converse with them. Our interpreter called them over, but they did not reply and after they had looked over our vessel they went back to shore.

On August 7 I sailed aboard the sloop in the direction from which the baidaras had come so I could look over the dwellings. We saw two empty iurts excavated into the ground and constructed of whale bones. They were old and run down. From there we returned to the vessel. As we left we saw two men on shore who spotted us and ran to the cliffs. We reached the *Sv. Gavriil* safely.

We stood at anchor from August 5 to 8, and on the 8th we had a favorable wind. At 4:00 A.M. we raised anchor, set sail and sailed, following Moshkov's directions, to search for the island.

On August 9 the assistant navigator Ivan Fedorov gave me his written opinion. It stated that in accordance with the order we had received we had not yet reached the place known as Bolshaia Zemlia. [He felt that] these islands were south of Cape Chukotsk, and he wanted me to add my opinion to his written statement, if Moshkov failed to find the islands he said he had seen toward the Anadyr. In accordance with the opinion of the assistant navigator, and by general consent, we went to the place where we had previously anchored. We reached the place, anchored and sent the small sloop ashore to take on fresh water.

On August 11 at 10:00 A.M. a good wind came up, so we raised anchor, set sails and proceeded on our way.

On August 13 at 5:00 A.M. the weather was calm. We lay at anchor and observed the iurts on shore. I went aboard the small sloop, and as we approached the shore and the iurts, three baidaras paddled out from the iurts. They saw us and paddled farther along the shore away from us. We rowed up to the iurts. There was a small river near the iurts. Our sloops entered the river, we went ashore and saw six iurts. They were built into the ground and were made of fir. Then we saw that one of the baidaras was paddling back toward us. Since there were only a few of us on our sloop, we rowed away from the iurt and returned to the vessel. When we reached it, I took 20 servitors and we rowed back to the iurts and put ashore.

The Chukchi left their iurts, got in their baidaras and paddled off toward a cliff opposite the iurts. There were only six men on the cliff. I sent a servitor and an interpreter to summon them to submit to Her Imperial Majesty's autocratic authority and to pay iasak, but the Chukchi replied, "We do not know about iasak and will not pay and we will not hunt."

Three times I sent the interpreter to summon them to pay iasak. They told the interpreter to send the prikashchik, and that then they would pay iasak in parkas. I sent the servitor Permiakov with an interpreter. Permiakov went to them and returned, saying they had asked him for a knife and had given him a parka made of marten. [One Chukchi man] had asked the interpreter, "What kind of iasak do you ask from us? Our tribe is quite large and I rule over them. What kind of iasak do you want? We fought against the captain and you did not force us then." Then he brandished his spear at the interpreter. By all appearances it was evident that they eat whales and walrus, for [Permiakov] did not see any other food. There is no forest except tundra. Our men returned to the vessel after midnight on August 15.

At 11:00 A.M. a favorable wind came up and we raised anchor, set sails and put out to sea.

On August 17 at about 7:00 A.M. we sighted an island. There was a head wind and because of that we maneuvered our vessel into the wind. That same day at 3:00 A.M. the sea became calm. We saw iurts at Cape Chukotsk, and I went in the small sloop toward the iurts, rowing to shore. The Chukchi fled from their iurts to the cliff, but because of the distance we could not converse with them so we turned back toward the vessel. The Chukchi paddled after us in two baidaras and caught up with us but would not come close.

There were about 20 men in each baidara. They observed us and then turned back. Through an interpreter I asked them what people live on the island, but they did not reply. In regard to themselves, they said they are "tooth Chukchi," and that their habitation is on Cape Chukotsk itself. Then we rowed back to the vessel.

The wind continued to be favorable, so we set sail and proceeded to the northern end of the island, then rowed the sloop up to the island. As we approached the shore we saw iurts and moved in to row closer to shore. The natives fired arrows at us, so we retaliated by firing three guns.

I ordered the interpreter to ask them what people they were and they replied that they were Chukchi. They added, "Our tribesmen joined the reindeer Chukchi to fight the Captain and they were all killed." We also asked them about Bolshaia Zemlia, but they did not say anything about that land, how large it is, or whether it is an island. As for the people who live on that land, they said, "They are our Chukchi," and over there "are more of our Chukchi who have run away from their iurts. . . ."

After we had inspected the iurts we returned to our vessel and sailed along the island to the southern tip where we saw more iurts. We stood at anchor and rowed to shore near the iurts, of which there were about 20. From their iurts the Chukchi shouted to us not to come ashore. I put the interpreter ashore and one man from a iurt came up to him. The interpreter asked about Bolshaia Zemlia and what people live there. The Chukchi did not tell him anything about the land or the people there. Then, in accordance with our orders, we summoned them to pay iasak. But the Chukchi said, "We do not know anything about iasak. We have never paid." Seeing that they were not inclined to pay, we returned to the vessel. The island is not large and there are no trees.

On August 20 at 1:00 A.M. we raised anchor and went on our way. At 7:00 A.M. there was a calm and we anchored opposite the second island. The distance between the first and the second is about half a mile. The second island is smaller then the first. We sent the sloop to the island to find out whether any people live there. When it returned, the crew said there were people. When we approached the island they began to shoot at us with bows and arrows, and for that reason we returned and there was no conversation with them.

At 3:00 A.M. on August 21 the wind came up so we raised anchor, set sail and sailed toward Bolshaia Zemlia. We reached land and dropped anchor but did not see any habitations. Ivan Fedorov, the assistant navigator, ordered the anchor raised and we sailed along land to the southern tip. There, on the west side, we saw inhabited iurts at a distance of a verst and a half. Because of headwinds it was impossible to approach close to the habitations. The water was shallow, only six or seven sazhens deep, so we returned and sailed close to the wind in order not to move off from land. The wind came up strong from the north, and the assistant navigator ordered the course held at southwest. Because of the strong wind we pulled away from shore and reached a fourth island on August 22. Because of heavy weather it was impossible to anchor at that island. When we approached the fourth island we lowered sails, and without sails, were carried away from the fourth island.

The seaman Lavrentii Smetanin and his companions suggested that we return to Kamchatka since time was growing late and the winds were becoming ever stronger. I told them that, in accordance with the formal orders, they should deal with the assistant navigator, because while sailing at sea he alone had authority. I said they should propose this to him, for without his concurrence I could not order that we turn back.

From the fourth island a Chukchi in a small boat rowed up to our vessel. The small boat he used is called a *kukhta* in their language. The kukhta was made entirely of hide, the upper part was also of hide. It could hold only one man, who sat in it. He wore a shirtlike garment made of whale gut which fastened both around him and around the kukhta. It came up under his arms and almost to his head, so that water could not get in. Even when a wave washed over him the water could not come inside to his body or into the kukhta. A large inflated bladder was attached to the kukhta so that a big wave could not overturn the kukhta.

Through an interpreter we asked him about Bolshaia Zemlia, inquiring what the land is like, what kind of people live there, whether there is forest, what rivers there are, and what kind of animals. The Chukchi spoke about Bolshaia Zemlia through our interpreter and said that their Chukchi live there, that there is a coniferous forest there, and that there are reindeer, marten, fox and river beaver there.

After we had spoken, the Chukchi paddled to the island. The island is small, round in appearance, and has no forest. Then the servitors Efim Permiakov, Lavrentii Poliakov, Fedor Paranchin, Aleksei Malyshev and their companions came to me and wanted to return to Kamchatka because our provisions were in short supply and they could no longer keep the water bailed out of the vessel. I replied that we could not turn back unless the assistant navigator agreed. Then the sailors, the navigator and the servitors submitted a signed petition to me and to the assistant navigator in which they detailed many needs and requested that because of these needs and the fact that it was late in the season, we return to Kamchatka from our voyage.

On the basis of their petition, and with the agreement of the assistant navigator, we returned to the mouth of the Kamchatka River, which we reached on September 28. We could not observe or learn anything more during this voyage beyond the information about the islands and other matters which I have reported here.

In this report I am not writing anything about rhumbs and the degrees in which the islands which we discovered and surveyed are located, because I sent the ship's logbook and the journal, which the assistant navigator and I kept, to the administration in Okhotsk with a report on July 22, 1733, before the maps were prepared. It was impossible to prepare the maps because when we left Kamchatka the assistant navigator Fedorov, for reasons I do not understand, would not allow me access to the journal except [for the pages] for two days, and on those days Fedorov had not made any entries.

Furthermore, during the voyage, there were many watch periods when Fedorov did not make any entries. For that reason, soon after I returned from the voyage to Kamchatka on November 10, 1732, I sent Fedorov a letter in which I wrote that he and I should prepare a map based on the journal, which would include places we visited and things we saw. However Fedorov would not bring the journal up to date, nor would he let me help in preparing the maps.

On November 28 of the same year I received a letter in reply, asking whether I did not realize that he had been sent by the State Admiralty College not to prepare land maps, but to perform the duty of assistant navigator on the voyage, and that therefore, on the basis of the responsibility of the navigator, sea maps rather than land maps were to be prepared. Neither he nor I had asked anyone to assist us at sea during our expedition, nor did we later request anyone from other ranks familiar with naval affairs and navigational duties. Therefore I took it on myself, and considered it my responsibility, to prepare a land map. As noted above, because of Fedorov's lack of cooperation in giving me access to the ship's journal, it was impossible for me to prepare the map. For that reason, I left that preparation and everthing contained in the journal for review by [the authorities of] the Port of Okhotsk, and sent it there. Consequently at the present time I do not have the journal and have not been able to recall everything in detail for this report.

I herewith humbly conclude my report to Your Excellency.

[signed] Geodesist Mikhailo Gvozdev

Reference: TsGAVMF, f. 216 (Beringa), d. 53, 11. 722–733 ob.

See: A. V. Efimov, ed. *Iz istorii russkikh ekspeditsii na Tikhom okeans. Pervaia polovina XVIII veka* (Moscow: 1948), 244–249.

33

FEBRUARY 28, 1744

AN EYEWITNESS ACCOUNT OF HARDSHIPS SUFFERED BY NATIVES IN
NORTHEASTERN SIBERIA DURING BERING'S GREAT KAMCHATKA EXPE-
DITION, 1735–1744, AS REPORTED BY HEINRICH VON FÜCH, FORMER
VICE PRESIDENT OF THE COMMERCE COLLEGE, NOW A POLITICAL
EXILE

Almost all the Iakuts, as well as many of the Russian farm peasants who live along the Lena River, and even those who live as far away as the Irkutsk and Ilimsk uezds, have been ruined by the Kamchatka Expedition, for the following reasons.

1.

Every year Russian peasants are required to transport provisions over a distance of 2,000 to 3,000 versts to the town of Iakutsk for this expedition. If there are not enough persons who have been exiled into hard labor, others have to transport provisions even farther, all the way to the mouth of the Maia River. Consequently, many of the peasants are away from their homes for as long as three years at a time. When they return they have to live on charity or by hiring themselves out.

Likewise the Iakuts are required to send several hundred fully equipped horses to Iakutsk in the spring, plus one man to care for every five horses. These horses are used to transport provisions and supplies overland to Okhotsk. Because the land between Iakutsk and Okhotsk is marshy and barren steppe, very few of the horses come back. The officials who are sent out to requisition these horses burden the Iakuts in every possible way in order to enrich themselves. They will not accept good mares or colts and they reject many good stallions so that the Iakuts will have to give them twice or three times the value in livestock or goods. Then these officials and their accomplices send their own horses to town, horses which are supposedly better than the ones they could have accepted from the Iakuts. Furthermore, the officials do not look only to the wealthier Iakuts for the necessary number of horses, but levy the same requirement on each Iakut. One Iakut may own 50 or 100 horses [and thus be able to supply the required number], while another [may be so poor he] cannot buy either horse or wife; in order to fulfill his iasak requirement he has to become a servant to the Russians or to other Iakuts. To buy one horse he has to pay an amount which is usually equal to the value of his iasak assessment.

Although the Treasury of Her Imperial Majesty pays a delivery fee for the horses, the Iakuts who bring in the horses, or from whom the horses are taken, receive nothing. Only those who are sent [to Okhotsk] with these horses receive some part of the fee for their care and maintenance en route.

If the newly commenced Kamchatka Expedition continues to burden the local people, it will obviously become necessary to [take measures to] prevent them from completely ruining the local population, which is happening in spite of the large Treasury outlays Her Imperial Majesty has to make. Since I have little information about the intentions of this expedition, I cannot offer any suggestions. However, I certainly do know these facts: in undertaking such an expensive, destructive and ruinous long term enterprise, three questions should have been discussed and resolved, according to basic rules of economics.

1. Can it be anticipated that the enterprise can be completed?

2. If so, will future benefits exceed the vast expenditures and the inescapable ruin of subject peoples?

3. If there is absolutely no doubt of this, will it be possible to maintain and defend these advantages against the envy and power of foreign neighbors and other sea powers?

I know definitely that it is absolutely impossible, traveling via Iakutsk and Okhotsk, to take possession of land in the Japanese Empire or in any other part of the world, or to establish trade, let alone maintain it. And eventually we must analyze the needs of Russian merchants and find the best possible means and opportunities for them to benefit from [trade with] those areas located between the Russian and Chinese empires from the mighty Amur River to Japan, China and all of southern Asia.

2.

It must also be perceived that a new policy of iasak collection must be adopted for the Iakutsk Tungus and others. When they are stricken with smallpox they die like flies. Nine years ago I saw one nomadic settlement where only two out of ten men survived; the survivors had to pay the arrears for all those who had died, and not just for an entire uezd or district of some collector, but also for their relatives. I personally knew several wealthy Iakuts who had to pay for four or five of their dead relatives. They were so impoverished that before I left they had had to forfeit all their livestock and horses, and sometimes pawn their wives and children [to Russian officials]. Some of them hang or drown themselves. This is a natural consequence because a local native works very hard in the forest all through the winter and suffers hunger and cold until he traps enough to pay his iasak and make a gift [of furs] to the iasak collector and his assistants. If in addition to this he is forced to pay the iasak for those who have died or who have run off, first he loses all his livestock, then his wives and children. He cannot hunt without horses, so he commits suicide or runs off. Then the collectors find his relatives and force them to pay. The collectors take everything, until the natives are destitute.

3.

The third principal reason the local natives are ruined is that from the time they first came under Russian control they have been forced to pay tribute. Some have paid in sables, others in red foxes, still others in cash. At first there were plenty of furbearing animals there, but now there are no sables and not many foxes in those Iakut lands, from the shores of the [Arctic] ocean all the way south to the great Lena River. Moreover, almost half the natives cannot hunt because they have no horses. The instructions to the collectors always imply that they are to collect for the Treasury on the basis of the [original] assessment of one sable from each person on whom one sable was originally levied, and one fox from each person on whom one fox was levied. But the collectors know ahead of time that the natives do not have these furs and so they bring out from town a number of sable and fox pelts to sell [to the natives]. Then, even if the natives manage to trap sables and foxes before the collectors arrive, the collectors do not accept them, but force the natives to purchase the furs they have brought out, paying double or treble the value. The highest price in town for a Kamchatka sable is four rubles, and two rubles for a fox. But a collector will get 400 squirrels for a sable and 200 for a fox, and then can sell the squirrels in town at the rate of three rubles per 100 skins. The collector profits, the native loses, and there is no profit at all for the Imperial Treasury.

Twice during my eleven-year stay there, deputations of natives went to town with a petition to be allowed to pay their iasak obligations in squirrels and wolverines instead of sables and foxes. On the basis of their petition the office issued an ukaz that collectors were to accept 100 squirrels or 40 wolverines in place of one fox or sable. In that particular year the natives achieved some reduction of their burden, but the next year their suffering began again because the new official had to act on the basis of the original instructions unless the natives could obtain a new ukaz for relief in that year. As a result, these people experience great hardship, as is evident from the following points.

1. These natives live great distances from one another and a great deal of time is required for them to gather and choose their representatives and collect enough funds for travel and office expenses.

2. These inhabitants comprise groups made up of small families, each of whom has its own princeling. Some are prosperous, others are wretched in their subordination. Some are able to meet their iasak obligations, others cannot. One princeling may have established credit in town and can readily pay for sables and foxes for his family and then the collector tries to find his wealth. Therefore these collectors have arguments with the princelings many times a year as the collectors attempt to appropriate the natives' wealth. Other princelings may not have such means or credit and will fall into the hands of the collector.

It would be possible to halt all native complaints if Her Imperial Majesty would graciously order a stipulation in the iasak collection rule to the effect that if there were no sables or red foxes, 80 wolverines or 100 squirrels could be substituted for one sable or for two [non-red] foxes or for four rubles; half that amount for red foxes. If the iasak were payable in wolverines and squirrels, the Treasury would not lose and the natives would have a great reprieve. If Her Imperial Majesty were to allow the collectors to accept the substitution for sables and foxes to be paid into the Treasury, they would still make a considerable profit, which they justly deserve, because they are sent into designated places at their own expense.

4.

The fourth factor that completely ruins poor natives and bur-

Tattoos such as those shown were thought to enhance the beauty of Tungus women. Reduced to desperation through the confiscation of their goods and by the excessive iasak demands of Russian servitors, Tungus men were often forced to sell their wives and daughters. Sauer, *Billings' Expedition to Russia*. (OHS neg. 80232)

dens all others is that every year a new official or collector is sent out to each ostrog or district with a scribe, an interpreter, a tselovalnik and four to eight servitors. Each of these expects a gift. The gift to the official often equals the iasak due the Treasury.

However, there are officials so lacking in conscience that when a native brings a fox or 100 squirrels or two rubles in cash as iasak, the official will take it for himself and tell the native to go out hunting to obtain his isask pelts, even though the native declares he must pay the iasak to Her Imperial Majesty. Still, in order to escape a beating, the native will later bring in a gift if God gives him good fortune during the spring hunt for wolverines and squirrels. The officials, however, will not accept any excuses. The scribe comes after the official and receives half as much as the official, or sometimes the same amount. The interpreter gets a little less, the tselovalnik less than that, and the servitors receive their share as an *artel* [organized group]. When the official takes his share before the others do, it often happens that the poor natives cannot satisfy the other servitors, who then take the natives' wives and grown children to work for them. They also take the nets, axes, tools, boats, bows and arrows. Sometimes they take the clothes right off the backs of the natives, and beat and torture them secretly in their iurts.

Finally, I do not know of any [other] land where native inhabitants live without any protection and representation. When the voevodas dispense justice in town, then although the natives have some satisfaction for their complaints, nevertheless it often happens that they do not obtain whatever it is they seek. They do not receive a satisfactory response to their petition. Furthermore, no native can petition [a Russian official] in town until he has secured a town interpreter, who is nearly always related to the official, or at least is of one mind with him. Consequently, instead of reporting their grievances, the interpreter will upbraid the natives viciously and threaten to beat them. Sometimes he actually does flog them and sends them back. And if the voevoda is a greedy scoundrel, he mistreats them even more viciously.

On the basis of such complaints, the governors sometimes appoint commissions from among local officers to provide the Iakuts and other natives with the justice they seek, in which case they come to the city in great numbers with their petitions. However the [greedy] officials and their associates watch the petitioners as they come along the roads and rivers, and seize them and take them home where they reach some agreement and make peace. The officials give back half of what they have taken, and in this way avoid petitions and punishment.

About five years ago a young [Russian] man 20 years old was sent as an official to collect iasak in the town where I was staying. He remained there and for two years took everything he could. Since his father was the chief official, no one could complain. Many times I warned him he should not take so much, but rather be satisfied with what the natives gave him of their own accord, after they had paid their iasak; that way he would still have plenty for himself, and yet be safe. I told him that if he kept on as he was doing, he would be in danger of having everything confiscated and then being hanged.

He answered me, "There is a time to seize and a time to be hanged. Now is the time to seize. If I live in fear of being hanged, I will never be rich. If necessary, I can buy my way free."

When I tried to have further discourse with him he told me to stop bothering him with such lectures, that he was tired of these frequent admonitions. He was later sent to another, more prosperous ostrog, where he behaved more wickedly and greedily than before. But when he was ready to send his plundered wealth of horses, livestock and women to town, the Iakuts assembled in great numbers, hunted down the pillager and took everything back, without either a battle or an uprising. Because this young official had protection in town, nothing further happened to him.

It should be noted that the Iakuts are quiet, peaceful and punctual in paying, as are the Kamchatka and other natives [under Russian colonial rule]. The Tungus are also quiet and peaceful people and punctual in the payment of their iasak. However, when the officials try to ruin and pillage them, they go off with their entire settlements into the far reaches of the forest, and from there send their chosen representatives to town. When they are treated with violence and injustice, they resist.

In a word, the interest of Your Imperial Majesty, and the well-being of those productive subjects, are sufficient reasons that good order be maintained for them and that they be placed under strong protection. Common sense gives reason to believe that all neighboring free peoples will come to find out in every possible way how Russian servitors in those places treat those who have come under Russian jurisdiction and pay iasak. If these neighboring people see justice being done, they will subordinate themselves; otherwise they will defend themselves. A local tribe called the Chukchi are even now providing a clear example of what can happen.*

5.

An example of the terrible oppression of iasak-paying subjects is that the iasak collectors deliberately reject sable and fox pelts which the natives have prepared for iasak. This happens whenever the officials receive an inadequate number of gifts, or when they wish to realize a large profit by selling [to the natives] their own sables or foxes. When the natives arrive [in towns to pay their iasak] almost all the officials forbid them to exchange or purchase sables or foxes from anyone but themselves. If a native gives the collector a sable which has been bartered from one of the servitor's retinue or from anyone else, the collector will order the native to give back the sable and [trade or buy] only from him; or he may simply discard such sables and foxes, saying that they are worthless.

Such action is contrary to Your Imperial Majesty's interest and to natural law, which grants every native the freedom to hunt or barter or purchase anything he needs, wherever he finds it most cheaply, or to have it on credit if necessary. Such lawlessness and injurious collecting by the official could be terminated if, in a new regulation concerning iasak collection, it were stipulated that in accepting the iasak, the scribe, the interpreter and the tselovalnik must be present and voice their opinions as to whether these sables or foxes are acceptable as iasak or not. The matter should be resolved by majority vote.

Furthermore, they should not ask the natives from whom they have acquired the sable or fox, but be satisfied that the natives are giving Your Imperial Majesty the required iasak punctually, and in good quality furs. In a word, the best way to achieve this is to end the abuse of power by officials who pretend they have full authority and demand absolute submission, as if in battle. When servitors are sent on a military campaign, such authority is absolutely necessary, but in economic and civil matters it is counterproductive because these officials use that authority to harm Your Imperial Majesty's interests and to ruin Your subjects.

---

*von Füch is here referring to a prolonged and bloody struggle between the Russians and the Chukchi which lasted until the 1770's.—Eds.

6.

When a new official arrives from a town, he immediately orders that everyone in his district be informed that he will provide transportation for a certain day which he will designate. As noted above, he and his retinue set out and travel throughout the district from one family to another, under the guise of collecting iasak. This journey is very burdensome to the natives because they have to supply horses and food for everyone. During this travel the officials do not collect iasak, but rather, their own gifts, so that the natives rarely have enough left to pay their iasak. Thus they are allowed to postpone their iasak payment until the following spring. Then the officials report that there has been a bad hunting season and that the natives have asked to be allowed to postpone payment until the following fall. This is a deliberate lie. The iasak has been made ready, but the officials have extorted it from the natives in the form of gifts. When a new official arrives the next winter, he will not find anything, because the previous official is still there collecting his shortfall from the autumn hunt. The new official and his assistants now have the job of collecting their gifts, just as the former ones did. This results in the fact that Treasury revenues cannot be sent to Irkutsk for another year. As a result of these officials' misappropriations, Your Imperial Majesty's interests are delayed for another year.

In a period of eleven years I saw only one official who behaved properly; this was the syn boiarskii Matvei Tarlykov. When he arrived and the natives came to him with gifts, he announced to all of them that he had not been sent to collect gifts for himself, but to collect iasak for Your Imperial Majesty. Thus the natives brought in their iasak in good time, and it was in fine quality furs. When the iasak was paid in full, if they had furs left over and wished to give him something as a gift, he said he would be grateful to anyone who gave him something, but he would not penalize any who did not. He actually abided by this, collected the iasak in three months, took it to town on time and sought nothing for himself. Tarlykov is an educated man, a writer, a man who leads a good life and is quick to dispense justice. It would be desirable to have many more such men there.

7.

Almost all the Tungus are under the jurisdiction of certain

Iakut ostrogs or of the small districts ruled by the officials who collect their iasak. Some have three uluses, others more. Each ulus sends one hostage to the ostrog every year, and then these are usually exchanged when the new official arrives. This is done for the more probable collection of Your Imperial Majesty's revenues, because these Tungus live in the forest and roam for some 1,000 versts in search of food and hunting animals. If they did not give hostages, they would never come back to pay their iasak. Many have complained because they have been wrongfully attacked by certain officials. Some officials use the hostages for their own benefit unconscionably.

These hostages are supposedly taken from among the children of the leaders and the princelings. However, because the natives are so much afraid of smallpox, instead of giving over their own children, they bribe poor tribesmen to give up their children as hostages. This practice may be detrimental to the interests of Your Imperial Majesty, because if the Tungus can deliver substitute hostages in every ostrog, they themselves may disappear deep into the forest and completely abandon the hostages. They are cunning and brave people, very skillful with the bow and arrow. They sometimes wage intertribal wars, as when the Turukhansk Tungus came too near the territory of the Olensk Tungus to hunt.

Each hostage is supposed to receive several puds of flour from the government warehouse, but sometimes the officials take this for their own use. The Iakuts must send one ruble's worth of frozen or smoked fish from each nomadic settlement for the sustenance of the hostages. Eight such amounts are needed for each hostage.

In Zhigansk I saw an official who came down with smallpox and took no precautions to send the hostages away. All four hostages died within two weeks. This nearly led to a confrontation because the Tungus refused to pay iasak in the future until they had secured their hostages. The Iakuts are almost destitute because of the necessity of providing this enormous amount of provisions, especially in spring when they usually deliver, because at that time they have need of the provisions for themselves and often have to resort to eating roots and the bark of fir trees.

The matter could be resolved in this way: if there were no children of princelings available, then in the future, children of princelings' brothers would be taken as hostages. These hostages could be assigned to the homes of prosperous Iakuts, either baptized or not. They would be assigned singly, so there would be less fear of smallpox and it would be easier to feed them. The households that take them should receive the flour allotted for hostages from the warehouses, and the eight rations of preserved fish from the ostrog, as mentioned above. However, these households would be required to give assurance that they would still provide for these hostages when a new official arrived. Such an order would satisfy the Tungus, who would then pay their iasak on time.

If it were decided that the hostages should be kept in the ostrogs with officials, as previously, this could be done; however provisions should be made for their sustenance, and precautions taken to prevent smallpox. An ukaz should be issued to local voevodas not to send servitors as iasak collectors from any household where there has recently been smallpox, nor are they to send them for any other assignment into any uezd or any household where there has recently been a case of smallpox. Here more natives die of smallpox than people in other places die of pestilential infections. If the number of iasak-paying subjects should decrease, Your Imperial Majesty's interests would suffer substantially.

As soon as the Iakuts learn that smallpox or other contagious diseases are in town, they set up sentries along all the roads, armed with bows and arrows, and they will not allow anyone to come into their settlements from town. Likewise, they will not accept Russian flour or other gifts, lest these be contaminated with smallpox. The disease spreads in those places because no precautions are taken. There is no medication or any other way to treat it. It affects these natives more than plagues affect European countries at the present time.

8.

Some officials have the temerity to force these Iakuts to perform personal service for them without giving them any food or clothing. Several years ago there was an official who was like an Egyptian supervisor over the Israelites. He made all the inhabitants of his district who lived along one bank of the river build a home for himself 20 versts away from the ostrog. At the same time he ordered them to build an enclosure for his personal horses which was 20 versts in circumference and looked like a royal menagerie. This only happened in one year, since these officials are replaced every year. He had no cause to burden these people in this way, because there are living quarters in the ostrogs for the Sovereign's servitors, and only persons who have actually been there can understand the oppression these subject people suffer under such conditions.

There is no way the official can force prosperous and high-ranking Iakuts to work, because they occasionally go into town and can submit an official complaint. For that reason it is the poor and the lowly ones who are rounded up for such labor. These poor people have wives and children in their iurts who suffer constant famine when the head of the household is absent for a few days. Moreover, each poor householder during the summer has to prepare enough fish and hay for his own iurt for the winter. So when an official or a subordinate sends him on some task, he and his family suffer great need and hunger all winter long and have to search for food.

This evil lawlessness causes serious illness and the natives disappear like flies. It should also be noted that the natives do not use any medication when they are ill, and have no one to care for them. Rather, their custom is to leave any sick persons behind so those who leave will not fall ill. When infants take sick, or if they are not loved, the parents hang them in boxes on trees in the forest. If a Iakut woman gives birth to a deformed child, the infant is abandoned under the ice in the water. I personally saw a baptized Iakut do this, and I also witnessed numerous other tragic acts which could eventually be corrected through public concern, if [Russian] servitors would be more involved with increasing benefits for the Treasury, and if they had proper concern for these subjects, rather than being so involved in increasing their own private funds.

9.

When natives' horses are requisitioned to be sent off on some public works, it is the well-to-do and those who are far away who escape the burden of these gifts. The entire burden thus falls on the poor and those who are near.

10.

When, as noted above, the officials first collect gifts for themselves and their subordinates, and thus postpone the collection of iasak for a year, it follows that they have to continue to live there with their wives and children and servants. If another official and his subordinates arrive, then both the old and new officials travel through the uluses. The previous official collects his due, and the new official collects gifts for himself and his subordinates. In this improper manner they consume the entire Iakut food supply.

If the voevodas in town are selfish and greedy, then all during the summer fair they are interested only in one thing: who will give the most, regardless of whether he is old or young, has fulfilled his obligation correctly, has rank and position and can read and write. The only thing that matters is how much he promises to give. On the basis of this, servitors are sent out by water as early as September, and by the overland routes in January. Consequently, there are often times when those who go by water accomplish only half of their travel by the time the riverways freeze over. They have to abandon their boats and requisition enough horses and dogs to reach their destinations with their wives and children and baggage and provisions.

Because this practice burdens the subject peoples, the following procedures should be adopted to alleviate the situation.

1. In the future such officials should not be selected from among the convicts. The Governor of Siberia established a rule when he arrived that he would not appoint anyone himself, but would delegate that responsibility to the leader of the servitors, the nobles and the deti boiarskie and others, who are instructed to select experienced persons who will be good, law-abiding officials. If there are not enough such persons among the ranks, or if those chosen have been fined or are leading dissolute lives, then in such cases they must appoint experienced servitors from the lower ranks who are not convicts.

2. In ostrogs situated near large rivers these officials should be selected prior to June 1, and sent out with their assistants by water aboard their own vessels prior to June 20. To ensure that they are out of town before July 1, there should be a fine of 30 rubles for the voevoda and 10 rubles for the official for each day they are delinquent in meeting the specified date. On the basis of such an arrangement these officials would arrive at the designated

place in good time and would be able to prepare hay and fish for themselves for the winter without burdening the local subjects.

3. Servitors who take the overland route using their own means of transport should also be sent at the same time, and be subject to the same penalty so that they too would be able to prepare hay and fish for the winter in good time.

4. Veteran officials, under the same penalty, are to set out from their ostrogs before July 1 with the official iasak they have collected throughout the winter, without any deviation from their instructions, in order to make way for the arrival of new officials.

5. Newly arrived officials should be instructed to travel to the designated uluses in December or January for the first time in order to collect iasak from the fall hunt which takes place in October and November. Any shortfalls may be postponed until the spring hunt which takes place in March and April. They will thus be in a position to collect in full by June, and then leave. At the same time they should be ordered not to travel to local uluses, but rather, when they reach the official residence they should authorize local princelings to bring in iasak from all of their uluses for that winter by May 1. They should bring it in to the ostrog and hand it over there. Under this arrangement the collected treasury could be delivered to Irkutsk that same summer and would be preserved from the damage of a year's time, as has previously been the case.

11.

Either out of need or through deceit, the Iakuts sometimes leave their habitations and move several hundred versts away, which causes a problem. If an official knows where they have gone, he sometimes has to send his servitors 100 versts or more after them, and this in order to collect from just two iasak natives. If he cannot find them, the relatives of the runaways have to pay iasak for them. It often happens that there are people who are forced to go to work for others in order to pay their own iasak. Because this is difficult for both sides, it should be corrected in the following manner.

1. An order should be issued that no Iakut, under threat of a fine, can leave his ulus without advance notice to his official as to where he is going. When he reaches his destination he must immediately inform the official there so the officials can keep records

of the arrival and departure of these Iakuts, and can report to the main office.

2. Servitors should not be sent out more often than necessary. Each official should collect the iasak from the nomadic people, record it in his books and send the iasak to the main office. If this method of collecting registered iasak should prove unworkable then:

3. The collection of iasak should be organized in such a manner that officials to whom the Iakuts come when they reach town will accept their iasak, but turn it over to the officials from whom the Iakuts have run away. Revenue books should be kept as before, and travel to all the uluses would continue as before. This would greatly reduce the tremendous ruin and labor. Previously there was an effort to send the runaway Iakuts back to their original settlements, but it was impossible to enforce. It might be detrimental to Your Imperial Majesty's interests as well as to the well-being of those people. There are years when neither hunting nor fishing is good. In other years the grass may not grow and hay cannot be prepared. In such cases those people and their families and all their livestock would die if they were not permitted to seek help from their relatives and acquaintances in other uluses.

12.

There are some officials who dispense justice improperly, whose eyes are blinded by gifts and who thus make unlawful judgments. This could be corrected in the following manner:

1. There should be a rule that when Iakuts complain or petition against servitors, the official should appoint three other servitors to investigate.

2. A scribe should keep a brief protocol of the litigation. He should carefully note the complaint, the reply, the testimony and the verdict, and at the end of the year submit the case for review to the office in town.

3. The Iakuts should be permitted to appeal the official's decision in the main office.

4. Unjust officials should be fined appropriately. Persons who petition against an unjust decision, as well as witnesses summoned to testify in town, should be compensated for travel expenses if it is ascertained that officials decided the case unjustly and contrary to the iasak regulations, and that they treated the natives cruelly.

The Chukchi of northeastern Siberia suffered great hardship during the Second Kamchatka Expedition. Reindeer and sledding equipment were requisitioned to assist Bering's passage, and iasak quotas were increased. Sarychev, *Voyage of Discovery*. (OHS neg. 80251)

13.

Generally the well-to-do Iakuts and Tungus are appointed as judges, and in uluses the princelings are assigned for the same purpose. Some of these persons harass their subordinates. Some cause violence if they happen to have patrons in town, or operate in unison with [Russian] officials and make it impossible for a wronged person to seek redress against them. However this injustice could be terminated if the miscreant were forced to pay double to the injured party for a first offence, fined and meted bodily punishment for a second offence and hanged for a third. This would be an example for all the other native judges in the uezd.

14.

In order to prevent all manner of deceptions and abuses, there should be a policy that an official sent on assignment should be accompanied by only the necessary number of subordinate servitors from town, and not by his wife or any other relatives.

15.

Officials who travel overland with a retinue burden the Iakuts with their demands for working horses. As soon as they reach an ostrog they immediately summon the nearby Iakuts, requisition their horses and use them for sentry purposes and for the collection of forage. If any of these horses are lost in the forest or injure themselves while they are tied to trees, or die of old age, then even though the Iakuts have had to buy hay many times they now have to give up everything and pay double the usual price for such a horse. This loss could be prevented if officials would go out on assignment in good time and prepare their own hay, or if they were helped by the *zakazchik* [overseer] who has been left behind by the previous official.

16.

Iakuts and other subject peoples are also devastated by the fact that provisions are requisitioned from them for iasak servitors, liquor control officials and influential exiles who are sent out from town via the water route. It also happens that deputies and agents of various ranks will force Iakuts who are living near rivers to hunt or fish or do other work for them. Often they take them so far away that during the best part of summer [the natives] cannot prepare food for their own winter needs.

In contrast to this, soldiers and servitors aboard the river vessels waste time playing cards, sleeping and debauching rather than working. This could be stopped if, when the chief administrators send persons out on the service of Her Imperial Majesty they would assign, in addition to the soldiers and servitors, the required number of workers from among those who are in penal servitude. If such persons were not available, they could hire either baptized or unbaptized Iakuts in return for relieving them of half or all of their iasak obligation. They would then be paid on a definite rate by the verst. However, this small expense would be raised from the Iakuts themselves by having them contribute one kopeck each, or one and a half, which would not be too great a burden. As it is, those who are taken by force from their fishing and hunting are bearing the burden for the entire uezd, which is detrimental to the well-being of the economy.

17.

Thievery and plunder along the overland and water travel routes are committed by evil persons and also by those who have become skilled thieves. These people do not start by deliberately committing crimes; rather, this happens by chance, as opportunity presents itself, as for example, when hard labor prisoners cordelled Admiralty vessels from Iakutsk to Shigan and were then sent back overland and along the way pillaged some Iakut iurts.

When soldiers who are assigned to guard prisoners complete their official duties in town and return with provisions, some of them steal anything they find along the banks of the rivers on their way: garments, fur cloaks, sashes, nets, fishing equipment, ropes, boats and the like. They are pleased with their booty and return home. They are not in the least concerned with how damaging this is to these subject people, when the equipment they need to procure their winter provisions is stolen. Some steal livestock and slaughter it for food. This can be prevented by forceful ukazes. First, the office from which the vessel is sent out should issue strict orders to the commanding officer, or if there is none, to the senior soldiers. Second, the servitor who is usually sent out in place of an interpreter should also have strict orders and should take an oath that while his group is en route the men will be absolutely forbidden to be rude or insolent [to the natives].

18.

Similar situations have been reported by noted Russians and foreigners [in Russian service] who have been sent to those regions from St. Petersburg for the Kamchatka Expedition and on other assignments. The officers whom the Governor sent to Iakutsk have treated the subjects of Her Imperial Majesty with violence and oppression. These were malicious cases. These things happen because persons who went on these assignments were not subject to local authorities. If they committed some violence or abuse, a civil petition was sent to the local authorities who then responded in a like manner. In this way the matter was concluded. The subject peoples were better off simply by bearing this violence and mistreatment than by traveling a thousand versts in order to present a petition protesting it.

185

This abuse could be controlled in two ways. First, all European powers have a rule that wherever persons travel and stop, including colonels and generals, they must submit to local authorities in any legal grievance except' in regard to their assignments, and must respond to queries without complaint. Consequently, in those countries one does not hear anything about violence and other forms of oppression. Officials of any province represent their sovereign's authority. There are cases, however, where a governor or vice governor may arrest a general if he does not call upon the governor or vice governor within 24 hours of his arrival. Such governors, of course, have high ranks and positions.

If this example were not applicable or tenable, then another regulation could terminate violence and lawlessness and offer the subject people protection and security. In that case, a rule should be passed and made public, directing that every person in a command postion or on a special mission must follow instructions according to existing rules, and loyally and diligently carry out the assignment on which he has been sent, without committing any violence or oppression against either the persons or property of subject peoples; neither must his associates be permitted to harass these people.

If this rule were to be violated, then local authorities could receive a written complaint from the injured parties, demand a response and have the matter investigated. A written report should be sent to the governor and from there to higher authorities and then on to the particular department [in St. Petersburg] which had dispatched the violator. If the complaint should concern debts or actual pillage, it would be obvious the debtor must make immediate restitution. If the matter were subject to a fine, higher authorities should be informed.

19.

There also are dishonest and unconscionable, cheating servitors who collect iasak from the Iakuts for their own benefit, without permission, by beating and torturing the Iakuts to force them to comply. Thus, when a dishonest iasak collector comes, a Iakut is forced to pay again. There are other servitors who collect the iasak and use it to engage in high living, drinking and gambling. Yet iasak is desirable, and the Treasury does not wish to lose it. In short, there is so much thievery and dishonesty that it is difficult to describe and terminate it. Thus various methods must be used.

This entire problem is due to the fact that there is neither order nor quick justice in those remote places. Although sometimes stern ukazes are issued to deal with this problem in those areas, and although the governors send officials there to receive petitions and investigate matters pertaining to Her Imperial Majesty's interest, they themselves may fall into evil ways and cause violence. They often accept gifts, fill their own pockets and cause the inhabitants of those remote places to be in the same miserable circumstances as before.

My own humble observation on this matter is that if these remote places were to have a low-ranking procurator or an executor with full authority who could protect these natives, accept their grievances and have the power to make decisions right then and there, as well as to investigate general problems in the areas along rivers where iasak is collected and to look after other aspects of Her Imperial Majesty's rights and interests, and if this person would conduct himself loyally and conscientiously in all matters, in the future there would be no further need to send officers or other servitors out from Irkutsk to those places, at great expense, and everything would gradually be brought under control.

There are examples in other places that at various times especially assigned officials were sent by the court to remote regions to investigate local conditions and oversee the behavior of the servitors in order to keep them in hand. When I left the region I promised the Iakuts and Tungus, who had petitioned me, that I would report these conditions to Imperial authorities. I assured them that Her Imperial Majesty's Empire would provide them mercy, justice and protection. My conscience and my respect for order, justice and good economic conditions force me to carry out this promise I made to them. I submit before the court of God that I am not reporting anything more than what I have personally heard, seen or witnessed. I submit all of this to the highest and most mature judgment for consideration.

20.

In conclusion, in order to reveal the evil conditons that exist there, I would like to submit three further points for Imperial consideration.

1. In those places there is a rule that when town dwellers elect liquor control officials from amongst themselves, they are answerable for their conduct. This is a good rule but it does not benefit the voevoda. A few years ago there was a voevoda in Iakutsk who recommended a certain thief for that post. Although the town dwellers were aware of this and had the right to vote on the man, they did not dare vote contrary to the will and intention of the voevoda. The person who was then Governor of Irkutsk planned to make use of the huge liquor revenues. In one year he sent to Iakutsk enough liquor for a ten-year period. The thief and the officials arranged the matter in such a way that not only did he dilute the liquor with water, but he never accounted for the 20,000 rubles he collected [as duty]. He soon afterward died in prison, and the lost revenue was never given to the Treasury.

2. Before I arrived, there was a young man named Stepan Guliaev. He was the town interpreter, a very important position since all the natives had to depend on him. He very quickly became rich by local standards. He became so wealthy, in fact, that he was able to bring the voevoda into his schemes. When the new governor came to Irkutsk, he ordered all the prosperous persons in Iakutsk to report to him. Guliaev arranged that in his important post of interpreter he had the rank of colonel and thus supervised the servitors. Furthermore, he arranged to have a permanent assignment to collect iasak from the two most prosperous districts.

And what happened then? Using his official status Guliaev oppressed and abused the natives, whose only recourse in such matters was to complain to the colonel through the interpreter. And Gulaiev held all three positions. The voevoda was his patron and protector, so he managed to amass a goodly fortune until the last governor, [L. L.] Lange, divided up the jurisdiction so it was no longer under the control of one person.

3. When servitors are sent with the finest iasak collections to Moscow or to St. Petersburg, they usually petition to be assigned to the uezds as permanent officials, and often this is granted. Such a reward is obviously proper and laudable. But there ought to be a stipulation in the ukaz that the servitor can hold that office only if he has served without infractions in the past, and con-

188

tinues to serve without infractions in the future. Otherwise there may be harmful consequences if the servitors try to be independent of supervisors and then pillage the subject peoples without harm to themselves.

I knew such a person in Irkutsk. In two years he stole 100 rubles and 500 head of horses and livestock from Russian subjects. When the present governor reached a decision in the matter and ordered that he be arrested and brought to judgment, the guilty person relied on the ukaz and persuaded a prisoner sentenced to hard labor to testify publicly against the governor, so that if the accused were sent to Moscow with the prisoner he would be able to secure freedom for both of them through influential patrons there. However the prisoner finally confessed and incriminated the accused of conspiracy. From this it is obvious that strict precautions must be observed in granting such rewards.

Reference: GPBOR. Ermitazhnoe sobranie, No. 360, 11. 1–36.

See: F. G. Safronov. "Iz istorii iakutskoi ssylki pervoi poloviny XVIII veka," in *Uchennye zapiski iakutskogo universiteta*. Seriia istorii, 1963, vyp. 14, 99–110.

34

A DECREE FROM THE SENATE SENDING AN INFANTRY COLONEL AND OTHER OFFICERS TO SIBERIA TO INVESTIGATE ABUSES AND MISTREATMENT OF NATIVES BY RUSSIAN IASAK COLLECTORS

This decree is to be announced in Siberia for general information.

1. In accordance with an ukaz of Her Imperial Majesty, Colonel Wolf of the Kabardinsk Infantry Regiment is being dispatched to Siberia with senior and junior officers to investigate the protection of the loyal subjects of Her Imperial Majesty, especially the Kamchadals, against officials assigned there to collect iasak, and from their subordinates who inflict abuse and ruin upon these people. This is to be done so that in the future no one, under any circumstances, will inflict abuse and ruin on local people (except for the collection of Treasury-imposed obligations).

Likewise, henceforth no one is to take any of the newly baptized or unbaptized natives into forced servitude under the pretext of punishment for debt, forgery or any other false accusation. Anyone who takes such baptized or unbaptized persons into servitude, or who has written acknowledgments of indebtedness, [is to be informed that] such debts are not to be recovered through force except for those which have been incurred through obligations during normal trade transactions, and which, upon careful examination, are seen to be bona fide. Such obligations can and should be enforced. In the future, however, any illegal statements of debt are not to be contracted.

If in the future, subsequent to this prohibition, anyone should hold such persons as slaves, or should have any written document of indebtedness, he will be treated as a violator of this ukaz.

2. If any local natives have been abused, they should submit their petitions to Colonel Wolf. In these petitions they should state the simple truth, without any embroidery. Upon receipt of the petitions, Wolf is authorized to investigate, in accordance with this ukaz, without exception. If investigations show that anyone has collected any additional [iasak] from local natives, this is to be confiscated from the usurious person, and returned to the natives from whom it was taken, without delay.

3. This generosity on the part of Her Imperial Majesty is extended to the local natives, as loyal subjects of Her Imperial Majesty, so they will not be impoverished. In return, those people, as subjects of Her Imperial Majesty, receiving such generosity from Her Imperial Majesty, are forever to perform loyal service to Her Imperial Majesty, and unhesitatingly pay the iasak imposed on them into the Treasury.

Reference: Russia. *Polnoe sobranie zakonov rossiiskoi imperii s 1649 goda.* First series (St. Petersburg: 1830), 452–453.

35

OCTOBER, 1747

A REPORT FROM CAPTAIN ALEKSEI I. CHIRIKOV TO THE ADMIRALTY COLLEGE REGARDING THE POSSIBILITY OF FURTHER EXPLORATIONS IN THE NORTH PACIFIC OCEAN TO AUGMENT INFORMATION OBTAINED BY THE GREAT KAMCHATKA EXPEDITION (1735–1741)

The Sibirskii Prikaz has requested precise information and opinions regarding lands and islands near Kamchatka. For this reason I am writing the following.

First, it should be ascertained whether or not the [Admiralty] College will release the information to the Sibirskii Prikaz about the areas near Kamchatka, as well as the map showing the natives who live in Kamchatka along the eastern part of the harbor of Petropavlovsk, and the map of the entire east coast from Kamchatka out to the east, where the late Captain Commander [Bering] and I sailed.

We did not find any [inhabited] land closer than 1,500 versts on a direct line. Between the nearest inhabited place we discovered and Kamchatka, near an island located 900 versts from the harbor of Petropavlovsk, we saw sea otters, seals, fur seals and whales, both near the island and in other places nearer and farther, in great numbers. We also saw them at the island where Captain Commander Bering died [Bering Island], and there were many sea otters in the place where Waxell, Khitrov and Ovtsyn, the surviving lieutenants, and the crew wintered over. There were also many sea lions, sea cows and other marine creatures. Consequently, it may be supposed that on other islands in the vicinity there also are sea otters, seals, fur seals and whales, and that the land which the geodesist Gvozdev apparently saw [in 1732] is inhabited, and is on a direct line, not less than 1,700 versts from the mouth of the Kamchatka River. It is more than 1,100 versts from the nearest Russian ostrog, Anadyrsk, by way of the Anadyr River and the sea. It is more than 600 versts from the mouth of the Anadyr River by sea. Captain Laptev's report, which he prepared after his voyage there, indicates the Anadyr River is quite inadequate for seagoing vessels.

In accordance with Her Majesty's personal ukaz of October 1, 1743, neither Captain Spanberg nor I may go to sea until a fur-

The bull fur seal was important for fur, hide, whiskers, and meat. Henry Elliott made this drawing of "Old John" at Gorbotch Rookery in July 1872 and was kind enough to include inset portraits of "his two wives." Elliot, *An Arctic Province*. (OHS neg. 80244)

ther ukaz is issued. The servitors have been ordered to move from these places to Siberian locations in order to protect [Russian] inhabitants of Siberian towns. Accordingly, they have been moved to Eniseisk and Tomsk and are awaiting orders. If further expeditions are authorized, then the Sibirskii Prikaz may decide to send volunteers from among the servitors and the Kamchadals who hunt sea otters to these islands near the Kamchatka ostrogs and to the larger islands to the east.

The sea otter, most highly prized of the marine furbearers. Chirikov's report to the Admiralty detailing the wealth of fur-bearing animals observed during the Kamchatka Expedition into North Pacific waters spurred subsequent hunting expeditions. Elliot, *An Arctic Province*. (OHS neg. 80243)

It is rumored that as early as 1744 servitors went from Kamchatka to the nearest island to the east, and made a good profit from sea otters. For such expeditions [in the future] they should have permission to use the vessels left in Okhotsk after the [Bering] expedition (except for the packetboat, which requires quite a large crew to sail to such places) and any available men. If more men are needed, then another new vessel should be built, similar in size to the brigantine *Mikhail*. It should be built on the Kamchatka River by shipwrights and carpenters who will later stay near Okhotsk. These vessels should be fitted with anchors left from the expedition. Anchor cable should be provided at the expense of the Sibirskii [Prikaz] from the Kazan Admiralty, two seven-inch cables, one six-inch cable and one five-inch per vessel; all must be 120 sazhens long. The Kazan Admiralty should also send stays, rope for rigging and lanyards. The rest of the equipment should be prepared on site. The vessels should be kept in Petropavlovsk harbor for safety. I will have more to say in regard to major repairs, but the following information is essential.

It is necessary to appoint two navigators and four assistants, two apprentice navigators, a boatswain and six seamen, all to be financed by the Siberian gubernia [office]. The vessels should be fitted with compasses and other navigational equipment.

It is very important that the commander or the voevoda, whoever is in charge, be a conscientious man, neither greedy for personal gain nor extortionate. He should be helpful, concerned with the interests of Her Imperial Majesty and the general wellbeing of the local natives as well as of the Russians under his jurisdiction. Such a man is necessary, not only for the expedition to be dispatched to the island in good order, but also for the expedition members to be well taken care of in Okhotsk and Kamchatka. Since both Okhotsk and Kamchatka are coastal areas, it would be useful if the local commanding officer could care for office matters and also be familiar with navigational affairs. For this reason it would be helpful to send retired naval officers there as commanding officers, men who have attained the rank of major or fleet lieutenant by the time of their retirement, men who are well-informed. They would be replaced every three or four years.

At the present time the men who are sent to Kamchatka as administrators are inhabitants of Iakutsk and are volunteer servitors. They are replaced every year and it is very difficult to single out even one of them who is really qualified. However, there is a nobleman from Iakutsk named Fedor Amosov. The Iakut leaders say that there has never been a complaint against him or by him, and that no matter what he does the inhabitants of that area have always been pleased with him and request that he be reappointed. Would it not be appropriate to send Amosov to Kamchatka as administrator? The commanding officer or voevoda should be entrusted with matters pertaining to the sea.

1. The servitor-navigators who are assigned to the Okhotsk command should be sent along the coast for 200 or 300 versts east of Okhotsk, and then west from the Ud River to make a systematic description of the coast. They should use geodetic measurements, show the configuration of the coast and search for good harbor sites in order to provide better protection for seagoing vessels than is presently afforded by the area at the mouth of the Okhota River. Large vessels are now kept there out of necessity, but at low tide they are out of the water. Large ships cannot enter the river because it is very shallow. The [Second] Kamchatka Expedition did send persons to describe that coast and search for coastal harbors, but it is not as productive to conduct such a search from the sea as it is if one goes right along the coast.

When harbor sites are found, it is then possible to examine the passage to the sea, to measure and survey, and to describe the kind of forest located near the harbors and its extent. For this, a geodesist should be sent out from Irkutsk province so that he and the servitor-navigators can make a description of the coast. If harbors are found that are better than Okhotsk, seagoing vessels should be docked there and harbor facilities built.

2. When the two vessels go out from Kamchatka to the nearby islands, fifteen servitors should be sent in each vessel to hunt, in addition to the sailors. These should be volunteers, under the command of the navigators, and they should be instructed to proceed to the islands near Kamchatka: first to the east, then the next year or whenever possible, to the south. They should hunt on any island where they find sea otters or land animals such as fox and sable. They also should collect whale whiskers. Wherever they find good hunting they should make a good and accurate description of the place. They should surrender two-thirds of their take of sea otters, sables, foxes and whale whiskers to the Treasury, and divide the remainder among all the promyshlenniks and crew aboard the ships. This one-third should be evenly divided. All pelts of seals and fur seals and all blubber are to be divided among the servitors and crew.

3. If they find natives anywhere they are to treat them with kindness and not harm them. They are to encourage them to come under the sovereignty of Her Imperial Majesty, using kindness, and promise them Her Imperial Majesty's generosity and protection. They should give the natives inexpensive gifts such as iron pots, small bells, glass beads, needles and such, and see if they cannot be attracted by this kindly approach. With that in mind, the commanding officer of Okhotsk should issue these or similar items when the occasion arises, as he may judge prudent, and local inhabitants should be requested but not forced to contribute to the Treasury to pay for them. However, if they do not wish to make a good will offering, but have furs or other items of value, these things are not to be taken from them, lest they become embittered.

4. In moving from one island to another, and returning to winter in Petropavlovsk, by the second or third summer they should reach the land which our servitors had discovered and which lies 1,500 versts from Petropavlovsk, south and east, in 65°

east. The native inhabitants should be treated as described above, with every kindness. If they are numerous it is important to be cautious lest suddenly, through inadvertance and presumed good will, our people are deceived and fall into their hands. Our people should take note of everything: what they have in abundance, what their clothing is, their food, dwellings, weapons. They should search for harbors near the islands as well as near the mainland and also safe places where one can retreat in bad weather.

5. They should look for a likely place to build a small fort near that inhabited land, and notice where our people could live and whether or not they would be welcome there. They should try to find a well situated small island near the land where a fortress could be built, which could be defended against attack because of the advantage of being surrounded by water.

6. They should make note and record islands where forest is to be found, and what kind of trees grow there.

7. Navigators and their assistants should keep an accurate journal during their voyages from one island to another so that a reliable map can be prepared.

8. After islands in this area have been explored, the island which Gvozdev sighted should also be investigated for a detailed description at some time in the future. That land lies above 64° northern latitude and is rumored to have many sables and other fur-bearing animals although it is far from Kamchatka and has such a cold climate that crops cannot be grown.

9. Upon their return every year a substantial report about everything should be sent to the Okhotsk administration, and from there a report should go to the Admiralty College [in St. Petersburg].

10. Ships should be sent out from Kamchatka every year, and the commanding officer there should see that they have all necessary provisions. If the Kamchatka Expedition has not been disbanded, ships should be sent only to the islands nearest Kamchatka to hunt sea otters and other animals. For this purpose they should have the smallest vessel from the expedition, the *Berezovka*, and supplement it with another vessel built in Okhotsk by Captain Walton. Otherwise two new ones, the size of *Berezovka*, should be built in Kamchatka. Boatswains or good quartermasters should be assigned as officers aboard these vessels, men who are skilled in the art of navigation. In addition, two sailors, ser-

The famous rock pillars, Three Brothers, which mark the entry to Avacha Bay on the southeast coast of Kamchatka. This magnificent natural harbor became the principal embarcation point for Russian fur hunters and government expeditions. 19th Century French lithograph. Private collection.

vitors and Kamchadals who know how to hunt sea otters should be sent with them.

Reference: TsGAVMF, f. 216 (Beringa), d. 48, 11. 741–744 ob.
See: V. A. Divin, ed. *Russkaia tikhookeanskaia epopeia* (Khabarovsk: 1979), 300–303.

36

A REPORT FROM FEDOR I. SOIMONOV, GOVERNOR OF SIBERIA, TO THE
GOVERNING SENATE, CONCERNING PREPARATIONS FOR AN EXPEDI-
TION TO THE PACIFIC AND ARCTIC OCEANS, UNDER THE COMMAND OF
IVAN BECHEVIN, A MERCHANT FROM IRKUTSK

On January 20, 1757, Ivan Bechevin, a merchant of Irkutsk, sent a statement of his intentions to Tobolsk, to Admiral and Cavalier Vasilii A. Miatlev, then Governor of Siberia. Hoping that Her Imperial Majesty would approve it, Bechevin submitted firm plans to sail on a vessel he had had especially built, out past the Kuril Islands, around the southern cape of Kamchatka and out into the open Pacific Ocean. He plans to sail to previously discovered areas both south and north, and also to any new unknown lands and islands he may discover, all the way to the mouth of the Anadyr River. If God grants him the opportunity, he also intends to sail around Cape Chukotka to rivers which empty into the Arctic Ocean and on to the mouth of the Lena River.

1. Bechevin intends that his men will hunt all manner of animals and birds on these islands, along the coast and on the mainland, and that they will also perform other useful tasks. He will commence this voyage in 1758 if possible, otherwise in 1759. In his statement he asks authorization for the following.

Two quartermasters from Okhotsk, Gavriil Pushkarev and Prokopii Lobashkov, have already been assigned to sail out into the open sea for their own interests as well as for the general benefit of the state and the nation, and to augment the mighty interests of Her Imperial Majesty. Now Bechevin asks permission to assign the *michman* [a midshipman] Andreian Iurlov to that voyage also, to keep a journal and to describe the coastline and do other essential work. If it is impossible to release him from his present assignments, then another navigator or someone of another rank should be assigned, provided he has the necessary navigational experience.

If there are no reliable volunteers, then two sailors, Andreian Ushokov and Iakov Sharapov, and the cossack Semen Tropinin, who is stationed in Kamchatka, should be assigned. They should also have an interpreter from the Okhotsk office to enable them to converse with the local heathens. The choice is Ivan Matveev, the son of Mokhnachevskii. He should have double pay and regular provisions, and during the voyage, in accordance with Naval Regulations, he should have appropriate rations, paid for from the funds left by the previous expedition. These men and the quartermasters who were previously assigned, as well as any naval personnel who may be assigned in the future, or any special replacements, will be with Bechevin constantly.

During the voyage these servitors should not attempt to issue any orders other than those which lie within their competence, without the consent and permission of the prikashchiks and supervisory personnel. While they are hunting animals, Bechevin's agents and laborers are not to be hindered, nor is anyone to interfere with their private lives.

2. To make repairs and perform routine maintenance, Bechevin requests Osip Leontev, a carpenter promyshlennik from the town of Iarensk, who by virtue of a permit and an ukaz from the Irkutsk office was engaged as a shipwright to build this vessel in Okhotsk, and in September of 1756 left Okhotsk aboard this vessel as a sailor, bound for the Kamchatka ostrogs. Up to 50 free workers from Irkutsk and Okhotsk and Kamchatka should be assigned to Bechevin's ship to hunt, in addition to the prikashchiks and agents. They should have properly authorized passports. However, if some of these men have papers with irregularities, then by reason of Her Imperial Majesty's lenience toward Her loyal servants, and because of the remoteness of this region and the shortage of personnel capable of undertaking the voyage, such irregularities should not weigh too heavily against them.

3. [Bechevin] also asks that two small bronze or cast iron cannon, two to three puds in weight, with appropriate cannon balls or shot, be issued from Her Imperial Majesty's government warehouses in Irkutsk or Iakutsk, with authorization from the voevoda's office. These would be used to insure the safe return of Bechevin's ship from its voyages at sea, and in case of attack, to defend the ship and men against unknown heathen natives in places where they put into shore. If there are enough cannon in the port of Okhotsk, then in addition to these two necessary cannon, he asks for two more. He also asks permission to purchase fifteen puds of gunpowder and two puds of cannon powder in

Irkutsk. Further, he requests that an official permit be issued to allow him to purchase up to 100 *vedros* [pails] of double-distilled spirits from the officials in the tax collection office in Iakutsk at the official price. This would be used for crew and workers during the voyage, and would not be resold in taverns.

4. If Bechevin should need assistance in preparing his vessel for the voyage, he asks that both in Okhotsk and in Kamchatka he might be supplied with temporary help by government craftsmen, blacksmiths and ropemakers, all with their own tools. He also asks for the use of the local lifting jacks.

In accordance with the rules and instructions of Her Imperial Majesty, all local commanding officers, prikashchiks and village elders, as well as naval and Admiralty people who may be there, should provide immediate assistance to Bechevin in helping him with his needs and necessities for the voyage. There should be no discord. On the voyage they should be permitted to enter government harbors and the vessel should not be denied anchorage anywhere.

Official permission from Her Imperial Majesty should be issued to deal with these problems. Wherever necessary, subordinate officials should be issued appropriate ukazes for instruction.

In 1755 Admiral and Cavalier [and Governor Vasilii A.] Miatlev granted permission to the Ustiug merchants Ivan Bakhov and Nikita Shalaurov to explore. Bakhov had a seagoing vessel built at his own expense in the Chechuisk *volost* [administrative unit] near the village of Veshniakovo. In this vessel Bakhov and Shalaurov voyaged from the mouth of the Lena River out into the Arctic Ocean and on to the Kolyma River. From there they continued around the Chukotsk Cape as far as Kamchatka and other places. Their aim was to increase and expand the benefits of government interest in Russian seafaring, to seek new unknown lands and islands and to hunt all kinds of new animals and birds in those places. Miatlev granted permission, although it was not certain they could find a passage from the mouth of the Lena via the Arctic Ocean around Chukotsk Cape to Kamchatka, where Captain Laptev had been dispatched. Nevertheless, the merchants Bakhov and Shalaurov undertook this at their own personal expense, without compulsion, willingly and without any governmental loss and with no detriment to important government interests.

Because of their desire to profit from hunting animals which abound in these places, they may perhaps discover a route which will be more advantageous than the present route to Anadyrsk and Kamchatka. Further, if an accurate description can be made during one of their voyages around Chukotsk Cape, that will be no mean accomplishment, and it will benefit everyone in the future.

On February 18, 1754, the Siberian gubernia sent to the Irkutsk office, with a copy of the ukaz from the Governing Senate, orders pertaining to a Senate project for merchants. These orders do not prohibit them from sailing to Japan and the nearby islands, nor indeed are they to be deprived of hunting privileges, in order that they may spread out over a greater area. It is very encouraging that merchants and promyshlenniks themselves are looking for a route to remote places, without any government loss, just as merchants and promyshlenniks sought Kamchatka and other previously unkown places.

In accordance with an ukaz of Her Imperial Majesty's Governing Senate of April 13, 1755, this was approved. Therefore no problem is foreseen in granting permission to the requests of this Irkutsk merchant, Bechevin.

I have written to the Irkutsk office about this. In accordance with the project of the Governing Senate and Her Imperial Majesty's ukaz, and for the purposes of Imperial and national benefits which may be secured from such new developments, I have authorized Bechevin to undertake this voyage aboard a ship which he has had especially built at his own expense.

He may sail beyond the Kuril Islands, around Cape Kamchatka into the open Pacific Ocean, to southern and northern lands which have already been visited, as well as to those he may discover, and also to unknown lands and islands all the way to the mouth of the Anadyr, or around Cape Chukotsk to the mouths of rivers which fall into the Arctic Ocean, and to the mouth of the Lena River. He may hunt on those islands, along the coasts and in the lands, using his own resources. He and his agents and workers may proceed in this present year of 1758, or, barring insoluble problems, in 1759. For the purpose of the voyage and of hunting, in addition to his prikashchiks and agents, he may take up to 50 men from among the free workers now located in Irkutsk, Okhotsk and Kamchatka. These are to be persons with authorized passports, not runaways or persons without passports.

The carpenter Osip Leontev (son of Zinin), one of the promyshlenniks in the town of Iarensk, is to be made available to Bechevin to make any needed repairs to his vessel. Leontev was assigned by an ukaz from the Irkutsk office to build Bechevin's ship in Okhotsk and in September of 1756 he sailed as a seaman aboard the ship to Kamchatka ostrog. Likewise, to ensure Bechevin's safe return from the voyage, and so he may defend himself if necessary when his ship stops in unknown heathen places, I have authorized that two small bronze or cast iron cannon of two or three puds, with appropriate cannon balls or shot be issued from the warehouse of Her Imperial Majesty in Irkutsk province or from the Iakutsk voevoda's office, with a receipt. It would be preferable to have him take any other cannon he needs from disabled expedition ships, since he will be sailing past the islands where these cannon are located, and he will be readily able to pick them up there, rather than to give him others from the port of Okhotsk.

On his return voyage past these places he should be authorized to bring with him all the cannon which have been left behind from damaged expedition ships, wherever they may be. He is authorized to purchase fifteen puds of musket powder and two puds of cannon powder in Irkutsk, at the authorized price. Likewise, if it is not contrary to Her Imperial Majesty's ukaz, he should be permitted to purchase in Iakutsk from the tax collection office up to 100 vedros of double distilled spirits, at the authorized price, for the servitors and laborers on the voyage. However, he is to be strictly prohibited from secretly reselling this, under the threat of a very heavy fine.

At the time of Bechevin's departure he should be instructed to be certain to have enough provisions to feed the workers for at least one year, and also to be sure to have everything else he will need.

In order to permit Bechevin and his prikashchiks free passage and uninterrupted assistance through designated places, an ukaz has been sent to the Irkutsk office to levy and collect appropriate fees, as requested by the petition. However, if at any time that office feels local circumstances require that these fees be raised, this can be done immediately.

In addition, Bechevin or anyone he selects as his prikashchik is to be obligated, under penalty of death, for the duration of this voyage, not to cause any harm or even the slightest resentment among the inhabitants of the islands who are iasak subjects. Bechevin and his men also have a further obligation. If they find any tribes who are not yet under the authority of the Russian Empire, they are absolutely not to take away from them any animals which they have killed for their own use. They are to treat them with every kindness, as circumstances may permit. In addition, provided there are no problems which might prevent it, they are to keep faithful notes or a daily journal all during the voyage so that when they return, or if necessary before that, they could send this report to the Irkutsk office, from where it would be sent on to me.

I have also sent an order to Navy Captain Lieutenant Rtishchev in Okhotsk authorizing that two quartermasters, Gavriil Pushkarev and Prokopii Lobashkov, who were previously assigned to Okhotsk, now, in accordance with the request of the Irkutsk merchant, Bechevin, be assigned to him. They will sail out into the open sea for both Imperial and national benefit and for the enhancement of Her Imperial Majesty's interests. In addition, they are to keep a journal and describe the coastline. The skipper Andreian Iurlov is also to be assigned to Bechevin for various purposes.

If Iurlov cannot be taken away from the crew, then another navigator or someone of another rank who is experienced in navigation should be assigned. If no reliable volunteers are to be found, then two other sailors should be assigned, either Andrei Zhdanov and Iakov Sharapov or others, as well as the cossack Semen Zropin, who was left in Kamchatka. The Okhotsk office is to assign Mokhnachevskii's son, Ivan Matveev, as interpreter to talk with local heathen natives during stops at lands or islands, provided he is not needed in Okhotsk at the present nor will be in the future, and that Mokhnachevskii himself is willing to go. According to his father's report which was sent here, concerning his own and his son's assignments to sail from Kamchatka aboard a hunting vessel to the foreign islands known as the Aleutians, and to bring under the suzerainty of Her Imperial Majesty the people who live there and to collect iasak from them (which matter was assigned for review in accordance with instructions to the Okhotsk commanding officer, Collegiate Councillor Shipilov), he does not wish to wait for a resolution. All naval personnel assigned to him should be forbidden to carry on any unauthorized activity during the voyage (except that which pertains to their assignments) without Bechevin's authorization and consent. Prikashchiks and overseers are not to interfere in any way with Bechevin's workers in their hunting or in his affairs.

Bechevin is to give all the servitors double pay, and normal rations in accordance with naval regulations, paid for from his own funds, just as has been done for the crews of previous expeditions. Bechevin is to sign a written statement of obligation to this effect. The government servitors and the two quartermasters who were previously assigned to him, as well as those who are presently being assigned, should remain with him until he replaces them with persons to be trained, or until they are no longer needed for the expedition.

Finally, when Bechevin needs assistance in preparing his vessel for the voyage, both in Okhotsk and Kamchatka, he should receive temporary help from government craftsmen, blacksmiths and ropemakers, with appropriate equipment. Bechevin should also have use of a jack which is available there. All of these things should be issued to him at the price they cost when they were made, or their present value. I humbly submit this report to the Governing Senate.

[Signed] Fedor Soimonov
Dmitrii Kalugin
Office clerk Vasilii Lazarev

Reference: TsGADA, f. 259 (I Department Senata), op. 22, d. 485a, 11. 436–441 ob.
See: V. A. Divin, ed. *Russkaia tikhookeanskaia epopeia* (Khabarovsk: 1979), 306–311.

37

THE ACCOUNT OF THE TOTMA MERCHANT, STEPAN CHEREPANOV, CONCERNING HIS STAY IN THE ALEUTIAN ISLANDS, 1759–1762

On August 3, 1762, in the office of the port of Okhotsk, Stepan Iakovlev, son of Cherepanov, a merchant from Totma, submitted the following account.

In the year 1759, because of a shortage of seamen in Kamchatka, I, Cherepanov, was hired there for a voyage with the company organized by the Touisk merchant, Stefan Posnikov, the Tula merchant Semen Krasilnikov, the Vologda merchant Semen Kulkov and the Iarensk merchant Stefan Tiurin. The voyage was to be made aboard a ship called the *Zakharii i Elisaveta*, which they had had built on the Kamchatka River with the permission of the Bolsheretsk office. The ship was six sazhens long and the deck was six-and-a-half arshins wide.

On September 29 of that year we set out on the voyage from the mouth of the lower [Kamchatka] river. The crew consisted of 42 men and one Kamchadal youth who went with his father. I, Cherepanov, held a course of ESE. After some time we reached the Komandorskie Islands and there, because it was late in the season, we stopped and spent the winter. During the winter we hunted sea cows for food. The island is about 100 versts long, but variable in width; in some places it is about 20 versts, in others 15 or less. The island is barren. There are no animals there with the exception of the blue fox, because there is no forest. There is an abundance of grass for hay and there are cloudberries, crowberries and sarana root. The mountains are rocky and have steep cliffs.

There are rivers: one on the northern side is called the Kamennaia, which is about 15 or 20 sazhens wide at its mouth and is shallow. It rises from a lake which is about 15 versts long and 10 versts wide or less. It is about 10 sazhens deep and has fish that come in from the sea, salmon and cod, of a sort that are also found in Okhotsk. These are abundant there. They migrate there from the end of May until Christmas and then they die. There is another river on the southern side which is small and also has migratory fish, but not as many as the Kamennaia River.

In regard to marine animals, there are many sea cows, sea lions and whales, but very few sea otters. Only the sea cow is hunted for food. The hunt takes place when the sea is calm and there is no wind. Ten men paddle out to sea in a hide baidara. One or two men are at the rudder. When they sight a sea cow floating in some place at sea, which they sometimes do when they are eating or sleeping or nursing a calf, the men quietly paddle out and come within two sazhens of it or even closer; then they harpoon it in the chest between its front flippers. The instant the harpoon strikes, all the men in the baidara paddle away from the cow as fast as they can so they will not be drowned, for when the harpoon strikes the cow beats its flippers as many as ten times, and if the men are too close and do not paddle away fast enough, they are in danger of being caught in the tumult.

After this, the sea cow moves off not far from shore, going slowly. At that point the men in the baidara turn to pursue it. When they again approach it they harpoon it with iron barbs which are about six *vershoks* [1 vershok=1.75 inches] long, fastened to a pole. There is a rope fastened to the middle of the hook; the rope is two or three inches thick and fifteen sazhens in length or less. When the harpoon strikes the hook remains in the cow's body and the men hold on to the rope and pursue the cow until it becomes exhausted. Then the men haul it into shore. When the tide goes out they butcher the cow for food.

A sea cow is four sazhens long or more and is two-and-a-half or three arshins in girth. There are two flippers on the front of the chest; the flippers are an arshin long or less and about an arshin in circumference. Instead of a hoof, such as a camel has, the cow has a soft flipper like a whale. Under the front flippers there are two teats like mammals have, but they are not white. They are about the size of a hen's egg. One cow yields about 150 puds of meat plus about 60 puds of blubber. There are two kidneys, each weighing about seven puds. Both the kidneys and the intestines of the cow are similar to those of land cattle. The meat and the blubber are very tasty and nutritious and the kidneys are particularly delicious.

After we had dried the meat of a cow and rendered the fat, we sailed on June 2 and proceeded on a course ESE. We reached one of the Aleutian islands on June 26, where we stopped and hunted sea otters. That island is called Ottaku and is approximately 100

This Choris drawing of an Aleut couple affords a fine view of the hunting visor with its special decorations of beads, bones, and walrus or sea lion whiskers. The man's waterproof gut parka and hood are designed for eight to twelve hours of paddling in his baidarka. The dressing of the woman's hair indicates high rank. Choris, *Voyage Pittoresque.* . . . (OHS neg. 80253)

versts long and 20 wide. There are no forests there. During the winter we used driftwood from the sea, such as old oak, which very rarely comes up, and beech and cedar, but the pieces were neither long nor large. This wood is so broken up in the sea between the sharp rock promontories that it can only be used for firewood. Fir and larch are also carried up by the waves, but in lesser amount. There is plenty of grass. There are steep rocky mountains on which the snow remains all summer. The blue fox is the most prevalent of the winter animals.

On that island live natives called Aleuts. There are two other islands nearby; the distance to the first is about 40 versts and to the next, another 20 versts. Both are small; the first is some 20 or more versts long, and the other about 50 or less. Both islands are narrow. There are no trees on them. The mountains are rocky but not high.

There are about 40 male Aleuts on these islands and more females. [The males] have one, two or sometimes three wives, and *toions* [chieftains] have four. They live in earthen iurts, the same as Kamchadals do. They enter them from above, and from one to three live in each one. A toion will use the wives and children of his dead relatives as slaves, and is called their father. When they return from hunting with a good catch, or even without, but when they wish to celebrate, they assemble in one large iurt and then make merry, beat drums and sing. The wives and daughters dance around in a circle in the iurt. The dancing goes on from evening until midnight, or as long as they wish or are able to continue. When it is over they go back to their own iurts.

In their dwellings they have small wooden bowls from which they drink water. They use small bags woven of grass to store meat. They do not have any other tableware. They eat the meat of marine animals such as sea lions, walrus and sea otters, when they can procure them. They also eat salmon and a whale which is similar to those found in Kamchatka but is not very abundant. They also eat halibut and *terpuk* [rock cod]. They usually eat this raw, but sometimes they cook it over a wood fire. They have become accustomed to eating raw food and it is natural for them. Necessity has forced them to resort to this because there are no trees on the island and thus nothing to burn. They use driftwood for fire in the same way the Kamchadals do.

They have no weapons but knives, which are a chetvert long and two fingers wide. One end is embedded in a four-sided wooden handle; they are very thin. They make these knives from nails which they find, cast up on the island from wrecked ships. When they find such a nail or some other small bit of iron, they put it on a rock and pound it with another rock, pour water on it and make it very thin, but they do not forge it in fire.

They fish for terpuk and halibut in the sea, about two versts out from shore. They spear terpuk with a bone harpoon about a vershok long. Both ends are sharpened, and in the middle they tie bait of sea lion or bird meat. They fish for halibut with bone hooks which are similar in appearance to the iron hooks used by

Russians. They use meat as bait. They use sharp points to spear salmon which migrate from the sea into the rivers. They use no other methods of fishing.

They hunt sea otters out at sea using slender arrows about an arshin-and-a-half long. At the end is fastened a sharp bone arrowhead a chetvert long, ridged on both sides. These they hurl from throwing boards. Once a sea otter has been hit, they pursue the animal in small hide baidarkas with one, two or three men in each, following the animal wherever it goes until it is exhausted.

We could not tell whether the natives had any faith or religion, nor did we see any shamans. They have leaders similar to the Kamchadal toions, whom they obey. I did not observe whether they punish persons involved in disputes; we were only told that when a toion becomes angry because of some misdeed on the part of his relatives they do not speak to each other for some time, but apparently there is no punishment. With this exception these people are very kind to each other.

They live in iurts in winter but in summer they have no dwellings. At that time they roam over the entire island hunting. When a person catches something edible, he stays in that place. If he cannot catch anything, he eats shellfish carried up from the sea.

Their clothing consists of parkas made from sea lion intestines and from the skins of a bird called the *uril* [cormorant]. They make their footwear from the throat of the sea lion, using the flippers to make soles. When it is bitterly cold in winter they wear blankets woven of grass over the birdskin garment.

The people very much like the foods the Russians eat, and they are also very fond of Russian clothing, of which our group gave them a few pieces as gifts. We did not have enough food to give them any [large amount], but when we ate we would always share the food with these Aleuts. We always did this, and as a result, we established a special friendship with them.

We did not learn anything about their religion because there was no opportunity to observe it. They live simply and everything they make is basic. Just as when we Russians go anywhere on business we always invoke the name of God to assist us, or when we set out sailing or go out in baidaras to hunt, we offer a silent prayer and ask God's help, and trusting in His mercy we say "God help us," so these natives speak the prayer, "God bless us," when they go out hunting. When they go out in their baidaras they all fall silent and then say the same thing we do, "God help us."

They are quite familiar with the Orthodox Christian faith and they do not think that we are wrong, because on one special occasion God's blessing was clearly demonstrated. In 1761 a native named Leontii (about whom I shall have more to say later) was confined to his dwelling with a severe injury to his arm. The wound was so terrible you could see the bone. Everyone thought he would never recover. He could not even stand up unless he was helped. Leontii's father, Makuzhan, came to us on the ship and said that his son wanted to be baptized, and that perhaps he would be better then. We replied that we had hope, because our God is great and merciful and readily gives His blessing to anyone who will accept His faith. In response Makuzhan said, "If your God is good, then my son will be healed."

Accordingly, in the year 1761 he received the sacrament of Holy Baptism at that island aboard the ship belonging to the Lalsk merchant Vasilii Popov. As soon as he had been baptized, he immediately improved and later made a complete recovery. Leontii's father, Makuzhan, rejoiced and said to us, "Your God is very good; indeed, He is great."

I do not know whether there are other islands whose people come to these people to trade; no one told me anything about this and I did not overhear anything.

There is no forest on the second island. There are berries such as the cloudberry, service berry and black crowberry, but not in abundance. The only animal is the blue fox. Of birds, there are geese and ducks, but not in abundance. The Aleuts trap two birds, one which the Kamchadals call the *toporka* [*Alca arctica*], which has two long white feathers on its head; the other is the *ipatka* [pochard, similar to redhead duck] which lives in the rocks but is not plentiful. The Aleuts trap these using nooses which they make from whale baleen and put in crevices on rocky cliffs where the birds go at night to sleep or to nest. When they emerge they are trapped in these nooses. The Aleuts as well as I, Cherepanov, and the men, use these birds for food and find them delicious. These two birds which are trapped are not of the same species, but are different. They nest in these rocky crevices and lay two eggs, never more. Some spend the winter in the crevices; others fly away.

On the first large island, the one called Attaku, blue foxes have increased. In the year 1750 a Selenginsk merchant, Andreian Tolstykh, took a family of foxes aboard his ship from the Komandorskie Islands and turned them loose on the Aleutian island of Attaku. In a few years they had increased to a thousand, and promyshlenniks now hunt them. Prior to that transplanting there had been no foxes on that island.

The promyshlenniks also hunt sea otters in the spring from mid-March until November. They hunt them in bays where the animals can be found between headlands. They put string nets into the water to trap them. It takes about 20 pounds of fine string to make such a net. They also use guns to shoot them. When they spot the animals lying on rocks or swimming in the water, they creep up next to them in baidaras. There are not many sea otters around these three Aleutian islands. They do not always hunt with nets; it depends on the time of year. If the weather is quiet and there is no wind, they do not set out nets, because the sea otters go out into the sea in calm weather. But when there is a moderate wind and waves, the natives put out into the sea in the evening, using baidaras made of hide, and they set their nets, because in windy weather the sea otters come into land, and thus they are caught.

The promyshlenniks themselves live on provisions they make from fish in the summer and from dog cabbage roots. They also eat the meat of the sea lions they shoot, for there are a few of them there. They also use the meat from sea otters. At the present time the group has made a seine, which they use along the islands to catch cod for food.

If possible, one should bring provisions from Kamchatka. It is impossible to find any locally and there is nowhere to buy any. Consequently the men have to sail without adequate provisions aboard.

The baidaras are made of hide, not wood. The hide baidaras are very light, strong and maneuverable. When they have to go in among the headlands approaching shore, it is easy to go ashore and carry these light craft in their arms. Wooden craft are difficult to handle. They draw more water and are unwieldly and therefore are not used there.

In regard to all of the above, Cherepanov spoke the whole truth in a sworn statement, acknowledging that he would be in trouble if an investigation revealed he had lied.

The Totma merchant Stepan Cherepanov has signed this account, and Fedor Kulkov, a merchant from Vologda who was aboard the ship, has also attested to this account.

Reference: TsGADA, portfeli Millera, No. 534, ch. 1, ll. 21–27 ob.
See: A. I. Andreev, ed. *Russkie otkrytiia v Tikhom okeane i v Severnoi Amerike v XVIII veke* (Moscow: 1948), 113–120.

38

A REPORT BY THE COSSACK SAVIN T. PONOMAREV AND THE PRO-
MYSHLENNIK STEPAN G. GLOTOV, CONCERNING THEIR DISCOVERY OF
NEW ISLANDS IN THE ALEUTIAN CHAIN

On August 27, 1758, I, cossack Ponomarev, received orders from the office at the Nizhnekamchatsk ostrog, based on an ukaz from Her Imperial Majesty dated February 8, 1757, which has been sent to the ostrog from the Bolsheretsk office.

My orders were to proceed on the vessel *Iulian*, which belonged to the late Moscow merchant Nikiforov, to unknown islands in the [North Pacific] ocean to bring the non-iasak-paying natives there under the suzerainty of Russia and to have them pay iasak. While on those islands with Nikiforov's crew, if we found such non-iasak-paying natives, we were to use kindness and cordiality if possible to encourage them to come under the suzerainty of Her Imperial Majesty's autocratic might, and to pay iasak. We were to collect the iasak from them and record it in an official book under seal, which I had received from the Treasury Office in Bolsheretsk.

In accordance with this order, the vessel was outfitted, and on September 2, 1758, we sailed from the mouth of the Kamchatka River into the open sea on a voyage along the designated route to discover new islands and peoples. The *peredovshchik* [foreman] Glotov and I were in command of the vessel.

On our initial voyage we set sail in the fall, and in nine days we reached one of the Komandorskie islands named Mednyi Island. This is a small island where with God's mercy we anchored and spent the winter. We procured food for ourselves and prepared supplies for our future voyage to search for distant unknown islands. Then we hunted and took 83 sea otters, including prime, young and immature, and 1,263 blue fox, all of which have been made up into cloaks and blankets, a list of which we are submitting with this report.

Between the time we sailed out of the mouth of the Kamchatka River and the time the vessel was beached on Mednyi Island, we lost two anchors because of autumn storms at sea. Consequently, the other crew members and I decided together that in order to save the vessel and the men and not to die before we had carried out our planned search for islands in the sea, we would take about fifteen puds of iron from the timbers of a packetboat which had been shipwrecked on the Komandorskie Island. The vessel had been part of the earlier Kamchatka Expedition. With no small effort we forged two anchors which our vessel still has at the present time. Each has lost a fluke because of storms at sea. We spent the winter on Copper Island and hunted sea cows for food, as well as walrus and sea lions, and prepared dried meat. On August 1, 1759, we again set out on our voyage to search [for islands] and to follow our set route.

After August 1 we sailed northeast toward the Aleutian chain, but did not sight land. Due to favorable weather we continued sailing until September 1, when, thanks to God's blessing and Her Imperial Majesty's good fortune, we successfully reached an island in the northeast part. We found an anchorage for the ship and so dropped anchor in soft sand south of the rocks of the island. We beached the vessel on shore with no damage. The name of the island in native language is Unimak. The natives favor it as the primary, main island over another one located nearby. This first island has about 400 inhabitants and two chieftains who, like the Kamchadals, are called toions. The first, Shashuk, has three children and the second, Akitakul, has five.

Not far from that island, about fifteen versts away, there is a second island larger than the first which is called Unalaska. There are about 300 native inhabitants on that island. It was impossible to make an accurate count because of the size of the island and also because these people move about from one island to another very often. These inhabitants said that beyond these two islands there are eight more still farther east, one of which is forested. They could not tell us what kind of trees it has, however, because they do not speak Russian.

There are also animals in abundance on all of these islands: sea otters, black-brown and brown fox, cross fox and red fox. On the forested island there are also reindeer, bears, wolves and ermine. All of these eight islands are inhabited by unknown people who are governed by their own leaders who, as they themselves say, attack the people from the two islands. They wage internecine battles and take prisoners, of whom there are several, even at the present time. Because of the distance we did not go there either by ship or by baidarka.

When we came to the first island, the natives met us with arrows which they hurl from throwing boards as the Aleuts do. The arrows have sharp points of bone or stone. They tried to kill us all, but only managed to wound me, Ponomarev, in the right shoulder, Glotov in his chest and left shoulder, and the Kamchadal Ignatii Uvarovskii in the right upper leg. They killed a Kamchadal from the upper ostrog, Stepan Uvarovskii, but God saved the rest. They took our baidara which had food, clothing and other things, including two axes.

We saved ourselves by putting up shields made of our clothes and various other items and boards. After this the natives ran off. But then, seeing that we were not vengeful because of their attack and had only kindness for them, they came to our vessel a second time, and this time without discord and without attacking. They met us in the customary manner. With them, they brought for our sustenance meat and dried cod. In return we gave them whatever small gifts we could, such as needles, a leather punch and the like. During this encounter they were friendly toward us and we were kind and courteous to them. They gave back our baidara which they had taken, and everything was still in it.

Because of our kindness and courtesy during this amicable encounter, we and all our crew were able to bring the people on those two islands under the mighty hand of Her Imperial Majesty so they would pay iasak. Although we did not know their language, we found from persons who had been there that their language is closely related to that of the Aleuts, except for those farthest away, and so we could converse with a translation into Russian.

The natives on the first large island, Unimak, who agreed to pay iasak, were under two toions. The first was Shashuk, whose son is Ugagolak; the second was Akitakul, whose son is Alikhshukhukh. They command eleven others, for a total of fifteen. On the second island, Unalaska, the toions are Aluzikh, whose sons are Aluzkhuchag and Chikilazhak; Sedan and Umakush. One toion lives on the second island in a bay called Kalchinsk. There are 28 men on both islands, including the toions. Their names have been entered into the official record book. Because of their willingness to submit, iasak was collected from these people

Aleut halibut fishermen show off bone hook and line technique and the clubbing style which survived the centuries.
Elliott, *An Arctic Province*. (OHS neg. 80248)

for the Treasury of Her Imperial Majesty for the years 1761 and
1762. Information on the kinds of furs collected is being submitted with this report. I am also reporting the same information
in the above-mentioned official record book which was given to us
from the Bolsheretsk office.

It has not been possible to measure the dimensions of these
islands, or everything about them, because time is so short.

Animals are found on both islands: sea otters, black-brown
foxes, brown foxes, blue, cross and red foxes of various qualities.
There are also lakes on these islands, from which flow small
streams that empty into the sea and have the same kinds of sea
fish one catches in Kamchatka, such as salmon and white loach,
and in the sea, halibut and cod. The local natives catch these fish
with fish hooks made of the ribs of sea otters and from the jaw-
bone of the sea lion. They live on this fish which they catch both
in the sea and in streams, using nets made of thin cord, 20 sazhens
long or more. When they catch the fish they cut it up with knives
which they make from iron. The iron is procured from the islands
previously mentioned which have forests. They obtain it when
they attack other natives, and also when they exchange furs and

clothing. They hang the cut fish up to dry on poles so they can eat it during the winter, just as the Kamchadals do. This dried fish, together with marine animals they take such as sea otters, sea lions, seals and fur seals, provides them with their supply of meat.

Throughout the extent of these islands there is no forest. The inhabitants use only driftwood brought in by the sea to build their dwellings, which are earthen iurts about 40 sazhens or more long. They also use this wood to heat, and they make fire by using a white rock which is found near the sea. They break a small rock in two pieces and strike one piece against the other. Instead of tinder they use dried grass and leaves as well as feathers and combustible brimstone. But since we did not know their language we were unable to find out where they procure sulphur. These people are not accustomed to cleanliness and they do not observe sanitation.

Both of these islands have birds such as the cormorant, puffin, diver, duck, pratincole, river duck, woodcock, merganser, teal and white goose which spend the winter there and then fly away in spring and do not return until the following winter. There are also migratory grey and black geese and an abundance of seagulls all year long. There are also eagles. Sometimes they catch these birds with nooses or arrows, but more often they use nets. They skin the birds, leaving the feathers on the skin, and make their parkas from these skins. They also make garments from sea otter pelts.

In 1761 I, cossack Ponomarev, went from the first to the second island with the promyshlennik from the crew, Ivan Solovev of Tobolsk, and with other workers whom Solovev had brought. While Solovev was hunting on the second island the local natives gave him a sparkling silvery substance which weighted 48 zolotniks. These people use this substance to paint their faces. Solovev does not know where the substance comes from, whether from the sea or the land.

Because of my brief stay on that first island, I, Ponomarev, did not have time to make observations. Moreover, I was quite ill from the wound in my shoulder which had been inflicted by these natives, which did not heal for a long time. However, I did send the Bolsheretsk office some of the pigment so they could examine it.

Inhabitants of the island of Unalaska. The woman wears walrus "teeth," labrets, an elaborately decorated parka and no
shoes. Women went about on land unshod. The man wears his
hunting visor and carries his waterproof parka. Sarychev, *Voyage of Discovery*. (OHS neg. 80265)

From 1759 to the present year, 1762, on both of those islands
we hunted sea otter, fur seal and black-brown, brown and cross
fox. I have appended to this report information on the number of
animals killed, the variety, quality, and the year in which they
were taken. Since I did not know the official procedures, I did not
make any entries in the official record books I had received from
the Bolsheretsk office, and I was also hampered by my wound.
But I did not hide any information about these animals and I
made a sworn statement at the Bolsheretsk office.

When we left these islands, because of the willingness of these
people to become subjects [of Russia], and because of our kindness and cordiality to them, some natives who want to become
subjects in the future expressed the desire that Russians always
come to them by ship, and said they will always pay iasak. They
voluntarily gave us a hostage from the first island, a relative of the
toion Shashuk. He is a young boy named Mushkal, whom we call

Ivan. He is about twelve or thirteen years old. We looked after him on our voyage as much as possible, and are now reporting this to the Bolsheretsk office. He has brought with him a parka sewed of birdskins in their manner, and a hat.

With God's help we set out on May 26, 1762, on our return voyage to the mouth of the Kamchatka River. En route we experienced desperate shortages of water and food. We finally had to take the boots from our feet and boil them for food. Although we encountered many problems, we exerted ourselves and reached the mouth of the Kamchatka on August 31. We managed to beach our vessel successfully, although there was some damage and the sand covered half the deck. This caused considerable damage to the furs which we had on board, which now have to be dried out.

One of the workers who was on the islands has died. His name was Petr Stroganov, a peasant from Sol Vychegodskaia. Ivan Svitsov, a Kamchadal from Bolsheretsk ostrog, died at sea. I am hereby submitting for your review the list of Russian workers and Kamchadals who returned on the ship, the wages due them and the contract for the entire company undertaking.

To this report and the above information the cossack Savin Ponomarev has put his hand, as has the peredovshchik from Iarensk, Stepan Glotov.

NAMES OF THE COMPANY OWNERS
1. Tobolsk merchant Ilia Snigirev
2. Vologda merchant Ivan Burenin
3. Iarensk merchant Ivan Tomilov
4. Tula merchant Semen Krasilnikov
5. Lalsk merchant Afonasii Chebaevskoi
6. Vologda merchant Vasilii Kulkov
7. Moscow merchant Egor Sabinin
8. Totma merchants Grigorii and Petr Panovykh and prikashchik Semen Shergin

Upon its return from its voyage, the *Sv. Iulian*, belonging to the above company owners, reported [the following furs]

Sea otters, prime, males and females and yearlings	1,389
Young sea otters, males, females and cubs	280
Cross fox of various qualities	1,100
Red fox	400

Pieces of cross fox	26
Blue fox sewed into garments and blankets:	
Blankets for Russian workers	21
Parkas and furs	8
Worn sea otter parka	1
Sea otter pieced [blankets?]	5
Fur seal blanket	1
Kamchadal blankets	8
Parka and furs	8
Walrus ivory	22 puds 10 pounds

1/10 of the above, at local prices, was valued at 3,344 rubles 23 kopecks.

THE NAMES OF THE ISLANDS
AND THE PEOPLE AND ANIMALS ON THEM,
ACCORDING TO INFORMATION FROM
THE INHABITANTS OF THE ISLANDS OF UNALASKA AND UMNAK

1. Umnak	On which one can hunt black and black-brown fox; unforested; the
2. Unalaska	people live in large encampments, and have bone bows and arrows.

The Far Islands

3. Unalga	There are foxes.
4. Akutanak	Sea lions.
5. Akunak	Sea otters.
6. Akugist	Foxes.
7. Kygalgist	Foxes.
8. Unimak	Foxes.
9. Alakhshak	Many people, large standing forest, foxes, bears, reindeer, indications of marten, wild boar; where the ship belonging to the merchant Bechevin wintered.
10. Directly beyond Kuchuk	Sea lions, some sea otter.
11. Tanilak	Sea lions, sea otter.
12. Kodiak, to the south	Foxes, sea lions, standing forest, the south trees of a girth to encompass five [men?].
13. Shugach Tany	Animals are bears, reindeer; there is forest;

	the people have huts and bows, glass and inkpots.
14. Uligis	Many sea otters; many people from Island Shugach Tany come here.
15. Atakhtak	There are people on this island, but who they are is not known.
16. Chikhmil	Not large, an abandoned foreign island ship was found there, evidently two-masted, but nothing is known of the people.

THE NAMES OF THE ISLANDS TO THE RIGHT OF UNALASKA,
INFORMATION ABOUT THE POPULATION AND ANIMALS,
ACCORDING TO PERSONS WHO RETURNED
FROM VOYAGES THERE AND SAW THEM.

1. Amukhta	Sea otters, sea lions, seals.
2. Chugindana	Sea lions, sea otters and seals.
3. Iunaskha	Sea otters, seals.
4. Chigula	Sea otters, seals.
5. Uliaga	Sea otters, sea lions.
6. Tanaaguna	Sea otters and sea lions.
7. Khagamilia	Sea otters and seals.
8. Chugidana	Sea otters, seals.
9. Samalga	Sea otters, seals.
10. Atkha	Sea otters, sea lions and seals.
11. Uiukana	Sea otters, sea lions and seals.
12. Nakunalashka	Sea otters, sea lions.
13. Unialga	Sea otters, sea lions.

The people on each island have dwellings, and all are populous.

[Signed] Denis Chicherin

Reference: *Arkhiv admirala P. B. Chichagova*, vyp. 1 (St. Petersburg: 1885), 127–134.

See: V. A. Divin, ed. *Russkaia tikhookeanskaia epopeia* (Khabarovsk: 1978), 314–320.

39

A DECREE FROM THE GOVERNING SENATE CANCELLING THE IASAK
OBLIGATION OF CHILDREN OF NEWLY BAPTIZED KAMCHADALS, ORDER-
ING THAT THOSE CHILDREN ATTEND SCHOOLS AND THEN BE ASSIGNED
TO SERVICE, AND PROVIDING PAY FOR THEM FROM KAMCHATKA
REVENUES

January 13, 1764. Upon the advice of the Holy Governing Synod, the Governing Senate has passed the following decree.

In the year 1742 an expedition was organized to spread the word of God in Kamchatka and to persuade the heathen peoples there to accept the Christian faith. The members of the expedition were an arkhimandrit, who is now Ioasaf, Bishop of Irkutsk; two ieromonks, one ierodiakon and students from the Moscow [Theological] Academy who were sent there to teach the Russian language to young boys from various tribes, in three schools which were established.

In these schools the children of newly baptized Kamchadals were well trained in reading and writing Russian, and some of them showed ability in drafting and were commended by members of the expedition. For that reason the suggestion has been made that in order to provide an example for other boys there who show promise, those who are presently students and those who will become students in the future, all of whom are children of newly baptized Kamchadals, should be freed from the regular iasak obligation. Those who have learned will teach others, as is the case in the garrison schools, and will earn some pay.

When they have completed their schooling they may be assigned to a clerical rank if they wish, and in accordance with local customs (as Ioasaf, Bishop of Irkutsk, and the ieromonk Pakhomii suggest), they may be assigned to cossack or other civilian service without delay. Through such means there is hope that in that country Orthodox Christianity can be firmly rooted, and the civil service will benefit and in the future the expenses for their education will not be in vain.

Upon review, the Governing Senate has passed the following decree:

To improve the condition of children of newly baptized Kamchadals who are presently studying in schools, and to provide incentive for other children of newly baptized Kamchadals who will enter schools in the future and become good students, those who are assigned into local cossack service or who are capable of becoming priests are to be excluded from regular iasak obligation. They are to receive recompense similar to that provided in garrison schools, in accordance with the Army regulations for 1731, consisting of money, food, clothing and boots to be issued out of local Kamchatka revenues, on the account of the College of Economy. However, those who complete their schooling but choose to live in their previous ways, with their parents, and are not to be assigned into any service, will not be excused from payment of iasak.

Reference: Russia. *Polnoe sobranie zakonov rossiiskoi imperii s 1649 goda.* First series. (St. Petersburg: 1830), 493–494.

40

NOT AFTER MAY 14, 1764

A REPORT DICTATED IN ST. PETERSBURG BY FEDOR AFANSEVICH
KULKOV CONCERNING HIS 1762 VOYAGE TO THE ALEUTIAN ISLANDS

Kulkov observed as much as he could concerning the location of these islands which [Russian promyshlenniks] usually call the Komandorskie, when he voyaged from Bering Island toward the coast of America. As one proceeds directly on one's voyage, the islands are on the right and the distance from [Bering] Island is three or four times greater than the distance from Bering Island to Kamchatka. In good weather with a strong wind, some promyshlenniks have managed to reach those islands from Bering Island in seven, eight or nine days; but in bad weather and with a head wind, many have had to spend five, six or even seven weeks at sea. Kulkov spent nearly four weeks on his voyage.

The islands which are now known as the Aleutians are three in number and are located not far from one another. In calm weather one can paddle in the local hide baidaras and easily travel from one to another in one summer day. The natives who roam about these islands often do this. At present most of the natives, like our promyshlenniks, are more likely to stay on the same island on which Kulkov and his men lived for two years. According to his statement, the best and safest time to travel to and return from these islands is the four-month period of June, July, August and most of September. The inhabitants of the island [where Kulkov stayed] number about 100, including both males and females. Many of these at the present time have been brought to pay iasak, and one of them has even been converted to our Greek Orthodox Russian faith. Kulkov took that man to Okhotsk, had him baptized and then sent him back to his homeland. I personally saw this in the instructions which he received from the Okhotsk office.

This island consists primarily of rocky mountain ridges. According to Kulkov it is about 90 versts long and some 19 wide. The base of the range, especially close to the coast, around most of its circumference, is covered with soil that has washed down and is quite rich. It is about ¼ arshin deep, and in some places is nearly ½ arshin deep. It is about 1½ versts from the shore to the

225

base of the mountains. A great many kinds of beautifully colored grasses grow on the mountains. Some of these have large roots like our carrots and parsley, which give a very delicious flavor to any food they are cooked with, and the roots themselves are tasty and tender. Other roots, although they look identical, can only be used for food in their raw state, because when they are cooked they lose their flavor and become too woody and tough to be used.

The mountains, especially the upper parts, consist almost entirely of rock, and throughout the entire island no trees of any kind have been observed growing on this rock, nor any grass except for a little moss. Even at the base of the mountains where there is soil, there are no trees except for small scrubby mountain ash. These are so thin and supple, and the berries which are borne in summer are so abundant and large and heavy, that in the strong winds and storms in winter the trees bend over to the ground and in fact almost lie along the ground. For this reason our promyshlenniks call this *slanets* [ground cedar or stone pine]. The berries are much larger and juicier and more flavorful than ours.

Although there are no trees suitable for construction or for fuel for cooking, as is true here [in Russia's Asian possessions] nevertheless our people almost never had a lack of wood because there is plenty of driftwood. Sometimes a storm brought in whole logs. This may be evidence that there are forests not too far distant from that place. Among the various pieces of driftwood they found on shore one large piece was apparently from the stern of some foreign vessel that had been shipwrecked. Large letters had been carved and gilded, but the men could not determine what language they were. They brought the piece they found to the Okhotsk office where hopefully it has been preserved.

There is no shortage of fresh water there because there are many streams which flow from the mountains. As for salt, our people evaporate as much as they need from seawater. Until the Russians came, the natives had been completely unaware of the process of evaporating salt.

They saw no land animals on that island except for polar foxes. These had been introduced by chance, when one pair was left there by our promyshlenniks some time previously. Some persons may not believe the following information about this animal, but I have been told that it is absolutely true. One pair of these polar foxes in a few years has produced so many offspring that now not only the local people but even our promyshlenniks often suffer extreme discomfort from their attacks. Sometimes they cannot even protect their belongings from them, because they will carry off and devour anything they find except for rock, iron and wood. They certainly damage things, especially baidaras which are made of sea lion hides, and often a baidara constitutes the only wealth of a poor native. The foxes frequently devour the clothing of people who are sleeping, since the animals are in an almost barren land and starve, especially in winter. At night when people are asleep they will creep up silently and bite a hand or foot, sometimes even a nose. In this way they often disfigure the body of a human. This is an account of how polar foxes were introduced on this island. According to the natives, there were no animals there at all previously.

There are only two kinds of marine animals which are abundant: sea otters and sea lions. Our promyshlenniks hunt the former with firearms, nets and special harpoons. The latter are hunted with various weapons, but usually with firearms. Whales appear seldom, sea cows even more rarely. The promyshlenniks call these "Komandorskii cows" because for the most part they are found near Bering or [one of the] Komandorskie Islands. On that island there are many varieties of birds, especially sea birds. Fish are enormously abundant. All kinds, such as cod and the like, are especially plentiful when the weather is calm and they are found in the creeks and streams.

In reference to ores and minerals, I could not obtain any reliable information from Kulkov, for he is a man who knows nothing of such matters. He did tell me that in many places in the sand and driftwood he saw bright white and yellow particles about the size of the head of a mace, and some twice that size. These were hard little balls which they tried to smelt, but in spite of their expectations, nothing useful developed. It all burned up and turned into ash. However there is much pure sulphur, in some places whole mounds of it, on the mountains. The local people obtain it in rock-size pieces and use it to make fire. They knew how to do this before the Russians arrived.

This is how they make fire with the sulphur pieces. They spread pieces of dry sedge or seaweed on the ground, sprinkle powdered sulphur over it, then take two stones or flints in their hands and strike one against the other until sparks fly onto the

227

sulphur, which then ignites and sets the sedge or seaweed afire.

Our people found the air on this island clear and healthy. Few of those who went with Kulkov became ill. Everyone aboard his ship, with the exception of one person who drowned, was remarkably healthy. Furthermore, during the two years they stayed there, they all lived exclusively on fish, sea otter and sea lion meat. They only ate bread five or six times.

Summer is quite warm and lasts almost nine months. Winter begins early in March or at the end of February and lasts only three months: March, April and May. Sometimes, according to statements made by some of the promyshlenniks, it continues on into June. Nevertheless, even then the cold is quite bearable, so that the local people endure it without great distress. They go barefoot, and instead of heavy clothing, they wear only simple thin apparel made like a shirt with a hood, sewed from sea lion intestines or fish bladders.

The snow is sometimes 1/4 arshin deep but it does not stay long, and our people did not encounter any severe frost. On the basis of this, it is possible to visualize in what climate or latitude these islands must be located.

Sometimes there are severe earthquakes, so that in some places mountain ranges not only separate but totally collapse. In winter there are frequent storms, blizzards and terrible floods. At such times the winds are so strong that even a large man cannot stand on his feet. On one occasion Kulkov had such an experience: a sudden wind grabbed him up, whirled him about and dragged him along on his back for a good half-verst.

In regard to the population and the customs of the local inhabitants, their number on that island is rather insignificant, in his opinion. As noted above, the total number of men and women is just over 100. For the most part they are of medium stature. Very few are tall, but they are broad-shouldered and powerful. The men's faces are dark and their noses are flat. They do not have beards. They always cut their hair around their heads, using stones and even more amazingly, bone knives. Women paint their faces red, but they are clean and comely. They tie their black hair in braids. To enhance their appearance in accordance with local customs, among other things, they insert two large teeth made of fish or sea lion bones into special slits cut in their lips while they are still young.

The men's dispositions are peaceful, simple and guileless. When they carry out any task they are very reliable and attentive to detail. In contrast, the women are perceived to be very merry, frivolous and quite inclined to infinitely improprietous behavior with the men. Men and women wear almost identical garments in both winter and summer, as I have reported to the present Imperial Kunstkamer [museum, St. Petersburg]. In their language they call their garment a *kamlei* [hooded, waterproof garment]. They wear no footcovering, but go barefoot both winter and summer. They have no luxuries and they do not subscribe to cleanliness; for that reason they reek and have lice.

Even now they eat almost only raw food. Prior to the time our people went there they never thought of cooking food. For the most part they live on fish, sea otters and sea lions, and from time to time they eat whale if the sea carries a dead one up on shore. (Our promyshlenniks eat the same food, but they usually cook it.) In summer they also eat roots, as noted above. When they have enough food, they eat heartily and are usually quite fat.

In contrast, in winter there is not enough food and they become very thin and sometimes suffer great famine, especially if the winter is stormy and the snow lingers for a long time. At such a time almost all of them lie hopelessly in the mountains. They are not familiar with iurts or huts, so they seek shelter in burrows and clefts in the mountains and use reeds or sedge for bedding.

They wrap newborn infants in blankets woven of this sedge instead of using swaddling clothes. Those who are more industrious wrap their infants in sea lion intestines or fish bladders.

In spite of such a barren and difficult life they are nearly always healthy, and furthermore, as our people have noted, they live a long time. In their own language they call themselves Aleut. They have no conception of the eternal and mighty creator of the world; however, nothing has been observed of idol worship other than shamanism. Our people did not observe any special ceremonies among women in their relations with the men. Whenever a couple shows signs of being attracted to one another and love appears, they begin to live together as man and wife. It often happens that a sister lives with her blood brother as her husband. Girls are married very young, at the age of thirteen or fourteen, at most fifteen. These people speak a language which has never previously been heard within the confines of the Russian Empire.

The Kamchadals may be their close neighbors, but they do not understand much of their language. Those of the Aleuts who accompany our promyshlenniks frequently and serve them are already able to express their thoughts in our language.

This is everything I can remember from Kulkov's firsthand accounts about one of the Aleutian islands. However, he also told me the following story which he had heard.

Certain promyshlenniks sailed on that sea a distance four or five times farther than these Aleutian Islands are located from the Komandorskie Islands, and as a result they discovered many islands both large and small; however, they could not go ashore on any of them because they saw a great many people on all of the islands. They themselves were few in number and had no weapons except for spears and handguns. He said that if promyshlenniks were allowed to have cannon on their vessels they would dare not only to survey these islands, but they would proceed on to the mainland of America. It is possible that certain promyshlenniks, especially those who previously searched for the Aleutian Islands and wandered for a long time at sea and went great distances, might know the routes.

Reference: AVPR, f. 339, op. 888, d. 17, 11. 245–251.
See: R. G. Liapunova. "Novyi dokument o rannikh plavaniiakh na Aleutskie Ostrova ('Izvestiia' Fedora Afanasevich Kulkova 1764g.)" in *Strany i narody vostoka*, vyp. XX: *Strany i narody basseina Tikhogo Okeana*, kn. 4 (Moscow: 1979), 97–105.

41

A SECRET PERSONAL UKAZ FROM EMPRESS CATHERINE II TO THE ADMIRALTY COLLEGE CONCERNING ORGANIZATION OF AN EXPEDITION TO SEARCH FOR A SEA ROUTE TO KAMCHATKA BY WAY OF THE ARCTIC OCEAN

For the benefit of navigation and trade in the East by Our loyal subjects, We have resolved that it would be useful to search for a sea route by way of the Arctic Ocean to Kamchatka and beyond. For that purpose We graciously decree that this project be undertaken without delay in this year, under the guise of resuming the hunt for whales, fish and other marine animals, in the following manner, starting from Spitzbergen.

1. This voyage is to commence from the town of Arkhangelsk and proceed to the west coast of the large island of Spitzbergen. From there [the expedition members] are to proceed into the open sea to the west, bearing north to the nearest coast of Greenland. From there they are to proceed along this coast to the right, to the Northwest cape of North America, insofar as time and other circumstances permit.

2. For this voyage an experienced and reliable officer is to be assigned as commander-in-chief. He is to be accompanied by two other experienced and knowledgeable men. They will proceed on three small seagoing vessels capable of this voyage. These vessels are to be requisitioned, if available, from the Admiralty College, or purchased, or hired from local promyshlenniks.

3. These officers are to be given the required number of non-commissioned officers skilled in navigation, seamen and experienced local pilots and navigators for each vessel. These are to be taken from Spitzbergen and Novaia Zemlia, as available.

4. Each vessel is to take on, from some convenient place, materials to build an izba like the ones used by local promyshlenniks. This can be used as a zimov'e.

5. These vessels are to be fitted out with provisions enough for two or three years and also with all necessary equipment, with no shortages.

6. To carry out his project a sum of 20,000 rubles has been

authorized and is to be taken from the account of the Admiralty College.

7. The officers who are being sent on this voyage are to be upgraded in rank upon their departure. When they determine they have safely reached their destination, they are to invoke Our name and elevate themselves another rank. When they return from that expedition, upon review they will be rewarded with a third upgrade in rank.

8. During the voyage all officers, noncommissioned officers and ranks are to receive double pay. Hired personnel are also to be paid double, and their pay is to be issued to them a year or two in advance.

9. If this expedition is successful We graciously pledge that all those present on that voyage will receive special remuneration until they die, notwithstanding the fact that in the course of their service they will be receiving their normal salaries according to their ranks.

10. The wives of any who may die on that expedition will receive compensation until they die, and the children until they reach adulthood, The amount will depend on the rank of the deceased.

11. Concerning this matter and all other related questions, appropriate instructions are to be drawn up and given to the com-

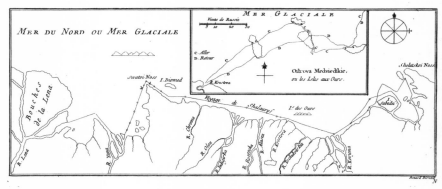

A beautifully clear description of the northern voyage of P. N. Shalaurov in the 1750s. He left the maze of the Lena River mouth, proceeding along the Arctic coast of Siberia to the Kolyma River, thence around the Chukotsk Peninsula to Kamchatka. His secret instructions ordered this voyage "for the benefit of Russian navigation." Courtesy of Department des Cartes, Bibliothèque Nationale, Paris.

mander-in-chief, for the orderly command and for all other unexpected developments which may be encountered en route.

12. State Councillor and Professor Mikhail Lomonosov is to participate in the preparation of this expedition.

13. This entire undertaking is to be kept secret, and for that reason, this, Our ukaz, is not to be revealed, even to Our Governing Senate.

14. To keep a written account of this undertaking, a senior secretary and one of the office servitors who knows how to transcribe notes is to be employed.

Reference: TsGAVMF, f. 315, d. 381, 11. 5–6 ob.

See: V.A. Divin, ed. *Russkaia tikhookeanskaia epopeia* (Khabarovsk: 1979), 334–335.

42

MARCH 2, 1766

A PERSONAL MEMORANDUM FROM EMPRESS CATHERINE II TO DENIS
IVANOVICH CHICHERIN, GOVERNOR OF SIBERIA, REGARDING BRING-
ING SIX OF THE ALEUTIAN ISLANDS UNDER RUSSIAN SUZERAINTY

D enis Ivanovich! I have read with satisfaction your account of
the discovery of six hitherto unknown Aleutian Islands
which have been brought under My scepter, as well as the copy of
the report from the cossack Vasiutinskii and his comrades. This
discovery is most pleasing to Me. I am only sorry that the detailed
description and the registry books for the natives have been lost.
The promise you made on My behalf to the merchant [Andreian]
Tolstykh for his sea voyage, consisting of privileges for his company and one-tenth of the iasak he collects from these islands, is
to be carried out. I approve it, and order that this be done.

Likewise, to encourage the cossacks Vasiutinskii and Lazarev,
they are to be promoted to the rank of local nobles. May God
permit that the voyage which they plan for this spring will be successfully carried out! I should like to know whether they heard
from the inhabitants of these islands that either Europeans or persons from other nations have visited them, or whether they have
ever seen the wreck of a European ship?

In regard to the items which you have sent from these islands,
many persons here feel that the piece of wood is actually seaweed,
which they say generally grows like this, although it seems to
be petrified. The bags woven of grass, the thread made of fish
gut and the bone hooks are very skillfully made. I have ordered
that the beans be planted; We will see what kind of harvest they
produce.

You have given orders to obtain garments and other curiosities
from the natives, and these are to be brought in because I am
eager to see everything. Also, have one of the local natives brought
back, but give orders that no one is to be brought unwillingly or
by any force whatsoever, only someone who is willing to come. I
have promoted the adjutant Miakinin, whom you sent here, to the
rank of Captain.

I have received the bird skins which you sent in with your last
report. They are fairly good, but if they had been better prepared

and ornamented, they might have been worth 60 rubles in the shops. The ones you sent go for 1 1/2 rubles. I am sending you a muff which was sewn here from one of the skins you sent; this may serve as an example of how the skins should be prepared. Local women of fashion wear flounces and edging on their garments made of furs. It would be a good idea if you were to select some, especially those that are colorful, and send them here.

If you do not know what flounces are, ask your wife, and she will inform you.

With good wishes, always,
[signed] Catherine

[In the margin Catherine II added a handwritten note:] Instruct the promyshlenniks to treat the inhabitants of the new islands with kindness and not to deceive or mistreat them when they collect iasak from them.

Reference: Russia. *Polnoe sobranie zakonov rossiiskoi imperii s 1649 goda*. First series (St. Petersburg: 1830), XVII, 603–604.

43

A REPORT FROM ADAM BRIL, GOVERNOR OF IRKUTSK, DESCRIBING THE
NATIVE PEOPLES OF KAMCHATKA AND THE NEARBY ISLANDS IN THE
NORTH PACIFIC OCEAN

Under the jurisdiction of the Okhotsk administrative district there are 80 nomadic Koriaks who pay their iasak obligations to Iamsk ostrog. According to the iasak books, 20 of these people pay iasak consisting of 24 *mautas*, which are 30-sazhen-long strips of seal hide; 27 men pay iasak of one reindeer hide parka each; the remaining 33 pay one red fox pelt each, for a total of 24 mautas, 27 parkas and 33 red fox. Each item is valued at one ruble, a total of 80 rubles.

These people recount the legend of their origins, saying that their ancestor Kokkuniakh and his wife Khakhila begot a son and heir named Amamkhut, who went to live in the sea and that he begot [the Koriak people]. In December they prepare a mixture of berries and grasses with seal or whale fat and fish. They put this in their iurts under the ladder which they use to go up out of the iurt. At night they take this prepared mixture out of the iurt and as they leave, they smear the ladder. At the top of the ladder they place an idol with a human-like face in the belief that their ancestor Kokkuniakh will come there unseen and eat the offering. When they take the food outside, they put it in special containers and leave it overnight. [The next day] they bring it back inside the iurt and invite their friends to come. As a gesture of hospitality, they offer the guests this food which has been tasted by their idols.

When they are ill and when they are on a hunt, they ask assistance from those who have died at sea.

These Koriaks are both courageous and vengeful. They will steadfastly endure hunger and all other deprivations. They are not afraid of death. They are quick and bold in their actions against their rivals or enemies. They procure their food at sea, using baidaras to catch marine creatures such as whales, sturgeon, sea lions and seals. They also take all kinds of land animals. They eat all the offal of any sea creature they take, with no sense of revulsion. They are quite expert in taking animals and have invented various trapping equipment.

To catch fish they make nets from roots, animal sinew or whale whiskers, and they also make other clever pieces of equipment with which they procure abundant amounts of fish. They dry goodly quantities of food for winter. The women are very industrious and skillful in sewing and are very good at preparing supplies of food. They gather grasses, roots, and berries to preserve for food.

Men and women wear the same kinds of garments and foot covering. Women wear garments made of reindeer and sealskin; their parkas are made of birdskins. They do not keep any livestock [other than reindeer], nor do they have herds of horses. As weapons they use the slingshot with which they skillfully hurl stones and kill good-sized birds; the bow and arrow; the lance and firearms which they like very much. Their axes used to be made of stone and bone, and could be used to split logs their entire length.

The nomadic Koriaks live along the coast all of the time, for which reason they are called the sedentary Koriaks. In winter they live in earthen iurts which they can only enter through an opening at the top which serves as a window, like the lookout on a ship, and also provides light and a place for smoke to escape when they build a fire inside. Many families live together in such iurts.

In summer they leave the iurts and live as separate families in huts, mostly along the seashore, where they hunt sea creatures from their baidaras. Each man has one wife; they live together until death. They respect their relatives and know who their ancestors were, back to the third generation on both sides of the family. When somone dies, they dress the corpse in fancy clothing and then burn it, believing that the dead person will go up in the smoke to live in heaven. If someone drowns at sea, or dies and is not burned, they believe that person was unhappy on earth and that in death he will not live in society but will dwell under the earth.

According to the iasak books, the reindeer Koriaks who live along the shore of the Sea of Okhotsk pay their iasak to the Gizhiga ostrog, under the jurisdiction of the Okhotsk administration. On November 2, 1769, the following information about them was sent from Gizhiga to the Okhotsk office. There are 259 nomadic Koriaks living along the shore of the Sea of Okhotsk and along various rivers who are under the jurisdiction of that ostrog. Their annual iasak obligation is one red fox pelt per man. If they do not have a fox pelt, they must pay 1 ruble 50 kopecks in cash. There are 366 reindeer Koriaks, each of whom pays one fox per year, or if they have no fox, pay 1 ruble 50 kopecks. In all there are 625 persons. On September 9 of that same year, 1769, at the request of the Irkutsk gubernia office, . . . a report indicated that there were 831 men each of whom paid one red fox into the treasury. Since each fox is worth one ruble, that number of pelts was worth 831 rubles.

Because of a very severe smallpox epidemic there (which is still prevalent), many of those people went off into the mountains to escape this deadly plague and many others died of it. No one knows how many have survived, since because of the epidemic the information has not been collected and sent from Gizhiga ostrog, as directed by the ukaz, to the Okhotsk office.

These people, as indicated previously, . . . are nomadic, speak the same language and have similar customs. The reindeer nomads have large herds of reindeer which they use to travel from one encampment to another in summer. In winter they harness them to sleds. Sometimes, if they are in a place where there is abundant grass for their herds for forage, they will remain for two or even three months in one location. They have tent iurts made of reindeer hide. Both men and women wear the same type of garments made of reindeer hide, and they also use the hide to make parkas. Both men and women hunt wild reindeer and kill a substantial number of them for food. Their weapons are bows, arrows and lances. In battle they use kuiaks made of animal bone and whale whiskers. Some of them have some iron. They are brave and have a passion for fighting.

To become intoxicated these Koriaks eat mushrooms called *mukhomor* instead of liquor. They gulp the mushrooms whole, which makes them very intoxicated and causes drunken behavior.

When someone dies they dress the corpse in finery, and following the instructions of the family, they put the body on a sled, harness several reindeer to it, and take it to a suitable place and burn it. They believe the dead person ascends into heaven and will live there. But they turn loose the reindeer that pulled the corpse, for no one wants to take these animals into his own herd.

There are iasak-paying Aleuts under the jurisdiction of the Okhotsk office who live on a nearby Aleutian island called Attu, located in the Bering Sea. There is an official record book regarding this, which a company vessel called the *Sv. Vladimir* brought back in 1769. The vessel belongs to the Tula merchant Semen Krasilnikov. It was under the command of the cossack Aleksei Sapozhnikov, the navigator of the vessel. Sapozhnikov had received the record book from the Lower Kamchatka prikaz office. The book registers 47 iasak-paying male Aleuts, each of whom paid one sea otter per year, the value of which has not been established.

From that island of Attu, the company brought in 84 sea otter pelts, both male and female, for the year 1769 and for previous years. These pelts were sent to the office of the Irkutsk gubernia, where they were appraised at 1,454 rubles. However the iasak collection does not come in every year from these Aleuts; it is collected only when company vessels are sent out to sea to hunt, and when they go to that island.

These people . . . provide their living by traveling in small sealskin baidarkas which they use to go from one island to another, up to 50 versts in distance. One man sits in the baidarka and fastens to it an inflated bladder from a whale or another sea creature; then he puts his wife in the bladder. They can then move about the sea boldly and freely and take great pride in doing this. They will put to sea during the worst storms, and teach [this skill to] their children as young as twelve years of age.

They sail out to sea in those baidarkas . . . hunting sea otters and seals which they take by hurling bone darts, which are spears made from walrus tusks one vershok long. They attach stone harpoons to these to stab the animals. They skin them at sea from the baidarkas and always eat the meat raw.

In winter they live on the island in earthen iurts, several families in one iurt. In summer each family lives in a tent. Their food consists of sea animals and fish and shellfish—whatever they happen to find or catch. They always eat meat and fish raw, and drink the blood of sea creatures uncooked. They do not eat any cooked food.

Men and women wear similar clothing, parkas sewn from bird skins. Neither men nor women wear foot covering in either winter or summer. They never prepare food supplies ahead, not even enough for five days, either summer or winter. When they do secure food from a sea creature, they do not go out after another one until they have consumed the meat from the first one. When they are out of food, they go hunting.

Their weapons consist of short arrows with bone or stone heads, which they shoot very skillfully up to 20 sazhens from small throwing boards. Their spears are made of bone. They do not often have fires, but they can make them by rubbing wood. Their knives and axes are made of stone and their needles are made of bird bones, by using stone. The women sew very skillfully with these needles. They do not have any extra clothing, garments for special occasion, extra utensils or anything else. They do not value things. They do not prepare beds in their iurts in either summer or winter. They sleep sitting up, with their wives, in an excavation in the ground. Their wealth and worldly goods consist of a single baidarka made of hide, which they use to go to sea to hunt, both summer and winter, and arrows which they throw by hand from the above described throwing boards.

They have no gods; they honor only shamans, who are never males. All shamans are women who leave their dwellings to go up into the mountains to spend several nights in solitude. When they return they report about visions they have had. Aleuts do not have any accounts of their ancestors, they only say that their forefathers came to the islands in baidaras, but they do not know from which direction they came. In their own families they know only the father, mother and siblings. They do not live with any one wife very long, but rather, often change wives. Friends will take on wives who have been discarded. If anyone becomes ill he is taken some distance away from his habitation; a special little tent is prepared for him and a little food is left for him. If he dies, the tent is folded over his body and this is the only funeral ceremony.

There are also Oliutors under the jurisdiction of the Okhotsk administration. They are part of the Gizhiga ostrog tribute district, but presently they pay their iasak to the Nizhnekamchatsk ostrog. They live along the coast of the [Pacific] ocean in one area. They live in earthen iurts they have made near the smaller ostrogs, as the Koriaks do. Until the above mentioned smallpox epidemic, they were registered in the iasak books as having 280 men paying iasak. From them the Treasury obtained 154 red fox, each worth one ruble, for a total of 154 rubles.

These Oliutors relate an ancestry similar to that of the nomadic Koriaks. They originate from Kokkuniakh and his son Amamkhut. These people are coarse and large in stature. They are not friendly with other tribes and do not visit them. They disdain everyone who comes to them. They do not take their wives from other tribes, nor do they give their children [in marriage] to outsiders. They marry only among themselves.

The attire is the same for men and women. They wear identical parkas made of reindeer or seal or bird skins. They eat various marine creatures such as whales, walrus, sturgeon and seal. When they hunt these creatures they go to sea in large baidaras with ten, fifteen or more men in each. Sometimes they catch fish with nets made of whale sinew. They also eat various grass roots. They eagerly consume intoxicating wild mushrooms and when they are in a drunken state they pretend to be shamans and discuss all kinds of supposed dreams and visions.

They use the same weapons as the Koriaks, the slingshot, bow, arrow and spear. When one of them dies, the eyes are removed from the corpse and the corpse itself is cut up into small pieces and burned, with the same superstitions as the Koriaks.

Kamchadals under the jurisdiction of the Bolsheretsk administration who pay their iasak at Nizhnekamchatsk ostrog live along the Kamchatka River and along the sea coast. There are 799 Kamchadal men in various locations and in their small fortified settlements. They pay their iasak into the treasury in the Nizhnekamchatsk prikaz office. At their own request, 552 of them pay 267 sables and 318 red fox, valued at 852 rubles.

On Karagin Island live the Karagin people, previously known as Kamchadals. They left Kamchatka for this island in the sea which has the name Karagin because it is about 40 versts from the mouth of the Karagin River, which flows from Kamchatka into the sea. This island is about 500 versts from Nizhnekamchatsk ostrog, and is under that administrative jurisdiction. There are 111 men who pay an annual iasak of 69 red fox valued at 69 rubles. These Karagin people are coarse [in appearance]. They seldom visit the mainland of Kamchatka and do not allow many outsiders to visit them. They hunt fox and eat sea creatures such as walrus, seal and the like. Both men and women wear garments made of bird skins. Their manner of living is similar to that of the Kamchadals and they use the same kinds of weapons. However, they are quite dissimilar in their habits and customs. Their language is also distinctly different from that of the Kamchadals and the Oliutors. It is impossible to know more about their other ways, because there has been no detailed report about them from the Bolsheretsk office in Kamchatka.

The Kamchadals who live near the Tigil ostrog along the coast of the Sea of Okhotsk in sixteen small fortified encampments are also under the iasak-collecting jurisdiction of this administration. There are 940 men; 619 of them by their request pay an annual iasak into the treasury consisting of 220 sables, 1 cross fox and 406 red fox, for a total value of 832 rubles.

There are 507 Kamchadals from Upper Kamchatka ostrog who live along the Kamchatka River and along the shores of the Pacific Ocean, and they are also under the jurisdiction of the Bolsheretsk administration. They pay 266 sables and 108 red fox, for a value of 640 rubles. Their customs, habits and manners are similar to those noted below; they differ from one another in their language from one small ostrog to another.

There are 1196 Kamchadal men under the jurisdiction of Bolsheretsk ostrog who live along the coast of the Pacific Ocean and the Sea of Okhotsk, along various rivers and on Cape Lopatka in fortified strongholds. The annual iasak collected from them for the Treasury is 267 sables and 612 red fox, valued at 1,146 rubles. These people are small in stature and not very bold.

In winter they live in earthen iurts, many families together. In summer they inhabit balagans built on posts. They hunt all throughout Kamchatka for sable and fox. They have a plentiful supply of sweet grass which is highly valued there, and from which they distill government spirits. They eat fish which is abundant there, as well as various grasses and roots which are suitable for human consumption. These Kamchadals are greatly addicted to smoking tobacco. Their weapons consist of bows, arrows and spears, but these are weaker and lighter than those of the Lamut and Koriak tribes.

They describe their ancestry by saying that they descended from an ancestor by the name of Kutys and his wife Khakhil, whom they used to worship. They cast spells on each other in whispers. They live in various places. Men and women wear the same clothing, parkas sewn of reindeer and dog hide and from bird skins, but they also greatly admire Russian clothing. It is impossible to know anything accurate about their customs and habits and manners because no reports have been sent out from the Bolsheretsk office; however the Bolsheretsk office will be reporting about this, because an ukaz to that effect has been sent there.

Under the jurisdiction of this same Bolsheretsk ostrog live the Kurils, who are like the Kamchadals but live on the Kuril Islands in the strait between the North Pacific Ocean and the Sea of Okhotsk. There are 262 men; annual iasak is collected from 183 at their own request, amounting to 1 sable, 65 red fox, 65 sea otters [prime male], 2 female sea otters and 50 immature, for a total value of 734 rubles. These people inhabit four of the Kuril Islands. In their baidaras they travel across the strait from one island to another. Both summer and winter their food consists of various marine creatures which are cast up on shore from the sea, and they also hunt these same creatures. They hunt sea otters at sea and foxes on the islands. Their clothing is similar to that of the Kamchadals.

These people differ from the Kamchadals who live on mainland Kamchatka by virtue of their dark complexions; they are quite bearded and hirsute. They are kindly and reliable. Like the Kamchadals, in winter they live in earthen iurts, but in summer, fall and spring they live under their baidaras, in which ten or more men voyage to the shores of islands in the sea in their constant hunt for animals.

Their other habits are impossible to ascertain because the Bolsheretsk office has not sent any information, although iasak is collected from them every year. The Bolsheretsk office in Kamchatka should report in a special dispatch to the Irkutsk gubernia office.

In conclusion: the population total for all these ostrogs— Kamchatka, Upper and Lower Bolsheretsk and Tigil—and for the Kuril Islands, in 73 small fortified Kamchadal iasak settlements and in the non-iasak-paying settlements, is 3,704 adult males. From them the following amount of imposed iasak is collected: 1,013 sables, 1 cross fox, 1,509 red fox, 65 sea otters [prime males], 2 young female sea otters and 50 immature sea otters, for a total value of 4,204 rubles.

Reference: F. I. Tumanskii, ed. "Opisanie narodov, nakhodiashchikhsia okolo Iakutska, Okhotska i v Kamchatke" in *Rossiiskii magazin* (St. Petersburg: 1792), ch. 1, 385–401.

See: T. K. Shafranovskaia, "Narody Kamchatki i prelegaiushchikh ostrovov (izvestie 1770 goda)", in *Strany i narody vostoka*, vyp. VI, *Strany i narody basseina Tikhoko Okeana* (Moscow: 1968), 62–67.

44

AN EXTRACT FROM THE JOURNALS OF CAPTAIN PETR KUZMICH KRE-
NITSYN AND CAPTAIN LIEUTENANT MIKHAIL DMITRIEVICH LEVASHEV
DESCRIBING RUSSIAN HUNTING TECHNIQUES AND NATIVES ENCOUN-
TERED IN THE ALEUTIAN ISLANDS DURING THEIR VOYAGES COM-
MENCING IN 1764

After the [Russian promyshlenniks] leave Kamchatka, their first stop is usually at one of the [Komandorskie] islands near Kamchatka, [Bering] or Mednyi Island, where they are able to enter shallow bays because of the small size of their vessels. (It is not yet known whether there are harbors for large ships on these islands). They will then remain there or spend the winter on low-lying parts of the shore preparing the pelts and throats of fur seals and sea lions. The flesh is also prepared for use as meat. The sea lion hides are used for covering baidaras and for making soles for boots. Sealskins are used for parkas and cloaks and the throats are made into kamleis and boots for use during future winters on distant islands, to which they will voyage from this island. When they reach these [more distant] islands, they put into bays where they can spend the winter. They beach their vessels and try to take hostages, children from that island or nearby islands. If they cannot do this peacefully they will use force.

Once this is done they issue traps to the natives to use to take foxes. They give the natives seal and sea lion hides called *lavtaks*, which the natives use to cover their baidarkas, and they also give glass beads, goat wool and small copper kettles. The natives become so indebted to the Russians that all the while the Russians are on the island the natives must provide them with fish and edible roots. No matter where the natives hunt, on shore or at sea, they must give everything to the promyshlenniks. In this manner the promyshlenniks augment their hunt, for although they also make a definite effort to hunt these animals, there are so few promyshlenniks it is dangerous to send them out hunting in some places.

This is apparent in a report dated October 1, 1768, from an apprentice navigator named [Afanasii] Ocheredin. He reported that fifteen men from his vessel were killed because they hunted in groups of too few men. There is another example: in the year 1763 on the islands of Unimak, Unalaska and Aliaksa [the peninsula of Alaska, then thought to be a large island], four vessels were completely burned and the crews killed. Because of this the promyshlenniks could not personally take over the hunting; the natives had to help them. Otherwise the promyshlenniks would have been forced to hunt only in the bays, using government-issued traps. They could not have ventured farther even though they had 50 traps. They gave more than half of the traps to the island natives whose children they held hostage.

Both the Russians and the American natives hunted all winter long but took only five black-brown foxes, twelve blue and one red. The Russian promyshlenniks complained about the poor hunt as compared to previous years. They said it seemed there were not even a tenth as many animals as previously, either because of the bad winter weather or because the island was so small the animals had been trapped out. Fox hunting begins at the end of November and continues until April.

On April 5 [1768?] Ocheredin returned with his merchant vessel from a winter stop on Umnak and brought with him the iasak he had collected for the Treasury over a three-year period from the natives on the islands of Umnak and Unalaska. The iasak consisted of 51 sea otters and 47 foxes of various sorts. This iasak was accepted.

On [April] 22 a galiot named the *Sv. Ekaterina*, which had been dispatched on March 27 from the island of Unalaska to the island of Unimak, returned, bringing in a toion from the Makushinsk settlement and ten baidarkas. There were four native converts aboard. The toion stated that about 100 baidarkas had gathered together to make the voyage, but when they reached the island of Kugalga the inhabitants there told them that the Unimak men intended to kill everyone who went out to the Russian vessel. More than half the natives were frightened by this news and dispersed to their dwellings. But the Makushinsk toion disregarded the threat and took 30 baidarkas to the island of Unimak. There the inhabitants detained him, confiscated buttons and beads from him and told him if he and his men dared go to that vessel again they would all be killed. The Makushinsk toion observed, having been informed of it, that there was indeed a Russian vessel at that island, but even after voyaging for two days he did not come to it. In calm weather he would be able to make 100 versts [in that period of time]. The Unimak men did not go to that vessel, but they supposedly had killed one of the crew. They would not let [the toion] go further, so he returned to the hooker [*Sv. Pavel*].

On August 31, 1768, both vessels [Krenitsyn's galiot *Sv. Ekaterina* and Levashev's hooker *Sv. Pavel*] were still there together. By general agreement with Captain Krenitsyn they decided that if necessary they would winter over in bays between Unimak and Aliaksa while they were en route to Kodiak Island. They decided Captain Krenitsyn would winter there. In order to load [Krenitsyn's] vessel and ready it for its voyage as quickly as possible, they careened the hooker and unloaded provisions and heavy equipment onto shore.

From the 9th [of September 1768] on, natives from various islands brought in iasak consisting of two black-brown foxes and one small brown fox, for which they were given receipts and gifts.

All during April [1769] there were intermittent winds with overcast skies and stormy weather. There were only six days free of rain; the rest of the month had either snow or rain which often continued for 24 hours or more without a letup. Thus it was very difficult to careen the vessel. On the first of May the wind was strong all day, there was heavy rain and then wet snow; consequently no one could perform any work.

In regard to the native inhabitants of that island, these people have no laws, do not believe in any god and have no concept of a god. They do not perform any service nor make obeisance. But they do have persons who foretell the future and reveal anything they wish to know. These people are called shamans; they claim the devil reveals everything to them.

When they have festive dances they put on masks made of wood and painted in various colors. Judging by their appearance, they make these masks to resemble the devils that appear to them while they perform the rites of shamanism. In their language they call these *kugakh*. While they dance they beat drums which look like barrel hoops, these are covered with thin sealskin. Everyone, men and women alike, sing songs in loud voices. The men sit in one group, the women in another. They dance alone, starting with small children, then women alone or in pairs, holding an inflated bladder. This festivity begins after the fur seal hunt starts, around the middle of December. It continues until April.

The men have as many wives as they need: one, two, three, four or more. They also have a man called a *zhupan* [transvestite], as noted in the Kamchatka history [S. P. Krasneninnikov, *Opisanie zemli Kamchatki*, St. Petersburg: 1755]. A man may have as many wives as he can provide parkas for. When a husband dies his wife is required to sit in a dark place for 40 days, not going out at all into daylight. Other persons bring her food and necessities. If a wife dies, her husband must observe the same rites.

If a husband does not love his wife, he may sell or exchange her for another woman. In case of famine a husband may trade his wife for a bladder of whale fat weighing two pounds. By the same token, if the husband does love his wife, he will try to steal her back. If he is not successful, he will be killed.

The men wear garments made of various bird skins with the feathers on. The garment is called a parka and reaches down to the heels. Over this parka they wear a garment called a kamlei when they go out in their baidarkas, or if they go out in rain. The kamlei is made of thin whale intestines. On their heads they wear wooden hats to which feathers and sea lion whiskers are fastened. Some are decorated with variously colored beads and small carved figures made of bone or soft stone.

In the lower lip they place items made of this stone; others insert bits of colored bone that look like large teeth. They make a hole between their nostrils into which they insert black grass or a bone resembling a pin. In good times when they are engaged in festivities they put beads and small bits of amber in their ears and between the labrets in the lower lip. They obtain these things from the island of Aliaksa in exchange for arrows and kamleis, but more often through battle. They also procure there the women and young girls whom they make their slaves; in their language these are called *kalga*.

The men's hair is cut above their eyes over their forehead and is straight in back. Most of them have the hair cut off the top of the head so it looks as if they had been tonsured.

The women's garments are the same length as the men's, but are made of sealskin. The women sew with bone needles and their thread is made of whale sinew. They wear no head covering.

Their hair is cut in front like the men's, but is tied into a knot in back. They have two or three rows of blue pigmented tatoos on their cheeks. Like the men, they make an incision in their noses, into which they insert bone ornaments from two to three-and-a-half inches long. At the ends of this ornament and around the mouth and in the ears they wear beads and small bits of amber. They do not have any domestic crafts. Around their necks they wear beads which they obtain from the Russian promyshlenniks in exchange for the pelts of sea otters and foxes. On their wrists and ankles they wear narrow ornamented strips called *nagovshki* which are made of walrus or whale skin.

These people are of medium height. Their hair is black and coarse, and their faces are dark and their bodies are swarthy. . . .

Whenever they wish to color something red, they use blood from their noses. A man or a woman who is ill or wounded lies down for three or four days without any food; the person is then bled with a stone implement made from black jasper which looks like a lancet. The skin is pierced in places where there is pain; the stone is inserted between the skin and the body and manipulated in all directions, letting the blood flow.

They live in earthen iurts with supports made of driftwood. They also use driftwood for cooking, but they cook very little. They eat a good deal of raw fish, mussels, sea cabbage and other wild things. They also eat whales which have been washed up on shore; sometimes they eat roots, sarana, snakeweed and angelica, but only with fat or fish. It is not possible to use one particular root which is extremely bitter.

They make fire when they need it by putting dry grass or birds' down on a rock; they then sprinkle fine sulphur over that and strike one stone against another, so that sparks fly. The sulphur on the rock ignites the grass and the down. Some make fire by twirling wood as if it were a drill.

Their baidarkas look like little boats; they are made with thin wooden boards which are covered with whale or sealskin, both top and bottom. These baidarkas are 16 to 18 feet long and 1½ feet wide. Others are a little larger. They are 14 inches deep. There is a circular opening in the middle where a man sits on the bottom of the baidarka. He has a double-bladed paddle in his hands and paddles on both sides with this. When it is stormy he pulls a wide whaleskin covering over the circular opening and over himself, so water will not get into the baidarka. In cold weather these natives stay warm in their iurts; then, when the weather passes, they come out onto shore.

They warm themselves by placing a saucer of whale oil between their feet; they light it and put dry grass in it, and warm themselves from the resulting heat.

They use bone hooks to catch fish; these are tied to long lengths of sea cabbage which they first fill with whale oil or some other oil and then dry out.

They kill animals and birds with bone arrows which they place in thin wooden boards and throw from the board with the right hand. They do not hunt fox, nor do they use fox pelts for clothing. They use stone arrowheads inserted in wooden shafts. They use these in battle because the arrow shaft is so thin that when it is shot forcefully, the shaft breaks off and the stone arrowhead is lodged in the body of the enemy.

Although the third point of the secret instructions states that the islands of Unimak and Unalaska have been brought under the suzerainty of Her Imperial Majesty and pay iasak, it is now apparent that the only ones who bring in iasak, as it is called in the Russian language, are the ones whose children have been taken hostage. They only pay iasak out of fear that they or their children will be killed. They do not know where the pelts are sent, nor do they care about the future.

They used to think that the only people in the world were on the islands they knew; now they have some small comprehension about Kamchatka because of all the people who come to them who live in Kamchatka. Beyond that [they believe] there is no other place. For that reason it is not possible to bring genuine order among them or to collect iasak from them because of the small number [of Russians there].

They subscribe to one thing: if their side is stronger, they will kill everyone without exception, not realizing that the following year many [more] persons will come. They think the ones they kill are the only ones, and that no more will come. And although at the present time they know through the accounts of their interpreters that the Russian people are numerous, it is impossible to bring them into a consistent life style because of their natural barbaric malice and envy for all kinds of trivial possessions. . . .

The people on these islands are called by the following [tribal] names: On the island of Unalaska—Kogolags; on the island of Akutan and farther east to Unimak—Kigigus; on the island of Unimak and Aliaksa—Katagaeguks. Why they are called thus, they do not know; they say that they have long been called by these names. Russian promyshlenniks call these people Aleuts, a name taken from the islands closest to Kamchatka which were named by the assistant navigator [Mikhail] Nevodchikov during his stay on these islands, but for what reason we do not know. The inhabitants of these islands themselves were queried about these names; they did not know about Russian promyshlenniks or what the name Aleut meant, but now even they call themselves Aleuts.

On the 24th of the month a nephew of the toion of Akutan island was taken hostage. He had no father. He observed the orderly existence [among the Russians] and the fact that two young lads whom the commanding officer had bought were outfitted with footwear and were well clothed. Seeing this, he expressed his desire and asked the commanding officer to accept him into service. This hostage speaks Russian well enough so that he can understand almost everything necessary. The commanding officer agreed to this request and accepted him into service. The lad is sixteen years old and is named Semen . . .

We asked the inhabitants of Unimak and Unalaska, as well as those of other islands, if they know whether there are islands either to the north or south such as are mentioned in the journals. We also asked if they know whether Aliaksa is an island or part of the mainland. But they know absolutely nothing of the islands which have been recorded in the journal, or where these people originated or how they dispersed through the islands. We were unable to ascertain these things through the interpreters because of their lack of knowledge.

We sailed to the middle of the harbor to await a wind that would take us out to sea. The crew of the hooker, including all ranks, numbered 60 men. From the provisions which had been stocked for the crew, each man received one pud of flour, eight pounds of groats, ten pounds of meat and five pounds of butter. Island inhabitants brought 70 bundles of dried cod, each bundle containing 50 fish. We salted six barrels of cod and took on 41 barrels of fresh water. We also had four sazhens of wood from dismantled iurts.

While we were in the harbor, at various times when the weather was clear we used the geodetic quadrant and the astrolabe to ascertain the latitude of the harbor, which was 53°29' N. For the longitude of this harbor we took the first meridian and the correction of the inclination of the sun. For the variance of the length we used the calculations that the company had made in 1768. This island is located 204°36' from Ferro; the compass deviation was established at the meridian line two rhumbs East.

In the harbor of Saint Paul, at high tide during the new moon, the water rises from six to seven feet; at half moon, from four to five feet. Igunok Bay is located N and W by an uncorrected compass. The harbor of Saint Paul and Igunok Bay have already been described. It would have been desirable to describe the entire island of Unalaska, but because so many of the servitors were ill, there was no one to do this . . .

Reference: TsGADA, f. Gosarkhiv, r. X, op. 3, d. 15, 11. 36 ob.-40; 44–44 ob.

See: V. A. Divin, ed. *Russkaia tikhookeanskaia epopeia* (Khabarovsk: 1979), 357–362.

45

AN ACCOUNT BASED ON THE JOURNAL OF IVAN KOBELEV, A COSSACK
SOTNIK, CONCERNING HIS VOYAGE TO ISLANDS LOCATED BETWEEN
NORTHEASTERN ASIA AND NORTHWESTERN AMERICA

On May 28, [Ivan] Kobelev was near a rocky mountain called Serdtse. He maintains that the land of the settled Koriaks begins there, that is, Koriaks who do not possess reindeer. He says that the reindeer Chukchi treat the settled Chukchi in the same way as nobles in Russia treat their peasants. The settled Chukchi are responsible for preparing whale oil for the reindeer Chukchi, as well as walrus meat. In exchange, the reindeer Chukchi give them reindeer meat. The place [where he was] is identified [on his map] with the red letter "A" and is located in 65°10″ northern latitude and 195°0′0″ from Ferro Island.

The rocky mountain named Serdtse was called this by Captain Bering. . . . The name comes from the fact that the mountain looks rather like a heart.

On July 2 Kobelev was along a creek called the Krapivnaia at the Vutein settlement. The iurts there he describes as being built around whale jaws and ribs [as supports], and covered over with earth. Such iurts are used by all settled Koriaks along the coast of the Arctic Ocean.

On July 17 Kobelev was in the small ostrog of Iagageinsk located not far from a small island called Nunemginsk. There is an inlet of the sea there; the mouth is about eight versts wide and narrows as it penetrates the island. According to natives two English ships anchored there in the year 1778 [belonging to the Cook Expedition]. They anchored for some time. Crew members went ashore in three small boats and bartered with the natives, trading glass beads for fox pelts. The English also traded a length of red fabric with white dots. The location is 65°18′ northern latitude and 206°30′ longtitude. These same natives also stated that in past years two other ships similar to the English vessels had come to their settlement, but they do not know who those people were.

It is apparent that Captain Bering stopped there on his return voyage [1728]. He reported, "Our seafarers returned there. On our return voyage nothing remarkable happened; however on Au-

By the time of Kobelev's 1779 voyage, geographical knowledge extended to most of the islands in the Aleutian archipelago, based partly on information from Russian explorers as well
as Captain Cook's celebrated voyages. Pallas, *Neue Nordische
Beytrage. . . .* (OHS neg. 80258)

gust 20, 40 Chukchi men in four baidaras came to our ship and
brought gifts of reindeer meat, fish, fresh water, fox and polar fox
pelts and walrus teeth; in return we gave them needles, fire flints,
iron and other such items."

Kobelev's remarks about his stay on these islands follow.

On July 26 Kobelev voyaged from the mainland of the Chukchi land to the first island, called Imoglin [Imagli, Ratmanov Is-
land] which is about 40 versts from the mainland. The island is
some five versts long and two wide; there are two settlements on
it, in which 203 men and 195 women live; these include both
young and old persons. Their language is the same as that of the
nomadic Chukchi. There is no forest on the island. The only animal is the blue fox. The inhabitants eat the meat of whale, seal
and walrus.

On July 31 Kobelev went on to the second island called Igellin
[Kruzenstern Island], which is located about three versts from the
previous one. The island is about three versts long and one-and-
one-half wide. There are 85 males and 79 females, including
youths. There is no forest there, and they eat the same food as on
the first island. To cook their food they use whale bones which
they sprinkle with seal oil [and ignite]. The only animals are a few
polar foxes.

254

From that island to the coast of North America the distance is about 30 versts. One can see the American coast from there, both near and in the distance, and one can also see the Chukchi coast.

The chief elder of that island is named Kaigun Momokhunin, who identifies himself as a native American, born on American soil, but not on that island; he had moved there some time previously. In conversation he revealed that on American territory, along the Kherven River [Yukon], there is a small ostrog called Kymgov where Russian people live. They speak Russian, read and write, worship icons, and have different features from native Americans; the latter have sparse beards which they pluck out, while the Russians who live there have big heavy beards.

The cossack sotnik Kobelev asked the elder to take him to the American coast to these Russian people, but the elder would not agree to do this.

Kobelev also states that when he left the Chukchi coast to voyage to the first island, the iasak-paying Chukchi under Russian jurisdiction warned the island inhabitants not to take Kobelev beyond the second island, that is to the coast of America. This was undoubtedly because the iasak-paying Chukchi were afraid that Kobelev would be killed or detained on American land, which could lead to an inquiry or trouble [with Russian authorities].

The elder agreed to take a letter from Kobelev to the Russians at first opportunity. Kobelev wrote a letter and gave it to the elder. He wrote:

"My beloved flesh and blood brothers who live on the great American land, if you are of Greek [Orthodox] faith and believe in the crucifixion of Our Lord Jesus Christ, and if you have been baptized in Holy Baptism, then I make myself known to you. First, I was sent from the Gizhiginsk fortress to the Chukotsk land to survey it. From that land I went to Imagli Island, opposite Cape Chukotsk. From the local elder, Kaigun Mamakhunin, I have learned about you, that you are people like us, that you write, bow to the holy icon, and live along the Kherven River in an ostrozhek called Kyngiuvei. If this is true, when you receive my letter, try if possible to come to Imagli Island every summer, or send a letter with someone telling me along which river you actually do live, and whether that river empties into the sea or falls into a bay. Erect a tall wooden cross at the river mouth or bay, on a clear spot which can be seen from the sea or from the bay, and if you happen to be in these islands, [you should be aware that although] these islanders have been friendly to me, nevertheless you should be careful because they have not yet been brought into full submission and cannot be trusted.

"I would also like to include in this letter the fact that when I was in Anadyrsk I heard from my predecessors that long ago seven koches, as they were then called, sailed from the mouth of the Lena River to the sea. They sailed along the coast of the Arctic Ocean and managed to reach the Kolyma River. They then proceeded along the Arctic coast around Cape Chukotsk. Opposite that cape a storm came up and separated these koches. We know the fate of four of them, but not the other three. The natives who live there at the present time do not know anything about this. [Dezhnev's expedition of 1649–1651].

"Signed by the cossack sotnik Kobelev."

Kobelev also heard in the Kangun Evunminsk ostrozhek, from a nomadic Chukchi named Ekhipk Opukhin, who had supposedly been in America five times, both to wage war and to trade, that he had a friend on the island of Ukipan. The friend came from that island to Imagli Island and brought Ekhipk a message written on a piece of wood about three chetverts long and five wide and one vershok thick. On one side of the board words were carved and painted red, and on the other side they were painted black. When he delivered the board he said that he had been sent by bearded people who live along that river whose language is similar to that of the Nangunch. They asked that this message be delivered to the Russians. At that time there was a Russian crew in Anadyrsk.

The message read that they had no iron and wanted the Russians to send them iron. The bearded people said that they had enough of everthing except iron. Ekhipk not only took the message; he also indicated that when they pray they make the sign of the cross, showing clearly how they do it. They gather in a large chapel and pray. They also have a place in a field where they set up wooden boards with writing; they face these boards, the tallest man first and the rest behind.

Kobelev's journal says he heard that from these islands to the north, along the coast of the American mainland, a great distance from there, there are supposedly people who have two faces—one in the usual place and the other in the back of the head. Both faces have ordinary eyes, noses, lips, tongue and teeth. They speak freely from both faces, but not at the same time. The rest of the body is normal. They use one mouth to eat, and they live in a special ostrozhek called Tapkhan.

He also reports that there are supposedly cannibals living in warm places in the south who are from these islands.

Kobelev says that [on a clear day] the American coast is visible from the Chukotsk coast, and that one can see both coasts from the islands—the coasts of both Eastern Asia and America. His journal includes a map, showing his track.

The same elder also told Kobelev that there are many bays, rivers and lakes along the American mainland. There are also islands formed by rivers; he identified them by name but did not show their location. For that reason it was impossible to locate them accurately on the map; however, for informational purposes they have been provisionally placed on the map according to descriptions by the English seafarers.

He also stated that along the American coast there are many people, an abundance of many kinds of fish, many reindeer and many people in the interior. Two English ships [Cook] circled three times around the islands of Imagli and Igellin.

The elder also told Kobelev that he had heard that English ships had anchored in the south at the ostrozhek of Uneglekhlen, where they spent four days. The commanding officer of these ships went ashore and received gifts of marten pelts; then the ships sailed north.

According to Kobelev's statement, it is noteworthy and in fact surprising that there is no tide in such a narrow area between the Chukotsk coast and the American mainland and islands, and that only in the narrows between islands is there a current, and even that is not very rapid. The current runs all summer long from the Pacific to the Arctic ocean; in August it turns south and brings ice. Also according to Kobelev's report, near the coast of the Chukotsk peninsula and in other northern places, there is a tide up to six feet in height.

In all justice it should be noted that the cossack sotnik Kobelev was the first of the Russians to have the good fortune to see, from the islands of Imaglin and Igellin, the end of eastern Asia and the coast of North America. The islands are in the narrow strait between Asia and America, a distance of no more than 77 versts, located in 65°30' northern latitude and 208° longitude, from the island of Ferro.

The geodesist [Mikhail] Gvozdev voyaged along the same part of the American coast on the vessel *Sv. Gavriil* in 1730 [*sic.*, voyage was in 1732], sailing in northern latitudes between 65° and 66°.

[signed] Second Major Mikhail Tatarinov

Reference: TsGADA, 1-e otdelenie, d. No. 2539, 1779 i 1785, 11. 62–64.
See: A. V. Efimov, ed. *Iz istorii russkikh ekspeditsii na Tikhom okeane. Pervaia polovina XVIII veka* (Moscow: 1948), 228–233.

46

A REPORT ON THE VOYAGE OF POTAP K. ZAIKOV TO ISLANDS IN THE
NORTH PACIFIC OCEAN BETWEEN ASIA AND AMERICA, ABOARD THE
MERCHANT VESSEL *SV. VLADIMIR*, AS DESCRIBED FOR THE ACADEMY
OF SCIENCES BY FRANZ NIKOLAEVICH KLICHKA, GOVERNOR OF IRKUTSK

A certain amount of information on the islands between Asia and America has already been published, but full information can only be obtained through familiarity with the various voyages there, particularly those accounts that give detailed descriptions of everything beheld by the traveler's eye. One such account is that of the voyage of Navigator [Potap K.] Zaikov, which His Excellency, the Governor of Irkutsk and Cavalier [Franz N.] Klichka has sent to the Academy of Sciences. Accordingly, his account is being published here as an appendix to previously published information.

The vessel on which Navigator Zaikov undertook his voyage belonged to the Tula armorer, Oregkhov, and his associates. There were 69 men aboard including Zaikov, the peredovshchik, 57 Russian workers and 10 Iakut men. The latter are hired for voyages such as this because they are not so likely to contract scurvy [as Russians are]. Their vessel, the *Sv. Vladimir*, set out from the port of Okhotsk on September 22, 1772 and proceeded to Kamchatka with a favorable wind until October 1. From that date on, they sailed against a head wind for a long time, and with a change of wind, a general consensus of those aboard forced Zaikov to return to Kamchatka. On October 19 he managed to enter the mouth of the Vorovskaia River, about 160 versts north of Bolsheretsk. At the time he reached Kamchatka the land was already covered with snow and therefore they built iurts patterned after the Kamchadal style in which to live during the winter.

When the ice in the river broke up on June 12, 1773, the boat put out to sea from the mouth of the Vorovskaia River. They sailed along the coast of Kamchatka and on July 7 reached the second Kuril strait where on July 10 they took on water. From there they had favorable winds and sailed southeast and east but found no islands. At last, because of changing winds, on July 26 they sailed to Mednyi Island, approaching from the north, and

259

anchored in a sandy bay where boats of promyshlenniks had previously anchored. Here, after they unloaded supplies, they pulled the vessel up on its beams. Then they built iurts to use for living quarters, as they were to do in all the places where Zaikov and his men had to spend the winter, and constructed baidaras, or hide boats. Each such craft could accommodate ten men for hunting [marine animals].

Mednyi Island is uninhabited and stretches from northwest to southwest for about 50 versts, and is from 3 to 10 versts in width. On all sides there are cliffs 40 to 50 sazhens high. There are small bays and two small streams on the northern side. On the western side of the island at low tide one can pick up chunks of red copper along the shore. Opposite that place is a cliff that looks as if it contains copper ore. The island has no forest except for small rose willows which grow sparsely in tundra and swamplands. Sarana grows at lower levels; it tastes rather like ground-apples. There are also edible roots about the size of small carrots. The grass grows more than an arshin tall and is used for food. The most frequent animals are the sea lions, fur seals and [other] seals which come here from the sea in great herds. Sea otters appear on shore from May 10 on; they multiply here and remain until November. At that time sea lions and fur seals leave the island completely, but the sea otters winter along the coast. They are hunted in September and October, when they are in prime condition. The meat is used as food; dried meat is taken on voyages to distant islands.

Fall on Mednyi Island begins in September, and the air is warm. Winds from the north and northwest bring snow. Winter begins in mid-December. There is no more than one arshin of snow, which remains until the middle of March, when southeasterly winds bring rains which melt the snow. The north winds bring clear weather. In the winter on the island there are three kinds of seagulls which Zaikov differentiates only in size, calling them large, medium, and small. Spring begins in March with warm clear air and moderate but changeable winds. In summer, from the middle of June to the middle of August, there are heavy clouds which are dispersed by north and northwest winds. At higher elevations the snow remains until July.

By the time summer came Zaikov had secured sufficient provisions to enable him to continue his voyage. So with general consent on July 7 [1774] they proceeded to other islands. On July 30 they reached the Aleutian island of Attu, entering a bay which was hidden on the northern side by three small islands. Both the shore and the bottom were sandy. A short distance to the west there is a small creek called the Gavan. It is about 1/2 verst long, 7 feet wide and 1-1/2 feet deep. It flows out of a small lake which has a circumference of about 1/2 verst and a depth of some 2 feet. The Gavan can accommodate large boats. Here the men used driftwood to build everything they needed to winter over and then they separated to go to various places to hunt sea otters.

The island of Attu extends from west to east and is about 99 versts long and 10 to 30 versts wide. It is mountainous, like Mednyi Island. Rose willow grows in a very few places. On the northern side not far from the Gavan creek there is a small river called the Sarana, because there is quite a bit of sarana growing nearby. This creek comes from a lake similar in size to the lake that gives rise to the Gavan creek. On the southern side, from the eastern cape to the west there is a third creek, the Ubienna. It is similar to the first two, and like them, has its source in a lake.

This island was discovered by the Tobolsk merchant Mikhail Nevodchikov. It was brought under Russian suzerainty in 1748 and today there are 27 men who pay iasak, in addition to children and women [who do not]. They are united in their customs and relations. Each has one wife, they speak Russian, were baptized by the Russians and are friendly toward them. Like the Russians they wear shirts, soft reindeer-skin boots with stockings, and both men and women wear parkas made of polar fox and other garments made of bird skins. From the Russians they obtain footwear, stockings, kerchiefs, caps, garments and copper kettles. Both sexes use tobacco eagerly, and they receive all of this in exchange for sea otters. As food they use fish taken from rivers and lakes. These fish include various types of salmon which come from the sea in May and remain until September. They gather the edible roots of angelica and sarana, and in the fall and winter fish for cod and halibut. Sometimes the sea carries up [dead] whales whose blubber and meat they use for food. They take a few sea otters and blue fox, and a very few sea lions, fur seals and [other] seals. For dwellings they build iurts similar to those in Kamchatka, for which they use driftwood which washes up on shore. The air and weather are similar to that on Copper Island. About

This dynamic group of North Pacific traders appears eager for a lively trading session, perhaps with a European ship in their waters. Here they offer pelts in exchange for highly desired goods such as metal tools, kettles, and clothing. Huish, *The Voyage of Capt. Beechey....* (OHS neg. 80226)

35 versts away from this island there is another one called Agata. The people there lead a life similar to that of the inhabitants of the island of Attu.

Zaikov left ten men with provisions on the island of Attu to hunt animals, and on July 4, 1775 the ship set sail for the chain of islands, proceeding along their northern side. On July 19 they stopped at the island of Unimak, entering a small bay where they encountered a ship at anchor, the *Sv. Evpl*, which belonged to a Vologda merchant, [Fedor] Burenin, and his company. In order to achieve greater success, the two companies agreed to cooperate in hunting on the following basis: one ship with 60 men and all necessary supplies would proceed east to discover islands and hunt; the other ship with 35 men would hunt on the island of Unimak until the first ship returned. They would divide the entire catch equally. On August 3, 1775 Zaikov and the *Sv. Vladimir* sailed east from Unimak and, with various winds, on August 17 were opposite Unimak and entered the strait of Isanok which separates the island of Unimak from the American cape of Alaska. Finally they went into the same bay where Captain [Petr] Krenitsyn had anchored. The strait is about 3 versts wide on the northern side and the depth ranges from 9, 10, 12, 14 to 16 feet. The tides are very fast.

The promyshlenniks remained on this island about three years and consequently were able to obtain the desired information about the people who live there, Because of their kind behavior toward the inhabitants of the island of Unimak, they established friendship with the Aleuts who live across the bay on the American peninsula of Alaska. They frequently came to the dwellings of the Russian promyshlenniks and were given presents of the things they like best: Cherkassian tobacco, various colored beads, copper kettles, shirts and sealskins. Seeing that they were well-disposed toward the Russians, Zaikov assured them of Her Imperial Majesty's kindness and endeavored to bring them under Russian suzerainty, in token of which they willingly gave iasak.

When the English Captain [James] Cook was there, the English asked these people to whose Empire they belonged. The inhabitants, as a sign of their allegiance to Russia, showed [the English] the receipts which Zaikov had given them when he accepted their pelts. Being assured of Russian friendship, the natives gave the Russians their children and relatives as hostages, who were treated well. Zaikov saw that relations were harmonious between the company and the natives, and he sailed from Isanok Strait to the island of Ssiulatys, in order to describe it and other nearby islands.

The island of Unimak extends from east-northeast to west-southwest for about 90 versts and is 25 to 30 versts wide. There are cliffs on both sides of a cape on the west side of the island. Away from the cliffs the coast is sandy, sloping and shallow. There is a mountain range in the middle of the island where there is volcanic activity from time to time. On the northern side there are two small creeks; one has its source in a lake. The fish in these lakes come in from the sea in summer. On the western side of the island small numbers of sea lions, seals and sea otters are found, and on the island itself there are black bears, mink, river otters and ground squirrels. The inhabitants live in iurts in family groups. On the eastern coast where the vessel anchored alder grows, but it is no more than 1-1/2 sazhens tall and 4 inches in girth. To build iurts, baidaras and other things, they use driftwood brought up by the sea, of which there are various deciduous varieties such as aspen, poplar, birch, pine and fir.

In the wintertime in Isanok Strait the strong southeasterly winds and rain break up the ice, which the incoming and outgoing tides carry back and forth, thereby causing the termination of communication with Alaska. The strait is about 20 versts long and from 3 to 7 versts wide. Along the shore on the northern side, halfway to the strait, there is a sandy harbor. The southern part is dominated by cliffs.

At a distance of about 6½ miles from Isanok Strait to the south, Sannakh Island is located, surrounded by small islets. It is about 20 versts long and 7 to 9 versts wide. Its shore is almost completely lined with cliffs with small bays and submerged rocks near shore. On these islands there are black-brown foxes, cross foxes and red foxes. Along the shore there are sea otters and seals. The inhabitants of Sannakh Island are well supplied with driftwood brought in by the sea.

The island of Ungin is located about 22 miles from this strait. It is rounded on the southwest, extending to the northeast. The shore has many cliffs with sandy bays. The inhabitants of the island are Aleuts, similar to those on previously mentioned islands. In addition to foxes, sea otters and seals, they hunt reindeer, otter and ground squirrels.

The western cape of Alaska is inhabited by Aleuts of the same stock, who live in family groups. The south coast of Alaska as far as Ssiulatys Island for about 200 versts has cliffs with sandy bays. The forest that grows there is alder. Near the shore they hunt sea otters, sea lions and seals; on the mainland the hunt is for bears, wolves, reindeer, red fox, otter, wolverine, mink and ground squirrel.

The islands described thus far are identified on the map in red by Zaikov, who inspected them personally; however, information on the coast, which is noted in various points, Zaikov obtained from leading Aleuts who have hunted along both coasts of Alaska in baidaras on the sea. From Isanok Strait to the north side of Alaska the coast is sandy, sloping and has shallow water, and extends for about 200 versts. Kodiak Island is located south of Ssiulatys Island about 400 versts distant. The width of the Alaska peninsula gradually increases toward Kodiak, from 30 to 70 versts. Starting at Kodiak the forest is deciduous and includes pine, birch, aspen and poplar. Among animals found there are the bear, reindeer, wolf, fox, otter and wolverine.

The inhabitants of Kodiak Island are called Koniags; they speak a different language from the Aleuts who live on the islands and on the peninsula of Alaska. Their settlements stretch along the coast east for about 600 versts. They live in iurts. Beyond them live the Chugach people, and beyond that, the bearded people. All are separated from one another by great distances. Each tribe lives in a special society and speaks a different language. On the northern shore of Alaska, opposite Kodiak, where the mainland turns north, the inhabitants are called Koniag Kenais, while the Russians refer to them as the *zubatye* or "tooth people" who are related to the Chukchi. These people war against one another. They take only women and small children into captivity; they kill men. They keep prisoners of war as slaves.

The older leading inhabitants of the American peninsula of Alaska believe that the Aleuts descended from them and that in ancient times they moved from one island to another and freely moved onto the islands adjacent to Kamchatka, that is, to Attu and Agatu. They do not have any organized religion. They call on evil spirits through a shaman, but they do not offer any sacrifices nor do they deify anything. In order to pass time during the winter men and women gather together in a iurt and put on painted wooden masks. Also, on certain high places they put up carved figures resembling humans, birds and sea animals, but they do not worship these figures. They beat drums, sing songs and dance. Their garments are made of birdskins and sealskins. Their hats are made of wood, painted and decorated with beads, feathers and bone ornaments. They have long hair; the women tie their hair back in a club and cut it across the forehead in front. In order to beautify the faces of young children they tatoo them with a fine needle which has been rubbed over black stone. Men and women wear white beads in their ears and around their necks, four strings or more. They collect flame-colored amber which is brought up on shore. From the Koniags they receive shells from lake creatures, which they consider a great treasure.

In winter the leading inhabitants wear boots made of reindeer hide which are sewn with gut from sea lions, fur seals or seals. Persons without means walk barefoot. They hunt sea lions, fur seal and sea otters on the islands, and walrus opposite the Alaska peninsula. They put out into the sea to hunt in 10 to 20 baidar-kas, each with one man. They kill the animals with arrows made of bone and stone harpoons. Instead of a bow they use a throwing board which is 9 vershoks long and 1 vershok wide. In one throw, this can shoot an arrow a distance of 20 sazhens. They do not have any other hunting equipment.

The leading men, called *tosny* [toions], have three or four male slaves. The person who catches the most sea animals commands the largest number of slaves. The wives occupy themselves making thread from sinew. They sew clothes and footwear for their men and for themselves. They make small coverlets for beds out of grass, and they make baskets to hold all kinds of things. They make needles from bird bones. In addition to their apparel, they have become accustomed to wearing shirts and silk, cotton and linen kerchiefs to tie around their necks. They consider themselves impoverished if they do not have a kettle to cook their own food in. Both men and women enjoy Cherkassian tobacco, and they treasure blue beads as well as beads of all other colors. They obtain all these things through barter with the Russians.

In summer they eat fish that comes into the streams from the sea. They catch fish with nets made of whale sinew, and they also spear fish with small bone harpoons. At sea they use fishpoles to catch cod and halibut. Often whales which have been brought ashore by the sea also serve as food. Of land produce, they eat sarana and dog cabbage. On the Alaskan peninsula raspberries grow as well as blueberries and blackberries.

If the wife of a toion dies, or one of his best servants, on some of the islands it is customary to kill a favorite male or female slave to bury with the dead wife or servant. But since the Russians' arrival this practice has been discouraged. The following custom, however, is still preserved: if a toion's favorite wife dies, they re-move the organs from her body, put the body into a box, tie it firmly with cinctures and place it in the iurt opposite their sleep-ing place. The belongings of the deceased are burned completely. The same practice is observed if a favorite child dies.

Zaikov and his men left Unimak Island for their return voy-age on May 27, 1778 and reached Umnak on July 20, anchoring in the same harbor where they had previously been. When other promyshlenniks reached the island, both companies divided the catch, in accordance with the terms they had agreed upon, and then each group set out for additional hunting. Umnak Island extends from east-northeast to west-southwest. It has cliffs with small bays and is some 90 versts long and from 7 to 20 versts wide.

On May 19, 1779, after they had repaired their vessel and loaded it with all their furs and with their necessary provisions, Zaikov went to the island of Attu to pick up ten men who had been left there to hunt. As they sailed along the northern coast of the island they sighted the island of Situin which had been placed on the map by Captain Krenitsyn. Islands identified in red were placed on the map by Zaikov in accordance with readings he took on his return voyage, while the islands of Adar, Kanaga, Tanaga, Amat, Gnak, Goreloi, Semisoloshkoi, Amachitka, Krysei, Sitkhin, Chekhula-Kyska and Byldyr are identified in yellow because it was impossible to describe them accurately on account of winds. These islands have been located on the map on the basis of information supplied by the promyshlenniks who visited those islands and who had been aboard the *Sv. Vladimir*. According to Zaikov's calculation, it appears that these islands are located four degrees farther east than Krenitsyn had indicated.

On May 30 [1779] Zaikov reached the island of Attu, from which place, having picked up the promyshlenniks who had been left on that island, on June 12 he proceeded to [one of] the Komandorskie Island[s] to hunt fur seals for food. He left there on June 23 and reached Okhotsk harbor on September 6 [1779]. He lost twelve men during the course of his voyage.

The ship belonging to the armorer Orekhov and his company brought back iasak for the Treasury and in addition they returned with 2679 large and medium sea otters, 1159 small sea otters, 2874 tails from large and medium sea otters, 583 tails from small sea otters, 549 black-brown fox, 1099 cross fox, 1204 red fox, 92 river otters, 1 wolverine, 3 wolves, 18 mink, 1725 grey fur seals, 1104 blue polar fox and 9 puds 8 pounds of walrus teeth.

See: Russia, Akademiia Nauk. *Sobranie sochinenii vybrannykh iz "Mesiatsoslovov" na raznye gody.* T. 5 (St. Petersburg: 1790) 146–164.

47

1785

INSTRUCTIONS FROM CATHERINE II AND THE ADMIRALTY COLLEGE TO
CAPTAIN LIEUTENANT JOSEPH BILLINGS FOR HIS EXPEDITION [1785–
94] TO NORTHERN RUSSIA AND THE NORTH PACIFIC OCEAN

To Joseph Billings, Captain Lieutenant of the fleet, commanding the geographical and astronomical expedition to the northeastern part of the Russian Empire.

Her Imperial Majesty, extending Her maternal and constant concern for the well-being of Her subjects to all parts of Her vast dominions, even the most distant, wishes to provide them with a better way of life and to make them happier and provide them more advantages. She is also most interested in the important advancement of science. Hence She has been graciously pleased to order an expedition of discovery to the easternmost coasts and seas of Her Empire. This expedition is to make an exact determination of the longitude and latitude of the mouth of the Kolyma River and the location of the Chukotsk Peninsula as far as East Cape. It is also to prepare an accurate chart of the islands in the Pacific Ocean extending to the coast of America. In short, the expedition is to complete the knowledge acquired during Her glorious reign of the seas lying between Siberia and the coast opposite Siberia.

The command of Her Majesty's expedition is entrusted to you, as an experienced officer who zealously serves Her Imperial Majesty. She has full confidence that the importance of this mission in regard to the glory of Her Majesty's sacred name, and the best interests of Her Empire, will inspire you to fulfill the great expectations She holds for your ability.

Her Imperial Majesty's gracious and generous maternal concern grants you the rank of Captain Lieutenant of the fleet, to encourage you to further zealous service. You have taken the oath of this office and received your papers. The officers and petty officers you have requested are assigned to you; the list is appended.

Her Imperial Majesty has also graciously ordered that from this day until your return to St. Petersburg, you and all the men under your command will be given double pay, in accordance with rank: to you, on the basis of the rank now granted; to your subalterns on the basis of the rank they will receive in Irkutsk. All will receive one year's pay in advance, plus a bonus of one year's pay to provide yourselves with travel necessities.

Our Most Gracious Sovereign has also generously ordered that when you reach Irkutsk, before you carry out the following instructions, you are to announce to all the officers and petty officers under your command that they have been promoted. Have them take the oath, except for those who will receive only monetary recognition. The list is appended.

After you have carried out your instructions regarding the Kolyma River, Her Imperial Majesty graciously orders you to declare yourself Captain of the fleet, Second Rank, and to take your oath.

You are to complete your assignments on the Kolyma River and along the Chukotsk coast and return to Okhotsk, where all preparations will have been made for your voyage to the coast of America. The moment you go aboard your ship you are to announce to all the men in your command that Her Imperial Majesty has promoted them in rank. Have the oath administered to yourself and to them, according to the above-mentioned list. Finally, when you reach Cape St. Elias, you are to declare yourself Captain of the First Rank.

Any of your subalterns who, according to their rank, fill the positions of any who die a natural or an accidental death, and who are breveted to the new rank either by you or by your successor, will be confirmed in that rank at the Admiralty College when they return to St. Petersburg, provided their Commander-in-Chief has given them a certificate of good behavior and zealous service. They will be accorded that rank from the day they were so appointed. This will hold for petty officers. Senior officers will likewise be advanced, in accordance with the order of advancement.

In case any member of the expedition should die or be disabled while along the Chukotsk coast or en route from Okhotsk to the coast of America, the following payments shall be made: half-pay shall go to a widow until she remarries or dies, and to children of a deceased man until they reach adulthood. Any man who is disabled will also receive half pay for life.

When you have carried out your assignment and have successfully returned to St. Petersburg, you and all the men under your command will receive the balance of double pay, according to rank achieved during the expedition. Further, each will be granted a year's double pay for the rank in which they return. Finally, you and all your subalterns who return safely will receive for life the single pay received during the expedition, in addition to any recompense for future services.

These gracious grants and promises of patronage, and most of all the importance of the assignment entrusted to you will inspire in you a noble zeal to execute it worthily. You must endeavor to do everything in your power to carry out the Articles of this instruction which Her Imperial Majesty has confirmed. You must set an example to all your subalterns by your own incessant efforts.

ARTICLE I.

For your information fourteen charts are appended; these were drawn up by previous navigators in the Arctic and Pacific oceans and along those coasts, and also by overland travelers. Also appended are short extracts from their journals. The plan for the ship which you presented for approval is herewith returned; you may use that plan to construct vessels at Okhotsk, if there are no vessels there suitable for your expedition. Also appended is a list of towns in Russia, and for some the latitude and longitude has been determined. There is also an example of the way in which you are to record the vocabularies of various peoples. You are also being given medals made especially for you to use with such peoples, according to instructions below.

A sum of 5,000 rubles is granted to you to use to buy beads, knives, other implements, small copper pots and other trifles as presents for the savages who want these things.

You are also given mathematical and astronomical instruments, in addition to others. You and all your Command are given a year's advance of double pay; you are also given the previously described bounty granted by Her Imperial Majesty for you and all your men. Distribute this and keep receipts in the official receipt book. Twenty of these books are given to you for this purpose from the Admiralty. You are also to keep records of all future receipts and expenditures.

When you have outfitted yourself with everything necessary for the journey, take all your men to Irkutsk via the shortest and best route. Exercise great care not to break your oath of secrecy in regard to your assignment. Do not exceed the 1724 ukaz in this regard;* a copy is appended for your reference. Do not on any account reveal to anyone matters pertaining to your expedition unless you are expressly ordered to do so. Further, you are especially ordered not to reveal to any person either this instruction or any other which you receive. You are to give all the men in your command the strictest possible orders in this regard.

If any important event happens to you during your travels, send notice to the Admiralty College by express; routine reports, however, are to be sent by post. From the day you leave St. Petersburg until the day your expedition ends you are to keep a very detailed journal; order your officers to do the same.

ARTICLE II.

When you reach Irkutsk you are to give [Ivan V.] Iakobii, Governor General of Irkutsk and Kolyvan, or if he is absent, the Vice Governor, Her Majesty's ukaz to him, and a copy of these instructions to you. The ukaz directs him to give you all possible assistance for the service of Her Majesty. The Governor is to give you directions for your journey to Iakutsk, Okhotsk, Gizhiginsk and the Kolyma River. He is also to provide you with an open [not secret] ukaz directing all officials and government officers of all places to which you or your men (to whom you must give instructions for travel) may journey to give you all necessary assistance in both manpower and in provisions and supplies. Further, Governor General Iakobii is instructed by Her Majesty to give you a second open ukaz so you may receive up to 10,000 rubles for unexpected and unusual expenses which may arise during your travels. This is for travel expense and for pay to any men you may employ in or near Irkutsk. You may draw as much of this sum as you need, whenever and wherever you judge best, but you and your most senior officer are to enter the amount in your books so you will know how much you have received and how much more is available. Whenever you draw funds have the payor endorse the ukaz indicating where, when and in what amount the funds have been paid.

---

*This reference is undoubtedly to secret instructions from Peter I to Bering, which scholars have to date been unable to locate.—Eds.

Expenses and a description of them are to be noted in the official book you received from the Admiralty. Keep all receipts. You are to receive supplies and provisions with the agreement of your subalterns. Note in the receipts you give both the quality and quantity of the goods you receive. On no account demand any unusual or unnecessary items, only those things mentioned above or others which are absolutely necessary to carry out Her Majesty's assignment. Do not spend money on unnecessary items, because you will be held responsible.

In Irkutsk, with the assistance of the Governor General, you are to provide yourself with everything necessary as quickly as possible, and have everything transported to its proper place. In order to forward materials you may detach senior and junior officers from your command to inspect, prepare and transport these stores to their proper destinations.

When you examine the Governor General's list [of supplies held in government depots], if you see that in the warehouses at Okhotsk there are not enough provisions and supplies necessary to arm and victual the ships you need for your expedition and for your overland travel to the Kolyma River and down the Chukotsk coast, then you are to request the Governor General to use every possible means to supply the warehouses with what you will need by the time you reach there. He may send an express order to the Commander of Okhotsk to supply you if he has such goods, or to halt the vessel that takes provisions to Gizhiginsk ostrog every June or July. Thus you could take that vessel to Gizhiginsk. And finally, the Commander of Okhotsk is to send orders to Petropavlovsk or to some preferred Kamchatka harbor to prepare enough dried fish, wild roots and vegetables for your voyages to the coast of America. There should also be ready at that harbor about twenty Kamchadal natives who are accustomed to life at sea and are skilled in hunting and fishing; these natives should accompany you on your voyage at the usual rate of pay.

At Irkutsk you may choose five or six of the best students of the Navigation School and take them with you to survey and make maps and charts. They are to remain with you until the end of the expedition, on the same basis as petty officers who go with you from St. Petersburg. The students who went with Captain [P. K.] Krenitsyn were paid 54 rubles per year. You may give your students a year's pay for their equipment.

From Irkutsk you are to take with you a naturalist, Mr. Patrin, who will remain with you until you return to St. Petersburg. He will describe all natural curiosities encountered during the expedition. He will receive specific instructions for what he is to do and how to describe various things. You are to assist him, upon his request, with men, instruments and money needed to carry out his orders. Allow him to stop to make observations if possible, and take him with you when you go off to distant places. If you think it necessary, you may draw from the Governor General at Irkutsk another year's double pay in advance for all your command, by the terms of the Imperial ukaz.

When you have received from the Governor General everything you need for the expedition and all possible information, and when you have carried out all your assignments in Irkutsk and carefully thought through your further travels, then without losing any time you are to take all in your command, excluding those detached to other duties, and proceed either by land or via the Lena River as you judge best, to Iakutsk, or to whatever place you think best for the purposes of the expedition. You are to follow the instructions of the Governor General, and you are also to send him reports of your progress. Include information on unforeseen problems en route to Okhotsk, Gizhiginsk and to the Kolyma River, so that if necessary he may send you instructions on how to proceed.

Finally, make it clear to the Governor General that he is to give the strictest orders throughout his region that absolutely no one but himself is to open letters and private reports sent by messenger. This happened during Captain Krenitsyn's expedition when the Okhotsk Commander Colonel Fedor Plenisner opened private mail on April 10, 1768, at Okhotsk.

It is especially important now in the eastern parts of the Russian Empire, particularly in the region beyond the Lena River, however far you travel by land or by sea, that you determine as accurately as possible the longitude and latitude of noteworthy places, also the variation of the compass. Make surveys and charts. Sketch identifiable coast profiles. Indicate bays, inlets and roadsteads. Mark advantageous sites for trade, fisheries and the like. Observe and describe the time, strength, rising, and irregularity of tides and currents. Make note of underwater rocks, shoals, and other hazards. Record prevailing, variable, and trade

The striking dancing masks of the Unalaska native as seen by Billings during his Russian expedition to the North Pacific convey a power felt to this day. The throwing darts are bone and stone tipped, propelled with great force from throwing boards. Sauer, *Billings' Expedition to Russia*. (OHS neg. 80233)

winds. Note the changes of weather. Describe meteors, especially the Aurora Borealis, and describe the condition of the electricity of the air during meteors and their influence on the compass. Finally, record changes in the barometer and the thermometer.

Mr. Patrin will have detailed instructions regarding his observations, but you are also to make observations, especially when he is absent. Observe the condition of the soil and of produce. Collect seeds, ripe fruits, dried plants, branches and wood samples from interesting trees, as well as samples of bark, resin and gum. Also collect sea weeds, zoophytes, shells, fish and amphibious creatures, insects, birds, and animals. Remove the skins of some and stuff them; preserve others in spirits. Also collect samples of various ores, fossils, rocks, salt, soil, and sulphur, and make careful note of where and when each sample was obtained.

In order to prevent your collections from being accidentally spoiled, you may leave them in places you judge proper, and then pick them up on your way back to St. Petersburg. If there is a commander in such place, give the collection to him and obtain a receipt. If the place is uninhabited, cache the collection in a safe place, secure from weather and destruction, or, preferably, send the collection, with your reports and descriptions, under seal, to the Governor General of Irkutsk.

You are also, if possible, to make descriptions and drawings of natural curiosities. Ascertain accurate information about the inhabitants of unknown places: their number, strength, customs, manners and occupations. Record vocabularies of their language, following the sample given to you. Try to express their own pronunciation as best you can, using both the Latin and Russian alphabets. Finally, procure if possible, or draw or describe the furs, garments, weapons and crafted items of these peoples.

ARTICLE III.

When you reach Iakutsk, immediately carry out any instructions from the Governor General in preparation for your journey on to Okhotsk. While you are there, use your blanket ukaz, which orders all commanders and local officials of towns on your route to give you all assistance you may require. Obtain from them abstracts of accounts from the archives of earlier navigators which may have information pertaining to your assignment on the Kolyma River and on the Chukchi coast. If you find information in these abstracts which is more complete than that communicated to you in St. Petersburg, have the documents copied if you need them. You may also have any maps or charts copied.

Wherever you use the blanket ukaz from the Governor General of Irkutsk, you may permit copies to be made of it, if necessary, by persons from whom you require assistance. Wherever you and the Governor General think it best, either at Iakutsk, Okhotsk, Gizhiginsk, or even at the Kolyma River ostrogs, you may select the necessary number of cossacks, soldiers, interpreters and guides. Give preference to hunters, persons who are experienced and reliable and those who have already been on the Kolyma. Choose soldiers who have been in the Anadyrsk garrison, who have been among the Chukchi and have been in their settlements around the Kolyma and the Arctic coast; some may even be Chukchi by birth. In the presence of the commander of the town you may either pay them or agree to pay them double the usual amount for persons hired to serve a term at sea in that region. They will receive pay from the time they enter under your command until you dismiss them at the end of the expedition, or until they die. Enter the terms of pay in the official book. In the name of Her Majesty you may promise volunteers that upon the successful conclusion of the expedition they will receive a bonus of one year's pay for their service.

In order to expedite matters, you may follow the precedent of Captain Krenitsyn who was sent to those seas in 1764; you may order, as he did in 1765, that in Iakutsk rope is to be tarred and provisions are to be packed in bags and cases, with no more than two and one-half puds in each. When the provisions are ready, send part of them off under the command of an officer to whom you have given instructions and everything necessary. Load each horse with no more than five puds because of the many bogs, rivers and mountains along the route. You may follow in the same way with the rest of the provisions, supplies and men. To prevent delays en route to Okhotsk, you may request the Commandant of Iakutsk to send orders by express to have everything ready for your journey.

ARTICLE IV.

When you have completely outfitted yourself at Iakutsk, make arrangements to complete the transport of provisions necessary to maintain your men during your journey to the Kolyma and the

Arctic coast. If you think it best to use cossacks for this, if possible choose those who have already been to that river or coast. Select them either at Okhotsk or at Gizhiginsk.

ARTICLE V.

Finally, so as to use your time to best advantage, try to reach Okhotsk close to the same time as your subalterns. There you may select the sailors and cossacks who will follow your expedition by land and by sea. You are also to choose two or three of the pilots at that port who are knowledgeable about those seas, and whose experience you feel will contribute to the success of your voyage. Upon your recommendation, they will have the same advantages as the rest of your men. Each of these men is to choose one of the students from the Okhotsk Navigation School as his assistant.

At Okhotsk you are to make all necessary preparations for your voyage, as detailed in Article X. In case none of the vessels in service there are safe enough for such a long voyage, you are to construct two ships of the requisite size and strength to serve your purpose and provide safety for the crew. You will command one of these vessels while you are along the coast of America; your second-in-command will have the other. Both the safety of the crew and the success of the sailing depend on having a second vessel accompany yours.

In order to enforce construction, orders are immediately being given to the Governor of Irkutsk that the best ship timber available near Okhotsk is to be prepared and all necessary equipment to fit out a ship of 80 feet in keel are to be prepared, as well as enough for a second smaller ship. The blanket ukaz from the Governor General of Irkutsk and Kolyvan will provide for this. Ask the Okhotsk Commandant for the carpenters you need, and all necessary assistance in building and fitting out the vessels. You may make one of your subalterns superintendent of the docks, along with your shipbuilder, so that construction may be done as quickly as possible and according to your plans. You are also to order at Okhotsk some stout posts [for markers] which you will erect on lands you discover. Stow these posts in your ship when you sail for America.

ARTICLE VI.

When the preparations for your travel are completed, and when you have obtained all relevant information and accounts from the archives in Okhotsk, then you are to proceed without delay to the Kolyma, via the most convenient route. You will take the naturalist Mr. Patrin with you, as well as the part of your command whom you will have chosen at Okhotsk. It will be best to travel with as little baggage as possible on board the vessel which sails every June or July with provisions for the garrison at Gizhiginsk. It is there that you will find the best cossacks and soldiers to go with you; some of them have previously been assigned to the garrison at Anadyrsk and have dealt with the Chukchi; indeed some of them have been born and traveled among them. Take these men and proceed over to the Omolon River, then go by raft down that river to the Kolyma. When you reach the Kolyma you are to make geographical and astronomical observations of the latitude and longitude of both the upper and lower Kolyma ostrogs, as well as of the mouth of the river. Make an accurate survey of it, and describe the soil and the inhabitants of the area near the river.

ARTICLE VII.

When you have determined the location of the Kolyma as accurately as possible, and have made a description of its course and the land through which it flows, then if circumstances permit you are to use shitiks [a sewn seagoing vessel], constructed as strong as possible, to proceed along the coast of the Chukotsk Peninsula from the mouth of the Kolyma to East Cape. However, if it is impossible to proceed in this manner, and if local information leads you to believe you can reach the cape by an overland route, you may then proceed by land to map these coasts, traveling in winter on the ice. It may be that you will discover lands or islands north of these coasts, and north of Bering Strait. If so, you may extend your travel and investigations by whatever means in your judgment are consonant with the safety of your men and the benefit of the service. Make an accurate chart indicating noteworthy places. Make views of the coast and drawings of unusual objects. Likewise try to get as much information as possible about the country from the Chukchi, and also about their strength and their customs. Whenever possible, do everything in your power to encourage these people to become subjects of Russia, and impress upon them the generous nature of this government.

ARTICLE VIII.

When you have expended all possible zeal to conclude your assignments along the Kolyma and along the coast of the Arctic Ocean, return to Okhotsk by the best route. There you are to complete the final preparations for your voyage in the Pacific Ocean. You will take command of the men and of the ships which have been built or selected for the expedition. Give all necessary helmsmen and sailors, instruments, provisions and other necessary supplies to the officer who will command the second ship. He is to follow your orders, signals and instructions implicitly.

ARTICLE IX.

If perchance the ships are not ready, while you are waiting for them to be completed you may use this time and employ your abilities to make useful discoveries in the sea between the Kuril Islands, Japan, China and even Korea. Do everything possible to perfect the charts of these almost unknown parts. For this purpose you may use any of the government packet boats or galiots at Okhotsk which best suits your purpose; and you may use a detachment of your men. However do not let this secondary assignment make you lose sight of the prime object of the expedition, which you are to endeavor to carry out implicitly.

ARTICLE X.

When your ships are completely loaded, armed and provisioned at Okhotsk, you are to proceed, with your second vessel and also with ships of any merchants who wish to join the convoy, and set out at the best time for rounding the tip of Kamchatka. Stop at the port of Petropavlovsk or at Kamchatka [ostrog], wherever the provisions outlined in Article II can be taken on. Distribute these to both ships, and also divide up the Kamchadal natives who have been ordered to be ready there. Then continue your voyage and survey the entire chain of known islands extending to America, and also try to discover new ones.

One of your most important duties is to draw up an accurate chart of these islands. Take frequent observations to determine their location. Continue your surveys right up to the coast of

America in order to acquire knowledge of the best harbors and roadsteads. Take special note of the islands least frequented and least well-known, which lie along the coast and south of it, east of the island of Unimak and of the Alaska peninsula. These will include islands such as Sanajak, Kodiak, Lesnoi and the islands of Shumagin and Tumanoi which Bering and others also sighted.

While you are at sea, if you meet other ships under the English, French or some other European flag, you are to behave in a friendly manner and not cause any disputes.

ARTICLE XI.

After you have spent the summer pursuing these questions, when autumn storms begin you may search for an appropriate harbor, either on the American coast, on the islands in the North Pacific, or on Kamchatka, where you may spend the winter and rest your men. You may recommence your work when the season of good weather returns.

ARTICLE XII.

When Bering sailed toward America he made certain observations which were later confirmed by the English captains [C.] Clerke and [J.] Gore when they returned from the Sandwich Islands to Kamchatka. These observations lead one to suppose there are islands south of those known to be in the archipelago, and east of the Kamchatka meridian, between 40° and 50° northern latitude. Either on your outward or return voyage you may try to discover these unknown islands, and to obtain information about them for the purpose of the Kamchatka trade. However, you are not to spend too much time on these uncertain assignments.

ARTICLE XIII.

You are also authorized to make inquiries about any parts of the American continent which previous navigators could not survey because of bad weather. Try most of all to find the best harbors, since these may eventually serve to open the fur trade with the native inhabitants. Wherever you go try to obtain knowledge of the various goods produced on the mainland and on the islands, as outlined in Article II.

Article XIV.

For this reason you are to give Mr. Patrin full liberty whenever he wishes, and provide him with all necessary assistance and with opportunities to carry out his assignments. Leave him ashore for as long as possible in those places he thinks worthy of study. The observations, descriptions and collections which he will make at such times are to be at his disposal until you reach St. Petersburg, and he is to travel there with you to deliver these things in person.

Mr. Patrin is to be able to take advantage of the same opportunities you have to investigate matters for your reports. He will give you extracts of his observations and his conclusions, to be written in whichever language he can best express himself. If through accident or illness Mr. Patrin is unable to take care of his research materials you are to care for his manuscripts and collections, keeping them sealed in the best possible condition until he recovers, or if necessary until you return.

Article XV.

All coasts and islands, inhabited or not, of which you are indisputably the first discoverer, and which are not subject to any European power, you are to claim, with the consent of any inhabitants. Take possession of all places, harbors and other sites you think advantageous, in the name of Her Imperial Majesty, the Sovereign of all the Russias, in the manner described in the following Article.

Article XVI.

When you bring newly discovered and independent lands and peoples under Russian suzerainty you are to observe the following instructions. Since such people have probably never been abused by any Europeans, your first responsibility is to see to it that they have a favorable opinion of the Russians. When you discover such a coast or island or promontory you are to send one or two baidaras, with armed men, under the command of an experienced helmsman. Send interpreters and small gifts with them. Have them look for a harbor or bay where vessels may safely be anchored, then take soundings and proceed into these. However if no harbor is to be found, then send baidaras or boats with part of your men ashore to see if there are inhabitants, forests, animals etc. They are not all to put ashore together. A guard is to remain with the boats, and those who go ashore are to stay together, not to spread out.

If there are inhabitants, your men are to communicate with them through interpreters, but such persons are never to be sent ashore alone. They are always to be accompanied by men who are armed either secretly or openly. It has happened in the past that savages have killed interpreters or taken them prisoner, which is a great loss to the explorers.

The interpreter is to speak to them of your friendly intentions. To prove this, he is to allow them to choose presents, and invite them in a friendly manner to accept these gifts. He is to invite the chieftains on board the ships. To flatter these chieftains, they may be given medals to hang around their necks; you have been provided such medals for this purpose. Tell the savages that these medals are tokens of eternal friendship of the Russians. Ask them for tokens in return, and accept whatever they choose to give you. Persuade them to tell all their fellow inhabitants that the Russians wish to be their friends. Learn their [tribal] name and its origin or meaning. Discover whether their population is large, especially in men. Ask about their religion and their idols, and be careful that none of your men go near these idols or destroy them. Find out about their food and their crafts, where and how they travel, the names of the places they frequent and what their compass locations are, and whether these places are islands or on the mainland. When they point directions with their hands, observe secretly but accurately the compass directions and note in your journal how far distant these places are. If you do not understand their terms of measurement, ask how many days it takes to travel to these places, so that if you find it necessary to travel there by land or by sea, you will know how to set your course.

Ask if there are large bays on any of the islands or on the coast, and whether large ships with one or two or three masts and sails go there, or go to their own islands or those nearby, or to the coasts. If you see that they have any article of European or Asian workmanship, ask them how they came by it. Make all necessary observations so you can describe the place, and ask their permission to come ashore often. Learn how they greet one another, and greet them in that way when you meet.

When they come to like you because of your generosity and friendship, if you are certain they are not subject to any European power, tell them you wish to find other friends like them. Ask them to let you erect some mark on a high place on shore, as your friends in other places do, so you will be able to find again this place where the friends of the Russians live. This should be done in accordance with your own customary ceremonies. When they give permission for this, order that one of the posts you have had prepared at Okhotsk be marked with the arms of Russia and that letters be cut into it indicating the date of discovery, a brief account of the native people and of their voluntary submission to Russian suzerainty. State that this has been done by your efforts during the glorious reign of Catherine II, the Great.

If the islands and lands you discover have no name, you are authorized to name them. When the post is ready, let the inhabitants know that you are coming ashore to establish your mark, and do this with proper ceremony and caution. Afterward give the inhabitants small things of which they are fond. Give medals to the chieftains so they can hang them about their necks. Finally, persuade the inhabitants that if they elect to continue being friends of the Russians they are never to permit their own people or any others to remove or efface this marker. They are to preserve it whole, as well as the medals about their necks.

Such ceremonial proceedings are always effective with savages, and conquests made by these means are always the most enduring.

Article XVII.

As you survey the islands, coasts and promontories under Russian subjection, in additon to obtaining the above information, you are to ascertain as accurately as possible the number of male inhabitants so you can begin to collect iasak from them. However, you are forbidden to use force in this regard, or even to avenge savage acts. On the contrary, do not kill them unless it is absolutely necessary, even if they attack you boldly, as islanders on Akutan, Umnak, Unalga, Akun and others have often done to Russian promyshlenniks, without any provocation. In such cases have your interpreters remonstrate with them. Tell them it is quite unreasonable to attack persons who wish to be friendly.

Promise them small presents, and give these to them. But order all your men to show their force from a distance, in order to frighten them but prevent bloodshed, which is sometimes almost unavoidable.

Explain to them that if they will not heed your kindly behavior toward them, you have frightful weapons which will kill masses of them all at one time, and that if they are not peaceful you will be obliged to use these weapons. The only reason they may be belligerent and unfriendly toward Europeans is that they are very fearful and overly cautious. This is very often the fault of the explorers, for they attack these people with fire and sword and cause them to despair, whereas on the other hand humane and amicable behavior keeps them peaceful. You are, therefore, strongly urged to proceed gently with them. Do not change your ways unless open and unavoidable danger force you to shed blood. However, you must be constantly on the alert.

Use your weapons only to frighten them, not [to] kill them. Try to take one of them alive. When you have a prisoner, you may be very kind to him, give him presents, hang a medal about his neck and explain to him that in this way you are making him your friend, and you will recognize him when he comes to you in the future. Do not keep him prisoner any longer than necessary. When you release him give him goods and persuade him to tell his fellow inhabitants of your kindness to him. Allow him to return to the ship with anyone he pleases, without fear. Promise him, if he will come, animal traps or anything else he wishes. Persuade him he will be recieved in a friendly manner by all your men if he displays the medal around his neck.

When he brings other natives to your ship, have the interpreters tell them that the same guns which terrified them so much will be turned into harmless thunder if they choose, and will serve as an expression of joy over the return of friends.

Then give them their favorite presents. Give them brandy, sugar or tobacco, which most of them like very much. Give them traps and guns, small copper kettles, knives, needles and nets, and explain how to use them. Ask them to bring you furs, animal fat, fish or whatever they have. Also tell them that when others [Russians] come with goods, they will give the natives what they wish. Once you have made them want to visit you, you will have laid the foundation for collecting iasak. Make them eager to trade and to hunt assiduously and to have a friendly relationship with you. You will thus carry out a prime part of your assignment, to the glory of Her Imperial Majesty, and to your own honor.

ARTICLE XVIII.

As you sail along these islands, coasts and promontories which you are to describe, when you reach Cape St. Elias you may declare yourself Captain, First Rank, in the name of Her Imperial Majesty. After you have made the same observations on this cape as in other places, and are on your return voyage, if when you are near Unimak Island or the point of Alaska and encounter weather which marks the approach of winter and makes it inadvisable to continue your voyage, you may look for a suitable place to winter over, either on Unalaska or Unimak island. On Unalaska you may anchor in the bay Captain Lieutenant [M. D.] Levashev named St. Paul's Harbor; on Unimak, in the sound opposite Alaska, a verst and a half distant from Alaska. If these anchorages are not appropriate, go into any of the bays on the Alaska coast, either east or west, where Captain Krenitsyn reported many fine bays within 150 versts.

Choose a safe and suitable wintering place and immediately set about building one or more habitations. Take every precaution against scurvy so you will not suffer as Captain Krenitsyn did when he wintered there. He lost some 60 men to this disease, and he himself was so ill that if Captain Lieutenant Levashev had not come to his assistance with his men, Krenitsyn would not have had enough men to handle his ship.

To protect yourselves you may take guns and ammunition. The island natives have made fierce attacks against Russian promyshlenniks, and also against Captain Krenitsyn when he spent the winter on Unimak. You must be as cautious as Krenitsyn was, especially against night attacks. He had four guard posts manned every night and ordered guns and small arms to be fired at stipulated times, every few minutes, to frighten the savages; but more than once they tried to kill the guards and all the men.

For your safety you must also attempt to persuade the American chieftains to give you some of their children as hostages. You may use kindly ways and presents to this end. Behave in a friendly manner toward them, but do not take too many hostages, for they could become a burden to you, especially if your provisions should run short. It is true that their own parents generally bring them food, but if there is a delay you will have to feed them from your own supply.

Be certain to warn any of your men who have recent wounds or any intestinal disorder or who have at any time had a venereal disease not to eat whale meat. Captain Krenitsyn reported in his journal that if such persons do eat whale meat, wounds will re-open and there will be a recurrence of the venereal disease within three days.

While you are on the island of Unalaska, try to make a more complete description of the natives. Inquire of them where they originated and why they call themselves Kogolach, as those on Umnak call themselves Kigigoos and those on Alaska are called Kartagaeguk. The pilot [Mikhail] Nevodchikov started calling them Aleuts, using the name of islands near Kamchatka. Also, while you are on Unimak, observe (out of curiosity) whether the wooden cross with a copper crucifix set in it which Captain Krenitsyn set up near his winter quarters is still standing. If so, look for a paper he left in a slit in the cross; the paper may help you in your dealings with the island people.

Article XIX.

If you find it necessary to repair your ship en route, or if you have an accident which makes it impossible for your ship to continue sailing, you are to go aboard the ship commanded by your second-in-command [Lieutenant G. A. Sarychev]. You are to take command yourself and continue your voyage and your observations in it. Likewise, if the second ship encounters such problems, take your second-in-command and his men aboard your ship. For this reason, the officer in command of the second ship is never to separate from you or lag behind, except for a very small distance, unless you give him express orders to the contrary. If he should become separated from you in a storm, he is to make every effort to rejoin you as quickly as possible. For greater safety you are to set frequent rendezvous points so that in case you do become separated you may more easily rejoin. You are to decide upon signals, both day and night, to be used for various accidents that may occur during the voyage. If you are unable to perform your duties because of illness or any other reason, your second is to take command and carry out your instructions, signed by you, which you will give him when you set sail from Okhotsk.

ARTICLE XX.

It often happens in those waters that heavy fogs move in during the month of October, when it is almost impossible to sail without danger of becoming lost. This happened to all the ships in 1767 during Captain Krenitsyn's expedition, especially to the one commanded by the pilot Duding. His ship was wrecked on the seventh Kuril island, Siashkuta, and not only the ship was lost, but most of the crew as well. Therefore you must watch carefully, especially in unfamiliar places, so that no misfortune befalls either the ship or yourself, for this would be a loss to the Treasury and a setback to Her Majesty's plans.

ARTICLE XXI.

You are to conduct yourself in Her Imperial Majesty's service as a reliable and experienced officer. You and your subalterns are to do your best to be worthy of the largesse she has given you, and that which she has promised for the future. For this reason you are to give clear and articulate directions to your subalterns when you send them on separate assignments. These instructions should be in accord with those given to you. They are to be held responsible, as you are, for any misfeasance or malfeasance of these instructions, whether deliberate or accidental.

ARTICLE XXII.

Once you have concluded your survey of the islands, if it is not a favorable time of the year and if the condition of your men, ships and provisions make it possible to spend another year in those seas, you are to set your course directly for Bering Strait in order to complete your knowledge of the Chukotsk coast. Try to sail to Chaunskaia Bay or to the Kolyma River, if you have not previously acquired such complete information that a further voyage is unnecessary.

If you find it is not practical to take large vessels to the Kolyma, you are to complete your work in the Pacific Ocean and along the coast of America and reach an anchorage on the Chukotsk coast. If it seems promising, land the necessary number of men and instruments there and give orders to the commanding officer who is to remain with the ships as to how long he is to wait for you (if indeed you feel it is advisable to have the ships remain). After that time they are to return to Kamchatka or Okhotsk where they will wait for your further orders.

If the sea is clear of ice along the coast, you may take some small boats from the ships, but be certain to leave some with the ships. Or you may build baidaras there from previously prepared materials. Using these you may proceed by land and by water and attempt to reach the Kolyma River. Map your route and make all possible observations in order to complete those things not yet mapped.

However if after these northern attempts you return in your frigates to Kamchatka or Okhotsk, you are to try to make your return voyage as useful to geography as possible by sailing along the coast around the bay of the Anadyr, and by touching on any islands you could not include in your outward voyage.

Article XXIII.

When you reach Kamchatka and then proceed on to Okhotsk, you will dismiss the helmsmen, cossacks, interpreters and Kamchadals so they may return to their own posts and homes within the government of Irkutsk. With each man send a written certificate of his conduct and your recommendations for what he deserves.

At that time you will also hand over your ships, supplies, ammunition and any remaining provisions to the Commander of Okhotsk, obtaining a receipt. If you can spare any instruments without detriment to your further investigations, you may also leave those in Okhotsk, obtaining a receipt, so they may be used in navigation there.

Article XXIV.

When you have completed the main part of your expedition, assemble the men who are to return to St. Petersburg with you and prepare to return without delay. Choose your return route with a view to adding to geographical knowledge of various parts of Siberia. You may wish to send some of your men on a different route from your own. They should take all necessary instruments with them. They might proceed up the Vilui River with Mr. Patrin, and from there via the Lower or Stony Tunguska rivers to the Enisei in order to survey unexplored places of interest in those areas. It would be advantageous if they could obtain some knowledge of the northernmost part of Siberia between the Olenek and Enisei rivers, on the Taimyr Peninsula north of the Khatanga Gulf.

If you have the opportunity to do so, you should determine or correct the longitude and latitude of interesting places not given in the appended list. Be certain to survey all rivers of interest.

ARTICLE XXV.

To conclude this instruction, which has been approved by Her Imperial Majesty, in order that your zeal be fully encouraged, Her Imperial Majesty has graciously ordered that you be entrusted with an important privilege. You may make changes in the orders contained within these Articles, depending on your best judgment and the circumstances you encounter, with the consent of your officers. This is primarily to be done, however, in order that clear advantages will accrue to the expedition, to the service and to the Empire. This great trust will inspire you to emulate nobly other great men who have had the honor to be employed in such a capacity as you, and will encourage you to devote all your energies so you can commence this important assignment with zeal, carry it out with good judgment and conclude it with honor.

ADDITIONAL ARTICLE

To the Instructions for Captain Lieutenant Billings.

On the map, opposite the Kolyma River and north of Bear Islands, the coast is shown extending out as a continuation of the American mainland. This is taken from a map Governor [D. I.] Chicherin sent in 1764. From the last of the Bear Islands, Sergeant Andreev saw, far in the distance, what was supposed to be a large island. They proceeded toward it over the ice on dogsleds, but stopped 20 versts from it. They found fresh footprints indicating that a great number of people had been along there using reindeer-drawn sleds. Since [the Russians] were few in number, they returned to the Kolyma.

We have not had any word of this large island or continent since that time; therefore it is deemed essential that you investigate this. You will be on the Kolyma River, not far from there, and it would be useful if you could survey and describe this land, or at least make closer observations of it. Determine whether it is an island or part of the American continent. If it is inhabited, how many persons are there? In general, make all the inquiries you would make for a newly discovered land. However, this is merely a recommendation, and must not interfere with your primary assignment.

See: Martin Sauer. *An Account of a Geographical and Astronomical Expedition to the Northern Parts of Russia* . . . (London: 1802), Appendix V, [29–49]. We have adapted this account into modern English. Martin Sauer was the official Secretary to the Billings-Sarychev Expedition.

48

1785

INSTRUCTIONS FROM PETER SIMON PALLAS, MEMBER OF THE ACAD-
EMY OF SCIENCES, FOR THE NATURALIST ON THE BILLINGS-SARYCHEV
EXPEDITION [1785–94].

I nstructions for the naturalist, Mr. Patrin,* who is to accompany the Expedition destined for the Kolyma River and the
Arctic Ocean.

Her Imperial Majesty has graciously appointed you to the
position of naturalist on the voyage of discovery which is about to
commence under the command of Captain Lieutenant [Joseph]
Billings and will proceed to the Kolyma River and to the Pacific
and Arctic oceans. You are to exercise all the zeal concomitant
with your honor and devotion to your special sciences and your
service to Her Imperial Majesty. This is all the more important
since Her Imperial Majesty has graciously advanced you one rank
above that which you now hold in the mining division in order to
encourage you. This will take effect on the day you join the expedition. You will also be given a sum of rubles to cover the cost of
your equipment and you will receive double pay during the expedition. You will have many opportunities to make discoveries and
perform services, and this will bring you further favor from Her
Imperial Majesty.

In order to give you a full understanding of your duties, Her
Imperial Majesty has graciously approved the following articles,
which comprise your instructions.

ARTICLE I.

When Captain Lieutenant Billings reaches Irkutsk, you will
advance from your present service into the expedition under his
command. You will continue with the expedition until its conclusion, and return with it to St. Petersburg. There you will hand
over your journals, observations and collections, including all

---

*Patrin became seriously ill in Siberia and never actually joined the expe-
dition. His place was taken by a German physician, Dr. Carl Heinrich
Merck, who was working at the hospital in Irkutsk when Billings halted
there.

specimens of natural history you have gathered. These will be given to the department Her Imperial Majesty will name to receive them.

ARTICLE II.

You are to accompany the Commander of the expedition on all overland journeys and sea voyages beyond the Lena River. You are to follow carefully all instructions as set forth herein, especially in those parts of Siberia as well as various coasts and islands which have never been explored by naturalists. This includes the banks of the Kolyma River, the coastline of the Arctic and Pacific oceans and Kamchatka and the various islands you will visit. You are to keep a detailed journal of the voyage, along with a topographical description of the lands you explore, including rivers, lakes and mountains. Include descriptions of the three realms of nature and of the inhabitants. You are also to make meteorological observations and descriptions of unique aspects of the lands you visit, using the most accurate information you can obtain.

ARTICLE III.

You are to pay particular attention to describing the extent, direction and interconnections of the mountain ranges. Describe their shapes, surfaces, declivities and heights, their rocks and soil, strata, and the directions in which the strata lie. Include descriptions of any craters, inactive volcanoes and all active volcanoes. Collect specimens of all sorts of rocks, soils, petrified material, lava, fossils, animal skeletons, minerals, salts and sulfurs. Number specimens carefully, making note of precisely where they were taken. Also collect any interesting stones and pebbles brought down by rivers or cast up by the sea, as well as any that are being used by the inhabitants.

Describe the surface of the country, any irregularities, the layers of soil at various depths. Mention whether the land is low or high. Describe forests and undergrowth, animals, birds, marshes, lakes, large and small rivers and the quality of the waters, any fish to be found in them, and every other interesting fact.

ARTICLE IV.

With regard to the people you encounter, observe their dispositions and physical makeup. Describe their manner of govern-

This fine drawing of a man and woman from Unalaska provides some of the knowledge Empress Catherine the Great and the Academy of Sciences were hungry for. The Billings-Sarychev Expedition carried precise instructions for ethnographic studies coveted by the Academicians. Sauer, *Billings' Expedition to Russia*. (OHS neg. 80262)

ment, their customs, crafts, ceremonies and religious superstitions. Observe their traditions, education, how they treat their women. Describe useful plants, medicines, dyes, food and manner of preparing it, dwellings, utensils, means of travel. Make notes on their way of life, how they hunt, fish, make war, whether they have domesticated any animals. In regard to languages, you are to collect vocabularies, using the example sent with the expedition. Mark pronunciation using Latin spelling. Try to obtain examples of their garments, ornaments, utensils, and weapons; if that is not possible, make drawings of them. Also describe burial places and any monuments.

Article V.

Pay special attention to trees, shrubs and land and aquatic plants. Preserve as many specimens as possible, especially of any that are unusual or new. Use your leisure time making complete descriptions of these. Note when they grow, flower and ripen. Lose no opportunity to make detailed notes of everything which may be useful to society, either as food for people or forage for animals or as medicines. Investigate how they prepare dyes and pelts. Collect specimens of wood, bark, gum, resin, seeds, bulbs, and roots. Also, collect things that may be raised in European gardens, and make note both of their scientific and local names.

Article VI.

Collect all interesting quadrupeds, birds, fish, amphibious animals, insects, shellfish, and zoophytes, and have them either stuffed or preserved. Observe carefully their habits, food, manner of propagation, the sounds they make, their migrations, their habitations, how they are caught, and gather information on any equipment used for trapping and techniques used. Collect examples of eggs of as many species of birds as possible. Animals and birds of both sexes and various ages are to be stuffed. Fish, amphibious animals, and zoophytes are to be preserved in spirits. Insects, shells, and skeletons are to be carefully packed in special cases.

Article VII.

Pay most careful attention to meteorological observations, especially those done with thermometer and barometer, and particularly in places where you winter over or spend any period of time. Make tables from these observations in the standard way. Note any phenomena such as parhelia, Aurora Borealis and the circumstances surrounding them. Observe the action of mercury in different temperatures of both natural and artificial cold. Use the spirit thermometer to determine the actual temperature of congelation. Establish the height of mountains by using barometrical heights.

The Commander will observe predominant and variable winds, changes and directions of tides, currents and other nautical matters, but you also are to make any observations you can, and note them in your journal.

Article VIII.

Gather information on all illnesses, both endemic and epidemic, which occur in specific latitudes or among certain peoples. Observe ailments of domestic animals and of horned cattle, and the remedies used to treat or prevent these ailments.

Article IX.

Use great care in preserving specimens you collect. Number them, keep a catalog of the places where each was found, along with descriptions and any other information. Instead, you may write this information on the label of each specimen. Stuffed birds and animals are to be dried carefully and smoked with sulfur before they are packed up. Boxes or packets are also to be smoked. Cases are to be covered first with pitch and then with hide. Pay particular attention to items vulnerable to insects or dampness.

When the Commander makes his reports, you are also to send in your observations and any collections that are convenient to send. Other collections are to be kept with you until you return to St. Petersburg.

Article X.

You may obtain from the Commander of the expedition all assistance of men, horses, instruments and money which you need for your assignment. When you are not needed, you may make excursions into nearby country, with the consent of the Commander, where you hope to find objects worthy of study, or interesting historical material. The Commander of the expedition is to render you every possible assistance for this purpose, and you may take a draftsman with you if he is not needed for other important business.

See: Martin Sauer. *An Account of a Geographical and Astronomical Expedition to the Northern Parts of Russia* . . . (London: 1802), Appendix VI, [50–54]. We have adapted this account into modern English.

49

THE ACCOUNT OF THE VOYAGE OF GRIGORII I. SHELIKHOV AND HIS
WIFE, NATALIA SHELIKHOVA, FROM OKHOTSK TO THE COAST OF
NORTHWEST AMERICA AND RETURN, INCLUDING A DESCRIPTION OF
ISLANDS AND NATIVE PEOPLES ENCOUNTERED

In the year 1783 the [Shelikhov-Golikov] company had three galiots built at the port of Okhotsk: the *Tri Sviatitelia*, *Sv. Simeon Bogopriemets i Anna Propochitnaia* and the *Sv. Mikhail*. With a crew of 192 men we thus set out for the Pacific Ocean on August 16, 1783, from the mouth of the Urak River which empties into the Sea of Okhotsk. I was aboard the first galiot with my wife [Natalia Alekseevna], who always went everywhere with me and was never daunted by any hardships. I gave instructions that in case the ships became separated because of head winds, we would rendezvous on Bering Island. We overcame various problems which made sailing difficult, and on August 31 reached the first of the Kuril Islands [Shumsha], but head winds prevented us from anchoring there until September 2. On that date we did anchor, went onto the island and took on fresh water. On September 3 we were able to continue on our way and on September 12 we ran into a storm which lasted two days. At that time the three galiots became separated. The storm was so bad that we almost despaired of our lives, but on the 14th the first two galiots met and on September 24 we anchored on Bering Island.

We decided to spend the winter there waiting for the third galiot which was carrying 62 men. However there were such bad winds while we were on Bering Island that we could not wait for it. On September 25 I sent several men from both ships, aboard baidaras which we had brought with us, to reconnoitre the island perimeter, being curious as to whether they would find anything worthy of investigating. The men whom I sent returned on the 27th without having found anything.

We did not hunt on that island all during the winter, except for a few foxes, because there were no other animals there. Food which is available on that island consists of all kinds of ocean fish and the meat from marine animals such as sea lions, fur seals and seal. Birds are there, too, including geese, ducks, swans, mergan-

This scene inside an Unalaska earth-covered dwelling depicts the natives scarcely affected by contact with the Russians and others; a situation soon to change. Cook, *Atlas*, 1789. (OHS neg. 80245)

sers, seagulls, murres and partridge. Edible roots include dog cabbage and sarana. The winter wore on; there were more strong northeasterly winds and snow and blizzards were almost daily occurrences.

Because we could not prevent scurvy, we had to find ways to cure it. For this reason during blizzards we walked along the sea, and on clear days we went into the mountains on skis, going into more distant regions.

Using observations made there we found the declination of the magnetic needle to be 1¼ rhumbs East.

We left the island on June 16, 1784. In the event that we again became separated, I designated the Island of Unalaska, one of the islands in the Fox Island group, as the rendezvous. In order to let the third boat, which had previously become separated from the first two, know of the new meeting place so it could proceed there from Bering Island, I left a written message. We sailed until June 19 without excessive wind. Occasionally there was a head wind, but we sailed quite calmly. On the 19th there was a dense fog and we lost sight of the galiot *Sv. Simeon*. On the 20th our own ship anchored on Copper Island. We took on fresh water, obtained fur seal meat, and then on the 23rd set out again. On July 6 we passed Atkha Island, one of the Andreanovskii group, and on the 7th, Amla. On the 8th and 9th we sighted the islands of Siugam and Amukhta, and later, Chetyrie Sopochnye [Unigun]. On the 10th we sailed through the strait by Chetyrie Sopochnye, which runs south to north. On July 12, a short distance north of the islands we met up with the galiot *Sv. Simeon*. We continued our voyage and on the 13th passed the island of Unalaska and entered Natykinsk Bay. On the 14th we led the galiots into Captain's Harbor [named for Captain Mikhail Levashev], where we reefed the sails, took on all necessary items and remained until the 22nd.

In sailing past these islands we could only observe that the entire Aleutian chain, from Bering Island to the island of Kyktak, about which I will have more to say, consists of high rocky mountains, among which there are many active volcanoes. There are no standing forests; in some places rose willow, alder and mountain ash grow on the rocks. The inhabitants pick up driftwood along the shore to use for firewood and for building purposes.

I had made all necessary preparations while we were on the island of Unalaska, so without waiting for the third galiot on July 22 I took two interpreters and ten Aleut men, who were all willing to serve, and we set out again on our voyage. I left instructions for the *Sv. Mikhail* to anchor at the island of Kyktak, also called Kodiak, which had been designated as the group meeting place. We sailed from the northern part of the Fox Island chain to the southern part, through the strait between the islands of Unimak and Akun. The strait poses no problem for navigation because it is clear, wide and free of hazards, except during the high and low tides when there is a very strong current.

On August 3 we went to Kyktak Island, and on the southern side led the galiots into harbor and anchored. On August 4 we sent the working crews in on two baidaras fastened together, to ascertain whether there were any inhabitants on the island. That same day two baidaras returned and reported they had not seen any islanders. Soon after that the two baidaras sent one back to the harbor with the news that they had encountered a number of inhabitants. The other baidara returned later, bringing aboard one of the island inhabitants.

I did my best to put him at ease, gave him some presents, talked with him, and the next day sent him back. He later returned and lived with us until we went back. He guided us in all our forays, and not only would he not permit even the slightest treason, but he also warned other ill-intentioned islanders not to try to kill us. We could see from their actions that they were plotting some evil, which will be enlarged upon later. The third day after we arrived at this island three of the Koniag people our men had seen came to us in three baidaras. We received them aboard the ship with all signs of friendship and amicability, and gave them some things they wanted in exchange for a few furs. During their visit to us on August 5, at 2:00 in the afternoon there commenced an eclipse of the sun which lasted for an hour and a half. The Koniags, like other people who do not have the slightest idea of the cause of this phenomenon, were profoundly astonished, but nothing out of the ordinary took place.

On August 7 once again I sent out workmen, in four baidaras, to survey animal habitats and more particularly to survey the island itself. I instructed them to encircle the island as far as they could. On August 9 they sighted a multitude of savages about 40 versts from the harbor; these savages had gathered together on a big cliff which was inaccessible from the sea. They were on a huge rock which is about five sazhens high on one side and more than seven sazhens high on the other side. The men I sent there tried to talk with the savages so they would receive us in a friendly manner, but the savages paid no attention and threatened us, shouting to us that we must leave their shores if we wanted to remain alive. No one was bold enough to sail past them.

When I learned of this I immediately set out from there with my workers and tried to persuade them to abandon any resistance, but instead to work for a friendly relationship, reassuring the savages that we had not come to cause discord or to oppress them, but that in order to have friendly relations with them we had to have their friendly cooperation. As evidence of this I promised that to the best of my ability I would provide them with gifts which they would find desirable. There was a great multitude of them, at least 4,000. They did not look favorably on my words and began to use their bows and arrows to shoot at us. I had to retreat, very fearful because I did not know how this trouble would end. However, I saw their determined attack against us and realized that they wanted us to leave their shore and that they would kill us if we did not. I tried to take all the precautions I could.

At midnight on August 12, the time when the workers were changing sentries, the savages left the rock and attacked us en masse with such ferocity it was possible to see that they would carry out their intention; this would not have been difficult if we had been less wary and more timid. We were emboldened by facing death and so defended ourselves with our weapons and forced them into flight. The struggle went on for a quarter of an hour. When the sun rose we did not see a single man, not even one dead warrior, because they had carried off all their dead with them. We were very fortunate in the fact that not one of our men was killed or wounded, which I attributed to God's benevolence.

Soon after that a [native] deserter came to us. He was a member of the Tagagut tribe, whom the Russians call the Fox Aleuts; he had been a prisoner of the Koniags. From him we learned that the next day, as had also been the case the previous days, the Koniags were expecting assistance from large numbers of other warriors from the settlements of Iliuk, Ugashik, Ugaatak and Chinigak and many other places, all of whom would meet at the same gathering place on the rock. They intended to join forces and attack us there and also attack our vessel in the harbor and destroy everything. They were not daunted by their earlier failure; on the contrary it served to embolden them. They agreed that if any of us were still alive they would distribute us among them as slaves and divide up our possessions. Since they consider the boards from the ships as very precious items, they wanted these also.

We immediately realized the danger these ferocious savages posed to us and resolved to forestall their plot. We decided to seize control of the rock where they had fortified themselves before their reinforcements could reach them. But all this time the Koniags kept making forays against us. To counter this, although we were fewer in number, I had to take all my men to attack their stronghold in order to drive them off. To accomplish this we approached using our firearms, but this was not effective. They attacked fiercely with bows and arrows, which forced me to resort to firing the five two-pound cannons I had brought with me. I ordered that these be trained on the rocky points and their huts, so that the consequent destruction would strike terror into these people who have never seen such weapons.

This experience which was new and extraordinary for them quickly instilled fear and terror in them and gave them an awesome impression of us. They fled from their stronghold, relinquishing it to us; we had no fatalities and only five men were wounded, severely but not mortally. Although I tried to avoid bloodshed, it is nonetheless necessary to assume that a number of the natives were killed. I tried to learn about this, but could not because they carried off their dead on one side and from the other side, hurled them into the sea. We took more than 1,000 Koniag men prisoner. The rest, at least 3,000, fled. We brought more than 400 prisoners to the harbor and released the rest. I selected one leader from the prisoners, who in the Koniag language is called *khaskak* [elder], and put him in charge of all the other prisoners. I gave them baidaras, baidarkas, nets and every other necessity, but kept 20 young men as hostages to ensure the loyal behavior of the others.

The prisoners wanted to live within fifteen versts of the harbor, which I permitted. For a time they proved loyal. From them we learned that we would not have been able to avoid extreme danger, or indeed total massacre, from the great multitude of savages whom the Koniags awaited from other settlements, who had already drawn near the settlement, if it had not been that the natives who ran off from the encounter had related a more horrifying account [of us] than was actually the case. They believed we had completely destroyed the rock and their dwellings with our firearms. They were so intimidated that they had immediately dispersed.

Shortly after this, however, the natives, including the prisoners I had settled, made another attack one night during a wind and rain storm. They assembled in a great multitude and made a fierce attack using lances and arrows against the baidaras which had been left in Ugatak Bay. We managed to repulse them with guns. I do not know how many of them were killed. Six of our men were wounded but were quickly rescued. The Koniags wrecked our baidaras by slashing them with spears. Their attack was so fierce some of the baidaras had been slashed nearly 100 times.

I had already been warned about the hostility of the Koniags, and about how they had easily managed to drive off all the Russians who had previously tried to stop there. But I was determined to bring benefit to the fatherland and this encouraged me to counter any fears instilled by previous reports from persons who had been on the cape of this island they call Agaekhtalik. This information had come from promyshlenniks who knew and had personally experienced their ferocity. I countered all preconceived notions about this, and since my associates, Captain Mikhail Sergeev [Golikov], the Kursk merchant Larionov, Golikov's sons and I had agreed that our first responsibility in pacifying the savages was to consider benefits to the government, I convinced my workers of this.

The Koniags felt they could easily force all of us off Kodiak Island, down to the last man, even if we made a stubborn resistance to their attacks, or that they could make us their slaves, which is their usual practice when they carry on incessant warfare. They use prisoners for all kinds of work and consider them permanent possessions. To achieve all of this they were relying on:

1. Our small numbers, since there were only 130 of us.

2. Previous successes which they had had, such as in 1761 when a vessel belonging to several companies, carrying promyshlenniks, unexpectedly put in at Cape Agaekhtalik to winter over. The savages would not let the men go more than five versts from their vessel, prevented them from any hunting whatsoever and forced them to sail off ahead of time.

3. The occasion in 1776 when the Kholodilovsk company vessel anchored on the island and they managed to force it off in eleven days.

4. Another occasion when in 1780 a ship belonging to the Panov company under the command of the navigator [Afanasii] Ocheredin had put in at that same cape, Agaekhtalik; the crew had planned to spend the winter there, but had such difficulties with the natives and lost so many men they finally had to beat a hasty retreat.

5. The occasion in 1785 when promyshlenniks from various companies outfitted three ships and sailed from the Fox Islands to the coast of North America with 300 men. The ships were under the overall command of Potap Zaikov. In late August they reached the coast of North America at Chugach Bay, which Cook later named Sandwich Sound. They anchored and prepared to

spend the winter. Because of their numbers they believed they could stand up against the savages but in the end they found they were completely mistaken. The local inhabitants would not let them hunt and they could not go even one verst away in small unarmed groups. They barely survived the winter and then abandoned all their earlier plans and retreated, having lost a number of men through starvation.

These seafarers, having learned of my intention to go to Kodiak Island, tried in every possible way to dissuade me. They described the natives as bloodthirsty and extremely hostile, pointing to the incidents just described and their own experience on Chugach Bay with the natives. I, however, paid little attention to them and ignored all dangers so as to achieve my goal, the intentions of society as well as my own.

Although we had removed the immediate threat of attack, this did not mean we were immune from future attack, especially since they never stopped attacking the baidaras we sent out for reconnaissance, even though they gave hostages after such [unsuccessful] attempts. Since we planned to spend the winter on this island which they inhabited, we tried to establish amicable relations with them through kindness, generosity, hospitality and gifts. However, they deprived themselves of peace through their own savagery by killing one another. Thus, in order to show them a way of life unfamiliar to them, I devoted all my efforts to building small dwellings and constructing a fortress, even though this was at first just hurriedly lashed together. We managed to do this, although it was very difficult.

Still, they did not cease their attacks against the baidaras which I sent out to survey and describe places, and against us personally. In an effort to prevent bloodshed as much as possible, and to protect ourselves better, I demonstrated the force and results of our gunpowder by drilling a hole in a huge rock, filling the hole with gunpowder and fastening a firing mechanism from a rifle to it. Then I attached a long cord under another rock to ensure the safety of the man who was to fire this. I ordered that this rock be blown to bits at the same moment another man fired his gun in the presence of a great mass of peaceful Koniags. This demonstration immediately gave rise to the tale that spread among their people of the incredible force of our "little arrows," as they called our guns.

As a result of this and other things they could not understand, things they found both wondrous and awesome, all the Koniags on the island ceased trying to force us to leave. I tried to assure them I wanted to live in friendship with them, not in a state of war; but that if my intentions were the opposite, they would not be able to escape the force of my weapons. I told them also that our merciful Sovereign Empress wished to protect them and give them a peaceful and secure life.

This and many examples of kindly behavior and small gifts completely pacified them. Through interpreters I tried to instill in them some understanding of the peacefulness, greatness, power and beauty of everything in Russia, as well as the mercy of our Empress. I realized that word of this was spreading and that they were curious, so I tried even more to reassure them, sometimes by talking to them and other times by showing them things which they could readily come to appreciate. I tried to bring them gradually into an awareness of their heathen condition. As a result I gained such respect that at last they began to call me their father. They trusted me, and obeyed me willingly. They considered the rapid construction of our dwellings miraculous, because it would take years to make one of their own little huts, using sharp bits of iron to split the boards. This is the reason they consider finished structures of such great value. Their heathen beliefs are so profound that when at night we put out a lamp made by a Russian mechanic [I. P. Kulibin], they thought we had captured the sun. They think this is what causes overcast days.

It was deplorable to see how ignorant they were. I resolved not to let them remain in this condition and tried as much as I could to explain that the lamp had been made by a person much the same as they, but with the difference that they would not be able to learn anything until they turned to peaceful ways and began to adopt our customs and way of life. I showed them the quality and advantages of Russian homes, clothing and the preparation of food. They saw the labors of my workers when they dug up the garden and planted seeds. When the produce was ready to be harvested, I gave instructions that it be divided among them. They evinced nothing but surprise, so I then ordered that they be given food my workers had prepared, and they developed a great fondness for this.

Such conduct on my part toward them from time to time bonded them increasingly to me. Not knowing how to please me, they brought me a great many of their children as hostages; I had neither asked for hostages, nor did I need them, but in order not to disappoint them, I accepted many of them and sent the others back after giving them appropriate trinkets. After they had showed me such affection, I tried to understand their religious beliefs. I did not find that their hearts were infected with idolatry. They believe in the existence of only two beings in the world, one good and the other evil; this added to their absurdity and inclination to ignorance and savagery. Seeing this, I tried as best I could, using the simplest terms, to explain the Christian faith to them. When I detected great interest, I tried to make use of the moment. I was so interested that in my free time I began to give them a more precise understanding of our faith, and to guide them toward truth. I was successful in exciting their interest. In short, before I left I converted about 40 of their men to Christianity. They were baptized in the same manner as those [in Russia] who are baptized without a priest.

I observed that they began to abandon their tribal brothers. Even more surprising, they began to adopt the customs and actions of the Russians and to ridicule other savages, considering them complete heathens. Since I received many of them in a room which had just been finished, they saw the portrait of Her Imperial Merciful Majesty, our Empress, and they observed certain books I was using. I noted their desire to learn about things they considered amazing, so I explained to them with great enthusiasm about Her Majesty, Her mercy, authority and power, and how fortunate those persons are who come under Her authority and find themselves under Her laws, and conversely, how miserable those are who desert Her or act contrary to Her instructions. As much as I could, I tried to instill in them the need for peacefulness and security for every person, so each may go where he wishes and travel alone without fear that someone will attack him or steal his possessions. I chose this small example so they might understand it better. Actually I managed to make such an impression on them that they desired this and asked me to expel all [foreign] persons who might come to their island. They entrusted themselves into my protection and pledged to obey me.

When these poor people came to my settlement sometimes they saw how my workers obeyed me and carried out my instructions and felt there could not be anyone more powerful then I. But I led them out of this unfortunate misconception and gave them to understand that I am the very lowest subject of my Empress, that she has established various governmental authorities who see to it that no one anywhere suffers from oppression or violence. In every possible way I explained to them how happy they would be if they were to become the beloved and loyal subjects of Her Majesty, Our Most Merciful Sovereign, but that She could also punish them if they disobeyed Her.

I often told them about order in Russia, order among people, and order in buildings, and I instilled in a number of them such curiosity that 40, both men and women, wanted to visit Russian settlements. There were even children in this group, who were given to me by the savages when I left so they could see everything in Russia, even though their parents could not see it. This group went with me to Okhotsk and fifteen went on to Irkutsk; this latter group returned aboard my ship and were given clothing and other presents.

As far as books are concerned, I could not make them understand anything at all. But sometimes I would send some of them with notes to artels which I had left in other parts of this island, and they were amazed that by means of my notes everything would be done which I had told them about beforehand. Therefore they considered written notes more powerful than human beings. For example, I sent one of them with a note to pick up some prunes and other dried fruits from my prikashchik. The man I sent to get these items ate half of them on the way, which I realized through the note and told him so. He was astonished and said, "It is true that this piece of paper watched me when I ate them but I know how I can avoid this in the future." To test his ingenuity I sent him off again, but as before, by means of the note and the scales, I realized that fully half were missing. I again received an acknowledgement of his greedy appetite from him. He was amazed because, although he had eaten the fruit, he had hidden the note in the sand. Still it was obvious to him that the paper had observed him even through the sand.

A second example. In the room which I had built there was a large mirror where these savages would come and look and be utterly amazed that they were seeing someone who looked so much like them. Not comprehending who the person was, they considered all this sorcery which they did not understand. In this way I started to introduce them to some understanding of books, promising to teach their children, if they would agree to it, so they could partake of such knowledge. Several volunteers brought their children and entrusted them to me. One must give these people credit for sharpness of mind, because their children quickly took to their lessons, and before I left some had learned to speak Russian so well that one could understand them without difficulty. I left 25 children studying basic subjects; these children very much preferred being with the Russians to being with their savage fathers.

In these ways I tried to guide them so they would realize their ignorance. I always struggled with my [native] workers who were inclined to fight, and finally I showed them the usefulness of learning. After the savages had learned the power of the notes I gave them, I would give them receipts when they were sent on distant hunting trips. They could show these in case they met men from my artels in distant places; this would be evidence that they were peaceful and well-intentioned toward us. By protecting them with my people from attacks by natives from other places, I gave them to understand how good it is to live in peace [with Russians], because after that their enemies did not dare attack them. They also saw that they were rewarded for their service to me, and they expressed the desire that I would remain with them forever. I can say, and I am proud of this, that when they learned I was leaving, they were as unhappy as if they had lost everything. But when I left I entrusted all business to the administrator I had left there, the merchant [K.A.] Samoilov, a man who I hoped would follow all my orders. I gave him complete instructions.

Prior to my departure I had information from the savages, who, although they cannot provide even the slightest information about the number of peaceful Koniags, are completely friendly toward me. From their accounts and my own observations, one may make a fairly accurate estimate that more than 5,000 males and females have become subjects of Her Imperial Majesty. I never mentioned to them the matter of iasak payment, so as not to create mistrust or an obstacle. I only tried to instill in them a favorable attitude toward the Russians and gradually to introduce them to our customs so they would not only not resist them, but would understand them. I left the question of iasak, however, for the consideration of higher authorities.

In 1785 my workers suffered from scurvy which finally became so severe that by the middle of winter some of them had died and the survivors were very weak. Word of this spread everywhere, and we learned from some of the friendly Koniags that savages in the more distant parts [of the island] were gathering together in great numbers with the intention of attacking us. To counter this, without waiting for my instructions, the Koniags themselves had immediately gone out and brought the leaders of the conspiracy to me. When I realized what they intended, I had to keep them near me under guard. On April 9 I sent out one of the Russians, a man named Rasetnyi, in charge of a thousand of the peaceful Koniags who out of loyalty to me volunteered to protect this single Russian on his assignment to the Uginsk Islands, which Bering had called the Shumagin Islands. Rasetnyi carried letters to the hunting artels there, informing them of our situation, the scurvy, illness and inauspicious developments, and asking them to help in every way possible. After Rasetnyi and his band departed, the scurvy problem began to improve.

On May 2 I sent 52 Russian workers, 11 Fox Island Aleuts in four baidaras and 110 Koniags in baidarkas off to the east to contact persons who lived on the islands along the American mainland, as far as Kenai and Chugach bays. They were to ascertain potentially profitable locations and make note of everything of importance. I ordered them to continue exploring as long as the summer weather would permit. They returned late in August. They had voyaged along the northern side of the strait between the American mainland and Kodiak Island and had not experienced any attacks from the Koniag, the Chugach or the Kenais all during the summer. On the contrary, these people gave them twenty hostages.

Local trade at this time was almost nonexistent because the natives were not familiar with us and were afraid to trade, in spite of the fact that they had given us hostages. When the group I had sent out reached Kodiak Island they decided to spend the winter at a well populated place called Karluk. During the winter they went in baidaras to the northern and western parts of the island, and along the American coast from Katmak to Kamysh [Cook]

Inlet. They had peaceful relations with the natives and constantly befriended them, treated them well, gave them gifts and were thus able to bring them into alliance, took hostages from them and traded with them, and there was not the slightest discord.

All winter long I sent out reconnaissance parties from the harbor to proceed around Kodiak Island from the south and the east, and also to explore along the islands off these coasts. We established friendly relations with a large number of Koniags through kindly treatment and trade. We also took hostages, and brought these people fully under the complete suzerainty of the Russian Empire. At the end of December I sent two of my workers out from the harbor with an interpreter to go to Kenai Bay. They went in the guise of traders to collect information. I gave them some goods to barter and charged the overseer of the hostages on the island of Shuiak with their safety.

On January 10, 1786, I sent eleven workers to the east coast of Kodiak Island to a fir forest some 160 versts from the [Three Saints] harbor, near the settlement of Chinigatsk with instructions to build small sloops. The men I sent built a zimov'e, carried out their instructions and also purchased some furs. They returned to the harbor on May 1.

On February 25 I received a letter dated February 19 from Katmak settlement, from the Greek, Evstrat Delarov. He informed me that our company's galiot *Sv. Mikhail* had put out to sea on May 12, 1785 from the harbor on Unalaska, in accordance with my instructions, but that because of headwinds it had been delayed for six weeks near Unalaska. Finally, during a storm its mast was broken below the crosstree and it had to return to Unalaska. The mast was repaired, and in August when it again attempted to put out to sea it experienced new difficulties and was damaged. An error by the assistant navigator was responsible for the galiot hitting rocks. The crew had to spend the winter on Unalaska, but when they received our communication they sent 30 men in baidaras to help us. However these men encountered storms en route and had to spend six weeks on the American coast. Six of them died of cold and starvation. Delarov reported that the rest were saved by men sent from our company, but five of those rescued died by the time they reached the harbor.

Having decided to leave America, on March 7 I sent five Russians to Cape St. Elias to make descriptions of the more distant parts which had not been completed the previous year. They were also instructed to build a fortress on that cape, which would assist them in their undertaking. This was of course to be done with the consent of the local inhabitants. They were to go as far as 47° latitude, and to be accompanied by a thousand Koniags from Kodiak and other islands and 70 Fox Island Aleuts who volunteered for that service. I instructed them to put up crosses along the coast and to bury pieces of pottery, birchbark and coal in the ground.

At the end of March these men sent me two persons from the Chinigak settlement who informed me that the toion of Shuekh had betrayed me and killed the workers and the interpreter I had entrusted to his care. I had sent the men there to survey Kenai Bay.

The toion was now demanding from me enough men to repel the Kenais who had come from the American mainland near Shuekh; there were some thousand Kenais. When I received this information I sent two groups there from the harbor. There were 30 Russian workmen and a leader in the first group; the second was under the direction of a special administrator and consisted of Koniags and Fox Island Aleuts who were serving voluntarily. I ordered them to appropriate a suitable place for a harbor on the island of Afognak, opposite the island of Shuekh, and to build a fortress there on the basis of a plan I gave them. Meanwhile they were to prepare the galiot *Tri Sviatitelia*, which was in the harbor, for an expedition. On May 19 we received word from Afognak and Shuekh that when our forces had united, the Kenais had abandoned their plot. A fort was later built on Afognak, and eventually, in accordance with my instructions, a similar one was also built at Kenai Bay. We then set out from the American coast for Cape St. Elias. We left a special party behind to finish building the forts. Afognak Island and the American coast opposite it and Kodiak Island all have excellent harbors. The land is suitable for agriculture and there is a great abundance of all varieties of fish and birds. The meadows are covered with grass and pasture and there is timber suitable for building ships and other structures. All of this is found in great abundance on Shuekh Island and on the American coast.

That same year [1786] the inhabitants of the American coast and the islands came to the harbor and to all of our artels daily, more often than during the first winter. They came both simply and ceremoniously. On these occasions we did not miss any opportunity to express signs of friendship and our peaceful intentions. There have been more strong winds out of the north and west this year. They are light from the east, and there have been no south winds all winter long. There has been little rain this winter, but quite a bit of snow. Where there are no winds, the snow was more than one arshin deep; but where the winds blow the snow does not remain on the ground very long.

On May 22 I put out to sea aboard the galiot *Tri Sviatitelia*. I was accompanied by Koniag toions and leaders from Kodiak and from other islands along the American coast. That same day we sighted our company's third galiot, *Sv. Mikhail*, out at sea with sails spread, approaching the harbor. When we were close enough I put my navigator aboard to take them into the harbor. I instructed the administrator that when the persons who had been on Shuiakh and Afognak islands returned, they were to be put aboard the galiot and assigned to the fort on Afognak.

I should also review here the basis on which the galiots were left behind. I put Samoilov in charge of one and ordered him to sail in longitudes between 40° and 73°, counting from the Okhotsk meridian which I used in my calculations, and between 60° and 40° latitude in open seas. I dispatched the other galiot north with instructions to proceed to the region where the two continents are closest, to search for new places and islands. The third, on which I sailed from Kodiak, I transformed into a transport ship which I take every year to carry out what I consider my pleasant duty to inform the goverment about the affairs of that region.

We left America with the intention of passing the 45th parallel and sailing along that line directly west. When we reached the latitude of Cape Kamchatka we would proceed toward that cape and once we had sailed through the Kuril strait we would proceed to Okhotsk. I intended to do this in order to ascertain whether I would encounter any unknown islands along that line between 40° and 50°. Unfortunately, however, the winds were from the west all summer long, which prevented us from carrying out this intention. For that reason it was only possible to sail directly to Okhotsk. Even there the headwinds hindered us.

While on this voyage along the islands in the chain we sighted the Chetyrie Sopochnye and Amukhta. The latter island, because of its volcanic peaks, appeared to be engulfed in flame. As we sailed along we also sighted Siuga, Amliu, Akhta and other islands in the Andreanovskii chain. We reached the first Kuril island and anchored there on July 30. Since twelve of the Russian workers with me had contracted scurvy and were extremely weak, the seamen's responsibilities on board the ship were taken over by American natives who were sailing with me to Okhotsk out of curiosity. On July 31 they brought 40 barrels of fresh water aboard the galiot from the first of the Kuril Islands.

As far as conditions of the sea are concerned, no precise observations can be stated except that the current is very strong near Kamchatka and there are waves there, not only when the wind is blowing, but even when there is no wind at all. The wave action is so strong that the boat rocks and the decks touch the water.

On August 1 we took the galiot into the first Kuril strait. There was a strong wind which held us there until August 5, when we went through the second Kuril strait [between Shumshu and Paramushir] and into the harbor. On August 7 we left the harbor and proceeded to the mouth of the Bolshaia River. On August 8 we stood at anchor at the mouth of the river. I went ashore in a baidara and sent it back to the ship while I remained ashore to buy fresh fish. When I had done this I wanted to return to the ship but encountered various problems. While I was ashore strong winds had torn the galiot from its anchor. The men aboard were so weak they could not handle the ship, and it became separated still farther from me. Finally I hired a boat and went to the settlement of Bolsheretsk, which I reached on August 15. From there I decided to proceed overland to Okhotsk, using three horses which I bought there for 200 rubles. But just then news came to Bolsheretsk from Petropavlovsk harbor that on August 9 an English ship had put in there and intended to stop for not more than 20 days. I very much wanted to find out where this ship had come from and why, as well as to see if we might gain some useful information, so I had to postpone my departure for Okhotsk in order to visit Petropavlovsk harbor.

On August 20 I set out on my horses and reached there on the 23rd. The English had noticed from their ship that I had arrived with my men, and they immediately sent several of their men ashore in a small sloop. The captain and two officers were very courteous; they persuaded me to leave the government office and join them on the ship where they showed me examples of their trade goods which they said they had brought from the [East] India Company to the commanding officer of Kamchatka. They had also brought letters expressing the desire of that Company to establish trade in Kamchatka and asking permission to do so from Russia.

Without revealing anything about myself, I tried to learn where they had come from and where they had voyaged, since they did not hide their maps from me. I discovered that according to our reckoning on March 20 they had left Bengal [Calcutta], which is located in 23° northern latitude. They had left the Straits of Malacca on April 16, reached Canton on May 29, left Canton July 28 and reached the harbor of Petropavlovsk on August 9. There were three English officers on the ship and one Portuguese; the sailors were English, Indian, Arabian and Chinese. The crew numbered 70 men in all. The ship was entirely built of a red wood and was sheathed with metal. It had two masts, 28 sails, at the keel 65 *gruz* [3½ feet] and had twelve cannons on the deck.

While I was on the ship I was given various beverages all day long up until suppertime, then at 10:00 P.M. after supper the ship's captain, William Peters, and his officers accompanied me on a small sloop to the government building, postponing trading until the commanding officer of Kamchatka should arrive. Baron [Ivan] Steingel, the Kamchatka commandant, arrived on the 25th; on the 26th and 27th they carried on conversations in French and agreed on duties on trade, but stipulated that if higher authorities should decide otherwise, they would pay without question. They then would begin to carry on trade. On the 28th they agreed about the kinds of goods they would bring to Kamchatka in the future and the kind of goods they would like to receive from us in return, and the prices. On August 29, 30, and 31 I received the goods which I had purchased from the English, and the transaction was completed on September 1. The total value of goods I received was 6,611 rubles. Of this sum I paid them 1,000 rubles in cash, and gave them a check for the rest, saying that in two months it would be paid in Moscow with interest at 6% per annum. On September 3, taking leave of the English, I set out from the harbor in boats. The English planned to leave on the

4th. I reached Bolsheretsk on September 8 and sold all the goods I had bought from the English to the Totma merchants, the Panovs' prikashchiks, Petr and Grigorii, and to others. The profit on the goods was 50 kopecks per ruble, [a 50% markup].

From Bolsheretsk I set out for the Tigil River, proceeding along the coast; I reached Tigilsk ostrog on October 2 and set out from there with dogs on November 18. I reached Okhotsk on January 27, 1787, obviously much later than the galiot I had been on reached there. From Okhotsk my wife and I again used dogs, leaving there February 8 and continuing our journey, with reindeer in some places and with horses and oxen in others. Everywhere we suffered unspeakable difficulties and dangers. I reached Iakutsk on March 11. On the 12th I set out from Iakutsk *oblast* [fort] in sleds. From the time I left Kamchatka, traveling by dog and by reindeer in many desolate places, I suffered extreme and unbearable difficulties. I was threatened with fearful torture on many occasions, and my life all that while was in great danger.

In the first place, the Koriak tribes between the Tigil River and Gizhiga were very unreliable. Second, the winter was extremely cold and the terribly fierce north winds continued with almost no let-up. Third, purgas often stranded us in desolate places so we were unable to travel. We would hitch the sleds together with leather thongs and on such occasions only saved our lives by lying in the snow for two, three or even five days, without leaving, without water, without cooking food. Since it was impossible to build a fire, we ate snow to quench our thirst. In place of any other food, we ate dry biscuits or iukola, which we chewed while lying in the snow.

The last part of the journey from the Aldan to Irkutsk was so difficult the dogs and reindeer were exhausted. The horses too were exhausted by the snowdrifts, often to the point of collapse. In order to make the journey more quickly, I went on foot. In spite of all these difficulties I finally managed to reach Irkutsk, the oblast town, at noon on April 6 [1787]. I consider it an obligation to express publicly my gratitude to two honorable men who have served the Empire and the fatherland for years without blemish—the brothers, captains Timofei and Vasilii Shmalev, who saved me from all manner of dangers at the hands of local savages. One of these brothers was stationed in the Tigilsk fortress and the other between Tigil and Gizhiga, among the Koriaks, so they could subdue the Koriak and Chukchi tribes in the Kamensk settlement. In addition, my successful journey was generously assisted by Corporal Nikolai Popov of the Tigil command outpost, and by the Koriak interpreter, the cossack Ivan Suzdalev, who, as interpreter, accompanied me from Tigilsk ostrog to the town of Gizhiga. Both Popov and Suzdalev have Koriak relatives, and for that reason I traveled there safely, for which I am obliged to the two brothers, the Captains Shmalev, and to Corporal Popov and the interpreter Ivan Suzdalev. I wish to take this opportunity to express to them my gratitude for having saved my life. . . .

Now it is necessary to describe the land of the American islands, the people who inhabit it, their customs, habits, clothing and to tell about the animals and birds there.

The islands which lie near the American coast and extend from Kodiak to the east, and also those off the coast of Northwest America, are quite rocky and mountainous; but they are good, and are appropriate for agricultural pursuits. I became convinced of this through my own experiments of planting there millet, peas, beans, pumpkins, carrots, mustard, beets, potatoes, radish and rhubarb. Everything grew very well except the millet. The peas, beans and pumpkins did not go to seed, but only because they were planted too late. There are many meadows ideal for hay and good grass, and in some places livestock can live without hay all winter long. I did not see any sizable stands of timber, but there are fine small stands of trees. The local vegetation which the natives use for food are roots such as sarana, snakeweed, yellow fern and angelica. This latter deserves special attention because on islands where there are no mice it grows and has a very fine flavor, but wherever there are mice the root is so bitter as to be inedible. There are also abundant quantities of raspberries, blueberries, blackberries, cloudberries, red cowberries, cranberries, and currants. In regard to trees, in the middle part of Kodiak Island and in America to the west I found five varieties: alder, rose willow, birch and mountain ash, and to the east on islands along the American coast near bays, there are fir, larch and the other trees just mentioned.

Birds which are to be found there include geese, various kinds of ducks, ravens, jackdaws, black canaries and magpies whose shrieks little resemble those of the same bird in Russia; they do not sing badly, but quite softly, almost like finches. There are also seagulls, cranes, herons, woodcock and auks. Marine animals include sea otters, sea lions, whales and seals. Riverine animals include the otter and beaver. There are various land animals such as foxes, wolves, bears, ermine, reindeer, sables, rabbits, wolverines, lynx, marmots, ground squirrels, wild sheep and porcupines. Saltwater fish include halibut, cod and herring; those to be found in rivers include king salmon, humpback salmon, red salmon, loach, chum, cuttlefish and a strange kind of shellfish.

The Koniag people are tall, healthy, stocky, with large round faces; but there are also some who have long faces. They are swarthy, have black or very occasionally light brown hair which both men and women wear cut off round. The wives of the leading men distinguish themselves from the rest by combing part of their hair over their foreheads and cutting it across at eyebrow level, and they also have braids. Others have tattooed beards on their chins and tattooed designs on their chests and backs.

Men, women and young girls pierce the middle part of the nose, and all pierce their ears and lower lips. A few men also have tattoos on their necks. Every male has his lower lip pierced so that at first glance it appears that he has two mouths. A long bone is inserted into the hole pierced through the nose; those who have large and small glass beads hang them from their ears, lips and nose and consider this a very fine beautification. They do not cut their beards; they do not have shirts; they go barefoot; in their dwellings they go about completely naked except that in front they gird themselves with a bit of fur or something made of grass and flowers.

They wear parkas made of sea otter, fox, bear, birdskins, ground squirrel, marmot, otter, sable, hare, reindeer, wolverine and lynx. The kamlei, which is similar to a parka, is made from the intestines of sea lion, seal and whale. On their heads they wear hats woven from fir roots and grass. They also wear curved hats carved from wood. When they hunt marine animals they use arrows which they hurl from a board, and for warfare they have bows and iron spears as well as copper, bone and stone weapons. Their iron axes are made of small pieces of iron. They have pipes, iron and bone knives and iron needles. . . . Prior to our arrival the women made their needles themselves. They use sinew for thread. They have utensils made of wood and of the horn of wild sheep, and also some made of clay pottery as well as stones that have been hollowed out.

The baidaras and baidarkas are covered on top with tightly stretched hide rather than with boards, except for the hatch. They use these when they go fishing or hunting marine animals. To procure food for their domestic needs and when they are on fishing expeditions they use bone hooks and fishing lines made of long pieces of dried sea cabbage. One stem of that cabbage can be 40 sazhens or more in length. In the rivers they take fish by using rock ponds and spearing the fish with harpoons which look like lances; at the dull end there is an opening in which is loosely placed a toothed blade made of bone, stone or iron, tied with sinew to a wooden shaft. In bays and inlets they kill salmon with arrows when the fish leap out of the water. They make fire by rubbing sticks together. For light they use the fat of seal, bear, sea lion, whale and fur seal; they put the oil in stone containers with grass wicks.

I know nothing about their marriage ceremonies, nor can I give any information about newborn babies except to say that they are given their names from whatever they first encounter, even though this may be an animal, a bird or some such.

Funerals differ from tribe to tribe among the Koniags. I did not see any myself, and for that reason I cannot say anything about this; however, it is true that some place their dead in a baidarka, especially influential persons who have died, and the baidarka is covered with earth. Others put a live prisoner, a for-mer slave, in with the dead person and bury them in the ground. The Kenais burn the bodies of the dead with animal pelts brought by the dead person's relatives.

As part of the funeral ceremony close relatives cut their hair and paint their faces black. This is done for a close relative such as one's father, mother, brother, sister or other close or beloved rela-tive, often even a close friend not related. However if the de-ceased was someone whom they did not like or with whom they were not friendly, even though he may have been a relative, then there will be no such mourning tradition.

They do not have the common diseases except for venereal

disease. They do not have nor ever have had smallpox. The people are basically of strong constitution and live to the age of 100 years.

To meet their guests they smear red pigment over themselves and wear their best garments. They beat on drums and dance with battle weapons in their hands. Guests arrive exactly as if they were coming to battle. As soon as they approach the shore the hosts leap into the water up to their chests. The baidaras and baidarkas are brought up on shore with all possible speed; then they hurriedly take the guests from the baidara and carry them one at a time on their backs to a place that has been prepared for games. They all sit together and everyone keeps silent until they have eaten and drunk.

The first and greatest honor is to be given cold water. Then young lads carry food, fat, *tolkusha* which is the mashed fat of seals, whales and sea lions, with berries such as red bilberries, cranberries, blackberries, currants and others, also various roots. They may also bring in berries alone, not mixed with anything. They will have dried fish which they call *iukola*, meat from animals and birds, whatever their best is. They do not use salt at all. The host must eat and drink before anyone else does; the guest will not eat anything until then. This may lead one to think that they might sometimes mix poison in the food. The host first eats some of each dish and then passes on to the next person, until it reaches the last person. The remaining food is returned to the first person, who puts it in its place. When the guests leave they take all of this with them.

When they have finished eating they continue conversing and then begin to play using drums and rattles. Some of them wear strange masks made of wood painted with various pigments. Then they carry the guests into a specially built large *kazhim* [communal structure] in which a multitude of people have gathered. This structure is similar to a small temple whose architecture is rather formless, crude and primitive. Here the games take place, according to customary ceremonies. The guests play there day and night without interruption. Those who become tired sleep there, and when they waken, start to play the games again. When they decide to disband, the games are over. When they leave, both sides exchange gifts and carry on barter. In these kazhim gatherings they take counsel, reach agreements and divide up things. When they are dealing with important matters women are not allowed in the kazhim.

The Koniags and Chugach have the same language, but the Kenais' life and language are entirely different.

They live in earthen dwellings that have walls lined with boards. There are windows at the top with panes made of intestines and bladders of various animals sewn together with thread made of sinew. They enter their dwellings from below. They have no stoves and they do not make fires inside because they are warm enough without fire. The same earthen structure is used for bathhouses, in which they beat themselves with grass and birch twigs. The heat comes from rocks which are heated in the cooking area and carried into the bathhouse. This creates extreme heat and there are never any fumes. The finest hunters are steambathed in this way. They have a common kitchen which has doors or openings around it. Their life, however, is one of thievery. Whoever most often best and most skillfully manages to steal, is the most esteemed.

They do not have many wives; two are rare. In contrast, good looking and adroit women have two or three husbands. In such an arrangement there is no jealousy among the husbands, who live in friendship.

They do not travel overland, and although there are many animals which could be used for overland transport, including many dogs, they do not employ them for this. The inhabitants of the American coast and of islands travel by rivers, creeks and lakes in their baidarkas. I do not know anything about the people in the interior of America.

They have not the slightest understanding of God, and although they say that there are two spirits in the world, one good and one evil, they do not have any images of them and they do not worship. In a word, they do not have idols. Concerning the existence of these beings, they cannot understand anything except that the good one taught them to make baidaras, and the evil one ruins and breaks these vessels. On the basis of this one may realize how much their minds are still in the dark. They also make considerable use of sorcery and shamanism. Justice and punishment are not only not orderly procedures; they are nonexistent. From all of this it is clear that their life is little different from that of animals. They are evidently hot-blooded, which can

319

be deduced when one approaches any of the local inhabitants. The women are particularly lusty. By nature they are clever and adaptable. When insulted they are vengeful and cruel, although on the surface they may appear calm. I cannot speak for their loyalty and honesty because I was there such a short time; I saw many indications of loyalty and constancy, but I also saw the opposite. When some task is suggested to them from which they will profit, they will willingly accept the labor; they will spare no effort if they are convinced of profit. Generally speaking these people are merry and carefree; their daily games are evidence of this. They live in such boundless and constant debauchery that their households are extremely slipshod, and they do not realize that this is often the reason they suffer famine and deprivation.

We made daily entries in our notes describing sea and weather conditions during our voyage and at places where we anchored. When I reached Okhotsk I gave them to the local oblast commander, Kozlov-Ugrenin; I suppose that he will not keep these, but will send them to the appropriate place if they contain some worthwhile observations.

See: G. I. Shelikhov. *Rossiiskogo kuptsa Grigoriia Shelikhova stranstvovaniia iz Okhotska po vostochnomu okeanu k amerikanskim beregam*, edited by B. P. Polevoi (Khabarovsk: 1971), 35–61.

50

NOT AFTER DECEMBER, 1786

A MEMORANDUM FROM COUNT ALEKSANDR R. VORONTOSOV, AND
COUNT ALEKSANDR A. BEZBORODKO, CONCERNING RUSSIA'S RIGHTS
TO THE ISLANDS AND COASTS OF NORTH AMERICA WHICH WERE DIS-
COVERED BY RUSSIAN SEAFARERS

On the basis of a memorandum from Major-General [P. P.] Soimonov to the President of the College of Commerce, concerning trade and hunting in the Pacific Ocean, Her Imperial Majesty has instructed us to submit our view to Her Imperial Majesty, which we have most humbly formulated and hereby submit.

The Northwest Coast of America and the islands in the archipelagos between there and Kamchatka, and from that peninsula to Japan, were discovered long ago by Russian seafarers. Their detailed notes bear witness to this. Major-General Soimonov has prepared an extract of these accounts, which extract is hereby dutifully appended.

According to a generally accepted rule, the first nation to discover an unknown land has the right to claim it. This has been true in earlier ages, and has been the general practice since the discovery of America. Thus when a European country discovered a previously unknown land, they claimed it. Indeed the popes of Rome, on behalf of Roman Catholic rulers, would issue papal bulls to reaffirm such a discovery and thereby finalize the right of possession.

Based on this precedent it is indisputable that the following should belong to Russia: 1) the American coast from 55°21′ north to the latitudes reached by captains Bering and Chirikov and other Russian seafarers; 2) all the islands near the mainland and the Alaskan peninsula, which were discovered by Bering and which [Captain James] Cook named after Montague—these include Sv. Stefan, Sv. Dalmatiia, Evdokiia, Shumagin and others which lie between the sailing course of our seafarers and the mainland; 3) all the islands west of these in the archipelagos known as the Fox and Aleutian islands, and others to the north which Russian promyshlenniks visited every year; 4) the archi-

The grave site of Captain Charles Clerke, who died of tuberculosis aboard H.M.S. *Resolution*. Not wishing to be buried "in the icy sea" as quoted from Vol. III of Captain Cook's voyages, he was carried to Petropavlovsk (1778) where his grave site is honored today by Soviet naval personnel. First view (above) is from Sauer, *Billings' Expedition to Russia*. The second, (below) from Krusenstern's voyage, reveals that the omnipresent "tree" has withered but the gravesite has flourished. La Pérouse also conducted ceremonies there before his own catastrophe. *Atlas k puteshestvie vokrug sveta Kapitana Kruzenshterna.* (OHS neg. 80240, 67272)

pelago of the Kuril Islands which extends to Japan, which islands were discovered by captains Spanberg and Walton.

For this reason there is no foundation to the claim of the English under the leadership of Captain Cook to a river which he named but which had previously been discovered by Captain Chirikov. Cook claimed this river under the jurisdiction and in the name of the English king, raised a flag and ordered that some English coins be buried in the land there. There is also no basis for his claim to Prince William Sound and the island of Kay. This is clearly documented by the naval journals of captains Bering and Chirikov, who sailed for a great distance along that coast. This can be more clearly seen in the map Major-General Soimonov has prepared.

The acquisition of all these previously unknown islands to Your Majesty's Empire is founded on the right of first discovery by the Russians. This was accomplished with great effort on the part of the government and also on the part of Your Majesty's individual subjects who were encouraged by their great profits from the fur trade and went on to make more and more discoveries. However, these acquisitions have not yet been officially claimed by the government. Thus in our view it is necessary that Your Majesty issue an Imperial decree, through Russian ministers accredited to the courts of all European seafaring nations, announcing that these lands which Russians have discovered must form an integral part of Russia as part of our Empire. For that reason the Empire cannot allow foreign seafarers and ships to sail there, just as other seafaring powers do not permit foreign nations into their settlements outside of Europe, considering these places as reserved exclusively for trade for their own subjects. For greater clarification they should be provided with the above mentioned map, which should be published and made available under the watchful supervision of Major-General Soimonov.

However, since such a declaration will be inadequate without considerable support, and might in some ways even undermine the dignity of the court, we, the undersigned, humbly submit to Your Imperial Majesty that it would be most beneficial if Your Majesty would decree that several naval vessels be sent into these regions belonging to Your Empire. A number of capable naval officers should be stationed aboard these vessels, as well as the appropriate number of lower ranking naval personnel, in order to be able to enforce the prohibition which would extend to all alien ships belonging to any European power who might proceed there to establish their own control or to carry on trade with the local people.

After such a declaration, out of respect for Your Imperial Majesty neither the English court nor any other like naval power would dare send their naval vessels there; however one should not assume that private merchants or privileged East Indian Company personnel or others would cease their efforts. This was evidenced by the fact that not long ago an English naval sloop belonging to private merchants attempted to trade in those regions to realize large profit through the fur trade. Although we too have commercial vessels, it is doubtful that they are equipped and built in such a manner that they could successfully prevent these private entrepreneurs from coming, without Your Majesty's mighty naval protection.

(Signed)
Count Aleksandr Vorontsov
Count Aleksandr Bezborodko

Reference: TsGAVMF, f. 296, 1. 131, 11. 53–55.
See: V. A. Divin, ed., *Russkaia tikhookeanskaia epopeia* (Khabarovsk: 1979), 373–375.

51

DECEMBER 22, 1786

AN UKAZ OF EMPRESS CATHERINE II TO THE ADMIRALTY COLLEGE
ORDERING THAT A NAVAL SQUADRON BE DISPATCHED TO THE NORTH
PACIFIC TO PROTECT RUSSIAN POSSESSIONS

I am attaching herewith a copy of Our ukaz sent to the College of Foreign Affairs, issued as a result of an attempt by English merchants to carry on trade and traffic in furs in the Pacific Ocean. This ukaz concerns the protection of Our rights on lands discovered by Russian seafarers.

I hereby authorize Our Admiralty College to send two ships from the Baltic Sea, armed in the same manner as those used by the English Captain Cook and other seafarers for similar discoveries, and two armed naval sloops or other vessels, as the Admiralty College may deem best. They are to be ordered to round the Cape of Good Hope, continue their voyage through the Sound, passing Japan on the left, and proceed to Kamchatka.

Subsequently the Admiralty College is to prepare appropriate instructions as to how to deal with this matter, and anything else they deem necessary to assure benefits to Our service. A director and his subordinates and servitors are to be appointed and efforts made to use as many volunteers as possible.

The Admiralty is also to issue instructions to assure the most rapid possible arming, suppplying and dispatching of these vessels. There is to be no delay in carrying out all matters which have been submitted for its review and approval.

Reference: TsGAVMF, f. 172 (I. G. Chernysheva), d. 408, ch. 2, 1. 791.
See: V. A. Divin, ed., *Russkaia Tikhookeanskaia epopeia* (Khabarovsk: 1979), 538.

52

APRIL 19, 1787

A REPORT FROM GRIGORII I. SHELIKHOV TO IVAN V. IAKOBII, GOVERNOR GENERAL OF IRKUTSK, REQUESTING GOVERNMENT AID TO STABILIZE AND EXPAND THE ALASKAN SETTLEMENTS AND ENTERPRISES

Men representing various companies have embarked on voyages to discover islands in the open sea extending toward the northern coast of America. When these men have succeeded and have returned [to Russia], from time to time both they and their sponsors have been encouraged in their efforts by being granted various privileges such as being excused from certain civil obligations, or being decorated with medals, thanks to the motherly munificence of Her Imperial Majesty. It is hoped that their efforts will provide an example to others to discover and lay claim to this distant territory for the Russian Empire, to find new lands and bring the native inhabitants under the suzerainty of Her Imperial Majesty.

In accordance with this Imperial approbation, I spent many years searching for ways to benefit [Russia]. However I did not wish to undertake such ventures alone, but rather in association with other companies so we could put our ships, goods, cargo and workers under the supervision of one of the leaders. I felt that equipment was inadequate without strong personal leadership. Thus one of the things our company provided was public support; but frequently there was also a loss of capital outlay. Those who have returned can provide practical evidence of this.

All this did not deter my desire to make a personal attempt, and because of my loyal and zealous obligation to Her Imperial Majesty, our most august Sovereign, and to Her motherly desires, I promised at the earliest opportunity to undertake an expedition from Russia along the American coast to the east of us where various American natives live, and bring them under the protection and authority of Her Imperial Majesty. In undertaking this venture I was impelled by nothing more than the desire to show its practical benefits.

I am inspired to undertake this because of the graciousness shown to my forebears by the Sovereign Emperor Peter I, the Great, of eternal and blessed memory, who gave them a golden *kovsh* [bowl] with silver inscriptions and a coat of arms. I myself have inherited this piece, and it inspires me to follow in the steps of my forebears. Consequently I have tried fervently to demonstrate my dedication to the fatherland, and have made every effort to establish a Russian settlement in the newly acquired lands as a first step in that direction. For that purpose when I was in St. Petersburg in 1781 to make a detailed exposition of my remarkable circumstances and the benefits that might accrue, I invited Captain Mikhail and the Kursk merchant, Ivan Golikov, to become members of the company to be organized in Okhotsk for the purpose of sending an expedition to the coast of America. I concluded a contract with them in which it is agreed that the company we organized would continue its activity for not less than ten years. When the appropriate number of ships initially would be outfitted, we would not trust any outsiders, but I personally would go with this expedition. We would agree as to the destination; I would make my own personal observations, and if our request were granted, we would establish settlements and forts on the mainland coast and on the islands off America.

After I returned from St. Petersburg I was in Irkutsk and inquired from the government about building seaworthy vessels in Okhotsk and about obtaining the necessary assistance. I hired the number of workmen we needed and took them to Okhotsk with the required cables, rigging, provisions and other goods. I built three galiots and on August 16, 1783, I sailed out from the mouth of the Urak River. There were strong headwinds, and it was already late in the season, so I anchored two galiots at Bering Island to spend the winter there. The third galiot, *Sv. Mikhail*, under the supervision of the assistant pilot Olesov, wintered on the first Kuril Island.

When winter was over and summer finally came, I did not wait for the *Sv. Mikhail*, but left instructions for it in various places. I then sailed toward the island of Kodiak near the American mainland. There, on August 3, 1784, I selected an appropriate harbor and decided to spend the winter and to build a fort. The fort was to be a gathering place, under the protection of our company, for half of the crew of our company, who, for future purposes, both for voyages and for wintering, would secure all the necessities for our company ships such as fresh local produce and staples, in adequate amounts.

Shelikhov spent the winter of 1784-5 building a rudimentary harbor and fort on Kodiak Island, battling hostile natives, weather, scurvy, and fatigue. The illustration shows the site as Billings saw it several years later, with a temporary church structure and the conventional astronomical tent. Sauer, *Billings' Expedition to Russia*. (OHS neg. 80234)

Thus in accordance with my instructions the first winter on the island of Kodiak was spent in preparing food and other chores. But the season was already late; also there were a great many hostile natives on this island and others nearby and on the American mainland itself, and in Kenai Bay. Furthermore the coastal climate at that new location was very damp. Thus many of our company workmen fell ill with scurvy and we encountered all manner of adversities which I tried to endure with a cheerful disposition and to ameliorate in every possible way. I concealed my weakness from the workmen and encouraged them in every possible way and never gave in to the terrible dangers. There was no doubt that the success of the venture depended on my conduct. In this dangerous situation there was no hope of assistance except to place ourselves at the mercy of God's providence. But in spite of our constant weakness, we had to be constantly vigilant because of the unceasing vicious attempts by the natives to attack us. We had to undertake every precaution and defense without fear or fatigue.

Prior to my arrival the local natives had earlier defeated the Russians and hence were emboldened and frequently attacked us with great force. Nevertheless in spite of our weakness with God's help we managed to drive them off. The natives tried especially to kill the workmen whom I sent to various locations on assignments in baidaras. They also attacked at night in heavy rainstorms and in wind, but thanks to my efforts and attention and vigilance they always failed, and lost some of their own men. These attemps did not have a favorable impact on them and they eventually gave up these evil schemes.

For our part, we also had great problems, but we tried to conceal our weakness and we gave the appearance of boldness and fearlessness. Fortunately we had some natives as interpreters. They were not well versed in our language, but by using various enticements and distributing little gifts, we managed to convince them that they should not fear us, but rather should establish friendly relations with us; that they should supply us with furs and trade with us in other goods. In all of this we hoped we would not offend them or any of their rivals, since all of these natives fight constantly among themselves and kill each other off. They will never be civilized. But if some of the native settlements which we may not know of were to be attacked by their enemies, and had already come under our protection, they would be both protected and saved. Once the Russians establish themselves there they will be there permanently.

Most important of all, I demostrated emphatically that the Humane Mother of our homeland is not only concerned about Her own loyal subjects, but also offers Her Imperial Majesty's protection to other peoples. She is also concerned with all people who live in proximity to the Russian Empire and suffer civil discord. She thinks of their well-being and expresses Her condolences. In all places that are not far from Her Majesty's frontiers, where there are people who are not under anyone else's protection, She will authorize Her appointed officials to work to bring and attract these unhappy people under the protection of Her mighty sceptre.

These officials are to obey the noble call of Her Imperial Majesty and during their voyages to America they are to carry out this and other assignments of Her motherly Imperial Majesty. They will summon the natives into friendship and call for trade, a policy which I set for myself as a firm obligation. I further assured the native interpreters that Her Imperial Majesty wishes that all people whom God has created can always live in peace under Her protection.

In order not to arouse fears about the payment of iasak, I did not mention it at first. I did not wish to leave them with any negative feelings. When the natives realized the potential benefits which I had tried to explain to them, and when I reassured them that there was nothing to fear, they were pacified and gradually abandoned their ancient deeply rooted animal instincts and obstinacy. They became inclined toward peaceful ways. Many of their leaders whom their language refers to as *khaskaks* started to give their children as hostages as a pledge of future loyalty and good relations. Upon seeing this the poor natives and their wives and children began to come to me as whole settlements. On these occasions I would give out little trinkets and reward them in other ways as well. For that reason, in all of the places where I settled artels, the natives became soft-hearted, and there is hope that they will remain peaceful in the future.

When our hopes were realized and the natives began to be peaceful and friendly so they could secure a more comfortable living for themselves, they left a large number of their children with me as hostages. This presented a future opportunity for our fatherland to take advantage of. I considered this the first step in raising these persons above their fellow natives. I decided to select certain ones of these hostages and to educate them. I chose those who seemed capable and bright and willing to be taught by my people to read and write Russian and to behave properly. For this purpose I built a school. Their fathers soon became favorably inclined, so that in this matter we are experiencing real success.

To cap this fine effort on their part, many have willingly agreed to embrace the Greek Orthodox faith. I immediately carried out this desire for those who wished. I admonished them to hold their Orthodox Catholic faith according to their instructions, and with great satisfaction I applauded their decision and revealed to them other steps leading to salvation, which they now constantly adhere to.

As a result of such amicable behavior on the part of the local natives, I was pleased to be able to develop trade with them. On all of these islands near Kodiak and along the American mainland there are many tribes of savage peoples who are independent and subject to no one. They have begun to establish peaceful accord with us.

For this reason I consider it necessary for future benefit and in order to hold these natives to take the necessary steps to choose appropriate places to establish settlements. Above all I sought to move as far south as possible along the American coast toward California to establish Russian settlements and to leave our marks on the land in order to forestall other nations who might have designs on this region, and to ensure that we were the first to claim these places.

In the reports I have submitted, Your Excellency may observe at Your convenience my dedication to the fatherland, my activities and discoveries, and my departure from the American coast.

The summer I left the American coast [1786] I had hoped for a quick voyage to Okhotsk so the vessel could return to America the same year to support my company. However fate decreed otherwise. When I left the ship to travel to Kamchatka by baidara, a storm carried the vessel off toward Okhotsk and I was left in Kamchatka with no ship. But by chance, at that time an English ship belonging to the [East] Indian Company came to the harbor of Petropavlovsk in Kamchatka. I have traded with that company, so I gave the English a list of goods we would need in the future. However I told the English that this arrangement would have to be approved as beneficial for the fatherland by our Great Sovereign. This is very clear in the instructions which I gave to the Kamchatka prikashchik, and in the bundle of letter copies which I have forwarded to Your Excellency for Your examination.

I also make bold to suggest that in reference to the stalemate in trade in Kiakhta, it might be a good thing if Your Excellency were to send one or two ships under some appropriate flags, carrying Kamchatka natives and furs from Okhotsk or Kamchatka to trade in Chinese ports.

I have evidence that the English are moving around Kamchatka, and along the coast of America in the North Pacific, and that they anticipate considerable profits. I make bold to explain this here. When I was at Petropavlovsk harbor in August last year, William Peters, a captain with the East Indian Company, came to trade, as did his English associates. In the year 1785 that company's ship was near our frontiers along the Northwest Coast of America in 50° latitude. Whether they traded with the consent of the Russian Empire or not, I do not know. They did trade for a brief time with American natives, and according to their reports, they acquired more than 800 sea otter pelts, I believe, and a substantial number of pelts from land animals. Not content with this, they sent five more ships in 1786. This is evidence that benefits due the Russian throne and its subjects are being siphoned off by people from other nations who are in no way proximate to those lands, and have not the slightest right in those seas.

For this reason, having finished my reports, I make bold to trouble Your Excellency: would You kindly permit me to send a ship back to the American coast without delay in order to reinforce our company's fort there? This would be the same ship which brought me to the port of Okhotsk this summer. It would carry workmen who used to belong to our company as well as newly hired ones. And it would carry all kinds of supplies and tackle and other useful items for the local inhabitants. The ship would be under the leadership of Evstrat Delarov, a Macedonian Greek whom I appointed to be administrator in my absence. I appointed the assistant navigator Gerasim Izmailov to assist him during his sailing on company business. Izmailov sailed there and back with me.

The administrators of that region should be given special instructions not to undertake any detrimental policy or attempt to change the administration, because of the great distances involved. And since the ship sailing back and forth will always be a transport vessel, in the future it should not be subject to the same government rules. Also, I would ask that except for police officials, no other government authority will intervene in any of my ships which are dispatched in the future.

In this regard I ask Your Excellency's wise advice and instructions in regard to the natives whom I have persuaded to be friendly, in order to strengthen their allegiance and friendship, as well as to assist my efforts and to approve them. I ask this so that the sacrifice which I have willingly made for the benefit of the fatherland will not be directed to the advantage of other companies, through negligent administrators, who send less carefully chosen workmen.

Please order that local warehouses supply food and naval goods such as rigging to those persons who are dispatched, in case they encounter any shortages between Irkutsk and Okhotsk. The quantities would be 150 puds of tarred rigging and 800 puds of food provisions. Please instruct Your local officials about this.

Likewise, to encourage Konstantin [A.] Samoilov and the apprentice navigator Dmitrii Bocharov and other dedicated people from our company who are along the coast of America, it would be helpful if You would write a letter praising their work and encouraging a reward from our Monarch.

Finally, if there are no objections, there should be a prohibition against any European ships coming to that part of the American coast or to Russian territorial possessions to trade or to hunt. I trust Your Excellency will report all of this to the proper quarter.

[Signed] Grigorii Shelikhov

If possible You should submit this request in Your Excellency's report.

Reference: LOII, sobr. Vorontsovykh, No. 476, 11. 381–382.

See: A. I. Andreev, ed., *Russkie otkrytiia v Tikhom okeane i v Severnoi Amerike v XVIII veke* (Moscow: 1948), 206–214.

53

SECRET INSTRUCTIONS FROM LIEUTENANT GENERAL IVAN V. IAKOBII,
GOVERNOR GENERAL OF SIBERIA, TO AGENTS OF GRIGORII I. SHELI-
KHOV, KONSTANTIN A. SAMOILOV AND EVSTRAT I. DELAROV, TO ES-
TABLISH RUSSIA'S CLAIM TO NEWLY DISCOVERED PARTS OF ALASKA

First. When you receive the packet which contains fifteen insignia of the Russian Empire and ten iron plates, on which
are a bronze cross and bronze letters proclaiming "This land belongs to the Russian Empire," immediately try to emplace these
on land in that part of western America known as Alaska. It is
desirable that the insignia be placed in the same location where an
English ship anchored in the year 1784 and engaged in a rich and
profitable trade. To the best of our knowledge that location is
in 50° 40′.

2. Wherever you emplace one of these insignia, within a few
paces you are to bury one of the plates as well, on which are to be
described not only the location but also a statement on which side
of the insigne it has been placed, and also the depth.

3. Use every possible means to chart the coastline. Note where
bays and inlets are located, their depth, names and configuration.

4. Try to bury the plates in such a manner that not only will
they not be seen by the natives, but so they are hidden from all of
our Russian workmen. This secret is to be preserved and the fact
that the plates have been buried is to be erased from the memory
of the natives.

5. If it should happen that ships of other nations should reach
those regions for the same purpose, you are empowered to declare
that the land and the commercial rights belong to the Russian Empire and that the land was first discovered by Russian seafarers.

6. The Company representative [G.I.] Shelikhov has asked
me for permission for the Company to hire workers from among
the native inhabitants because of the shortage of Russian workmen. I find no objection to this and so give my permission on this
condition: that every man be compensated for his work with decent pay, and that each be treated not only in a manner which
human beings deserve, but in a manner which will also carry out
the wish and intent of the wise and humane Autocrat. By treating

them justly and giving them honest pay for their labor, you will not only provide the Company with help needed in the business, but you will also use this as a means of making them contented subjects of Russia under the wise administration of our great Empress, and will inspire in them the desire to become subjects of the Russian scepter.

7. Whenever a special expedition is sent to a place you have discovered, when vessels carrying our promyshlenniks go there, you should instruct them to try diligently to find new places, places not previously discovered. Thus not only may they claim the discovery of these new areas and thereby gain better trade opportunities for themselves, but also their efforts may be recognized by the Crown with praise and respect. This will also eliminate the constant complaints from one company or another, and the abuse of native inhabitants. Further, it will eliminate the need to search for transgressors, which is required by law, if companies do not remain in one place.

8. Send a detailed description of all vegetation in areas your company visits. If you are in a forested area, identify the trees, state whether there are berries, whether there are fruit trees. Describe the animals and birds that live in that climate. Also describe the quality of the soil and state whether or not it may be possible to develop agriculture there.

[Signed] Ivan Iakobii

See: P.A. Tikhmenev. *Istoricheskoe obozrenie obrazovaniia Rossiisko-Amerikanskoi kompanii i deistvii eia do nastoiashchago vremeni* (St. Petersburg: 1861–63), II, Appendix, 21–23.

54

A PERSONAL UKAZ FROM EMPRESS CATHERINE II TO IVAN V. IAKOBII, GOVERNOR GENERAL OF SIBERIA, APPROVING HIS INVESTIGATION INTO CRUELTIES PERPETRATED BY RUSSIAN PROMYSHLENNIKS AGAINST NATIVES ON ISLANDS IN THE NORTH PACIFIC OCEAN

We have noted from your report to the Senate the information concerning pillaging, cruelty and inhumanity allegedly perpetrated by seagoing promyshlenniks against the inhabitants of the [North Pacific] islands. We fully approve your decision to investigate this matter, but at the same time We feel compelled to give you the following instructions.

1. You are to make a report about these cruelties, with all substantiated facts, to Navy Captain Lieutenant [Joseph] Billings when his voyages take him to any of these islands. We Ourselves will issue similar instructions to Navy Captain [Grigorii I.] Mulovskii at the time he departs on his voyage.

2. When your investigation is complete, those found guilty of violence and pillaging are not to escape their deserved lawful fine and punishment.

3. Those who have been accused of such transgressions, even though they are only under suspicion, [will be held] and neither their owners, prikashchiks or servitors will be allowed to hunt at sea while the investigation is being conducted.

4. Finally, all seagoing promyshlenniks and servitors who are sent out to collect iasak are to be given absolutely firm instructions not to perpetrate any cruelty against the native inhabitants of those regions, neither are they to pillage or inflict burdens on them, under the threat of immediate punishment. If a complaint is made, an immediate investigation is to be undertaken, and the guilty are to be punished accordingly.

Reference: Russia. *Polnoe sobranie zakonov rossiiskoi imperii s 1649 goda*. First Series (St. Petersburg: 1830), XXII, 881–882.

55

A MEMORANDUM BY GRIGORII I. SHELIKHOV ON A CONVERSATION
WITH JOHN LEDYARD, AN AMERICAN SERVING AS A MARINE CORPO-
RAL ON CAPTAIN COOK'S THIRD VOYAGE

First. He questioned me with intense curiosity as to where I
had been and in what place; whether [our] fur trade and commerce extend far into the Pacific from the Russian side and along
the American mainland. [He also asked] in what locations and
what latitudes our establishments are, *where our government markers have been placed*, in what years and by whom.

I replied that we have been trading for a long time in the
northern, southern and eastern parts of the Pacific, that we built
our establishments in many places during this time, and that the
government markers were placed at this time but that I do not
remember precisely in which years or which locations. I also said
that our trade commenced by means of the Bering and other
maritime expeditions, *along the American mainland beginning from
Cape St. Hermogenes*, which he was familiar with. I said that at the
present time our [North Eastern] company has brought these establishments into complete order and that our settlements extend
to Cape St. Elias, on down the coast toward California and inland, and that the people in these places have come under Russian
authority. Furthermore, in order to keep watch over the new islands, *for three years two of our company ships* have been cruising in
the waters between California, Unalaska and Cape St. Hermogenes on Kodiak Island—a triangle extending from 65° northern
latitude down to 40°.

2. He was also eager to learn from me whether at the present
time many of our Russian ships are trading with these islands,
and how many Russians are on the ships. He asked how many
people I had left on the American mainland. He stated that there
are more than 10,000 Europeans along the coast north of California, and that they have for a long time held the coast from California north to Cape St. Elias in 50° northern latitude. He conveyed
this information as if to alarm me, so I parried with the reply that
people from other powers were not to be in these places without
the permission of the Russian monarch.

3. He also said that he had been with [Captain James] Cook near Cape Chukotsk in 73° northern latitude, and that they had taken iasak from the Chukchi consisting of sea otter pelts. [He also said] that some of the people had supposedly been brought under the suzerainty of the English crown. Here his inaccuracy was apparent, for the people known as Chukchi who live in the vicinity of Cape Chukotsk, and especially those who live in 73° northern latitude, never hunt sea otters. Instead, they buy them from Gizhiginsk at very high prices through the barter of marten pelts, and make them into garments. From this it is obvious that he mistakenly considers many persons as subjects of the English crown who have long belonged to our Russian scepter.

4. He stated that he had been with Cook on his last voyage, for which reason he could have been in Kamchatka. But upon further investigation of his claims, and in considering reports of Cook's visit made by persons known to me, I find that he was never there at all. He speaks either of things he has heard related, or that he has learned through the reports of other persons. For example, he maintained that some of the Aleuts and Russians from the Aleutian Islands came to him aboard the ship and left a note. But when I questioned him further as to precisely which island, what people, old or young, he immediately remembered that he was not there himself, but had been sent off to another ship. He made similar evasive and vague replies to many other questions I posed.

5. Concerning [Joseph] Billings, he said that it was imperative that he meet with him, and through him to reach the American mainland. Then he plans to go inland alone, on foot, across North America. But then I mentioned to him that the native peoples of the northern part of America, from the cape of Alaska from where he proposes to walk along the coast of Canada, and especially those in the interior, are warlike and constantly carry on internecine battles. [I said that] from what I had *heard* it would be dangerous for a lone European to cross there. He appeared to yield on this matter, and then revealed his intention of going on to California and following the coast from 49° down to 40°.

6. The [rest of the] conversation concerned matters supposedly less important to him such as: the Kuril Islands at the present time, whether there are Russian settlements on the islands, [and if so] how large they are, whether they have been es-

tablished there for a long time, on precisely which island the main Russian settlement is located, and whether the Russians there communicate with the Japanese.

To these questions I gave brief replies: on the Kuril Islands a large number of Russians have always lived near the Japanese limits. I observed from this that he evidently is quite interested in this matter.

Reference: Library of Congress, Manuscript Division. Yudin Collection, Box 2, Folder 29.

See: N.N. Bashkina et al., eds. *Rossiia i SShA: Stanovlenie otnoshenii, 1765–1815* (Moscow: 1980), 156–157.

56

NOVEMBER 7, 1787

A REPORT FROM IVAN V. IAKOBII, GOVERNOR GENERAL OF SIBERIA,
TO ALEKSANDR A. BEZBORODKO, COLLEGE OF FOREIGN AFFAIRS, CON-
CERNING THE TRAVELS OF JOHN LEDYARD

First, before I have the honor of presenting to Your Excellency
my remarks regarding the outcome of the earlier visit here of
the American gentleman John Ledyard, I must make a point of
describing his arrival.

This occurred in the middle of August this year, and since a
foreigner was involved, it was immediately reported to me. His
title of *dvorian* [nobleman] aroused my intense curiosity to find
out, as prudently as possible, his intentions in such a remote region. Through the report of the Governor of Kolyvan, Lieutenant
General Meller, which referred briefly only to his stay in Bar-
naul, I felt it would not be out of order to ask about everything
that had prompted his visit here.

He presented me with the travel papers and passport given to
him in St. Petersburg: the first from the post office there, and the
second from the gubernia administration, dated May 7 [1787]. In
these papers he is referred to as an American dvorian being sent
to Moscow to request permission to travel to America by way of
Ekaterinburg, Korkina, Kolyvan, Irkutsk and Okhotsk. I cannot
give Your Excellency any assurance of whether or not he has actually been in any of these places, however, because there was no
validation on either the travel papers or the passport.

From this I conclude that he obtained the passport from the
gubernia administration in St. Petersburg and then later also received travel papers from the post office, which gave him free passage to this town by way of the mentioned places. His primary
goal, which he may have discussed in an earlier meeting with the
gubernia administration and for that reason noted in his passport,
and which he also announced to me, is basically that he is traveling here and visiting this region to collect information pertaining
to natural history. I have since realized that he has another purpose, which Your Excellency will see from the following account.

While he was here I extended the usual courtesies to him and
inquired of him about his travels. My first question was how he

hoped to accomplish his goal [of reaching America] via the extremely difficult route to Okhotsk, and the voyage from there by sea? He replied that in order to voyage from Okhotsk to the coast of America he would need the assistance of a certain secret Northeastern Expediton [Billings-Sarychev Expedition, 1785–1793], and that for this it would only be necessary for him to meet with the leader of the expedition, Navy Captain of the second rank [Joseph] Billings. [He said that] the islands in the North Pacific are well-known to him because when [Captain James] Cook visited that region he [Ledyard] had voyaged with him during the entire expedition. Ledyard's ultimate destination of this present travel is the coast of North America; from thence he will travel overland.

As soon as I informed him that although the people who live along that coast are subjects of Russia, they are fierce and could be a problem for him, he seemed inclined to alter his route. He immediately shifted his plans so that he would proceed toward 49° northern latitude, toward California, and then proceed across the continent from there.

After this discussion he was very curious about islands in the North Pacific. He asked complex questions in order to learn as much as he could about when they were occupied by the Russian state, how many of the local inhabitants are engaged in the fur trade there, and what establishments they have on the islands. He did not manage to learn all he wished, however, for I only told him that Russia took possession of these places long ago and that she has received *dan* [tribute paid by conquered peoples] from the local [native] people, for which they have receipts.

The American, however, then slyly shifted the conversation and maintained that the coast from California north to 50°, to Cape St. Elias, has long been occupied by the English, and that there are some 10,000 persons from various European countries there. Cook's expedition voyaged as far north as 73°, in the vicinity of the Chukotsk people, some of whom were brought under English suzerainty, and as proof of this [the English] collected iasak from them in sea otter pelts. However, as Your Excellency is aware, it was our Russian expeditions that discovered not only Cape St. Elias but also the area from California north to Unalaska and Cape Hermogenes on Kodiak, a triangle extending south to 40° and north to 65°. And I can assure you that the crews of our companies are even now engaged in the fur trade there. In the land of the Chukotsk people, as far as I know, there does not even exist such fur trade as [Ledyard] speaks of, in which Cook supposedly received iasak in sea otters from the local people. Instead, the natives there actually obtain sea otter pelts from the Gizhiginsk region, and in a rather small amount at that.

In conclusion he tried to substantiate his presence on Cook's voyage by declaring that the native people who live on the Aleutian Islands came out to their ship. But he had no proof of this and he suddenly started asking questions about the Kuril Islands and Russian establishments there. When he could not obtain information on this, he finally made the pronouncement that whoever is the stronger of course has the very first right to occupy these islands.

In order not to prolong my report to Your Excellency of other lesser plans of the foreigner, I will not burden you further. In regard to the present matter I will only venture most humbly to ask your kind consideration of whether I have done the right thing in this situation. His confused travel pattern and way of putting his thoughts into words were sufficiently strong grounds for me to doubt him, especially since he does not have a proper passport even to this place; he only has travel papers.

It is not necessary to assure Your Excellency that this American is not English, because his actions as well as his conversation make it clear that he is not. It is entirely possible however that he was sent here by the English to obtain information on these places.

Because of the unsophisticated condition of people here, which Your Excellency knows, this traveler would easily be able to obtain any information he wished from them. [For this reason] I have decided to send him to Iakutsk, where it will be more difficult for him to put his plans into action. I have sent a secret directive there to the Commandant, [Grigorii A.] Marklovskii, so that he will welcome [Ledyard] courteously but will not overlook even the least of his crafty activities. In the meantime he is to try to persuade Ledyard to remain in Iakutsk because it is so difficult to travel to Okhotsk from there during the winter. In this way he can be detained there unobtrusively until I am able to obtain more detailed information about him; however he should be assured that as soon as it is possible to travel he will be sent on to Okhotsk.

The immediate result of my directive is that Marklovskii has informed me that the American arrived in Iakutsk. Ledyard maintained his composure when he learned from navy Captain Lieutenant [Christian, grandson of Vitus] Bering, who was there with the [Billings] expedition, that Billings, the expedition leader, had already left Okhotsk.

Ledyard's plans are not known as yet. For this reason, having brought this matter to Your Excellency's attention, I must reveal to you that when the American left Irkutsk he left a letter with me for Professor [Peter Simon] Pallas in St. Petersburg, and in it he enclosed another letter to England. I have the letter here, as well as another one to Collegiate Councillor [Aleksandr M.] Karamyshev. Since I am reluctant to send the second letter to England I have decided to send it to Your Excellency. If you find my comments on this situation worthy of your attention, my dear sir, perusal of the letter may more conveniently disclose this man's previously secret intentions.

I have not felt it necessary to impose this matter upon Her Imperial Majesty, realizing full well how busy the Most Gracious Sovereign is with state matters of the greatest importance. However at the present time I leave it to Your Excellency to decide [whether or not to inform Her] about the travels of this dvorian Ledyard. I make bold to add that should it be necessary to send him back to St. Petersburg from here, this will not present a problem, for there is plenty of time.

With this, I conclude, my dear sir, most Illustrious Count.

Your most devoted servant,
Ivan Iakobii

Reference: TsGADA, f. 24, d. 62, ch. 2, ll. 419–422.
See: N. N. Bashkina et al., eds. *Rossiia i SShA: stanovlenie otnoshenii 1765–1815* (Moscow: 1980), 162–164.

57

MAY—NOVEMBER, 1787

A REPORT FROM GRIGORII I. SHELIKHOV, REQUESTING SPECIAL PRIVI-
LEGES FOR HIS COMPANY IN NORTH AMERICA

A decision has been reached by my companions who were with me on a voyage in the North Pacific Ocean where our purpose was to discover previously unknown islands near the American mainland. Although those islands and their inhabitants, who are very numerous, have been studied a little, nevertheless in order to make a full and comprehensive report to Her Imperial Majesty, the Most August Monarch and Autocrat of All Russia, and to authorities appointed by Imperial authority, the following privileges are necessary.

1. In order for our company to make a thorough survey of the American mainland and its peoples, and as quickly as possible submit complete (and hitherto unknown) information, which we will supplement in the future to include information on everything we encounter there, we need to be assured that there will be no outside interference from anyone, either authorities in the Okhotsk oblast or those in Kamchatka. To enable the company to carry out this important undertaking to discover unknown places and inhabitants, in spite of the great distances involved, and also to bring benefit to the company, we ask the all merciful Imperial Majesty, through Her grand Imperial benevolence toward Her subjects, to decree that the company be under the leadership of the official who is closest, that is, the Governor General of Irkutsk, the head of this gubernia. We also request that no one but he have any authority over company matters.

2. Assistance is imperative for future endeavors by the company. It needs to have full control over the fortified positions it will build, and it also needs to have the right to defend and protect peoples whom I have brought under the command of the company as subjects of Her Imperial Majesty. We need to have military personnel who will establish and maintain discipline; for this purpose we will need as many as 100 men. Upon approval of this request, the following persons should be among those designated for company service: six men who are experienced cannoneers, six cannon foundry men, coppersmiths, wagoneers, two

master gunsmiths from Tula, two master anchor makers, one surveyor who is experienced in mining operations, and two army officers to be selected by the company. The mining officer can also be in charge of describing the natural history of the area. We will also need persons familiar with shipbuilding: two shipwrights or apprentices, two sailors who know rigging, and one who understands cloud formations.

In addition to these, we need two priests and a deacon to educate people who have come into the Greek-Catholic faith, or who may desire to embrace it in the future. This should cause no difficulty whatsoever. The company will maintain all these people at its own expense under one condition: that none of them is to engage in trade which does not rightfully belong to him under any pretext.

3. Because of the distance [from Russia], the company should be allowed to hire any Russian workers, even those who may have false passports, to perform all manner of work, both on land and at sea. Every year the company will pay the state taxes for these persons, to the place from which they have run away. However, there should be an ukaz prohibiting the hiring of persons who have unpaid debts with payments of 24 [or more] rubles per year.

4. While the company is on American soil it should be permitted to bring into suzerainty persons wishing to become subjects of Her Imperial Majesty's throne, by buying American natives who have been slaves for a long time. According to my information, there are a great many such persons there.

If the company finds enough of these people, then for the benefit of the fatherland, and in order to spread the glory of the All Russian Autocratic Throne, the company should be permitted to settle these people. They might go to the harbor of Petropavlovsk [Kamchatka] or to the Kuril Islands or other islands, to places the company selects, where they could become useful. The company should have the right freely to hire Aleuts and Kurils for sea duty and for other company work. The company should also be allowed to have its own harbor and office near the Ud River, and to manage all of its affairs. That office should be supplied from Irkutsk via Iakutsk, by water. Supplies should include things required for navigation and for establishment of the harbor, as well as those items which would be transported from there to the newly discovered places on American islands and on the American mainland. The company should be allowed to select 50 exiles from the gubernia city of Irkutsk to deliver these items from Irkutsk to the new harbor, wherever it may be designated.

5. To manage these affairs the company should depend on the person selected by the will of Her Imperial Majesty and by the Governor General of Irkutsk as the head of that gubernia. However, should it sometimes be necessary to dispatch urgent reports, the company should be allowed to send such reports direct to Her Imperial Majesty, using the company's own couriers.

6. If matters develop in such a way as to serve to glorify Her Imperial Majesty's illustrious throne, the company, at its own expense, should be allowed to establish trade with Japan, China, Korea, India, the Philippines and other islands, and on the American mainland with the Spanish and with Americans. A consular post should be established to deal with all these matters, and should be handled by a person who is knowledgeable about such affairs, and also one who has a suitable bearing. The company should be granted the right to export spirits distilled from fruits and grape wine to Kamchatka, the port of Ud and other places for [tax-]free sale.

7. If the company, on its own initiative, should have the good fortune to find still more peoples and islands, in addition to those mentioned above, which are previously unknown and belong to no power, the company should bring these under the scepter of the Russian throne. If the places are suitable, the company should introduce agriculture and build mills and factories.

8. There are many unforeseen needs caused by the constant levies and by the fact that furs valued at many thousands of rubles are lying in warehouses, useless, because of the closure of the trade through Kiakhta. This is in effect inactive capital. Therefore, in order to assist the company's expectations in this undertaking which has already been started and will be developed further, Her Imperial Majesty should be asked to assist the company by means of a loan of 500,000 rubles for a period of 20 years, with interest, and with a government-owned ship which might be obtained from the port of Okhotsk at the earliest opportunity.

9. The company should have the right to reward its servitors who demonstrate excellence in their work under the supervision

These fine pieces collected by Cook at Nootka Sound now comprise part of the too few North Pacific artifacts preserved from the collections of early Pacific mariners. Shelikhov pressed for monopoly privileges in the North Pacific, but other nations soon established their rights. Cook, *Atlas*, 1784. (OHS neg. 80241)

of officials appointed over them, and under the protection of the company.

Reference: LOII, sobr. Vorontsovykh, No. 476, 11. 379–380 ob.
See: A. I. Andreev, ed. *Russkie otkrytiia v Tikhom Okeane i Severnoi Amerike v XVIII veke* (Moscow: 1948), 223–226.

58

NOVEMBER 30, 1787

REPORT FROM GOVERNOR GENERAL IVAN V. IAKOBII TO EMPRESS
CATHERINE II CONCERNING ACTIVITIES OF THE GOLIKOV-SHELKIHOV
COMPANY ON ISLANDS IN THE NORTH PACIFIC

Your Imperial Majesty's desire, expressed in Your gracious ukaz to me, concerning the establishment of Your authority in the Pacific Ocean, is a matter which will increase the glory of Your Majesty, Your interests, and the well-being of Your subjects.

The people who inhabit that part of America and the islands which extend from the shores of Asia almost all the way to Japan belong to the scepter of Your Majesty. This includes the 22nd island of the Kuril chain, called Atkis or Nadezhda. Their wealth was also acquired for Your Imperial Majesty by the indisputable right of first discovery. These lands were acquired through a substantial financial outlay from the Treasury, and by Russian promyshlenniks who sailed in that ocean. They proclaim [Russia's rights to them] to the entire world, and warn off all who would try to lay claim to those lands and waters. The profits Russian merchants make in trading in those places with the Chinese is evident from the enrichment of the traders whose revenues the Treasury has acquired. The goods they obtain from the Chinese have become necessities, almost indispensable to Your Empire. In return, they give the Chinese superfluous [Russian] goods.

For that reason, any encroachment on hunting and trading in America and on the islands which belong to the throne of Your Majesty not only will interfere with all of this, but in time may even terminate the sources of revenue which have brought into Russia a substantial treasure. This will certainly be apparent if other powers are not prevented from taking part in all such activities, and forbidden from the very outset. It is not only trade that will suffer. I also believe that without the significant presence of Your naval forces in these waters it will be impossible to maintain possession of many places which are now in Russian ownership, or even of just some of the best of them, which in time could be even more profitable, due to certain circumstances.

Consequently, Your Majesty's noble ambitions should be realized as soon as possible, in my opinion. There is no doubt that the route which the famous voyager, Cook, showed to his countrymen will be abandoned, now that Russia's acquisitions and gains will stimulate her imagination. Russia's actions in dispatching the fleet from the Baltic Sea, and in establishing port facilities on the Ud River, will effectively bar any outside interference.

Your Imperial Majesty most graciously assigned me the latter of these projects: on the basis of my local knowledge I was to ascertain the feasibility of carrying this out. I would like to assure Your Majesty that the harbor facilities on the Ud River are so much better than those in Okhotsk that a large part of the problems associated with that port will be eliminated, along with any ancillary details, and I will have the happy honor of reporting on this to Your Majesty in the future.

I believe the hardships of travel to Okhotsk are occasioned by the fact that our promyshlenniks' vessels cannot be armed to the same degree as the ships of merchants of other European powers. It is also true that up until now it has not been necessary to arm these vessels any more heavily than they are at present. They have really only had to defend themselves against the savages. And we cannot assume as probable every danger inherent in the acquisition of profit. When the route to the new harbor is improved and relations with foreign traders will persuade them to use it also, there is no doubt that all ships used by Your Majesty's subjects for sailing and trading will be better constructed than they are at present. This alone will help to strengthen and defend the territories in the Pacific Ocean. It is certainly true that the establishment of harbor facilities will serve to prevent any impulsive antagonistic actions. This will take a good bit of time because a new enterprise in such a distant place will have to have careful support.

In the meantime, in accordance with Your Imperial Majesty's instructions, I have issued preliminary warnings about subjects of other powers who may wish to carry on trade there. I have also given the necessary instructions to officials along the coast and to our promyshlenniks as to how to deal with these persons. However, I cannot assure Your Majesty that all of this has had the desired results, and that my efforts have convinced them that these lands belong to Russia by right of first discovery. Not satisfied with this action alone, at the first opportunity I sent 30 bronze plaques with the insigne of the Russian Empire, and an equal number of iron plates with bronze crosses, and with the following words engraved, "This land belongs to Russia." I entrusted half of these signs to be distributed by the company of Mikhail Golikov, the Kursk merchant Ivan Golikov and the Rylsk merchant, Grigorii Shelikhov, who on behalf of their company will voyage along the American coast between 61° and 47° latitude to survey and describe this coast and the nearby islands. I gave personal instructions on placing these plaques in appropriate places near harbor sites, in bays and on the mainland of the Alaska peninsula, in the same place where in the year 1784 an English ship anchored which had gained enormous wealth from hunting. I also ordered these plaques to be distributed farther south if possible, so that the first would be implanted in 44°. Shelikhov has been instructed to keep the plaques secret not only from the local people, but even from his own crew. He is also to bury a description of the landmarks of the places where he has emplaced a plaque; this to be done a few paces away. I sent the other half of these plaques to the commanding officer of the Okhotsk oblast, and instructed him to keep them there until there is an opportunity to emplace them in appropriate locations on the Kuril Islands.

I believe that immediate attention must be given to taking steps to prevent foreigners from visiting islands in the Pacific Ocean or the mainland itself. If the English come to consider that region as a new arm of their trade, it is possible other nations will follow. Profits already received by those who have an interest in the privileged East India Company will encourage them in such efforts. The more successful they become, the more difficult it will be to stop them. Consequently it appears absolutely imperative to declare to them [Russia's] rights to her discovered coast of America and the islands in the Pacific Ocean, this to be done through Your Majesty's ministers accredited to European courts.

Meanwhile, although it is possible that the English and other powers may not protest this just acquisition, in view of current attitudes on these matters, a premature termination of an agreement would involve needless losses. And at the same time, taking into account English interest in that territory and their ambitions to acquire wealth, I cannot waver in my view that other European naval powers would also be equally interested. The honor of Your Empire requires that such insolence result in shame and repentance. To prevent this it is necessary to have reliable protection consisting of several frigates which would be stationed in the Pacific Ocean. In my judgment this problem cannot be solved in any way other than by establishing a port here.

The present war with the Turks [1787–1792] poses certain difficulties such as the dire necessity to increase our strength in this sea directly from the Baltic fleet. No matter how vital the fleet under Captain [G.I.] Mulovskii's command could be for this region, it cannot accomplish more than just preventing new attempts by foreign merchants' ships, or bringing about an improved perception of Your Empire's strength on the part of the Chinese government.

In order to accomplish this while implementing measures already in existence or others that could be put into effect, I do see a need to postpone issuing formal notice to European powers concerning the islands in the North Pacific and the coasts of America being in the possession of the scepter of Your Majesty, until a new port has been established on the Sea of Okhotsk. Its construction will decrease the great expense and untold difficulties associated with the perils of the route to Okhotsk which have in the past hindered the construction of even a single naval vessel. This new facility will facilitate strengthening the naval fleet here. It appears that the mere presence of the fleet here will warn them of our rights, and the brusque action will temper their enthusiasm. This is necessary for their own good and information. On the other hand, it will also be an indication that in spite of their protestations we will protect our hunting in places they are attempting to occupy.

However, I consider hunting profits a temporary matter. Merciful Sovereign, we know from many examples that the hunting has decreased substantially each year. There is absolutely no doubt, when one realizes that millions of animals have been taken here. The increased number of promyshlenniks is certainly responsible for this. One can therefore suppose that in a few years the animals will be completely depleted, or at the very least, that the great expenses associated with hunting will not continue to be rewarded at the same level.

Neither the islands nor the American coast inhabited by savages have yet been explored by naturalists. Previously this has been virtually impossible. If information does exist about certain areas, it was not obtained by experts or well-informed persons.

However, if an eagerness to acquire knowledge were to be applied diligently, it is possible new wealth might be found there, which has never previously been known. It is also possible we could compensate for the decrease in hunting.

I will not dwell further on these matters because I do not wish to burden Your Majesty, and indeed, this has already been stated.

Your Imperial Majesty is greatly concerned about educating Your subjects so that they can fully appreciate their well-being. I therefore turn now to the conduct of the Rylsk merchant, Shelikhov, and the things he has done on the islands of Kodiak, Afognak and other places during his voyage there. All the actions he and his men have taken affect hunting in America, and its protection.

This merchant Shelikhov, along with Captain Mikhail [Golikov] and the merchant Golikov, have entered into an agreement concerning hunting in the Pacific Ocean. They pledge that Shelikhov is to take on the responsibility of building ships and sending them there, as well as husbanding their joint capital. The chief goal of this agreement is to discover new islands and other places in that ocean. If land is discovered, they are to use any available means not contrary to law to make the native inhabitants understand their heathen condition, and to improve their savage ways and crude habits. They are to show the natives Your Imperial Majesty's concern for them, and guide them in improving their ways.

On the basis of this agreement the merchant Shelikhov made all the necessary preparations, took three galiots for his voyage and sailed out from the mouth of the Urak River on August 16, 1783. He returned from that voyage more than three years later. When he reached Irkutsk, he submitted to me papers concerning his voyage. The most important papers are the notes which he kept about various places he visited, both those previously known and those which he discovered; a chart of his voyage to which is appended a chart of the islands of Kodiak (also known as Kykhtak), Afognak and a number of others located nearby. For Your Imperial Majesty's review I am submitting this map with the plan, as well as his notes and observations about the islands he discovered and places where he has pacified the native inhabitants.

I have kept these notes in the same condition in which he submitted them to me, so Your Majesty may see more precisely all of his actions as a whole, rather than in extracts which of course would not include all the circumstances he encountered. From these notes and the map it is apparent that his course took him to the first of the known islands, in spite of the fact that other promyshlenniks had warned him of how dangerous the islanders are. In the past they have been considered hostile and bloodthirsty because of their huge numbers. He received this warning from various promyshlenniks who had been in Chugach Bay on three vessels, aboard which there were 300 men. They attempted to spend the winter there in 1783, but were constantly harassed by the Chugach, who are related to the inhabitants of Kodiak and Afognak. The promyshlenniks lost many men and were never allowed to hunt.

Shelikhov and his men arrived on two galiots, the third having been left on the island of Kodiak with its crew of 130 men. No sooner had Shelikhov and his men gone ashore than the savages, who had gathered together in a seething mass, attacked him during the night. He had to use all the resources at his disposal to defend himself against them. Although he succeeded, there was still danger that all the promyshlenniks would be killed, for the natives were enraged by the failure of their attack and began to gather reinforcements from many distant places so they could carry out their plan. When Shelikhov learned of this he was determined not to let all these savages unify, and to that end he dispersed those who were awaiting assistance by destroying their naturally protected fortification. These two major instances and several lesser attempts by the island natives against Shelikhov were the only ones that posed serious danger to him.

However in the end all of his activities in that part of the world, as can be seen from his notes, reveal his intelligence and great moderation in working for his own profit; he has also been concerned for Your Imperial Majesty's interests. His ability to bring hostile, rude, and savage people to realize the benefits of peace is testimony to his character and wisdom. He not only pacified them, but even persuaded them to protect him and defend his interests.

Another testimony to his ability is the fact that they have voluntarily surrendered their children as hostages as a sign of their loyalty to him; I am also inclined to think that these savages agreed to this so their children could be taught Russian, which has previously been unknown to them. This reveals their endurance as well as their realization of their own mental shortcomings. When he told them about everything to be found in Russia—the structure, order, beauty, the multitude of people, the administration, peace and security—they all were overcome with curiosity and 40 of them, both men and women, agreed to visit Russian settlements. They went to Okhotsk with Shelikhov on his return voyage. Fifteen of these people are now en route to Irkutsk in order to see the city, its inhabitants and their way of life. The rest of the 40 have been sent back to their original homes.

I believe [what he has written of] his voyages as well as the circumstances he encountered while he was there and new ways that he introduced there. I also believe his statement that some of these savages have accepted the [Christian] faith which he has propagated among them, and have been baptized in accordance with rituals permitted in case there is no priest available. I cannot verify that they were convinced of the necessity of doing this, for they knew the consequences of their action. But I mention this in regard to all that has been written. The inhabitants of those lands are gentle by nature, and they are willing and agreeable when they realize they are being treated with kindness and generosity. Later I will be pleased to report how much support Sheilikhov's efforts will require in order to prevent corrupt profit-seeking and ignorance from arousing these people, and to help Shelikhov create a beneficial situation there which will correspond with the intent of Your Majesty.

There is not the slightest doubt that these American natives must be protected from all foreign interference, and if this is done they will always belong to the Empire of Your Majesty. But their brutish minds still cannot conceive the same kind of sincerity and loyalty that all of Your other subjects so zealously exhibit. They themselves must perceive the need to become loyal subjects of Your Majesty. Since they are the unfortunate victims of total ignorance, they do not and cannot understand what a priceless benefit it is to be Your subjects. They will destroy themselves if they refuse to be brought into harmony with Your thoughts and no other, which is proposed as a means for ending the imposition of iasak.

Now I will turn to Shelikhov's acquisitions on the islands of Kodiak and Afognak, as well as his stay on the American mainland between 50° and 62° northern latitude. He has made a considerable outlay for fortifications. I submit sketches of these for Your Imperial review. He has also incurred expense for construction necessary to persuade the Koniag, Kenai and Chugach people [to become friendly]. He has maintained these people there at his own expense and that of his associates. I conclude from all of this that we see the loyalty of this association, and above all of Shelikhov himself, who is its guiding spirit and is zealous in the service of the throne of Your Imperial Majesty.

When he left there he instructed his deputy, who was to remain, to use the two galiots to carry on explorations for unknown islands. One of the galiots was instructed to sail in the longitudes between 49° and 73° from Okhotsk meridian, which he had adopted for his own calculations, and in open sea between the latitudes of 60° and 40°. The other galiot, when he departed from the Sea of Okhotsk, had been carried by headwinds in another direction but finally reached the island of Kodiak; its instructions were then to sail north between the closest point of Asia and America. The third galiot will be turned back into a transport vessel.

Taking all of this into account, I believe this zeal should be encouraged through formal recognition and the granting of certain privileges which their own capital and labor can exploit there. This could be achieved by granting exclusive rights, within certain time limits as may be deemed wise, to hunt furbearing animals in those places which they have discovered through sailing their ships there, or in places where the inhabitants have become friendly toward them, between 51° and 65° latitude and 53° and 73° longitude, calculating the latter from the Okhotsk meridian which was first indicated on Shelikhov's chart of his voyage.

I am aware of how much Your Imperial Majesty in Your monarchical heart is opposed to anything that might be called a monopoly that could give the impression of oppressing any of Your subjects. I would not have presumed even to suggest such a proposal if it did not seem to me that great benefit would accrue to Your interests and those of Your Majesty's subjects. But I do see the need for exclusive hunting rights for Shelikhov and his associates in the places I have mentioned. This might enable Shelikhov to bring the people of Kodiak, Afognak and other islands into a good relationship with him. It is evident from his travel notes that he managed to put a thousand willing savages under the command of one Russian, without danger. If he could bring all of these people into friendship, his relationship with them and his zeal to prove his loyalty will be even more effective among these people. And in turn they will trust him and follow the course he sets for them.

Because of their devotion to him they will adopt Russian customs and have a better understanding of peaceful conduct, both public and private. Thus they will also have a better perception of the Russians than they have now, and also a better understanding of themselves. This in turn may lead them finally to seek means to please Russian subjects, and they themselves, understanding the greater glory and might of Your Majesty, will become loyal and zealous subjects. However, they must be led in that direction gradually, in my judgment, through someone they trust. Time will show them that not only Shelikhov but his people as well are necessary to them, and that they understand how to treat them. This, however, will come about only when they have been prepared and made ready.

While I am dwelling on this awaited success, I would like to elaborate on the reasons that have led me to suggest to Your Majesty that Shelikhov and his associates be granted exclusive privileges. In light of the benefits and advantages which I shall mention presently, I will now deal with the regions and territories which European commercial associations have acquired in various distant parts of the world. I shall omit accounts of barbarism which have occurred in a number of places where there have been such establishments, for these are not suitable to be mentioned to Your Majesty and, furthermore, the times and superstitions which caused these have now come to an end.

Another factor which prompts me to recommend that Shelikhov and his associates be granted privileges is that the area is far distant from the interior of Russia where there is such a multitude of merchants and where every person can easily benefit from the fruits of his own labors. There, the very idea of a monopoly would be a restraint to Your Majesty's subjects.

In contrast, hunting in the North Pacific Ocean requires a great expenditure of capital, much more than hunting within the Empire. As far as we know, no promyshlennik has ever hunted in the region where Shelikhov has established his enterprise, although there were a few vessels in 1761, 1776 and 1780 on a cape on Kodiak Island called Agaekhtalik; these vessels, however, were forced back and driven off by the savages, with great losses. They were not allowed to hunt, even though the vessels had large enough crews to offer opposition and to defend themselves against attack. Further, even if the island natives are presently inclined to peaceful behavior and ready to be well-disposed [to the Russians], it is impossible to state categorically that they will not destroy and undo everything. All promyshlenniks will visit these islands, and one simply cannot suppose that all, in the multitude who will visit the islands, will behave in the same manner. This diversity will be inimical to Shelikhov's enterprise, for it appears that the savages will defend themselves by killing [the Russians] and waging incessant battles against them.

This leads me to believe that it will be better to entrust the matter to one man who is well-known and respected, rather than to many persons. Accordingly, if Your Imperial Majesty were pleased to approve this plan, and grant exclusive rights to Shelikhov and his associates to hunt and trade in the reported vastness of the ocean and in America, then it would seem necessary to provision Shelikhov, so as not to hinder what he has begun. If this is to be the case, he should be given complete instructions on how he is to proceed regarding the establishment of new enterprises.

I believe his most important responsibility, and the very first point to be made, is to see to it that all reasonable means are used to ameliorate the savagery of the natives, and to work on behalf of their needs, using all available means to improve their life. At the same time every effort should be made to give them some real education as quickly as possible and to establish agriculture there in the future. These two factors can have a great impact on sailing in the Pacific Ocean. Shelikhov has made observations concerning the superb climate in the places he has visited in America as well as on Kodiak and Afognak and other islands nearby. He has both observed and experienced success in planting various seeds. In the notes on his voyage he has mentioned the abundance of wild animals, fish, birds, fine meadows, rich soil and the amount of forest on the island of Afognak and on the American coast which is suitable for shipbuilding. He has also written of the excellent harbors. All of this appears to me extremely important, and of great interest to Your Majesty. Basing my judgment on all of this, I most humbly report my views, and how I believe it is possible to strengthen the security of this region and the safety of Your subjects who will sail there.

Meanwhile, since as soon as the fleet there is reinforced, all doubts on the part of European courts as to the possession of this region by Your Majesty will be favorably resolved, I will now turn to the matter of Afognak Island and the American mainland. I propose building fortifications, one on the American coast as far south as possible, and another on the island which Shelikhov says has the best harbor for ships, and also has timber suitable for ship construction.

The fortifications should be just field fortifications with deep moats and parapets. I believe that such a stronghold on the mainland could protect the entire American coast all the way north to Cape St. Elias. It would at least prevent any minor attempt to encroach, and above all it could hold the local natives in complete submission and obedience. Afognak and the other islands there will be responsible for suppressing any attempted encroachments. Further, it goes without saying that such measures will aid the fleet proceeding there to cruise in those waters by providing protection so they will be less exposed to danger.

I do not see the need to build further fortifications, because before Shelikhov left Kodiak he sent a detachment of his men to build fortifications on Cape St. Elias. They are to be assisted by a thousand Koniag natives from Kodiak and other islands. There will also be 70 Aleuts from the Fox Islands. They have volunteered for this service and will point out [appropriate] places and persuade local tribes to behave peacefully. In time this fortification will extend its influence north and will support the other two. Judging from Shelikhov's plan for construction and from his notes, it is apparent that he has already decided to build a stronghold on the island of Afognak. Indeed, as he points out, it may be now be completed. For that reason there would be no need to build a new one there. However, it will be built of wood and therefore will be unable to withstand a heavy attack. For that reason it will only be effective in protecting the local people. I therefore propose that a real fort be built on the mainland, in the 47th parallel, unless it is possible to build it farther south.

Two questions must now be addressed. First, who should build these; second, who should maintain them. These questions are very important because the answers depend on Your Most Gracious Majesty's approval of the preferential rights of the company. However, if [these fortifications] should be of benefit to Your Imperial Grace, then any apparent difficulty will be resolved. The company will use every means to protect its own interests and will also use every effort to assist hunting. It will use the same people both for hunting and building these fortifications. As for maintaining these fortified places, the government should send 50 men into each fort, both cossacks and soldiers. These should be taken from the Okhotsk and Iakutsk oblast commands, so they will be men who have already become accustomed to the local diet in the region and will not be burdened by being assigned to these places.

For better protection of these forts I suggest that they be provided with an adequate number of artillery pieces and all supplies, and that experienced gunners make up a good part of the complement of men.

Since all servitors will be more involved in protecting the interests of the company for the duration of their service, they should be compensated by being maintained at company expense for the duration of their service, and receiving double pay.

I believe there should be one staff officer in charge of the garrison command in each fort. These officers should not use their authority beyond the responsibility of their command. They should exercise their authority in accordance with the precise instructions they will have received. Should need arise they would act in accord with Shelikhov himself. Shelikhov should be responsible for locating fortification sites, since he has already stated that the entire territory is familiar to him. He should be assigned one man experienced in engineering so the fortifications will be properly constructed in accordance with the rules of fort construction. Shelikhov has agreed to send annual reports back via his transport vessel, and will include information on all matters there.

Earlier I was pleased to submit to Your Majesty a special recommendation concerning Shelikhov's conduct on the islands and in America and his concern in dealing with these savages in such a way that they can be brought out of their primitive ways. To accomplish this and to soften their hearts, I suggest sending two educated priests there to propagate the Christian faith among them. In my judgment this is the [best] way to accelerate the humanitarian interests of Your Majesty. If they are converted to Christianity in this manner, these people will recognize their own deficiencies, and the examples [set by the priests] may transform them into good citizens and ardent subjects of Your Imperial Majesty. I believe that priests appointed for this work would have to go of their own free will and would have to be men impelled by a zealous spirit to spread the word of God. Considering the great distance they would be sent, they should receive double salary, and the religious authorities should supply them with everything they need for their mission. If it is possible to build a church, it should be provisioned. The priests should be permitted to spend as much time there as they deem necessary.

Merciful Sovereign, the ideas which I have proposed appear to me to be easily achievable within a few years. In that distant place it is possible to have settlements of obvious importance, especially if the proposed port is opened, for this will enable more merchants, who are subjects of Your Majesty, to sail in that sea.

According to Shelikhov, the local natives will not reject anything if they are convinced they will benefit from it. Thus a good example may serve to engender favorable attitudes in them as well as patience toward everything which will improve their present condition and serve to benefit them. Furthermore, a good start in that direction, handled reasonably, would be a definite hindrance toward any outside attempts [to encroach on Russia's claims].

I hasten to endorse all Shelikhov's useful proposals. Meanwhile, until such time as Your Imperial Majesty may deign to review all of this, on the basis of my responsibilities I have authorized that Shelikhov's request be granted and that there be put aboard the ship he is sending to Kodiak 500 puds of rye flour from Okhotsk and 300 puds of rigging, which he has agreed to pay for in due time either in goods or in cash, depending on the needs of the Treasury.

Finally, believing that Your Majesty may wish to have Shelikhov himself enlarge on matters pertaining to his travels and adventures, I have decided to send him personally to You with his report.

In conclusion, in submitting all of the above for Your Majesty's wisdom and insight, I cannot add anything beyond this which I have already had the audacity to attempt to submit herein, which is the result of my most humble and sincere devotion to Your Imperial Throne, to which I shall forever remain most steadfast.

Lieutenant General Ivan Iakobii
Irkutsk, November 30, 1787.

Reference: TsGADA, f. Senata, No. 4383/812, 11. 701–776.
See: A. I. Andreev, ed. *Russkie otkrytiia v Tikhom okeane i Severnoi Amerike v XVIII veke* (Moscow: 1948), 250–265.

59

FEBRUARY, 1788

A PETITION TO EMPRESS CATHERINE II FROM GRIGORII I. SHELIKHOV
AND IVAN L. GOLIKOV, REQUESTING SUPPORT FOR THEIR COMPANY IN
NORTH AMERICA

Most Gracious Sovereign. Lieutenant General and Cavalier [Ivan V.] Iakobii, Governor General of Irkutsk, has already informed You in detail of the discoveries made by our company ships in the North Pacific. Consequently, our humble report to Your Majesty concerning our activities will be brief.

In 1781 Grigorii Shelikhov, a member of our company, began preparations and in 1783 at our expense and at the risk of his life he set out with three galiots that had been built at the port of Okhotsk. He overcame many difficulties and hardships, but following our plans, he reached the island of Kodiak, the prime objective of his voyage. There he constructed a fort in a suitable place and brought the local inhabitants under the suzerainty of Your Imperial Majesty.

From there he continued his voyage and took possession of another island nearby called Afognak. He built a fort there also and brought the natives under [Your Imperial Majesty's] suzerainty. He followed the same procedure with a number of other small islands which extend right up to the coast of the American mainland. He also surveyed the regions nearby, including the coast of the American mainland, and he brought some 50,000 islanders and coastal dwellers under Russian suzerainty. He took some 500 children of leading families as hostages. Finally, through practical observations, he correctly located the islands on a map.

During the nearly two years he was on the main island, he used every means to induce the natives to obey him willingly, not from fear or necessity, but because of his regard for them and concern for their well-being. The means he used to accomplish this were in conformity with humanitarianism and human rights, and as a result his efforts brought complete success. He ended the discord and internecine warfare which had resulted in their killing one another for as long as anyone could remember. He showed them ways of procuring food which they had not known before. In the past lack of food had often threatened their existence. He also gave them the tools they needed for this.

Because he cared for their needs and was concerned for their welfare, he won their respect, gained their trust and persuaded them that the presence of Russians on their territory would bring them many benefits, security and prosperity. At the present time many of them serve us willingly, work for us, assist our people, live alongside them and are provided for by us.

In making this a reality, we exposed ourselves to many dangers and hazards, but never sought anything other than to prove our loyalty to the fatherland and our desire for the public good. These motives have guided us in all our undertakings and they have ameliorated our hardships. We have postponed any thought of personal gain until our ventures prove successful in the future.

As a result of our zeal for the public good the following have taken place:

1. Our associate who was mentioned above [Shelikhov] outfitted two vessels for further explorations. One voyaged from California to the Kuril Islands, between 40° and 55° northern latitude; the other sailed the waters between Asia and America from the Aleutian Island chain, between 55° and 68°.

2. We felt it was imperative [to protect Russian interests and] to prevent outside powers from infringing and we therefore decided to build a fort and harbor facilities on either the 21st or 22nd Kuril island to facilitate the establishment of trade with China and Japan, to assist in further discoveries, and to bring under the mighty power of Your Imperial Majesty nearby islands which were not under any foreign jurisdiction and which as far as we know are at present still not claimed by any nation.

3. We also resolved to lose no time in moving south as far as we could along the coast of the American mainland, and to build settlements in suitable places there so as to thwart any foreign claims to that territory, and also to bring the local inhabitants under Russian suzerainty in the most useful way.

4. In order to send reports on our progress to the government, we decided to organize a postal service, one part of which would go from the American mainland across the strait near Chukotsk Cape, then overland through Atlansk and Zhigansk to the Okhotsk oblast. The other route would be across the ocean via a transport vessel. Before Shelikhov left to return to Russia, he made the necessary preparations and authorized our agents to carry out his plans until he returned.

The ship on which he went to Okhotsk last summer he sent back to America with the necessary provisions for our people there as well as with equipment to build a new packetboat there.

Thus, we have put our trust in God, who favors good intentions, and we do not envision problems. However we believe it is essential for Shelikhov to go there again this summer in order to improve the administration. For that purpose we are outfitting a fourth galiot in Okhotsk.

To carry out these plans we will need more than 250,000 rubles, and cannot expect the return of even one kopeck on this sum. Further we believe that in order to realize all our other enterprises, many of which have already been started, and to place on a solid foundation those that have already been organized with such effort and expense, we will need at least that much in additional funding. Unfortunately our resources are inadequate to carry out our plans. We have spent our capital on the projects we have realized thus far. Furthermore, the closure of the Kiakhta trade leaves us with little hope of recovering expenses in the near future. Consequently the only hope we have left is to appeal to the generosity of Your Imperial Majesty and humbly request that in accordance with Your most gracious manifesto of 1786 You allocate to us from the funds of the Loan Bank a sum of 200,000 rubles.

We also humbly request that You protect us and our property from infringement by others who would like to capitalize on our discoveries. [This would protect us] in places where we have established our enterprises, through our own work and resources, so that no persons will bring about violence or oppression nor will they bring destruction or chaos where we have already built or intend to build.

We also deign to request another favor of Your Imperial Majesty: to single us out in our work, and to honor our achievements with Your Imperial Majesty's special public ukaz which by its force and importance would enable us in that remote area to secure assistance and protection from government authorities against any possible intimidation, and safeguard our enterprises.

In addition, since we plan to build new fortifications, we request a military force of some 100 men, including at least four gunners and two master gunsmiths. We need these men not so much for the islands of Kodiak and Afognak, as for the forts which we intend to build on the coast of the American mainland and on the Kuril Islands, especially in the early stages of our settling there, until the local inhabitants are persuaded to adopt a friendly attitude toward the Russians.

To assist the military personnel we can utilize several thousand island people. They are courageous, strong, adept at coping with difficulties, very skillful and fearless. Further, they obey Russian authorities and have demonstrated their genuine loyalty to Russia and to Your Imperial Majesty. We have witnessed this on many occasions.

Because of their genuine zeal toward Russia, we deign to report to Your Imperial Majesty in all honesty that the islands of Kodiak, Afognak and others nearby, which these people inhabit, are not only devoid of internal disorder, but can be expected to provide firm support for us if any foreign powers exhibit hostile intentions there. Moreover, we can also utilize these people to navigate in local waters if there is a shortage of Russian sailors. The islanders are brave seafarers by nature. They eagerly take up that work and learn seafaring skills more readily than the Russians do.

Most Gracious Majesty, we submit this petition to You most humbly and reverently kiss the dust under the blessed feet of Your Imperial Majesty.

Your Imperial Majesty's most loyal subjects
Ivan Golikov, merchant of Kursk
Grigorii Shelikhov, merchant of Rylsk

Reference: TsGADA, f. 248, d. 4383, 11. 738–740 ob.
See: N. N. Bashkina et al., eds. *Rossiia i SShA: stanovlenie otnoshenii, 1765–1815* (Moscow: 1980), 165–167.

60

A DECREE FROM THE GOVERNING SENATE GRANTING GOLIKOV AND
SHELIKHOV MEDALS AND PROHIBITING PROMYSHLENNIKS FROM PRO-
VOKING ARGUMENTS WITH THE CHINESE

The Procurator General, Cavalier Prince Aleksandr Alekseevich Viazemskii, informed the Governing Senate in writing
that Her Imperial Majesty had reviewed a report prepared by the
Commission on Commerce. The report is appended hereto, in
the original, with all appendices. It concerns navigation and trade
in the Pacific Ocean and along the coast of North America carried
on by the golova and merchant of Kursk, Ivan Golikov, and the
merchant of Rylsk, Grigorii Shelikhov. It also concerns Shelikhov's discovery of a number of unknown islands in the region
and the fact that he has brought native inhabitants under the
suzerainty of Her Majesty. Consequently Her Imperial Highness
has deigned to make the following decisions.

1. Her Imperial Majesty rejects the petition of these merchants in which they ask that the Treasury issue them 200,000
rubles to assist in supporting their newly organized enterprises as
well as their future activity.

2. Her Imperial Majesty does not consider it beneficial to
grant them exclusive rights for these voyages and trade because
such exclusive permission would be contrary to Her Majesty's
policies concerning the elimination of all kinds of monoplies.

3. It will also be impossible to supply them with a military
detachment of up to 100 men and artillery personnel, in view of
the fact that there are scarcely enough military personnel to meet
present needs.

4. However, to reward the zealous efforts of these merchants
on behalf of Her Imperial benefit, through the discovery of unknown lands and peoples, and the inauguration of commercial relations with them, Her Imperial Majesty most graciously grants
each of them a sash and gold medal to wear around their necks
with a portrait of Her Majesty on one side and on the other, a
statement as to why the medals were given. She has also been
pleased to decree that the Governing Senate shall issue them cer-

tificates of honor indicating all the efforts and noble activities they have carried on on behalf of Society.

In addition, Her Imperial Majesty wishes to be informed on this matter: on the basis of what ukaz has iasak been imposed on the Aleutian Islands? If no such ukaz exists, then the merchants are forbidden to collect iasak, for it will not have been legally authorized. Strict orders are to be issued to promyshlenniks operating in the Kuril Islands not to provoke any disputes with the Chinese over territorial jurisdiction in these islands. Further, they are not to encroach on islands under the rule of other powers. And finally, they are to be asked to submit maps and detailed notes about all the places which they have discovered, indicating from where the island inhabitants receive iron, copper and other necessary items; and they are to make extensive descriptions of the American mainland.

In accordance with this the Governing Senate has ordered:

1. The merchants Golikov and Shelikhov are to be summoned to the Senate where they will be informed of Her Imperial Majesty's gracious generosity which She is bestowing on them. At this time they will be asked to submit maps and detailed reports on all the places they have discovered, with an indication from where the island inhabitants receive iron, copper and other necessary items, and they are to make extensive descriptions of the American mainland.

2. The Office of Heraldry is to prepare certificates of honor for them, first submitting a copy for the approval of the Governing Senate.

3. The St. Petersburg Mint is to be instructed to cast the gold medals; the medals are to be equal, and are to be prepared in accordance with previous similar cases, and correspond with point 4 of the Imperial ukaz.

4. The silver sashes are to be purchased with funds from the Senate expense account.

5. Concerning the information requested by Her Majesty as to which ukaz was the basis for imposing iasak on the Aleutian Islands, the Senate is to prepare a brief and the office of the Irkutsk *Namestnichestvo* [administrative unit] is to be asked for information.

6. The office of the Irkutsk Namestnichestvo is to be instructed to carry out Imperial instructions by issuing a firm order

to all promyshlenniks regarding the Kuril Islands. They are not to provoke discords with the Chinese concerning island possession. They are not to infringe on islands which are under the jurisdiction of other powers. And they are to be requested to submit maps and detailed reports on all places which they have discovered, with an indication as to where the island inhabitants procure iron, copper and other necessities. They are also to provide extensive information about the American mainland. After securing this information, the Irkutsk Namestnichestvo office is to submit it to the Senate.

Reference: Russia. *Polnoe sobranie zakonov rossiiskoi imperii s 1649 goda*. First series (St. Petersburg: 1830), XXII, 1105–1107.

61

COMPLAINTS MADE BY NATIVES OF THE UNALASKA DISTRICT TO RUS-
SIAN GOVERNMENT INSPECTORS ABOUT TREATMENT BY RUSSIAN
PROMYSHLENNIKS AND SEAMEN; RESPONSES TO THESE CHARGES
FROM THOSE NAMED BY THE NATIVES

On June 7, 1789, testimony was taken from three Aleuts of Unalaska Island concerning treatment by Russian promy-shlenniks. The Aleuts were: the toion Algamalinag whose baptismal name is Mikhail; the interpreter Saguakh whom the Russians at first called "monkey", but whose baptismal name is Ivan Chuloshnikov; and a woman, Anshiges. They testified that when the pilots Ocheredin and Orekhov and their assistants Izmailov, Gogolev and Lukanin wintered over, there was a quarrel over the allocation of hunting sites. Ocheredin and Polutov were the strongest and so took most of the Aleut laborers and forced them to hunt even during the worst winter storms. As a result three of the Aleuts were drowned.

When Ocheredin and Polutov left Unalaska for the mainland of Alaska, Ocheredin and Polutov took more than 100 Aleut men and women with them and from the Aleuts who remained on the islands they took all their baidarkas, arrows, parkas and provisions. After four years of deprivation of food and clothing, only a few hundred of the Aleuts remained alive.

Among the worst oppressors on Unalaska was the *baidarshchik* [baidara and baidarka supervisor] Pshenichnoi who "treated the islanders tyrannically, kept several Aleut women and young girls as his mistresses and mercilessly beat the Aleuts with ropes and clubs." Six Aleuts were beaten to death and sixteen died of starvation. During two months in winter more than 300 Aleuts died of starvation because the promyshlenniks had taken their provisions.

The Aleuts suffered similar treatment from Polutov, Panin and Popov. Popov stabbed to death every Aleut girl and two men in the Bobrovoi settlement.

[The testimony continued,] "After that the hunting ships of the Greek, Delarov, and of Cherepanov and Nagaev visited Unalaska. Shishaev also came there as well as Potap Zaikov, a pilot for the Orekhov company. Shelikhov also stopped briefly but left the same summer. Delarov spent the winter, then took the best Aleut men from Kigolgan and Unimak and went to Kodiak. Shishaev and Zaikov from Orekhov's company took off some 30 men and 20 women and they never returned. Cherepanov and Nagaev remained on the islands.

"Now the companies of Cherepanov and Nagaev do not inflict such cruel abuse and murder but they send us out to hunt against our will and force us to provide food and do domestic work without pay. From Cherepanov's company we receive in exchange for each sea otter pelt either a kettle, shirt, knife, kerchief, a tool to make arrows, ten strings of coral or five, six or ten tobacco leaves and a handful of beads . . . The difference between these two companies is that . . . Nagaev's pays less for a sea otter and does not supply any clothing either to those who become domestic servants or to hunters who are often sent out naked to hunt and to fish. Because of this many run away to Cherepanov's company, seeking relief from these unbearable conditions.

"We also suffer greatly when our young girls, wives, daughters and sisters are taken, which all companies do except for Panov's which is more orderly than others who were here before and after his company. Although we see our women forced to become sexual partners and treated cruelly, and although we know the terrible tempers of the hunters, we cannot fight back and we cannot even speak out against this. We have to endure because we are afraid of what may happen. When the peredovshchik Solovev came he plundered the islands of Unalaska, Sannak, Akun, Akutan, Asutan and Igilga and shot all the men on them. And as a final outrage he lined up men one behind the other to see how many could be killed by one shot from his firearm. All the companies know their promyshlenniks treat us cruelly. Sergeant Builov who came to collect taxes said the Government forbids such treament. He promised us that when he returned to Russia he would help stop this cruelty, but nothing has happened.

"We have learned that your ship is not a company ship, but has been sent by the Russian Empress and that its commander is higher in rank than the navigators of company ships. We thought they were the highest because they were so cruel and because they said there were none higher. But now we see that the promyshlenniks and their leaders obey you, and so we make bold to report to you about these abuses on the part of the promyshlen-niks and traders. We ask that you protect us from them."

On June 25, 1790, the promyshlennik Egor Purtov, citizen of Irkutsk, employed by the Kursk merchant Golikov and the Rylsk merchant Shelikhov, testified in an inquiry on Nagai Island say-ing that he had not taken part in the acquisition of Kodiak Island, that he had come to Kodiak when the Greek, Delarov was there, after Shelikhov had gone. He could not relate any information about that company except that the company's agents send the is-land natives out to hunt for animals and are paid for pelts with shirts, parkas, kamleis and other items.

According to rumors Shelikhov reported to the government that there were nearly 20,000 people on the islands, and that 500 paid taxes. He said the Russians want to settle these islands. These reports however are not true. The total number of natives on all the nearby islands is no more than 3,000; not more than 50 pay taxes. Concerning the desire of Russians to settle there per-manently, perhaps men who have married native women from these islands and have children by them will wish to do so. Pur-tov further said that the truth of his statement about the number of island natives can be proved by the navigator and assistant pilot of the Lebedev-Lastochkin company ship, Gavrilo Pribylov, who visited them and made notes of the population in his journal and reported this to the Okhotsk authorities. Also, this can be sub-stantiated by Shelikhov's promyshlenniks who have to pay four times the Okhotsk price for everything they buy from him. . . . This is why we run up debts we cannot pay and cannot return home before our contracts are up. Shelikhov foresaw this and says we all have to remain on this island.

On July 1, 1790, Gerasim Grigoriev Izmailov, assistant pilot, was questioned at Kodiak about assistant surgeon Bratikov's re-port. He testified that when Shelikhov came to these islands he never said that he was empowered to punish and hang island na-tives and Russian subjects.

Izmailov never heard and does not know whether 150 to 200 native men and women and Russians were killed during the at-tack on Kodiak when the islanders refused to give up hostages. He thought that perhaps the natives might have jumped from cliffs into the ocean and into their baidaras and drowned. He said they found out about this when their bodies washed up on shore. Six Russians were wounded in that foray, and between 200 and 300 natives were taken prisoner. Shelikhov ordered that six to ten of the old men be taken out to the tundra and speared to death. The rest were kept in the harbor for a month-and-a-half. Many were given presents. Shelikhov then chose the best man to be their leader and entrusted all the women and children to him. When husbands came to visit wives, or fathers or relatives to see the children, Shelikhov returned each, and eventually let them all go.

Izmailov says it is not true that Shelikhov shot one man and speared another, and to prove this he said that one of these men supposedly killed lives in Kodiak and his son attends the Russian school. Izmailov admits that he himself shot two native traitors by order of Shelikhov, and further states that Konstantin Samoilov and Vasilii Malakhov put to death the leaders of the uprising against the Russians on Afognak and Shuyak islands. Izmailov says that he reported all events from this inquiry to the Okhotsk Government Office in 1787.

The original testimony was signed by the navigator Gerasim Izmailov. His testimony was taken down in writing by Vasilii Diakonov, the acting secretary and gubernatorial registrar. The Priest Vasilii Svitsov was witness to this.

On July 4, 1790, on Kodiak Island, Captain of the Second Rank Joseph Billings ordered that Vasilii Petrov Merkurlev, an agent of the Golikov-Shelikhov Company from Tomsk, be questioned. Merkurlev stated that he does not know anything about the affairs of the company, that he had not taken part in any of these events, and that the only person who can report in detail about all of this is the local administrator, the Greek Evstrat Delarov.

On July 5, 1790, on Kodiak Island, the navigator Gerasim Izmailov was again questioned by Navy Captain of the Second Rank, Gavrilo Sarychev . . . and testified that Delarov's peredovshchik, Purtov, took 20, not 200 baidarkas on his hunting trip, and that Delarov used to send as many as 600 baidarkas out to hunt sea otters. . . . He also said that the promyshlennik who is assigned to trade with the islanders is given beads, coral pieces and iron hatchets about four inches long from the company.

Izmailov was not present during the hunt and does not know how many animals were taken. New baidarkas are generally ordered to be ready by April 15, when they are sent out to hunt.

Reference: Library of Congress, Manuscript Division. Yudin Collection, Box 2, Folder 23. Translation adapted.

62

A LETTER FROM GRIGORII I. SHELIKHOV TO EVSTRAT I. DELAROV, CHIEF ADMINISTRATOR OF SHELIKHOV'S COMPANY IN THE ALEUTIAN ISLANDS, CONVEYING INFORMATION AND INSTRUCTIONS

M y dear Evstrat Ivanovich!
I have been pleased to receive the letters you have sent on to me. [Gerasim L.] Pribylov's letter written last year reached me August 16 this year through Potap [Zaikov, a helmsman]; I received the one from Dmitrii Ivanovich Bacharov on August 7. I very much appreciate your sending this correspondence, and I especially appreciate your efforts for the general good [of the company] and for sending the ships with the fine furs.

Our ship *Sv. Tri Sviatitelia* reached the mouth of the Okhota River from America on July 26 and stood at anchor during a strong east wind. I immediately sent 27 volunteer hired men with supplies to assist the expedition crew, as requested. However because of the strong wind they could not get the ship into the mouth of the river, and that evening it slipped anchor. Twelve of the men I sent were carried along the coast by the storm and reached Okhotsk in very bad condition. The rest of the men aboard our ship were carried off from Okhotsk toward the Ud River by the strong east and northeast winds for some 400 versts, which continued without ceasing for ten days. When the wind changed the vessel managed to reach the Okhota River safely on August 7. We divided the furs. Because the ship's crew were weak, I let them rest. The trade goods, tackle and supplies which have been delivered to me are in sufficient quantities for me to outfit two ships rather than just one. If God permits, next summer I will send out two ships earlier [than this year], one to you and the other in another direction.

When Pribylov was about halfway to Aglits, he discovered two small islands not more than 200 versts from Unalaska. From those two islands, still others are visible. On the two he discovered, he left 20 Russians and 20 Aleuts to hunt, and the rest went back by ship to good harbors. In two years the 40 men took more than 2,000 sea otters, 40,000 fur seals, 6,000 blue fox, 1,000 puds of walrus tusks and 500 puds of whiskers which, for want of

The Pribylov Islands were one of the primary breeding areas for seals (top). Shelikhov reported at the end of the 18th century that in two years 40 of his Russian and Aleut hunters took 40,000 fur seal pelts, as well as thousands of sea otter and fox pelts. On the left, a sealer is dressed for a day's hunting. To the right, the fruits of his labor, the carcass and pelt. By the late 19th century, seals were a threatened species and an international protest finally curbed the depredations. Elliott, *An Arctic Province*. (OHS negs. 80227, 80228 and 80247)

space on the ships, they had to leave on the islands. Pribylov's two hunting vessels will set out in 1791 with Potap in charge of one and Lukaniev of the other.

When I talked with Osip Osipovich [Billings], the leader of the expedition, he assured me that he would give you all aid and assistance in port. He said that along the northern part of the islands, as well as on the Pribylov Islands and along the coast of North America they saw millions of sea otters, fur seals and sea lions basking.

I am sorry that you did not follow my instructions to send a ship to the north. What is done cannot be undone. But I urgently request that when you receive this letter you send 25 Russian men to the north. Hire 400 American natives to help them. Send them all there to hunt sea otters, fur seals, fox, and to take walrus whiskers and tusks, as much as possible. The catch is to be sent to Petropavlovsk harbor or to Okhotsk without losing any precious time. If you do this quickly, the same price will prevail. Please try not to let this opportunity pass by.

Then, do not change our previous pursuits and plans. If God brings the expedition to Kodiak before our ship arrives, you are immediately to render them every assistance.

If possible, while the shipwrights are there, build a ship about 85 feet long which would be suitable for trade with Macao. We will soon have no hope for the Kiakhta trade, either now or in the future because of various circumstances. I am sending aboard my ship extra iron, bolts, tackle and everything I know will be needed to build that ship. If you cannot build it, then take counsel with Osip Osipovich Billings, the leader of the expedition, and send the ship Izmailov commands to Macao to trade furs for Cantonese and other goods. Do this upon Billings' recommendation, and send some gratuity for an interpreter. Appoint Polomoshnyi as prikashchik. He has assured me that he will assist you with the hunt in the north.

Meanwhile, rely on your men, but be efficient and careful yourself. Above all avoid discord.

I am sending you and the Company two puds of white and blue beads which Billings is carrying, as well as three packs of tobacco to Merkulev. In addition to this, ask that 20 puds of tobacco be put on my account until our ship arrives. Perhaps Billings will be so kind as to do that favor for us.

I advise you to be moderate in everything you do. Under no circumstances let anyone become drunk. Dmitrii Ivanovich Bacharov has been drinking ever since he came [with us], and I do not expect any improvement in the future. I have not been at all successful in sobering him up.

There is a new Governor General in Irkutsk, Ivan Alferevich Pil, a noble gentleman. I have sent your report on to him.

Be wary of foreigners. The English, Prussians, Swedes, Dutch and Turks are enemies of Russia and they can fly false flags. For that reason you should beware of all foreigners and be vigilant in all cases and heed all these precautions.

From here on you are not to reveal or disclose to anyone secrets which are entrusted to you. Remember the holy words: be as clever as a serpent and as safe as a dove.

Because of the current slump in the market our shares are selling for less than 700 rubles. I have been supporting this because I have been given 100,000 rubles in cash. If I had not kept the price up, no one would have bought even at 400 rubles. However do not worry about this because the time will come when the price of goods will not drop.

Since the government does not have transport vessels at the present time, I am sending the *Sv. Tri Sviatitelia* to Kamchatka with trade goods. In spring, with God's help, when accounts are more accurate, I will dispatch her to you in America with goods, and upon your request, with supplies for the company. I will send the other ship in another direction. I also think that I myself may join you. If I cannot come personally I will send a plenipotentiary. In accordance with your request, I will send one ship to Okhotsk.

On matters affecting the company and everything else, consult only with the Governor General and with me, not with anyone else. Do not allow anyone, no matter who, to harm the company. Do not let anyone take advantage of you, and do not take advantage of anyone else.

You should know that last year Ivan Larionovich Golikov and I were most generously rewarded by the Empress and we hope that everyone in the company may be so rewarded by our Monarch for their outstanding achievements. The present unexpected war with the Swedes and others has interfered.* However, in the

---

*Shelikhov refers here to Russia's war with Sweden (1789–90) and with the Ottoman Empire (1787–92).—Eds.

future, the workers [of our company] will not go unrewarded for their efforts on behalf of the Empire.

Last year the Empress decided to end the collection of iasak on all the islands. You are therefore not to collect any iasak, for fear of legal fines.

Our associate, Mikhail Sergeevich Golikov, died early in 1788 and will not be sailing on the *Sv. Tri Sviatitelia*.

I have retrieved your contract which was given to the unscrupulous Menevskii for two shares, and I am returning it to you aboard the ship.

Last year [Miron] Britukov made malicious accusations against me. For this malice, when the investigation is completed, he is to be punished in accordance with the law. Even though he has already expressed his regret a hundred times, no one can help him because his charges have gone to the highest authorities where true justice will prevail.

God has given us a great Empress in Catherine Pavlovna.

In concluding these lines, I want you to keep the workers in firm control and order. Do not make any concessions to them, that is, do not permit any trading among them. And do not allow any quarrels or arguments, and do not let the American natives become at all oppressed or embittered.

In order to control venereal diseases, allow any single men who wish, to marry [native women]. God, not we, will judge them. Because of natural weakness, no one can long refrain from having relations with women.

Please do your best to teach reading, writing, singing and arithmetic to more of your young native lads, so that in time they can learn to become seafarers and good sailors. They should also be taught various crafts, especially carpentry. The young natives who have been brought here are studying music in Irkutsk, and we are paying 50 rubles for each of them to the choir master. We are going to supply good musicians and drummers to America. I will try to send all the church necessities. I will send you primers and books on mining, navigation and other subjects in large numbers. And I will send gifts on the ship for everyone who does well in his studies.

Finally, please convey my best wishes and my greetings to all your good young men.

I remain in every way your sincere well-wisher and ready servant, Grigorii Shelikhov, citizen of the town of Rylsk and head of the North Eastern American Company.

P. S. According to Osip Osipovich [Billings], there is another island about 350 versts southeast of Unalaska. He and his men saw it personally when they were there.

Reference: P. A. Tikhmenev. *Istoricheskoe obozrenie obrazovanie Rossiisko-Amerikanskoi kompanii* (St. Petersburg: 1863), II, Appendix, 23–26.

63

SEPTEMBER 19, 1789

A CONFIDENTIAL REPORT TO THE GOVERNING SENATE FROM IVAN ALFEREVICH PIL, ACTING GOVERNOR GENERAL OF IRKUTSK AND KOLYVAN, TRANSMITTING INFORMATION ON CONDITIONS IN RUSSIAN POSSESSIONS IN ALASKA AND THE ALEUTIAN ISLANDS

Herewith, I enclose a copy of a report made by Assistant Surgeon Miron Britukov to Navy Captain Second Rank [Joseph] Billings, dated Iakutsk, November 2, 1788.

"In 1783 I was transferred by the government from the Okhotsk Office to the Rylsk merchant Grigorii Shelikhov, who headed a company which was about to set off on an expedition in a hunting vessel. I was assigned to care for him and his men. We set out on August 15 of that year, and from that day on I was completely under his orders.

"We spent the winter on one of the Komandorskie Islands and then continued on to America. When we reached the first island, Kodiak, the following events took place.

"Shelikhov, as master of the ship and in command of all persons aboard, proclaimed that he had great authority to punish and hang not only island natives but even us, loyal subjects of our Most Merciful Empress. We were frightened and acknowledged him as a man who had been given power by the highest authorities and who had been entrusted with important secret instructions which he was not to disclose. We obeyed all his orders.

"When we sailed into the harbor on this island, the men were sent ashore on five baidarkas to find island natives. When the natives saw our men approach, they ran off from their settlements. Our men pursued them and discovered that island natives from other settlements had also run off and had left all their belongings behind. The Russians managed to capture two natives, who led them to the place where a large group had gathered together. These people had gathered on a detached headland surrounded by rocks so that even from the water it could not be approached except when the tide was out, when there was a neck of dry land that connected it with the shore. I do not remember the name of the place.

"Our men spent five days in their baidarkas just off that headland. They wanted to take hostages to keep us from being attacked and in order to become friendly with the natives; however the natives refused to give hostages. Our men informed Shelikhov, who had remained in the harbor, of what had transpired.

"One night our sentries spotted natives creeping up in the dark. The sentries fired but did not kill any of the natives. Since the natives did nothing more, the sentries paid no more attention to the event. However Shelikhov took two baidaras filled with his men and at dawn the next morning, during a low tide, took them across the neck of land to the headland. He and his armed men killed about 500 of the natives. If one counts the natives who ran to their baidarkas and were killed by drowning or being trampled to death while trying to escape, there would be more than 500. Many men and women were taken captive.

"Upon Shelikhov's orders the men were taken out into the tundra and speared to death. Then he took the 600 or so women and children with him to the harbor where he kept them for three weeks. The men who had managed to escape being killed began to come, and Shelikhov gave their wives back to them but kept one child from each family as a hostage. At last he let the rest of the women and children go.

"During this same time he sent his men in five baidarkas to the east coast of the island to find natives. The men were gone for an entire month. I do not know how they treated the natives. When they returned they reported that the natives had attacked them and had wounded six [Russians] with spears. I do not know how many of the natives were killed and wounded.

"When these Russians returned to the harbor, they captured two of the men who had been leaders of the attack and brought them to Shelikhov. He had them tortured with whalebone and with gun butts to make them confess, but they would not. Perhaps they did not know what they were being asked. Finally, Shelikhov shot one of them with his pistol. He ordered that the other be killed with a sword and that their bodies be taken out into the tundra.

"During the time the Russians were voyaging to various islands to the east, two native men came from the west by baidarka and said they had been sent by their leaders to establish friendship and trade with the Russians. They announced that a large number of natives would be coming, but that the Russians should not fear them and should not fire on them. Shelikhov received the two natives courteously, took down their names and agreed to their wishes. But when they had gone we waited all winter for others to come and nothing happened.

"In the spring of 1785 Russians took baidarkas to the west side of the island to explore and take hostages. They returned with children who had been taken from the leading natives, and then their fathers had to come to see their children. Shelikhov asked whether they were the ones who had sent the two natives the previous summer to establish friendship ahd trade relations, but these natives replied they had not done this. Shelikhov told them the names of the two natives and ordered these leaders to find the men and bring them to him, which they did. Shelikhov questioned them about whether they had been truthful in what they had told him, and then he ordered the navigator Izmailov to shoot both men with a single rifle shot, which he did.

"But this was not the end. There were some chiefs who came from Shuiakh Island to visit their children being held hostage. When they were ready to return home, two Russians were sent with them, taking various small trading goods. The Shuiakh natives killed the two Russians, either because they wanted the trade goods the Russians were carrying or because they had developed a hatred for Russians. We did not hear about this until a native from Afognak learned of it. He was afraid to tell the Russians and so he told the Kodiak natives who went with the Russians to Afognak and Shuiakh. He swore he was telling the truth but said he did not dare tell the Russians. When the Russians learned of the incident from the Kodiak natives, they sent the Afognak man to Shelikhov. Shelikhov asked him whether he had taken part in the murder. The native denied this and said he only wanted to tell the Russians about it. Shelikhov then asked him whether anyone else knew about it; the native replied that another native from Afognak also knew of it. Shelikhov immediately sent for that native, who also said that neither he nor the other native had had anything to do with the murder. Then they were accused of not having told the Russians earlier. Shelikhov ordered that they stand together so he could shoot them both with a single shot. He fired his gun and killed the first and wounded the second, whom he then ordered beheaded.

"Shelikhov sent Russians in three baidaras to Afognak and Shuiakh to kill the natives and find the chief with whom his two Russian traders had been sent. We later heard that all the people from one settlement were completely destroyed and the people from other villages had run off. I do not know what happened there after we left.

"Such acts horrified me, and although Shelikhov said that he had been given authority to put to death not only natives but Russians as well, I have no proof that he actually was given this authority. I myself was afraid of what he might do, and so I did not dare testify against him in a government office when I first returned. However, the oath I took will not permit me to remain silent. I have heard that you, Sir, have been empowered by Our Empress to investigate all matters of abuse and oppression in this remote region, and that you treat those under your protection with great mercy. Therefore, I beg you to investigate this matter to judge whether it should be reported to higher authorities, and to see precisely how Shelikhov reported this affair in his journal. I have no doubt that he made a glowing report to Our Empress.

"I do not know whether he was actually granted the powers by the highest authorities which he claims. My oath obliges me to report these terrible acts, and I do not wish to be delinquent by not doing so, although my role is unimportant. Therefore I beg you to accept this report, and either forward it to the proper authorities or keep it among your papers so that in case I should at some future time be accused of concealing information, I may use it to defend myself."

Reference: Library of Congress, Manuscript Division. Golder Collection, Transcripts, Box 3. Russian Archives of the State, St. Petersburg, 1789, VII, #2742. Translation adapted.

64

FEBRUARY 14, 1790

A REPORT FROM IVAN A. PIL, GOVERNING GENERAL OF IRKUTSK AND
KOLYVAN, TO EMPRESS CATHERINE II, CONCERNING EUROPEAN IN-
TRUSION INTO NORTH PACIFIC WATERS AND MEASURES TO COUNTER-
ACT THIS

The persistent and bold attempts of Europeans to participate
with Russia in hunting and trade along the coasts of the Pacific Ocean which belong exclusively to Russia are not limited to
the particular success of the East Indian Company. These efforts
are increasing in momentum, in spite of all the difficulties encountered, into the most distant parts of North America where
Russian promyshlenniks are only now beginning to attain the
goal which has been their chief objective: to benefit from the new
and extremely profitable hunting and trade with the savage islanders. Their increased navigation in those waters and the fact
that they are holding back for themselves a substantial part of the
wealth they are plundering from that region are evidence of the
true nature of their activity, and is clear proof of the loss to our
seafarers.

In the first report on this matter which I humbly made bold
to submit to Your Imperial Majesty, I detailed the efforts made
along the coast of America by the company of the well-known
citizens, Golikov of Kursk and Shelikhov of Rylsk, and about the
submission of that part of the region, along with other islands, to
the Russian Empire.

In this report, however, I hope that the Most Merciful Sovereign will deign to consider my remarks concerning earlier activities by European ships navigating along various parts of America,
along the coasts and among the islands. In submitting this report,
I am absolutely obliged not to remain silent before Your Majesty;
I must say that the Russian promyshlenniks who are working in
that part of the vast ocean have met with well earned success, and
moreover have actually created, through the amicable relationship
between themselves and the island natives, such useful cooperation that the numerous attempts by Europeans to encroach on this
area with armed vessels have been rebuffed, and have failed to attain their intended goal. The reason the Russians did not arm

themselves against the Europeans was not that they feared them, but rather that the Russians wished to avoid armed conflict. The Russians have tried to navigate in those waters where they could attain their goal and where they could solicit cooperation from Your subjects.

The English and Spanish intrusions along the coasts of the Kuril and Aleutian islands, and along the coast of North America itself, must now be acknowledged by Your Majesty as very bold attempts by those powers to enable them to be joint powers in these regions, from which they should be completely prohibited by the right of first discovery by Your expeditions.

These European navigators have gone fearlessly into these waters and have strengthened their relationships with the savage tribes to such an extent that trade and hunting are really in their hands, and are thus an infringement on the rights of Your Empire. Thus, Most August Empress, I shall detail herein the basic consequences of this which compel me to submit this present report.

I have previously noted the accomplishments of the promyshlenniks of the Russian ships. As my first point I submit that the seafarers who are aboard these vessels were obliged, as part of their service, to observe all things worthy of note during their voyage and to report these observations to the officials in Okhotsk. They have reported the following events.

1. On March 1, 1788 the navigator [Gerasim G.] Izmailov, employed by the company of Golikov and Shelikhov, set out from Okhotsk aboard a galiot across the strait which separated the Kuril Islands from the Aleutians, to North America. When he reached Kodiak he learned from the promyshlenniks there that in 1786 two large foreign vessels identified as English had stopped in Kenai Bay, and that two other ships had been cruising in sight of Kodiak itself. With the approach of the winter of 1787 three more vessels stopped with the local Chugach people, and a wherry carried on trade with the Kenais. It was reported that when that vessel left to return to the Chugach region it supposedly lost six men to Chugach attacks and had to leave two men behind who were taken prisoner. Then another vessel appeared in that region and had no better luck since its men were killed by the islanders and the ship was burned. It appears to have been the wherry which was burned, although the navigator does not state this. Everything

seems to point to this, however, because many of the Russian workers paid several visits to the vessels which were anchored in Kenai Bay.

2. The navigator [Dmitrii I.] Bocharov, serving in the same company, made a report almost identical to Izmailov's, on February 28, 1789. He stated that when the foreign vessels put back out to sea the Russians did not have even the slightest amount of the trade which they might have had with the islanders, because the foreigners were the only ones who made a good profit when they exchanged their goods for those of the American natives. Bocharov maintains that the English set out eagerly to procure furs there and tried to make contact with the promyshlenniks through written communications, hoping to attract them under the pretext of trading. However once they discovered that the promyshlenniks were subjects of Your Majesty, and not just any people, they rapidly took their ship back out to sea.

3. The Chief Administrator of this company, a Greek named [Evstrat] Delarov, reported on April 28 of last year that in May of 1788 a foreign two-masted vessel came into Kenai Bay, anchored there for about six days, entrusted an unsealed letter to Delarov and put back out to sea. In June and July two more ships came. One anchored near Shelidak Island, the other at Tugidak Island. They gave various European items to the islanders and also handed out silver medals. Delarov says both ships were Spanish; when they addressed their commanding officers they called them "Capitan." He verified this through the under officers and also learned that they had sailed from Acapulco to the northern Chukotsk seas and that at Tugidak Island they had given the Russians a sealed letter signed by Don Antonio Valdez, one of the ministers of naval affairs with the Indians, as well as six unsealed letters, and that they also showed Delarov three medals which he had given the natives [previously] in barter. The conclusion of his report details how the Kenai natives, apparently emboldened by the appearance of the foreign vessels, attacked the Russian promyshlenniks. They killed ten of the Golikov-Shelikhov Company's men on the Alaska mainland, and in another place killed four workmen from the company of the Iakutsk merchants Lebedev and Lastochkin.

In addition, the following information came here from the navigator [Potap K.] Zaikov who sailed there on a galiot belonging to the Tula merchant Arekhov. Zaikov stated that in August of 1781 he put to sea with 70 workmen. He wintered on Bering Island and then reached Unalaska where he joined with the company of the Totma merchant Kholodilov until the spring of 1783. He then set out on a course of east by south proceeding along the American coast with the same intention as before, to sail to the strait of Isanok from the Okhotsk meridian to 71°, in order to add to his discoveries both there and farther. However, while he was sailing in various places along America, he spent some time in Chugach Bay near Sukli Island, located in 60°10' northern latitude and along the eastern meridian of 68°08'. Here the inhabitants, the Chugach who are still hostile, tried to kill the Russian promyshlenniks. Because of inadequate precautions on the part of the Russians, they did kill eight men, and another eight died of illnesses which they contracted there. Nevertheless trade was quite profitable, since the seafarers obtained 250 sea otters in addition to other animals.

In 1784 both of these vessels returned to Unalaska and Isanok Strait. While they continued to hunt and trade there, in 1786 there came to Captain's Bay a two-masted English frigate armed with fourteen guns, the *Nootka*. In addition to [John] Meares, captain of the vessel, there was a crew of 35, of whom half were Indians. The sailors said they had sailed from the East Indies in six frigates, and that they were proceeding along the American coast to Nootka Bay, which, according to maps, lay between 48° and 49° northern latitude, and where they proposed to trade the European goods they were carrying. The sailors wanted to trade for sea otters which they coveted avidly, but they finally realized [the natives] were unwilling to trade. Therefore when the English saw the Russian insignia displayed by a toion who lived on Unalaska, they hurriedly put out to sea, where their smaller vessel cruised near the island of Unimak. They then headed due east.

Early in the summer of 1788 in Captain's Bay and Kalekhtinsk Bay a Spanish frigate and packetboat appeared; they were armed and had about 130 crew members including 80 American natives. There were two commanding officers, the first of whom was Don Gonzalo Lopez de Haro. Although they all appeared friendly and refrained from trading and hunting, nonetheless their numbers were so much superior to those of the Russians that our men were prevented from behaving in any other way. For that reason the Spaniards and the Russians spent some time in a mutually friendly relationship. Through conversation with the Spaniards, and in particular with an officer from Ragusa [Dubrovnik], Stefan Mondofii, our men discovered that these foreigners had put out to sea from California by orders of the Viceroy of Mexico in order to survey the Chukotsk cape and to stop at Petropavlovsk harbor. Since they had failed in this, they had to return. The leader of the expedition, Don [Esteban] Martinez, had already sailed along the coast of America in the same area where Captain Chirikov had sailed in 1741 on behalf of the Russians. Don Martinez had found items which the Russians had left there for the island natives. When these men left for California they left two letters for Zaikov. One was unsealed, and the other in an envelope. Both were signed by the above-mentioned minister Valdez.

Before I offer my observations on this information, I will make bold, All Gracious Sovereign, to ask Your most careful attention to these letters and notes which were given by these foreigners to the Russian seafarers, and the three medals which had been bartered to the island natives. With Your Imperial Majesty's insight, You will realize that the Europeans gave the letters and notes to Your Majesty's subjects, not because they were attempting to establish peaceful relations with them, but in order to hide from them the evidence of the plunder they had committed. There is no need to document this, because just one look at their voyage proves that it was not a bona fide expedition which would have special imperial significance.

They were spreading out along the American coast and among the islands which are indisputably subject only to Russia, and they tried to conceal their voyage and avoid contact with Your subjects in order to profit more from their trade with the island natives and to procure the best furs. Then, when they were forced to make contact with the Russians, they identified themselves falsely. Once they identified themselves as sailors, not merchants. At other times they revealed their true purpose. Reserving judgment on their entire system, I nevertheless find that the English, following the route Captain Cook showed them, are experiencing considerable success, and will soon be able to establish trade with Japan and with China. The Chinese Empire, because of its obstinate behavior toward Your Imperial Court, now has a great need of goods which it used to receive through Kiakhta. Obviously this has in no way frustrated the intention of the English, if for no other reason than to gloss over the action taken in the well-known Ulaldzaev affair. It seems to me that if they were unable to establish new ways of trade with Europeans, they could not have rejected the methods proposed by Your Majesty.

The problem stemming from the imbalance between Japan and China is further aggravated by [China's] cavalier treatment of Russian subjects. These [native] inhabitants [along the Amur River] are technically Russian subjects, but they have not yet been given the formal opportunity to become subjects of Your Imperial Court.

I would have thought about handling this, but only if naval forces worthy of Your Empire could quickly be brought together and demonstrate the firmness of Your Majesty's resolve. It is obviously impossible to conceive that such an undertaking would escape the notice of all Europeans, as well as of the Chinese who are accustomed to follow the nature of their policies. However, all of this, pertaining to this territory, through quick and direct action on Your part, would not be difficult to manage, if the possibility presented itself and time permitted.

However, the enlightenment which presently pervades Europe permits the Europeans to know of even the slightest effort Your Majesty makes to provide for the well-being of Your subjects. Therefore it is very likely that if Your Imperial Order assigned a flotilla from the Baltic and another from the Sea of Okhotsk, they would also immediately focus all of their military strength on the very areas [we have] concealed from them. For that reason, it would be prudent now not only to dispatch military forces to the planned port of Udinsk, but also to take steps to suggest a better goal for private Russian promyshlenniks who sometimes become wearied on their ocean voyages.

In the present instance there is a very important motive for closing the Kiakhta trade, and for military action on the part of foreign courts inimical to Russia. However, we should not join in this extreme situation, which may be considered merely a local closure, and the difficulty arising from it as an unusual price on all goods and commodities.

Comparing the successes of previous Russian expeditions with those which have been made by private promyshlenniks, one may come to the conclusion that this does not in any way affect Your Treasury, nor does it rouse Europeans to overt action. I therefore conclude that Your Imperial Majesty is well aware that from the introduction of seafaring by private Russian companies on the Sea of Okhotsk until the present time, there has been no basis for expecting important results from their voyages. The interest of Your Treasury and its profit require that with the introduction of such efforts there will be created the means for private entrepreneurs to maintain themselves and their system without worrying about building and outfitting their ships as if for the first voyage.

The efforts of those who sailed were of course rather redundant, for in extending their ventures to the islands nearest the Kamchatka peninsula, they not only willingly paid taxes into Your Treasury, but also ventured to use their own capital prematurely to move from one corner of the earth to another, aboard government vessels, since there were not enough [private vessels] at the Okhotsk roadstead. Because of the prolongation of the Kiakhta trade all of this seemed quite secure to them, but at the same time less profitable. Thus their only need was to increase hunting and trading in these islands in the open ocean, and to build up the supply of materials they needed to build ships. Each of them risked everything to luck, everything to the unknown. As a result some failed completely in their efforts and decided to terminate all the transactions and activities which they had previously undertaken.

It is possible that the inadequacy of the Okhotsk harbor and the difficulty of reaching it hindered them in carrying out their intentions for the public good as implied, and that consequently the primary concern of these companies appeared to be to seek volunteers to go to sea. But if one sets aside these two reasons from the present issue, then it appears that the lack of enterprise of these seafarers stemmed for the most part from inexperience in these regions. For if they had been zealous in trying to build up their knowledge of that part of the coast which they needed to know about, they would have acquired both knowledge and an understanding of how to use it so as not to obstruct their aspirations. But since from the government's point of view it could have been difficult and quite dangerous to devote large amounts of money from Your Treasury without favorable time and opportunity, consequently, it is now proposed that they be protected in the present military circumstances and that a new method be found to establish a basic [educational] institution of seafaring.

I personally believe the most pressing problem is to choose an appropriate site for a harbor, in regard to which Your Illustrious Majesty has already expressed Your intentions, and to allow any seafarers who wish to do so to introduce and build a special wharf there, along the lines of other harbors within Your Empire. These aspiring persons should be granted freedom to hire the workers they need, to establish factories and other enterprises which could be of vital use to them in the future. There should be certain restrictions so that these would be organized in accordance with Your generous decrees. Initially one might expect that there would arise various difficulties caused by the natural problems of this territory. These however could be overcome by appropriate instructions from the government, avoiding as much as possible even the smallest expenditures which could prove a burden to Your Treasury. I believe that time will show that the eagerness for profits and benefits on the part of subjects of Your Majesty will certainly lead them to venture on such an enterprise and not be sparing of their own capital when the opportunity arises.

I am certain that such a shipyard would inspire many of them to involve themselves in this present trade, and in due course this reinforcement would seem to be well within reach. With such earnest and zealous efforts on the part of these seafarers, all Your Imperial Majesty would have to do would be to bring in a large part of this endeavor through naval forces and trade, which can easily and successfully develop. Once that takes place, it would not be necessary for Your Treasury to continue to absorb so many difficulties and problems through such substantial expenditures. Definite profit will result from the continued construction of ships at the Okhotsk site which will be used for transport. The appreciable increase in Your interest must be held inviolate, since either the seafarers or the company which will maintain the shipyard will be obligated to take on the expense of distributing at a reasonable cost, those provisions which are necessary to human existence, to towns and forts along the coast of Kamchatka. At the same time, in return for lending Your support, this will bring into Your Treasury a sum which will actually compensate You for current expenditures. Payment for one part of the share would be transferred to the Treasury, and from this should be paid the costs of transporting merchants and their goods and the maintenance of the shipyard.

In addition, I believe one of the most important things of interest to Your Imperial Majesty in this matter is that by putting even a very small structure in this newly proposed harbor at that location, it would subsequently be possible to expand it, which Your Imperial Majesty may acknowledge would be beneficial. Then a start could be made to build a new road leading to the port. These two problems, especially the latter, deserve special attention. Although I have no doubt that a satisfactory location for a port can be found, as well as an easy access to it, nonetheless it will take a good deal of time and effort to realize it using Treasury funds.

I am not here concerning myself with the plan which, in accordance with Your Imperial Majesty's permission, was submitted by my predecessor, Lieutenant General [Ivan V.] Iakobii, and I dare not consider that he was anything but worthy of Your Imperial Majesty's attention. However, in regard to anything concerning the location of the road charted in his plan, I can only stress here that it should be mapped on the other side. Instead of the Ud River it should be possible to find another more accessible river. Even Navy Captain Fomin who was sent to that area to gather information does not endorse the choice of the mouth of the Ud because of its unsuitability and low water. I will try very hard to report in good time to Your Majesty on any success here in finding a closer and better location for a new port. I now have plans and preliminary descriptions of all these places, which Fomin made during his investigation of Udsk ostrog, following Your instructions given him by my predecessor; however, these drawings are not complete. I do have other descriptions and drawings of the entire coast from Okhotsk to the Ud River, and because of that I will review these in terms of their natural locations. I will try to submit these for Your Imperial Majesty's benevolent review as soon as possible.

Finally, since at the present time I am not in a position to do anything to stop the Europeans sailing in the Pacific Ocean, the only thing I have done is to give instructions to the Okhotsk administrator, as I outlined in my first report on this matter to Your Imperial Majesty. I instructed him that he must emphasize that private promyshlenniks everywhere must treat Europeans with every courtesy, and at the same time they must protect Your Imperial Majesty's rights to the best of their ability, and keep that right unchanged in that part of the world. I have also suggested to him special rules and possibilities regarding the activities of foreigners. As soon as some new success develops in this matter, which will bring beneficial results, I will consider it my responsibility and obligation to report to Your Majesty immediately about it. Therefore I am submitting all of this information for Your most careful review.

Ivan Pil

Reference: LOII, sobr. Vorontsovykh, No. 476, 11. 352–360 ob.
See: A. I. Andreev, ed. *Russkie otkrytiia v Tikhom okeane i v Severnoi Amerike v XVIII veke* (Moscow: 1948), 305–315.

65

1791

DESCRIPTION OF THE ALEUTIAN ISLANDS AND THE NATIVE INHABI-
TANTS, FROM THE JOURNAL OF CAPTAIN JOSEPH BILLINGS, ABOARD
THE *SLAVA ROSSII*, IN THE SECOND PHASE (1789–1791) OF THE
BILLINGS-SARYCHEV EXPEDITION

The inhabitants of Unalaska say that the first man and the first woman were borne by a lusty woman, and that this occurred about the time of an eclipse of the sun. When the land became populated with their descendents, many people went east in search of better land. In this way all the neighboring islands, the Alaskan lands and regions farther off were peopled.

Names. They call themselves, and the inhabitants of the island of Umnak, Kaugalins. The inhabitants of Uniagun, "The Island of Four Volcanoes," are called Akokhtin. This island is presently uninhabited, and there are many other such islands. But what these names mean, and why they are called this, they themselves do not know. They refer to the inhabitants of Alaska and the islands around Alaska as Kagataiiakungs, that is, eastern people.

Appearance. They are of medium build or slightly smaller. I have not seen a single Unalaska man of more than medium height. They are all quite dark and swarthy. Their faces are broad; their eyes small for the size of the face and deep-set. Their hair, eyebrows and body hair are black and coarse. They have high cheekbones, and the mouth is in proportion. They pierce two holes in the lower lip into which they insert feathers or carved bones as decorations. Some do not pierce their ears, but others do and insert beads in the holes. Some men wear a kind of amber in their ears, but such men are few. I have noticed that they pierce a small hole through the septum of the nose. The chin is small and round.

Generally speaking their appearance is pleasing. They are stately and very adroit in their small baidaras, which they keep very clean. They do not paint their bodies with pigments, and they do keep themselves as neat as they can. The women are strongly built and sturdy. They never cover their heads. On each cheek they have two tattooed streaks from the ear to the nose. The women tattoo their jaws with small regular black dots.

Russians were impressed with the skills of the Aleut hunters who skimmed out to sea in their light, manueverable baidarkas or baidaras. The low profile of the patient, wave-tossed hunter in his bird-like visor gave advantage in stalking wily sea otters through a day long hunt. *La Corvette Senavine.* (OHS neg. 80239)

Clothing. The men wear parkas made of bird skins; sometimes the feathers are on the outside, sometimes inside. The hide side is completely decorated. For finery they sew on small thongs and very skillfully cover all the seams on the back by sewing two rows of these thongs on the back and two more in front. There is a well made narrow border of seal fur. Around the neck they all have a wide collar made of any fine fur. They wear a kamlei over the parka in bad weather or when they go out in a baidara. . . .

[June 6] As we proceeded on for another hour, four hours of rowing in all, we sighted a settlement located in a distant bay with a flat shore of white sand. It was nine or ten miles from the place where our ship was anchored, and somewhat north of east. The entire land appeared to us to be flat and was covered for some distance with water during the tide. However the settlement was located on a rocky hill which protruded out into the sea; on each side of this rocky hill there was a lake with small creeks flowing to the sea. It seems to me that such a place was chosen by the inhabitants with the thought that it would protect them against attack by hostile people, because there is no other way to reach it than by water. This settlement was large, for it consisted of many iurts. Here we encountered about 100 women and young girls, but only four or five men. They received us courteously and immediately tidied one iurt, spreading some grass and covering the ground with bast matting so we would have a place to sit. Then an elder came to us and announced that Shelikhov had made him the head of this settlement. After he had spoken these words he reached into a box and carefully took out a small ordinary icon on paper, framed in lead, which Shelikhov had given him as a sign of his authority so he might show it to indicate he was the local chieftain. We noted many old women with suppurating wounds on their heads and faces which resembled the sores we call cancer. . . .

They entertained us with dancing, for which the women painted their faces and put on their best clothing.

Iurts. Their iurts are built in the following manner. Four to six posts are set into the ground, leaving a height of about four arshins above the ground. Then two long posts are fastened to the ones set in the ground, and two more are placed perpendicularly at both ends. In the corners of each iurt there are more poles which are set into the ground. From the middle to the corners there are four more posts, forming a rectangle. To these are fastened boards, and above this dry grass is spread, and then either dirt or mud is spread over everything. On the east side of the iurt there is an entry made of two upright posts set into the ground. Atop these there are two small posts to which the hide of a sea lion is tied. This protects the inhabitants of the iurt from wind and rain as well as our doors do.

The hearth is a pit seven or eight inches deep in the middle of the iurt; the smoke escapes through an opening made in the roof over the fire.

On all sides of the iurt there are small partitions similar to the kind we have in our stables for horses. In these partitions each family lives separately, eats there, and keeps its own possessions. In addition, each family has its own separate sleeping quarters. Of course this is all very crowded. Each little cavern is covered with fish skin so the light may penetrate; the people crawl in through a little window on their hands and knees. Their beds are made of various reed mats, and their own clothing serves them as covering. However, their dwellings are warm because they heat them as well as Russian bath houses are heated, by pouring water on hot rocks which are set in a fire. This provides hot air throughout.

The inhabitants complained to us about the problems caused by the Russian promyshlenniks who force them to travel far off to hunt animals, and then take all their furs away from them. For their hard work the promyshlenniks give them only what is convenient, for example, a few glass beads, which they wear as decoration, or a few leaves of tobacco.

They told us that the Russians took away from them all their large baidaras in which they transport all of their possessions from one settlement to another, and that now the Russians will not let them have any large baidaras. During the time we were there all of them were divided into artels and were sent out to hunt by the Greek [Evstrat I. Delarov], who administers Shelikhov's company. In all there were about 600 baidaras with two or three men in each one. These 600 baidaras were divided into units, and each unit was sent to a particular island under the leadership of one or two Russians.

Inhabitants of Kodiak Island. On Kodiak Island and the small islands nearby there are about 1300 adult men and some 1200 lads. One may suppose there is about the same number of females. These islanders both in their outward appearance and in their general outlook resemble the inhabitants of Unalaska. Both groups decorate their faces by slitting the lower lip and the nasal cartilage, into which they insert various small bones and other small things which they consider finery. The Kodiak women tattoo their bodies with various designs as do the women living on other islands.

Their clothing is made of bird skins but they also use furs such as marmot, ground squirrel, reindeer and wild sheep which they obtain from the mainland. Generally they use small shells, amber and the beaks of birds called sea parrots for ornaments, but they prefer the amber above all else. Their customs and behavior are similar to those of the inhabitants of the island of Unalaska; however the Kodiak people are coarser and not as smart.

They do not have any family customs. Marriage sometimes is arranged by purchasing a wife; however, in general, one can say that any man who is lucky in hunting will always find himself a wife without having to pay for her. She will give herself to him as soon as he asks for her from her father. Once he accepts her he takes her to bed. In the morning when he awakes he goes out for wood, warms up the bath house, and then he and his bride and all the guests, of both sexes, steam and wash without shame. The young man lives with his father-in-law until his wife gives birth to their first child. Then he is allowed to live with his wife wherever he wishes. They practice polygamy; however, in that case the first wife may leave her husband and marry another, provided she does not have any children by the first man.

Some islanders have an object for unnatural love which they dress in women's clothing and adorn just like a woman [in Kamchatka, called *koekchuchami*]. . . .

Funerals. They bury a dead person in the ground in his best clothing. They put all of his belongings, adornments, arrows, even his baidara into the grave; they break everything into small pieces. If the dead person was poor and died out in the open, they dig a hole into which they place the hides of sea animals which they use to cover the body of the dead person. They then pile dirt over the body. The hide on the baidara is torn to bits and the wooden frame is broken into small pieces. All of this is put together with arrows on the grave; they also put rocks on the grave. If the person died in a iurt, they perform his funeral in his sleeping quarters and break up his baidara and all his possessions, and bury everything with him as noted above. When a rich person dies, they kill his favorite servant and bury them together. If a wealthy woman dies, her favorite servant must expect the same fate—they kill and bury her together with her mistress.

Work and hunting. At the end of February they go out to hunt fur seals and sea lions, south of Kodiak. In April they move from their winter settlements to their summer ones, located in places where fish and whales are caught. During April and May they hunt sea otters around the entire island of Kodiak, and sometimes they leave the coast and go out to sea for great distances. In June when there are few sea otters they catch fish and hunt sea lions. The primary fish which they like is halibut; this comes close to shore in search of its own food which is small fish. There, the islanders kill the halibut with a spear which they use instead of a harpoon. Often the waves will carry the fish up onto shore, where they are deposited in great abundance. Other fish are the humpback salmon, a red fish, the dog salmon and the silver salmon. These fish are caught in great numbers until September and they are all delicious.

In July, either early or late in the month depending on how hot or cool the weather is, they gather sarana and prepare it by cooking and storing it in small containers covered with fish oil. In a similar manner they collect a large-leafed variety of grass, *Kislitsa*, dig a hole like a small well, line it with grass and layer kislitsa and whale meat, layer upon layer, until the hole is full. They cover this heavily with grass, and on top of that, dirt; this will be used for winter food.

In October all of their hunting comes to an end. Then they set out to return to their winter settlements. Each person brings his provisions with which he can sustain himself and not be dependent on the others.

Treatment of outsiders. Kodiak inhabitants are generous in receiving persons who come to visit them, but they are more cordial to the rich than to the poor. They seat a guest at the entrance of the iurt and bring him a cup of cold water. Shortly afterward the host brings him a piece of whale fin and places it in front of him. The women bring small pieces of fish, sarana, berries, sea lion meat and whale blubber. In fact, they place before him ten or fifteen kinds of delicacies, and the guest either eats it all or takes it with him.

Festivities. At the beginning of November they begin their festivities which continue on throughout the winter. The festival consists entirely of eating. One person invites all his neighbors and all his friends, even those who live 100 or 200 versts away. On that occasion he presents his guests with all the food he has been able to prepare. Dancing and singing and drum beating culminate these celebrations. The dancers paint their faces and hold rattles in their hands; the rattles are made from two or three hoops of various widths, which are fastened by a band decorated with feathers, used in place of a handle. Many sea parrot beaks are tied to these hoops so that when they shake the rattle to the drum beats, a very loud sound is produced which unless one is accustomed to it, is not very pleasant to hear. The next day a new celebration begins at a neighbor's dwelling, with the same kind of merrymaking. This continues on to the next, right down to the last inhabitant, for each must take his turn in entertaining until it is time to go hunting or until they run out of food. Then the merrymaking ends and everyone goes along the seashore searching for food such as shellfish and the like. However, it sometimes happens that in winter they also catch sea lions of various sorts out at sea.

Household utensils. We have observed the following utensils and household items among the islanders. Their dishes and plates are made of wood, carved from a flat block of wood and decorated with small bones, pieces of glass, beads, teeth of various creatures and other such things. They also have baskets woven of grass and sea weed that are so tightly woven they can even hold water. They cook their food in these by putting hot rocks in the water along with fish or meat. They do not eat fish raw, except for the head of the halibut, which has cartilage. They also make clay pots, but these are not very attractive because they are rather coarse; they are so soft they do not last long. They make knives of jasper or of hard slate. They also have knives made of iron with round handles which are made from a hard stone. They do not have any ordinary knives.

They have spears or lances almost two sazhens long. On one end they fasten [inflated] bladders to keep them on top of the water; at the other end there are various skillfully made sharp points embedded to stab whales and sea lions. For the whales they have a special long weapon made of hard slate which resembles a wide double-edged knife. When such a knife strikes a whale it remains in the body. Hunters hope that the whale in a short time will be washed up on the shore, dead.

For other sea animals such as sea lions they use smaller weapons made of stone or from the sharpened skull of a shellfish. They also have hand lances with feathers, bows and arrows for hunting birds, sea otters and other sea creatures. The tips of arrows are made from sharpened stone or bone. For hunting fish they make hooks of small bones and the line is made of sea weed and is tied with whale whiskers.

Their lodkas or baidaras, both single and double, are much heavier and larger than those of the Unalaska people, but they are made in much the same manner.

They wear hats made of grass, woven and decorated with various colors set in patterns; however, they also have wooden hats

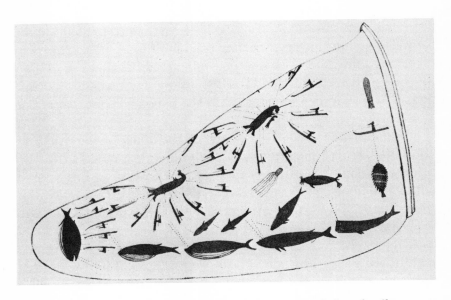

This extraordinary drawing of an Aleut hunter's hat details
the various marine animals, whales, halibut, and squid, and
the techniques to capture sea otter, seals and large denizens.
Choris, *Voyage Pittoresque*. . . . (OHS neg. 80250)

that have heads of various sea creatures carved on them. During
their dances they decorate these in a very dandy fashion. They
also make very lovely hats for their children.

From the inhabitants of the American mainland they receive,
through trade, hide clothing called kamleis and parkas made from
the skins of various land animals. In return they give them whatever trivia they have, sometimes even sea lion hides and the
like. . . .

Reference: GPB im. M. E. Saltykova-Shchedrina, otdel rukopisei, OSRK,
IV, No. 814, tetr. 6 i 8.
See: V. A. Divin, ed., *Russkaia tikhookeanskaia epopeia* (Khabarovsk: 1979),
379–380, 383–388.

66

A LETTER FROM KYRILL [ERIC] LAKSMAN TO COUNT ALEKSANDR R. VORONTSOV CONCERNING THE PLIGHT OF JAPANESE CASTAWAYS RESCUED IN THE ALEUTIANS BY RUSSIAN PROMYSHLENNIKS

Most Gracious Lord, Your Excellency, Count [Vorontsov]! Although I am certain that Your Excellency is aware of the unfortunate plight of the Japanese seafarers, nevertheless I am presuming to present their situation to you in brief detail.

On December 13, 1783, seventeen Japanese men sailed out from the town of Shiroko to trade in the capitol city of Yedo. At the halfway point of their voyage they, like many similar vessels, stopped to spend the night in Semioda Bay. During a violent windstorm another vessel hit them and broke off their rudder. Without the rudder they had to cut the mast, and thus they drifted at the mercy of the waves for more than seven months, drifting in various directions. At last on July 20, 1784 they came to the Aleutian island of Amisachka where they dropped anchor and went ashore in a smallboat. They found seven Aleut men there who were hunting wild geese. The Aleuts invited the five Japanese into their earthen iurts and gave them cooked goose and fish to eat. Toward evening Russian promyshlenniks came to the island from a vessel which had been wrecked on the island, a vessel which belonged to the Totma merchant, Khodilov. The Russians went to the Japanese vessel and spent the night in a cabin on shore, but during the night there was a storm at sea and the anchor broke away on some sharp rocks underwater. The ship was cast adrift and then was wrecked on the coast. Thus, deprived of their last hope, the men had to remain on that island for three years and a month, during which time the Russian promyshlenniks used planks from their wrecked vessel, and the remains of the Japanese vessel, which had been built of redwood and camphor, to build a new vessel. In September of 1787 they took the remaining nine Japanese men with them to Nizhnekamchatsk ostrog. Seven of the Japanese had died while they were on the Aleutian island, and an eighth was killed during a storm at sea.

During their stay at Nizhnekamchatsk ostrog, they were maintained at government expense until June of 1788. In that

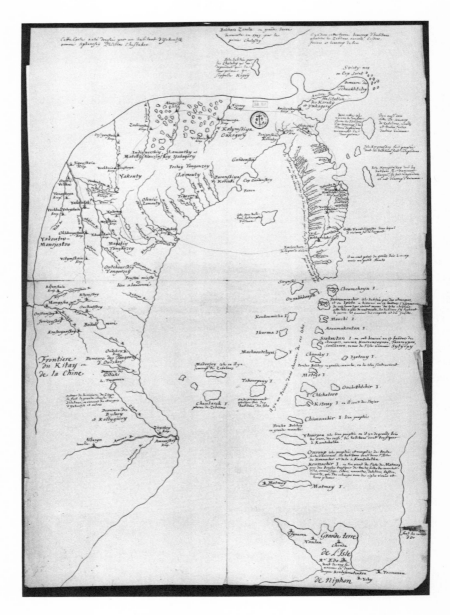

This map by the Kuril explorer V. A. Shestakov (c. 1730) gives a richly detailed view looking north from Hokkaido. The Amur River empties at the lower left. Individual islands are named and were located accurately as hydrography improved. The line across the sea defines the route between Okhotsk and Bolsheretsk. Imperial advisers early urged trade with the Japanese islands south of the newly discovered Kurils. Courtesy Bibliothèque Nationale, Paris.

year six of them, because three died at the ostrog, were brought to Irkutsk at government expense. They reached Irkutsk on January 19, 1789, and were maintained here at government expense until 1790. In that year, as a result of the report about them issued from the Irkutsk Government Office, the Governing Senate issued an ukaz that the Treasury would not support them any longer, and that means should be found to return them to their homeland.

During their stay in Irkutsk I tried to become acquainted with the former captain of the Japanese vessel, Koodai, a person who had been a prominent merchant in Japan. I wanted to obtain a good deal of information from him about Japanese trade and about his homeland in general. He believes the best way to return is to go to Nagasaki with the help of Dutch captains who go there each year. But since when I left Irkutsk for St. Petersburg he expressed a desire to learn about the Russian Empire, I took him with me in order to show him our capitol cities [Moscow and St. Petersburg] and other major cities.

For that reason I am presuming to make a humble suggestion to Your Excellency, as to whether it might not be possible to make use of this situation for our fatherland, and establish contact with the Japanese to benefit our trade. I believe that the first and most hopeful approach would be to deliver these Japanese to their homeland, if we could, on one of our transport or merchant vessels, taking them to Matsumai, where their countrymen constantly come to trade.

I am confident that an initial attempt such as this to establish friendship and trade with the Japanese will be successful, especially if Her Imperial Majesty, our Most Gracious Empress, the Most Generous Patroness of the unfortunate, would consent to reinforce this initial contact by sending a few gifts to the Japanese government, woolen fabrics and goods such as the Dutch bring to Nagasaki, where they exchange them for gold ingots. Our own merchants could annually trade for Japanese tea, millet, silk and cotton fabrics, gold and the like from the southern Kurils in exchange for fabrics, hides and beaver and lynx pelts.

Finally, I am also presuming to submit for Your Excellency's consideration a route hitherto unknown to us, without the opening of which, Russian possessions in the Pacific Ocean cannot bring as much profit as they actually should. I am referring to the fact that we need to possess the Amur River, which appears not too difficult to explore and survey, if circumstances will permit the construction of two seagoing vessels on the Shilka River. If these were outfitted with all necessities they could proceed down the Amur from its source to the sea, and from there to designated destinations.

If Your Excellency believes that adequate information about Japan could be obtained from Koodai, the former Japanese captain, whom I brought here, then I will introduce him to you upon your request.

I would be complimented if Your Excellency would deign to forward these suggestions which I have submitted to Her Imperial Majesty, our Most Gracious Sovereign, and I have the deepest honor, gracious Sir, to remain Your Excellency's Most Humble

Kyrill Laksman.

Reference: Petr Bartenev, ed. *Arkhiv kniazia Vorontsova* (Moscow; 1880), vol. 24, 188–191.

67

SEPTEMBER 13, 1791

INSTRUCTIONS FROM EMPRESS CATHERINE II TO IVAN A. PIL, GOVER-
NOR GENERAL OF IRKUTSK, CONCERNING THE LAKSMAN PROPOSAL TO
RETURN THE JAPANESE CASTAWAYS

T o Our Lieutenant General Pil, who is currently serving as
Governor General of Irkutsk and the Kolyvan Namestnichestvo.

You know the way in which the Japanese merchants were rescued on the Aleutian Islands after having been shipwrecked.
They were at first provided for by local promyshlenniks and then
were taken to Irkutsk, where for a time they were maintained at
Treasury expense. The chance of returning these Japanese to
their homeland opens the possibility of establishing commercial
relations with their Empire, especially since no European nation
has as many advantages for this as Russia, thanks to the fact that
not only are We in close proximity by sea, but in fact are neighbors. We therefore concur with the proposal of Court Counselor
Professor Laksman, who has brought Koodai, the leader of these
Japanese, here to St. Petersburg; his proposal for establishing
trade with Japan is appended. Considering the tremendous benefit Our empire would derive from such trade, We are submitting
his plan for your attention and We authorize you to put it into
effect.

1. For the voyage to Japan, either there should be hired at
Treasury expense a seaworthy vessel at the port of Okhotsk, with
an experienced pilot and the necessary number of skilled workers
and servitors; or if Captain [Joseph] Billings has by then returned
from the expedition you are well-informed about, instead of hiring
a ship, one of his ships and crew should be used. Make certain
that the leader of the expedition is a native Russian. If none can be
found who is qualified, use a foreigner, but do not employ an
Englishman or Dutchman.

2. The Japanese are to be sent aboard this vessel at the full
expense of the Treasury, but the two who have become Christians
are to be left behind. Mention will be made further on as to how
they are to be utilized.

405

3. To accompany these Japanese to their homeland, one of Professor Laksman's sons should be chosen. They are presently serving as officials in the Irkutsk Namestnichestvo, and they are familiar with both astronomy and navigation. The one chosen should be instructed that during his voyage and stay in Japan he is to make astronomical, physical and geographical observations both at sea and on the islands and mainland, and he is also to inform himself on local commercial possibilities.

4. The leader is to be given clear and detailed instructions on establishing order and direction for the expedition. All necessary advice and counsel are to be solicited from Professor Laksman, who is well-informed on this matter.

5. With this expedition to return the Japanese to their homeland, send an open letter to the Japanese government extending greetings and describing everything that has taken place. Describe how these men were brought to the Russian territories, and the attentions they have received here. State that We have given these attentions very willingly because We have always desired to have relations and commercial ties with the Japanese Empire. Assure them that We will extend all possible assistance and generosity to all subjects of Japan who may come to Our ports and territories.

6. In order to gain the most favorable response from the Japanese government, you may use as much as 2,000 rubles from the Treasury to buy various useful items which may then be sent to Japan as a gift from you.

7. You are to try to persuade some of Our best merchants from Irkutsk to go along on this expedition, or to send some of their prikashchiks who will gain experience aboard this vessel. It will be sent out from Okhotsk to Japan carrying a certain amount of choice goods which the inhabitants of that country may find useful. After the [Russian] merchants sell their goods, they can purchase Japanese goods. With this experience it will be possible to obtain knowledge which can be used in the future in Our commercial dealings with Japan.

8. In regard to Professor Laksman's proposal to find a new route along the Amur River, that project must be considered impractical at the present time because of the circumstances between us and the Chinese. In order not to arouse any suspicion on the part of the Chinese through Our activity and Our negotia-

tions to open mutually advantageous trade, this proposal is not to be implemented, lest new difficulties are caused.

9. Since two of the Japanese have accepted Our Christian faith, they are not to be returned to their fatherland. They can be used to teach the Japanese language which will be necessary once trade is established with Japan. You are to see to it that they are placed in public schools in Irkutsk and given reasonable compensation. At the earliest opportunity they should be assigned five or six young lads selected from among the local seminary students; these lads will study the Japanese language so that eventually they can serve as interpreters when the desired contact which We are seeking with the Japanese Empire has materialized. You are also to see that these lads [later] help to teach the Japanese language.

10. You should submit to Us the figures for the total cost of the salaries of the expedition leader and his subordinates and servitors, the cost of outfitting the expedition with everything needed for its success, and the cost of providing for the Japanese en route. We will issue authorization that these funds be released. Meanwhile, use Treasury funds for the necessary preliminary preparation expenses.

11. Draw the funds needed to provide for the Japanese en route from the Treasury before they actually embark. Then, when they are dispatched, give them more presents and enclose with the gifts an inventory which will also note that their leader Koodai has also received funds and goods from My Own Office. We trust your zealous attention to ensure that all instructions detailed herein will be carried out precisely. Our Imperial Majesty will be most grateful to you.

Reference: Petr Bartnev, ed. *Arkhiv Kniazia Vorontsova* (Moscow; 1880), Vol. 24, 201–204.

68

A REPORT FROM IVAN A. PIL, GOVERNOR GENERAL OF IRKUTSK, TO
EMPRESS CATHERINE II, CONCERNING IMPLEMENTATION OF PLANS TO
RETURN THE JAPANESE TO THEIR HOMELAND

I have been implementing Your Imperial Majesty's personal
ukaz of September 13, 1791 which You have most graciously
issued to me, concerning the return of the Japanese to their homeland. I herewith hasten to report to Your Majesty most humbly as
to the manner in which I have carried out this assignment.

1. Your Majesty instructed me to hire a suitable seagoing vessel for this voyage at the port of Okhotsk at government expense,
or to use one of the ships from the secret naval expedition [Bil-
lings]. Most Gracious Majesty, I have learned from reliable information that there are no such ships in Okhotsk that could be
requisitioned for this voyage. Although private companies do
build ships there for voyages at sea, these are sent out to hunt marine animals and seldom return to Okhotsk in less than ten years,
even if they are not shipwrecked. Thus having been in use for
such a long time, they are not seaworthy for further voyages. And
there are never private ships docking in Okhotsk which are not
already designated for another purpose. For this reason it would
be necessary to use a vessel from Captain Billings' expedition.

However, Most Merciful Sovereign, at present I do not know
where he is sailing with his squadron as he carries out his instructions, nor whether he will return in time to send the Japanese to
their homeland. The tremendous distances, the difficulty of the
voyage, and the sailing conditions in the vast local waters make it
impossible to obtain information, and consequently while I wait
for this expedition, Your Imperial Majesty's instructions must remain unfulfilled for the time being. Furthermore, even if this expedition were to return to the [Okhotsk] coast in time, it would
not have a vessel appropriate for the assignment. The expedition
vessels are large and require a large crew; consequently to requisition one of them to send the Japanese home would require a substantial sum of money from Your Majesty's Treasury, larger than
the amount I have at my disposal. First, a considerable number of
men would have to be assigned to the vessel, much larger than

would be required for some other ship. Second, it would be necessary to prepare extra provisions for them, which are very expensive in Okhostk. And, moreover, such a vessel would be carrying a great deal of heavy equipment and instruments which we would not need. Thus it would not be as suitable for this proposed voyage as a ship specially built for the purpose.

Because of these circumstances, and specifically in order to carry out Your Imperial Majesty's Imperial intention without losing time, I have felt it best to approach a distinguished citizen of Rylsk who is here now, [Grigorii I.] Shelikhov, the owner of the overseas American Company, and to ask him to sell us a ship he has just had built in Okhotsk. The ship is named the *Dobroe Predpriatie Sviatia Aleksandry*; the ship seems most suitable for that assignment, and is an ideal size for that voyage. With my strong persuasion, Shelikhov agreed to sell it for 5,000 rubles.

Since the ship is just a hull, and has not yet been rigged, I instructed the Okhotsk administrator, Collegiate Assessor Koch, that he should accept the vessel from Shelikhov as state property and make it ready for the voyage, rigging it in the best possible manner and fitting it out with all provisions, tackle and other supplies for the voyage, using everything he needs from the things left behind from preparations for the secret expedition and from other government supplies located in Okhotsk. He is to purchase from private individuals any items not available in government warehouses, paying careful attention to Treasury expenses. For this purpose, to cover immediate expenditures made in order to carry out Your Imperial Majesty's instructions, I have requisitioned from the Irkutsk Treasury Office a sum of 3,000 rubles which I have sent to Koch. Thus I may presume to assure Your Majesty that this vessel will be ready next summer to undertake the voyage and no further expenditure will be necessary, Most Merciful Sovereign. After it makes its successful voyage to Japan that vessel will remain in government service as a transport vessel, and these are outfitted by the Treasury from local customs collections.

2. In carrying out Your Imperial Majesty's instructions, I have decided to send this ship to Japan under the command of a navigator with the rank of ensign, [Grigorii] Lovtsov, who is currently on assignment at the port of Okhotsk. He is a native Russian, experienced in navigation, and a man who has conducted

himself well. As his assistants I have assigned two naval servitors who are non-commissioned officers, as well as other servitors, whose numbers You will see in the appended list.

I have appointed one of Professor Laksman's sons Lieutenant Adam Laksman, to accompany the Japanese, in accordance with the instructions in Your Majesty's ukaz. Lieutenant Laksman is currently on a civil assignment in the town of Gizhiginsk. I have assigned a geodesist-sergeant to him to carry out the mission, and I have set a reasonable salary for him. I have already issued instructions to both Laksman and Lovtsov to be ready for the voyage and await further instructions in Okhotsk. I have also prepared an open letter to the Japanese government, the content of which is in accordance with Your Imperial Majesty's instructions.

3. I have tried diligently to buy suitable gifts here with the 2,000 rubles which I was to obtain from Your Majesty's Treasury, but I have not been able to find anything. For this reason I have decided for the present to have them bought in Moscow, as well as certain astronomical and mathematical instruments which are necessary for the expedition. I am sending a personal envoy to Moscow to do this. I have instructed him to return here to Irkutsk this winter, which will be a good time to send him on to Okhotsk.

4. To carry out Your Imperial Majesty's instructions, I have been able to persuade some merchants to send prikashchiks aboard that ship with appropriate goods, which will help them gain experience. The above mentioned Shelikhov, the Kursk merchant Golikov and the Totma citizen Vasilii Rokhletsov have also sent personal agents to Moscow [to purchase goods] because of the lack of goods in Irkutsk. In good time these gifts will be delivered to Okhotsk.

5. I will submit my humble report to You for Your Majesty's personal attention on the amount of money necessary to pay salaries to all ranks for the expedition, the cost of equipping it with all necessities and providing for the maintenance of the Japanese en route. I hereby make bold to assure Your Majesty that I have prepared this report personally. I have estimated the costs on the basis of reliable information, and because of the high cost of all supplies in that region, it is impossible to reduce the cost. Further, although the cost of some goods may be higher than estimated because of unforeseen circumstances, in other instances supplies may be found for less than the estimated amount. But I

do want to assure Your Majesty again that the total cost of all preparations for the expedition will not exceed the sum which has been allocated. It is indeed possible there may be some funds left over because in my opinion everything will depend on the preparations Captain Koch makes in Okhotsk, and he is extremely eager to be in Your Imperial Majesty's service, is very efficient, will carry out his instructions with great precision and will constantly strive to save the government Treasury any possible expense. His diligence in all matters entrusted to him has been well-known to me from the moment I arrived in Irkutsk.

At this point I make bold to add the following for the attention of Your Majesty. There should be a sum of money of not less than 20,000 rubles aboard that vessel for the captain, Laksman, the Japanese and all the servitors, as well as for unforeseen circumstances. And since government assignats will be worthless in the regions they will be sailing, silver money should be sent. According to my personal investigations at the Irkutsk Treasury Office and all of its branches, there is no such amount of silver currency there at present. Consequently, Most Merciful Sovereign, would it not be helpful for You to give orders that the necessary sum of silver currency be delivered here?

I have ordered salaries and rations for officials on the planned voyage for only one year, beginning June 1, 1792, since that is the date on which the vessel is to be ready for the voyage. Even if the ship sets out in July, it can still return to Okhotsk the following July providing there are no unfortunate developments, because the distance between Russian possessions and Japan is not too great. If, however, Most Gracious Sovereign, this voyage cannot be completed in one year, then the ship's crew can use the funds set aside for unforeseen expenses to buy the supplies they need for the extra time they are aboard the ship.

I submit all of this for Your Imperial Highness' review, and most humbly request that Your Imperial Majesty authorize the approval of the sum requested.

Finally, Most Merciful Sovereign, the responsibility Your Imperial ukaz has assigned to me to use the two Christian Japanese to teach their language to young lads at a local school, and to care for the other Japanese until the time of their departure back to their fatherland—that assignment, I can assure You, will be carried out to the letter.

411

Most August Monarch, may I take this opportunity, since in all justice I cannot remain silent before Your Sacred Person, to mention the fact that Court Counsellor [Eric] Laksman has served in this assignment as a very close assistant. He has labored under my guidance in preparing the estimate, as well as the instructions for his own son and for the navigator, Lovtsov and the letter which I am sending to the Japanese government under my own name. For these reasons, and in appreciation of his work and diligence, I make bold to request most humbly that Your Imperial Majesty grant him the Order of the Apostolic Saint Prince Vladimir. Such an expression of Your personal Imperial favor to him would inspire in him in the future even greater zeal in carrying out the tasks assigned to him, which he will of course fulfill with dedication, timeliness and the desired benefit for the country.

Reference: Petr Bartnev, ed. *Arkhiv kniazia Vorontsova* (Moscow; 1880), Vol. 24, 207–213.

69

JUNE 20, 1793

A DECREE FROM THE GOVERNING SENATE APPROVING THE REQUEST
OF IVAN L. GOLIKOV AND GRIGORII I. SHELIKHOV TO BUILD CHURCHES
IN ORDER TO PROPAGATE THE ORTHODOX CHRISTIAN FAITH AMONG
NATIVES OF NORTH AMERICA

The Governing Senate has reviewed the report of the Holy Governing Synod, in which it is stated that on May 4 the Oberprocurator of the Holy Governing Synod and Cavalier [Count Aleksei I. Musin-Pushkin] received from a member of the Holy Synod, Gavriil, Metropolitan of Novgorod and St. Petersburg, a report to be presented to Her Imperial Majesty for approval. [This report was] an explanation of a petition from the distinguished citizens, Ivan Larionov Golikov of Kursk and Grigorii Ivanovich Shelikhov of Rylsk, requesting that they be given permission to build churches in the northern part of America which they have discovered, and that they be allowed to propagate the Christian faith.

The Oberprocurator and Cavalier stated that on the basis of this presentation Her Imperial Majesty had expressed Her most gratified satisfaction that the petitioners wished to propagate Christianity and that they were so zealous in serving their fatherland. She instructed the Holy Synod to approve their request and authorized this worthy affair to be entrusted to the jurisdiction of Gavriil, a member of the Holy Synod and Metropolitan of Novgorod and St. Petersburg, with the understanding that when he received word of the benefits expected to accrue from the dissemination of the Holy Faith, he would report to the Synod, who would then submit the report for the attention of Her Imperial Majesty.

The petition of the distinguished citizens, Golikov and Shelikhov, states that in the year 1781 they established a company for hunting on the islands in the North Pacific Ocean, and that after they had voyaged through the Aleutian Islands they came to North America. The people they discovered there are called the Kikhtan, Afognak, Koniag, Kinaits, Chugach, Akmokhtet and Koliuzh. They befriended them. The advantages which the natives saw in the Russian way of life fascinated them, and in due

413

time they desired to become Christians and Russians. [Russian] workers conduct evening and morning services and prayers on holidays, and this creates an intense desire to become Christians among natives who have no religion. Many of them have already been baptized by lay Christians and a great many of them have already learned to read and write Russian. Because of this these citizens [Golikov and Shelikhov] request that they be sent an ieromonk qualified to teach the faith to the natives, and that he be authorized to consecrate as priests those whom he teaches to read and write Russian, so they in turn may become the interpreters of his teaching. Thus his exemplary conduct will open for the natives the true nature of Orthodox Christianity.

[Golikov and Shelikhov] want [the newly literate native priest-candidates] to be educated at their expense at the Irkutsk Seminary, the better to be prepared for the priesthood. They also ask that they be permitted to build churches and a field church. The relics for these church structures should be brought by the ieromonk. The petitioners will assume the responsibility for building the churches, providing the vestments and maintaining the clergy.

To implement this noble undertaking which Her Imperial Majesty has approved, the support of the Holy Synod is necessary, and has been obtained as requested.

[The Senate therefore] has decreed that information about this matter should be forwarded to Lieutenant General Pil, who is serving as Governor General of Irkutsk and the Kolyvan region, and also to the administration of the Irkutsk Namestnichestvo in an appropriate ukaz.

Reference: *Polnoe sobranie zakonov rossiiskoi imperii s 1649 goda*. First series (St. Petersburg: 1830), XXIII, 440–441.

70

DECEMBER 31, 1793

PERSONAL INSTRUCTIONS FROM EMPRESS CATHERINE II TO IVAN A.
PIL, GOVERNOR GENERAL OF IRKUTSK, AUTHORIZING HIM TO ASSIGN
SIBERIAN EXILES TO THE SHELIKHOV-GOLIKOV COMPANY AS ARTI-
SANS AND FARM SETTLERS.

From your report dated September 28 [1793] We note with satisfaction the diligence and zeal with which the company of the Rylsk citizen [Grigorii I.] Shelikhov and the Kursk citizen [Ivan L.] Golikov continues its efforts to extend new discoveries in the North Pacific Ocean and along the coast of North America; and its intention, in order to achieve even greater success, to establish a shipyard at Cape St. Elias at its own cost, as well as to develop agriculture at appropriate places on the American mainland and the Kuril Islands. All they request from the government to realize this is to be assigned certain criminals who have been exiled to the Irkutsk gubernia. These would include men who have a knowledge of blacksmithing, carpentry, copper smelting and coppersmithing, as well as ten families of agricultural workers. They pledge to pay the legal taxes for these persons.

Since We find the enterprises of the company of Shelikhov and Golikov very profitable for Our Empire, We desire that they continue to meet with all possible success; therefore We authorize you, in accordance with the request of that company, to assign to it, from among the exiles, up to twenty artisans and ten farming families to begin with. Be certain that you periodically inform Us of the progress of this company, and send Us reports and maps regarding its future distant voyages, discoveries, and all matters pertaining to that region.

Reference: *Polnoe sobranie zakonov rossiiskoi imperii s 1649 goda.* First series (St. Petersburg: 1830), XXIII, 478.

71

MARCH 1, 1794

A REPORT FROM IVAN A. PIL, GOVERNOR GENERAL OF IRKUTSK, TO
EMPRESS CATHERINE II, CONCERNING SENDING EXILES TO SETTLE IN
AREAS CLAIMED BY RUSSIA IN AMERICA AND ON THE KURIL ISLANDS.

I recently had the pleasure of receiving Your Imperial Majesty's
ukaz of December 31, 1793, which authorized me to send
exiled convicts and their families to the maritime company of the
distinguished citizens [Grigorii I.] Shelikhov and [Ivan L.] Golikov: some twenty artisans and families will build shipyard facilities near Cape St. Elias and ten farmers will engage in agriculture
in suitable places on the American mainland and on the Kuril
Islands.

In executing Your Imperial Majesty's decree I will carry out
the order with the greatest care. I will diligently report to Your
Imperial Majesty on the progress of this worthy project as soon as
I have information on it, and also on any future voyages and discoveries of this company.

Reference: TsGAVMF, f. 179, op. 1, d. 131, 1. 195–195 ob.
See: N. N. Bashkina et al., eds. *Rossiia i SShA: stanovlenie otnoshenii 1765–
1815* (Moscow: 1980), 191–192.

72

APRIL 30, 1794

A LETTER FROM GRIGORII I. SHELIKHOV AND THE PAVEL S. LEBEDEV-
LASTOCHKIN COMPANY TO ARKHIMANDRIT IOASAF REQUESTING AS-
SISTANCE WITH A PERSONNEL PROBLEM IN NORTH AMERICA.

Reverend Father Arkhimandrit Ioasaf, Merciful Lord! Thanks be to God that you have been given the destiny, from the hand of the Almighty, to implant the evangelical truth in America, a land which is still completely ignorant of the Christian faith. Your efforts there will serve to curb much violence, because your exemplary life will compel everyone living there to be meek and to fulfill his spiritual and civic obligations and obey laws, including those persons who have already been brought up in the Christian spirit and are presently there on temporary assignment.

This is especially true now when we presume to say that in thinking about the future of that distant land we have strong hopes for your success. In this regard we would like to give you the following assignment. In September, 1790, Lebedev-Lastochkin sent out a vessel, the *Sv. Georgii Pobedonosets*, to hunt marine animals. Shelikhov has quite an important enterprise there with a number of persons working. When Shelikhov had concluded his work and discovered a route to America, he established various sites in Kenai Bay where he has a settlement, and promyshlenniks on the mainland have built a small fort for the purpose of hunting furbearing animals. They have also built living quarters completely separate from their American Company settlement. This is the same company where you will stay and carry on your religious work.

Your stay there will be under the direction of Lebedev-Lastochkin, as the primary sponsor of the ship just mentioned, and of the commanding officer of that ship, the chief navigator, who is a man from Eniseisk named Grigorii Konovalov. Great benefits have been expected, but have unfortunately failed to materialize because of problems. It is impossible to assess the true consequences of this misfortune at the present time, because we do not have any concrete evidence as to who was responsible for these problems and how they happened. One thing is clear, however, that promyshlenniks on that company vessel prevented Ko-

417

novalov from carrying out his responsibility. He was shackled and transferred to the American Company, then sent back here to Okhotsk in 1792 aboard the ship *Mikhail*.

Whether the cause of this was some transgression against the faith on Konovalov's part, or violence by the promyshlenniks, or perhaps the actions of other persons, we do not know. But regardless of the cause, we [Shelikhov and Lebedev-Lastochkin] have taken counsel together and have agreed with other members participating in the ownership of this vessel, and have decided to send Konovalov back this summer. He will leave from Okhotsk aboard a ship belonging to the American Company. If his subordinates removed him from command of the ship without cause, that was an action detrimental to the interests of the company and all of its participants, and we would like to reappoint him as commanding officer of that ship.

However, since a review of the circumstances of this event cannot be entrusted to anyone there, your benevolent presence there in close proximity to the company ship may perhaps enable you to find some way to discover what happened during these events which affected Konovalov.

Therefore, we are counting on your just and open-minded review and we appeal to you and your sincerity to take on this burden and look into the circumstances of Konovalov's situation. Your inquiry may indicate that he was not guilty of any wrongdoing, as accused, which would have brought harm to the company's interests, have been contrary to rules regarding promyshlenniks or have made him unsuitable to take charge of a company vessel. If there are no clear violations of government rules, such as treason or extortion, if the company interests there will be in a state of chaos without his leadership, and if there is absolutely no hope for successful hunting, then you are hereby authorized by us, Shelikhov [and Lebedev-Lastochkin] to reinstate Konovalov as skipper of that ship. Further, those promyshlenniks who unjustly shackled him are to be seized and taken from the company and sent to Okhotsk; if their behavior can now be tolerated they should be transferred to another company, the American Company, to repay their debts.

In order to prevent future chaos, the company is to be supplied with everything it needs so that shareholders of the company can expect to receive fruits from their investment and can anticipate that everything requested by Shelikhov has been done.

However, if you find Konovalov guilty and unworthy to serve in that company, you should deprive him of his freedom and find another person to take his place.

In short, we have complete trust in your judgment and fairness, and we beg you to organize matters in accordance with your best judgment. All that is necessary for you to do is to decide who should be put in charge and how matters should then be organized. We trust that you will inform us how you have done this.

Finally, we entrust this company as well as ourselves into your prayers, and we have the honor to remain Your Gracious Lord's humble servants.

[Signed] Grigorii Shelikhov
Pavel Lebedev-Lastochkin

Reference: Petr A. Tikhmenev. *Istoricheskoe obozrenie obrazovaniia Rossiisko-Amerikanskoi Kompanii* (St. Petersburg: 1861–1863), II, Supplement, 56–58.

73

MAY 11, 1794

INSTRUCTIONS FROM IVAN A. PIL, GOVERNOR GENERAL OF IRKUTSK,
TO GRIGORII I. SHELIKHOV, CONCERNING ESTABLISHMENT OF SETTLE-
MENTS IN NORTH AMERICA.

Her Imperial Majesty, our Most Gracious Sovereign, has responded to your petition to Her Imperial Majesty of September 28, 1793, which I transmitted in a special report to Her. Now, in a personal ukaz to me, dated December 31, 1793, She has authorized me to state the following.

She supports your request to build a shipyard at your own expense near Cape St. Elias, and to introduce agriculture in suitable places on the American mainland and on the Kuril Islands, and to settle up to twenty exiled artisans and ten agricultural families (which I have already ordered assigned to you). Her Imperial Majesty considers your enterprises very beneficial to the Empire and desires that they be accorded every possible assistance to be successful. She has further authorized me to tell you that I will report periodically to Her Imperial Majesty about the progress of these enterprises, and about everything that happens in that region. I am also authorized to tell you that Her All Merciful Imperial Majesty is most pleased to approve the activities of your Company.

I am certain that you will not lessen your zeal in continuing your work, through your company administrators in America, in making new discoveries in the North Pacific Ocean and along the coast of the northern part of America. I am confident that you will make full use of the master artisans and the agricultural workers who have been assigned to you, and that in the near future we will see good results both in shipbuilding and agriculture there. Nevertheless, I still consider it my duty to submit certain rules to you which can serve as guides to maintain peace and tranquillity in that region so that any potential disorder or disobedience by the exiled artisans and peasants will be quickly halted and resolved, especially since they will not be the only persons who will have to live there; along with these people a religious entourage is being assigned to your company. Furthermore, native Americans will eventually be attracted to come under your jurisdiction.

Consequently, the economic situation of the new settlers should initially be based on such sound material incentives that without any pressure from you they will themselves work to become good entrepreneurs. To accomplish this, taking into account all the measures that might be introduced presently in the new settlements in America and on the Kuril Islands, I feel that it is imperative that you do the following:

First, the measures pertaining to America:

1. As soon as your company administrator in America carries out your instructions and selects a suitable new place where a settlement should be established, then his first obligation should be that as soon as he reaches that place he should construct a fort, just as quickly as possible. The location will depend on local circumstances. That fort, as well as others you have already built in other places for your promyshlenniks, can serve as a defensive outpost to protect all the inhabitants who will settle there now as well as those who may come in the future. It will serve as a guardian of company property and will protect those people from potentially harmful actions on the part of American natives either in the immediate vicinity or farther away, until any misconceptions these unlearned people may have had in regard to Russian intentions there have been resolved. For this purpose also there should immediately be organized a strong sentry unit made up of settlers and some of the promyshlenniks in the fort. The administrator himself must supervise this; if any sentry should leave his post or be irresponsible in carrying out his sentry duties, he should be considered a traitor to public safety and be punished accordingly.

In order that all settlers and promyshlenniks living there realize the importance of zealously fulfilling sentry duty, they should be frequently reminded that their own safety depends on it and that Imperial interest demands it.

I am certain you have already briefed your local administrator on how vitally important a defensive fort is, and all the rules for locating it in as suitable a place as possible, and that you have instructed him to build it as quickly as he can, and have told him which persons should build it. You are more familiar with local conditions than I am and you already know the areas and the people.

I will leave any further details concerning this matter to your zeal which you have already demonstrated on behalf of Imperial glory.

2. As soon as the fort has been completed, or at least is in condition so that you do not need to fear a sudden attack, the second responsibility of your administrator is the following. Either inside the fort or outside, on the side which the fort itself can protect, dwellings should be built for the agricultural workers and the artisans and all other personnel. Instruct your administrator to pattern these dwellings after those that are built in [Russian] towns. Everything should be comfortable, peaceful, and pleasing in appearance. They should be located a safe distance apart from each other in case of fire. The streets should be straight and wide and divided into blocks. In appropriate places there should be squares set aside for possible future construction of public buildings. In short, order these matters on the basis of your knowledge of local places so that the first settlement in America will be built and organized on the same lines as any ordinary [Russian] city. Anything resembling winding or narrow or impassable streets or walkways would be inappropriate, for in time this first settlement can create a sense of beauty among the people and the Russian inhabitants will not lose their respect and love for art and good taste.

In accordance with an ukaz of Her Imperial Majesty, a religious entourage will be sent to the place where the new settlement is to be founded. They will have their own living quarters; depending on when and how they are to reach America, you are to instruct your administrator to have living quarters built for them. These should be similar to the quarters of the other inhabitants. A church should be constructed where they will conduct services. Both the church and their dwelling should be built at the same time, not after, the dwellings for the settlers are built, so that they can be used as soon as possible in the new settlement, circumstances permitting.

3. Although it may take a great deal of effort and diligence to build these dwellings and other structures to satisfy the basic needs of the settlers, nevertheless no time should be lost in preparing grains and other garden produce and vegetables, for these are as vital as the dwellings for the immediate needs of the people.

For this reason draw up detailed instructions for your admin-

422

istrator. Use your experience of the climate there to tell him when the first plantings should take place, especially in regard to grains for bread and garden vegetables. This is information that you will determine, in your eagerness to introduce agriculture and to supply the new settlers with seeds. However, you must order that the first harvest not be used for food until there is enough grain for a second planting, and so that in case of a poor harvest there will be some surplus left. Moreover, you will need to provide for feeding all the persons who live there and for enough to sell to your Company or to send on to Okhotsk and Kamchatka.

It would also be wise to give orders that a special warehouse be built which could be used for permanent grain storage. Such grain could be used for the next planting in case of a poor harvest. If such a building were constructed it would be permanent, and very useful for persons who decide to settle there. Likewise, seeds for garden produce should be saved at first until there are enough so that in case of a poor harvest some could be used for planting and some for food, and still have some left over as surplus. When this system has increased the amount of grain for making bread, and results in plenty of bread to eat, the rest of the harvest should be allotted to the settlers as their personal property in compensation for their work. They should be allowed to sell some of it to Kamchatka and Okhotsk. If your company can encourage the settlers in this, you should pay them 50 kopecks per pud for the grain. Meanwhile, until an amount of grain necessary for the settlement has been produced, instruct your administrator that the settlers should look for all possible ways of getting food from local sources, and eat the same thing the company promyshlenniks do—all varieties of fish, marine animals, local birds and edible roots can be eaten with the bread your company provides for them. You should have your administrator give special consideration to solving this problem as well as the previous one. He should serve as the chief economic administrator for all matters, and supervise the benefit which the Empire expects from the establishment of the settlement and from agriculture.

Follow these same rules to increase livestock and domestic fowl. Make every effort to increase them as much as possible; do not use them for food; rather, find other edible things which can be acquired through diligence and effort.

4. Speaking of exercising economy in the use of grain, there

are other ways in which the settlers could be transformed into good providers by following certain rules. If each of them can acquire things through work, they will be pleased, and will use this means to bring further satisfactions. If the place where they live is well-organized and has all these advantages which are necessary for them, as well as the opportunity to acquire other things right there, then one can already foresee various means to promote their satisfaction and prosperity. But at present we do not know all the sources, except for the sea and the rivers and the wintering places, which can provide them with meat and fish; and so I believe that initially it is the responsibility of your administrator in America to search out the resources which could be had there from the land itself. The settlers should be given freedom so that following your administrator's suggestions based on the local circumstances, they could develop the trade in furs of both land and marine animals.

They will have food from the meat and fat of sea animals and from fish, and can make clothing and footwear from the pelts, as also from the pelts of land animals. They can use various minerals to tan the hides. For that reason you should give instructions that if the settlers do not know how to use minerals to tan hides and make food and soap from the fat, any promyshlenniks who know how to do this should be assigned for a time to teach the settlers the art of tanning hides for clothing and footwear, making soap and other skills.

If your administrator there is a very attentive and enterprising person, he will try to care for all of these things. He will see to it that this matter is successfully carried out, so the settlers will be able to fill their own needs for clothing and footwear and will be able to sell the surplus results of their labor and thus acquire property. They will thereby improve their own well-being and gain other economic benefits for themselves. Further, they will not need to be outfitted with clothing and footwear from Russia by your company.

In addition, appropriate attention must be given to planting hemp and flax. Those who are not familiar with how to process it should be instructed; those who know how to treat it should be assigned to weave fabric and other necessary items. When the planting of these two grasses is successful, there will be no need to bring materials for ships' sails and rigging, for they will produce it themselves.

There is no doubt that there are ores there, especially iron ore. For that reason you should see to it that every effort is made to prospect for these ores. The settlers should smelt iron which could be used not only in the present settlements but also for your company ships, and in general for future basic needs. If iron ore is found and processed, the final product should belong to the settlers, and there will be no need to import anchors, bolts and shipbuilding nails which are manufactured here. The discovery of other ores will enrich the settlement there also.

In short, you should order that everything the settlers produce through their own labor will be their own property, except that they are not to purchase furs from American natives and resell them to others. This enterprise is not to be part of their livelihood because it could divert them from agriculture and other beneficial economic activity, and furthermore, this [fur trade] should continue to be the exclusive prerogative of your company. You should give orders that this prohibition be strictly observed. Anyone who attempts to purchase furs from the American natives is to be treated as a suspected transgressor, whose punishment will be detailed below.

I leave it to you to decide on the basis of your own judgment and your knowledge of local circumstances whether they may acquire property individually or as a group. It is still not clear whether the settlers will be safe from the American natives when they travel about to take care of their necessities. I do think that it would not be a bad idea if you were to instruct the settlers to form several large groups at first, with several families in each group, taking into account those who will be congenial and may live together harmoniously as an artel.

Each such family group should be obliged to make all their own equipment and work together in such a manner as a large household of good peasants would. Each such family should be assigned a leading American native, a person who expresses a desire to live with them willingly, in the same way as Russian people do. These American natives should be treated as well and as generously as possible. Every effort should be made to accustom them to doing the same tasks, using the same equipment and practices which the settlers themselves do, so that in due time these American natives can not only become citizens of this first settlement in America, but also serve aboard vessels for reasonable wages, or in due time be engaged in other work. Eventually there would thus be no need to send Russian craftsmen or agricultural workers there from Russia.

In order for all of this to be accomplished with the desired speed, your administrator must oversee this diligently, and both suggest and try various means to accomplish it so that the anticipated economic success will not be replaced by disorder.

In time, when the settlers perceive their benefits, when the land is producing and grain is growing in abundance, it will be possible to divide them into smaller groups, so that each Russian and each American native will have his own household.

It also would be very useful, while these economic benefits are in the process of being realized, if bachelor settlers would take native American women as their wives and teach them how to perform all household tasks. This could be done with the help of Russian women and young girls who are members of families there now. Likewise, efforts should be made to arrange marriages between native American men and young Russian girls and with Russian widows, so that mutually beneficial ties will be established.

5. Every reasonable and well-intentioned person realizes that authority over him is for his own good, and that it is to his own advantage to obey that authority, as well as necessary for the good of others close to him. For that reason persons who violate the rules are disturbers of peace and transgressors, and must not go unpunished. Consequently, from the time of your departure from Kyktak, the administration of all matters in America has been in the hands of the person you designated. I want to impose on him the obligation of maintaining peace and tranquility throughout that region, and preserving the well-being of all persons. To that end I, therefore, order that if any of the original settlers, or any Russians who may live with them in the future, including promyshlenniks who may be assigned there on company business, in any way cause disharmony or violence, or are lazy, or disobey company orders or orders from your administrator, or perpetrate any other harmful deed and thereby interfere with the good habits of the native Americans and set a poor example for them while

they are trying to learn proper ways, or if any persons disobey my personal instructions—such persons are to be dealt with by the administrator. He will first try to persuade them by verbal counsel and minor fines to keep them from further wrongdoing. But if any of them continue to misbehave, then, because of the distant situation of the region, the administrator has the right to punish such persons right then and there, on the basis of lawful rules, in accordance with the transgression. However, the punishment is not to be witnessed by American natives. The punishment is to be meted out with some moderation, and there is to be a written account of the guilty parties and their transgressions.

In the case of serious problems, and especially in any criminal cases, once the investigation has been conducted and all possible evidence assembled, you are to send it to me. Keep the transgressor shackled and under guard, or send him, under guard, to Okhotsk to face judgment. This should all be done with great care, and all such matters should be taken to the arkhimandrit assigned to the settlement for his advice. He is a spiritual man, a learned man, and one who understands the customs and habits of people. For this reason both he and all his brothers are to be accorded proper respect and dignity. They are to be protected from any pranks the settlers or other inhabitants might devise. They are to have a peaceful life with full freedom to employ all their monastic talents, in addition to their present responsibilities, in various artistic endeavors and in searching for ores, precious stones, unusual vegetation and all other such beneficial activities, and they should have all possible support in such efforts.

Your administrator would be very wise to observe carefully the behavior of each of the servitors in the new settlement. He should immediately resolve any quarrels among the settlers so that the American natives will not be influenced by this bad habit.

In short, he should attempt to bring about a situation where all the Russians will live in complete harmony, friendship and cooperation among themselves as well as with the American natives, so that the uneducated minds of the native Americans will be conditioned by the examples of the good lives of the Russians.

6. In point 4 I said that the native Americans should be treated with kindness and good will. Now I want to enlarge on this point and emphasize that the prime objective of all your

efforts is the following. Try to transform the native Americans from savages into civilized persons. Change them from persons who do not comprehend the need for education into those who value learning; from those who have no faith, no knowledge of the existence of God, into Christians. In short, bring them into a state of awareness and instill in them a feeling for the work Russians perform and the positions they hold. The activities of your company, which are known at the present time, have already demonstrated good progress. The kindly attitudes of your promyshlenniks toward them encourages them to come frequently and in large numbers to harbors, artels and various places where the promyshlenniks are based.

Hostages who are accepted from [the natives] as a sign of their trust are introduced to Russian life and try to imitate the Russians in all ways, even to willingly accepting baptism. Their children are learning to speak Russian and also to read and write. Some are already studying mathematics. In 1792 you sent two of them [on a voyage] to Japan to study navigation, and seven other young lads are studying this in [Russian] America. Thus it is important that your administrator carry out this important matter completely, and that he also take every measure on his own initiative to seek the realization of this goal through kindly treatment, justice, and by caring for the needs of both men and women so that they can become acquainted with the way of life, the customs, sciences and arts [of the Russians]. These can be taught to them at the very beginning, as well as agricultural methods and how to breed livestock. American natives are by nature quick-witted; they understand well, are dexterous and have strong constitutions; they are well able to learn these matters.

In regard to inculcating the Christian faith and its practices in them, this is the task of the religious personnel. Their efforts should instill a meek attitude and good behavior in the American natives, as mentioned earlier.

If there are any doubts about their loyalty, you should take hostages from them. Select bright young persons so that once they develop a taste for the life style of the Russians they will become closely tied to them, as well as to their own people, in whom they will instill the advantages of our way of life and thus help establish that way of life among them. All of these matters, however, should be undertaken only in accordance with their willingness, without any pressure whatsoever.

Furthermore, while showing them kindness and advantages, one must nevertheless always be vigilant in order to avoid any acts of treason and subsequent bloodshed. For that reason it is essential to be vigilant and give judicious orders that security be maintained and that we have informers everywhere among the American natives, choosing these from among those natives who have shown an inclination toward us. These persons and all others who are well-disposed toward us should be singled out and given certain recognitions.

All the needs of such persons should be cared for, and in the future there should always be special food allowances on hand for them, a practice which you have already initiated.

7. When a suitable place is found for a shipyard, or if you have already decided upon a place for such a facility, Russian settlers should be used to build all company ships. To compensate them for their work, so their labor is not in vain, all workers should at the outset be paid by the year so they can be counted on to work on future construction. The rate of pay is to be 36 rubles per year. They are to be able to spend their pay however they wish.

It would be very desirable if your administrator, while building company vessels for voyages at sea, were also to teach the settlers how to build small boats such as lodkas and baidaras and boats for their own use. Using these they can become accustomed to sailing at sea and occasionally they can learn to hunt marine animals for themselves.

8. Judging by experience in past years it is quite unlikely that foreign ships will visit these new settlements or even be in the vicinity very often. Sometimes when this does occur there will be a great desire to buy things from the foreigners, and to visit them on board their ships; however, detrimental consequences may result from this if the visiting ships belong to a nation hostile to Russia, and if news of their hostility has not yet reached the settlers.

For this reason it is hereby decreed that not only settlers and all other Russians, but even your administrators are forbidden to have contacts with foreign ships, until you ascertain through friendly and loyal American natives why the ships have come and any other pertinent information which will assure you that there is not the slightest doubt about the foreigners. But even if there are no vital Empire and company interests and aspects involved, you should avoid contact as much as possible, and conduct any business through American natives.

If it is impossible to avoid contact and you have to go aboard their ships and permit them to visit your settlement, try to adhere to all the rules of hospitality and show them every possible courtesy; assist them in their needs but at the same time prevent them from seeing the true condition of your settlement. Most of all, use any excuse to avoid letting them see your fortifications, buildings and other things that should be concealed. Use your good judgment and take counsel with the arkhimandrit in this regard; in such a situation he should make the decision as to how to receive the foreign visitors.

Be especially careful about any English, Swedish or French ships. Because of the current situation in Europe the French should not be permitted to come to you under any circumstances. They should be considered enemies of Russia until such time as legal authority is reestablished in France. If they resort to the use of force and you are not able to prevent them from coming, then treat them as enemies and take all of your belongings and withdraw to a safe place.

You should also follow these rules during voyages at sea and surveys in those waters, when you search for islands not yet known.

9. Now I will try to give you some information about the Kuril Islands. You have expressed the intention of sending some of the agricultural peasants who have been sent to you to the eighteenth of the Kuril Islands, the one called Urup. You want them to develop agriculture there because of the favorable location of the island, and to hunt animals with the promyshlenniks who have been sent there. Except for the hairy Kuril people [Ainus] who come there on a temporary basis from the nineteenth island to hunt, there are no native inhabitants. Likewise, at the present time there are no Russian promyshlenniks there.

Consequently, concerning the establishment of a settlement and order on this eighteenth island, I shall refer to the rules previously stated, which are enclosed with the copy of my orders. You should so inform the person whom you will appoint as your chief administrator on that island. Moreover, since this island is located in the vicinity of the possessions of the Japanese Empire, where as you know in the year 1792 an embassy was sent from Russia to establish friendship and trade, therefore it is necessary that your administrator try his best to establish contact with the Japanese and show them signs of friendship and treat them with kindness and consideration, and not give them even the slightest reason for suspicion.

At the same time, try to obtain information from the hairy Kurils who visit this eighteenth island and other islands where they hunt; and if the situation permits the Russians to undertake naval observation, obtain information from them. The effort to be made is to ascertain, in as detailed a manner as possible, the position of the Japanese Empire and others of the Kuril Islands located close to and belonging to Japan. Ascertain what resources they have in plenty, what shortages they face and everything else such as their military strength, population, fortifications, commerce, customs, habits, laws and their opinions about the Russians. Above all, try, through kind treatment of the hairy ones to establish trade with them so it will be possible to obtain goods and grain from Japan through them.

Likewise, through kind treatment of the hairy Kurils from the nineteenth island, and other islands, try to establish settlements and introduce agriculture, for it is known on the basis of certain information that the hairy islanders on the nineteenth and twentieth islands live in discord among themselves and have no genuine loyalty to the Japanese. Furthermore, it is also known from certain reports that the hairy Kurils are inclined to barbarism; thus, your administrator and the people under his care must always be extremely careful so the hairy Kurils from the nineteenth and twentieth islands will not come in large bands and kill the Russians.

For a situation such as this I should give better and more detailed instructions, but the circumstances of these places is still very little known. Consequently the only other thing I can say is that I leave everything to the good judgment and experience of your administrator there. You will give him your own counsel and advice as well, so that your intentions for the Kuril Islands will be carried out with the desired success. Equip and arm your Kuril

While hardly the geometrically platted cityscape envisioned and ordered by Empress Catherine, Shelikhov's settlement at Pavlovsk on Kodiak Island was a remarkable outpost in the wilderness, and had a distinctively Russian appearance. More important, it afforded good anchorage for the fur trade bonanza. Yefimov, *Atlas of Geographical Discoveries. . . .* (OHS neg. 80223)

detachment with everything they will need, as best you can.

Finally, 10. In regard to organizing all of this in America and on the eighteenth Kuril Island, and subsequent events there, and the success with which all of this is organized, please have your administrators keep you informed of everything. In turn, you are to inform me directly from time to time by using the transport vessels which will depart from there for Okhotsk. On these sailings they should bring back maps, journals, economic analyses and reports on nature. They should also bring for my attention reports on all kinds of unusual occurrences which are worthy of note, so that on the basis of such information I can then prepare my reports for Her Imperial Majesty.

Reference: LOTsIA, f. 1147, op. 1, d. No. 140, 11. 10–23 ob. Also Library of Congress, Manuscript Division. Yudin Collection, Box 2.
See: A. I. Andreev, ed. *Russkie otkrytiia v Tikhom okeane i v Severnoi Amerike v XVIII veke* (Moscow: 1948), 323–336.

74

AUGUST 9, 1794

A LETTER FROM GRIGORII I. SHELIKHOV TO ALEKSANDR A. BARANOV, ADMINISTRATOR OF THE NORTH-EASTERN COMPANY, INSTRUCTING HIM TO ESTABLISH A SETTLEMENT, BUILD A SHIPYARD AND INTRODUCE AGRICULTURE IN NORTH AMERICA

My dear Aleksandr Andreevich!

I am dispatching to you two new ships built at this port: a 63-foot double-deck two-masted vessel called *Tri Ierarkhi*, and a 51-foot double-masted single-deck vessel called the *Sviataia Veliko-muchenitsa Ekaterina*, named in honor of our ruling Autocrat and Benefactress. I am most pleased to announce to you the visitors who are coming to you on these ships. They are the Arkhi-mandrit Ioasaf and his brothers, all of whom have been assigned in accordance with the will of Her Imperial Majesty, as you will see from the papers appended to this letter. One is a copy of the ukaz from the Governing Senate concerning spreading the word of God in America and teaching local people about the Christian faith and making them aware of their responsibilities in well orga-nized societies. These ecclesiastics have been especially chosen by that very wise person, His Eminence, Gavriil, Metropolitan of St. Petersburg. They have been exemplary as monks, leading gentle, quiet and orderly lives.

The second group of visitors have also been assigned to my company in accordance with Her Imperial Majesty's will. They are to build ships near Cape St. Elias. There are also 30 families of unfortunates [exiles] who are to introduce agriculture there. I am appending a list of their names.

Having given you this news, which you probably had not ex-pected at this time, I am certain that you will be pleased, as I am, that this land where I worked before you and where you now work, for the glory of our fatherland, will now realize through these guests who are coming to you, the desired support for fu-ture benefits. May God grant that this be realized soon, while we have the good fortune to be able to carry out certain noble inten-tions of Our Wise Benefactress. You yourself will judge how im-portant this is, because it is primarily you who will build and carry out this undertaking.

433

His Excellency, Lieutenant General Ivan Alferevich Pil, Cavalier and Governor General of Irkutsk and the Kolyvan Province, has given me the original order, which I am sending to you. You will see that through you, as the Administrator of the company, I have been authorized to carry out the following tasks. Before you build the shipyard and introduce agriculture, you are to build a church and living quarters and provide other necessities which will ensure the well-being of my company and bring glory to the [Russian] Empire. I consider myself obliged, through this friendly letter to you, to indicate all the means by which you can carry out these assignments and fulfill the task that has been set for you. I shall observe the same order in which this assignment from His Excellency [Governor General Pil] is presented.

In the first point I am instructed to designate the site for a settlement and build a fort. I will explain my reaction, which I have submitted to the government, concerning establishing shipbuilding and agriculture near Cape St. Elias. While I was on Kodiak I learned that the mainland coast of America, from the limits of habitation of the Ugalakhmut people above the island of Suklia on which Cape St. Elias is located, down to the limits of habitation of the Kenai people, has a better climate than Kodiak because the winter there is quite brief and very mild, there is little snow and spring begins early so that by mid-April the wildflowers are blooming as well as the berry plants in the forest. Summer is hot and long. The soil is friable and there are a number of areas suitable for planting grains. There are larch and other trees which are necessary for shipbuilding as you know, and these are plentiful.

This area has a clear advantage over Kodiak Island, for although the latter also has an early spring, a good summer and a moderate winter, nevertheless there is little land suitable for growing grains, and the location is less favorable. As an example, after I left Kodiak, from the earlier harbor of Tri Sviatiteli, I experimented with planting grains and I also had a vegetable garden. Both areas were flooded by an unexpected rise of seawater. There is also another important point, namely, that with the exception of fir, there are absolutely no trees suitable for ship construction. Therefore I believe that it would be infinitely better to establish a permanent Russian settlement on the mainland than on the island, where foreigners could always come. In case of necessity one could find better protection from them on the mainland. Further, for political reasons you should know that you must devote more effort to holding the mainland than the island.

In certain places near Cape St. Elias, where you stopped in 1793, you saw quite a number of natives whom you wished to befriend and from whom you planned to take hostages. It is possible that since your last letter you have succeeded in this. This is where I propose establishing the first Russian settlement and shipyard. For that reason, please let me know if during your travels along this part of the American coast you have located places where this would be possible, a site where all necessary advantages exist to establish the settlement and shipyard. We must find such a place by the fall of this year. When I go there in large baidaras I plan to take with me the Arkhimandrit and his staff, as well as craftsmen and farm workers and all necessary equipment, tools, grain and vegetable seeds, livestock, artillery and everything else which will be indispensable.

I do not need to remind you that such a settlement will best be established on a good navigable river where shipbuilding lumber can easily be procured, and where the shipyard itself can be located. It should be near a lake, or at least near fresh water springs. Likewise, the site should be near construction lumber, meadows for grazing livestock and fields for cultivating grain. In accordance with the wishes of the arkhimandrit, the place should have a healthy climate, be suitable for agriculture and offer protection against enemy attack. If you do not find such a place near Cape St. Elias, toward the region of the Ugalakhmuts, or if you do find a place but for some unforeseen reason it is impossible to establish a settlement there, then you should look for a site in the region of the Chugach or the Kenais, where the air, climate, land and water are also good [Cook Inlet].

Once you have found the place, you are to prepare it for settlement in the following manner. First, all of the people there must live together, and the place and its environs are to be identified with the name of Her Imperial Majesty, Autocrat of All Russia. It is to be both formally and symbolically taken with arms, using a salvo of guns, and loudly proclaiming in the presence of everyone with you that *this territory is under the possession of the Russian Empire.*

On the site where the fort is to be built, a large Russian flag should be raised immediately, and a large cross erected where living quarters are to be built. Certainly the arkhimandrit should conduct an appropriate religious ceremony on the occasion, and he should offer a special prayer, beseeching the Almighty Creator to grant good health to Her Imperial Majesty, the entire Imperial Family and all loyal subjects of the Russian Throne. . . . Then you are to consult with the Reverend Father about all matters. He is an educated person, familiar with the local economy, and has good judgment. The two of you should decide on a location where the settlement will be established.

Once you have done all this, immediately prepare a plan for both a fort and the settlement. As quickly as possible establish an enclosure fenced by a *chevaux de frise* and boards with sharp iron spikes, which the Company has, and which you and I have used. Station sentries in appropriate places and assign people to cut lumber. The rest should prepare the other necessary materials. They should be protected by armed men in case of danger.

Once the lumber and other materials are ready for construction, invoke God's blessing and start to build the fort. When the foundation is complete, name it Fort St. Catherine in honor of the Empress. If there are to be redoubts, they should also be named in honor of the Imperial Family. I cannot give you exact instructions at this point on the size of the fort, how it should be laid out and whether redoubts should be built. I will entrust this matter to your experience and judgment. You should refer to information in the books on fortifications. A good number of these have been sent to you. I do ask that in laying out the fort you consult the ieromonk Iuvenalii and the ierodiakon Stefan, both of whom worked in mining operations in civilian life and are well versed in mathematics. When they were here they both promised to assist you in this.

In regard to further details for carrying out this first point rapidly, I recommend that you act in precise accord with the counsel of His Excellency [Governor General Pil]. Entrust the supervision of the people, construction, economic matters, property and everything else to Ivan Grigorevich Polomoshnyi, whom I have sent to you especially to help you in all your projects. He is to be under your leadership, and in this new settlement he will be the chief supervisor and overseer of order, peace and tranquility. You will be busy with many other matters, such as mapping and exploring, and will not always be able to be in the settlement.

436

Give Polomoshnyi His Excellency's directions and this letter from me, in the form of instructions. Also give him all the appended materials, in the original, to guide him in carrying out his instructions. Keep an exact copy of all of this for yourself for reference. However, as time and opportunity permit, be certain to make inquiries and personally oversee everything that is happening in the settlement. If matters need improvement, use your own best judgment and take counsel with the arkhimandrit.

At first this important undertaking may be hampered by a shortage of men to work and to stand sentry duty, and there will be a shortage of construction and farm workers. To assist these persons, you are to select 30 of the promyshlenniks who are well armed and equipped. Choose them on the basis of their good behavior and their knowledge of carpentry and cabinetry, and other skills such as tanning, soapmaking, brick-making, pottery and other crafts. Do this at the earliest opportunity in order to establish economic and craft pursuits. These persons may be assisted, as need arises, by up to 100 of the best Kodiak men who speak Russian, or by other American natives or Aleuts. As far as possible, these men should be fed, and some agreement should be made with them about additional payment. They should be kept in this settlement until all living needs are met, and until the economy of the place is established.

In consideration of this you should issue appropriate instructions concerning the preparation of provisions and other necessities. When the fort or the redoubts have been built, they should be fitted out with artillery if possible, and with everything else they need. All of this should be done in a manner suitable for defense. Polomoshnyi is to be instructed to supervise this. Equipment and materials for building the fort are to be taken from the Company. When you have finished building it, have a drawing of the facade and profile made, and send it to me by the first available transport. Also send your journal so I can transmit these things to the government.

In accordance with the second point, when you have completed the fort, you are to start building living quarters and the church, either inside or outside the fort. I cannot predict whether you will be able to build everything at the same time or not, or whether the dwellings will be inside or outside the fort, because I am not familiar with the location, the proximity of forest and other necessities, and for that reason I cannot give you specific instructions. But I am relying on your judgment, skill, knowledge and feelings. You will be the founder of a well built settlement on land which has never before had one. I am confident that you will do everything in your power to see that comfortable buildings and a place of worship are built there as soon as possible.

For this reason there is nothing more for me to say except the following.

1. I ask that in locating streets and dwellings, you follow His Excellency's [Pil's] instruction in every detail, having first made plans for all the construction necessities. Abide by the counsel and views of the arkhimandrit and the priests Iuvenalii and Stefan, who are experienced in surveying and architecture, and are there to help you.

2. If the dwellings are built outside the fort, you are to call this settlement, until new instructions from authorities are forthcoming, Slavorossiia, in honor of the Glory of Russia.

I have submitted to the arkhimandrit and his staff the plan for the church which was prepared in Irkutsk. Initially it calls for two chapels, church furnishings and vestments. These may be increased or decreased as circumstances dictate. The first chapel is to be unheated, and is to be named Voskresenie Khristovo [Christ's Resurrection]; the second is to be heated in winter and dedicated to the Uspenie Bozhei Materi [Ascension of the Holy Mother]. The site for the construction of the church should be chosen so that as far as possible half of it will be either inside the settlement or facing the dwellings, so that it can be entered from the dwellings without going into the part outside the settlement. It is to be protected by a strong high fence, which will enclose a large enough space to accommodate the cells for the arkhimandrit and the other monks, as well as the necessary service buildings, a garden and a school for young American natives.

Be certain to send the plans and drawings of the facades of these buildings when they are completed. It seems to me that the homes for the settlers should be built so that each has a *belaia izba* [windowed cabin], a hall with a pantry and a cool room or a storeroom adjacent. Other buildings such as sheds, livestock shelters and cellars should be built as wings, but in such a manner that the exterior appearance is not unattractive but rather with a pleasing appearance when viewed from the streets. In drawing up the plan for this settlement, designate three or four places where it will eventually be possible to erect obelisks in honor of Russian patriots. Let me know whether you have any porphyry or some other appropriate building material in the vicinity.

Concerning the third point which deals with growing grain and garden produce, you are to issue instructions so as not to miss the earliest planting opportunity. This matter is clearly and fully explained in His Excellency's instructions. Regarding this I want to say that you should use your own judgment, and not wait for instructions from me, as to the months in which this very important assignment should be carried out. You have had experience with the climate on Kodiak, and you should ask God's assistance first of all. I have given Polomoshnyi grain seeds from here: 59 puds 39 pounds of rye seed; 10 puds 15 pounds of *iadritsa* [groats]; 2 puds 4 pounds of oats; 7 puds 12 pounds of barley; 33 pounds of hemp; 23 pounds of buckwheat; 10 puds 35 pounds of millet; 8 puds 10 pounds of peas; also various vegetable seeds such as radishes, carrots, turnips, rutabagas, beets, cabbages, cucumbers, pumpkins, melons, salad greens, spinach, purslaine, parsley, celery, onions and many others. The Father Arkhimandrit has also been given a great amount of these same seeds. Only seed potatoes are lacking, but you can obtain these from Kodiak, since potatoes grow well there. All seeds both grain and vegetable, are to be divided into two equal parts. Use half for the first harvest and save the other half for a second planting in case the first fails. You have many garden books on Kodiak which will give planting directions. Your own experience as well as that of the clergy and the farm workers who have been sent there will guide you in approaching this vital matter with diligence and will help you use the best possible methods.

I have also given Polomoshnyi farm tools. You should immediately order that other wooden tools which you will need be made. I have also sent livestock with Polomoshnyi. There are two male and five female goats, three rams, four ewes, one colt and one filly. When you leave to establish the settlement, take these animals with you, as well as animals presently on Kodiak, but leave one pair of each there to reproduce.

In regard to cultivating the new land, if there are no full-grown oxen on Kodiak, then I suggest you use any available personnel to cultivate the ground with iron picks and shovels, because the present sowing of grain will not be enough for all the workers and other servitors. It would be best if you could devise a piece of equipment to plow the land.

In order to alleviate these labor problems and shortages in the future, I will try to send more livestock and seed grain on a future transport. I would have liked to send you full grown horses, but the lack of space on the ships obviated this. We had nearly 130 men on one ship and 80 on the other, plus their effects and company goods.

Most of all I am relying on your judgement. I trust you will carry out the intentions of the illustrious Empress in our initial enterprises as far as possible. I will await your recommendations and detailed news about all of this, reporting how this vital matter has commenced. His Excellency's instructions give details about caring for the grain, livestock and equipment; all you have to do is follow these instructions. Since you are familiar with local circumstances, I rely on you and Polomoshnyi. Give him your wise advice on matters, including how to attract American natives to settle there and be useful to our people.

Try to arrange marriages between the bachelor settlers who are being sent you and good American native women. For this purpose I am sending you special gifts for the brides and future wives—various items of apparel—which you may present to each one who marries.

The fourth point of His Excellency's instructions quite clearly instructs that new settlers are to be given the right to acquire everything they need for their comfort. I cannot add anything to this, except to point out that the people who inhabit that area under consideration are backward; and since we want to gain control of the new settlement area on land and sea, this should be done by our promyshlenniks, with the consent of the [Russian] settlers. When these people have time free from farm work and household tasks, they may attempt to hunt, especially for their own uses; however any surplus they have they should sell to the company. Give them every opportunity, means and instructions to enable them to do this.

If iron, copper, silver or other valuable ores are discovered, even if they are outside the boundaries of the settlement, you may be able to obtain these by using local natives, or if not, by using settlers, who, however, are not to neglect their primary agricultural responsibilities. You may procure these metal ores on the basis of arrangements you and Polomoshnyi will make, using your judgement of local circumstances; you should pay settlers for the ore they bring in, which the company will then take over. It would be helpful to ascertain first of all whether there are any iron and copper ores nearby which could be used for the needs of the new settlement and for shipbuilding. Fathers Iuvenalii and Stefan will advise you on how to smelt the ores and how to build smelting furnaces and all other related matters. These fathers are experienced in mining and extracting, and you are to ask their advice on such matters. As far as I know they will not be prospecting for ores personally. However, you should provide them with everything they need, through Polomoshnyi, and be sure to keep me informed about the progress of this undertaking.

There are so many urgent projects which require mutual agreement that I feel you should try your best to persuade more native American men and women to settle there with you. By using many people work will go faster and it will be easier to finish everything. Furthermore, this will enable the American natives to adjust more quickly and easily to our way of life. For this purpose you should use captives whom you may buy; by virtue of their having been bought they may be more reliable than others and more obedient to the settlers. The settlers should use these persons for labor, but under strict supervision so that proper measures will be taken to attract them and make them loyal.

I do not see that I need to add anything to the fifth point of His Excellency's instructions except that a company office should be built to help keep proper records about all developments in the new settlement and other business matters. In this building there should be a room where persons suspected of violations could be detained occasionally. In this office structure you could easily settle all manner of affairs, as could Polomoshnyi when you are away, far better than in your own quarters or in his. This would also provide a safe storage place for the various pieces of communal equipment, plans and models, as opposed to private property. I believe this structure will be respected and treated properly both by the Russians and especially by the American natives, if you are certain to see that any native who has been wronged is justly compensated. Give Polomoshnyi detailed instructions on what to do to carry out investigations; make certain he has the proper respect for the authority he has been given in this new settlement.

The sixth point of His Excellency's instructions is so clear and well set forth that I do not think I need to add anything to it except for the following. If either you or Polomoshnyi take young American natives as hostages, or if either of you or some of the settlers entice young natives to come to the new settlement, and they express a desire to live there, then all of these young natives like those young natives on Kodiak who are being taught to read and write, should be taught to read and write and cipher under the guidance of the Father Arkhimandrit. Some of his monks are able to teach and have expressed their willingness to do so, especially Father Makarii. For this purpose I have given the arkhimandrit the books I have selected to be sent to America, concerning classics, history, mathematics, morals and economics. Add to this collection all the books you have on Kodiak in the artels and in the company office. Give all of these to the arkhimandrit when he arrives. If necessary you may obtain from him any book you need, but then you are to return it to him.

In regard to the propagation of the Christian faith, leave this completely in the hands of the arkhimandrit. Try to send to him all the American natives from various places who express a desire to become Christians. You and your associate should just try to supply provisions for all who wish to be in the new settlement; toward that goal apply wise measures of economy.

In the seventh point His Excellency advises that Russian settlers should be used to build company vessels, and thanks to the great generosity of Her Imperial Majesty I have received twenty shipwrights for that task. Your last letter of July 24, 1793, from Chugach Bay, which I received last June 22 via the ship *Simeon* which you dispatched, informed me that following my instructions the keel had already been laid in Chugatsk Bay for a 66-foot vessel. You do not however give a detailed description of the place you have chosen for that project. You only note that you are procuring lumber for ship construction on Greek Island, and that the lumber is brought by boat. Consequently it appears that the place you have chosen to build the vessel is not completely suitable. I therefore surmise that this place is only suitable for launching ships, keeping them safe and rigging them out and dispatching them to sea, but that it does not have suitable construction lumber and that is the reason you have to bring this in from the small Greek Island.

If I understand the actual situation of your present shipbuilding accurately, I must conclude that your shipyard is not completely suitable, or that you have not yet had time to find a good location with all advantages. When you set out to establish a new settlement, ideally there should be plenty of construction quality lumber nearby in order for you to be able easily to build, maintain, rig and launch a ship. But if there is no such source of lumber nearby, then you must try to find such a site suitable for ship construction out beyond the settlement site. I trust your judgment in this; my only instruction is that you must not fail to have young American natives study with master shipwrights, carpenters, blacksmiths, artisans and navigators. Generally speaking American natives make very capable seafarers; all they need is practical experience, especially with the compass which is so necessary; then they can master this. You may reward Russian master builders, who have been sent to construct ships, over and above the payment designated by His Excellency, especially those who are the most industrious and have distinguished themselves through their work.

Point eight of His Excellency's instructions deals with [Russians] who desert after meeting foreigners. It would be superfluous for me to enlarge on His Excellency's instructions and on the earlier government decrees you receive in 1790. All of these are sufficiently detailed and clear so that for the present you and your associate need only carry them out fully, in the case of the English skipper [Hugh] Moore coming to you, the man you met on his forfeited ship *Phoenix* in Chugach Bay. You know the cost of letting foreigners take advantage of us and our weakness. We must therefore try desperately to do as much shipbuilding as possible.

For that reason I once again advise you that on Kodiak, in the new settlement and if possible in other places, you have several of the most loyal American natives chosen to be your spies and bring you information about any foreigners who may come. If a French naval or merchant vessel should appear, they could cleverly sink it by drilling a hole in the vessel or by setting it afire or by luring it into a harbor, bay or inlet where it would be wrecked on underwater rocks and reefs. In brief, I leave this subject to your judgment, but I hope that you will continue to act on your infor-

Shelikhov's instructions to Baranov included orders to use "loyal American natives" as spies to bring news of intrusion by any foreign ships. The natives should sabotage such vessels by sinking, setting them afire or luring them onto reefs to be wrecked! Private collection.

mation so as to bring benefit, right, and profit to our Russian Empire, and that you will give instructions and authority to your associate to accomplish this same goal.

In point 10 His Excellency instructs you to send me complete information about successful projects entrusted to you. Send thorough and accurate information to me personally, and obtain information from everyone who has been authorized to carry out his work. Polomoshnyi is appointed as your necessary administrator, builder, and overseer for the new settlement. He must keep you informed of his progress and give you his advice and counsel in case it is impossible to send a ship here from the settlement.

Now that I have given you my observations, I conclude with a friendly request that you continue to explore the expanses of the sea and discover new places on the American mainland. Make orderly descriptions of these places, and locate them on maps. I also want you to know that with God's help I have completed a matter which I undertook long ago. I have sent the ship *Simeon* back to you with a crew of something more than 70 men under the leadership of Merkulev. The ship arrived here in Okhotsk on June 22 last year, dispatched from you. I have also organized a company named the North American Company, on precisely the same rules as the North Eastern American Company which you are administering. This company will merge with my other companies where there are presently 140 workers, in addition to those I am sending. Next summer I will send another ship, the *Mikhail*, and this will further increase the number of men there. I would like to occupy all the northern part of America from the island of Unalaska, meaning everything opposite the Chukotsk territory. After I have designated the place where this company should have its posts for trading with the natives, I will establish ties and commercial relations with them. The ship *Simeon* will stop first on the islands of St. Paul and St. George.

From my plan you will now see that both sides of the coast of the American cape opposite the Chukotsk land can be surveyed. However, I believe that the exploration of those areas, especially in the north, will best be undertaken by the company you administer. Your reports coincide with my thoughts. You propose using a shorter and more convenient route from north to south, via the Iagyk River and the lake, and the shortest overland route, which the navigator Bocharov discovered in 1791, which goes across Alaska in the place where the Alaska Cape begins to jut off from the mainland as an isthmus.

I will be very pleased to hear that this survey has been made, because after receiving the letters and plans from you via the *Mikhail* in 1793 concerning the discovery of a shorter and better route across Alaska, I reported this to the government and to Her

Imperial Majesty. This route would have the advantage of making it possible to place artels along the way, and to have a large vessel on the northern coast as well as the baidaras. If you request it, I can outfit the vessel from the funds of the recently organized North [American] Company. I plan to build a warehouse for company equipment on that coast to protect myself from occasional hostile Europeans who might try to harm the company.

I will not enlarge on how much there is to be done quickly, since I am fully aware of your eagerness and know that I do not need to remind you to do everything you can to prevent foreign powers from doing anything to cause trouble for us on the American coast. However, I do beg you to accelerate this expedition as soon as you are free. I know that you have a great deal of business now. In addition to surveying the coast all the way to Nootka, you are also responsible for organizing the Russian settlement of Slavorossiia and construction on Kodiak. Nevertheless, although you are occupied with this important matter, do not let the Europeans beat you to Ltuya Bay. I ask that you send at least two of the four ships presently at your disposal to carry on the discoveries you have begun. [Your four ships are] the *Severnoi Orel*, the two I am sending you from here, and the one you will build in Chugach Bay.

You write that you have a shortage of men and that the crew is quite inadequate. Let me assure you that you will have plenty, since, in addition to the 149 men you presently have, 123 newly acquired promyshlenniks are being sent to you on the two vessels and you can supplement these with American natives and Aleuts. I have agreed to use the five older experienced men on the *Simeon*; I will hire them as company sailors. I will pay them up to 200 rubles per year in cash, but will not pay them hunting shares. You may employ them to work with navigators on voyages to make surveys, but do not use them in any other capacity.

I am also sending you and the company a sufficient quantity of various goods, supplies, weapons, powder, shot and the like, which we value at some 300,000 rubles. With all of this you will be able to carry out the plans which you have undertaken and establish commerce with the [native] peoples you subdue.

In regard to the problems which the ill-mannered Lebedev workmen caused in Kenai, all your reports will undoubtedly be reviewed in Irkutsk. There will be a fair resolution to this problem, but not before the transport vessel arrives, which I hope you will send next summer if possible, considering all your responsibilities.

I have not yet informed you of another very important matter. You will see from His Excellency's instructions that I am to send several families of farm workers, who have been assigned to me, to the 18th Kuril Island, because it has been and continues to be my intention gradually to introduce the Russian way of life there also. For that purpose, in accordance with the orders to me personally, on the official list I am assigning four families who are now being sent on the new vessels I am dispatching to you. They are on the smaller vessel. The instructions are that when these people are put ashore on the first of the Kuril Islands, the ship is to continue on its way to you. However, I realize that from now on, strong winds will be blowing in that region and the Kuril Straits are quite dangerous at such times, as you yourself know. Because of the strong currents, tides, and the surge of water toward the shore, I have been persuaded to give prime consideration to the safety of the capital, the people, and the disembarkation of the settlers, who must be protected by twenty chosen promy-shlenniks. If it should be impossible to land them [on the Kurils], they would have to be brought to you in America, which would be pointless. Consequently, I have devised another means of doing this by sending them from here aboard a government trans-port ship and paying for their passage. This ship left here a few days ago bound for Petropavlovsk harbor in Kamchatka. I de-cided to do this because the ship has to sail past the first Kuril Island, and it may be possible to land them there, which would be desirable. But if this is not possible, they will be taken to Kam-chatka and next spring can be sent from one [Kuril] island to an-other by baidara until they reach the eighteenth. As you yourself know, this is possible to do.

I explained my plan and asked for help from [Colonel von] Witten, the local commandant [of Okhotsk]. Unfortunately, he decided not to send them on a navy vessel even though there was plenty of space, and the ship had some 2,000 puds of ballast. In place of the ballast it could have taken my people, their belong-ings, supplies, grain and the tools, which would have been more useful. However, it seemed to Witten that it would be difficult to make out new papers for the ship's cargo. Consequently, I now find it necessary to provide for wintering these four families of settlers and twenty workers here, where there is no food. Next spring I will try to send them to the Kurils on the *Mikhail*. The biggest problem for me is not the expense of providing for these people through the winter, but not being able to begin farming next year because they will reach the island too late in the season and will have to spend another winter without having started to farm. Now that I have informed you about this, I will reveal my further ideas for you.

I intend to have a company on the 18th Kuril Island, in addition to farming there. But since I will not always be able to have Russians there, I have decided to engage Aleuts and native Americans to hunt, as many as 50 men at first. The Russians will only be there to be administrators, and to protect them from the hairy Kuril [Ainu] people, with whom it is unsafe even to associate. Consequently, when you send the first ship, be certain to persuade healthy young American natives and Aleuts, up to 50 men and their families, to agree to come. Give them what they need, reach agreement on pay, and send them to the first Kuril Island, from where they can proceed in baidaras to the eighteenth. These American natives and Aleuts can periodically be replaced by others whom you may send there. Send one Russian man with them, who can guide them to the eighteenth island, having first procured all necessities and built large wooden baidaras. Please make every effort to do this.

Then, I urge you to provide as well as you can for the Holy Father Arkhimandrit and his monks in every possible way. Provide for them on Kodiak and en route, giving them everything they need and enough provisions of local origin for their sustenance. As far as clothing is concerned, and other needs, as well as food and other necessities, both for themselves and for the church, I have already provided for these here and I believe they will receive these things within three years. I do not think they will be idle on Kodiak. I believe they will want to have a church on Kodiak Island. Thus, if in your new harbor, Sv. Pavel [Pavlovsk], where I have sent you greetings via the transport vessel, there is still no adequate structure where Mass can be said and where the liturgy can be read, you should give instructions for a small house of prayer to be built, and organize a church in it. You

A rendering of the natives of Sitka. Ever optimistic, Shelikhov assigned hard-driving Baranov to carve company headquarters in the rocks and rain forests of Sitka. Timber suitable for their company fleet was abundant, and Shelikhov hoped the town "would have a healthy climate, be suitable for agriculture and offer protection against attack." The forests and ravens still reign. *La Corvette Senavine*. (OHS neg. 80235)

will give the fathers much comfort through this. They are all very fine people and sincere monks.

Finally, I send you my most sincere regards, and wish you good health, happiness, and success in all your ventures.

I remain, as always, your obedient servant,

[signed] Grigorii Shelikhov

Reference: LOTsIA, f. 1147, op. 1, d. No. 140, ll. 24–35 ob.

See: A. I. Andreev, ed. *Russkie otkrytiia v Tikhom okeane i v Severnoi Amerike v XVIII veke* (Moscow: 1948), 336–353.

75

NOVEMBER 18, 1794

A REPORT FROM GRIGORII I. SHELIKHOV TO IVAN A. PIL, GOVERNOR GENERAL OF IRKUTSK, CONCERNING THE ESTABLISHMENT OF SETTLEMENTS ON THE NORTHWEST COAST OF NORTH AMERICA

Last May I received Your Excellency's instructions pertaining to the settlements near Cape St. Elias on the coast of the American mainland and on the Kuril Islands. I have been given settlers to farm and to build ships [in these settlements]. To carry out these instructions I prepared a supplementary order for the merchant [Aleksandr A.] Baranov from Kargopol, who is presently my Company administrator. I sent this order to him aboard two ships which were also carrying the settlers and the religious entourage. I had built the ships for that very purpose. They set out from the Okhotsk harbor on August 13 and 14. I now submit my report for Your Excellency's gracious review, and humbly request that if there are any shortcomings in my instructions in regard to establishing a better settlement or in sound business economic arrangements, please do not hesitate to bring this to my attention, so that when the transport vessels set out for America next summer, I will be able to carry out Your Excellency's wishes.

In my instructions to Baranov please note that I only sent that group to America. I have nothing to report about the Kuril Islands because I have done nothing there for the following reasons.

1. It would have been difficult to put the Kuril detachment aboard these two ships because the first vessel, the *Tri Ierarkhi*, although the larger of the two and double-decked, already had 126 passengers including 9 ecclesiastics, 5 American natives, 45 persons of both sexes who were to become settlers, the navigator, an assistant, the Administrator Baranov, 2 company prikashchiks and 62 experienced veteran workers. Also aboard that vessel we loaded livestock, domestic fowl, seed grain, agricultural implements, provisions for passengers and for workers, and supplies for their maintenance in America, the belongings of all these people, company trade goods, supplies, materials and weapons. Thus in addition to the people and the equipment and 120 barrels of fresh water, the absolutely necessary cargo weighed some

13,000 puds. Both the interior and part of the center of the deck were filled to capacity.

The other vessel, the *Sv. Ekaterina*, carried 67 men including the navigator, two company prikashchiks, 5 American natives and 59 experienced veteran workers, and it too was loaded to capacity with its passengers, goods, company cargo and supplies that could not be accommodated aboard the first vessel.

2. If it had been absolutely necessary we could have sent on these vessels the group who were to go to the Kurils. I chose six settlers, both men and women, and 20 of the best promyshlenniks to protect them. I planned to land all of these on the first Kuril island so they could proceed from there to the eighteenth island in baidaras. However, it seemed unwise to send these people aboard these vessels because the first island, like many others in that archipelago, has a very dangerous coastline, and the straits between the islands have strong currents and seasonal fall storm winds, which would have made it impossible to land these people safely. Thus, the Kuril group would have had to proceed on to America without any benefit to the American destination.

Because of this, in order not to expose the ship to danger and so as not to have to leave the Kuril group for a long period of time in a place other than its destination, and, above all, in order to carry out the Imperial desires to have agriculture introduced on the Kurils, I decided to ask Colonel [von] Witten, the commanding officer of Okhotsk, that the entire group be carried on a government transport vessel which was about to leave for the harbor of Petropavlovsk. I would pay the Treasury for the transport of the personnel and their property, with the understanding that, since this vessel would be sailing near the first Kuril island, it would land them there. If this could not be done because of headwinds or some other unforeseen circumstances, then the people would be brought to the harbor of Petropavlovsk which is only 200 versts from the first Kuril island. The settlers and promyshlenniks could spend the winter there and the next spring set out in baidaras for the first Kuril island, then move from one island to the next until they reached their destination. But since the cargo vessel was ready to depart, the commanding officer could not carry out my request. Consequently, I have been forced to keep this Kuril-bound group in Okhotsk until next summer.

For this same purpose I make bold to request a helping hand from Your Excellency. Could you kindly instruct the commanding officer of Okhotsk, to assign to me early next spring one of the three small government transport vessels presently wintering in Okhotsk—the one called the *Aleksei Chelovek Bozhii*. I would have the Kuril-bound settlers and the 20 promyshlennik sentries put aboard and taken to the eighteenth Kuril island, along with company property, agricultural tools, seed grain, livestock and other necessary supplies, equipment and weapons. The vessel could return to Okhotsk that same summer and still serve as a transport, or winter over in Okhotsk, since there are enough transport vessels.

This depends on your decision, because government ships are kept in Okhotsk in order to transport only government cargo and personnel. It would be no greater distance for the vessel to sail to the eighteenth Kuril island than to sail to the harbor of Petropavlovsk on Kamchatka or to the town of Gizhiga. In fact, it would be closer than to go to Nizhnekamchatsk. I would pay here in Okhotsk to the Treasury the cost of transporting our cargo and passengers.

In addition to this I feel obliged to bring to Your Excellency's attention the fact that during my stay in Okhotsk this past summer I received a report from my company administrator Baranov, from Chugach Bay in America. His report came to me aboard the company vessel *Simeon*; he had sent the report in August of 1793, but the vessel wintered over on the island of Unalaska in the Aleutians. Baranov informed me that everything is going well in the region, thanks to God's blessings. He mentioned, by the way, that in June of 1792 when he was traveling along the coast of mainland America from Kenai Bay to Nootka, in Kanashak Bay he came on a two-masted English ship, the *Phoenix*, which has about a 75-foot keel. The skipper is an Irishman by the name of [Hugh] Moore. He had set out from the East Indies [actually Bengal], then had been in Manila and Canton, and reached America, having held a course near Nootka in order to sail along the coast to Chugach Bay and exchange goods with the American natives, because he had a substantial amount of bartered furs. From there he intended to return to Canton as soon as he had repaired his mast which had been broken by a savage storm.

Baranov spent five days aboard that vessel. Skipper Moore treated him in a friendly fashion, and as a sign of his friendship, gave Baranov a young [East] Indian. In conversation, Baranov gave Moore to understand that the American coast all the way to Ltyua Bay near Nootka belongs to Russia by virtue of first discovery in the year 1740. Although Moore countered this by claiming that England claimed first discovery of Kenai and Chugach Bays because of the efforts of the famous Captain [James] Cook, Baranov rejected this, claiming that previous Russian sea voyages have not yet been made public and that he had an order to report to his government any interference by foreign vessels in those waters.

From Moore Baranov learned that the famous English Archbishop [William] Coxe who had been in Kamchatka with Cook's vessel, had died in Canton. Thanks to him England now knows all the activities of our latest secret astronomical [Billings-Sarychev] expedition.

A second ship, also English, was three-masted. It was seen in July of that year in Chugach Bay by a group of my company promyshlenniks whom Baranov had sent to Yakutat Bay to determine the best method of hunting sea otters. The ship had come from Boston (but which Boston, the British port or the other one by the same name located in America under British jurisdiction, has not yet been made clear), but it had come to that bay from Macao to trade with the savages along the American coast and proceed all the way to Nootka. The skipper of this vessel was named James; he received these promyshlenniks with courtesy and kindness.

A third vessel came in 1793 to the islands of St. Paul and St. George, located north of the Aleutian Island chain toward the Arctic Ocean, where the crew of my ship, the *Ioann Predtecha*, had been working before the ship was wrecked in 1792. The leader of the crew of the *Predtecha*, Popov, did not mention the size of the vessel, its name or its skipper; however the skipper [of the *Predtecha*] heard rumors that it was a merchant vessel sent out from Isle de France, but whether the French administrative region or the island Isle de France off Africa and under French jurisdiction, is impossible to ascertain. The men aboard that vessel were dying of starvation and scurvy. There were only eleven men including the skipper and his son. All except the skipper and his son were ill with scurvy; when they reached these islands no one could raise the sails or do other necessary tasks. They were in dire need of provisions; the sailors had been issued only extremely small rations. They anchored there for a day or so and then put back out to sea. The skipper gave into the care of the peredovshchik Popov three of his desperately sick sailors, with the hope that he would send them back to him in due time, recovered. But this had not yet happened, judging by the news from Popov which he sent me this year. Two of the sick men are English; thanks to Popov's care they have recovered and are now under his supervision; the third was a Spaniard who died.

Over the course of the winter the two recovered Englishmen learned a little Russian and told Popov about their skipper's background. About seven years ago his master, a wealthy merchant had sent him from America in a large vessel to the island of Simpol (?) on a whaling expedition. But he betrayed his master's trust and took the vessel and the oil to India where he sold the cargo and bought two small vessels and set out for the island [Hawaii] where Cook had been killed. There misfortune overtook him. The island people killed the commanding officer of one of the vessels, his son, and all the sailors aboard the vessel, and then destroyed the vessel itself. Following this tragic event, another ill omen followed when he left that island. His own ship was wrecked at sea and sank with all hands except for the skipper, and a few of his men who were saved by being taken on board a third vessel captained by another of his sons. But they were unable to salvage anything from the wreck.

Aboard that last vessel he anchored at Isle de France, hired additional sailors for nine rubles per month, purchased various trinkets and set out from there for the coast of America where he traded on the islands off Nootka toward the Arctic Ocean. He traded beads, necklaces, knives, scissors, colorful textiles, kerchiefs and other cheap items for sea otter pelts and other furs. On this last voyage he had too little food and gave the sailors such inadequate rations that they became very ill. Enduring many hardships, he finally reached the islands of St. Paul and St. George by chance. Popov noticed that the skipper had a map of the Aleutian island of Unalaska and other islands under Russian jurisdiction, and that the map showed all the harbors and bays.

Considering the desperate state of health of the sailors, and the shortage of provisions, Popov felt the vessel was doomed.

I wrote to Popov instructing him to send the two sailors who had recovered from their illness to Okhotsk, and in the meantime to give them proper treatment but not to disclose to them the routes of my company or other matters.

Among the various dispatches from Baranov in America, there is one which states that when he was away along the coast of the mainland he attempted to befriend the native inhabitants. After he encountered the English vessels, on June 20, 1792 he was on the island of Nuchek or Tkhalkha where he spent two days with sixteen Russian men and several natives who live peacefully with us; he sent the rest of his crew to survey another island called Siukliu.

In the middle of the night of June 21 he was surrounded in his camp by a great number of armed savages who had come by water from the distant places on the American mainland where they live. They attacked from every side and killed American natives who were living peacefully with us. Although Baranov had five sentries in his camp, nevertheless under the cover of darkness the attackers were able to advance close before they were spotted at a distance of ten paces. In the first attack, when all the men except the sentries were sleeping soundly, the attackers killed two Russians and nine of the peaceful American natives. They wounded fifteen others. The Russian crew repulsed the attack courageously with their guns, and the American natives used bows and arrows and handknives. But this was unsuccessful because the attackers were dressed in three or four layers of shields made of woven slats of wood, or as we might say, interlaced slats, which were covered with heavy elkhide. On their heads they wore heavy wood helmets which were decorated with various frightening faces. The result was that neither bullets nor buckshot nor arrows nor blades could penetrate. If it had not been for the fact that our crew had with them a one-pound cannon, they would all have become victims, because the attackers fought with great ferocity until dawn. They were commanded by the voice of one person whom no one had noticed before among the savages. Any who were killed were replaced by new braves.

Finally, thanks to the use of the cannon and the dispatch aboard a baidara of new men from my ship, the *Simeon*, which was nearby, the attackers were driven back to their baidaras, of which there were six, filled to capacity with warriors. On the site of the encounter, twelve attackers were found dead, and one wounded. It is possible that attackers took their dead and wounded with them, carrying them during the attack to their baidaras, a distance of at least two versts. As noted above, we suffered two Russian promyshlenniks killed and nine peaceful natives who had been in the Baranov party. Fifteen were wounded. Baranov writes that he himself was almost killed. During the initial attack he rushed out from his quarters to direct the defense. He was wearing only a shirt, which was pierced by a spear. A multitude of arrows fell about him, but thanks to the fearlessness of his men he was victorious.

Baranov took a wounded attacker prisoner and from him learned that the attackers were American natives from the interior of the country, from Yakutat Bay, and Ugalegmuts from Cape St. Elias who belonged to the Kolosh [Tlingit] tribe. They had come to avenge an affront by the Chugach which had occurred in 1791. As they were looking for the Chugach, they saw Baranov and his party from a high mountain. They resolved to destroy the Russians who prided themselves on being invincible, or to die there in the attempt, all of them. They had expected to be reinforced by ten baidaras with men from the Copper River; together they had intended to wipe out the Chugach people and move on to the Kenai region.

With his report Baranov also sent me an example of warrior's regalia. He sent another example with his report to the Okhotsk adminstration, and I hope they will send it on to Your Excellency for your inspection. All of this compelled Baranov to return across Kenai Bay where a company promyshlennik artel is located, before he proceeded home. He stopped on the island of Kodiak to issue the rules necessary to prevent barbarism on the part of the savages.

Baranov also informed me that in accordance with my instructions he had laid the keel for a 66-foot vessel which he is building in Chugach Bay, from where he sent word to me. For quite some time I have waited for the chance to start this kind of construction there, in order to cut the expenses associated with the Okhotsk facilities, and to have the advantage of having a number of ships there to carry on future explorations. My work will be greatly assisted by the new settlement there and by the various craftsmen who have been assigned to me. I will report my progress to Your Excellency in due time.

Baranov has not claimed any new lands in those waters during the past two years, although he sent out two ships to explore in 1792 and 1793. At the present time he has sent one ship to Okhotsk with his reports and has kept the other in company service. As noted above, he is building a new vessel.

The foreign vessel which I mentioned having stopped at St. George Island appears to have been more likely French than English. I believe that on the basis of my own knowledge of current affairs in Europe some means should be found to protect Russian hunting interests in the northern islands; however, my stay in Okhotsk was too brief for me to do this.

For some time I have intended to establish my hunting interests firmly in the north, from the Aleutian island of Unalaska all the way to the Arctic Ocean. I foresaw that creating another larger permanent company in this huge region, such as my North Eastern Company, would help in establishing trade with the natives living along the coast of the American mainland opposite the Chukotsk territory, which, at one point, is no more than 80 versts distant, as well as in Chukotsk itself. At the present time the Chukchi do not have the walrus tusks, whale whiskers and other fur trade goods which they once traded with the Russians. Now they obtain these items from neighboring American natives across this strait.

I have also thought that by establishing such a company it would be possible to make certain discoveries along the American cape directly opposite the Chukchi, proceeding along the coast to the north and northeast. One would search especially for a passage to Baffin Bay, even if one had to cross some small part of the mainland. One might also explore along the northern coast of the Alaskan peninsula (previously called the Alaskan Cape by the Americans), as a result of the 1791 discovery of a very short route from the southern coast of that peninsula. I was pleased to present a plan about that to Your Excellency in 1793, to build a structure there so that in case hostile Europeans should come to Kodiak Island it would be possible to provide safety for company property and personnel.

A good opportunity has now presented itself and I felt it necessary to act; some time ago I organized this kind of company on the very same lines as the North Eastern Company. I have decided to call it the new North American Company.

As soon as I could, on August 2 I sent a vessel to St. Paul and St. George islands, with 70 promyshlenniks and a company administrator. I gave them various trade goods as well as provisions for the workers, equipment and other necessary items. These people will be joined by several volunteer promyshlenniks and other men who are returning to Okhotsk from other companies. In addition to this, God willing, next summer I will send several promyshlenniks and another vessel, so that for the first time in the vast northern waters and lands this company can carry on its activities free of fear.

Now that I have completed this report about the American situation, I will take this opportunity to submit my thoughts concerning the methods that I feel may benefit Russian commerce. I hope that Your Excellency will participate in my oceanic ventures as you have in the past, by assisting me with your official patronage, and by giving this your attention and approval.

Your Excellency knows how much effort I have devoted to strengthening Russian interests in the north and northeastern parts of America, in increasing benefits to the local natives, and in increasing hunting and other activities that may benefit trade. But even if all of this should result only in delivering furs to Russia and bringing needed items here from Russia, especially until good agriculture and livestock production are established here, and if no metals or other products are developed which will be beneficial to the public, then all of this will not amount to much without contacts with other natives living on the shores of the Pacific Ocean; it cannot be viewed as a triumph of our trade in that part of the world; in fact, nothing will result except that Russia will command glory by virtue of controlling the many islands there and part of the American mainland.

Therefore, in order to increase the glory of the Empire in that part of the world, and to increase the benefits that should accrue, as well as to increase Russian trade opportunities to the greatest possible extent, I believe that we must extend our voyages in the Pacific Ocean beyond the present confines. With the acquisition of the Kuril and Aleutian islands, and of resources on the American mainland, and with the development of products of Russian manufacture, we should be able to travel to Canton, Macao, Batavia, the Philippine and Mariana Islands and from there, to bring to America and the Aleutian Islands necessary items of apparel, textiles, food such as millet and other necessities. We should also import canvas and rope for use in outfitting ships there and in Russia as well. It will be necessary to increase the amount of goods we import from China and other places.

This important topic is becoming most urgent. If everything that is needed on our [Pacific] islands and in America is delivered [from Siberia] every year, not only must we deal with the high cost of goods being supplied at present, but the transport to the Sea of Okhotsk is enormously difficult. As Your Excellency knows, the Iakuts carry goods from Iakutsk to Okhotsk by horse, a distance of 1,013 versts, at a cost of at least six rubles per pud. Sometimes one would not object to paying even more, if one could be assured that the goods would actually be delivered. But it frequently happens that heavy downpours cause the Iakuts to abandon freight en route, which spoils or is completely lost. Desert areas, mountains, swamps, impassable stretches and rivers mean that it takes the most tremendous efforts to reach Okhotsk, and very often in these problem areas the Iakuts lose many horses. Consequently, the delivery of goods from Russia to America is both expensive and difficult, and, moreover, not everything that is needed can be delivered all the time, especially heavy goods. Thus freight that could be delivered by sea [from sources other than Russia] would be less expensive in America and could be sold on the islands as well; and further, such goods could be supplied in sufficient quantity to satisfy all needs there. Any surplus not needed in America or on the islands could be transported to Kamchatka and to Okhotsk as well as to other places that are in great need of them.

This enterprise could be realized only if, with God's help, shipbuilding is undertaken in America. As the above report indicates, Your Excellency knows that the foundation for this enterprise has already been established. I will devote all of my energies and resources to bring it to fruition. But I cannot undertake this without the approval of the authorities, especially if my ships are to sail to Canton and Macao and other places which are under the jurisdiction of the Chinese Empire. We must not create any concern on the part of our neighbors by the sudden appearance of a new merchant ship; this matter has thus far not been dealt with in any treaty between ourselves and the Chinese.

For this reason we must not only obtain a permit from the government, but we must also inform the Chinese court beforehand so they will not suspect Russian vessels of anything. I sincerely hope that Your Excellency, having graciously received this important thought and my humble explanation, will use your official position to forward it to the attention of the throne for approval, and request permission for Russian maritime companies on the Pacific Ocean to sail to the above mentioned Chinese ports and other places to search for things that might benefit out commerce.

Now that I have explained my intentions, I should also like to consider another important possibility that could fulfill a need of domestic Russian trade.

As Your Excellency knows, the port of Okhotsk, where government transport ships are presently being constructed as well as privately owned ships, is very inconvenient. The port has not been put into condition really to be designated a port. In the first place, with the exception of lumber, almost all the materials and supplies needed for ship construction, such as iron, hemp, cable, sails and other necessities, especially provisions, are delivered to Okhotsk along the route with all the difficulties that have been explained above, and consequently these items are extremely expensive. Secondly, Okhotsk has neither harbor nor roadstead for ships. The mouth of the Okhota River is particularly dangerous because there is a narrow passage that separates the rocky and sandy banks for several versts; this has given rise to the saying that anyone who manages to sail through this has already completed half of his voyage. The many shipwrecks in and before the mouth of the river are sufficient testimony of this.

In the third place, Okhotsk has been built in an extremely dangerous location. The sandbar which has been built up by the waves coming in from the sea is about eight versts long and only a quarter of a verst at the widest part. The height is perhaps two sazhens. The end of the sandbar is at the Okhota River and this is where the town stands. It is neither attractive nor safe. For the past three years the riverside bank of this sandbar has been eroded and three streets have become very dangerous and the people there are imperiled during heavy storms at sea when the waves break over the sandbar into the Okhota River, right across the entire width of the bar where the town stands. The very poorly built structures in Okhotsk are flooded, and on these occasions the people's lives are threatened. There is no way of saving them during a sudden sea storm, for there are no small vessels available to rescue them except for the dangerous and useless *batas* [Tlingit boat] which are made of a single log and are used for fishing. There are no large vessels, and even if there were, they could not be used because there is no place to go for safety aboard them. Furthermore, the vessels that are anchored there are generally used to protect government interests. They are either pulled up on shore on their beams, or they have not yet been rigged and launched into the water, or they are in the process of being rigged but have not yet been needed for transport.

The poor and disadvantageous condition of the port of Okhotsk is even worse because there is no other satisfactory place suitable for harbor facilities in the vicinity. For the more than twenty years that I have been dealing with the affairs of Okhotsk, Kamchatka and other isolated places, I have not personally encountered nor have I heard of anyone else finding a site on the coast of that sea where a more convenient port could be built. Some persons feel that the area around Udsk ostrog is the only place where one could find or build a harbor for Russian ships which sail in the Pacific Ocean. However I have never been in that area myself and therefore I cannot express a personal view, except to say that because of the inconvenience and difficulty of the Okhotsk route and the disadvantages associated with developing shipyards and trade facilities in Okhotsk, an effort should be made to find a good location on the coast of the Sea of Okhotsk and also an overland route to that place which would be better and more convenient.

For a long time I have had to send a number of my ships into the Pacific Ocean on company business and have always suffered the hardships I have just described on the Okhotsk route, and the disadvantages of Okhotsk itself. Thus on many occasions I have tried at my own expense, to find some place other than Okhotsk which is suitable for anchorage and for constructing a wharf where I could have my company ships built. But, when I tried to solve that problem, I encountered obstacles from the very persons who could have assisted me, even though I was willing to spare no

461

expense. Therefore, I put aside this very important matter for future consideration.

At the present time, however, in accordance with Her Imperial Majesty's approval and permission, Russian possessions are being established in the Pacific Ocean and in America, and close ties with Russia are being created, as evidenced by the founding in America of a permanent settlement and farming; in time this will also be true in the Kuril Islands. For that reason I consider it necessary to realize my long sought ambitions which I have described above, so as to be able, by building ships, to establish a link with all the Russian possessions in the Pacific.

I have also most humbly asked that I receive permission to sail to Canton, Macao, Batavia and the Philippine and Mariana islands. However the problem is that I have no experienced people whom I could organize and send along the summit of the mountain range which extends from Lake Baikal east to the coast of the Sea of Okhotsk, with the Amur River on the right and the Ud on the left. Tungus natives assure me that one can proceed along the summit of that range and that on the upper slopes there are many fine dry places suitable for travel routes. The route along the summit to the sea is shorter than the present Okhotsk route. If this route should be opened, then one could probably anticipate that a suitable ship anchorage on the coast could be found, perhaps even quite close to the mouth of the Amur River. Even if no suitable anchorage were discovered, at least such an expedition would bring one benefit, namely, that we would come to know the territory between the Amur and the upper reaches of the Vitim, Olekma, Aldan and Maia rivers, since these places are still quite unexplored and undescribed to the very present day.

For these reasons I make bold to inquire of Your Excellency whether it would not be useful to organize an expedition consisting of experienced land surveyors to search for suitable sites along the summit of the mountain range, and once they reach the sea, to proceed along the coast to look for a place suitable for building ship construction facilities. Since such an expedition would need financial backing for all its necessary expenses, I will assume that responsibility, and voluntarily will offer the necessary sum for the good of the fatherland. I will not ask anything from the Treasury for this expedition. I hope for a favorable response from Your Excellency in this regard.

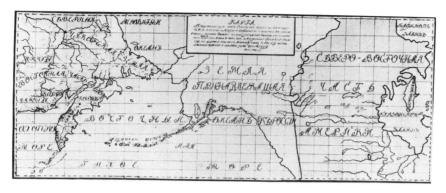

A 1796 map drawn by Shelikhov's company reveals large scale thinking. Written in the large center section, "Land Belonging to Russia," and to the right, "the Northeastern Part of America." Eastern Siberia and Kamchatka are to the left. Yefimov, *Atlas of Geographical Discoveries*. . . . (OHS neg. 80257)

Meanwhile, until an appropriate shipbuilding site is found, out of absolute necessity I will undertake to build a small wharf in addition to the present Okhotsk port for the following reasons. First, as I have reported, Okhotsk does not have either a good or a safe anchorage. Second, although this problem could be delayed for a while, the sale of spirits in Okhotsk, the major town of this oblast, is causing great delays and unsatisfactory performance of company work because company laborers and supervisors spend all the money they earn on drink. They become involved in so many dissolute activities during working hours that there is no way to deter them. The work on ships is left to be done in the brief summertime. In some years there are very few dry clear days, without the usual and almost incessant rain or storms at sea. To build this small wharf, where a new ship could be built or an old one repaired, I have selected a place at the mouth of the Ul River, about 100 versts from Okhotsk, a river that empties into the sea. The place is not much better than the mouth of the Okhota River because it also has many sandbars, but at least it is far from the sale of spirits and there is no settlement there.

Because of this I most humbly request Your Excellency to instruct the commandant of Okhotsk to allow me to undertake to build a wharf at the mouth of the Ul River, and not to prevent me from maintaining company servitors there and all the master artisans who are necessary for my maritime enterprises. I will keep all of these persons at my own expense. I will prohibit the sale of spirits at that wharf in order to keep the laborers in good condition. And so that the government will not be deprived of its due revenues, in return for the prohibition of the sale of liquor there, if you will kindly issue an order that I pay an equitable sum of money to the government, I will willingly pay this every year. I also humbly ask Your Excellency's favorable consideration of this matter.

Distinguished citizen of Rylsk,
Grigorii Shelikhov

Reference: LOTsIA, f. 1147, op. 1, d. No. 140, 11. 36–45.
See: A. I. Andreev, ed. *Russkie otkrytiia v Tikhom okeane i v Severnoi Amerike v XVIII veke* (Moscow: 1948), 353–368.

76

MAY 18, 1795

A REPORT FROM ARKHIMANDRIT IOASAF TO GRIGORII I. SHELIKHOV
REGARDING ACTIVITIES OF THE RUSSIAN ORTHODOX CLERGY IN
ALASKA, AND PROBLEMS WITH ALEKSANDR A. BARANOV

My dear Sir, gracious friend and generous benefactor, Grigorii Ivanovich [Shelikhov]:

I cannot adequately express in writing the respect and devotion I feel for you. I will not try to express this for it needs no proof of sincerity. Therefore, dispensing with empty compliments, I will tell you the following. We left Okhotsk on August 13 and reached Kodiak safely on September 24. Throughout the winter we have baptized all the Kodiak, Alaska, Kenai and Chugach natives who came here voluntarily, of whom there were a large number. We have no church building here as yet. I have asked the administrator Aleksandr Andreevich [Baranov] about this but have not received any response. He offered to build a small church here soon, which would be four sazhens by one and one-half sazhens and would have an altar. But although the foundation was laid on November 21, not even the walls are finished yet. I have put off reporting about this to the Most Reverend Metropolitan [of St. Petersburg].

Since I arrived at this harbor I have not seen anything done to carry out your noble intentions. The only satisfaction I have is the fact that the American natives come in droves from everywhere to be baptized, but not only do the Russians make no effort to encourage them in this, indeed they do everything possible to discourage them; the reason is that the good behavior of the American natives shows up the corrupt ways of [the Russians]. I have barely succeeded in urging some of the promyshlenniks to be [legally] married, but others will not consider such an idea. Everyone openly keeps one or more mistresses, which is very offensive to the American natives. As you know, they are jealous of their women and can wreak havoc out of vengeance.

I cannot ascertain whether my arrival here or your sharp reprimand to Baranov angered him. It appears to us all that he agitates the promyshlenniks. He is unfavorably disposed toward you, makes written complaints against you and persuades others to sign them. He opposes you constantly. He announces that everything belongs to the company and not to the shareholders. He views ships and other company property as detrimental to the interests of the settlers and the Empire. He misinterprets all Imperial policies so they will be deleterious to our company. [He says] the 30 men who have been assigned here should be reassigned to the settlements, that hunting will suffer because 500 versts of land along the coast are being set aside for the settlers; that the newly arrived promyshlenniks are inexperienced; that the shareholders alone will get rich but not the company; that the greatest number of shares belong to persons who have died and that by right the total assets of the company do not belong to the present shareholders; and similar statements. You can verify all of this through persons who have left for Okhotsk, a number of whom left here unwillingly, and some of it you will learn from this report.

In regard to our own situation, there is little to be said. Ever since we arrived there has been a shortage of food throughout the entire winter. People avidly consumed three-year-old rotted iukola, which we cleaned. There were still fish to be had when we arrived, but no one would catch them. There was also a run of herring in the fall, but people only fished for them two or three times. Baranov would not order the Aleuts to fish for halibut, saying that it was not his job to feed settlers who did not work. Nets lay on the ground by the shore all winter long. The hides which had been brought in by ship were ruined. Two of the calves we had brought were eaten by dogs. Nearly all the goats are dead, and one of the last two sheep was also eaten by the dogs. A great deal has been lost. Filip will elaborate on this for you; it is obvious that the livestock are not doing well.

The cooks are barefoot, half-naked and dirty. They work all day long to feed people, and at night they go out to gather firewood. We carry our own wood on our backs from the forest. Even more ludicrous, not even [Baranov] has been provided with a single bit of firewood all year long. When he orders tea, his servants rush about to break some wood off the corner of some structure or other in the settlement, or they will rip a log out of a lean-to, or even take coal from the blacksmith to use to prepare the tea. I have never seen him go out from his quarters on inspection. He sits day and night and formulates his complaints.

He has not conducted any experiments in growing grain or produce. Filip has planted turnips and potatoes with good success. Sapozhnikov reports that he has tried to grow barley at his home near the bay. He planted a pound of seed and harvested one and one-half puds. I have advised that various seeds be planted next spring even if only as an experiment, but whether the people will do this, I do not know. I would like to raise potatoes and cabbage and other garden vegetables here, but what a problem! No one knows anything about how to do this. I have asked for shovels and hoes, but I do not have much hope of getting them. At present we are using sticks to dig with.

There are only five children in the school, and former students are almost completely unsupervised. They are going back to their savage customs and now there is little difference between them and other Aleuts. One of them was punished for taking up with Baranov's woman. His head and eyebrows were shaved, and the front of his parka was torn. He was exiled to Iadryshnikov's settlement where he works and is rewarded by being whipped.

I do not know where to teach my five students. Our quarters are always swarming with people. Aleuts come to be baptized or married. Some people come just to talk. Further, because there is no church building, we hold services in our quarters. I have received only a few church books from the company, and ten of these are so decomposed that we cannot use them. We have not seen the rest.

Baptism of the American natives should pose no problems for the company: *kaiurs* [native workers] remain kaiurs, hostages remain hostages, and each promyshlennik continues to perform his assignment. It should not matter to anyone that these people are baptized, but there are always complaints. In some settlements if I baptize an Aleut, I have to marry him to his woman. But sometimes the Russians take some of these married women as sexual partners or kaiurs or hostages, just to provoke me. However I endure, waiting for your orders.

In one village I performed a marriage between an Aleut and his woman. She then came to me with an interpreter and told me that previously, during a war between their settlements, she had been taken prisoner by a toion, but was subsequently captured by another toion. She had been taken from the latter by a Russian. When the Russian abandoned her, she had taken up with the Aleut to whom I had married her. I was asked why I had performed the ceremonies of baptism and marriage for a toion's prisoner. I explained that I had not known the circumstances. But they criticized me. They said the toion, who had taken her prisoner, owed the company a feather parka and a skin of blubber. Since she was a prisoner of war, either she or the Aleut whom she had married must pay the debt, or else she would have to be returned to the toion. I said I would pay the debt to the company, even though I did not have to. But then Aleksandr Andreevich said, "If you do this, we will be through." That is how he manipulates things. This is not sound reasoning, and this is just one example which I am citing. There are a hundred more as bad or worse. If I were by myself I would ignore it; but this is humiliating in front of my own retinue and others who see this peculiar situation. I should be criticizing their sinful behavior, but they are the ones who are tormenting me and deliberately trying to provoke me so I will criticize their barbaric treatment of the American natives.

Now I will not perform a marriage ceremony for a single Aleut without reporting it to [Baranov], but even this does not satisfy him. He constantly tries to rouse the promyshlenniks against me. He tells them they should not be ashamed of what they do. He says that Shelikhov has ordered me to be strict with the clergy, to get them used to the local food and have them work in various jobs. This we would do in any case, even if you did not order it, for there is not any too much food. If we did not provide ourselves with food from the shore by collecting shellfish, we would have had only bread to eat, and that would long since have been gone.

Baranov and his favorites have no problem: people shoot birds, sea lions and seals for him. They bring him reindeer meat from Alaska, and he always has milk. It is true that Filip provided us with milk all winter, although we only had two cows. We always had milk for our tea. But now the cows have calved and there is only one cup of milk a day for all ten of us, and none on fast days.

It is very difficult to get whale blubber to burn for light. We do not have the time or the materials to engage in handicrafts, and we cannot send you anything to sell. All day long we have to be busy searching for food. We have to walk some five versts to find clams and mussels. There are no clams in the harbor. There are a few mussels, but not enough even for the kaiurs. And we also have to carry wood in, make our own shirts and breeches and do our own laundry. There are about 100 girls and kaiurs in the harbor, but they do not work for us. We were miserable all winter with the very cold weather, the leaking roofs and the drafty windows.

It is true that when I came here [Baranov] gave me a house for myself which was well built; but he sent the brothers off to the barracks where the laborers live with their women. I felt it best not to leave the brothers alone, so I moved to the other building with them. Not only are the barracks filled with loose women, but there are very often gatherings and games there, and they will dance all night long. This goes on every Sunday and holiday, and sometimes even on working days. [Baranov] tells me this is to bring good weather, and that we had the games yesterday to bring an end to the rain. Women and dancing amuse him, and he claims to be a Christian!

His men are not ashamed to follow this minister. They publicly ridicule the rules of the church, and curse and argue with me. They say they think rules are made for fools. In addition to being immoral, [Baranov] and Iakov Egorovich [James George Shields] favor free French thinking. [Baranov] has told the baidarshchiks that not only the veteran promyshlenniks, but also those who have just recently come, should openly keep women without fear. At the present time anyone who does not have a woman is made the butt of jokes. It happened that right after we had baptized a native woman, the promyshlenniks came and dragged young girls from their homes off to the barracks. They often trade girls, even though some of the girls are scarcely ten years old. Some of these men could be encouraged to marry, but Baranov says, "A married man makes a poor promyshlennik." Some have married, and lost their credit and had to leave to go back to Russia.

I observe that the promyshlenniks always take their women with them when they go out. If they married they would be more useful for the company. Married men buy more things, and other men follow their example and buy things for their women. Before we arrived the girls wore only feather parkas, but now each one has a skirt and a blouse. Eventually when the promyshelnniks have children they will perhaps have no wish to return to Russia.

If I were to write a detailed account of everything [Baranov] does, it would make a whole book, not just a letter. According to my instructions I should have reported his conduct to His Eminence the Metropolitan or to the Holy Synod, but my devotion and regard for you have restrained me. I hope that you will use your good judgment to try to remedy the problem. However, bearing in mind that wisdom cannot exist in an evil soul, I feel that no good will come from your instructions to Baranov if he learns that I wrote about him to you and that he still retained his position. I repeat the maxim that evil does not remedy evil.

Although he has pledged 1,500 rubles for the church and the clergy, I would rather have had him manage his own affairs here better. I mention this to you not because I am afraid of him if he learns that I have written to you, but because I know that when he does find out, he will persecute me more than ever and I may lose my patience and quarrel with him. So far, for my part I have not revealed to anyone my feelings about Baranov, although I have told my friends of his hostility toward me. I would like to suggest that you send Ivan Osipivich here, or someone else who has his managerial skills. I could consult privately with a man like that and put things in order as much as possible. I do not ask for a complete change, but at least the beginning of some kind of order is necessary. Afterward, with God's help, the rest may also be put into order.

It is not possible to consult with Baranov. He goes his own way. I do not presume to give him open suggestions, but hold my patience and suffer in silence. There is no point in asking him for a meeting because I realize that he wants just such an occasion to wear out my patience and show me to the shareholders to be as ungrateful as he is. Even if you had to pay someone else 4,000 rubles a year to become Chief Administrator, it would be less expensive. Such a man would have no shares in the company and he would not be trading with the promyshlenniks and putting them into debt by selling them his own goods. He sold his own tobacco for more than 400 rubles per pud even though more than 20 puds of the company's tobacco were available here. And still the people blame you for the high price. You of course are better able than I to handle this, so I will continue my report.

The Chief Administrator gives his permission for the pro- myshlenniks to take the children whom Russians have fathered from their [native] mothers, although they may be only a year or two old. They [promyshlenniks] plan to send the children to Rus- sia. I do not approve of this. If the children are sent to Russia this will indicate the sinful conduct of our promyshlenniks and the blame will fall on you. Furthermore this would be disastrous for such young children. If they were raised here as Russians and educated to the best of their abilities in various skills, they would become good promyshlenniks, better than those who come from Russia. This would also be beneficial to Imperial interest. I would like to know your views on this matter. I visualize that it could be possible to bring up these children properly if we have a good Chief Administrator. In the meantime they should be cared for by the Russians while they are here, not sent off to Russia. I would like to ask His Eminence the Metropolitan for his instruc- tions in this matter, but first I need to know whether you agree with me.

I am concerned about the French spirit of freedom that agi- tates here. Even here at the harbor, where the people are less frenzied, and where many good people live, it is impossible to pass a group of roguish young fellows without being castigated as a collaborator of the company. They curse the company share- holders and their wives in the bazaar right in front of the shop- keepers and other people, for they hope that Baranov will protect them because of his relationship to Shelikov. What will it be like at Yakutat? Baranov is forever making trouble for me and Ivan Grigorivich [Polomoshnyi, manager at Yakutat]. He says he is not interested in Ivan Grigorivich's work, but that he wants to let him and the arkhimandrit establish the settlement.

Last fall Baranov promised to send boards to the settlement but now he refuses because he says he needs the boards himself. He says he will send Shields to Ltuya Bay with the Company's supplies and then he and his men will go there along the coast. He will leave us at Yakutat and take the settlers to various places. Some will go to Kenai, some to Chugach and some to Yakutat.

This sounds all right, but I worry that he may treat us as he did the Lebedev party. Zaikov told me that the Chugach killed his artel and that Baranov had incited them to this murder. The killers were apprehended and said Baranov had instructed them. They gave him everything they had taken, the sea otter pelts, the gunpowder and the rest. Lebedev's men then wrote Baranov and Iakov Egorovich about this and asked them to make a report to the Government, but this was not done. Furthermore they did not even report it to you. If you have heard about this, it is not because they reported it. Lebedev's men have imprisoned the Chugach who testified against Baranov. I do not know whether Baranov actually ordered them to kill, but I do know that he took the furs from them.

Although he will not give orders that we be killed, he might leave us without any help, and in that case they might kill us of their own volition. I do not know what Baranov plans to do, but he is very much set against you. He criticizes you for selling shares, saying this was dishonest. Iakov Egorovich and Baranov used to quarrel and fight but now they are friends. This sudden accord is strange. I have heard from some people that Baranov frequently says to his freebooters, "If only we could send the arkhimandrit and Juvenal to the next world we could swat the others like flies." I do not believe all of this, but I do not trust him. Such a cruel man can do anything. He has already sent many people into the next world, and he would not hesitate to dispatch me. This Easter he made one of the kaiurs run the gauntlet until he was beaten to death with whalebones. If authorities hear of this, I will have a hard time explaining it, even though I could do nothing to prevent it. He is very cruel to all the Aleuts here, especially the ones who attempt to intervene in his treatment of the young women.

Do not neglect to find some reason to reprimand [Egor] Purtov, one of the rebels. He makes trouble on Baranov's orders among both the promyshlenniks and the settlers. He tells them all manner of lies and he curses you everywhere, saying that you deceived the Empress. He also spreads other lies. Last year when the English expedition was here he gave them complete information about the Russian settlements and he even gave them a list of the names of the promyshlenniks. They gave him presents and showed him much kindness, but he was such a dolt that when he went visiting them at their frigate he would shout, "Quick! Tell the captain I want to drink coffee!" Of course they gave him all the coffee he wanted.

There are rumors here that Iakov Egorovich's people sighted new islands between Chugach and Kodiak. When Baranov returned he also said that on a clear day he had sighted a volcano and an island opposite Ukamok to the south. The Aleuts also told me that they had sighted it. Last winter they saw sea otter near there. One toion told me that he would volunteer to go aboard a vessel searching for the islands, if they would take him. I do not know whether or not an expedition will go out this summer. I am sorry that we have no experienced navigators. [Gerasim A.] Izmailov is in Okhotsk, Shields is far away in the land of the Kolosh, and Gavriil Loginovich [Pribylov] is at Yakutat.

I am suspicious of their plan to gather information about these new islands and to keep the discovery secret. Sometimes I overhear them talking about new partners. At first we thought that Shields planned to set up a new company because he organized an artel and recruited promyshlenniks. Then Aleksandr Andreevich [Baranov] heard of this and looked into it. Nothing was said, but they still talk about new partners and try to keep it secret from me. You can get better information from the people who have left here to go to Okhotsk, because people here are afraid to say anything.

I believe you need someone here who can manage your affairs efficiently and who will be loyal to you. I understand that Lebedev's men found out about the islands from our promyshlenniks and plan to search for them. [Potap Kuzmich] Zaikov was here; he bribed the navigators with gifts to give him the needed information and maps. Kiselev's men will also have access to this information and the maps. I feel that Izmailov may be planning to transfer to Kiselev's group.

When Pribylov was in difficulty at sea between Kodiak and the Chugach his men sighted something, and Maksim and Avaev, a clerk and an intelligent person, insisted it was an island. Pribylov denies it because he is embarrassed to expose his lack of knowledge of navigational routes around Kodiak.

On April 30 [Petr] Kolomin, an interpreter for Lebedev, came here. I have heard that he is being sent to Okhotsk. On May 5 Balushin arrived, and he is also being sent to Okhotsk by order of the commandant. In investigating the affair of Konovalov, I had misgivings about sending him as an interpreter on the ship *Georgii*, because I knew the stormy tempers of the promyshlenniks, but circumstances forced me to do it. Without him there would have been no one to take charge of the ship. Perhaps the promyshlenniks will change their minds and realize their mistake and treat him in a friendly way. I hope, too, that Konovalov will behave better and will try to bring about peace and friendship through his good treatment of them.

I am enclosing Balushin's letters to me for your information. They are the same as those which Baranov sent you via Konovalov. If Konovalov's action was not well-taken, it was harmful to Kolomin but not to the promyshlenniks. Kolomin deserves such treatment or even worse. You will have further information about their activity from Aleksandr Andreevich's report.

You have informed me that you plan to assign a white [parish] clergyman to help us, and that His Eminence the Metropolitan has approved this. I suggest Osip Prianishnikov, a man who knows the local language and wishes to become a member of the clergy. Attempt to determine his reaction before making the appointment. He wanted to remain with me to serve as an interpreter but I did not dare to keep him because Baranov could not tolerate him once he was married.

I would not advise you to export bricks from here. It would not be very profitable, and here not only the Aleuts would complain, but so would the Russians, even more. Persons ill-disposed toward you try to suggest brutal consequences to the kaiurs here. It is quite true that it is unavoidably difficult to make bricks for use here. Clay is brought from a small island, dried, crushed and sifted and then made into bricks. Both the Russians and the kaiurs are busy with this work.

Do not be angry that I am writing so openly. I am really trying to protect your honor. Because of the present slander which Lebedev is spreading, it is necessary to be extremely cautious. In trying to justify their depraved actions against the Kenaits and the Chugach, they may slander you to the government over some trifle.

Please do not be annoyed that I am writing so much. I hope that you do not doubt that I wish you well. If I did not I would have tried to be more flattering and not write about everything. Besides, I must write to you what I think, and you are free to read what pleases you and tear up the rest and ignore it. I will not take offense, for this is what I am thinking. For the rest, I shall always wish you well, and I always pray to God for your good health.

[signed] Arkhimandrit Ioasaf and brothers.

Please give my best wishes to Natalia Alekseevna [Shelikhov's wife], and to all your family I send my respectful greetings. Please kiss Vasilii Grigorevich for me. My most humble regards to Ivan Petrovich.

Please give Ieromonk Ieronim the letter I wrote to him in Rostov. Please open it in his presence and write down for him the address to which he should send his letter to be sent on to me.

If Kulikalov takes his child to Okhotsk, please try to have the child sent back here. He has legitimate children in Irkutsk. The presence of this illegitimate child will bear witness to the sinful life of the promyshlenniks here, and this will dishonor you. I would have to report all cases of corruption here to the authorities. But if the children remain here, then I can keep silent about it and meanwhile God may correct matters. Many have already redeemed their sins by marrying the women by whom they have had children.

May 18, 1795

On Kodiak Island

Reference: Library of Congress, Manuscript Division. Yudin Collection, Box 1. Alaska History Documents, v. III: Archive of the Holy Synod, 1795–1804.

77

MAY 19, 1795

A REPORT FROM ARKHIMANDRIT IOASAF TO HIS ARCHBISHOP CON-
CERNING CONDITIONS IN THE RUSSIAN SETTLEMENT ON KODIAK
ISLAND

Your Eminence, my lord, Most Gracious Archbishop and
Father.

We put out to sea from Okhotsk on August 13, 1794. Although we suffered several storms, nonetheless with the aid of
your blessed prayers we all arrived safely in northeastern [i.e.,
northeast of Russia] America on Kodiak Island on September 24.
In accordance with Your Eminence's directives to us, we have
tried to give the American natives some elementary understanding of God and His holy law, through interpreters. There are,
however, many problems that hinder them from accepting Holy
Baptism. In insisting that they leave a number of their wives, they
are deprived of many advantages. However, in acknowledging the
sanctity of Christian law, they have agreed to distribute the extra
wives among other men, legally.

I had intended not to baptize them until they had learned and
understood the true evangelical precepts. However, because of
their persistent pleas, I did not wait until a proper time to baptize
them. I also observed that those scheduled to be baptized had not
abandoned their former practices, but continued to worship their
shamans and play their usual heathen games. They justify their
behavior by saying that they have not yet been baptized. They
also cite the unusual behavior of the newly baptized.

The baptized ones, although they habitually subscribe to all
of these [heathen practices], are fearful of the Russian promyshlenniks who live in almost every [native] settlement to hunt.
The natives do not wish to antagonize the promyshlenniks and
consequently they voluntarily abandon all their shamanistic beliefs without any pressure. Thus, I have baptized everyone who
came to the harbor and asked to be baptized. I only tried to ascertain how much they understood. I explained the rules of Christian life to them. Because of the distance from the harbor of 300
versts or more, the rest of the natives, both young and old, were

baptized by the two ieromonks, Makarii and Iuvenalii, who were sent around the island for that purpose. They prepared a special report which has been sent to His Eminence, Veniamin, Bishop of Irkutsk and Nerchinsk.

If we could understand the local dialect, our progress in propagating the faith would obviously be greater, but unfortunately even the interpreters cannot explain the concepts of our teaching to the natives in their own language. And we have had no opportunity yet to study the language. Every locality has its own tongue: Kodiak, Alaska, Kenai, Chugan, Koliuzh and and other tribes along the coast have different languages and none are similar.

We have no opportunity of speaking about Christian life more frequently with the newly baptized Kodiak natives because there are only a few of them in the harbor. On the other hand, those who have been assigned for company service, or the temporary hostages who have been brought here from the American mainland, are in a few sparsely populated settlements which are dispersed around the entire island. The weather does not permit us to visit them more frequently and there are no overland roads here at all. Everywhere one encounters insurmountable high mountains and volcanoes, and there are precipitous bays along the coast.

There are more than 6,000 who have been baptized on Kodiak. These include nearly everyone except for those about whom we have strong reservations, namely:

1. The zhupans. These are men who have been brought up from childhood as women. They perform women's duties and the American native males keep them in addition to their wives. They wish to be baptized, but do not want to give up this dreadful custom.

2. In all local settlements the natives practice polygamy. When a man takes a young woman he keeps her as long as he wishes, then they go their separate ways if they no longer wish to live together. They may freely take other mates. Such persons come to us to be baptized, but when they hear that we do not tolerate polygamy, even those who have children will abandon both the children and their previous wives. They then state that since they may have only one wife, who will be permanent until death, they will choose a new wife and then come to be baptized and married

to this new young woman. The previous wives and children are left without any support.

3. There are American natives who have close relatives as their mates: cousins, nieces, some even cohabit with their own daughters and are raising children by them. Such persons also come and ask to be baptized, but only for the purpose of being allowed to marry those with whom they have already been living, even though they are blood relatives.

4. There are a number of Russian promyshlenniks who have lived here for fifteen years or more. They have left wives behind in Russia, and keep women here by whom they have begotten children whom they are raising. They ask that their women be baptized and that they be allowed to marry them. They give us as the reason the fact that they have no intention or hope of returning to Russia. They will openly admit that they left for this distant land without ever having a disagreement with their wives.

Unfortunately, I do not have any authority from Your Eminence to baptize these American natives or to perform marriage ceremonies. For that reason, will you kindly send me special instructions on how to handle such matters.

As far as the inhabitants of Kodiak are concerned, one can say that they are good people and that there is hope that they will accept Russian customs; but, unfortunately, there is scarcely a family which is not afflicted with venereal disease, and they do not even have houses to live in. Their belongings consist of a baidarka which they use for hunting to procure food and clothing. For the most part their clothing is made of bird skins. The garment is long, reaching all the way to the ankle. It resembles the kitaika kamlei which the company gave out to many people when we came here. The company also gives them necessary metal utensils such as copper kettles in exchange for various furs. In view of this, it appears they could be quite attracted to the Russian promyshlenniks. However, every promyshlennik is under the influence of the company administrator, the Kargopol merchant, Aleksandr Baranov, and has great contempt for American natives. They [promyshlenniks] consider our preaching a means of making the natives useless. Moreover, they openly keep women companions, a practice which did not exist when Grigorii Ivanovich Shelikhov was here.

I have not imposed any legal obstacles against marriage, at least for those who do not already have wives in Russia, but not many agree with me. Therefore, I beg of Your Eminence fatherly instructions as to how to end this sinful condition here. I have also written to Grigorii Ivanovich Shelikhov about this, asking him to recall or replace the administrator. But it appears that this practice is not going to end, and therefore I submit this matter for your judgment.

I would like to organize an orphanage for the children born out of wedlock. I believe this idea would be favorably received by Company officials, because they maintain and train capable young American natives near the harbor, and some of these orphans could be taught to read and write. Then depending on their abilities, they could be trained in crafts and would be useful not only for this society but for the Company as well. However, many promyshlenniks intend to take their illegitimate children to Russia with them, and since I do not have any special instructions on this matter from Your Eminence, I feel I must mention it here. I have tried to issue some prohibitions but since [Baranov] is accustomed to living as he pleases, not only would he not listen to me, but he expressed no desire to take my advice. I do not know whether he will adhere to this stand. For the future, I beg you to send me instructions as to whether I am permitted to keep here these illegitimate children of Russian fathers, and especially those of fathers who also have legitimate wives and children in Russia.

This spring I intended to travel to the American mainland, to Kenai Bay, and from there to the Chugach and beyond Cape St. Elias where, in accordance with the orders of the Governor General [Pil] of Irkutsk, a Russian settlement is to be established. We will introduce education there and spread Holy Baptism, at least among those American natives in the places where Russian companies have established a foothold.

I do not know where a suitable and safe site for the settlement will be selected. There is the possibility that the Kenai Bay settlement which is already established will be chosen. But if so, governmental instructions will not have been carried out, because the personal Imperial decree [of Catherine II] orders that the settlement be beyond Cape St. Elias or even farther south if possible. However, there is not a single good harbor site for shipbuilding all the way to the Kolosh region, and thus the local company is trying to push farther south to Yakutat Bay to establish the settlement there. Also, we already have hostages from there, as well as from the distant Ltuya and Chilkha bays. But putting a settlement among them in the near future is not without danger because they are still savage people who know how to fight. Furthermore, through the sea otter trade, the English have supplied them with firearms and powder.

We will ascertain this summer whether it will be possible to establish friendly relations with them and to settle there. I plan to return to Kodiak for the winter, where the rest of the brothers will remain to teach the Christian faith to the newly baptized persons.

In the course of our travels in 1794 in the Aleutian archipelago, we stopped at the Fox Islands. We also stopped on the island of Unalaska to take on fresh water, but we only stayed two days. The native inhabitants there have been accustomed to the Russians for quite some time. There are even some there who have been baptized, and some were taken to Okhotsk for baptism. We were able to baptize about 100 of them who earnestly desire

The Russian Orthodox Church with its distinctive onion dome occupies a prominent place in most early settlements in Alaska, and remains a dynamic religious force. This 19th century view of Unalaska looks west from the cemetery along the treeless strand. Elliott, *An Arctic Province*. (OHS neg. 80246)

to receive Holy Baptism. Many of them pleaded with me to leave an ieromonk with them to baptize others, but for various reasons we did not do this. Next spring an ieromonk will go by transport vessel to Okhotsk. Ieromonk Makarii will go to Unalaska. In the winter he may be able to go on by baidarka along the Fox Islands, returning to the Fox Islands and to Kodiak.

The construction of the church on Kodiak Island is nearly complete. By the time it is finished a place will have been chosen on the American mainland for a small church. This will be a place where Russians will be settled, which is suitable for building harbor facilities. By the next available transport I will send Your Eminence a letter in which I will report in full any new developments and the progress we are having in spreading the holy faith along the American mainland. With this present letter I am appending for your information a map which has been drawn up here showing the location of various places on Kenai and Chugach bays, and beyond the bay of St. Elias.

All the brothers are working very hard to spread the holy faith. Thanks to your holy prayers they are living in peace, in love, and harmony. They are very busy here.

Finally, I entrust myself to the protection of your holy prayers and I humbly beg your fatherly person to give me your blessing and your grace. I consider it an honor and a pleasure to be forever completely dedicated and loyal to you. Your Eminence, most Merciful Shepherd-Bishop and Father, I remain your humble servant, the sinner Arkhimandrit Ioasaf and brothers.

May 19, 1795, from Northeastern America on Kodiak Island at the harbor of Pavlovsk.

Reference: Library of Congress, Manuscript Division. Yudin Collection, Archive of the Holy Synod, Box 643, 38–49.

78

MAY 19, 1795

A REPORT BY THE MONK HERMAN TO FATHER NAZARII CONCERNING
THE WORK OF THE RUSSIAN ORTHODOX MISSIONARIES ON KODIAK
AND OTHER ISLANDS IN THE NORTH PACIFIC OCEAN.

M ost eminient and most honorable Lord, Father Nazarii, and all the Brothers in Christ, praise the Lord.

Nothing can take away the fatherly counsel you have given to me, a humble person. Neither the awesome desolate places in Siberia which I have crossed, nor the dark forests which have embedded themselves in my heart, nor the swift currents of the great rivers of Siberia could change me; not even the awesome ocean could cool my ardor. In my mind I visualize my beloved Valaam. I envision it always across the great ocean, but I cannot see it with my own eyes because of the great distance, [and thus my eyes] cannot express to you my deep gratitude. However, by means of this little piece of paper I shall try, insofar as possible, to express my gratitude to you, my dear Father, and at the same time I will try to give you a little news of myself.

First, thanks to the blessing of Almighty God and all the saints, and thanks to your prayers, all ten of us arrived safely in our American regions. Time will not permit me to write in detail about such a long journey; suffice it to say that our travel took us almost a whole year. We did not encounter any unusual situations except for a few minor occurrences.

The journey was quite picturesque. The only event worthy of comment occurred on the Okhotsk section of our trip where we were attacked by bears while crossing the mountains. The attack was terrifying, yet funny. In the ocean we saw various marine animals such as whales, dolphins, porpoises, sea lions and others, in great numbers. We experienced only one major storm.

Second, we are presently on Kodiak Island, but we are not yet in the place which is to be our final destination. Our intention is to proceed on to the mainland, but we do not know whether we will encounter American natives. They come willingly to be baptized. On Kodiak Island we baptized almost 7,000, and on Unalaska during our voyage through the Aleutian Islands, a headwind forced us into a bay where the Aleut natives surprised us completely by their hospitality and their desire to be baptized.

Third, at present Father Makarii is being dispatched to spread the Gospel and to baptize natives in the Aleutian, Fox and Andreanovskii islands. He also is carrying a copy of this letter. In the near future Father Iuvenalii will go to the mainland, beginning at Kenai Bay, to move among the Chugach, Alegmut and the distant Kolosh and a great many other tribes, all the way to Chilkat [Sound; Lynn Canal].

I myself, having temporarily settled here in spirit, to be brief and to continue the story of the time, stole a brief moment in order to take care of a few important matters. We found ourselves between joy and boredom, plenty and need, poverty and wealth, food and famine, warmth and cold. But in spite of all these problems my spirits are greatly uplifted when I hear my brothers talking about their sermons and about dividing the regions among themselves. I especially like to hear conversations between the ieromonks Makarii and Iuvenalii, because they plan to go around Kodiak in the winter in little skin boats, oblivious to all the dangers of the sea. Father Arkhimandrit remained with us in the harbor, as if we were little children and the ieromonkhs wandered in their thoughts and sometimes focused on the bay where I, the sinner, happened to be with them.

We climbed a small hill to the south and viewed the ocean. In between, we began to talk of where each of us should go to spread the gospel, because the time was approaching when the ships on which we would travel were to be sent out. On that occasion a lively and joyous debate arose concerning information placed on the maps of Captain [James] Cook indicating that Russian people live to the north along a river. We have heard many rumors about them. As we talked, we expressed the desire to meet them.

Father Makarii started to say that if God permits, when I go to the Aleutian Islands and perchance am given the opportunity to go to Alaska near where those Russians are supposed to be, I should find some way to obtain reliable information about them. But Father Iuvenalii, having heard about Alaska and not wishing to discuss it any further, hastily said, "Alaska belongs to me. Consequently I beg you not to trouble me. Since the ship is not being sent to Yakutat, the spreading of the gospel should start in the south. Then moving on the ocean to the north around Kenai Bay, one should proceed directly to this harbor. Then one must go on to Alaska." Listening to this, Father Makarii flushed and his face became sad. Slowly but firmly he said, "No, Father, you will not exclude me. You know that the Aleutian chain is grouped with Alaska, and for that reason it belongs to me, and the entire northern coast as well. On the other hand, if you wish, the southern part of America will belong to you for the rest of your life."

I listened with joy to this conversation, which did not develop into an argument. Father, I am sorry that because of lack of time I cannot relate more, nor do I even have time to discuss customs and habits and all the developments of our life in this distant country, or to tell you about our brothers. But I will report to you periodically.

Kuzma Alekseevich has received the tonsure and the name Iosaf. We met him in the bakehouse. Forgive me my dear Father, forgive me that I cannot write more, but I beg your saintly fatherly prayers and blessings.

[signed] Your humble Herman

Reference: Library of Congress, Manuscript Division. Yudin Collection, Archive of the Holy Synod, Box 643, 53–58.

79

NOVEMBER 22, 1795

A LETTER FROM NATALIA ALEKSEEVNA SHELIKHOVA TO FIELD
MARSHAL COUNT PLATON ALEKSANDROVICH ZUBOV, REPORTING ON
CONDITIONS IN ALASKA SINCE THE DEATH OF HER HUSBAND, GRI-
GORII I. SHELIKHOV.

Illustrious Count, Most Merciful Lord: . . .
On August 6 of this year, 1795, the frigate *Phoenix* which belongs to the American Russian Company, arrived in Okhotsk,
bearing news and the following information.

As a result of Your Excellency's intervention, farm laborers
were assigned to the company in 1793. My late husband sent
them from Okhotsk on August 13, 1794 aboard two ships which
had been built by order of the local commandant. These ships,
which also carried the religious entourage assigned to him, landed
on the coast of the American island of Kodiak on September 24 of
that same year. The people spent the winter at Pavlovsk Harbor
on that island, and at the present time the main headquarters of
the company are located there, as well as an office in the fort.

Although my husband had given written instructions to the
local administrator of the company that during that same fall he
should send the farm workers to the mainland to Chugach or
Kenai Bay to establish settlements, those instructions were not
carried out, not because it was late in the season but because the
ships were wrecked in a storm. However the men were sent there
this spring, with instructions to look for a suitable place for their
settlement, searching as far as Ltyua Bay below 58° northern latitude. Information regarding the progress of this venture should
be forthcoming next year.

Meanwhile, the leader of the religious entourage, Arkhimandrit Ioasaf, has baptized and married many American natives
at the zimov'e on Kodiak, persons who came to him from the
mainland and from the islands. He has sent a report of this to me,
to the local bishop [in Irkutsk] and to His Eminence, Metropolitan Gavriil of St. Petersburg and Novgorod. He also reports
that the foundation for a wooden church has been completed at
that same harbor, but that the church itself had not been com-

pleted by the time the ship sailed. Another such church is being built in a settlement on the coast of the mainland. Both of these churches, including the iconostases and church plate, have been donated by my late husband, with the exception of food supplies which the government has allotted for the arkhimandrit.

Seven of the Russian farm laborers have married American natives. The company Administrator [Aleksandr A. Baranov] complains, however, that the agricultural workers made a rash decision. They had no desire to work to make all the necessary preparations and they did not provide all the food they would need. They thus made unreasonable demands to be supplied with food and other necessities. My late husband provided food and other needs for them in Okhotsk prior to their departure. He also sent a special official with them with enough goods to supply them with all reasonable needs. However, they finally threatened to kill the official and then conspired to use the weapons, which they had been given to defend themselves against savage natives, to seize the ship in which they were to be taken to the coast of the mainland. They planned to sail to the Kuril Islands.

They also plotted to choose one of their own men to be their navigator. They managed to hide provisions and three guns, but the company official uncovered the plot. The local official punished the three chief conspirators by having them flogged, and he sent a warning to the artels of the rest of the promyshlenniks and this foiled the plot.

The English expedition, which was publicized in the newspapers in 1793, was in Chugach, Kenai and Yakutat bays in 1794, where the artels of my company promyshlenniks are located. [The English expedition consisted of] two frigates, one, the three-masted *Discovery*, and the other, the two-masted *Chatham*. Captain [George] Vancouver commanded the former, and Captain [Peter] Puget the latter. These men made observations about everything they encountered in those harbors. They measured the depth of the water all the way into the inland bays and at the harbors of those bays. There was a third ship, a merchant vessel, at Yakutat Bay.

They visited my company and asked the promyshlennik [Egor] Purtov and his associates such questions as how long the Russians had controlled these regions. My men answered that these regions and the land beyond Ltyua Bay had belonged to

Russia since 1741. The English disputed this, stating that *they* were the first to acquire the land, as a result of the work of their famous Captain Cook.

Other than this, they associated with our people in a friendly manner, and they were hospitably received. They expressed a desire to meet the administrator of the company in order to delineate the frontier with him and establish how far they should control the American shore as neighbors. They were unable to meet with him, however, since he was elsewhere. Some members of that expedition knew a few words of Russian and said that we should expect five or six English vessels to take possession of Kenai Bay within two years. However, if the English vessels do not come within two years, these areas will belong to us permanently.

This information which they gave to the Russian promyshlenniks, along with three letters which no one there could translate and the above mentioned detailed report from the administrator, were all sent to the oblast commandant in Okhotsk and then on to the local administrator of the namestnichestvo [in Irkutsk]. The latter made a report of this and asked for administrative instructions on how to lay claim to the coast of the mainland beyond Ltyua Bay up to the point from where the earlier Russian expedition under Captain [Aleksei I.] Chirikov returned from America. It was in this place that he lost seventeen persons he had sent ashore; however he did not wish to leave there to go beyond Ltyua Bay for observations in order to bury the secret plates which the Company received from the government.

My husband instructed the administrator, Baranov, to try to build seagoing vessels there. Consequently in 1793 he built a port in the land of the Chugach which he named Voskresenskii Harbor. He used native trees, called *spruce* in English, to build a frigate with three masts and two decks. It is 73 feet long, 23 feet high and 79 feet deep. The space between the lower and upper decks is 13½ feet. This was completed in September, 1794, in spite of the company's severe shortage of iron and tar. Instead of oakum and tar he caulked with a substance made from the entrails and offal of fish mixed with whale blubber.

He left for Kodiak on his frigate, and from there sent to Okhotsk the pelts from three years of hunting furbearing animals. He also built two small craft for more convenient use in making a reconnaissance along the coast of America and for travel to headquarters. I am pleased to enclose the plans and drawings of Voskresenskii Harbor where these vessels and the frigate were built.

Even before the craftsmen who had been assigned arrived there, my late husband had directed that the preparations for shipbuilding be carried out meticulously. As a result, by the time the craftsmen came the drydock was ready, thanks to the attention and efforts of my late husband.

The report also mentions iron ore. There is a goodly quantity of it on Kodiak and at Kenai Bay. [Baranov] himself made an attempt to smelt a small amount of iron, which he sent to me, but there is no one there who knows how to forge iron. He asks that an expert be sent to him and I will of course try to fulfill this request.

[Baranov] also informs me that after an earlier encounter with a large number of savages from the American contintent, all of them have been registered. In 1793 and 1794 he succeeded in teaching a little Russian to some families of the Agalakhmiuts, Kamuzh, and Alaksins who live some distance away. He has registered all of them. He also surveyed a previously unknown island which can be seen from Kodiak. It has never been carefully explored, although he very much wishes to have this done. He sent company vessels there in 1793 and 1794, but storms prevented them from sailing close to shore and so the exploration has not been completed. I have the honor humbly to submit a map to Your Excellency for your examination.

In addition to these American enterprises and the voyage to Okhotsk last August 6 by the newly built American Russian Company frigate called the *Phoenix*, another ship which belonged to my late husband also sailed from the Aleutian Islands to Okhotsk. This ship, the *Sv. Aleksandr*, carried furs. While it was anchored on the island of Atka, it unexpectedly took aboard fifteen Japanese whose ship was completely wrecked on that island. They had been driven there by a storm which took them from one bay to another. Their cargo had been Sarachinsk buckwheat. When they left the coast they lost their navigational direction as a result of a storm and were carried to the Aleutian Islands. Three of the men are being sent here on their way to Irkutsk.

Last year when the agricultural workers were sent to America my late husband did not have enough ships to send any of them to the Kuril Islands. However, this summer four families of these workers, as well as 32 promyshlenniks with firearms and other equipment, food supplies for the families, livestock and other necessities, were sent from Okhotsk to the sixteenth island aboard a government ship. This year I hope to receive news of their successful arrival there. As soon as I do, I will have the honor of reporting this to Your Excellency.

I have written all of this to Your Excellency for your careful consideration, since you are the patron of my company. I would like to submit humbly that although I am not wholly familiar with all matters, nonetheless, I do believe the time has come to decide on establishing a line between the Russian and the English possessions—the sooner the better—in order to prevent them from using devious means to eject us from our present possessions, which we have acquired by our determination and zeal.

We must attempt to go beyond Ltyua Bay, which is beyond Kenai and Chugach bays where our settlement of farm laborers is presently being planned, and where the two English frigates were sighted. We have the right to that territory because it was acquired by the Russian sailors who were along the American coast as far as 58° northern latitude. Moreover, it was also claimed by previous Russian expeditions and subsequently placed on the map, as the English know very well, because in 1741 the navigator Dementev and seventeen Russian sailors were put ashore among the savages between 57° and 58° latitude. Further, even more emphatic testimony is the fact that the copper plates inscribed "This land belongs to Russia", which the government gave my company, were secretly placed in the ground. I hereby submit for Your Excellency's careful consideration five secret plans made at various times by navigators of my company to indicate the locations in America in which these plates were emplaced. The plates were not placed beyond Ltuya Bay, but they will be, this summer, by the administrator of my company.

In submitting this information for your consideration, I beg Your Excellency's gracious intervention with Her Imperial Majesty, for Her approval. This problem is vitally important to the Empire if the planned settlement of farm workers beyond Cape St. Elias is to be successful.

In addition, I also humbly submit to Your Excellency a request that you will continue your patronage of the American Company. My need at the present time is for navigators because currently there is only one navigator aboard the company vessels in America, and he is ill. Because of this, navigators for long voyages and explorations and reconnaissance and transport to America are in very short supply, especially now that shipbuilding has already begun in America. This should produce good results, and a large number of ships will be built to use for governmental needs as well as for the needs of the Russian settlement. My late husband, while he was alive, asked the present Governor General to secure navigators from high authorities, and although the Governor did submit such a request to the Governing Senate, the request has not yet been approved.

Navigators are now needed even more than previously. The frigate *Phoenix* which arrived there this year will have no navigator to take her back to America, where next year a large quantity of goods, livestock, grain and other necessities must be sent to the settlers and the religious entourage which went there last year. The navigator who returned to Okhotsk with that frigate must remain in the port of Okhotsk to care for government transport because of the dire shortage of manpower.

In regard to this matter, I hereby humbly submit a copy of the request which has been forwarded to the Governing Senate, and humbly beg Your Excellency to intercede with a single word to the Empress, pointing out at that time what benefits the activity of my company has brought, so that Her Imperial Majesty will give Her approval to my request.

Whenever the navigators are dispatched, at least one of them should be empowered to meet with the English to delineate the boundary [between our respective claims]. If discord should develop at some time in the future among the farm people there, or the company promyshlenniks, this chief navigator, as the official representing the crown, should be empowered to overrule any objections by the administrator of the company and subject the guilty party to punishment in the presence of Arkhimandrit Ioasaf, the leader of the religious entourage, whose rank is presently higher than that of anyone else.

Finally, I humbly beg you to forgive me for disturbing Your Excellency's peace with these requests of mine, but to whom am I now to turn, if not to you, Your Excellency, since I am now a widow with young children? From whom can I secure patronage, if not from you, Your Excellency?

With the very deepest respect for the person of Your Excellency and with the most sincere and total devotion to you for all my life, I remain, Sire, Your Excellency's most devoted servant,

Natalia Shelikhova.

See: P. A. Tikhmenev. *Istoricheskoe obozrenie obrazovaniia Rossiisko-Amerikanskoi kompanii i deistvii eia do nastoiashchago vremeni* (St. Petersburg: 1861–63), II, Supplement, 108–113.

80

NOVEMBER 22, 1795

A REPORT FROM VENIAMIN, BISHOP OF IRKUTSK AND NERCHISNK, TO THE ARCHBISHOP OF IRKUTSK, CONCERNING BAPTISM OF NATIVES ON KODIAK ISLAND BY RUSSIAN ORTHODOX MISSIONARIES

Your Eminence, Gracious Archbishop and Father:
On November 18 [1795] the American Company people delivered to me a parcel addressed to Your Holiness from Father Arkhimandrit Ioasaf, along with news concerning the acceptance of the Christian faith by the Kodiak Island natives. This parcel and this news I hereby faithfully forward to Your Holiness, as well as to the Holy Synod, via this mail. In a letter addressed to me, Father Arkhimandrit writes that they left Okhotsk on August 13, 1794 and safely reached northeastern [i.e. northeast of Siberia] America, and the island of Kodiak: and as Shelikhov's brother told me, they spent 40 days of the winter in the company settlement of the late Shelikhov.

They have baptized more than 6,000 American natives who sincerely desired to accept the Christian faith. However, since the natives are scattered about the island, [our Russian clergy] are not able to travel around in order to teach them the Holy Gospel and administer Holy Baptism because of the distances from the harbor. Thus, in order to perform this service for the young and the old, two ieromonks have been sent who will travel around the island.

Because of the bad weather all winter long it has been impossible to build a field church. A church on Kodiak is under construction now and is nearly completed.

Moreover, Father Arkhimandrit writes that this spring he plans to go along the coast of the mainland of America, through the land of the Kenais and the Chugach, beyond Cape St. Elias to Yakutat Bay where a Russian settlement is to be established by order of the Governor General [Pil]. Once he familiarizes himself with the circumstances, it is likely that the Russians will need to build a church there. However, if circumstances are such that no fort is built before winter sets in, he will return to Kodiak in the fall. He has left the other brothers on Kodiak.

Finally, Father Arkhimandrit writes that in his opinion the inhabitants of Kodiak Island are good people, and there is hope that they can be taught to accept Russian customs; however, unfortunately there is hardly a family of them who are not afflicted with venereal disease. None of them have dwellings; their belongings consist of the baidarkas in which they hunt and travel about to secure food and clothing [which they make from] birdskins. When we arrived there, many natives received Chinese kamleis from the company. The company also gave them metal utensils they need such as copper kettles, in exchange for furs.

Kodiak Island is as much as 5,000 versts in circumference. The Company people believe that some 30,000 natives live on this island and on other small islands nearby.

Thanks to the blessed prayers of Your Eminence, the enterprise is meeting with as much success as might be expected.

Father Arkhimandrit complains about the local Russians and especially about the administrator [Baranov]: to the utter disbelief of the newly baptized, and contrary to the Gospel being taught to the natives, the Russians are keeping female companions, and he is unable to persuade them to discontinue this practice. Father Arkhimandrit wrote personally to Shelikhov asking that the administrator be recalled, and he asks my assistance in this.

Although Father Arkhimandrit has not mentioned the name of the administrator there, I have made inquiries here and have learned that the administrator is [Aleksandr A.] Baranov, about whom I have received letters from other priests concerning the same problem. I will try to persuade him that he must stop setting a bad example. Whether or not the company will decide to recall him I do not know, for he is a capable person and indispensable for local business matters.

However our endeavors will be successful only if they are blessed by the divinity of Your Eminence, to whose protection I also always entrust myself, to Your Holy Person, with the deepest trust and loyalty, Your Eminence, Merciful Archbishop and Father, I remain your humble servant and pilgrim,

Veniamin

Bishop of Irkutsk and Nerchinsk.

Reference: Library of Congress, Manuscript Division. Yudin Collection, Archive of the Holy Synod, Box 643, 33–37.

81

A REPORT FROM METROPOLITAN GAVRIIL OF NOVGOROD TO FIELD MARSHAL COUNT PLATON ALEKSANDROVICH ZUBOV CONCERNING THE ACTIVITY OF IVAN L. GOLIKOV IN ALASKA AND THE WORK OF RUSSIAN ORTHODOX MISSIONARIES.

Most Illustrious Count Platon Aleksandrovich, Gracious Sir: The accomplishment of the distinguished citizen of Kursk, Ivan Larionovich Golikov, has greatly enhanced the scepter of our Illustrious Monarch by bringing various large islands and an important part of the native peoples along the shores of North America [under Russian control]. He has already built seagoing vessels from American lumber and has established trade with China; it appears that in time he will also be able to establish trade with Japan.

He also has tried very hard to care for another extremely important matter, to send a group of missionaries there to convert the American natives to the Christian faith. Accordingly, I have sent five [missionaries]. Their efforts in a very short time have resulted in the conversion of more than 6,000 American natives to Orthodoxy.

The local arkhimandrit and his brothers are maintained at Golikov's expense, and he has introduced the Christian faith there and has built a chapel in which he glorifies the name of the Empress. He has submitted to me a report about this.

The merchant Shelikhov who personally supervised the organization of this important American enterprise there, and whom Golikov took from among the prikashchiks as his associate, tried to promote this, but he has died. This has caused the ruin of this company, and if the Company does not receive help and official guidance, it will collapse, as will the efforts which have spread the glory of Russia. For that reason it would be very useful to induce Golikov to return as soon as possible to Irkutsk so as to bring order into the present chaotic situation.

I have received information from those places that in the year 1794 the English demanded the delineation of the frontiers, but one of Golikov's company prikashchiks, who was in charge of administering the American enterprises, refused to take upon him-

494

self this responsibility, which appropriately belonged within the competence of the government of the Russian Empire. He informed the English that in two years five or six [Russian] naval vessels would come and take complete possession of these places. That news has already been published in English newspapers.

This attempt by the English may compel this American Company to bring the American natives into the Christian faith. From the letters I have received from the above mentioned [arkhimandrit] I turn with a humble plea to Your Excellency that you, Most Merciful Sir, will take on this task which would enhance the glory of the fatherland and the church: to ask Her Illustrious Imperial Majesty to give Her permission and blessing to this.

With complete respect, I have the honor to be, Your Excellency, Most Merciful Sir, your zealous servant and pilgrim.

Reference: Library of Congress, Manuscript Division. Yudin Collection, Archive of the Holy Synod. Box 643, 30–32.

82

AUGUST 5, 1797

AN UKAZ FROM EMPEROR PAUL DIRECTING THAT RUSSIAN COMPANIES TRADING IN AMERICA BE UNDER THE SUPERVISION OF THE COMMERCE COLLEGE.

To the President of the Commerce College and General Procurator.

His Imperial Majesty has responded to my humble report based on information I received from the Privy Councillor and Civil Governor of Irkutsk, Governor Illarion Timofeevich Nagel. This report concerns a request by local citizens to establish an American trading company to carry on hunting in America similar to the existing company of Shelikhov and Golikov. To this request was appended personal testimony I had received from the members of this Shelikhov-Golikov Company, describing the harm the existence of a number of companies would bring, and arguing that the greatest benefits would result if all would unify.

His Imperial Majesty has decreed that the existing present company and those that may be organized in the future are to be placed under the direction of the Imperial Commerce College, with the proviso, however, that those desiring to establish enterprises similar to [those of Shelikhov and Golikov] be allowed only with the permission of those already in existence, and in accordance with terms previously agreed upon, and without contradiction.

Informing Your Excellency of this Imperial wish, for your attention and administration, I have the honor to submit to you copies of all the papers and reports which I have at my disposal concerning this matter.

Reference: *Polnoe sobranie zakonov rossiiskoi imperii s 1649 goda*. First Series (St. Petersburg: 1830), XXIV, 670.

83

OCTOBER 5, 1797

A REPORT FROM IEROMONK MAKARII, HEAD OF THE RUSSIAN ORTHO-
DOX MISSION IN ALASKA, TO THE HOLY GOVERNING SYNOD, DETAIL-
ING TREATMENT OF NATIVES BY RUSSIANS.

This humble report is submitted in accordance with the personal Imperial decree of Our Most Merciful Sovereign of
Illustrious Memory, the [late] All Wise Empress Catherine Alekseevna, and His Eminence Metropolitan Gavriil of Novgorod and
St. Petersburg, member of the Holy Governing Synod. The decree directs that Father Arkhimandrit and the now Bishop Ioasaf
and his brothers leave St. Petersburg on December 25, 1793, for
the northern part of America in order to convert the native
peoples to the Christian faith.

I [Makarii] was by my own request assigned by His Excellency the Archbishop, with his blessing, to go to Kodiak Island,
which I reached safely in September 1794. When the arkhimandrit arrived I was sent from Kodiak Island to settlements to
the natives of America to spread the Word of God and to exhort
those people to accept Holy Baptism. I continued this through
the first winter. On May 25, 1795, the arkhimandrit sent me from
Kodiak Island to the Aleuts on the Fox Islands to spread the Word
of God. I went there aboard the vessel *Phoenix* which belonged to
Shelikhov and Golikov, the company owners, who were voyaging
to the town of Okhotsk. The vessel was under the command of
the navigator [Gerasim A.] Izmailov, and it reached these islands
safely on June 13. I remained there until June 25, 1796. I baptized more than 1,000 men at the request of the natives themselves. While I was on those islands I was so badly treated by the
peredovshchik of the Golikov company, the town dweller of
Vologda Ivan Kotiutin, and his men, that I feared for my life. To
save my life I requested an armed guard of two men from the
peredovshchik of Okhotsk, the citizen Ivan Svinin who was employed by the Irkutsk merchant of the second guild Stefan Kiselev, a navigation company owner who was at that time working
on these islands.

These two men stood guard with weapons day and night
without fail and would not allow any member of the Shelikhov-

Golikov company to enter the iurt where I lived. I was in such danger that I would not let any person come to me without making inquiries about him.

The peredovshchik Kotiutin treated me in a most barbaric manner. He came to the door of the iurt where I lived but the sentry would not let him pass through the door. So then he came to the window, but again the sentry told him to leave. He would not obey, but tried again to come in through the window. He threatened me, shouting,

"We fed you *pirogi* [meat pies] in vain, and we tried to treat you nicely, the same as if you were our master, Grigorii Ivanovich [Shelikhov]." He also said, "You are a big man, you talk with the Bishop."

Meanwhile the sentry ran to the peredovshchik Svinin and told him that Kotiutin was trying to climb through the window into the ieromonk's room. When the peredovshchik heard this he immediately ran to Kotiutin and asked him why he has trying to climb through the window, "Don't you know who lives here? Get away from here!"

But Kotiutin would not go away, so Svinin quickly pushed him away but Kotiutin would not pay any attention to him. Svinin, seeing that he did not intend to leave the window and that he was being troublesome, had to hit Kotiutin in the face. He ordered his workers to carry Kotiutin away from the window. But then Kotiutin shouted to his comrades, "Fellows! They are beating me!"

From around the corner twelve men jumped up and ran toward the iurt where I lived. The peredovshchik Svinin then ordered his workers to ready their weapons. One of his workers grabbed a big oak staff and jumped on those who were attacking. If Svinin had not saved me, peredovshchik Kotiutin would either have killed me or perpetrated some other evil deed. This experience was the worst in my whole life.

I asked Svinin for a third man, and they stood guard day and night, constantly, with guns loaded and bayonets fixed, until I boarded the ship to leave these islands. This is what I suffered at the hands of the Shelikov-Golikov Company. Furthermore, an Aleut died and I did not dare perform his funeral service. I did give instructions that he be buried, and I read the service in the iurt where I lived. But this Aleut died without confession because

I did not dare hear his confession. In the iurt I performed marriages and baptized children in the presence of the guard. I was exposed to such danger that I did not dare go out of the iurt without a guard.

The Shelikhov-Golikov Company treats the native islanders in the most barbaric manner. They have no humane instincts. They take the wives and young daughters [of native men] as their sexual partners. They kill any who refuse to hunt sea otters, and early in the spring they send out the healthy and the sick alike, against their will. Many of these, especially those who are ill, die on the way and during the hunt which lasts until fall.

As a result the natives cannot prepare enough food for themselves, nor can they catch enough birds to make parkas. Because of the failure to prepare enough food they starve to death, and for lack of adequate clothing they suffer greatly from the cold. And because they are so severely beaten, many of them commit suicide. Any of the Aleuts who bring in too few foxes are stretched out on the ground and beaten with heavy sticks mercilessly and accused of laziness. The Russians take away from them for the company any sea otter and fox pelts which they have procured over and above their quotas. They even force men to work whose wives have died. These people cannot procure food for themselves and are forced to join the company. They are compelled to fish, cut lumber, and build baidarkas. Young people are forced to go to the desolate northern island to hunt for the company. They take the young children of these men as hostages, two from each family, so that there is no one to procure food.

They will take a native's baidarka to the coast and put him in it, and because he has no provisions he must go out to sea to catch fish for his own sustenance and for his family so they will be able to eat and not go hungry.

The prikashchik Maksim Krivdin took one very young girl, who had been baptized, as his enslaved sexual partner. One day he planned to commit a sexual atrocity against her. He called her to his bed and when she refused him he beat her so severely with a stick that her back bled. There was no one to prevent this. The Russians take whatever they want. The Aleuts have come to a point where they have no hope of Imperial mercy.

I did try as much as possible to encourage the natives to have hope in Imperial great mercy, but the Russians of the Shelikhov-

499

An Aleut from the island of Unalaska dressed for hunting in a waterproof gut *kamlei* and an intricate wooden headpiece which serves as a rainhat and eyeshade. It also presented a non-human profile to a curious sea otter or seal. The Shelikhov-Golikov Company forced male Aleuts to hunt every day from spring until autumnal storms. The death toll from beatings, starvation, hostage mistreatment and storms at sea was catastropic. Sarychev, *Atlas*. (OHS neg. 80225)

Golikov Company have behaved so dreadfully that one said he was a priest from Kodiak Island, and gave his priestly blessing to the Russians. He even tried to persuade the Aleuts by saying that the priest commits a sin if he says that Russian men should not keep women. One of them told the Aleuts that I was a Tatar. Another, talking to an Aleut, asked him facetiously whether a priest had baptized him. Using these confusing words, they put the newly baptized people into a state of bewilderment and pressure, and there is no one to stop them.

During my stay on these islands I was told about important government secrets which are being suppressed and not reported to His Imperial Majesty. These are secrets which no one but His Imperial Majesty should hear. In order to report directly [to the Emperor] I requested a vessel from peredovschik Ivan Svinin so I could leave the islands and make my report. Svinin himself should have an opportunity to leave the islands and go to the Russian harbor at the town of Okhotsk to report to the Okhotsk administration that he had been approached by more than 20 island toions who were seeking protection from the Shelikhov-Golikov Company. These toions had previously been rewarded with government medals. They could no longer endure the violent abuse and mistreatment perpetrated by the North American [Company] administrator, Vasilii Merkulev and the peredovshchik Kotiutin and their men.

The principal toions, Aleksei Shelikhov and Petr Mykhoplev, who work for the Shelikhov-Golikov Company on contract, are virtually enslaved. These toions who have been rewarded in the past pleaded with the peredovshchik Svinin to take them under his protection. One toion named Kusikh, another named Fedor Osetrobeznov, and another also named Osetrobeznov who walks with two crutches, in their settlement organized their own group of Aleuts and asked Svinin to come to their iurt. They knelt before Svinin and wept bitterly and asked him to accept them under his protection. Witnessing this emotional plea, I could not bear it; I too cried, and indeed Svinin himself wept.

Those who live well in the settlement are genuine rarities, and out of bitter experience they are very glad to avail themselves of protection. These island toions asked that the Okhotsk administration send Svinin to protect them in the islands, but they were given no assurance. Now they are left without any protection. Although the administration sends written instructions to the islands that the islanders are not to be abused and robbed, and that no other evil deeds are to be perpetrated against them, the Russians do not heed these instructions, but do as they please. On the islands they simply say, "The sky is high, the sovereign is far away, so do whatever you wish." They also say "As long as there are sea otters there will be no problems."

The newly baptized islanders cry not with tears but with blood. They expected justice. They thought they would have Svinin because they were greatly attached to him and loved him for his kindness toward them.

A toion named Elisei Puryshev and two Aleut interpreters, Nikolai Lukanin and Nikifor Svinin, came with me to go to His Imperial Majesty with secret reports and petitions. We left the islands on June 25, 1796 and reached the first of the Kuril Islands on September 7. We spent the winter in the harbor in the second strait. From there we sailed on June 30, 1797 and reached Okhotsk on July 28. We left Okhotsk on August 8 and reached Iakutsk on September 12. We have stopped in Iakutsk, and are waiting for the first winter route to be open. If God should so desire, and if we are still alive we will take that route from Iakutsk. Because I am in such great danger I am presuming to put this into my report. I find myself at present in great danger and in perilous circumstances. I suffered greatly in the islands, and do now as well.

When I reached the town of Okhotsk the Shelikov-Golikov Company office administrators there, the Kursk merchant Nikifor Shmatov and the Rylsk merchant Sidor Shelikhov, tried to detain me in Okhotsk so they could take me back to Kodiak Island with them. But I, your humble servant, submitted a statement in writing to Okhotsk commandant Prince Myshetskii, saying that I was carrying a secret report to His Imperial Majesty. Because of that they did not detain me further in Okhotsk. But I am afraid that in Irkutsk the request of the Shelikhov-Golikov Company people will not be honored. Thus, in order that the Aleut toions and I will not be detained, and so that the secret report and other papers will not be taken away from us, I am presenting this humble report to the Holy Governing Synod, so that these matters will be known to all.

[Signed] Ieromonk Makarii, humble servant of the Holy Governing Synod in the North American religious mission.

Reference: Library of Congress, Manuscript Division. Yudin Collection, Archive of the Holy Synod, Box 643, 13–24.

502

84

A PETITION FROM THE IAKUTSK MERCHANT, FEDOR STRUCHKOV, TO THE GOVERNOR OF IRKUTSK, ILLARION TIMOFEEVICH NAGEL, TO FORM A FUR TRADING COMPANY.

To the Most Noble and Esteemed Gospodin Privy Council-lor, Governor of Irkutsk and Cavalier, Illarion Timofeevich!

A humble petition from Fedor Struchkov, a merchant of the second guild in Iakutsk and city golova.

I have resolved to undertake the organization of a company within the jurisdiction of Udsk ostrog at the mouth of the Ud River. I plan to build a baidara there and send it not only to the unknown Shantar Island to hunt land and sea animals, but also to explore near this and other islands which hitherto, because of un-willingness on the part of promyshlenniks, have not yet been ex-plored or surveyed. This includes lands beyond the Tugur River which form the frontier between the Russian and Chinese em-pires, all the way to the Amur River and all the way to the sea-coast. I will do this with the help of the people who live all along the coast who are known as Giliaks.

If there is a possibility that this proposal will be approved, and no obstacles are encountered, and neither the Giliaks nor other people interfere, then I would even try to approach the large is-land of Sakhalin located at the mouth of the Amur River. I would like to survey not only its coastline but also its interior, in order to determine its geography, resources and settlements.

For this undertaking I need people not only capable of work-ing and hunting, but also those who have sound knowledge of the projected journey and exploration through both theory and prac-tical experience. I did not find enough such people among the vol-unteers and retired servitors, townsmen or iasak-paying peasants. Those I did find and who have freely agreed to travel with me on my voyage on the basis of published Imperial laws must receive appropriate passports. But since my undertaking is voluntary, and its only purpose is to explore fully that part of the territory which has not yet been fully described, I would like to provide a detailed description from which may be derived extensive bene-fits for my state and fatherland, and the acquisition of new islands.

To achieve this desired objective, it is necessary that my newly organized company receive full support in all of these places where there are lawfully established authorities and administrations. There must not be any hindrance or delay because even the briefest delay often negates the success of an undertaking and the opportunity for the anticipated benefit and advantages, once lost, does not occur again.

For that reason I am submitting to Your Excellency a proposal to create this new company which I am organizing, to be called the Shantar Hunting Company. I humbly request that you approve not only that I be allowed to accept volunteers who will sign contracts with me for this noble venture, but also that you will permit me to assign retired servitors, merchants and iasak-paying peasants, so that they can be released from their public and tax obligations and can be issued appropriate legal passports.

I also request that for a period of four months I may be free from all obligations so that I can prepare supplies and materials and everything else necessary for my newly organized company—in a word, all the essentials for a move to the Utur River, which is 600 versts or more from here.

I would appreciate it very much if you could intercede on my behalf with the Iakutsk administration and especially with the Udsk officials.

Reference: Library of Congress, Manuscript Division. Yudin Collection, Box 2.

85

NOT BEFORE AUGUST 3, 1798

NOTES BY NATALIA A. SHELIKHOVA PERTAINING TO THE ROLE OF GRI-
GORII I. SHELIKHOV IN THE ACHIEVEMENTS OF SHELIKHOV-GOLIKOV
FUR TRADING COMPANY

My husband, the late [Grigorii I.] Shelikhov, voyaged to America in 1784, 1785 and 1786 with three ships. He befriended the native inhabitants of Alaska and the islands of Kodiak and Afognak, as well as various tribes on the American mainland from Kenai Bay or Cook River down to Ltuya Bay in 57° northern latitude. He converted more than 120,000 of them into Russian subjects, those who wished this. Commercial ties have been established with these people and a fur trading company founded. All of this has been based on permanent and reliable rules.

When Shelikhov returned he empowered his company assistants to continue to carry on business. Accordingly, the following achievements have been made.

1. The Alaska peninsula has been fairly well surveyed and a shorter and better route has been discovered across the northern part to Bristol Bay. This obviates having to sail around the cape and in the dangerous strait between the peninsula and Unimak Island. In addition, [our people] have learned more about the Alaska natives and have brought them under better control.

2. The promyshlenniks have organized a hunting artel in Kenai Bay, which [Captain James] Cook named as a river, after himself.* Once the promyshlenniks had thoroughly befriended the natives they established trade and other communication with them.

3. An artel has also been established in Chugach Bay. In 1794 three ships were built there of local lumber. One is a fine frigate, *Phoenix*, with 24 guns; the other two are the smaller *Pegasus* and *Oleg*. [Our people] have become acquainted with many natives and have established [commercial] ties with them.

---

*Actually named for Cook by the Earl of Sandwich. Also called Cooks Inlet, Cook's Inlet, Cooks River, Baie de Cook, as well as several variations of "Kenai."—Eds.

4. On the island of Montague, or Siukliu, a small fortification has been erected at Cape St. Elias.

5. A school has been established on Kodiak where young native American boys learn to read and write Russian and study arithmetic and navigation. Ten boys were sent to Irkutsk where they learned to play various musical instruments. In 1793 they returned to Kodiak, to the delight of the native inhabitants who are fond of merrymaking.

6. Some exploration of the coast of the mainland at Yakutat and Ltuya bays has been undertaken. The natives there, as well as in other regions, are quite primitive. For that reason there was marginal success in trying to civilize them prior to 1795, but the situation is not hopeless. Trade with them continues without much fear.

Ltuya Bay is located slightly beyond 55° northern latitude, in the vicinity of Nootka, an English settlement. It should serve as the boundary for Russian possessions in America.

7. In all of these bays and in various other places, for political reasons, copper plates have been buried in the ground. They are inscribed with the words "This land belongs to Russia."

8. Many pacified American natives and islanders have been baptized without a priest, and many have already adopted the lifestyle of the Russians. Also, whole tribes have moved from faraway places to points where Russian trading artels are located. [These friendly natives] defend these sites from other natives who have the dreadful custom of robbing and killing one another over mere trifles.

9. When, as a result [of these efforts], the natives became familiar with the Russians and with our legal system, in 1793 my husband requested [Russian Orthodox] authorities to send missionaries there. In response, a group under the leadership of an arkhimandrit [Ioasaf] was sent at company expense. During the winter of 1794 and the spring of 1795 they baptized more than 8,000 souls on Kodiak, performed marriage ceremonies [to legalize unions] for a large number of American natives and married many Russians to native American women and taught them how to live peacefully and in a decent manner. The company also built a church on Kodiak.

In 1796, following these accomplishments, the arkhimandrit was consecrated as the local bishop with the title of vicar bishop.

St. Lawrence natives haul a huge tusked walrus above the tide by a "double purchase" technique (below). Shelikhov employed 200 men to hunt walrus for ivory (above). Elliott, *An Arctic Province*. (OHS neg. 80263, 80264)

This summer he is scheduled to arrive in Okhotsk for his consecration which will take place in Irkutsk. His achievements should be great.

10. During his stay on Kodiak, my husband successfully experimented with growing various grains and garden produce.

When he requested missionaries, he also asked that twenty families of exiled convicts be assigned to him for agricultural work, and that ten more, artisans, skilled blacksmiths and carpenters, be assigned to help him with shipbuilding. In 1794 these persons were sent, with instructions from the Governor General of Irkutsk [I. A. Pil] to settle near Cape St. Elias in Chugach Bay or farther on toward 55° northern latitude where they might find a likely site for a settlement.

When [Shelikhov] sent these settlers he supplied them with seed grain, tools, livestock and domestic poultry for breeding purposes; these were in addition to that which he had previously brought personally.

In 1795 these settlers left Kodiak with the religious entourage to go to the coast of the mainland in search of a suitable settlement site. Presently we are awaiting news from them as to where and how they have settled.

My husband ordered that another church be built in the new settlement, as well as a fort, homes, warehouses and everything necessary to provide a secure and satisfactory life. He named that settlement, and the entire region in fact, "Slavarossiia."

11. He also established another settlement, an agricultural and company outpost, on the 18th of the Kuril Islands [Urup], not far from Japan, in order to promote commercial relations with that country in due time.

12. He also organized a company consisting of 200 men on the northern Aleutian Islands [inhabited by the "tooth people"] to procure sea lion and walrus ivory and he set up the headquarters of that company on the island of Unalaska.

His aim in establishing this company was to lay claim to all the Aleutian Islands and to the islands to the north in Bering Strait as well as those bewteen the Chukotsk Peninsula on the Asian side and the American mainland opposite. He did this in order to establish trade with the natives and to build forts and organize settlements wherever possible, so as to prevent envious foreigners who procure rich furs from the islanders in exchange for trifles from coming here.

13. From that time until now Shelikhov built eleven ships to service these enterprises. In 1790 one of the ships was lost near Unalaska.

14. In 1794, in order to improve the operation of these enterprises, he established a company office in Irkutsk.

The total assets of the company, including property and goods, exceeded 1,500,000 rubles. He drew up specific rules on how the assets and the enterprise should be governed, under his own direct supervision.

In the midst of all this organizational activity, he died in 1795. In accordance with his will I assumed responsibility for running these companies . . .

Reference: TsGAVMF SSSR, f. 198, op. 1, d. 79, 11. 233–238.
See: N. N. Bashkina et al, eds. *Rossiia i SShA: stanovlenie otnoshenii 1765–1815* (Moscow: 1980), 208–209.

86

JANUARY 11, 1799

A REPORT TO EMPEROR PAUL I FROM THE COMMERCE COLLEGE CON-
CERNING A MERGER OF THE SHELIKHOV-GOLIKOV COMPANY AND THE
MYLNIKOV COMPANY TO FORM A UNITED FUR TRADING COMPANY.

Prince [Aleksei B.] Kurakin, former Procurator General and
Actual Privy Councillor, on August 7, 1797 submitted to the
President of this College a report based on Your Imperial Majesty's instructions concerning the desire of certain citizens of
Irkutsk to organize an American company patterned after the
existing Shelikhov-Golikov Company, for the purpose of hunting
furbearing animals in America. The instruction reads:

> The present company, as well as any company to be orga-
> nized in the future, is to be under the direction of the Com-
> merce College, with the proviso that no one may organize a
> similar enterprise without the consent of the present com-
> pany, and there must be a mutually binding agreement
> beforehand.

The information regarding this matter which Prince Kurakin
sent to the college included a letter he had received from the former Civil Governor of Irkutsk, Privy Councillor [Ivan O.] Seli-
fontov, with four proposals from merchants from Irkutsk and
other towns; a memorandum on Japanese trade which he appended to Your Imperial Majesty's report; a letter he had received
from Irkutsk Governor and Privy Councillor [Ilarion T.] Nagel,
with his report to Your Imperial Majesty; and his own cover letter,
appended to the Imperial report, concerning harm which might
result from having a number of companies in America, and benefits that could result if they joined forces.

Following Imperial instructions, the Commerce College reviewed this information as well as material from the archive of the
former commission on commerce. The Commerce College found
the information wholly inadequate to enable it to reach a judgment on this matter. Consequently, on September 7 the College
requested additional information from the Irkutsk governor, as
well as navigational charts from voyages in the North Pacific. It

also requested the governor to send proposals concerning new projects there; historical documents from former participants and from those presently involved in hunting there; mutual agreements and detailed descriptions of all hunting, trade, settlements and fortifications on the mainland of Northwest America and on the islands in that ocean; information about persons desiring to organize a company at the present time, with their terms and regulations; information on other promyshlenniks, such as their numbers and the current status of their hunting and trading; and finally, information concerning the recent attempt by Irkutsk merchants to open trade with Japan.

In implementing this, the President of the College reviewed the matter and on September 9 forwarded to the College a copy of a report from Irkutsk Governor Nagel which had been sent to His Imperial Majesty concerning the American trading company recently organized in Irkutsk. He also sent copies of two agreements contracted between them in accordance with the Imperial decree and requested the College's comments.

That same day the Commerce College had the pleasure of reporting to Your Imperial Majesty that it considered it useful to organize this company if the provisions relating to its management, to which Shelikhov's widow [Natalia A. Shelikhova] refers in her petition, are based on sound and solid foundations. However, since these two strong companies which have recently merged (one belonging to the honorable citizen of Kursk, Golikov, and the noblewoman Shelikhova, and the other belonging to the Irkutsk merchant, Mylnikov, and his associates) will command a very large part of the fur trade, it would perhaps be beneficial to allow other promyshlenniks who may be involved with them to merge with that company, in accordance with Your Imperial Majesty's permission and by mutual agreement among themselves.

In accordance with the statement from the Procurator General to the President of the College, and pursuant to Your Imperial Majesty's instructions, the Council of the Imperial Court examined this report, endorsed it and proposed that other promyshlenniks be allowed to join that company. The Council instructed the Governor of Irkutsk to invite them all to join that company and to inform them that the required contract was to be drawn up and transmitted for Imperial review and approval; and that by way of official blessing to this venture the Emperor would grant the company the privileges it requested for a period of twenty years.

Since Your Imperial Majesty graciously accepted the opinion of the Council, the Procurator General informed the President of the Commerce College that the College was to contact the Governor of Irkutsk and prepare a report for Imperial approval, setting forth the terms of the privileges which the company should have.

On November 16, in order to implement Your Imperial Majesty's instructions, the College requested of Governor Nagel information needed to prepare this report. On February 25 and March 26, 1798, the College received information from him stating that the present members of this company had given him oral information about the scope and importance of this undertaking, and had asked for enough time to draw up the required contract.

On July 12, Infantry General [Khristofor I.] Treiden, who by then had been appointed Civil Governor of Irkutsk, informed the College that not only had the present company members failed to submit any such document to him, but that there were serious disagreements between them, as well as among promyshlenniks.

The College felt this delay was not just the result of the great distances separating the company members from one another, but was evidence of mutual discord.

Meanwhile the College had not received the information it had requested, which would enable it to reach a judgment on such an important matter, and thus could not issue any basic regulations. Therefore the College felt obligated to ask the Governor again to send them information; they did this on July 19.

At last, on September 27, the College received from the Governor the document which had been adopted by the united company on August 3.

The College immediately examined this document and ascertained that the individuals participating in this company were of unanimous opinion, and that the document provided sufficient regulations to establish the company.

Your Imperial Majesty, however, desired that other promyshlenniks involved in the fur trade also be permitted to join this company. The noblewoman Shelikhova had stated in a report to the President of the College that not only promyshlenniks, but all loyal subjects of Your Imperial Majesty who might wish to join the company would be welcome to do so.

The College, considering Imperial will to be its prime concern, since it still did not have all the requisite information, on October 25 again requested it from the Governor. In order to carry out Your Imperial Majesty's will in the shortest possible time, the College gathered basic missing information wherever it could.

Always protecting the interests of the state, and benefits which might accrue to members of the company now and in the future, the College found it necessary to clarify the above mentioned document by writing regulations to serve as a basis for directing the company. The College hereby submits to Your Imperial Majesty the substance of the most important provisions.

The initial subscribed capital of the company consists of 724,000 rubles divided into 724 shares. This, however, is insufficient to accommodate all who may wish to invest in it. Furthermore, the financing is inadequate for such an ambitious undertaking, especially if it is to be utilized to bring substantial benefit to the Empire.

The College has recently received information which indicates that certain departments of the company have had considerable success and that its capital assets have increased substantially. Consequently the College proposes to make a complete inventory of the Company's property: ships, goods, enterprises and the like. This will be done in conjunction with the shareholders who have signed the present document and own shares from the initial capital investment. By dividing the entire sum by the number of shares presently issued, the value of each share will be calculated. At that time 1,000 shares will be offered for sale at the price determined by the amount of total assets. These shares will be offered to anyone who may wish to invest, except for foreigners who are not permanent Russian citizens.

This company, by virtue of the most gracious privileges granted to it and by the nature of its activity, will be called the Russian American Company.

By these means the College has established the initial rules for evaluating the shares on the basis of its present assets; furthermore, it has offered every Russian subject the right to enjoy

With the merger of the Shelikhov-Golikov Company and the Mylnikov Company, the Russian American Company was formed. The "Russian bear" appeared firmly established in North America. Private collection.

profits from it. Therefore the College believes it is necessary to establish rules pertaining to promyshlenniks who have previously operated in the area and have ships there, and who for some reason do not wish to join the Company. The College believes that if there are such persons, in accordance with the freedom of trade they enjoy under sovereign laws of Your Imperial Majesty, and because they were engaged in that trade long before the founding of this Company, they should be allowed to continue their activity, and reap profits from it, until their ships return to home port. After this time they would not participate in the fur trade under threat of forfeiting all their property to the new Company.

The rest of the articles of these regulations concern the distribution of profits accruing to the Company; the establishment of its main office in Irkutsk where all its affairs will be managed, and of local branch offices in various places under its jurisdiction; the election, oath and duties of its directors; and the right for the Company to amend this contract at some future time if it deems it necessary. All the articles of these regulations are to remain inviolable and are to be put into effect after they have been submitted to the Commerce College for approval.

The College has prepared these regulations and in conformity with them has proposed privileges for this Company in the area described. These privileges pertain to hunting, trade, the discovery of new territories, and include all other benefits stemming from the above. The College is pleased to submit herewith these regulations and the document itself, for the consideration of Your Imperial Majesty. The College also humbly reports that since the regulations governing the establishment of the Company's management stem from the document signed by all the participants, it is only necessary to add information pertaining to the additional shares of new individuals wishing to join the Company. The College believes that in this instance there should be a rule that not only the interests of the individual persons, but the good of the entire state should prevail.

The College believes there is no need to consult the present participating members of the Company concerning this matter. Such a procedure would only result in an enormous loss of time through correspondence over such a great distance, and the opinions received would only reaffirm what has already been set forth in the document itself. Therefore the College takes the liberty of submitting this for resolution by Your Majesty's will.

[Signed]
Petr Soimonov
Ivan Dolinskii
Antonii Kashcharev
Petr Litke
Petr Ilinskii
Fedosei Paikov
Sergei Benevolenskii
Iakov Beliavskii
Davyd Voronovskii
Secretary,   Mikhail Blagoskolnov

Reference: AVPR, f. RAK, d. 130, 11. 1–6 ob.
See: N. N. Bashkina et al., eds. *Rossiia i SShA: stanovlenie otnoshenii 1765–1815* (Moscow: 1980), 212–215.

SELECTED
BIBLIOGRAPHY

Bibliographies

Kerner, Robert J. *Northeast Asia: A Selected Bibliography. Contributions to the Bibliography of the Relations of China, Russia and Japan, with Special Reference to Korea, Manchuria, Mongolia and Eastern Siberia in Oriental and European Languages.* 2 vols. Berkeley, 1939.

Lada-Mocarski, Valerian. *Bibliography of Books on Alaska Published before 1868.* New Haven, 1969.

Sokolov, A. P. *Russkaia morskaia biblioteka, 1701–1851* . . . [Russian Naval Library, 1701–1851 . . .] St. Petersburg, 1883.

Tomashevskii, V. V. *Materialy k bibliografii Sibiri i Dalnego Vostoka (XV-pervaia polovina XIX veka)* [Sources for a Bibliography of Siberia and the Far East (Fifteenth to the first Half of the Nineteenth Century)]. Vladivostok, 1957.

Wickersham, James. *A Bibliography of Alaskan Literature 1724–1924.* Cordova, Alaska, 1927.

Sources

Andreev, A. I., ed. *Russkie otkrytiia v Tikhom okeane i v servnoi Amerike v XVIII veke* [Russian Discoveries in the Pacific Ocean and in North America in the Eighteenth Century]. Moscow, 1948.

——, ed. *Russkie otkrytiia v Tikhom okeane i v severnoi Amerike v XVIII–XIX vekakh: Sbornik materialov.* Moscow-Leningrad, 1944. Translated by Carl Ginsburg: *Russian Discoveries in the Pacific and in North America in the Eighteenth and Nineteenth Centuries: A Collection of Materials.* Ann Arbor, 1952.

Bartnev, P., ed. *Arkhiv Kniazia Vorontsova* [The Archive of Prince Vorontsov]. Vol. 24. Moscow, 1880.

Bashkina, N. N., et al., eds. *Rossiia I SShA: Stanovlenie otnoshenii 1765–1815* [The United States and Russia: The Beginning of Relations 1765–1815]. Published simultaneously in Moscow and Washington, D.C., 1980.

Benyowsky, Mauritius Augustus, Count de. *Memoirs and Travels* . . . . London, 1790.

Broughton, William R. *A Voyage of Discovery to the North Pacific Ocean* . . . . London, 1804.

Buache de la Neuville, Jean Nicolas. *Memoire sur les pays de l'Asie et de l'Amérique, sitúes au nord de la Mer du Sud* . . . Paris, 1775.

Cook, James and James King. *A Voyage to the Pacific Ocean* . . . *in his Majesty's Ships the "Resolution" and "Discovery," in the Years 1776, 1777, 1778, 1779, and 1780.* 3 vols. London, 1784.

————. *The Voyage of the "Resolution" and "Discovery," 1776–80.* J.D. Beaglehole, ed. 2 vols. Cambridge, England, 1967.

Divin, V. A., ed. *Russkaia tikhookeanskaia epopeia* [The Russian Epic in the Pacific Ocean]. Khabarovsk, 1979.

Gere, V. *Otnoshenie Leibnitsa k Rossii i Petru Velikomu, po neizdannym bumagam Leibnitsa v Gannoverskoi biblioteke* [The Relationship of Leibnitz to Russia and to Peter the Great, According to Unpublished Papers of Leibnitz in the Hanover Library]. St. Petersburg, 1871.

Gmelin, Johann, G. *Reise durch Sibirien, von den Jahr 1733 bis 1743.* 4 vols. Göttingen, 1751.

Gnucheva, Vera F. *Materialy dlia istorii ekspeditsii Akademii nauk v XVIII i XIX vekakh. Khronologicheskie obzory i opisanie arkhivnykh materialov* [Materials for the History of Expeditions of the Academy of Sciences in the Eighteenth and Nineteenth Centuries. A Chronological Survey and Description of Archival Materials]. Moscow, 1940.

Golder, Frank A. *Bering's Voyages: An Account of the Efforts of the Russians to Learn the Relation of Asia and America.* 2 vols. New York, 1922–1925.

Howay, Frederic W. *A List of Trading Vessels in the Maritime Fur Trade, 1785–1825.* Ottawa, 1930–34. Reprinted, edited by Richard Pierce, Kingston, Ontario, 1973.

Krasheninnikov, Stepan. *Opisanie zemli Kamchatki.* St. Petersburg, 1755. Translated with Introduction and notes by E.A.P. Crownhart Vaughan: *Explorations of Kamchatka, 1735–1741.* Portland, Oregon, 1972.

La Pérouse, Jean François Galaup de. *Voyage de La Pérouse autour du monde* . . . Paris, 1797.

Ledyard, John. *A Journal of Captain Cook's Last Voyage to the Pacific Ocean* . . . Hartford, 1783.

Markov, S. F., ed. *Ekspeditsiia Beringa: Sbornik dokumentov* [The Bering Expedition: A Collection of Documents]. Moscow, 1941.

"Materialy dlia istorii russkikh zaselenii po beregam Vostochnogo okeana" [Materials for the History of Russian Settlements along the Coasts of the Pacific Ocean]. Four fascicles in one, offprinted as a Supplement to *Morskoi Sbornik,* 1861, Nos. 1–4.

Meares, John. *Voyages Made in the Year 1788 and 1789, from China to the North West Coast of America* . . . London, 1790.

Mortimer, George. *Observations and Remarks Made during a Voyage to the* . . . *Fox Islands on the North West Coast of America* . . . London, 1791.

Müller, Gerhard Friedrich. *Bering's Voyages: The Reports From Russia*. Translated by Carol Urness. Fairbanks, 1986.

————. *Lettre d'un Officier de la Marine Russienne à un Seigneur de la Cour Concernant la Carte des Nouvelles Découvertes au Nord de la Mer du Sud et le Mémoire Qui y sert d'Explication, publié par M. de l'Isle a Paris en 1752*. Amsterdam, 1753.

————. *Nachrichten von Seereisen, und zur See gemachten Entdeckungen, die von Russland aus längst de Küsten des eismeeres und auf dem östlichen Weltmeere gegen Japon und America geschehen sind. Zur Erläuterung einer bey der Akademie der Wissenschaften verfertigten Landkarte* [News of the Sea Voyages and Discoveries at Sea that have been made from Russia along the coast of the Arctic Ocean and in the Pacific Toward Japan and America. For clarification a map, preferred by the Academy of Sciences is appended]. St. Petersburg, 1758.

————. *Voyages from Asia to America, for Completing the Discoveries of the Northwest Coast of America. To Which is Prefixed a Summary of the Voyages Made by the Russians on the Frozen Ocean. Serving as an Explanation of a Map of the Russian Discoveries, Published by the Academy of Sciences at Petersburgh*. London, 1764.

Nicholson, William. *The Memoirs and Travels of Mauritius Augustus Count de Benyowsky in Siberia, Kamchatka, Japan, the Liukiu Islands and Formosa from the Translation of His Original Manuscript* (1741–1771). Edited by Captain Pasfield Oliver. London, 1893.

Pallas, Peter Simon, ed. *Neue nordische Beytraege* . . . 7 vols. St. Petersburg and Leipzig, 1781–1796.

Pavlov, P. N., ed. *K istorii Rossiisko-amerikanskoi kompanii: Sbornik dokumentalnykh materialov* [Toward a History of the Russian-American Company: A Collection of Documentary Materials]. Krasnoiarsk, 1957.

Pavlov-Silvanskii, N. *Proekty reform v zapiskakh sovremennikov Petra Velikago* [Projects for Reform in the Memoirs of the Contemporaries of Peter the Great]. St. Petersburg, 1897.

Pierce, Richard A., ed. *The Russian Orthodox Religious Mission in America, 1794–1837. (With Materials concerning the life and works of the Monk Herman, and ethnographic notes by Hieromonk Gedeon)*. Translated by Colin Bearne. Kingston, Ontario, 1978.

Pokrovskii, A. A. *Ekspeditsiia Beringa: Sbornik dokumentov* [The Bering Expedition: a Collection of Documents]. Moscow, 1941.

Portlock, Nathaniel. *A Voyage Round the World; but More Particularly to the North-West Coast of America: Performed in 1785, 1786, 1787, and 1788*. London, 1789.

Russia. Academy of Sciences. *Sobranie sochinenii vybrannykh iz "Mesiatsoslovov" na 1781 god* [Selected Works taken from "Mesiatsoslov" for the Year 1781]. Vol. 4. St. Petersburg, 1790.

Russia. Arkheograficheskaia kommissia. *Dopolneniia k aktam istoricheskim* [Supplement to Historical Acts]. 12 vols. St. Petersburg, 1846–1872.

————. *Pamiatniki sibirskoi istorii XVIII veka* [Memorials of Siberian History of the Eighteenth Century]. 2 vols. St. Petersburg, 1882–1885.

————. *Polnoe sobranie zakonov rossiiskoi imperii s 1649 goda* [Complete Collection of the Laws of the Russian Empire from 1649]. 1st series. 44 vols. St. Petersburg, 1830.

————. *Sbornik dogovorov Rossii s Kitaem 1689–1881* [Collection of Treaties between Russia and China 1689–1881]. St. Petersburg, 1889.

Sarychev, Gavriil A. *Atlas severnoi chasti Vostochnogo okeana* [Atlas of the Northern Part of the Pacific Ocean]. St. Petersburg, 1826.

————. *Puteshestvie flota kapitana Sarycheva po severo-vostochnoi chasti Sibiri, Ledovitomu moriu i Vostochnomu okeanu v prodolzhenii osmi let pri Geograficheskoi i Astronomicheskoi morskoi ekspeditsii . . . kapitana Billingsa s 1785 po 1793 god* [The Travels of Naval Captain Sarychev in the North-eastern Part of Siberia, the Arctic Ocean and the Pacific Ocean during the Eight Years of the Geographic and Astronomical Expedition . . . of Captain Billings from 1785 to 1793]. St. Petersburg, 1802.

————. *Puteshestvie kapitana Billings chrez Chukotskuiu zemliu ot Beringova proliva do Nizhnekolymskogo ostroga i plavanie kapitana Galla na sudne "Chernom Orle" po Severo-vostochnomu okeanu v 1791 godu* [The Travels of Captain Billings across the Chukotsk land from Bering Strait to Lower Kolymsk Ostrog and the Voyage of Captain Hall on the ship *Chernyi Orel* in the North Pacific in 1791]. St. Petersburg, 1811.

Sauer, Martin. *An Account of a Geographical and Astronomical Expedition to the Northern Parts of Russia . . . and of the islands in the Eastern Ocean, Stretching to the American Coast . . .* London, 1802.

Shelikhov, Grigorii I. *Rossiiskago kuptsa Grigoriia Shelikhova stranstvovanniia iz Okhotska po Vostochnomy okeany k Amerikanskim beregam.* [The Journey of the Russian Merchant Grigorii Shelikhov from Okhotsk across the Pacific Ocean to the American Shores]. New edition edited by Boris Polevoi. Khabarovsk, 1971.

Steller, Georg Wilhelm. *Beschreibung von dem Lande Kamtschatka . . .* Frankfurt and Leipzig, 1774.

————. *Reise von Kamtschatka nach Amerika mit dem Kommander-Kapitan Bering . . .* St. Petersburg, 1793.

United States Hydrographic Office. *Sailing Directions, East Coast of Siberia.* Washington, 1951.

Vancouver, George. *A Voyage of Discovery to the North Pacific Ocean and Round the World . . .* 3 vols. London, 1798.

Waxell, Sven. *Vtoraia kamchatskaia ekspeditsiia Vitusa Beringa* [The Second Kamchatka Expedition of Vitus Bering]. Leningrad and Moscow, 1940.

Monographic Literature

Adamov, A. G. *Pervye russkie issledovateli Aliaski* [The First Russian Explorers of Alaska]. Moscow, 1950.

————. *Po neizvedannym putiam: Russkie issledovateli na Aliaske i Kalifornii* [Along Unexplored Ways: Russian Explorers in Alaska and California]. Moscow, 1950.

————. *Shelikhov.* Moscow, 1952.

————. *Shelikhov na Kadiake* [Shelikhov on Kodiak]. Moscow, 1948.

AN SSSR. *The Pacific: Russian Scientific Investigations*. Leningrad, 1926.

Alekseev, A. I. *Bratia Shmalevy* [The Shmalev Brothers]. Magadan, 1958.

————. *Kolumby rosskie* [Russian Columbuses]. Magadan, 1966.

————. *Okhotsk: Kolybel russkogo Tikhookeanskogo flota* [Okhotsk: Cradle of the Russian Pacific Fleet]. Khabarovsk, 1958.

————. *Osvoenie russkimi liudmi Dalnego Vostoka i Russkoi Ameriki do kontsa XIX veka* [The Conquest by the Russian People of the Far East and of Russian America until the end of the Nineteenth Century]. Moscow, 1982.

————. *Syny otvazhnye Rossii* [Brave Sons of Russia]. Magadan, 1970.

————. *Uchenyi Chukcha Nikolai Daurkin* [The Learned Chukchi Nikolai Daurkin]. Magadan, 1961.

Allan, Alexander. *Hunting the Sea Otter*. London, 1910.

Andreev, A. I. *Lomonosov i Krasheninnikov*. Moscow-Leningrad, 1940.

Arkticheskii Nauchno-issledovatelskii Institut. *Russkie morekhody v ledovitom i tikhom okeanakh* [Russian Seafarers in the Arctic and Pacific Oceans]. Moscow-Leningrad, 1952.

Bagrow, Leo. *A History of Russian Cartography up to 1800*. Wolfe Island, Ontario, 1975.

Baker, John N. L. *A History of Geographical Discovery and Exploration*. Boston and New York, 1937.

Bancroft, Hubert H. *History of Alaska, 1730–1885*. San Francisco, 1886.

Barratt, Glynn. *Russia in Pacific Waters, 1715–1825*. Vancouver, 1980.

Belov, Mikhail I. *Arkticheskoe moreplavanie s drevneishikh vremen do serediny XIX veka* [Arctic Seafaring from Ancient Times to the Middle of the Nineteenth Century]. Moscow, 1956.

————, ed. *Puteshestviia i geograficheskie otkrytiia v XV–XIX vv.* [Travels and Geographical Discoveries in the Fifteenth to Nineteenth Centuries]. Leningrad, 1965.

————, ed. *Russkie arkticheskie ekspeditsii XVII–XX vv.* [Russian Arctic Expeditions of the Seventeenth to the Twentieth Centuries]. Leningrad, 1964.

Berg, Lev S. *Istoriia russkikh geograficheskikh otkrytii* [History of Russian Geographical Discoveries]. Moscow, 1962.

————. *Ocherki po istorii russkikh geograficheskikh otkrytii* [Studies on the History of Russian Geographical Discoveries]. Moscow, 1946.

————. *Otkrytie Kamchatki i ekspeditsii Beringa (1725–1742)* [The Discovery of Kamchatka and the Bering Expeditions, 1725–1742]. Moscow-Leningrad, 1946.

Berkh, V. N. *Karta rossiiskikh vladenii v Severnoi Amerike* [Map of the Russian Possessions in North America]. St. Petersburg, 1842.

————. *Khronologicheskaia istoriia otkrytiia aleutskikh ostrovov ili podvigi rossiiskago kupechestva, s prisovokupleniem istoricheskago izvestiia o mekhovoi torgovle*. St. Petersburg, 1823. Translated by Dmitri Krenov, edited by

Richard A. Pierce: *A Chronological History of the Discovery of the Aleutian Islands; or, The Exploits of the Russian Merchants, with a Supplement of Historical Data on the Fur Trade*. Kingston, Ontario, 1974.

——. *Khronologicheskaia istoriia vsekh puteshestvii v severnyia poliarnyia strany* . . . [Chronological History of all the Voyages to the Northern Polar Lands . . .] Part 1. St. Petersburg, 1823.

——. *Pervoe morskoe puteshestvie rossiian, predpriniatoe dlia resheniia geograficheskoi zadachi: Soediniaetsia li Aziia s Amerikoiu?* . . . *pod nachalstvom Flota kapitana l-go ranga Vitusa Beringa* [The First Russian Maritime Voyage Undertaken to Resolve the Geographical Question: Is Asia Joined to America? . . . under the Command of Captain of the First Rank Vitus Bering]. St. Petersburg, 1823.

Black, Joseph Lawrence. *G. F. Müller and the Imperial Russian Academy of Sciences, 1725–1783*. Montreal, 1986.

Bludov, D. N. "Bunt Beniovskogo v Bolsheretskom ostroge" [Benyovsky's Insurrection in Bolsheretsk Ostrog]. In Egor P. Kovelevskii, *Graf Bludov i ego vremia* [Count Bludov and His Times]. St. Petersburg, 1866, pp. 200–218.

Bodnarskii, Mitrofan S. *Velikii severnyi morskii put: Istoriko-geograficheskii ocherk otkrytiia severo-vostochnogo prokhoda* [The Great Northern Sea Route: a Historical-Geographical study of the Discovery of the Northeastern Passage]. Moscow and Leningrad, 1926.

Bolkhovitinov, Nikolai N. *Stanovlenie russko-amerikanskikh otnoshenii, 1775–1815*. Moscow, 1966. Translated by Elena Levin: *The Beginnings of Russian-American Relations, 1775–1815*. Cambridge, 1975.

Brooks, Alfred H. *Blazing Alaska's Trails*. Washington, D. C., 1953.

Buache, Philippe. *Considerations géographiques et physiques sur les nouvelles découvertes au nord de la Grand Mer, appellée vulgairement la Mer du Sud; avec des Cartes qui y fond relatives*. Paris, 1753.

Burney, James. *A Chronological History of the North-eastern Voyages of Discovery; and of the Early Navigations of the Russians*. London, 1819.

Cahen, Gaston. *Histoire des relations de la Russie avec la Chine sous Pierre le grand (1689–1730)*. Paris, 1912.

Cook, Warren L. *Flood Tide of Empire: Spain and the Pacific Northwest, 1543–1819*. New Haven and London, 1973.

Coxe, William. *Account of the Russian discoveries between Asia and America*. London, 1780.

Dall, William H. *Early Explorations to the Regions of the Bering Sea and Strait*. Washington, 1891.

Delisle, Joseph N. *Explication de la carte des nouvelles découvertes au nord de la mer sud*. Paris, 1752.

——. *Nouvelles cartes des découvertes de l'Amiral de Fonté, et autre navigateurs Espagnols, Portugais, Anglois, Hollandois, François & Russes, dans les mers septentrionales* . . . Paris, 1753.

Divin, Vasilii A. *K beregam Ameriki; plavaniia i issledovannia M. S. Gvozdeva, pervootkryvatelia severo-zapadnoi Ameriki* [To the Shores of America; the Navigations and Explorations of M. S. Gvozdev, the First Discoverer of Northwestern America]. Moscow, 1956.

———. *Russkie moreplavaniia na tikhom okeane v XVIII veke* [Russian Seafaring on the Pacific Ocean in the Eighteenth Century]. Moscow, 1971.

———. *Velikii russkii moreplavatel A. I. Chirikov* [The Great Russian Navigator A. I. Chirikov]. Moscow, 1953.

Efimov, Aleksei V., ed. *Atlas geograficheskikh otkrytii v Sibiri i v severo-zapadnoi Amerike XVII–XVIII vv.* [Atlas of Geographical Discoveries in Siberia and Northwestern America in the Seventeenth and Eighteenth centuries]. Moscow, 1964.

———. *Iz istorii russkikh ekspeditsii na Tikhom okeane (pervaia polovina XVIII veka)* [History of Russian Expeditions on the Pacific Ocean (First Half of the Eighteenth Century)]. Moscow, 1948.

———. *Iz istorii velikikh russikikh geograficheskikh otkrytii v severnom ledovitom i tikhom okeanakh XVII-pervaia polovina XVIII v.* [History of the Great Russian Geographical Discoveries in the Arctic and Pacific Oceans from the Seventeenth to the First Half of the Eighteenth Century]. Moscow, 1950.

Engel, Samuel. *Anmerkungen über den Theil von Cap. Cooks Reise-Relation, so die Meerenge zwischen Asia und Amerika ansiehet . . .* [Observations Concerning the Portion of Captain Cook's Voyages Pertaining to the Strait Between Asia and America] [n.p.], 1780.

———. *Mémoires et observations géographiques et critiques sur la situation des pays septentrionaux de l'Asie et de l'Amérique, d'après les relations les plus recentes . . .* Lausanne, 1765.

———. *. . . Neuer Versuch über die Lage der nördlichen Gegenden von Asia und Amerika . . .* [A New Attempt to Discover the Position of Northern Regions between Asia and America]. Basel, 1777.

Erdmann, H. *Alaska: Ein Beitrag zur Geschichte nordischer Kolonisation* [Alaska: A Treatise on the History of Northern Colonization] Berlin, 1909.

Evteev, O. A. *Pervye russkie geodezisty na Tikhom okeane* [The First Russian Geodesists on the Pacific Ocean]. Moscow, 1950.

Fainsberg, E. Ia. *Russko-iaponskie otnosheniia v 1697–1875 gg.* [Russo-Japanese Relations 1697–1875]. Moscow, 1960.

Farrar, V. J. *The Annexation of Russian America to the United States.* Washington, 1937.

———. *An Elementary Syllabus of Alaskan History.* Washington, 1924.

———. *The Purchase of Alaska.* Washington, 1934.

Fedorova, Svetlana G. *Russkoe naselenie Aliaski i Kalifornii, konets XVIIIv.—1867g.* Moscow, 1971. Translated and edited by Richard A. Pierce and Alton S. Donnelly: *The Russian Population in Alaska and California, Late Eighteenth Century—1867.* Kingston, Ontario, 1973.

Fel, Sergei E. *Kartografiia Rossii XVIII veka* [The Cartography of Russia of the Eighteenth Century]. Moscow, 1960.

Fisher, Raymond H. *Bering's Voyages: Whither and Why?* Seattle and London, 1977.

Fradkin, N. G. *S. P. Krasheninnikov*. Moscow, 1951.

Friis, Herman R., ed. *The Pacific Basin: a History of its Geographical Exploration*. New York, 1967.

Gibson, James R. *Feeding the Russian Fur Trade: Provisionment of the Okhotsk Seaboard and the Kamchatka Peninsula, 1639–1856*. Madison and London, 1969.

Gnucheva, Vera F. *Geograficheskii departament Akademii nauk XVIII veka* [The Geographical Department of the Academy of Sciences in the Eighteenth Century]. Moscow, 1946.

Goldenberg, L. A. *Fedor Ivanovich Soimonov, 1692–1780*. Moscow, 1966.

Golder, Frank A. *Russian Expansion on the Pacific, 1641–1850: An Account of the Earliest and Later Expeditions Made by the Russians along the Pacific Coast of Asia and North America, Including Some Related Expeditions to the Arctic Regions*. Cleveland, 1914.

Grekov, V. I. *Ocherki iz istorii russkikh geograficheskikh issledovanii v 1725–65 gg.* [Notes on the History of Russian Geographical Explorations 1725–1765]. Moscow, 1960.

Gsovski, V. *Russian Administration of Alaskan Natives*. Washington, 1950.

du Halde, Jean Baptiste [de la Compagnie de Jesus]. *Description géographique, historique, chronologique, politique, et physique de l'Empire de la Chine et de la Tatarie Chinoise*. 4 vols. Paris, 1735.

Harrison, John A. *The Founding of the Russian Empire in Asia and America*. Gainesville, 1971.

———. *Japan's Northern Frontier. A Preliminary Study in Colonization and Expansion with Special Reference to the Relations of Japan and Russia*. Gainesville, 1953.

Hrdlicka, Ales. *The Aleutian and Commander Islands and Their Inhabitants*. Philadelphia, 1945.

———. *Anthropology of Kodiak Island*. Philadelphia, 1944.

Ianikov, G. V. *Velikaia severnaia ekspeditsiia* [The Great Northern Expedition]. Moscow, 1949.

Jeffreys, Thomas, ed. *Voyages from Asia to America, for Completing the Discoveries of the North West Coast of America. To Which is Prefixed, a Summary of the Voyages Made by the Russians . . . Serving as an Explanation of a Map of the Russian Discoveries, Published by the Academy of Sciences at Petersburgh*. London, 1761

Jochelson, W. *History, Ethnology and Anthropology of the Aleut*. Washington, 1933.

Khlebnikov, Kyrill T. *Zhizhneopisanie Aleksandra Andreevicha Baranova, glavnogo pravitelia rossiiskikh kolonii v Amerike*. St. Petersburg, 1835. Translated by Melvin Ricks in *The Earliest History of Alaska*, Anchorage, 1963; and by Colin Bearne, edited by Richard A. Pierce: *Baranov: Chief Manager of the Russian Colonies in America*. Kigston, 1973.

Kushnarev, Evgenii V. *V poiskakh proliva: Pervaia kamchatskaia ekspeditsiia, 1725–1730*. Leningrad, 1976. Translated by E. A. P. Crownhart-Vaughan: *In Search of the Strait: The First Kamchatka Expedition, 1725–1730*. Oregon Historical Society, in press.

Lagus, Vilhelm. *Erik Laksman. Ego zhizn, puteshestviia, issledovaniia i perepiska* [Eric Laxman. His Life, Travels, Explorations and Correspondence]. St. Petersburg, 1890.

Lantzeff, George V. and Richard A. Pierce. *Eastward to Empire: Exploration and Conquest on the Russian Open Frontier, to 1750*. Montreal and London, 1973.

Lauridsen, Peter. *Vitus Bering: the Discoverer of Bering Strait*. [Translated from the Danish by Julius O. Olson]. Chicago, 1889.

Lebedev, Dmitrii M. *Geografiia v Rossii petrovskogo vremeni* [Geography in Russia in Petrine Times]. Moscow and Leningrad, 1950.

──────. *Ocherki po istorii geografii v Rossii XVIII v. (1725–1800 gg.)* [Essays on the History of Geography in Russia in the Eighteenth Century (1725–1800)]. Moscow, 1957.

──────. *Plavanie A. I. Chirikova na paketbote "Sv. Pavel" k poberezhiam Ameriki, s prilozheniem sudago zhurnala 1741 g.* [The Voyage of A. I. Chirikov on the Packetboat "St. Paul" to the Coast of America, with the Inclusion of the Ship's Journal for 1741]. Moscow, 1951.

──────. and Vasilii A. Esakov. *Russkie geograficheskie otkrytiia i issledovaniia s drevnykh vremen do 1917 goda* [Russian Geographical Discoveries and Explorations from Ancient Times to 1917]. Moscow, 1971.

Lensen, George A. *Report from Hokkaido: The Remains of Russian Culture in Northern Japan*. Hakodate, 1954.

──────. *The Russian Push toward Japan: Russo-Japanese Relations, 1697–1875*. Princeton, N. J., 1959.

Liapunova, Roza G. *Etnografiia narodov tikhookeanskogo severa Ameriki: Russkie i sovetskie issledovaniia* [The Ethnography of the Peoples of the North Pacific Regions of America: Russian and Soviet Research]. Leningrad, 1979.

──────. *Ocherki po etnografii Aleutov (Konets XVIII–pervaia polovina XIX v.)* [Essays on the Ethnography of the Aleuts (Late Eighteenth to the First Half of the Nineteenth Century)]. Leningrad, 1975.

Lomonosov, Mikhail V. *Trudy po russkoi istorii, obshchestvenno-ekonomicheskim voprosam i geografii, 1747–65g.* [Works on Russian History, Socio-economic Questions and Geography, 1745–65]. Vol. 6 of *Polnoe sobranie sochinenii* [Complete Collection of Works]. Moscow, 1952.

Lower, J. Arthur. *Ocean of Destiny: A Concise History of the North Pacific, 1500–1978*. Vancouver, B.C., 1978.

Magidovich, I. I. *Istoriia otkrytiia i issledovaniia severnoi Ameriki* [History of the Discovery and Exploration of North America]. Moscow, 1962.

Makarova, Raisa V. *Russkie na Tikhom okeane vo vtoroi polovine XVIII v.* Moscow 1968. Translated and edited by Richard A. Pierce and Alton S. Donnelly: *Russians on the Pacific, 1743–99*. Kingston, Ontario, 1975.

Marbault, E. *Essai sur le Commerce de Russie avec l'Histoire de Ses Découvertes*. Amsterdam, 1777.

Markov, Aleksei I. *Russkie na Vostochnom okeane . . .* [The Russians on the Pacific Ocean . . .]. Moscow, 1849.

——. *Vostochnaia Sibir, Aziia, Okhotsk, i russkie vladeniia v Amerike* [Eastern Siberia, Asia, Okhotsk and the Russian Possessions in America]. St. Petersburg, 1856.

Markov, Sergei N. *Letopis Aliaski* [The Chronicle of Alaska]. Moscow, 1948.

——. *Zemnoi Krug: Kniga o zemleprokhodtsakh i morekhodakh* [The Terrestrial Globe: A Book about Overland and Maritime Explorers]. Moscow, 1976.

Masterson, James R. and Helen Brower, eds. *Bering's Successors, 1745–80: Contributions of Peter Simon Pallas to the History of Russian Exploration toward Alaska*. Seattle, 1948.

Materialy dlia istorii russkago flota [Materials for a History of the Russian Navy]. 17 vols. St. Petersburg, 1865–1905.

Müller, Gerhard F. *Istoriia Akademii nauk G. F. Millera, s prodolzheniiami I. G. Shtrittera (1725–43)* [The History of the Academy of Sciences by F. G. Müller, with a sequel by J. G. Stritter (1725–43)]. St. Petersburg, 1890.

Novlianskaia, Mariia G. *Ivan Kirilovich Kirilov: geograf XVIII veka* [Ivan Kirilovich Kirilov: Geographer of the Eighteenth Century]. Leningrad, 1964.

Okun, Semen B. *Rossiisko-amerikanskaia kompaniia*. Moscow and Leningrad, 1939. Translated by Carl Ginsburg: *The Russian American Company*. Cambridge, Massachusetts, 1951.

Pallas, Peter Simon. *O rossiiskikh otkrytiiakh na moriakh mezhdu Azieiu i Amerikoiu* [Concerning the Russian Discoveries in the Seas between Asia and America]. Vol. IV of *Sobranie Sochinenii* . . . St. Petersburg, 1790.

Parker, Robert C. *Contributions of Peter Pallas to Science and Exploration in Russia*. M.A. Thesis, Portland, 1973.

Pasetskii, V. M. *Vitus Bering, 1681–1741*. Moscow, 1982.

Perevalov, V. A. *Lomonosov i arktika: iz istorii geograficheskikh nauk i geograficheskikh otkrytii* [Lomonosov and the Arctic: From the History of Geographical Sciences and Geographical Discoveries]. Moscow and Leningrad, 1949.

Petersen, Josef. *Vitus Bering, der Seefahrer*. Translated from the Danish by H. Kurtzweil. Hamburg, 1947.

Pilder, H. *Die Russisch-Amerikanischer Handels-Kompanie bis 1825*. Berlin, 1914.

Polevoi, Boris P. *Grigorii Shelikhov—"Kolumb rosskii"* [Grigorii Shelikhov—The "Russian Columbus"]. Magadan, 1960.

Polonsky, A. S. *Kurily* [The Kurils]. St. Petersburg, 1871.

Poniatowski, Michel. *Histoire de la Russe, d'Amérique et de l'Alaska*. Paris, 1958.

Ramming, Martin. *Reisen schiffbrüchiger Japaner im XVIII Jahrhundert* [Japanese Sea Voyages in the 18th century]. Berlin, 1931.

Raskin, N., and I. Shafranovskii. *Erik Gustavovich Laksman*. Leningrad, 1971.

Ratner-Shternberg, S. A. *Otdel Severnoi Ameriki—Putevoditel po muzeiu antropologii i etnografii AN SSSR* [The North American Department: A Guidebook to the Museum of Anthropology and Ethnography of the Academy of Sciences of the USSR]. Leningrad, 1929.

Robert de Vaugondy, Didier. *Lettre de M. Robert de Vaugondy a M.—au Sujet d'une Carte Systematique des pays Septentrionaux de l'Asie & de l'Amérique.* Paris, 1768.

————. *Mémoire sur les Pays de l'Asie et de l'Amérique sitúes au Nord de la Mer du Sud.* Paris, 1774.

Scherer, Jean-Benoit. *Récherche Historiques et Géographique sur le Nouveau-Monde.* Paris, 1777.

Senchenko, I. A., ed. *Issledovateli Sakhalina i Kuril* [Explorers of Sakhalin and the Kurils]. Iuzhno-Sakhalinsk, 1961.

Sherwood, Morgan B. *Alaska and Its History.* Washington, 1967.

Shirina, D. A. *Letopis ekspeditsii Akademii nauk v Severo-Vostok Azii v dorevoliutsionnyi period* [Chronicles of Expeditions of the Academy of Sciences to Northeast Asia during the Pre-revolutionary Period]. Novosibirsk, 1983.

Siebert, Erna G. *North American Indian Art.* London and New York, 1969.

Skalkovskii, K. A. *Russkaia tórgovlia v Tikhom okeane* [Russian Trade in the Pacific Ocean]. St. Petersburg, 1883.

Slodkevich, V. S. *Iz istorii otkrytiia i osvoeniia russkimi severo-zapadnoi Ameriki* [From the History of the Discovery and Conquest of Northwest America by the Russians]. Petrozavodsk, 1956.

Smith, Barbara. *A Preliminary Survey of Documents in the Archives of the Russian Orthodox Church in Alaska.* Boulder, Colorado, 1974.

————. *Russian Orthodoxy in Alaska; a History, Inventory and Analysis of the Church Archives in Alaska, with an Annotated Bibliography.* Alaska Historical Commission, 1980.

Solovev, A. I. *Kurilskie ostrova* [The Kuril Islands]. Moscow-Leningrad, 1945.

————. *Severnaia ekspeditsiia, 1733–1743* [The Northern Expedition, 1733–1743]. St. Petersburg, 1861.

Sparks, Jared. *The Life of John Ledyard, the American Traveler.* Cambridge, 1828.

Staehlin, Jakob von Stocksburg. *Das von den Russen in den Jahren 1765, 66, 67, entdekte nordliche Insel-meer, zwischen Kamtschatka und Nordamerika . . .* [Islands the Russians have Discovered in 1765, 66, 67 in the North Sea, Between Kamchatka and America]. Stuttgart, 1774.

Stejneger, Leonhard. *Georg Wilhelm Steller, the Pioneer of Alaskan Natural History.* Cambridge, Mass., 1936.

Stephan, John J. *The Kuril Islands, Russo-Japanese Frontiers in the Pacific.* Oxford, 1974.

Tebenkov, Mikhail D. *Atlas severo-zapadnykh beregov Ameriki ot Beringova proliva do mysa Korrientes i ostrovov Aleutskikh . . .* [Atlas of the Northwest Coasts of America from Bering Strait to Cape Corrientes and the Aleutian Islands]. St. Petersburg, 1852.

Tikhmenev, P. A. *Istoricheskoe obozrenie obrazovaniia Rossiisko-amerikanskoi kompanii i deistviia ee do nastoiashchego vremeni* [Historical Survey of the Formation and Activities of the Russian-American Company to the Present Time]. 2 vols. St. Petersburg, 1861, 1863. Translated and edited by Richard A. Pierce and Alton S. Donnelly: *A History of the Russian-American Company*. Seattle and London, 1978.

Tompkins, Stuart R. *Alaska: Promyshlennik and Sourdough*. Norman, Oklahoma, 1945.

Vakhtin, Vasilii V. *Russkie truzheniki moria. Pervaia morskaia ekspeditsiia Beringa dlia resheniia voprosa, soediniaetsia li Aziia s Amerikoi* [Russian Toilers of the Sea. The first Bering Maritime Expedition to Resolve the Question whether Asia is Joined to America]. St. Petersburg, 1890.

Vdovin, Innokentii S. *Ocherki istorii i etnografi Chukchei* [Studies of the History and Ethnography of the Chukchi]. Moscow and Leningrad, 1965.

Veselago, F. *Kratkaia istoriia russkogo flota* [A Brief History of the Russian Navy]. Moscow-Leningrad, 1939.

Vila Vilar, Enriqueta. *Los Rusos en America*. Seville, 1966.

Vize, Vladimir Iu. *Russkie poliarnye morekhody iz promyshlennykh, torgovykh i sluzhilykh liudei XVII–XIX vv. Biograficheskii slovar* [Russian Polar Seafarers of the Seventeenth to Nineteenth Centuries: Promyshlenniks, Traders and Servitors: A Biographical Dictionary]. Moscow and Leningrad, 1948.

Volkl, Ekkehard. *Russland und Latin-amerika, 1741–1841*. Wiesbaden, 1968.

Wagner, Henry R. *The Cartography of the Northwest Coast of America to the Year 1800*. 2 vols. Berkeley, 1937.

Watrous, Stephen D., ed. *John Ledyard's Journey through Russia and Siberia, 1787–1788: The Journal and Selected Documents*. Madison, 1966.

Yoshino, Sazuko. *Rokoku kikan no hyoru-min Kodayu* [The Castaway Kodayu Who returned from Russia]. Tokyo, 1924.

Znamenskii, S. *V poiskakh Iaponii. Iz istorii russkikh geograficheskikh otkrytii i morekhodstva v Tikhom okeane* [In Search of Japan. History of Russian Geographical Discovery and Navigation in the Pacific Ocean]. Vladivostok, 1929.

Zubkova, Z. *Aleutskie ostrova* [The Aleutian Islands]. Moscow, 1948.

Zubov, Nikolai. N. *Otechestvenny moreplavateli-issledovateli morei i okeanov* [The Nation's Navigator-Explorers of the Seas and Oceans]. Moscow, 1954.

Periodical Literature

Andreev, A. I. "Ekspeditsiia Beringa" [The Bering Expedition] in *Izvestiia Vsesoiuznogo Geograficheskogo Obshchestva* [hereafter *IVGO*], Vol. 75, no. 2 (March-April, 1943), pp. 3–44.

———. "Ekspeditsii na Vostok do Beringa (v sviazi s kartografiei Sibiri pervoi chetverti XVIII veka)" [Expeditions to the East before Bering (in Regard to the Cartography of Siberia in the First Quarter of the

Eighteenth Century)] in *Trudy Moskovskogo Gosudarstvennogo Istoriko-arkhivnogo Instituta*, Vol. 2 (1946), pp. 183–202.

———. "G. F. Miller o Vtoroi Kamchatskoi Ekspeditsii" [G. F. Müller on the Second Kamchatka Expedition] in *IVGO*, Vol. 91 [January-February, 1959), pp. 3–16.

———. "Novye materialy o russkikh plavaniiakh i otkrytiiakh v Severnom Ledovitom i Tikhom okeanakh v 18–19 v." [New Materials on Russian Voyages and Discoveries in the Arctic and Pacific oceans in the Eighteenth and Nineteenth Centuries] in *IVGO*, Vol. 75, no. 5 (1943).

———. "Pervye issledovateli Aleutskikh ostrovov" [First Explorers of the Aleutian Islands] in *Istoricheskie Zapiski*, Vol. 68 (1961).

———. "Rol russkogo voenno-morskogo flota v geograficheskikh otkrytiiakh XVIII veka" [The Role of the Russian Navy in the Geographical Discoveries of the Eighteenth Century] in *Morskoi Sbornik*, 1947, No. 4.

———. "Russkie otkrytiia v Tikhom okeane v pervoi polovine XVIII veka" [Russian Discoveries in the Pacific Ocean in the First Half of the eighteenth Century] in *IVGO*, Vol. 75, No. 3 (May-June, 1943), pp.35–52.

———. "Vtoraia Kamchatskaia ekspeditsiia 1733–1743 gg." [The Second Kamchatka Expedition, 1733–1743] in *IVGO*, Vol. 76, No. 1 (1944).

———. "Zhizn i nauchnye trudy Stepana Petrovicha Krasheninnikova" [The Life and Scholarly Works of Stepan Petrovich Krasheninnikov] in *Sovetskii Sever*, 1939.

Arkanev, A. "Russkie na Tikhom okeane: obzor literatury" [The Russians on the Pacific Ocean: a Survey of the Literature in *Nauka i Zhizn*, 1949, No. 3.

Baer, Karl E. von. "Zaslugi Petra velikago po chasti rasprostraniia geograficheskikh poznanii" [The Services of Peter the Great in Spreading Geographical Knowledge] in *Zapiski Imperatorskago Geograficheskago Obshchestva*, Vol. 3, 1849, pp. 217–53; Vol. 4, 1850, pp. 260–83.

Bagrow, Leo. "A Few Remarks on the Amur, Tartar Strait, Sakhalin," in *Imago Mundi*, Vol. 12, 1955, pp. 152–56.

Bartenev, Petr. "Graf Vladislavich o Kitae v XVIII veke" [Count Vladislavich on China in the Eighteenth Century] in *Russkii Arkhiv*, Vol. 2, 1900, pp. 572–80.

Baskin, Semen I. "Bolshoi chertezh kamchadalskoi zemli" [The Large Sketch-Map of the Kamchatka Land] in *IVGO*, Vol. 81, no. 2 (March–April, 1949), pp. 226–38.

———. "Puteshestvie Evreinova i Luzhina v Kurilskii arkhipelag (1719–22)" [The Voyage of Evreinov and Luzhin to the Kuril Archipelago (1719–22)] in *IVGO*, Vol. 84, No. 4 (July-August, 1952), pp. 363–79.

Berg, Lev S. "Ekspeditsiia Beringa" [The Bering Expedition] in *IVGO*, Vol. 74 (1942), pp. 5–15.

———. "Iz istorii otkrytiia Aleutskikh ostrovov" [From the History of the Discovery of the Aleutian Islands] in *Zemlevedenie*, Vol. 26, Nos. 2 and 3, 1924.

————. "Lomonosov: pervoe russkoe plavanie" [Lomonosov: the First Russian Voyage] in *IVGO* , Vol. 72, No. 6 (November-December, 1940), pp. 713–30.

Bering, Vitus J. "Donesenie Flota Kapitana Beringa ob ekspeditsii ego k vostochnym beregam Sibiri" [The Report of Navy Captain Bering Concerning His Expedition to the East Coast of Siberia] in *Zapiski Voenno-topograficheskago Depo*, Vol. 10 (1847), pp. 69–75.

Berkh, Vasilii. "Izvestiie o mekhovoi torgovle proizvodimoi Rossiianami pri ostrovakh Kurilskikh, Aleutskikh i servo-zapadnom beregu Ameriki" [Information on the Russian Fur Trade along the Kuril and Aleutian Islands and on the Northwest Coast of America] in *Syn Otechestva*, 1823, no. 88, pp. 243–64; 1823, no. 89, pp. 97–106.

————. "Pobeg grafa Beniovskogo" [The Escape of Count Benyovsky] in *Syn Otechestva*, Vols. 27 and 28, 1821.

Blashke, E. "Neskolko zamechanii o plavanii v baidarkakh i o lisevskikh aleutakh" [Some Remarks on voyaging in Baidarkas and on the Fox (Island) Aleuts] in *Morskoi Sbornik*, 1848, No. 3, pp. 115–24 and No. 4, pp. 160–65.

Bolkhovitinov, Nikolai N. "Zarubezhnye issledovaniia o russkoi Amerike" [Foreign Research on Russian America] in *SShA*, 1985, No. 4, pp. 87–95.

Breitfuss, L. "Early Maps of Northeastern Asia and the Lands around the North Pacific" in *Imago Mundi*, 1939, No. 3, pp. 87–99.

Burney, James. "A Memoir on the Geography of the North-eastern Part of Asia, and on the Question of Whether Asia and America are Contiguous, or Are Separated by the Sea" in *Philsophical Transactions of the Royal Society of London*, no. 108, 1818, Part 1, pp. 9–23.

Chernenko, M. B. "Puteshestviia po chukotskoi zemle i plavanie na Aliaske Kazachego sotnika Ivana Kobeleva v 1779 i 1789–1791 gg." [Travels through the Chukotsk Land and a Voyage to Alaska made by the Cossack Sotnik Ivan Kobelev in the Year 1779 and 1789–1791] in *Letopis Severa*, Vol. 2, 121–41.

Dall, William H. "A Critical Review of Bering's First Expedition, 1725–1730, together with a Translation of his Original Report on It" in *The National Geographic Magazine*, 1891, No. 2, pp. 111–166.

————. "Notes on an Original Manuscript Chart of Bering's Expedition of 1725–30, and on an Original Manuscript Chart of His Second Expedition; together with a Summary of a Journal of the First Expedition, Kept by Petr Chaplin . . . " in *Report of the Superintendent of the U.S. Coast and Geodetic Survey* . . . 1890, Appendix no. 19, pp. 759–74.

Divin, V. A. "Vklad russkikh moriakov v otkrytie severnoi chasti Tikhogo okeana v 17–18 vv." [The Contribution of Russian Seamen in Opening the Northern Part of the Pacific Ocean" in a supplement to *Morskoi Sbornik*, 1952, No. 1.

————. "Vtoraia Sibirsko-tikhookeanskaia ekspeditsiia i voprosy khoziaistvennogo osvoeniia Dalnego Vostoka" [The Second Siberia-Pacific Expedition and Questions on the Economic development of the Far East] in *Letopis Severa*, 1957, no. 11.

Domning, D. P. "Steller's Sea Cow and the Origin of North Pacific Aboriginal Whaling" in *Syesis*, 1972, No. 5, pp. 187–89.

Dvoichenko-Markova, E. "John Ledyard and the Russians" in *The Russian Review*, 1952, Vol. 11.

Dzeniskevich, Galina I. "Ecology and Chronology of Athapascan Settlement on the Southern Coast of Alaska" in *North America Indian Studies*, offprint from Forum 1, Götingen, n.d., pp. 123–28.

———. "Okhotnichii i rybolovnyi promysly u Tanaina (Aliaska) v XIX v." [Hunting and Fishing Trade among the Tanainas (Alaska) in the Nineteenth Century] in *Sbornik Muzeia Antropologii i Etnografii*, Vol. 31, 1975, pp. 52–68.

———. "Vklad russkikh puteshestvennikov v etnograffiu Atapaskov Aliaski (XVIII–XIX vv)" [The Contribution of Russian Travelers to the Ethnography of the Athapascans of Alaska (Eighteenth to Nineteenth Centuries)] in *Trudy Instituta Etnografii im. N. N. Miklukho-Maklaia*, New Series, Vol. 104, No. 7, 1977, pp. 77–88.

Efimov, A. V. "Rossiia i kolonizatsiia Ameriki v pervoi polovine XVIII veka" [Russia and the Colonization of America in the First Half of the Eighteenth Century] in *Izvestiia Akademii Nauk SSSR, Seriia Istorii i filisofii*, Vol. 4 No. 2, 1947.

Egerman, E. "Put do Iaponii" [The Road to Japan] in *Zapiski po Gidrografii*, 1914, Vol. 38, No. 3.

Emmons, George T. "The Meeting between La Pérouse and the Tlingit" in *American Anthropologist*, 1911, Vol. 13, pp. 294–98.

Fedorova, Svetlana G. "Issledovatel Chukotki i Aliaski kazachii sotnik Ivan Kobelev" [Cossack Sotnik Ivan Kobelev, Explorer of Chukotka and Alaska] in *Letopis Severa*, 1971, No. 5, pp. 156–72.

———. "K voprosu o rannikh russkikh poseleniiakh na Aliaske" [Concerning the Question of Early Russian Settlements in Alaska] in *Letopis Severa*, 1964, No. 4, pp. 97–113.

———. "Pervoe postoiannoe poselenie russkikh v Amerike i Dzh. Kuk" [The First Permanent Settlement of Russians in America and James Cook] in *Novoe v Izuchenii Avstralli i Okeanii*, 1972.

Fisher, Raymond H. "The Early Cartography of the Bering Strait Region" in *Arctic*, 1984, Vol. 37, No. 4, pp. 574–89.

———. "Kerner, Bering and the Amur" in *Jahrbücher für Geschichte Osteuropas*, 1969, Vol. 17, No. 3, pp. 397–407.

Gibson, James R. "European Dependence upon American Natives: The Case of Russian America" in *Ethnohistory*, 1978, Vol. 25, No. 4, pp. 359–85.

———. "Russian Expansion in Siberia and America" in *The Geographical Review*, 1980, Vol. 70, No. 2, pp. 127–36.

Glushankov, I. V. "Krenitsyn and Levashev's Aleutian Expedition" in *Alaska Journal*, 1973, Vol. 3, No. 4, pp. 204–11.

————. "Sekretnaia ekspeditsiia" [The Secret Expedition] in *Morskoi Flot*, 1969, No. 10, pp. 36–37.

Goldenberg, L. A. "Zdes byl geodezist Gvozdev 1732 goda" [The Geodesist Gvozdev Was Here in 1732] in *IVGO*, 1982, Vol. 114, No. 6, pp. 526–32.

Gorin, P., ed. "Iz istorii osvoeniia severnogo puti" [From the History of the Development of the Northern Route] in *Krasnyi Arkhiv*, 1935, Vol. 71, No. 4, pp. 137–69 and No. 5, pp. 160–81.

Gnucheva, V. F. "Materialy dlia istorii ekspeditsii Akademii nauk v XVIII i XIX vekakh" [Materials for the History of the Expeditions of the Academy of Sciences in the Eighteenth and Nineteenth Centuries] in *Trudy Arkhiva AN SSSR*, 1940, No. 4.

Grekov, Vadim I. "Naibolee rannee pechatnoe izvestie o pervoi kamchatskoi ekspeditsii (1725–30 gg.)" [The Earliest Printed Information about the First Kamchatka Expedition (1725–30)] in *Izvestiia AN SSSR, seriia geografii*, 1956, No. 6, pp. 108–12.

Hirabayashi, Hirondo. "The Discovery of Japan from the North" in *Japan Quarterly*, 1957, Vol. 4, No. 3, pp. 318–28.

Isnard, Albert. "Joseph-Nicolas Delisle, sa biographie et sa collection des cartes géographique a la Bibliothèque Nationale" in *Bulletin de la Section de Géographie du Comité des Travaux Historiques et Scientifiques*, 1916, Vol. 30, pp. 34–164.

Joppien, Rüdiger. "The Artistic Bequest of Captian Cook's Voyages—Popular Imagery in European Costume Books of the Late Eighteenth and Early Nineteenth Centuries" in Robin Fisher and Hugh Johnston, eds. *Captain James Cook and His Times*. Vancouver and London, 1979.

————. "Die Bildillustrationen zum Atlas der *Voyage de La Pérouse*. Zur Dokumemtation ihrer Entstehung" [Illustrations for the Atlas Voyages of La Pérouse. A Documentation of Their Origin] in the published papers of a Colloquium on *Die Buchillustration im 18 Jahrhundert*, Heidelberg, 1980.

Kerner, Robert J. "Russian Expansion to America: Its Bibliographical Foundations" in *Papers of the Bibliographical Society of America*, 1931, Vol. 25, pp. 111–29.

Khlebnikov, Kyrill T. "Pamiatniki G. I. Shelikhova" [Memorials of G. I. Shelikhov] in *Syn Otechestva*, 1839, Vol. 2, No. 7, pp. 20–21.

————. "Zhizneopisanie Gr. I. Shelekhova" [Biography of G. I. Shelikhov] in *Russkii Invalid*, 1838, pp. 77–84.

Konstantinov, V. M. "Sveditelstva Iapontsev o Rossii XVIII veka" [Japanese Testimonies Concerning Russia in the Eighteenth Century] in *Sovetskoe Vostokovedenie*, 1958, No. 2, pp. 76–81.

Kudashev, L. N. "Iz istorii Kurilskikh ostovov" [From the History of the Kuril Islands] in *Voprosy Istorii*, 1963, August, pp. 42–58.

Laughlin, William S. "Russian-American Bering Sea Relations: Research and Reciprocity" in *American Anthropologist*, 1985, Vol. 87, pp. 775–92.

Lensen, George A. "Early Russo-Japanese Relations" in *The Far Eastern Quarterly*, 1950, Vol. 10, No. 1, pp. 2–37.

Liapunova, Roza G. "Aleutskie Baidarki" [Aleut Baidarkas] in *Sbornik Muzeia Antropologii i Etnografii AN SSSR* [Hereafter: *Sbornik MAE*] 1963, Vol. 21.

———. "Etnograficheskoe znachenie ekspeditsii kapitanov P. K. Krenitsyna i M. D. Levashova na Aleutskie ostrova (1764–1769 gg.)" [The Ethnographic Importance of the Expedition of Captains P. K. Krenitsyn and M. D. Levashev to the Aleutian Islands (1764–1769)] in *Sovetskaia Etnografiia*, 1971, No. 6, pp. 67–79.

———. "K voprosu ob obshchestvennom stroe aleutov serediny XVIII v." [Concerning the Question of Social Structure among the Aleuts in the mid-Eighteenth Century] in *Okhotniki, Sobirateli, Rybolovy*. Leningrad, 1972, pp. 215–27.

———. "Morskoi zveroboinyi promysel aleutov XVIII–XIX vv." [The Maritime Fur Trade of the Aleuts in the Eighteenth and Nineteenth Centuries] in *Sbornik MAE*, 1964, Vol. 22.

———. "Novyi dokument o rannikh plavaniiakh na Aleutskie Ostrova" ('Izvestiia' Fedora Afanasevicha Kulkova 1764 g.)" [A New Document Concerning Early Voyages to the Aleutian Islands (the "Information" of Fedor Afanasevich Kulkov, 1764)] in *Strany i narody vostoka*, Vol. 20, No. 4, pp. 97–105.

———. "Orudiia okhoty aleutov" [Hunting Weapons of the Aleuts] in *Sbornik MAE*, 1963, Vol. 21.

Makarova, Raisa V. "Ekspeditsii russkikh promyshlennykh liudei v Tikhom okeane v 18 veke" [Expeditions of Russian Promyshlenniks to the Pacific Ocean in the Eighteenth Century] in *Voprosy Geografii*, 1950, Vol. 17.

———. "Rol Timofeia Shmaleva v izuchenii istorii russkikh geograficheskikh otkrytii v Tikhom okeane vo vtoroi polovine 18 veka" [The Roll of Timofei Shmalev in the Study of the History of Russian Geographical Discoveries in the Pacific Ocean in the Second Half of the Eighteenth Century] in *Trudy Moskovskogo Gosudarstvennog Istorikoarkhivnogo Instituta*, 1954, Vol. 6.

Mazour, Anatole G. "Russian-American Company: Private or Government Enterprise?" In *Pacific Historical Review*, 1944, Vol. 13, pp. 168–173.

Medushevskaia, O. M. "Kartograficheskie istochniki po istorii russkikh geograficheskikh otkrytii na Tikhom okeane vo vtoroi polovine XVIII veka" [Cartographic Source Materials for the History of Russian Geographic Discoveries in the Pacific Ocean in the Second Half of the Eighteenth Century] in *Trudy Moskovskogo Gosudarstvennogo Istorikoarkhivnogo Instituta*, 1954, Vol. 7.

Mikhelson, V. A. "Iz istorii russkogo putevogo ocherka XVIII veka" [From the History of a Russian Travel Account of the Eighteenth Century] in *Problemy Russkoi i Zarubezhnoi Literatury*, 1970, No. 4, pp. 148–156.

Nagrom, M. I. "Novyi variant itogovoi karty Pervoi Kamchatskoi ekspeditsii" [A New Variant of the Final Map of the First Kamchatka Expedition] in *Letopis Severa*, 1971, No. 5.

Ogloblin, N. N. "Dve 'skazi' Vl. Atlasova ob otkrytii Kamchatki" [Two "Accounts" of Vladimir Atlasov Concerning the Discovery of Kamchatka] in *Chteniia v Obshchestve Istorii i Drevnostei Rossiiskikh*, 1891, Vol. 158, Book 3, pp. 1–18.

———. "Pervyi iaponets v Rossii, 1701–1705" [The First Japanese in Russia, 1701–1705] in *Russkaia Starina*, 1891, Vol. 72, pp. 11–24.

———. "Putevye zapiski morekhoda I. M. Soloveva 1770–1775 gg." [The Travel Notes of the Seafarer I. M. Solovev, 1770–1775] in *Russkaia Starina*, 1892, Vol. 75.

Ogryzko, I. I. "Otkrytie kurilskikh ostrovov" [The Discovery of the Kuril Islands] in *Iazyki i istoriia narodnostei krainego severa SSSR*, 1953, pp. 167–207. [Uchenye Zapiski Leningradsokogo gosudarstvennogo universiteta, No. 157. Seriia Fakulteta narodov severa, No. 2]

Polevoi, Boris P. "Glavnaia zadacha pervoi kamchatskoi ekspeditsii po zamyslu Petra I. (O novoi interpretatsii instruktsii Vitusu Beringu 1725 g.)" [The Main Assignment of the First Kamchatka Expedition according to the Intention of Peter I. (A New Interpretation of the 1725 Instructions to Vitus Bering)] in *Voprosy Geografii Kamchatki*, 1964, No. 2, pp. 88–94.

———. "Kolumby russkie (K 250-letiiu ekspeditsii Vitusa Beringa)" [Russian Columbuses (For the 250th Anniversary of the Expedition of Vitus Bering)], in *Dalnyi Vostok*, 1975, No. 1, pp. 127–132.

———. "Novyi dokument o pervom russkom pokhode na Tikhom okeane" [A New Document Concerning the First Russian Expedition on the Pacific Ocean] in *Trudy Tomskogo Oblastnogo Kraevedcheskogo Muzeia*, 1963, Vol. 6, No. 2, pp. 21–27.

———. "250-letie otkrytiia Aliaski" [The 250th Anniversary of the Discovery of Alaska] in *IVGO*, 1982, Vol. 114, No. 5, pp. 409–15.

Polonskii, Aleksandr S. "Kurily" [The Kuril Islands] in *Zapiski Imperatorskago Russkago Geograficheskago Obshchestva po otdeleniiu Etnografii*, 1871, no. 4, pp. 367–576.

———. "Pervaia kamchatskaia ekspeditsiia Beringa, 1725–29 goda" [Bering's First Kamchatka Expedition, 1725–1729] in *Zapiski Gidrograficheskago Departamenta*, 1850, Vol. 8, No. 4, pp. 535–556.

———. "Pokhod geodezista Mikhaila Gvozdeva v Beringov proliv, 1732 goda" [The Voyage of the Geodesist Mikhail Gvozdev into the Bering Strait, 1732] in *Morskoi Sbornik*, 1850, Vol. 4, No. 11, pp. 389–402.

Sgibnev, A. "Bolshoi Kamchatskii nariad (Ekspeditsiia Elchina)" [The Great Kamchatka Command (The Elchin Expedition)] in *Morskoi Sbornik*, 1868, Vol. 99, No. 12, pp. 131–139.

———. "Bunt Benevskogo v Kamchatke v 1771 g." [The Benevskii Mutiny in Kamchatka in 1771] in *Russkaia Starina*, 1876, Vol. 15, pp. 526–542 and 757–769.

———. "Ekspeditsiia Shestakova" [The Shestakov Expedition] in *Morskoi Sbornik*, 1869, Vol. 100, No. 2.

———. "Istoricheskii ocherk glavneishikh sobytii v Kamchatke" [An Historical Essay on the Most Important Events in Kamchatka] in *Morskoi Sbornik*, 1869, Vol. 101, No. 4, pp. 65–142; 1869, Vol. 102, No. 5, pp. 53–84; No. 6, pp. 37–69; vol. 103, No. 7, pp. 1–129.

———. "Okhotskii port s 1649 po 1852 g." [The Port of Okhotsk from 1649 to 1852] in *Morskoi Sbornik*, 1869, Vol. 105, No. 11.

———. "Popytki russkikh k zavedeniiu torgovykh snoshenii s Iaponiei v XVIII i nachale XIX stoletii" [Russian Attempts to Establish Trade Relations with Japan in the Eighteenth and Early Nineteenth Centuries] in *Morskoi Sbornik*, 1869, Vol. 100, No. 1, pp. 37–72.

Shafranovskaia, T. K. "Narody Kamchatki i prelegaiushchikh ostrovov (izvestie 1770 goda)" [The Peoples of Kamchatka and the Nearby Islands (Acccording to Information from 1770)] In *Strany i Narody Vostoka*, 1968, No. 6, pp. 62–67.

Shirokii, V. F. "Iz istorii khoziaistvennoi deiatelnosti Rossiisko-Amerikanskoi Kompanii" [From the History of the Economic Activity of the Russian-American Company] in *Istoricheskie Zapiski*, 1942, Vol. 13, pp. 207–21.

Sokolov, A. "Ekspeditsiia k Aleutskim ostrovam kapitanov Krenitsyna i Levasheva, 1764–1769" [The Expedition of Captains Krenitsyn and Levashev to the Aleutian Islands, 1764–1769] in *Zapiski Gidrograficheskogo Departamenta*, 1852, Vol. 9, pp. 70–104.

———. "Ekspeditsiia na Medvezhye ostrova, serzhanta Andreeva, 1763–1764 g." [Sergeant Andreev's Expedition to Bear Island, 1763–64] in *Zapiski Gidrograficheskago Departamenta*, 1851.

———. "Pervyi pokhod Russkikh k Amerike 1732 goda" [The First Voyage of the Russians to America in 1732] in *Zapiski Gidrograficheskago Departamenta*, 1851, Vol. 9, pp. 78–107.

———. "Prigotovlenie krugosvetnoi ekspeditsii 1787 goda, pod nachalstvom Mulovskogo" [The Preparations for the 1787 Circumnavigation under the Command of Mulovskii] in *Zapiski Gidrograficheskogo Departamenta*, 1848, pp. 142–91.

———. "Severnaia ekspeditsiia 1733–1743 gg." [The Northern Expedition, 1733–1743] in *Zapiski Gidrograficheskogo Departamenta*, 1851, Vol. 9, pp. 190–469.

Sutton, Joseph L. "Territorial Claims of Russia and Japan on the Kurile Islands" in *Occasional Papers* (Univeristy of Michigan Center for Japanese Studies), 1951, No. 1, pp. 35–61.

Sykes, Godfrey. "The Mythical Straits of Anian" in *Bulletin of the American Geographical Society of New York*, 1915, Vol. 67, No. 3, pp. 161–72.

Szczesniak, B. "Russian Knowledge of Japanese Geography During the Reign of Peter the Great. A Bibliographical Note." in *Monumenta Nipponica*, 1956, Vol. 12, Nos. 3 and 4, pp. 131–40.

Takano, Akira. "Eburenor to Rujin no Chishima tanken ni tsuite" [Concerning Evreinov's and Luzhin's Kuril Explorations] in *Kaiji Shikenkyu*, 1968, Vol. 10, pp. 78–95.

Tompkins, Stuart R. and Max L. Moorhead. "Russia's Approach to America. Part I: From Russian Sources, 1741–61" in *British Columbia Historical Quarterly*, 1949, Vol. 13, No. 2, p. 55–66.

———. "Russia's Approach to America. Part II: From Spanish Sources, 1761–75." *British Columbia Historical Quarterly*, 1949, Vol. 13, Nos. 3 and 4, pp. 231–55.

Tumanski, F. I., ed. "Opisanie narodov nakhodiashchikhsia okolo Iakutska, Okhotska i v Kamchatke" [Description of the Peoples Found near Iakutsk, Okhotsk, and in Kamchatka] in *Rossiiskii Magazin*, 1792, Part 1, pp. 385–401.

Varep, Endel F. "O kartakh, sostavlennykh russkimi v atlase I. B. Gomana, 1725 g." [Concerning the Maps Drawn up by Russians in the J. B. Homann Atlas of 1725] in *IVGO*, 1959, Vol. 91, No. 3, pp. 290–98.

Voichenko-Markov, Euphesimia. "John Ledyard and the Russians" in *Russian Review*, Vol. 11 (October 1952) pp. 211–222.

Yamamoto, Hiroteru. "History of the Kuriles, Shikotan, and the Habomai Islands" in *Contemporary Japan*, 1951, Vol. 20, pp. 459–95.

Yarmolinsky, Avrahm. "Shelekhov's Voyage to Alaska. A Bibliographical Note" in *New York Public Library Bulletin*, 1932, No. 36, pp. 141–48.

Zhdanko, M. "Raboty russkikh moriakov v okhotskom more" [The Work of Russian Seamen in the Sea of Okhotsk] in *Zapiski po Gidrografii*, 1916, Vol. 40, no. 5.

Unpublished Materials

Crownhart-Vaughan, E. A. P. "Eighteenth Century Russian Scientific Expeditions to the North Pacific Ocean" in *Papers of the Third International Congress for Soviet and East European Studies, 1987*. In press.

Dmytryshyn, Basil. "Privately-financed Russian Expeditions to the North Pacific in the Eighteenth Century" in *Papers of the Third International Congress for Soviet and East European Studies, 1987*. In press.

Vaughan, Thomas. "Spanish, English, French and American Responses to Russian Activities in the North Pacific." *Papers of the Third International Congress for Soviet and East European Studies, 1987*. In press.

INDEX

536

Russian claim to, xxxix,
321–24, 384, 458–59, 509
Aleut people: culture, lvi–lvii, lxv,
135–38, 209–12, 217–18,
228–30, 239–40, 247–50,
261–62, 393–96; hostilities,
245–46, 283–84, 285; names,
251, 286, 393, *see also* Fox
Aleuts; relations with Russians,
lviii–lix, lx, 368–70, 472,
497–502; territory, lvi
Algamalinag ("Mikhail") (Aleut
toion), 368
Aliaska, *see* Alaska Peninsula
Alikhshukhukh (Aleut native), 216
Almodovar, Marques de, li–lii
Aluzikh (Aleut toion), 216
Aluzkhuchag (Aleut native), 216
Amat Island, 267
Amchitka (Amachitka, Amisachka)
Island, 267, 401
America, *see* North America
American Company, 492, 495
American Russian Company, 485,
488
Amlia (also Amla, Amliu) Island,
lviii, 298, 312
Amosov, Fedor, 195
Amukhta Island, 222, 298, 312
Amur Basin, lxvii
Amur River, xlvi, 11, 59, 62, 118,
119, 169, 387, 403–404, 406,
462, 503
Anadyr Cape, 162
Anadyr natives, 26–27
Anadyr River, 4, 23, 45, 57, 97, 98,
111, 132, 134, 162, 163, 192,
199, 202, 288
Anadyrsk, 17, 21, 25–30 *passim*,
54, 55, 57, 58, 161, 202, 256,
276, 278
Anadyrsk ostrog, 24, 25, 28, 36,
47, 48, 54, 55, 56, 159, 162,
192
Anadyrsk zimov'e, 3, 4, 12
Anagara River, *see* Angara River

Anaul, Oriavin (Koriak native), 54,
55
Andreanov (Andreanovskii)
Islands, xlii, xliii, 298, 312,
483
Andreev, — (sergeant), 289
Andreev, Aleksandr I., lxviii–lxix,
lxv
Angaman River, 61
Angara (Anagara, Angarka) River,
57, 62, 120
Aniui River, 4
Anna I, Empress of Russia, 79, 87:
instructions to Bering, 108–25
Anshiges (Aleut woman), 368
Antipin, Andrei, 57
Antsyforov, Danilo Iakovlev, 33,
42, 46
Apraskin, — (General Admiral), 79
Ara, 71
Arctic Ocean, 59, 113, 118, 170,
199, 201, 202, 253, 256, 257,
270, 291, 292: proposal of
Admiralty College to survey,
97, 98, 109; sea route to
Kamchatka, 231–33;
shipbuilding on coast, 97–98,
111; survey, 278–79
Arekhov, — (Tula merchant), 386
Argish, 55
Argunov, Mikhailo, 54
Argun River, 71
Arkhangelsk, 59, 97, 99, 109, 112,
231
Asia: question of land link to North
America, xxxv, xxxvi, 65, 69,
96–97, 111–14, 120, 258
Asutan Island, 369
Atakhtak Island, 222
Atamanov, Petr, 30
Atka (Atkha) Island, xlv, lviii, 222,
298, 312, 488
Atkis (Nadezhda) Island, 348
Atlansk, 362
Atlasov, Stefanida Fedorova, 32
Atlasov, Vladimir, 32: account of

Iagyk River, 445

Iaik River, *see* Ural River

Iakobii, Ivan V., 271, 326, 336, 361, 391: instructions to Shelikhov, Samoilov and Delarov, 334–35; report on John Ledyard, 340–43; report on Shelikhov-Golikov Company, 348–60

Iakut people, 81, 82, 110, 135, 195, 259, 459: abuses of, by Russians, 168–91

Iakutsk, 12, 18, 27, 40, 47, 48, 57–58, 64, 84, 110, 114, 119, 185, 187–88, 195: Ledyard at, 342–43; route to Kamchatka from, 3, 21, 22, 25–26, 49–51, 79–86, 98, 113, 120, 157, 168–69, 273, 275, 314, 459, 502; shipbuilding, 97, 111; supply depot for Pacific, 23, 35, 51, 83, 86, 87, 99, 121–22, 168, 200–201, 203, 276, 345, 358

Iakutsk ostrog, 59

Iamsk ostrog, 236

Iana River, 3

Iarensk, 200, 203, 206, 220

Iarmonga settlement, 4

Iasashna (vessel), xlix

Iasovilka River, 45

Ieronim (ieromonk), 475

Igellin Island, *see* Kruzenstern Island

Igilga Island, 369

Ignateev, Vasilii, 57

Igunok Bay, Unalaska Is., 252

Ikilav (Kamennoi native), 29

Ilim River, 80, 81

Ilimsk, 80, 86, 168

Ilinskii, Petr, 515

Iliuk, Kodiak Is., 300

Imoglin (Imagli) Island, *see* Ratmanov Island

Imperial Academy of Science, St. Petersburg, lxiii

Imperial Kunstkamer, St. Petersburg, 229

India, 12, 345, 454

Indigirka River, 3, 4, 23

Indigirsk ostrog, 3, 27

Ioann Predtecha (ship), 453

Ioasaf (arkhimandrit), 417, 433, 435, 485–86, 490, 497, 508: report on Kodiak Island, 476–81; report to Shelikhov, 465–75

Ioasaf (Bishop of Irkutsk), 223

Irkutsk, 64, 108, 122, 181, 187–89, 196, 199, 200, 202, 238, 239, 243, 269, 275, 288, 291, 306, 340, 352, 354, 366–67, 370, 403, 405, 415, 447, 475, 485, 496, 502, 503–504, 508: Ledyard at, 343; route to Okhotsk and Kamchatka, 159, 168, 271, 314; Shelikhov–Golikov Company office, 509, 510–14; supply depot for Pacific, xlvi, 80, 200–201, 271–77 *passim*, 327, 333, 345–46, 410

Irkutsk Navigation School, 272

Irkutsk Seminary, 414

Irtysh River, 62, 79, 97, 111

Isanok (also Isannok) Strait, 262, 263, 264, 386

Islands of the Four Mountains, *see* Unigun (Chetyrie Sopochnye) Island

Isle de France, 453–54

Istomin, Gavrilo, 24

Iudoma Cross, 49, 82, 83, 86, 121

Iudoma River, 49, 81, 82, 83

Iukagir people, 54–57

Iukalnikov, Sopina (Iukagir native), 55

Iulta (Penzhina native), 29

Iunaskha Island, 222

Iurevich, Mikhail, 16, 36

Iurlov, Andreian, 199, 204

Iurtin (Oplansk native), 40

Karagin people, 241–42
Karagin River, 241
Karamyshev, Aleksandr M., 343
Kargapol, Ivan, 53
Kargopol, 450
Karluk, Kodiak Is., 308
Karmakulov, Mikhail, 52
Karmanskii, Kuzma, 30
Kashcharev, Antonii, 515
Katagaeguk (Kartageuguk) Aleut people, 251
Katmak, 308, 309
Kaugalin people, 393
Kavanaev, Vasilii, 54
Kayak (also Sukli, Suklia) Island, 386, 434
Kay Island, 323
Kazan, 160
Kazan Admiralty, 194
Keltiaka, Gavrilo, 42, 46
Kenai Bay (Islet), lii, 310, 384–85, 447, 452–53, 481, 483, 487, 488: fort, xlv, 310, 417; natives, see Kenai people; settlement, 417, 456, 471, 479, 485–86, 489, 505
Kenai (Kenait, Kinait) people, lvi, lviii, 319, 384, 434, 435, 465, 474, 492: culture, 265–66, 317, 219–20; hostilities, 308, 310, 328, 385
Kenai Peninsula: natives, lvi, lix
Kendrick, John, liv
Kerner, Robert J., lxvi–lxvii
Ket River, 80
Khabarov, Fedor, 54
Khagamilia Island, 222
Khailov, Ivan, 24
Kharitonov, Ivan, 36, 37–38
Khatanga Gulf, 289
Kherven River, see Yukon River
Khimkon Tugurik, 75
Khitrov, Sofron, 139, 192
Khitsenkov, Fedor, 24
Khodyn tribe, 54
Kholodilov, (merchant), 386, 401

Kholodilovsk Company, 302
Kiakhta, 71, 332, 346, 363, 375, 387, 388, 389
Kiakhta River, 71, 73, 74
Kigigu (Kigigoo) Aleut people, 251
Kigolgan Island, 369
Kikhtan people, 413
Kinait (Kenait) people see Kenai people
King George's Sound, see Nootka Sound
Kiransk, 71
Kiselev, Stefan, xl, 473, 497
Kiukov, Matvei Leontev, 42, 46
Klichka, Franz Nikolaevich, 259
Kliuchevaia River, 9
Kobelev, Ivan: journal of voyage to Arctic, 253–58
Koch, — (Okhotsk administrator), 409, 410
Kodiak (Kyktak) Island, xlix, 221, 247, 264–65, 280, 337, 341, 369–71, 375, 379–82, 456, 465, 482, 487–88, 497, 505: agriculture, 439–40, 508; discovery, xxxviii; European ships at, lii, liii, 384, 443–44, 457; Ioasaf reports on, 476–81, 485–86, 492–93; Krenitsyn at, 247; natives, see Koniag people; Shelikhov-Golikov Company settlement, xlii, xliv, lx, 298, 303, 304, 327, 331, 358–64, 442, 443, 446, 448–49, 506; Shelikhov reports on, 298–311, 327–31, 352, 353
Kogolag (also Kogolach) Aleut people, 251
Kolesov, Stepan, 54
Kolesov, Vasilii, 44, 54, 55–56: Kuril Islands report, 22
Koliuzh people, 413
Kolmogor (ship), xlvii
Kolomin, Petr, 473, 474
Kolosh people, see Tlingit people

Ottoman Empire, 351, 376n
Ovan dzhan torzhi (Chinese
    official), 74
Ovan tanzhin torzhi (Chinese
    official), 74
Ovtsyn, — (lieutenant with
    Bering), 192

Pacific Ocean, 257, 279, 287, 296:
    coastal survey, 21, 59, 113,
    291–92; Europeans in North
    Pacific, 383–92; harbor for,
    110, 349, 461; maps, 270;
    natives along, 240, 242, 243;
    Russian claims in, 348–51,
    357, 462, search for islands,
    199, 202; trade, 321, 349, 356,
    365, 460; *see also* North
    America
Paikov, Fedosei, 515
Pakhomii, — (ieromonk), 223
Palamoshnoi, Andrei, 57
Pallas, Peter Simon, lxi, lxii–lxiii,
    343: instructions to
    Billings-Sarychev Expedition,
    291–95
Pallas (vessel), xlix, lxiii
Palomoshnyi, Ivan G., *see*
    Polomoshnyi, Ivan G.
Panin, — (promyshlennik on
    Unalaska Is.), 368
Paniutin, Evan, 16, 24
Panov, — (hunting company), 302,
    369
Panovykh, Grigorii, 220, 314
Panovykh, Petr, 220, 314
Paramushir Island, 312
Paranchin, Fedor, 166
Parensk natives, 24, 25
Paris, 120
Patrin, —, 272–73, 275, 278, 281,
    288, 291
Paul I, Emperor of Russia, xlv,
    496, 510
Pavlov, Ivan, 54, 55
Pavlovsk (Sv. Pavel) Harbor, 448,
    481, 485

Pavlutskii, Dmitrii I., xxxvii, 109,
    110, 114, 115, 126, 162
Pechora River, 112
Pegasus (vessel), 505
Peking, 72, 73
Penzhina River, 10, 11, 28, 29, 30
Penzhinsk ostrozhek, 29
Perez, Juan, lii
Permiakov, Efim, 133, 163–64, 166
Permiakov, Vasilii, 25
Persia, 62
Peter I, Emperor of Russia, xxv,
    xxxiii, xxxiv–xxxv, 16, 28,
    69n, 79, 85–86, 96, 111, 115,
    120, 126–28, 129, 271n,
    326–27: instructions
    concerning first Bering
    expedition, 66–67; instructions
    regarding Kamchatka, 18–27;
    instructions to Glebov
    regarding China trade, 13–14;
    instructions to Tatarinov,
    47–48; petitions to, for pardon,
    32–33, 34–42, 43–46; proposal
    to, regarding Arctic
    exploration, 59–63; ukaz
    concerning aid to Elchin's
    expedition, 64; ukaz concerning
    assistance to Bering, 68; ukaz
    concerning route to Kamchatka
    and Kuril Islands, 49–53
Peters, William, liv, 313, 332
Petropavlovsk, xxxvii, liii, liv, 139,
    140, 147–48, 155, 192, 194,
    196, 272, 279, 332, 345, 375:
    East India Company at,
    312–13, 332
Petrov, Afanasii, 54, 55, 56, 58
Petrov, Efim, 25, 28, 30, 36
Petrovich, Ivan, 475
Philippine Islands, 346, 459, 462
Phoenix (Moore's ship), 443, 452
Phoenix (Shelikhov-Golikov Co.
    frigate), 485, 488, 490, 497,
    505
Pierce, Richard A., lxviii
Pil, Ivan Alferevich, xliv, 376, 379,

550

552

Slavorossiia, 438, 446, 508
Smallpox, 12, 169–70, 177–78,
    237, 317
Smelyi (ship), xlviii
Smetanin, Lavrentii, 133, 166
Smith, Adam: influence on
    Catherine II, xliv
Snigirev, Ilia, 220
Soimonov, Fedor I., xlvi: report on
    Bechevin expedition, 199–205
Soimonov, Petr P., 221, 323, 515
Sokol (ship), xlviii
Sokolov, Aleksandr P., lxiv,
    lxv–lxvi
Sokolov, Kozma: instructions from
    Peter I, 49–53
Solovev, Ivan, xliii, lix, 218, 369
Solovki (ship), xlviii
Sol Vychegodskaia, 79, 220
Sonora (galiot), lii
Sorokoumov, Ivan, 49, 51
South Sea, 92
South Sea Company, liii
Spain, 61, 130, 345: colonial
    interests in North Pacific,
    xxxiv, xxxix, xlviii, li–liii;
    trade in North Pacific, 384,
    385, 386–87; trade with
    Americas, 92–93
Spanberg, Martyn Petrovich,
    xxxvi, 66,80, 81, 82, 83, 98,
    99, 109, 115, 120, 192–93, 323:
    report from Gvozdev, 161–67
Spaskii Monastery, Tobolsk, 87,
    159
Spitzbergen, 231
Ssiulatys Island, 263, 264
Stefan (ierodiakon), 436, 438, 441
Steingel, Ivan, 313
Steller, Georg Wilhelm, xxxvii,
    xxxviii
Strait of Gibraltar, 61
Strait of Malacca, 313
Strait of Vaigats, 61
Stroganov, Petr, 220
Struchkov, Fedor, 503

Sukli (Suklia) Island, *see* Kayak
    Island
Surgut, 80
Suzdalev, Ivan, 315
Sverev, — (naval lieutenant), 66
Sv. Aleksandr (ship), *see Dobroe
    Predpriatie Sviatia Aleksandr*
Sv. Dalmatiia Island, 321
Sv. Ekaterina (galiot), 246, 247
Sv. Evpl (vessel), 262
Sv. Gavriil (vessel), xxxvi, xxxvii,
    85, 161, 162, 163, 258: voyage
    to Alaska, 132–34
Sv. Georgii Pobedonosets (vessel), 417
Sv. Iulian (vessel), 214, 220
Sv. Lavrentii Island, *see* St.
    Lawrence Island
Sv. Mikhail (galiot), 296, 298, 309,
    311, 327
Sv. Pavel, Kodiak Is., *see* Pavlovsk
    Harbor
Sv. Pavel (Chirikov packetboat),
    xxxviii
Sv. Pavel (Lesvashev hooker), 247
Sv. Petr (packetboat), xxxvii, xxxviii
*Sv. Simeon Bogopriimets i Anna
    Prorochitsa* (galiot), 296, 297,
    298
Sv. Stefan Island, 321
Sv. Tri Sviatitelia (galiot), 296, 310,
    311, 373, 376, 377
Sv. Velikomuchenitsa Ekaterina
    (vessel), 433, 451
Sv. Vladimir (merchant vessel), 239,
    259, 262, 267
Sviatyi Nos, 59, 61
Svinin, Ivan, 497, 498, 501–502
Svinin, Nikifor (Aleut native), 502
Svistunov, Ivan, 66
Svitsov, Ivan (Kamchadal native),
    220
Svitsov, Vasilii, 371
Sweden, 61, 94, 376, 430

Tagagut Aleut people, *see* Fox
    Aleut people

von Verd, K. P., 66
von Witten, — (colonel at
    Okhotsk), 447–48, 451
Voronovskii, Davyd, 515
Vorontsov, Aleksandr R., xliv,
    321, 401
Vorovskaia River, 259
Voskresenskii Harbor, Chugach
    Bay, 487–88
Vutein, 253

Walton, — (Captain), 197, 323
Waxell, Sven, xxxvii, 139, 192
Weather: Aleutian Islands, 228,
    247, 296–97; Cape St. Elias,
    434–35; Kamchatka, 5, 10;
    Kodiak Island, 311, 328, 434;
    Kuril Islands, 5; Mednyi
    Island, 260; North Pacific,
    156–57; purgas, 28, 55, 84, 314
Witsen, Nicholas, xxiv
Wolf, — (colonel of Kabardinsk
    Infantry Regiment), 190

Yakutat Bay, lii, lvi, lix, 453, 456,
    486, 506: Russian settlement,
    471, 473, 480, 483, 492
Yedo (Edo), 401
Yukon River, 255

Zaikov, Potap Kuzmich, xliii,
    302–303, 368, 369, 373, 374,
    385–86, 387, 471, 473: report
    on voyage to North Pacific
    islands, 259–67
Zakharii i Elisaveta (vessel), 206
Zalesov, Ondrei, 24
Zalevin, Ivan, 133
Zankevich, Ioasaf, 159
Zashiversk ostrog, 27, 58
Zashiversk zimov'e, 24
Zershchikov, Fedor, 56
Zhdanov, Andrei, 204
Zhigansk, 177, 362
Zhupanova River, 34, 46
Zinin, Osip Leontev, 203

Zropin, Semen, 204
Zubov, Platon Aleksandrovich,
    485, 494
Zykov, Vasilii, 54
Zyrian, Vasilii, 133
Zyrian people, 8

COLOPHON

Designed and produced by the Oregon Historical Society Press, this volume is the tenth in the Oregon Historical Society's North Pacific Studies Series and second in a three volume set entitled *To Sibera and Russian America: Three Centuries of Russian Eastward Expansion, 1558-1867*.

The text and interior display typeface is Janson. This face, often confused with Jensen and mistakenly attributed to a Dutchman, Anton Janson, was cut during the last century by Nicholas Kis, a Hungarian who worked in Amsterdam. Janson is part of the Geralde family of typefaces with an oblique incline in all its letters, and a strong contrast between thick and thin strokes.

Deepdene is used for the display typography on the title page. Created in 1927 by the legendary American type designer, Frederick W. Goudy, Deepdene was one of the first classical faces designed with mechanized typesetting in mind — a merging of beauty and form with modern functions and needs.

The text was set by G&S Typesetters of Austin, Texas; Bookcrafters, Inc. of Chelsea, Michigan printed this volume on 70 lb. Warren Olde Style, an alkaline paper, using PMS 336 for the second color. A three-piece combination of Roxite cloth and Papan paper was used in the binding.

3

Сыскать изъ Ученивовъ,
Или изподмастерьевъ
которой бы могъ тамо,
здѣлать Стальовъ об̄
позвѣшнемъ примѣру,
какие есть прибольшихъ
наравяхъ. И для того
Сниямъ от̄правити 6,
плотинивовъ 4 сихъ
Инструменты, которые
молосе были, и
от̄ного партиямастера
и 8 чиниъ мастровъ.

От̄шаной Учивъ Федоръ
повловъ пишется, по
тпорой погерти самъ
обши Спальбамъ й об̄
Пал дѣлать мостр.

И потой препорцій от̄
пустить от̄сюда впо̄
тора: паруса, лопо.
шахъпъ, веревокъ, про̄
чаго. И 4 салшанети
снадшт ощъв. А м учи
цивъ, й от̄ного пих 2.
паруснихъ шеецъ.

тапиславъ Опустица

+ вдои

процевосфтри
шро